The Qur'ān and Its Biblical Subtext

This book challenges the dominant scholarly notion that the Qur'ān must be interpreted through the medieval commentaries shaped by the biography of the prophet Muḥammad, proposing instead that the text is best read in light of Christian and Jewish scripture. The Qur'ān, in its use of allusions, depends on the Biblical knowledge of its audience. However, medieval Muslim commentators, working in a context of religious rivalry, developed stories that separate Qur'ān and Bible, which this book brings back together.

In a series of studies involving the devil, Adam, Abraham, Jonah, Mary, and Muḥammad among others, Reynolds shows how modern translators of the Qur'ān have followed medieval Muslim commentary and demonstrates how an appreciation of the Qur'ān's Biblical subtext uncovers the richness of the Qur'ān's discourse. Presenting unique interpretations of thirteen different sections of the Qur'ān based on studies of earlier Jewish and Christian literature, the author substantially re-evaluates Muslim exegetical literature. Thus *The Qur'ān and Its Biblical Subtext*, a work based on a profound regard for the Qur'ān's literary structure and rhetorical strategy, poses a substantial challenge to the standard scholarship of Qur'ānic Studies. With an approach that bridges early Christian history and Islamic origins, the book will appeal not only to students of the Qur'ān but to students of the Bible, religious studies, and Islamic history.

Gabriel Said Reynolds is Associate Professor of Islamic Studies and Theology at the University of Notre Dame (USA). He works on Qur'ānic Studies and Muslim–Christian Relations and is the author of *A Muslim Theologian in the Sectarian Milieu*, the translator of ʿAbd al-Jabbār's *A Critique of Christian Origins*, and the editor of *The Qur'ān in Its Historical Context*.

Routledge studies in the Quran
Series Editor:
Andrew Rippin
University of Victoria, Canada

In its examination of critical issues in the scholarly study of the Quran and its commentaries, this series targets the disciplines of archaeology, history, textual history, anthropology, theology and literary criticism. The contemporary relevance of the Quran in the Muslim world, its role in politics and in legal debates are also dealt with, as are debates surrounding Quranic studies in the Muslim world.

Literary Structures of Religious Meaning in the Qur'ān
Edited by Issa J. Boullata

The Development of Exegesis in Early Islam
The authenticity of Muslim literature from the Formative Period
Herbert Berg

Biblical Prophets in the Qur'ān and Muslim Literature
Robert Tottoli

Moses in the Qur'ān and Islamic Exegesis
Brannon M. Wheeler

Logic, Rhetoric and Legal Reasoning in the Qur'ān
God's arguments
Rosalind Ward Gwynne

Textual Relations in the Qur'ān
Relevance, coherence and structure
Salwa M. El-Awa

Sūfī Commentaries on the Qur'ān in Classical Islam
Kristin Zahra Sands

The Qur'an in Its Historical Context
Gabriel Said Reynolds

Interpreting al-Tha'labi's *Tales of the Prophets*
Temptation, responsibility and loss
Marianna Klar

The Qur'ān and Its Biblical Subtext
Gabriel Said Reynolds

The Qur'ān and Its Biblical Subtext

Gabriel Said Reynolds

Routledge
Taylor & Francis Group
LONDON AND NEW YORK

First published 2010
by Routledge
2 Park Square, Milton Park, Abingdon, Oxon OX14 4RN

Simultaneously published in the USA and Canada
by Routledge
270 Madison Ave, New York, NY 10016

Routledge is an imprint of the Taylor & Francis Group, an informa business

Typeset in 10/12pt Times NR MT by
Graphicraft Limited, Hong Kong

British Library Cataloguing in Publication Data
A catalogue record for this book is available
from the British Library

Library of Congress Cataloging in Publication Data
Reynolds, Gabriel Said.
The Qur'an and its biblical subtext / Gabriel Said Reynolds.
p. cm. – (Routledge studies in the Qur'an; 10)
Includes bibliographical references and index.
1. Koran–Hermeneutics. 2. Koran–Criticism, interpretation, etc.–History. 3. Islam–Controversial literature. I. Title.
BP130.2.R49 2010
297.1′22601–dc22

2009035977

ISBN13: 978-0-415-77893-0 (hbk)
ISBN13: 978-0-203-85645-1 (ebk)
ISBN10: 0-415-77893-X (hbk)
ISBN10: 0-203-85645-7 (ebk)

To Luke, Emmanuel, and Theresa

Acknowledgements

Whatever contribution the present work makes, if any, will be in large part due to those scholars who have been my mentors during its composition. Christopher Melchert of Oxford University, Andrew Rippin of the University of Victoria, Sidney Griffith of the Catholic University of America, Fred Donner of the University of Chicago, and Tarif Khalidi of the American University of Beirut have all read the work at different stages. They critiqued it in a manner that allowed me both to correct errors in its details and to improve my thinking about the substantial issues it addresses. Throughout my work on this project John Cavadini of the University of Notre Dame has offered me guidance when I most needed it and supported me at the most difficult moments, not without cost. All of these scholars, in assisting me, have sacrificed time and energy that could have been kept for their own projects, and for no personal benefit. Their assistance has both humbled and inspired me.

I have also benefited from generous financial support during this project. During the 2006–7 academic year I was able to pursue research in Jerusalem and Beirut as a Henry Luce III Fellow in Theology. Later in 2007 I returned to both cities with the backing of a Fulbright Grant. During the summers of 2008 and 2009 my research travel was supported by the University of Notre Dame. Throughout my time at Notre Dame the Department of Theology in particular and the university in general have been extraordinarily supportive of my work and my academic vocation. In the course of editing this work I have benefited from the careful proofreading of Hannah Hemphill and from the professional and judicious guidance of Kathy Auger of Graphicraft. To her and to all of the supportive representatives of Routledge I am grateful.

Finally I would to thank my family: Lourdes, my lovely wife, and Luke Electious, Emmanuel Joshua, and Theresa Anne, our children. Together they have filled my life with laughter and taught me to live each day in thanksgiving.

Contents

Abbreviations

Sources

AEL	*An Arabic-English Lexicon*, ed. E. Lane, London: Williams and Norgate, 1863–93
BEQ	H. Speyer, *Die biblischen Erzählungen im Qoran*, Gräfenhainichen: Schulze, 1931 (reprint: Hildesheim: Olms, 1961). F. Rosenthal notes in "The history of Heinrich Speyer's *Die biblischen Erzählungen im Qoran*" (see bibliography entry) that the original publication information is false. The printing was only completed in 1937, and then under the direction of the Marcus family in Breslau
BT	Babylonian Talmud
BSOAS	*Bulletin of the School of Oriental and African Studies*
CSCO	*Corpus Scriptorum Christianorum Orientalium*
EI²	*The Encyclopaedia of Islam*, 2nd edition, Leiden: Brill, 1954–present
EQ	*The Encyclopaedia of the Qur'ān*, ed. J. McAuliffe, Leiden: Brill, 2001–6
FV	A. Jeffery, *The Foreign Vocabulary of the Qur'ān*, Baroda: Oriental Institute, 1938. Reprint: Leiden: Brill, 2007
GdQ1, 2, 3	*1*, 1st edition: T. Nöldeke, *Geschichte des Qorāns*, Göttingen: Verlag der Dieterichschen Buchhandlung, 1860; *2*, 2nd edition, Nöldeke's revised work being titled therein *Über den Ursprung des Qorāns* and including F. Schwally, *Die Sammlung des Qorāns*, ed. and revised F. Schwally, Leipzig: Weicher, 1909, 1919; *3*, 2nd edition including G. Bergsträsser and O. Pretzl, *Die Geschichte des Koran-texts*, Leipzig: Weicher, 1938; reprint: 3 vols. in 1, Hildesheim: Olms, 1970
JAOS	*Journal of the American Oriental Society*
JNES	*Journal of Near Eastern Studies*
JRAS	*Journal of the Royal Asiatic Society*
JSAI	*Jerusalem Studies in Arabic and Islam*
JSS	*Journal of Semitic Studies*

KU	J. Horovitz, *Koranische Untersuchungen*, Berlin: de Gruyter, 1926
LCD	*Comparative Dictionary of Ge'ez*, ed. W. Leslau, Wiesbadan: Harrassowitz, 1987
LJ	L. Ginzberg, *Legends of the Jews*, trans. H. Szold, Philadelphia: Jewish Publication Society of America, 1988
MIDEO	*Mélanges de l'Institut dominicain d'études orientales du Caire*
MQQ	*Mu'jam al-qirā'āt al-Qur'āniyya*, ed. Aḥmad 'Umar and 'Abd al-'Āl Mukarram, Tehran: Dār al-Uswa li-l-Ṭibā'a wa-l-Nashr, 1426
MW	*The Muslim* (or, in earlier volumes, *Moslem*) *World*
NTA	*New Testament Apocrypha*, ed. W. Schneemelcher, trans. R. Wilson, Cambridge: J. Clarke & Co., 1991
OC	*Oriens Christianus* (serial)
OIC	T. Andrae, *Les origines de l'islam et le christianisme*, trans. J. Roche, Paris: Adrien-Maisonneuve, 1955. Originally published in German as "Der Ursprung des Islams und das Christentum," *Kyrkshistorisk årsskrift* 23, 1923, 149–206; 24, 1924, 213–25; 25, 1925, 45–112
PG	*Patrologia Graeca*
PL	*Patrologia Latina*
PO	*Patrologia Orientalis*
QHC	*The Qur'ān in Its Historical Context*, ed. G.S. Reynolds, London: Routledge, 2007
QS	J. Wansbrough, *Quranic Studies: Sources and Methods of Scriptural Interpretation*, Oxford: Oxford University Press, 1977. Reprint: Amherst, NY: Prometheus, 2004
SI	*Studia Islamica*
TB	J. Kugel, *Traditions of the Bible: A Guide to the Bible as It Was at the Start of the Common Era*, Cambridge, MA: Harvard University Press, 1998
TS	R. Payne Smith, *Thesaurus Syriacus*, Tome I, Oxford: E Typographeo Clarendoniano, 1879; Tome 2, 1901
ZDMG	*Zeitschrift der deutschen morgenländischen Gesellschaft*

Biblical abbreviations

Gn	Genesis
Ex	Exodus
Chr.	Chronicles
Mt	Gospel of Matthew
Mk	Gospel of Mark
Lk	Gospel of Luke
Jn	Gospel of John
Acts	Acts of the Apostles

R.	*Rabba* (thus, e.g. *Gn R.* = *Genesis Rabba*)
LXX	Septuagint
Psh.	Peshitta

Language abbreviations

Ar.	Arabic
Gk.	Greek
Heb.	Hebrew
Syr.	Syriac

Other abbreviations

CS	Case Study

Nota bene

In the case studies (Chapter 2), italicized words are transliterations. Underlined words are provisional translations. Unless otherwise stated, Biblical translations are from the New Jerusalem Bible.

Introduction

Listening to the text

The present work is largely a response to the difficulties that scholars have in explaining large parts of the Qur'ān. Scholarly difficulties are nothing strange, of course, but there is something particularly intriguing about this case. For the most part, scholars of the Qur'ān accept the basic premise of the medieval Islamic sources that the Qur'ān is to be explained in light of the life of the Prophet Muḥammad. The life of the Prophet, meanwhile, is recorded in those sources with intricate detail. This detailed information, one might assume, should allow scholars to explain at least the literal meaning of the Qur'ān without difficulty. But it does not.

Perhaps the most salient example of this problem is the work of William Montgomery Watt. In his books *Muḥammad at Mecca* and *Muḥammad at Medina*,[1] Watt, following Islamic sources, provides details on every aspect of the Prophet's life, from his family, to his relations with his neighbors and friends, to his military and diplomatic strategies. Yet in his book *Bell's Introduction to the Qur'ān* Watt consistently notes how much is unknown about the Qur'ān, from the chronological order of its proclamation, to the mysterious letters that open 29 Sūras, to obscure vocabulary throughout the text.[2] The method of reading the Qur'ān through the life of the Prophet seems not to have served Watt well. Nevertheless, Watt and other scholars argue (or, in some cases, assume) that the Qur'ān must be viewed through the lens of Muḥammad's biography. For Watt this is not one method of reading the text; it is the only method.

The present work is meant as a challenge to this state of affairs, at least in part. This is not a work of history and I will not examine, let alone rewrite, the biography of the Prophet. My concern is only to develop a fruitful method of reading the Qur'ān. And yet the Qur'ān is not a text that renders its secret easily. There is, as has often been noted, nothing that approaches a true

1 W.M. Watt, *Muḥammad at Mecca*, Oxford: Oxford University Press, 1953; idem, *Muḥammad at Medina*, Oxford: Oxford University Press, 1956.
2 W.M. Watt and R. Bell, *Bell's Introduction to the Qur'ān*, 2nd edition, Edinburgh: Edinburgh University Press, 1977 (1st edition 1970).

narrative in the Qur'ān, the story of Joseph (Q 12) notwithstanding. Instead the Qur'ān seems to direct the reader, through allusions and references, to certain traditions which provide the basis for appreciating its message. The Qur'ān awakens the audience's memory of these traditions and then proceeds without pause to deliver its religious message. This means, in other words, that the task of reading the Qur'ān is a task of listening and response. The audience must follow the Qur'ān's lead to some subtext of traditions.

This dynamic is raised by Salwa El-Awa in a recent article. She comments, "If recipients of the Qur'ānic text lack access to the knowledge they need to process the meanings of its language, they are unlikely to succeed in uncovering the intended meanings."[3] El-Awa proceeds to illustrate her point with reference to *al-masad* (Q 111), wherein the Qur'ān rebukes a man named "father of flame" (*abū lahab*) along with this man's wife. The proper explanation of this chapter, she insists, is found among those medieval Muslim exegetes who explain it by describing a confrontation that Muḥammad had in Mecca with an uncle named Abū Lahab. And yet she adds that this explanation is not obvious in the Qur'ān itself: "If information about the historical situation is not available to interpreters, the meaning of the whole *sūra* may be turned into an image of man and his female partner being punished in hellfire for their disbelief."[4]

Thus El-Awa follows faithfully the manner in which the medieval exegetes use biographical material to explain the Qur'ān. I, on the other hand, will argue below (see Ch. 1) for the very position which she is relieved to avoid, that the Sūra is "an image of man and his female partner being punished in hellfire for their disbelief."

Accordingly, the general argument in the present work is that the connection made by medieval Muslim exegetes between the biography of Muḥammad and the Qur'ān should not form the basis of critical scholarship. Instead, the Qur'ān should be appreciated in light of its conversation with earlier literature, in particular Biblical literature (by which I mean the Bible, apocrypha, and Jewish and Christian exegetical works). This argument necessarily involves an examination of both the relationship of Muslim exegetical literature to the Qur'ān and the relationship of the Qur'ān to Biblical literature. Still it is the latter relationship that is of particular importance to me, since ultimately I will argue that the Qur'ān expects its audience to be familiar with Biblical literature. Whereas both Islamic tradition and the tradition of critical scholarship have tended to separate Qur'ān and Bible, the Qur'ān itself demands that they be kept together.

3 S.M.S. El-Awa, "Linguistic structure," in A. Rippin (ed.), *The Blackwell Companion to the Qur'ān*, London: Blackwell, 2006, (53–72) 67.

4 Ibid.

1 The crisis of Qur'ānic Studies

The scholarly conflict over the Qur'ān

The idea that the Qur'ān and Biblical literature are related is not a new one. Indeed there is a long tradition of critical scholarship dedicated to the search for sources of the Qur'ān in earlier Jewish and Christian writings. Yet for the most part the scholars who contributed to this tradition took for granted the connection made by medieval Muslim scholars between the biography of Muḥammad and the Qur'ān. In their search for sources, they tended to ask when, where, and how Muḥammad learned something from Biblical literature. In other words, these scholars generally assume that the Prophet, as it were, stood between the Bible and the Qur'ān.

The link between the Qur'ān and the Prophet's biography, or *sīra* (by which I mean not only works by this title but biographical information on Muḥammad generally), was generally taken for granted from the beginning of European scholarship of the Qur'ān.[1] The three most prominent translations of the Qur'ān in eighteenth-century Europe all include a biographical sketch of the Prophet Muḥammad.[2] The 1833 prize-winning work of Abraham Geiger, *Was hat Mohammed aus dem Judenthume aufgenommen*, includes frequent references to details of the Prophet's biography.[3] From its beginnings,

1 Regarding the dominance of this method see E. Gräf, "Zu den christlichen Einflüssen im Koran," *Al-Bāḥith* 28, *Festschrift Joseph Henninger zum 70 Geburtstag*, 1976, (111–44) 111. In a recent article N. Sinai refers to this method as the "authorial paradigm." See his "Orientalism, authorship, and the onset of revelation: Abraham Geiger and Theodor Nöldeke on Muḥammad and the Qur'ān," in D. Hartwig, W. Homolka, M. Marx, and A. Neuwirth (eds.), *Im vollen Licht der Geschichte: Die Wissenschaft des Judentums und die Anfänge der kritischen Koranforschung*, Würzburg: Ergon, 2008, 145–54.

2 These include the Latin translation of L. Marraccio (Padua: ex typographia Seminarii, 1698; see 1:10–32), the English translation of G. Sale (London: Ackers, 1734; see 33–56), and the French translation of C.-É. Savary (Paris: Knapen, 1783; see 1:1–248).

3 Thus Geiger writes, "Was aber die übrigen Abweichungen und vorzüglich Hinzufügungen betrifft, so rühren diese wiederum . . . von der Vermischung mit seiner Zeit und Person her." A. Geiger, *Was hat Mohammed aus dem Judenthume aufgenommen*, Leipzig: Kaufmann, 1902 (1st edition: Bonn: Baaden, 1833), 114. On Geiger see S. Heschel, *Abraham Geiger and the Jewish Jesus*, Chicago: Chicago University Press, 1998, ch. 2; J. Lassner, "Abraham Geiger:

in other words, the method of reading the Qur'ān through that biography was a *sine qua non* of European scholarship on the Qur'ān.

This method reached its most famous formulation in *Die Geschichte des Qorans*, a book in three volumes which evolved over seventy years, through the efforts of four different authors: Theodore Nöldeke, Friedrich Schwally, Gotthelf Bergsträsser, and Otto Pretzl. The earliest form of the *Geschichte* was a 1856 Latin essay by Nöldeke: *De origine et compositione Surarum Qoranicarum ipsiusque Qorani.*[4] Nöldeke submitted this essay to a competition hosted by the Académie des inscriptions et belles-lettres of Paris, a competition that asked participants to "déterminer autant qu'il est possible, avec l'aide des historiens arabes et des commentateurs et d'après l'examen des morceaux [coraniques] eux-mêmes, les moments de la vie de Mahomet auxquels ils se rapportent."[5] In other words, the competition to which Nöldeke submitted his work involved the assumption that a critical study of the Qur'ān means matching individual passages ("morceaux") of the Qur'ān with elements of the Prophet's biography.

Nöldeke's work, which would become the first volume of *Geschichte des Qorans*, is in fact almost completely taken up by a critical arrangement of the Sūras of the Qur'ān into four periods of the Prophet's life: 1st Meccan, 2nd Meccan, 3rd Meccan and Medinan. Nöldeke adopted the system of four periods from Gustav Weil,[6] but the idea that each Sūra, as a unity, can be placed in a certain moment of the Prophet's life is a tenet of Islamic religious tradition.[7] On the other hand, this idea is in no way obvious from the text of the Qur'ān. The text itself nowhere demands to be arranged according to the life experiences of an individual.[8]

Yet this idea had its attraction. The scholars of Nöldeke's era believed that the Prophet's biography, when read critically, was a reliable source of historical information.[9] It therefore seemed an optimal place to begin a

A nineteenth-century Jewish reformer on the origins of Islam," in M. Kramer (ed.), *The Jewish Discovery of Islam: Studies in Honor of Bernard Lewis*, Tel Aviv: Tel Aviv University, 1999, 103–35.

4 See *GdQ1*, v.

5 Quoted by Watt and Bell, *Bell's Introduction to the Qur'an*, 175.

6 See G. Weil, *Historisch-kritische Einleitung in den Koran*, Bielefeld: Velhagen and Klasing, 1844. Cf. *GdQ1*, 72, n. 1.

7 Thus the standard Egyptian edition of the Qur'ān, first published in 1924 and ubiquitous today, labels each Sūra "Meccan" or "Medinan."

8 Accordingly it is worth noting the observation of H.-C. Graf von Bothmer, that in the early Qur'ān manuscript fragments discovered in the Great Mosque of Ṣan'ā', Yemen, not a single Sūra is identified as Meccan or Medinan. See H.-C. Graf von Bothmer, K.-H. Ohlig, and G.-R. Puin, "Neue Wege der Koranforschung," *Magazin Forschung* 1, 1999, (33–46) 43–4.

9 Already in the middle of the nineteenth century E. Renan proclaimed: "One can say without exaggeration that the problem of the origins of Islam has definitely now been completely resolved." E. Rénan, "Mahomet et les origines de l'Islamisme," *Revue des deux mondes* 12, 1851, 1065. Reference and translation from R. Hoyland, "Writing the biography of the Prophet Muhammad: Problems and solutions," *History Compass* 5, 2007, (581–602) 582.

critical study of the Qur'ān, a text that is often not forthcoming with contextual details. Thereby scholars were able, for example, to explain Biblical material in the Qur'ān through reports in the Prophet's biography that connect him or his followers to Jews and Christians.[10] In this way Aloys Sprenger argues, on the basis of the reports in Islamic literature that the Prophet met a Christian monk (named Baḥīrā) during a childhood journey to Syria, that Muḥammad had a Christian informant.[11] Nöldeke devoted an article to the refutation of Sprenger's theory,[12] but tellingly he pursues this refutation only by pointing to other elements in the Prophet's biography (such as Muḥammad's relationship with Waraqa b. Nawfal) that render superfluous the search for a secret informant.[13] This Nöldeke does even while he acknowledges the questionable authority of such reports, admitting that "der einzige unverfälschte, durchaus zuverlässige Zeuge über Muḥammad und seine Lehre ist der Qur'ân."[14]

Karl Ahrens exhibits a similar method in his influential article, "Christliches im Qoran."[15] He argues that the Qur'ān was influenced more by Christianity than Judaism with reference to a report in Islamic literature, namely that Muḥammad's followers were distraught to hear of a defeat the Christian Byzantines had suffered at the hands of the Persians. Yet this report is evidently a story designed to give a context to *al-rūm* (30) 2–4a ("The Byzantines

10 See, for example, the comments of J. Obermann: "The situation becomes clear once we recognize that Muhammad had acquired his entire store of knowledge about Scripture, and about Judaism and Christianity in general, through oral channels and personal observation during a long period of association with the People of the Book. His was the case of a pagan converted to monotheism, who absorbed its theory and practice by attending services and pious assemblies of worshipers, by listening at the feet of popular preachers and missionaries, but who never read a line of Scripture, or a breviary, or even of a hymnbook." J. Obermann, "Islamic origins: A study in background and foundation," in J. Friedlander (ed.), *The Arab Heritage*, New York: Russell and Russell, 1963, (58–120) 95.

11 A. Sprenger, "Mohammad's journey to Syria and Professor [F.L.] Fleischer's opinion thereon," *Journal of the Asiatic Society of Bengal* 21, 1852, 576–92; cf. idem, *Das Leben und die Lehre des Moḥammad*, Berlin: Nicolai'sche Verlagsbuchandlung, 1861–5, 2:348–90.

12 Nöldeke,"Hatte Muḥammad christliche Lehrer?" *ZDMG* 12, 1858, 699–708. He opens by noting (p. 700), "Nun hat sich aber in neuster Zeit *Sprenger* zur Aufgabe gemacht, seine Ansicht, dass Muḥammad nicht der Stifter des Islâms, sondern – denn darauf läuft doch seine Beweisführung hinaus – ein unbedeutendes, halb betrogenes, halb betrügendes Werkzeug Anderer gewesen sei."

13 Nöldeke returns to this refutation in the *Geschichte*, commenting: "Wenn in den Legenden, welche Muhammed mit einem syrischen Mönche Bahira oder Nestorios Verbindung bringen auch ein wahrer Kern steckt, so kann doch eine solche Begegnung kaum eine ausschlaggebende Bedeutung für seine Prophetie gehabt haben. Und mag Muhammed noch so oft nach Syrien gekommen sein – Hunderte seiner Landsleute machten ja jahraus jahrein diese Reise: um die Offenbarungsreligionen kennen zu lernen, brauchte weder ein heidnischer Mekkaner nach Syrien oder Abessinien, noch ein syrischer oder abessinischer Christ nach Mekka zu kommen." *GdQ1*, 17–18.

14 Nöldeke, "Hatte Muḥammad christliche Lehrer?" 700.

15 K. Ahrens, "Christliches im Qoran," *ZDMG* 84, 1930, 15–68, 148–90.

have been defeated * in a nearer land. After their defeat they will inflict defeat * in a number of years.").[16] In other words, the Qur'ān seems to explain the story, not vice versa.

The link between the Qur'ān and the Prophet's biography also led scholars, confident that they knew the time and place in which the Qur'ān was written, to search outside of the Islamic canon for Jewish and Christian groups that might have influenced the Qur'ān.[17] Wilhelm Rudolph, for example, dedicates the first chapter of his *Die Abhängigkeit des Qorans von Judentum und Christentum* (1922) not to anything in the Qur'ān but rather to the nature

16 Wansbrough finds the logic of this explanation particularly wanting: "The primary motif, a natural alliance between Muḥammad's followers and the Byzantines (both being 'people of the book') against his opponents and the Persians (both being idolaters), became a constant in Quranic exegesis and a 'fact' of oriental history. The circular argumentation underlying that process is graphically illustrated by the manner in which Ahrens drew upon Wellhausen's assertion (itself apparently an inference from the haggadic interpretation of Q 30.1–4) that the Jews in Arabia (hence opponents of Muḥammad) had traditionally (!) sided with Persia against Byzantium to prove, conversely, that Islam was influenced in its development by the prophet's sympathetic attitude to Christianity." *QS*, 144–5. See Ahrens, "Christliches im Qoran," 148; J. Wellhausen, *Reste arabischen Heidentums*, Berlin: Reimer, 1897, 236. I personally heard this motif expressed in dramatic fashion by Irfan Shahid, who in a lecture I attended at the American University of Beirut in Spring 2001 proposed that Arab Christian and Muslim scholars unite against secular scholars in the West, as Christians and Muslims united in the days of the Prophet to combat the "fire-worshipping" Zoroastrians.

17 On the influence of Jewish groups see especially R. Dozy, *Die Israeliten zu Mekka von Davids Zeit*, Leipzig: Engelmann, 1864; A.J. Wensinck, *Mohammed en de Joden te Medina*, Leiden: Brill, 1908; English trans.: *Muhammad and the Jews of Medina*, trans. W. Behn, Freiburg: Schwarz, 1975; R. Leszynsky, *Die Juden in Arabien zur Zeit Mohammeds*, Berlin: Mayer and Müller, 1910; D.S. Margoliouth, *The Relations between Arabs and Israelites Prior to the Rise of Islam*, London: Oxford University Press, 1924; H. Hirschberg, *Judische und christliche Lehren im vor-und frühislamischen Arabien*, Krakow: Nakl. Polskiej Akademii Umiejetnosci, 1939; On the influence of Christian groups see especially L. Cheikho, *al-Naṣrāniyya wa-adabuhā bayna ʿarab al-Jāhiliyya*, Beirut: Dar al-Machreq, 1912–23; French trans.: *Le christianisme et la littérature chrétienne en Arabie avant l'Islam*, Beirut: Imprimerie Catholique, 1923; H. Lammens, *La Mecque à la veille de l'Hégire*, Beirut: Imprimerie Catholique, 1924; idem, *Les sanctuaires préislamites dans l'Arabie occidentale*, Beirut: Imprimerie Catholique, 1926; idem, *L'Arabie occidentale avant l'hégire*, Beirut: Imprimerie Catholique, 1928; R. Bell, *The Origin of Islam in Its Christian Environment*; London: Macmillan, 1926; F. Nau, *Les arabes chrétiens de Mésopotamie et Syrie du VIIe au VIIIe siècle*. Paris: Imprimerie Nationale, 1933; H. Charles, *Le christianisme des arabes nomades sur le limes et dans le désert syro-mésopotamien aux alentours de l'hégire*, Paris: Leroux, 1936; J.S. Trimingham, *Christianity among the Arabs in Pre-Islamic Times*, London: Longman, 1979; E. Rabbath, *L'orient chrétien à la veille de l'islam*, Beirut: Université Libanaise, 1980; R. Tardy, *Najrân: Chrétiens d'Arabie avant l'islam*, Beirut: Dar al-Machreq, 1999; I. Shahid, *Byzantium and the Arabs in the Fourth Century*, Washington, DC: Dumbarton Oaks, 1984 (and subsequently *Byzantium and the Arabs in the Fifth Century*, 1989; . . . *in the Sixth Century*, 1995); idem, *Byzantium and the Arabs: Late Antiquity*, Bruxelles: Byzantion, 2005–6.

of Judaism and Christianity in pre-Islamic Arabia.[18] Scholars frequently looked to Muḥammad's Arabian context to explain the idiosyncratic nature of Biblical material in the Qur'ān. The Arabian desert, they often assumed, must have been a sort of refuge for heretics and heterodoxy. Thus the anonymous English translator of Gustav Weil's nineteenth-century work *Biblischen Legenden der Muselmänner* explains:

> Many heresies respecting the Trinity and the Savior, the worship of saints and images, errors on the future state of the soul, etc., had so completely overrun the nominal church of that country that it is difficult to say whether one particle of truth was left in it. More especially the worship of Mary as the mother of God, whom the Marianites [!] considered as a divinity, and to whom the Collyridians even offered a stated sacrifice, was in general practice round Mohammed; and it is as curious as it is sad to observe how this idolatry affected him.[19]

Other scholars, more restrained in their judgment, often came to the conclusion that Muḥammad was influenced by some sort of Jewish Christianity. Sprenger, among others, proposed this idea in the nineteenth century.[20] Rudolph, Hans-Joachim Schoeps, Shlomo Goitein, and Yūsuf Durra al-Ḥaddād did so in the twentieth century,[21] and a number of contemporary

18 W. Rudolph, *Die Abhängigkeit des Qorans von Judentum und Christentum*, Stuttgart: Kohlhammer, 1922. The second chapter is dedicated to the question, "Wie ist die Übernahme jüdischer und christlicher Stoffe durch Muhammed zu denken?"

19 G. Weil, *The Bible, the Koran, and the Talmud or Biblical Legends of the Musselmans*, New York: Harper, 1846, 256. Weil himself was a Jew and presumably would not have thought of pre-Islamic Christianity in this manner.

20 Sprenger bases this conclusion in part on the traditions which relate that Zayd b. Thābit learned Hebrew. He therefore argues that Arab Christians in Muḥammad's day had translated the Bible into Judaeo-Arabic. *Leben*, 1:131. Similar ideas are proposed in Wellhausen, *Reste arabischen Heidentums* (see esp. p. 205), and in the work of the Protestant missionary S. Zwemer, *The Moslem Christ* (New York: American Tract Society, 1912). Cf. the conclusion of Nöldeke (*GdQ1*, 8), that Islam is "eine wesentlich in den Spuren des Christentums gehende Religionsstiftung."

21 Rudolph writes that the particular form of Christianity that influenced the Qur'ān, "wie überhaupt alle orientalischen Christensekten, einen starken jüdischen Einschlag hatte . . . deshalb kann vieles im Qoran stehen, was auf den ersten Blick als zweifellos jüdisch erscheint und doch aus christlicher Quelle geflossen sein kann" (*Abhängigkeit*, p. 27). Elsewhere (p. 51) Rudolph points to the fact that the Qur'ān has essentially nothing to say about the apostles, which he interprets as a reflection of Ebionite ecclesiology. Schoeps includes Islam in his larger survey of Jewish Christianity: *Theologie und Geschichte des Judenchristentums*, Tübingen: Mohr, 1949 (see pp. 334–43). S.D. Goitein describes the sect that influenced Muḥammad from the opposite direction. They were not Jewish Christians but rather Jews heavily influenced by Christianity. See S.D. Goitein, *Jews and Arabs*, New York: Schocken, 1955. Ḥaddād builds his argument on an analysis of the Qur'ān's use of the term Naṣārā, and reports of Nazarene sects in early Christian heresiographies. See Yūsuf Durra al-Ḥaddād, *Al-Injīl fī-l-Qur'ān*, Jounieh: Librairie pauliste, 1982; idem, *Al-Qur'ān da'wā naṣrāniyya*, Jounieh: Librairie pauliste, 1969.

scholars, including Joseph Azzi, François de Blois, Édouard Gallez, and Joachim Gnilka continue to hold to it in different forms today.[22] Still others looked to Manicheanism,[23] or the Qumran community.[24] Tor Andrae, for his part, concluded that Muḥammad was influenced by Nestorian (i.e. East Syrian) Christianity, which he asserts had become prominent in the southern Arabian peninsula due to the Persian triumph over the (Jacobite/monophysite) Ethiopians there.[25] More recently Günter Lüling has argued that the Qur'ān developed from the hymnal of a Christian sect that rejected both the Trinity and the divinity of Christ (holding him instead to be an angel of the divine council), a sect that had fled from Byzantine oppression to Mecca.[26] If these works reach wide-ranging and contradictory conclusions, they have one thing in common. They all work from the basic premise, inherited from Islamic tradition and enshrined by the work of Nöldeke, that the Qur'ān is to be understood in light of the biography Muḥammad.[27]

22 See Abū Mūsā al-Ḥarīrī, *Nabīy al-raḥma*, Beirut: Diyār 'Aql, 1990; idem, *Qass wa-nabīy*, Beirut: n.p., 1979; French trans.: J. Azzi, *Le prêtre et le prophète*, trans. M.S. Garnier, Paris: Maisonneuve et Larose, 2001; F. de Blois, "*Naṣrānī* and *ḥanīf*: Studies on the religious vocabulary of Christianity and Islam," *BSOAS* 65, 2002, 1–30; É. Gallez, *Le messie et son prophète: Aux origines de l'islam*, Versailles: Éditions de Paris, 2005; J. Gnilka, *Die Nazarener und der Koran, Eine Spurensuche*, Freiburg: Herder, 2007. See also A. Yousef, *Le moine de Mahomet: L'entourage judéo-chrétien à La Mecque au VIe siècle*, Monaco: Rocher, 2008.

23 See C. Clemens, "Muhammeds Abhängigkeit von der Gnosis," *Harnack-Ehrung*, Leipzig: Hinrichs, 1921, 249–62; and more recently, M. Gil, "The creed of Abū 'Āmir," *Israel Oriental Studies* 12, 1992, 9–47; F. de Blois, "Elchasai – Manes – Muhammad: Manichäismus und Islam in religionshistorischen Vergleich," *Der Islam* 81, 2004, 31–48; cf. M. Sfar, *Le Coran, la Bible et l'orient ancien*, Paris: Sfar, 1998, esp. 409–25.

24 See C. Rabin, "Islam and the Qumran Sect," in C. Rabin (ed.), *Qumran Studies*, London: Oxford University Press, 1957, 112–30. Rabin writes (p. 128), "To sum up, there can be little doubt that Muhammad had Jewish contacts before coming to Medina; it is highly probable that they were heretical, anti-rabbinic Jews; and a number of terminological and ideological details suggest the Qumran sect."

25 Andrae (*OIC*, 16) shows that the liturgical language of Yemeni Christians at the time of Islamic origins was Syriac. Elsewhere (*OIC*, 29–31) he argues (in less convincing fashion) that Muḥammad originally supported Nestorian/Persian Christianity due to an anti-Ethiopian sentiment among the Arabs (a sentiment Andrae proposes was connected to Abraha's campaign against Mecca).

26 See G. Lüling, *Über den Ur-Qur'ān: Ansätze zur Rekonstruktion vorislamischer christlicher Strophenlieder im Qur'ān*, Erlangen: Lüling, 1974; translated and expanded as *A Challenge to Islam for Reformation*, Delhi: Molital Banarsidass, 2003; idem, *Der christliche Kult an der vorislamischen Kaaba*, Erlangen: Lüling, 1977; idem, *Die Wiederentdeckung des Propheten Muḥammad: eine Kritik am "christlichen" Abendland*, Erlangen: Lüling, 1981; idem, "A new paradigm for the rise of Islam and its consequences for a new paradigm of the history of Israel," *Journal of Higher Criticism* 7, Spring 2000, 23–53; Irfan Shahid, on the other hand, argues that orthodox Chalcedonian Christianity was widespread among the Arabs by the rise of Islam. For example, I. Shahid, *The Martyrs of Najrân: New Documents, Subsidia Hagiographica* 49, Bruxelles: Société des Bollandistes, 1971; cf. idem, *Byzantium and the Arabs*.

27 Tellingly this premise can be found in works by scholars who otherwise disagree entirely. It is evident, for example, in the polemical work of the Christian missionary W. St. Clair

This premise is no less central to works which per se are dedicated not to history but to philological studies of the Qur'ān, such as the sober and scholarly works of Josef Horovitz, *Koranische Untersuchungen* (1926) and Heinrich Speyer (a student of Horovitz in Frankfurt), *Die biblischen Erzählungen im Qoran* (1931). Horovitz introduces the reader to Qur'ānic narratives not according to their appearance in the Qur'ān or their interior chronology (i.e. Adam before Noah before Abraham), but rather according to the supposed moment in Muḥammad's life when he proclaimed them.[28] Speyer, in this same vein, indicates one of Nöldeke's four periods (1st Meccan, 2nd Meccan, 3rd Meccan, Medinan) every time he mentions a Qur'ānic verse.

Meanwhile, the method of reading the Qur'ān through the Prophet's biography was questioned by a handful of scholars. In an article written fifty years after the first volume of *Geschichte des Qorāns*, the Belgian scholar Henri Lammens argues that the biography of Muḥammad is not something that the Islamic community remembered, but rather something that Muslim exegetes developed in order to explain the Qur'ān.[29] The *sīra* is itself a product of exegesis (*tafsīr*) of the Qur'ān, and therefore it can hardly be used to explain the Qur'ān.[30]

Tisdall, who finds in the division of the Qur'ān between Meccan and Medinan passages evidence for the corruption of Muḥammad's character: "The Qur'an is a faithful mirror of the life and character of its author. It breathes the air of the desert, it enables us to hear the battle-cries of the Prophet's followers as they rushed to the onset, it reveals the working of Muhammad's own mind, and shows the gradual declension of his character as he passed from the earnest and sincere though visionary enthusiast into the conscious impostor and open sensualist." W. St. Clair Tisdall, *The Original Sources of the Qur'an*, London: Society for Promoting Christian Knowledge, 1905, 27. It is no less evident in the apologetical work of the Muslim modernist M.H. Haykal, who comments: "I discovered that the most reliable source of information for the biography of Muhammad is the Holy Qur'an. It contains a reference to every event in the life of the Arab Prophet which can serve the investigator as a standard norm and as a guiding light in his analysis of the reports of the various biographies and of the Sunnah." M.H. Haykal, *The Life of Muḥammad*, trans. I.R.A. al-Fārūqī, n.p.: North American Trust, 1976, li–lii.

28 On Horovitz see G. Jäger, "Ein jüdischer Islamwissenschaftler an der Universität Frankfurt und der Hebrew University of Jerusalem," in Hartwig et al. (eds.), *Im vollen Licht der Geschichte*, 117–30.

29 H. Lammens, "Qoran et tradition: Comment fut composé la vie de Mahomet," *Recherches de Science Religieuse* 1 (1910) 25–51; English trans.: "The Koran and tradition: How the life of Muhammad was composed," in Ibn Warraq (ed.), *The Quest for the Historical Muhammad*, Amherst, NY: Prometheus, 2000, (169–87) 181. See also Lammens' work on the material in Islamic tradition regarding the age of the Prophet: "L'Age de Mahomet et la chronologie de la *sīra*," *Journal Asiatique* 17, 1911, 209–50; English trans.: "The age of Muhammad and the chronology of the sira," in Ibn Warraq (ed.), *Quest for the Historical Muhammad*, 188–217; cf. C.H. Becker, "Prinzipielles zu Lammens' Sirastudien," *Der Islam* 4, 1913, 263–9.

30 Lammens, "The Koran and tradition," 179. Describing the *sīra* Lammens writes elsewhere: "Autour du noyau, fourni par l'interprétation du Qoran, sont venues se superposer des couches inconsistantes, amas bizarre d'apports chrétiens et judaïques, amalgamé avec le

One of the few scholars to appreciate this insight was Régis Blachère. In his *Introduction au Coran* Blachère rejects the fundamental precept of the first volume of *Die Geschichte des Qorāns*:

> Il n'apparaît pas inutile de rappeler les principes qui, après Nöldeke et Schwally, semblent devoir inspirer désormais un regroupement acceptable des textes coraniques.
>
> En premier lieu, il faut renoncer pour toujours à l'idée d'un reclassement des sourates qui collerait à la biographie de Mahomet, fondée uniquement sur la Tradition. Seul le Coran pourrait être un guide sûr. . . . Puisque ni la biographie de Mahomet telle que l'ont imaginée les auteurs musulmans, ni celle qu'ont tenté d'établir les historiens occidentaux ne fournit une base sûre ou assez détaillée pour un regroupement chronologique des textes de la Vulgate.[31]

Thus Blachère objects to the manner in which Nöldeke established a chronology of the Qur'ān, that is, on the basis of reports in Islamic tradition. Yet he does not object to the idea of a chronology per se (indeed in the first version of his translation of the Qur'ān the Sūras are arranged according to a chronology). He simply argues that it must be achieved solely on a literary basis, that is, independently from *tafsīr* and *sīra*. This, of course, is problematic, inasmuch as the Qur'ān itself provides little evidence for the Prophet's life.[32]

In a similar fashion the English scholar Richard Bell, and thereafter his student Watt, proposed a modification, but not a rejection, of Nöldeke's method.[33] Bell leaves no doubt that the Qur'ān should be read in the light of the Prophet's biography.[34] He begins his study of the Qur'ān with a

théories dynastico-politiques, avec les rêveries théocratiques, les opinions des écoles de théologie et de droit, avec les tendances de cercles ascétiques et les aspirations de soufisme." H. Lammens, *Fāṭima et les filles de Mahomet*, Rome: Sumptibus pontificii instituti biblici, 1912, 139–40.

31 Blachère, *Introduction au Coran*, 2nd edition, Paris: Maisonneuve, 1959 (1st edition 1947), 252–3. Cf. R. Blachère, *Le problème de Mahomet*, Paris: Presses universitaires de France, 1952.

32 Thus R. Hoyland relates: "Régis Blachère tried to circumvent the problem by using the Qur'ān as his starting point. This text is generally considered to issue from Muhammad himself and in which case it is the key to his thought. But even if this is granted, it does not help us very much, for the Qur'ān makes scant reference to the historical environment in which it arose." R. Hoyland, "Writing the biography of the Prophet Muhammad: Problems and solutions," *History Compass* 5, 2007, (581–602) 584.

33 R. Bell, *Introduction to the Qur'ān*, Edinburgh: Edinburgh University Press, 1963; Watt and Bell, *Bell's Introduction to the Qur'ān*. The latter work is Watt's revision and commentary of the former work. Cf. W.M. Watt, "The dating of the Qur'ān: A review of Richard Bell's Theories," *JRAS* 1957, 46–56.

34 Thus A. Rippin accurately notes: "At this point it is worth noting that the highly praised work of Richard Bell, although supposedly using the biblical methodology consequent on

presentation of the historical context of pre-Islamic Arabia and historical reports of Muḥammad's life.[35] Regarding the chronological order of the Qur'ān, Bell criticizes Nöldeke's conviction that Sūras in their entirety can be placed into certain periods in the Prophet's biography,[36] and notes, like Lammens, the place of (haggadic) exegesis in shaping that biography:

> But in the great bulk of the Qur'ān there is either no reference to historical events, or the events and circumstances to which reference is made are not otherwise known. In regard to such passages there are often differing traditions, and as often as not the stories related to explain them turn out, when critically examined, to be imagined from the passages themselves. . . . There is, in effect, no reliable tradition as to the historical order of the Qur'ān.[37]

In his revision of Bell's views Watt notably edits this point, arguing that such traditions should nevertheless be seen as the fundamental basis for understanding the Qur'ān. After acknowledging the objections of Bell, Watt continues:

> Despite these deficiencies the traditional dating of passages by Muslim scholars is by no means valueless, and indeed forms the basis of all future work. In so far as it is consistent it gives a rough idea of the chronology of the Qur'ān; and any modern attempt to find a basis for dating must by and large be in agreement with the traditional views, even if in one or two points it contradicts them.[38]

The contrast between Bell and his student on this point is significant, inasmuch as later scholars largely follow Watt. The great exception to this

the Documentary Hypothesis, has, in fact, progressed not one iota beyond implicit notions in the traditional accounts of the revelation and the collection of the Qur'ān; he took the ideas of serial revelation and the collection after the death of Muḥammad (the common notions accepted by most Western students of the Qur'ān) and applied them literally to the text of the Qur'ān. However, the primary purpose of employing modern biblical methodologies must be to free oneself from age-old presuppositions and to apply new ones. This Bell did not do; in fact, he worked wholly within the presuppositions of the Islamic tradition." A. Rippin, "Literary analysis of Qur'ān, *tafsīr* and *sīra*: The methodologies of John Wansbrough," in R.C. Martin (ed.), *Approaches to Islam in Religious Studies*, Tucson: University of Arizona Press, 1985, (151–63) 156; reprint: *The Qur'ān and Its Interpretive Tradition*, ed. A. Rippin, Aldershot: Ashgate, 2001.

35 Bell, *Introduction to the Qur'ān*, 1–36; Watt and Bell, *Bell's Introduction to the Qur'ān*, 1–39. In the *Origin of Islam in Its Christian Environment*, Bell argues that the fundamental dynamic in the Qur'ān is Muḥammad's gradual discovery of Jewish and Christian teachings during his career. Bell, *Origin*, 68–9.

36 Regarding which see A. Rippin, "Reading the Qur'ān with Richard Bell," *JAOS* 112, 1992, (639–47) 643.

37 Bell, *Introduction to the Qur'ān*, 100.

38 Watt and Bell, *Bell's Introduction to the Qur'ān*, 109.

trend is John Wansbrough,[39] who argues trenchantly in *Qur'ānic Studies* that the stories which exegetes tell to explain the Qur'ān are not historical records, but rather the literary product of a community developing a salvation history in an environment charged with sectarian rivalry. The stories that involve Muḥammad, no less than the stories that involve Abraham, Moses, or Jesus, are literary, not historical.[40]

Now most critical scholars acknowledge that story-telling is a salient element in classical Qur'ānic exegesis. For Wansbrough, however, this acknowledgment leads to fundamentally different conclusions about the Qur'ānic text. First, the idea of a chronology of the Qur'ān according to Muḥammad's life is by his reading spurious, since the stories that would link a certain passage of the Qur'ān to a certain moment in that life have no historical authority. Second, and even more far-reaching, *tafsīr* literature in general, *even when it is read with a critical method*, cannot provide the scholar with privileged information on what the Qur'ān originally meant.[41] Instead,

39 The literary approach of Toshihiko Izutsu, followed more recently by Daniel Madigan, might also be considered an exception to the trend. Izutsu concerns himself only with an analysis of the language and semantics of the Qur'ān, setting aside the question of its relationship with the *sīra* for the sake of his method. In this, however, Izutsu provides no fundamental challenge to the dominant method of reading the Qur'ān through *sīra*, but rather frames his work as an alternative – but not contradictory – approach to the Qur'ānic text. See T. Izutsu, *The Structure of Ethical Terms in the Koran: A Study in Semantics*, Tokyo: Keio, 1959; idem, *God and Man in the Koran: Semantics of the Koranic Weltanschauung*, Tokyo: Keio, 1964; D. Madigan, *The Qur'ān's Self-Image: Writing and Authority in Islam's Scripture*, Princeton: Princeton University Press, 2001.

40 In this same line Patricia Crone argues that the fundamental process in the development of *tafsīr* is not remembering but story-telling: "Classical exegetes such as Ṭabarī may omit the story, having developed hermeneutical interests of a more sophisticated kind; but even when they do so, the story underlies the interpretation advanced. It is clear, then, that much of the classical Muslim understanding of the Qur'ān rests on the work of popular story tellers, such story tellers being the first to propose particular historical contexts for particular verses." P. Crone, *Meccan Trade and the Rise of Islam*, Princeton: Princeton University Press, 1987, 216. To this argument Uri Rubin responds that the exegetical elements of the *sīra* are secondary efforts to connect earlier stories about the Prophet to the material in the Qur'ān. See U. Rubin, *The Eye of the Beholder*, Princeton: Darwin, 1995, esp. pp. 226–33. Similar is the approach of M. Schöller, *Exegetisches Denken und Prophetenbiographie: Eine quellenkritische Analyse der Sīra-Überlieferung zu Muḥammads Konflikt mit den Juden*, Wiesbaden: Harrassowitz, 1998. It is also worth noting that Watt himself wrote a short work in response to Wansbrough and Crone, intended to show that the evidence in the Qur'ān itself verifies the basic outline of the *sīra*. See his *Muḥammad's Mecca: History in the Quran*, Edinburgh: Edinburgh University Press, 1988.

41 Noting the argument of Joseph Schacht that legal traditions attributed to Muḥammad are in fact the products of medieval Muslim scholars, Wansbrough comments, "It seems at least doubtful whether for exegetical (*tafsīr*) traditions a different origin can be claimed." *QS*, 179. Schacht himself makes this point forcefully in "A revaluation of Islamic traditions," *JRAS* 1949, 142–54; reprint: *Quest for the Historical Muhammad*, ed. Ibn Warraq, 358–67.

tafsīr literature is a remarkably successful intellectual enterprise to develop original and distinctive religious traditions in the face of competition from (above all) Jews and Christians. It is this second conclusion that is particularly important for the present work. I will argue that the Qur'ān – from a critical perspective at least – should not be read in conversation with what came after it (*tafsīr*) but with what came before it (Biblical literature).

In other respects, however, this work diverges from Wansbrough's theories. Wansbrough doubts that the Qur'ān had a unitary form before the 'Abbāsid period (instead of an Ur-text of the Qur'ān he imagines that various "prophetical *logoi*" first came together as a book in this period). In the present work, on the other hand, I have no concern for this question. Instead my concern is how the canonical text of the Qur'ān might best be read.

The answer to that question offered by the present work conflicts with the dominant scholarly method today. With some exceptions,[42] scholars in the field today continue to explain the Qur'ān by means of a critical reading of *tafsīr*. By dividing the Qur'ān according to Muḥammad's life they hope to find a historical context that will illuminate the passage at hand. By sorting through the traditions in *tafsīr* they hope to spot a valid tradition that preserves ancient material. This approach to the text, as Wansbrough points out, is essentially that of medieval Muslim scholars.[43]

In this regard the example of Angelika Neuwirth, a student of Anton Spitaler (the student of Bergsträsser and Pretzl in Munich), is particularly

42 Notably G. Hawting in various publications including *The Idea of Idolatry and the Emergence of Islam*, Cambridge: Cambridge University Press, 1999; "Qur'ānic exegesis and history," in J.D. McAuliffe, B. Walfish and J. Goering (eds.), *With Reverence for the Word: Medieval Scriptural Exegesis in Judaism, Christianity and Islam*, Oxford: Oxford University Press, 2003, 408–21; see also the article by J. Chabbi, "Histoire et tradition sacrée: la biographie impossible de Mahomet," *Arabica* 43, 1996, 189–205. Particularly noteworthy are the remarks of Fred Donner in his opening essay in the recent *Cambridge Companion to the Qur'ān*: "Taken together, these two facts – that the Qur'ān text crystallised at an early date, and that the *sīra* reports are sometimes exegetical – suggest that we must consider the relationship of the Qur'ān to its context in a manner that reverses the procedure normally adopted when studying the relationship of a text to its context. Rather than relying on the *sīra* reports about a presumed historical context to illuminate the meaning of the Qur'ān text, we must attempt to infer from the Qur'ānic text what its true historical context might have been, and in this way check on the historicity of the various reports in the *sīra*." F. Donner, "The historical context," in J.D. McAuliffe (ed.), *The Cambridge Companion to the Qur'ān*, Cambridge: Cambridge University Press, 2007, (23–39) 34.

43 On Nöldeke, Wansbrough comments: "His historical evaluation of traditional data did not bring him much beyond the position established and occupied by Sūyūṭī 400 years earlier." To this he adds: "Modifications of Nöldeke-Schwally by Bell and Blachère, respectively, exhibit refinement of detail but no critical assessment of the principle involved, namely, whether a chronology/topology of revelation is even feasible." *QS*, 126.

illuminating. Neuwirth argues that the Qur'ān should be studied for its literary forms and its internal indications of a community of believers, not on the basis of *tafsīr*.[44] Despite this, Neuwirth bases her work on the traditional division of the Qur'ān into Meccan and Medinan periods of Muḥammad's life.[45] Neuwirth, like Blachère, looks for evidence of a chronological development within the text.[46] In practice, however, her division of Sūras between Meccan and Medinan is essentially that proposed by Nöldeke in the middle of the nineteenth century. Indeed, in a recent publication Prof. Neuwirth laments that more scholars have not returned to Nöldeke's chronology, which she names the "foundation for any historical Qur'ān research."[47]

44 See, e.g., A. Neuwirth, "Qur'ānic literary structure revisited," in S. Leder (ed.), *Story-Telling in the Framework of Non-Fictional Arabic Literature*, Wiesbaden: Harrassowitz, 1998, 388–420; eadem, "Qur'ān and history–a disputed relationship: Some reflections on Qur'ānic history and history in the Qur'ān," *Journal of Qur'anic Studies* 5, 2003, 1–18.

45 Notice the title of her first book: *Studien zur Komposition der mekkanischen Suren*, Berlin: de Gruyter, 1981 (2nd edition 2007). See more recently her "Structural, linguistic and literary features," in McAuliffe (ed.), *Cambridge Companion to the Qur'ān*, 97–113. More recently Neuwirth has begun a major project to establish a critical edition of the Qur'ān with the evidence of manuscripts, a project once imagined by none other than Bergsträsser and Pretzl (along with the Australian Arthur Jeffery). I understand that the critical edition will be produced according to a supposed chronology of the Qur'ān, i.e. "Meccan" Sūras will be produced first. The project has been announced as *Corpus Coranicum: Edition und Kommentar des Korans* (the name *corpus coranicum* coming from Pretzl's description of the initial project; see O. Pretzl, *Die Fortführung des Apparatus Criticus zum Koran. Sitzungsberichte der Bayerischen Akademie der Wissenschaften 1934 (Heft 5)*, Munich: Verlag der Bayerischen Akademie der Wissenschaften, 1934, 12). For more details on the project and the proposed format of the online text see M. Marx, "Ein Koran-Forschungsprojekt in der Tradition der Wissenschaft des Judentums: Zur Programmatik des Akademienvorhabens *Corpus Coranicum*," in Hartwig et al. (eds.), *Im vollen Licht der Geschichte*, 41–53; and http://www.geschkult.fu-berlin.de/e/semiarab/arabistik/projekte/index.html. This project was in part the focus of a front page *Wall Street Journal* article: A. Higgins, "The Lost Archive," *Wall Street Journal*, January 12, 2008, A1.

46 She argues that Meccan Sūras are distinguished by liturgical concerns, while Medinan Sūras are distinguished by political and social concerns, along with the rejection of Judaism for a Meccan, Abrahamic cult. "Die Neureflexion des Koran als Diskursabfolge hat gegenüber der klassischen Periodisierung den Vorteil, dass sie nicht auf einer linearen Vorstellung von einem Informationszuwachs der einen Figur des Propheten und einer stilistischen Entwicklung der Texte aufbaut, sondern die Übermittler-Hörer-Kommunikation in ihrer Bedeutung erkennt und den Koran als einen Kommunikationsprozess zu beschreiben unternimmt." Neuwirth, "Zur Archäologie einer Heiligen Schrift: Überlegungen zum Koran vor seiner Kompilation," in C. Burgmer (ed.), *Streit um den Koran*, Berlin: Schiler, 2004, (82–97) 97.

47 "That not only critical analysis of previously formulated positions was abandoned, but also that even the foundation for any historical Qur'ān research was relinquished, namely the chronology of the suras elaborated by Nöldeke, has to be seen retrospectively as a perilous regression." "Im vollen Licht der Geschichte: Die Wissenschaft des Judentums und die Anfänge der kritischen Koranforschung," in Hartwig et al. (eds.), *Im vollen Licht der Geschichte* (25–39) 34 (quotation from English trans., p. 19).

The dominance of this perspective on the Qur'ān is particularly salient in the work of Karen Armstrong. One of the most popular authors on Islam,[48] Armstrong is often portrayed as a leading authority in the field,[49] even if she knows little if any Arabic (as suggested by the transliteration of Qur'ān as Qu'ran throughout [the second edition of!] her work on Muḥammad). Yet precisely because of this her work is an interesting case study, since it is entirely dependent on secondary sources in the field. It is noteworthy, then, that Armstrong accepts, apparently without questioning, the traditional notion of connecting individual passages with Muḥammad's biography. Regarding *al-ḍuḥā* (93), for example, she writes:

> We know very little about Muḥammad's early life. The Qu'ran [sic] gives us the most authoritative account of his experience before he received his prophetic vocation when he was forty years old: "Did he not find thee an orphan and shelter thee? Did he not find thee erring and guide thee? Did he not find thee needy and suffice thee? [Q 93.6–9; Arberry]"[50]

In fact, the Qur'ān never identifies the speaker or the intended audience of these questions. According to Islamic tradition, however, God is here speaking to Muḥammad. But certainly these verses could be something else altogether, such as the Qur'ān's exhortation to believers generally to be charitable to orphans ("Therefore do not oppress the orphan," Q 93.10) and to the needy ("and do not reject the needy," Q 93.11). In fact, it might be argued that the powerful moral argument of this Sūra, that mercy should be shown because God is merciful, is nullified when the reader imagines that the Qur'ān intends only Muḥammad here.

Armstrong explains *al-masad* (111) in a similar fashion:

> Abu Lahab's wife, who fancied herself as a poet, liked to shout insulting verses at the Prophet when he passed by. On one occasion she hurled an armful of prickly firewood in his path. It was probably at this time that Sūra 111 was revealed: "Perish the hands of Abu Lahab, and perish he! His wealth avails him not, neither what he has earned; he shall roast at a flaming fire; and his wife, the carrier of the firewood; upon her neck a rope of palm fibre [Arberry's translation]."[51]

48 On July 5, 2007, Karen Armstrong's *Muhammad: A Biography of the Prophet* (2nd edition, London: Phoenix, 2001 (1st edition 1993)) was ranked #8,481 of all books at amazon.com.

49 She was, for example, one of the few scholars called on to provide the basic commentary for the monumental Public Broadcasting (USA) special on Muḥammad broadcast on Sept. 25, 2002.

50 Armstrong, *Muḥammad*, 72.

51 Ibid., 130.

Read by itself *al-masad* hardly supports Armstrong's explanation. The Qur'ān never identifies Abū Lahab, "Father of Flame," as a historical figure. The phrase might in fact be an allusion to anyone who is doomed to hell (regarding which see Ch. 2, CS 13).[52] Similarly the reference to his wife as a carrier of firewood (*ḥaṭab*) seems to be a rather artful play on the theme of damnation. The rich, sinful woman will not carry her wealth to the afterlife (Q 111.2) but rather be dragged (Q 111.5) by her neck, as she carries instead firewood that will light the flames of her own punishment (Q 111.4). Nevertheless in *tafsīr* this passage is explained through the introduction of a historical figure named Abū Lahab, a relative of, and ultimately an antagonist to, the Prophet. His antagonism is encouraged by a spiteful wife, who is reported to have harassed Muḥammad by throwing firewood in his path. Armstrong adds the detail that the firewood was prickly.[53]

With Armstrong the reader has the sense that she has chosen the model of reading the Qur'ān through *tafsīr* without any serious reflection. With a second influential scholar, Muhammad Abdel Haleem, the results are the same but the tone is quite different. Abdel Haleem is professor of Qur'ānic Studies at the School of Oriental and African Studies of the University of London, and founder of the *Journal of Qur'ānic Studies.* His book *Understanding the Qur'ān* has become a standard resource for undergraduate instruction on the Qur'ān.[54] Therein it appears that Abdel Haleem, like Armstrong, inevitably views the Qur'ān through the lens of *tafsīr*.

This is seen, for example, in his commentary on *al-baqara* (2.223a), which reads: "Your women are your field. Go into your field as you wish." Abdel Haleem explains: "When the Muslims migrated from Mecca the men found the women of Medina bashful and only willing to sleep with their husbands lying on their side. So the Muslim men asked the Prophet if there was anything wrong with such sexual positions."[55] It perhaps goes without saying there is nothing in the Qur'ānic verses that connects this verse to the bashfulness, or the sexual habits, of the women in Medina.[56]

52 On this point cf. *KU*, 78, 88.

53 Almost all of Armstrong's work reflects this method. For example, she explains Q 96.1–5 with the story of Muḥammad and Mt. Ḥirā' (p. 83), Q 74.1–5 with the story of Muḥammad being wrapped up in a blanket after the first revelation (pp. 84–5, 91), and Q 53.19–26 and 22.51 with the story of the Satanic Verses (pp. 115–6), etc.

54 M. Abdel Haleem, *Understanding the Qur'an*, London: Tauris, 1999. See more recently the *Arabic–English Dictionary of Qur'ānic Usage*, ed. E.M. Badawi and M.A. Haleem, Leiden: Brill, 2008.

55 Abdel Haleem, *Understanding the Qur'an*, 44.

56 In a similar fashion Abdel Haleem argues that the Qur'ān's phrase in *al-baqara* (2) 109, "Forgive and pardon until God gives His command," is God's instruction to the Muslims in Mecca when they were facing persecution from pagans (*Understanding the Qur'ān*, 61). This is a strange argument, since the verse begins with a reference to the People of the Book (presumably Jews or Christians, but not pagans). More to the point, there is no detail in this verse itself, or any of the verses around it, that would give it the historical context that Abdel Haleem imagines.

With Armstrong and Abdel Haleem we have returned to a state that might be described as pre-Nöldeke. They assume, like Nöldeke, that *tafsīr* is the key that unlocks the Qur'ān's meaning, but unlike Nöldeke they offer little critical reading of *tafsīr*. In fact, if their works reflect a bias (namely modernism) that would not be found among the classical *mufassirūn*, their method is by no means different than that of medieval Muslim scholars.

Yet even those scholars who propose radical re-readings of the Qur'ān often rely on the presuppositions of *tafsīr*. The Lebanese scholar Joseph Azzi (also known under the pen name Abū Mūsā al-Ḥarīrī)[57] argues that Muḥammad was actually the disciple of Waraqa b. Nawfal (the cousin of Muḥammad's first wife Khadīja who, in the *sīra*, confirms Muḥammad's original revelation), by his view a Judaeo-Christian.[58] Such ideas reflect a radically (and for Muslims, unacceptable) different view of the Qur'ān. Yet Azzi still relies on the method of reading the Qur'ān through Muḥammad's life that is so central to *tafsīr*. He even cites Nöldeke's chronology of the Qur'ān as justification for his novel thesis:

> Cependant, si nous nous référons aux recherches des orientalistes, notamment à celles du professeur Nöldeke, qui a classé les sourates du Coran par ordre chronologique, nous découvrons une donnée extrêmement important et significative. Nous nous rendons compte que les enseignements du Coran de La Mecque sont les mêmes que ceux de l'Évangile des Hébreux.[59]

What is to account for the dominance of this method? In certain cases it seems to be connected with a particular religious orientation, but this hardly explains the dependence of supposedly secular scholars on *tafsīr*. To some extent this may be a case of academic inertia. The method of reading the Qur'ān through *tafsīr* has been taught by almost every western scholar, from Nöldeke to Neuwirth, and to doubt it might seem impudent. But it seems to me that this method is above all favored simply because it is useful, both

57 See Al-Ḥarīrī, *Qass wa-nabīy*; trans.: J. Azzi, *Le Prêtre et le Prophète*.

58 See Ibn Hishām, *Sīrat Rasūl Allāh*, ed. F. Wüstenfeld, Göttingen: Dieterich, 1858–60, 153–4; English trans.: Ibn Isḥāq, *The Life of Muḥammad*, trans. A. Guillaume, Oxford: Oxford University Press, 1955, 107. According to Azzi, however, Waraqa was actually the priest (*qass*) of a Jewish Christian community in Mecca, and the translator of the Hebrew Gospel of the Nazoraeans, which he incorporated into the Qur'ān. Nazoraeans (Ναζωραῖοι) is the name used by Epiphanius (d. 403), Theodoret of Cyrrhus (d. ca. 458) and John of Damascus (d. 749) for a Jewish-Christian sect that existed in the early Christian centuries in Palestine and the Decapolis. Azzi connects these references with the Qur'ānic term *naṣārā*. De Blois takes a similar approach in "*Naṣrānī* and *ḥanīf*," 1–17.

59 Azzi, *Le Prêtre et le prophète*, 121; Arabic: *Qass wa-nabīy*, 92. The more recent work of J. Chabbi, *Le Coran décrypté: Figures bibliques en Arabie* (Paris: Fayard, 2008), is similar in method. Chabbi pursues her (otherwise novel and scholarly) study of the Biblical background to the Qur'ān with the historical context of Muḥammad always in mind.

to apologetical scholars such as Armstrong and Abdel Haleem and polemical scholars such as Azzi. Without the library of *tafsīrs*, scholars might feel themselves in a sort of intellectual wilderness, with no orienting landmarks to guide their thought.

The remarks of Watt are revealing in this regard. On the one hand Watt seems to recognize that the traditions which match certain segments of the Qur'ān with elements in the Prophet's biography are the creation of *tafsīr*. Thus in discussing the question of whether *al-qalam* (or *'alaq*; 96) or *al-muddaththar* (74) was first revealed, he comments:

> In fact neither of these may be the first extant revelation, and the stories may be only the guesses of later Muslim scholars, since there are grounds for selecting each as first. Sura 96 begins with "recite", and this is appropriate for a book which is called "the recitation" or Qur'ān; and sura 74 after addressing Muḥammad has the words "rise and warn" – an appropriate beginning to the work of a messenger or warner.[60]

Despite this admission, Watt insists that the *tafsīr* method of dating the Qur'ān according to the Prophet's life is "by no means valueless, and indeed forms the basis of all future work."[61] Apparently what Watt means is that the traditional dating should be used because it is helpful to the scholar. But what if it is wrong?

What if, as John Burton puts it, "Exegesis aspiring to become history, gave us *sīra*"?[62] Indeed biographical reports on Muḥammad regularly serve the function of explaining unclear passages in the Qur'ān. The story of the Yemeni king Abraha's invasion of Mecca with one (!) elephant seems to be an exegesis on *al-fīl* (105).[63] The story of the angels who removed Muḥammad's heart from his body and washed it in a golden basin of melted snow seems to be an exegesis on *al-sharḥ* (94) 1–2.[64] The story of Muḥammad's first revelation on Mt. Ḥirā', according to which he saw the angel Gabriel as a massive form on the horizon, and then demanded that Khadīja wrap him in a blanket, seems to be an exegesis on *al-'alaq* (96) 1–5, *al-najm* (53) 1–18, and *al-muddaththar* (74.1; cf. 73.1).[65] The story of Muḥammad's night journey to Jerusalem seems to be an exegesis on *al-isrā* (17) 1 and so forth.[66] Now

60 Watt and Bell, *Bell's Introduction to the Qur'an*, 109.

61 Ibid.

62 J. Burton, "Law and exegesis: The penalty for adultery in Islam," in G.R. Hawting and A.A. Shareef (eds.), *Approaches to the Qur'an*, London: Routledge, 1993, (269–84) 271.

63 Ibn Hishām, *Sīrat Rasūl Allāh*, 29–42 (trans., 21–30).

64 Ibid., 105–7 (trans., 71–3).

65 Ibid., 152–4 (trans., 105–7).

66 Ibid., 263–71 (trans., 181–7). There is, of course, more that went into the Prophet's biography. The story of Mt. Ḥirā', as indicated by Waraqa's declaration that Muḥammad has received the *nāmūs* (cf. Gk νόμος, "the law"), is marked by a larger religious topos of the prophet receiving the revealed law on a mountain top, etc.

such traditions, it goes without saying, can be a proper guide for a pious reading of the Qur'ān. But to the critical scholar they should suggest that *tafsīr* is a remarkable literary achievement to be appreciated in its own right. These *tafsīr* traditions do not preserve the Qur'ān's ancient meaning, and to insist otherwise does a disservice both to *tafsīr* and to the Qur'ān.

The standard response to this perspective (much like Watt's reproach of Bell) is that there is no need to throw out the baby with the bath water. The works of the *mufassirūn* can still connect us with the time of the Qur'ān's origins. True, the interpretive traditions therein were affected by later legal, mystical, sectarian, and theological currents that flowed through the early Islamic community. Yet at a fundamental level the historical record is intact. All that is needed is a good critical reading to separate the exegesis from the history.

The problem with this view is that the *mufassirūn*, even the earliest *mufassirūn*, are unable to understand basic elements of the Qur'ān. Two examples might illuminate this point. First is the case of the disconnected letters (Ar. *al-aḥruf al-muqaṭṭa'a* or *fawātiḥ al-suwar*) that appear at the opening of 29 Sūras.[67] These letters seem to play an important role in the organization of the Qur'ān. For example, every consonantal form in the Arabic alphabet is represented at least once by these letters, while no form is used for more than one letter.[68] Meanwhile, Sūras that begin with the same or similar letters are grouped together, even when that grouping means violating the larger ordering principle of the Qur'ān (from longer to shorter Sūras).[69] Yet the classical *mufassirūn* do not know any of this. They do not demonstrate any memory of the role these letters played in the Qur'ān's organization. Instead their commentary reflects both confusion and creative speculation.[70]

67 On this topic see, e.g., A. Jeffery, "The mystic letters of the Qur'ān," *MW* 14, 1924, 247–60; J.A. Bellamy, "The mysterious letters of the Qur'ān: Old abbreviations of the *Basmalah*," *JAOS* 93, 1973, 267–85; M. Seale, *Qur'ān and Bible*, London: Helm, 1978, 38–60; The most impressive treatment of this topic, I believe, is the concise analysis of A. Welch, "Ḳur'ān," *EI*², 5:412–4.

68 Thus, e.g., *al-aḥruf al-muqaṭṭa'a* include ي but not ب, ت or ث; ح but not ج or خ; ر but not ز; س but not ش; ص but not ض; ط but not ظ; and ع but not غ.

69 Thus Sūras 13–15, which are part of the *a.l.(m.)r.* group of Q 10–15, are shorter than Q 16; Sūras 40 and 43, which are part of the *ḥ.m.* group of Q 40–6, are longer than Q 39.

70 Abū Ja'far al-Ṭabarī, for example, opens his discussion of this topic with the admission that "the interpreters of the Qur'ān differ over the meaning" of the disconnected letters. He then reports over fourteen different interpretations of these letters, and offers up to five traditions for each interpretation. These interpretations include that the letters represent different names for the Qur'ān, or names of different Sūras, or names for God, or a mystical way in which God makes a vow upon His own divinity, or that the letters are each abbreviations for different words, or a method of counting camels, or that each letter has a numerical value, thereby recording the length that certain nations will last, or that the letters are simply a mystery known only to God. In all, Ṭabarī's discussion of the first three disconnected letters takes over nine pages in the standard Beirut edition of his *tafsīr*. He concludes this discussion with his own view, that each letter is an abbreviation for more than one word. This is

It seems to me unlikely, to say the least, that the *mufassirūn* are reliable preservers of an unbroken chain of Qur'ānic interpretation, or that they remember perfectly the time and place and reason why individual verses were revealed, and yet at the same time totally fail to understand these letters. Watt's view, after all, stands on the premise that the *mufassirūn* might have forgotten obscure matters, and their presentation of controversial legal or sectarian matters might reflect certain biases, but in a fundamental way they have remembered the original context and meaning of Qur'ānic verses. Presumably, then, we should discover this sort of fundamental knowledge on matters that are neither obscure nor controversial. Yet when we turn to the disconnected letters we find nothing of the sort.

What is particularly illuminating about this case is that the letters themselves do not provide the sort of references that would allow an exegete to develop a haggadic interpretation. From the references in *al-fīl* (105), for example, one could write a story about Abraha's invasion. From the references in *al-masad* (111) one could write a story about Abū Lahab and his malevolent wife. But the letters provide no material for the storyteller to work with. So it is not that the *mufassirūn* somehow remembered the original context and meaning of *al-fīl* (105) and *al-masad* (111) but forgot the meaning of the letters. It is that the *mufassirūn* have stories for *al-fīl* and *al-masad*, but not for the letters.

The case of the Ṣābi'ūn seems to be similar. On two occasions the Qur'ān includes the Ṣābi'ūn among four groups (including also the believers, the Jews and the Christians) who "need have no fear, for they will not be sad" (Q 2.62; 5.69; cf. 22.17). On one occasion the Qur'ān mentions that these groups "have a reward with their Lord" (Q 2.62). In other words, the Qur'ān seems to be identifying the four groups who will be saved. This report is likewise no minor matter. If the Prophet announced such a thing it is hard to believe that the community would have forgotten it (while at the same time remembering the smallest details of other passages). In fact, the *mufassirūn* are totally incapable of remembering exactly what the Prophet said about the Ṣābi'ūn. Their proposals, as in the case of the disconnected letters, are matters of speculation and logical deduction.[71]

a perfectly logical deduction, since it explains why the Qur'ān might use a letter instead of a word (although Ṭabarī does not attempt to identify which words are intended by each letter). Abū Ja'far al-Ṭabarī, *Jāmi' al-bayān fī ta'wīl al-Qur'ān*, ed. Muḥammad Bayḍūn, Beirut: Dār al-Fikr, 1408/1988. (The pagination of this edition follows the 30 equal-part division of the Qur'ān, although it is bound in 15 volumes. References in the present work are to part:page, 1:86–96, on Q 2.2).

71 Ṭabarī records eight different opinions on this matter. The Ṣābi'ūn are either those who have left a religion, or those who have no religion, or a group "between" the Zoroastrians and the Jews, or a tribe in the Sudan, or a religion based in Mesopotamia that teaches the belief in one God but has no prophets and no book, or a religion that teaches the worship of angels, or a group of believers who pray in the direction of Mecca and use the Psalms as their scripture, or simply a group from the People of the Book. In the end Ṭabarī does

Thus it seems that when the *mufassirūn* began their work, they were dealing with a text that was fundamentally unfamiliar to them.[72] To this end Lawrence Conrad comments:

> Even words that would have been of great and immediate importance in the days of Muḥammad himself are argued over and guessed at, sometimes at great length, and with no satisfactory result. We might expect that comparisons of the work that proceeded in different regions would show that the scholars of the Ḥijāz had a better record in arriving at likely or compelling solutions, since their own forefathers, the first Muslims, would have known the truth of the matter and passed it down through their descendents. But this is not the case. Confusion and uncertainty seems to be the rule, and at the centre of it all, is a written text in which textual anomalies could not be solved, and for which oral tradition offered no help, and for which clarifying context was unknown.[73]

not even attempt a solution. Ṭabarī, 1:318–21. Meanwhile, the nature of the opinions he reports is telling. The first two proposals ("those who have left a religion, or those who have no religion") are related to the meaning of the Arabic root *ṣ.b.'*, "to leave" and hence "to leave a religion." Some traditions relate that the Quraysh called Muḥammad *al-ṣābi'* for leaving their pagan religion. See *AEL*, 1640, b–c. The tradition on Mesopotamia is presumably inspired by the Mandaeans, or the Christians of St. John, of Southern Iraq. They may indeed be the group whom the Qur'ān intends, if Ṣābi'ūn is seen as a transformation of *ṣābighūn*, i.e. "the baptizers," since baptism is a central part of Mandaean religious life. This explanation is proposed by Nöldeke (*Mandäische Grammatik*, Halle: Buchhandlung des Waisenhauses, 1875, 235) but doubted by Horovitz (*KU*, 121–2). Cf. more recently T. Fahd, "Ṣābi'a," *EI*[2], 8:675–8; and the article of F. de Blois ("Sabians," *EQ*, 4:511–12). As for the tradition related to the Psalms, in *al-ḥajj* (22) 17 the Qur'ān identifies six religious groups: believers, Jews, the Ṣābi'ūn, the Christians, the Zoroastrians (*majūs*), and the pagans. Of these the *mufassirūn* were unable to identify only the Ṣābi'ūn. The Qur'ān also refers to three different scriptures: the Tawrāt, the Injīl, and the Psalms (*al-zabūr*; e.g. Q 4.163; 17.55; 21.105). Of these the *mufassirūn* knew that the Tawrāt belonged to the Jews and the Injīl to the Christians, but they were left with the Psalms. It made perfect sense, therefore, to associate the unknown scripture, the Psalms, with the unknown religious group, the Ṣābi'ūn.

72 Accordingly Jeffery reflects, regarding the foreign vocabulary in the Qur'ān: "Now it is conceivable that there may have been correct tradition from the Prophet himself in many cases as to the interpretation of some of the strange words that meet us in the Qur'ān, but if so, it is evident that this tradition was soon lost, for by the time the classical exegetes came to compile their works there was a bewildering entanglement of elaborate lines of conflicting tradition as to the meaning of these words, all emanating from the same small circle of the Prophet's immediate Companions." Jeffery, *FV*, 3.

73 L. Conrad, "Qur'ānic studies: A historian's perspective," in M. Kropp (ed.), *Results of Contemporary Research on the Qur'ān* , Beirut: Ergon, 2007, (9–15) 13. After analyzing *tafsīr* on *quraysh* (106), Patricia Crone comes to a similar conclusion: "It is thus clear that the exegetes had no better knowledge of what this sura meant than we have today. What they are offering is not their recollection or what Muḥammad had in mind when he recited these verses but, on the contrary, so many guesses based on the verses themselves. The original meaning of these verses was unknown to them." Crone, *Meccan Trade*, 210.

Thus it seems that the *mufassirūn* were not involved in a process of remembering, but rather in a process of logical speculation. In this they may serve as inspiration for scholars of the Qur'ān today, inasmuch as we are involved in precisely the some process. Yet once it is recognized that a gap exists between the Qur'ān and the *mufassirūn*, then the *mufassirūn* no longer appear in a particularly privileged position. In fact, scholars today might with some justification feel themselves better qualified than the *mufassirūn* to study the original meaning of Qur'ānic passages. On the one hand the *mufassirūn*'s freedom to speculate was limited (to various degrees) by dogmatic and sectarian considerations. On the other hand they had considerably fewer resources. The *mufassirūn* as a rule did not know the other languages of the Qur'ān's historical context, that is, Syriac, Aramaic, Greek, Hebrew, Ethiopic, Pahlavi, and Ancient North/South Arabian. They were not familiar with the religious texts of those languages. They did not have studies in front of them such as Speyer's *Die biblischen Erzählungen im Qoran* or Jeffery's *Foreign Vocabulary of the Qur'ān*.[74]

It is these considerations that offered me the inspiration and confidence to pursue the present work. The task thereof is twofold. First, I hope to establish the nature of the Qur'ān/*tafsīr* relationship, demonstrating that *tafsīr* is the product of a society removed from the period of Islamic origins, and of scholars with their own intellectual and sectarian concerns. Second, and more importantly, I hope to demonstrate how the Qur'ān can be fruitfully read in the light of Biblical literature. As such my interest in the present work is explicitly literary and not historical. I do not ask questions of either the authorship or the redaction of the Qur'ān. In this the present work is unlike those works commonly labeled revisionist. It is more like the recent work edited by John Reeves: *Bible and Qur'ān: Essays in Scriptural Intertextuality*.[75] Like Reeves, my interest is not a historical deconstruction of the Qur'ān, but rather an appreciation of the canonical text of the Qur'ān in the light of Biblical literature.[76]

74 Jeffery himself makes a similar point elsewhere: "Modern scholars, however, have the advantage of knowledge of the environment of sixth century Arabia, particularly its cultural and religious environment, and the use of tools of comparative linguistics and comparative religion, which were not available to earlier generations." A. Jeffery, *The Qur'ān as Scripture*, New York: Moore, 1952, 7.

75 Atlanta: Society of Biblical Literature, 2003.

76 In addition to the aforementioned work of Reeves, some precedent to the present work is found in works such as U. Bonanate's *Bibbia e Corano: I Testi Sacri Confrontati*, Turin: Bollati Boringhieri, 1995. Therein Bonanate seeks above all to identify themes which appear in both the Qur'ān and the Bible. His concern, therefore, is less with the textual relationship of the Qur'ān and Biblical literature (as evidenced by his exclusion of non-canonical Biblical writings), and more with a comparison of the individual books as sacred scripture. Similar are C.M. Guzzetti, *Bibbia e Corano: Un Confronto Sinottico*, Cinisello Balsamo: Edizioni San Paolo, 1995; and S.J. Wimmer and S. Leimgruber, *Von Adam bis Muhammad. Bibel und Koran im Vergleich*, Stuttgart: Katholisches Bibelwerk, 2005.

The format of the present work

The present work is built around the following chapter, which consists of case studies on individual Qur'ānic passages. Each case study is divided into three sections: Qur'ān, interpreters, subtext. In the first section I present the passage at hand on the basis of Qur'ānic material alone. In the second section I describe the attempts of modern translators and classical *mufassirūn* to understand that passage. In the third section I analyze that passage in the light of the Qur'ānic subtext, that is, the larger literary and religious tradition in which the Qur'ān is participating. Thereby I hope to show how the Qur'ān itself depends on the reader's knowledge of that subtext for the expression of its own religious message.

The format of the case studies is inspired in part by a short article by Franz Rosenthal entitled "Some minor problems in the Qur'ān."[77] Therein Rosenthal analyzes three disputed lexical items in the Qur'ān: *al-jizya 'an yad* (Q 9.29), *al-ṣamad* (Q 112.2), and *al-shayṭān al-rajīm* (Q 3.36; 15.34; 16.98; 38.77). The method in his analysis of *al-ṣamad* seems to me particularly fruitful. Rosenthal describes the Qur'ānic context of *al-ṣamad*, then the debates among the *mufassirūn* over the term and various modern translations of it (in fact forty-six different translations, according to him a "brief survey"). Finally Rosenthal turns to a philological study, presenting first the meaning of the root *ṣ.m.d.* in other Semitic languages, and then the use of this root in the Bible (Numbers 25.3; Psalm 106.28). This method both respects the efforts of the *mufassirūn* and modern translators, and highlights the virtue of appreciating the Qur'ān's literary and historical context.

A second inspiration for this format is that of Speyer in his *Die biblischen Erzählungen im Qoran*. Speyer presents his detailed analysis of the Biblical material in the Qur'ān in a series of studies that follow a Biblical sequence, that is, he begins with the Pentateuch (the creation of the world, Adam, and so forth), then the Deuteronomic history (including David, Solomon, and so forth) and concludes with the prophets. For each individual study Speyer begins with an overview of the Qur'ānic material ("Die qoranische Darstellung") and then turns to an analysis of the Biblical background to individual elements of that material. In these two respects my method is similar to that of Speyer. On the other hand Speyer never concerns himself with *tafsīr*. This I find fully justifiable, although it renders awkward his decision (mentioned above) to identify each Qur'ānic passage with a certain period of the Prophet's life.

Meanwhile, Speyer's work approaches a comprehensive analysis of Biblical material in the Qur'ān and thus is vastly more exhaustive than the present study. The achievement of *Die biblischen Erzählungen im Qoran* is perhaps

77 F. Rosenthal, "Some minor problems in the Qur'ān," *The Joshua Starr Memorial Volume*, New York: n.p., 1953, 67–84; reprint: *What the Koran Really Says*, ed. Ibn Warraq, Amherst, NY: Prometheus, 2002, 322–42.

best described by (none other than) Franz Rosenthal, who edited the work in the midst of the turmoil (and, in Prof. Rosenthal's case, personal risk) of late 1930s Germany, Speyer himself having died at the age of 38 in 1935. In 1993 Rosenthal noted that Speyer's work "is still the most comprehensive and detailed work to deal with the Jewish, Christian, also the Gnostic and Samaritan, parallels to the biblical material in the Qur'ān."[78] Speyer's work is a monument. My work is an exercise.

Still the thirteen studies that I include in this work are meant to be comprehensive in a more limited sense; that is, they represent a wide range of topics and a number of different literary forms found within the Qur'ān. The case studies address the Qur'ānic accounts of characters including Adam, Satan, Abraham, Haman, Jonah, Mary, and the Companions of the Cave. Still other case studies, such as that on *ghulf* or *muḥammad*, involve the study of a single word, and yet still demonstrate that the Qur'ān is in conversation with a larger literary tradition. Thus the case studies are meant to be diverse enough, in content and form, to make the point that the issue at hand is not a few idiosyncratic Qur'ānic passages. There are, of course, certain types of Qur'ānic passages – notably legal material – that find no place here. They are missing only because of constraints of space and time. Whether or not such passages can be read in light of a Biblical subtext will have to be the subject of a future study. I suspect they can.

As for the present work, in the first section of each individual case study I generally present the Qur'ānic material at issue according to the 1924 Cairo Qur'ān edition, which has today become the standard text. I am not fully satisfied with this presentation, inasmuch as it gives the impression that the Cairo edition is a critical edition. In fact, the Cairo edition only came into being when the Egyptian government, having received complaints of the divergences between the versions of the Qur'ān being used in various secondary schools, appointed a committee to establish a standard text for Egyptian government schools.[79] The task of this committee was not to establish the most ancient form of the Qur'ān through the investigation of early Qur'ān manuscripts. Instead it sought to establish a text on the basis of one of the canonical *qirā'āt* (lit. "readings") of the Qur'ān, namely that of Ḥafṣ (d. 180/796) *'an* 'Āṣim (d. 127/745). Yet the very idea of *qirā'āt* is the product of later Islamic tradition. It was developed and sponsored, most

78 F. Rosenthal, "The history of Heinrich Speyer's *Die biblischen Erzählungen im Qoran*," in Hartwig et al. (eds.), *Im vollen Licht der Geschichte* (113–16) 113. This is the transcript of an address that Prof. Rosenthal delivered in Berkeley, California, in 1993.

79 See M. Albin, "Printing of the Qur'ān," *EQ*, 4:269–72. The committee was led by Muḥammad b. 'Alī al-Ḥusaynī al-Ḥaddād, a religious scholar otherwise known for his criticism of Ṭāhā Ḥusayn's *Fī l-shi'r al-jāhilī*. For further details see G. Bergsträsser, "Koranlesung in Kairo," *Der Islam* 20, 1932, 3–4. The Cairo text was edited twice thereafter, in 1924 and 1936, during the first year of King Fārūq's reign (r. 1936–52), for which reason it became known as the Fārūq edition.

famously by Ibn Mujāhid (d. 324/936),[80] in response to the disagreements over the shape of the Qur'ānic text in the third and fourth Islamic centuries.

In other words, the 1924 Cairo Qur'ān edition is the product of school administration, on the one hand, and religious tradition on the other. Nevertheless, due to the religious prestige of Egypt the Cairo edition eventually became almost ubiquitous in the Islamic world. In response western scholars took to using this text as well, and Gustav Flügel's 1834 edition, which had previously been the standard text of western scholarship, gradually became obsolete. My use of this edition in the case studies, then, is essentially a matter of convenience for author and reader.

In the first section of the case studies certain words, which are transliterations and not translations, are italicized. These are terms which are the center of scholarly dispute, for which reason I postpone translating them until the final section of the case study, where their meaning becomes evident in the light of the Qur'ān's subtext. Other words, which are translations, are underlined. These are terms for which I present the standard translation in the first section, for the sake of comparison, and a new translation in the final section.

Finally, I do not concern myself with *variae lectiones* in the first section of the case studies. Since I conclude that these variations are largely a product of exegetical speculation (a point that will be emphasized in the third chapter), I assign them to the history of the text and not its origin. In other words, since the *qirā'āt* belong to the study of *tafsīr* and not of the Qur'ān, they enter into the case studies only in the second section.

In that section I present the interpretations, when appropriate, of a number of modern Qur'ān translations, along with those of a select number of classical *mufassirūn*. Neither element is intended to be a comprehensive survey. Instead in both cases I have attempted to isolate a small yet diverse group of scholars.

In all I refer to seven different modern Qur'ān translations. The earliest is that of Marmeduke, later Muḥammad, Pickthall (d. 1936, translation published 1930), the English son of an Anglican priest and convert to Islam. Pickthall's translation, which was for much of the mid-twentieth century the most popular English translation of the Qur'ān, occasionally reflects his knowledge of the Bible. Elsewhere, however, it seems to reflect an effort to summarize Islamic exegesis (for example, he translates one word, *al-ṣamad* [Q 112.2], as "the eternally Besought of all.").

Whereas Pickthall was an Englishman who composed his translation in India (it was commissioned by the Muslim governor of Hyderabad), Abdullah Yusuf Ali (d. 1953, translation published 1938) was an Indian who composed his translation in England. Yusuf Ali was an Ismā'īlī Shī'ī, a fact that has

80 Regarding which see C. Melchert, "Ibn Mujāhid and the establishment of seven Qur'ānic readings," *SI* 91, 2000, 5–22.

led certain Muslims to question the orthodoxy of his translation. Meanwhile, that translation tends distinctly towards modernism, especially on topics relating to human rights, the treatment of women, slavery, and war. In a review article, Arthur Jeffery presents Yusuf Ali's perspective as an apologetical response to Christianity,[81] a not unreasonable presentation in light of the frequent comparisons that Yusuf Ali makes in his footnotes to show the superiority of Islam to Christianity. Yusuf Ali's original translation was later edited by a Saudi-sponsored committee. It is the Saudi version which has been widely published today (with funding from missionary organizations). In the present work, however, I refer to Yusuf Ali's original translation. That translation tends to reflect piety more than philology.[82] Perhaps because of this Yusuf Ali generally preserves the word order and the sentence structure of the Arabic text, producing at times long and awkward English sentences.

Like Pickthall, Yusuf Ali presents the translation as a single, continuous text. Neither translator ever indicates uncertainty (although Yusuf Ali regularly resorts to parenthetical additions in order to clarify his intention), suggests any emendations to the text, or provides anything approaching an *apparatus criticus*. The effect is of a text that is perfectly well understood.

The French translation of Régis Blachère (d. 1973, translation published 1949), on the other hand, is quite different. Blachère, like Richard Bell (d. 1952, translation published 1937) before him, shows great interest in both the literary forms and the redaction of the Qur'ān. Thus Blachère regularly sets texts off to the right, or places texts in italics, in order to indicate passages which he believes were added to the Qur'ān at a later date. In places where Blachère believes that two different versions of the same passage have been joined in the process of redaction he divides the text into two parallel columns. Thus Blachère's translation is a work of critical, if speculative, philological revision.

The German translation of Rudi Paret (d. 1983, translation published 1962) is likewise critical and philological but in a different manner. Paret generally accepts the Cairo edition as the *textus receptus*, and does not seek to identify layers of the Qur'ānic text. Yet he shows interest in both the

81 "Over and over again one can watch the translation being glossed in a Christian sense, and only too often when what we want in a note is information that will put a verse in its setting, what we get is an apologetic explaining away what may seem offensive to those brought up to observe the Christian standard of morality and the teaching of the Christian ethic." A. Jeffery, "Yusuf Ali's translation of the Qur'an," *MW* 30, 1940, (54–66) 63.

82 Jeffery comments: "The translator has not asked himself what these words would have meant to those to whom they were addressed, but what they can mean now to the believer who looks to the Qur'ān for help to live his religious life. His approach is thus all the way through didactic in this homiletic sense. He is interested in edifying his co-religionists, drawing moral lessons, suggesting topics for religious meditation, and strengthening their faith in the superior excellence of Islam. His interests are not in critical exegesis." Jeffery, "Yusuf Ali's translation of the Qur'an," 57.

etymology of Qur'ānic vocabulary and the religious symbolism thereof. In his translation Paret also demonstrates a rare quality: candor. Paret, unlike all of the other translators in my survey, acknowledges when he is uncertain of his translation with the addition of question marks in parentheses.

The translation of Arthur John Arberry (d. 1969, translation published 1955), on the other hand, reflects still another approach to the text.[83] Arberry, a professor of Arabic and Persian at Cambridge, sought above all to produce an English translation that demonstrates the formal and rhetorical qualities of the Arabic Qur'ān. For this reason Arberry's translation continues to be popular among Muslim and non-Muslim scholars who are concerned with the appreciation of the Qur'ān as scripture (although Arberry's translation is rendered cumbersome by his use of Flügel's verse divisions, and by the provision of numbers only every five verses).

Finally, the most recent translations in my survey, that of Fakhry (published 1996) and Abdel Haleem (published 2004) are chosen above all as examples of recent trends in translating the Qur'ān. Unlike Yusuf Ali, neither Fakhry nor Abdel Haleem introduce or frame their work as expressions of Islamic tradition or piety. On the contrary, they both claim to provide the original meaning of the text, arrived at through critical evaluation. Abdel Haleem, for example, declares, "It is the job of the translator to bring his or her reader as close as is possible to the meaning of the original Arabic, utilizing the tools of solid linguistic analysis and looking at it in the context of its own stylistic features."[84] Accordingly the works of Fakhry and Abdel Haleem seem to offer reasonable standards with which to compare my own attempts at the study of the Qur'ān in the present work.

Yet the majority of the second section of my case studies is focused not on modern translations but rather on medieval *mufassirūn*. Even then I work with a limited group of *tafsīr*s, since my aim is not to present a catalog of traditional Islamic interpretation but only to present evidence for my argument about the relationship of Qur'ān and *tafsir*. Accordingly I have chosen five different medieval *tafsīr*s with the aim of representing different periods as well as diverse sectarian and theological perspectives. The earliest *tafsīr* in my survey is that attributed to Muqātil b. Sulaymān (d. 150/767), but extant only in the recension of Abū Ṣāliḥ Hudhayl b. Ḥabīb (d. after 190/805; and then on the authority of ʿAbdallāh b. Thābit, d. 315/927).[85] In light of

83 On Blachère's and Arberry's translations see A. Bausani, "On some recent translations of the Qur'ān," *Numen* 4, 1957, 1, 75–81. Bausani himself composed a popular translation of the Qur'ān into Italian. On the general task of translating the Qur'ān he comments (76), "We can freely say that – with some minor exceptions – we substantially know pretty well what the Qur'an means, at least what it meant for centuries to the Muslim world. The only originality that the new translations may offer is an originality of approach."

84 M. Abdel Haleem, *The Qur'ān*, Oxford: Oxford University Press, 2004, xxvi.

85 Regarding the origin and development of *Tafsīr Muqātil* see I. Goldfeld, "Muqātil Ibn Sulaymān," *Bar-Ilan Arabic and Islamic Studies* 2, 1978, 13–30; C. Versteegh, "Grammar

questions surrounding its authenticity, I refer to the text as *Tafsīr Muqātil*, to indicate the status of Muqātil as the authority, but not the ultimate author, thereof.[86]

The *tafsīr* attributed to Abū l-Ḥasan Ibrāhīm al-Qummī (d. after 307/919) was likewise subjected to later revision, but it can be traced to the author with greater confidence.[87] Qummī was an Imāmī (Twelver) Shīʿī from Qumm (as his name suggests), whose father was a companion of ʿAlī b. al-Riḍā (d. 202/818), the 8th imam.[88] Qummī's *tafsīr* is an important example of early Shīʿī interpretation. However, unlike other early Shīʿī *mufassirūn*, he does not limit himself to those verses that are the traditional objects of Shīʿī exegesis on the Imāmate.

The commentary of Abū Jaʿfar al-Ṭabarī (d. 310/923), is the cardinal work of early Sunnī exegesis. Ṭabarī's work has little need of introduction, and my choice thereof has little need of justification. Still I might add that unlike *Tafsīr Muqātil* and Qummī, Ṭabarī is concerned in a fundamental way with the recording and analysis of earlier exegetical traditions (a method later referred to as *tafsīr bi-l-ma'thūr*), even if he regularly introduces his own contributions to the conversation. Ṭabarī's *tafsīr* also appears more comprehensive in his application of other elements, including

and exegesis: The origins of Kufan grammar and the *Tafsīr* Muqātil," *Der Islam* 67, 1990, 206–42; C. Gilliot, "Muqātil, grand exégète, traditionniste et théologien maudit," *Journal asiatique* 279, 1991, 39–92; J. van Ess, *Theologie und Gesellschaft im 2. und 3. Jahrhundert Hidschra*, Berlin: Walter de Gruyter, 1991–7, 2:516–32. A. Rippin concludes that early *tafsīr*s such as *Tafsīr Muqātil* "are late renditions at best, which have been filtered through several generations of editors, compilers and copyists. Theoretically, there may well be a 'historical kernel' of material that could be ascribed to a given person within these texts, but determining just what that kernel consists of is no longer possible. What is more, arbitrary and mythical ascriptions abound, rendering the entire ascription framework suspect." A. Rippin, "Studying early *tafsīr* texts," *Der Islam* 72, 1995, (310–23) 314; reprint: *The Qur'ān and Its Interpretive Tradition*, ed. Rippin. Cf. the response to Rippin of M. Muranyi, "Visionen des Skeptikers," *Der Islam* 81, 2004, 206–17. For his part John Wansbrough points out that *Tafsīr Muqātil* includes citations, for example on grammatical questions, from later figures such as al-Farrā' (d. 207/822) and Thaʿlab (d. 291/904). See QS, 143, and the response of Versteegh, "Grammar and exegesis," 220.

86 Still this text has certain features that suggest it represents a relatively early stage of *tafsīr*. It shows little concern for *isnād*s or *qirā'āt*, both standard features of later *tafsīr*s. Meanwhile *Tafsīr Muqātil* is greatly concerned with narrative. Thus dogmatic considerations, for example, rarely get in the way of telling a good story. As Versteegh points out, *Tafsīr Muqātil* begins his commentary on each Sūra with a summary of its contents under the title *ahdāf al-sūra wa-maqāṣiduhā*, suggesting he sees each Sūra as a coherent narrative (C. Versteegh, *Arabic Grammar and Qur'ānic Exegesis in Early Islam*, Leiden: Brill, 1993, 69). *Tafsīr Muqātil* was later considered to be dependent on Jewish and Christian sources and consequently heterodox. In fact the original edition of the *Tafsīr Muqātil* was censored in a 2002 reprint. A significant number of pages which once contained more controversial commentary are blank therein.

87 See M.M. Bar-Asher, *Scripture and Exegesis in Early Imāmī Shīʿism*, Leiden: Brill, 1999, 35, 46–50.

88 Ibid., 34.

qirā'āt, Jāhilī poetry, and grammatical analysis, to the commentary on individual passages.[89]

The work of Muḥammad al-Zamakhsharī (d. 538/1144) is different. Himself a Mu'tazilī *mutakallim*, Zamakhsharī is fundamentally concerned with an exegesis that is rational (a method later referred to as *tafsīr bi-l-ra'y*). While he cites the views of earlier scholars, and indeed prophetic *ḥadīth*, Zamakhsharī generally puts such citations at the service of his rational arguments. Zamakhsharī attempts to interpret the data of revelation in a manner that is compatible with the axioms of Mu'tazilī theology, beginning with the oneness and justness of God, the latter point involving human free will.[90]

The last *tafsīr* in our survey, that of Ibn Kathīr (d. 774/1373), is far removed from the rationalism of the Mu'tazila. Ibn Kathīr, a Shāfi'ī from Damascus, was strongly influenced by his Ḥanbalī teacher Ibn Taymiyya (d. 728/1328), who emphasized revelation above reason, and warned against the dangers of innovative and speculative rationalism. Accordingly, Ibn Kathīr insists that the proper litmus test for the data of revelation in the Qur'ān is the data of revelation in the *ḥadīth*.[91] This insistence means, of course, that order had to be made out of the mass of *ḥadīth* and *isnāds*,

89 Gilliot accordingly comments: "En effet, il s'agit pour l'exégète de mettre un savoir positif, la philologie et la grammaire au service de l'interprétation, afin de mettre en valeur la précellence du Livre, mais aussi, au besoin, de montrer que les philologues n'ont pas le dernier mot, celui-ci revenant, en définitive, aux 'anciens exégètes'. Par des voies diverses, notamment par des choix effectués dans le dépôt grammatical transmis, le commentateur manifeste que les deux traditions se rejoignent, la tradition grammaticale et la tradition exégétique." C. Gilliot, *Exégèse, langue, et théologie en Islam*, Paris: Vrin, 1990, 281. Ṭabarī is hardly without his own theological agenda. His interest in grammatical analysis of the text, and accordingly in following its literal meaning, is connected to his belief in the Qur'ān's inimitability. See Gilliot, *Exégèse, langue, et théologie en Islam*, 166. Ṭabarī also pointedly directs his interpretations against, as he sees it, heterodox Islamic movements, including the Shī'a, Ṣūfīs, and philosophers. Gilliot comments, "A part cela, l'enquête sur ces positions dogmatique en théologie n'a guère révélée de surprise. Toutefois, elle nous à montré là encore, à travers le dédale de questions abordées, que Ṭabarī, tout en suivant le Coran *ad litteram*, vise à enraciner dans la conscience musulmane une conception 'majoritaire' de l'islam." Gilliot, *Exégèse, langue, et théologie en Islam*, 281.

90 This, of course, is no easy task, particularly when elements of the Qur'ān appear irrational, or two different elements appear rational by themselves, but in conflict with one another (verses classically labeled *mutashābih*, "ambiguous"; cf. Q 3.7). Thus Zamakhsharī employs many of the interpretive elements found in Ṭabarī, such as *qirā'āt*, pre-Islamic poetry, and grammatical analysis. With Zamakhsharī, however, these elements are primarily tools for the task of shaping scripture according to the dictates of reason. On Zamakhsharī see A. Lane, *A Traditional Mu'tazilite Qur'ān Commentary: The Kashshāf of Jār Allāh al-Zamakhsharī*, Leiden: Brill, 2006.

91 Thus N. Calder comments, "The Islamic concept of revelation, as is well known, is dual: it includes the text of the Qur'ān, (*waḥy matlū*) and the words of the Prophet (*waḥy ghayr matlū*). . . . Ibn Kathīr's *Tafsīr* is a comparison of canons, a juxtaposition of the two modes of revelation." N. Calder, "Tafsir from Tabari to Ibn Kathir: Problems in the description of a genre, illustrated with reference to the story of Abraham," in Hawting and Shareef (eds.), *Approaches to the Qur'an*, (101–40) 130.

for which reason Ibn Kathīr counts on *ʿilm al-rijāl*, or the study of transmitters and their *isnād*s, to identify authentic reports. In this Ibn Kathīr's approach is the furthest from *Tafsīr Muqātil* not only in time, but also in method.[92]

These five *tafsīr*s hardly make for an exhaustive survey, especially since there are places in the case studies where one or more of the *tafsīr*s have no significant material to add to the question at hand. It is also worth noting that Qur'ānic exegesis is not limited to works properly known as *tafsīr*s, but can also be found, for example, in *qiṣaṣ al-anbiyā'* ("stories of the prophets"), and in the classical Sunni *ḥadīth* collections (and indeed in most Islamic sciences, including history, jurisprudence, and so on). Yet in the second section of the case studies my aim is not to be exhaustive but only to establish the main trends in the classical *tafsīr*s. Thereby I intend to create a background against which the reader can judge the third section of the case studies, which is dedicated to the Qur'ān's relationship to pre-Islamic literature.

Here it is appropriate to add that I do not place Jāhilī (so-called "pre-Islamic") poetry in this latter category. This is, I acknowledge, not a position that can be taken for granted, and therefore I will add some brief comments in its defense.[93] The basic point, of course, is that not a single line of Jāhilī poetry comes from a book written by a Jāhilī Arab. Instead the entire corpus is found in the works of Muslim scholars who lived long after the supposed society of Jāhiliyya had ceased to exist. And notably the earliest *tafsīr*s, such as *Tafsīr Muqātil*, have no recourse to Jāhilī poetry whatsoever.[94]

Thus the situation is strikingly analogous to the question of *ḥadīth*. Few critical scholars today would comfortably accept *ḥadīth*, even those in the *ṣiḥāḥ*, to be literal quotations of something said about 150 years earlier in the Ḥijāz. Presumably scholars should then feel even less comfortable about accepting the historicity of Jāhilī poetry, since much of it is supposed to date even before the time of the Prophet. Imru' al-Qays, for example, the most famous Jāhilī poet, is said to have died around the year 550, yet a written version of his famous poems in the *Muʿallaqāt* cannot be dated before the time of Aṣmāʿī (d. 213/828). Other cases are still more striking. The poet Zuhayr b. Abī Sulmā is also supposed to have lived in the sixth century, but his poems are extant only in the collection of al-Aʿlam al-Shantamarī (d. 476/1083). In light of this it is strange to read contemporary scholarship

92 For Ibn Kathīr see, besides Calder, J.D. McAuliffe, "The tasks and traditions of interpretation," in McAuliffe (ed.), *Cambridge Companion to the Qur'ān*, (181–209) 196–8; A. Saeed, *Interpreting the Qur'ān: Towards a Contemporary Approach*, London: Routledge, 2006, 61–3.

93 On this topic generally see D.S. Margoliouth, "The origins of Arabic poetry," *JRAS*, 1925, 415–49.

94 See *QS*, 142; Versteegh, *Arabic Grammar*, 71.

in which the historical nature of Jāhilī poetry is described with great confidence.[95]

Meanwhile, the historical discrepancy between the supposed poets and the recording of their poetry is only one reason to doubt the antiquity of Jāhilī poetry. No less important is the evidence of material in the poems themselves, as Ignaz Goldziher observes:

> Es ist eine wahre Plage für alle jene, die bei der Betrachtung dieser Verhältnisse auf die Überlieferung der altarabischen Poesie angewiesen sind, daß die Entscheidung der Frage nach der Echtheit oder Unechtheit der in Betracht kommendem Stellen – ganz abgesehen von Daten, deren apokrypher Charakter aus inneren Gründen auf der Hand liegt – oft nur auf den subjektiven Eindruck gestellt ist, den die fraglichen Gedichte auf den Beobachter machen.[96]

Jāhilī poetry often seems too good to be true; that is, it seems to reflect knowledge of the Qur'ān itself. Nevertheless a number of modern scholars explain the Qur'ān by citing this poetry (much as the *mufassirūn* once did).[97] Haim Hirschberg, for example, bases his analysis of the Qur'ān on evidence in Jāhilī poetry for the religious ideas of Arabs at the rise of Islam.[98] Hirschberg himself notes that it is peculiar to find so much Biblical and Qur'ānic material in Jāhilī poetry, and yet so few traces of paganism.

95 Navid Kermani, for examples, writes that in pre-Islamic Arabia, "The written word was not widely disseminated, and most people were, in fact, illiterate and the differences between dialects made communication difficult. Yet still, throughout the Arabic region, which was a third of the size of all Europe, and spread from Yemen in the south to Syria in the north, from the borders of modern Iraq to the borders of Egypt, old Arabic poetry with its formal language, sophisticated techniques and extremely strict norms and standards was identical. 'How this was achieved, we do not know and most probably shall never learn,' remarked the Israeli Orientalist, Shlomo D. Goitein, on this astonishing phenomenon." N. Kermani, "Poetry and language," in Rippin (ed.), *The Blackwell Companion to the Qur'ān*, (107–19) 108. The quotation from Goitein is from *Studies in Islamic History and Institutions*, Leiden: Brill, 1966, 6.

96 I. Goldziher, *Muhammedanische Studien*, Halle: Niemeyer, 1888–90, 1:90; English trans.: *Muslim Studies*, trans. C.R. Barber and S.M. Stern, New Brunswick, NJ: Aldine, 2006, 1:90. Cited by Hirschberg, *Judische und christliche Lehren*, 2–3.

97 Cf. the use of Jāhilī poetry in the article by K. Athamina, "Abraham in Islamic perspective: Reflections on the development of monotheism in pre-Islamic Arabia," *Der Islam* 81, 2004, 2, 184–205.

98 See Hirschberg, *Judische und christliche Lehren*, 4–8. He argues for the authenticity of this poetry by noting, one, that it contains more details on Biblical legends than the Qur'ān and, two, that no Muslim would later forge such poetry which would seem to put the originality (and thus the validity) of Qur'ānic revelation in doubt. Both of these arguments fail to account for the role that poetry plays in Islamic exegesis, where it both explains and justifies particular interpretations.

Jāhilī poetry, after all, is supposedly the product *par excellence* of a pagan culture.[99]

The most well-known case illustrating the problem of Jāhilī poetry is that of Umayya b. Abī l-Ṣalt, a poet who is described in the Islamic sources as a *ḥanīf* from the city of Ṭā'if and a contemporary of the Prophet.[100] Umayya's poems are distinguished both by references to Biblical narratives and by Qur'ānic vocabulary. In an article entitled "Une nouvelle source du Qorān," Clément Huart accordingly argues that these poems provide scholars with a clear literary source for the material in the Qur'ān.[101] Yet the matter can hardly be this simple. The earliest recorded compilation of Umayya's poems is that of Muḥammad b. Ḥabīb, who died in 244/859, about 250 years after the supposed death of Umayya.[102] Moreover, these poems seem to reflect not only the Qur'ān, but even *tafsīr*.[103] Most scholars, therefore, objected to Huart's thesis.[104] Andrae notes "la dependence manifest du poète à l'égard du Coran."[105] Nöldeke argues that material in Umayya's poems which closely reflects Qur'ānic expressions should be seen as a later forgery.[106] More recently Franz-Christoph Muth has shown the danger of using Jāhilī

99 Hirschberg, *Judische und christliche Lehren* (pp. 12–13) speculates that the Bedouins who wrote these poems were simply not religious types.

100 T. Seidensticker concludes that Umayya died at some point between AH 2 and 8, noting that a poem on the martyrs at Badr is attributed to Umayya (and according to Seidensticker correctly so), but that Umayya does not figure in the Islamic accounts of the Muslim conquest of Ṭā'if. See T. Seidensticker, "The authenticity of the poems ascribed to Umayya Ibn Abī al-Ṣalt," in J.R. Smart (ed.), *Tradition and Modernity in Arabic Language and Literature*, London: Curzon, 1996, (87–101) 88.

101 C. Huart, "Une nouvelle source du Qorān," *Journal Asiatique* 10, 1904, 4, 125–67. A similar attitude to Umayya's works was taken by L. Cheikho in his *Al-Naṣrāniyya wa-adabuhā bayna 'Arab al-jāhiliyya*.

102 Although Muḥammad b. Ḥabīb's compilation is not in fact extant. Most of Umayya's poems are taken from quotations in other works, most notably al-Muṭahhar b. Ṭāhir al-Maqdisī's (d. late 4th/10th century) *K. al-Bad' wa-l-ta'rīkh*.

103 Thus Seidensticker notes that while the Qur'ān (Q 21.91) has Jesus conceived when God breathes into Mary, Umayya follows *tafsīr* (with its wariness of anthropomorphism) in having the angel Gabriel do so. See Seidensticker, "Authenticity of the poems," 91.

104 See *GdQ1*, 19. The most comprehensive response is I. Frank-Kamenetzky, *Untersuchungen über das Verhältnis der dem Umajja b. Abi ṣ Ṣalt zugeschriebenen Gedichte zum Qorān*, Doctoral Dissertation, Königsberg, 1911. See also F. Schulthess, *Umajja ibn Abī ṣ Ṣalt: Die unter seinem Namen überlieferten Gedichtfragmente gesammelt und übersetzt*, Leipzig: Hinrichs, 1911.

105 *OIC*, 63. Elsewhere (p. 58) he writes: "Ainsi, à mon avis, les poésies d'*Umayya* sont à rejeter de la discussion de l'origine de la théologie coranique."

106 T. Nöldeke, "Umaija b. AbiṣṢalt," *Zeitschrift für Assyriologie* 27, 1912, (159–72) 163. One such example that he gives is *al-jūdī*, a *hapax legomenon* that appears in the Qur'ān (Q 11.44a) for the mountain on which Noah's ark landed. Although the form *al-jūdī* seems to be a corruption of the well-known Semitic term for that mountain, *qardū*, it is cited in a poem attributed to Umayya precisely in its Qur'ānic form, for which reason Nöldeke reasonably considers the poem suspect. Nöldeke, "Umaija b. AbiṣṢalt," 165.

poetry to explain Qur'ānic *hapax legomena*.[107] In light of all this it seems to me best not to assume that Jāhilī poetry is pre-Islamic poetry. The proper assumption is that proposed by Alphonse Mingana, that the Qur'ān is the first Arabic book.[108]

More generally it seems to me that scholars need not feel compelled to read the Qur'ān in light of a pagan culture that would have produced this poetry. The premise that the Qur'ān emerged amidst paganism has more than once left scholars confused by the fact that paganism is hardly evident in the Qur'ān. Rudolph, for example, writes:

> Es fällt immer wieder auf, wie weniges im Qoran an das arabische Heidentum erinnert. In der ganzen mekkanischen Zeit findet sich in ihm nichts Heidnisches, abgesehen vom Glauben an die Dämonen (*jinn*), von der nicht zu leugnenden, aber freilich nur ganz vorübergehenden Anerkennung der drei Göttinen Allāt, Manāt und al-'Uzza in S. 53 und von der einmaligen positive Erwähnung des Opfers in der frühmekkanischen S. 108."[109]

107 Muth examines the poetic witnesses to the term *abābīl* (Q 105.3), a *hapax legomenon* in the Qur'ān. This term is traditionally interpreted to mean "flocks," and is connected to the legend that God sent flocks of birds to destroy the army of the Yemeni king who invaded Mecca in the year of the Prophet's birth. Yet the use of this term in Jāhilī poetry usually presumes knowledge of this legend, i.e. the poetry and *tafsīr* match each other in a way that suggests they developed together. Jāhilī poetry might then be of interest for the study of *tafsīr* on the term *abābīl*, but it should not be used as the key to the ancient meaning of this term. See F.-C. Muth, "Reflections on the relationship of early Arabic poetry and the Qur'ān: Meaning and origin of the Qur'ānic term *ṭayran abābīla* according to early Arabic poetry and other sources," in Kropp (ed.), *Results of Contemporary Research on the Qur'ān*, 147–56.

108 See A. Mingana, "Syriac influence on the style of the Kur'ān," *Bulletin of the John Rylands Library* 11, January 1928, 1 (77–98) 78. This same conclusion, incidentally, is strongly suggested by the absence of any clear evidence that the Bible was translated into Arabic before Islam. There were, of course, many Arabic speaking Christians before Islam. Accordingly Sprenger and, most famously, A. Baumstark argued that these Christians must have had a Bible in their language. See Sprenger, *Leben*, 1:132; Baumstark, "Das Problem eines vorislamischen christlich-kirchlichen Schrifttums in arabischer Sprache," *Islamica* 4, 1931, 562–75; idem, "Eine frühislamische und eine vorislamische arabische Evangelienübersetzung aus dem Syrischen," *Atti del XIX Congresso Internazionlae degli Orientalisti* (1935), Rome: G. Bardi, 1938, 682–4. Yet Baumstark's theories are refuted by G. Graf, *Geschichte der christlichen arabischen Literatur*, Rome: Biblioteca Apostolica Vaticana, 1947, 1:143–5. Guillaume, basing himself on Islamic sources, also argues for the existence of an Arabic Bible in the Prophet's time. See A. Guillaume, "The version of the Gospels used in Medina," *Al-Andalus* 15, 1950, 289–96. Cf. the more comprehensive approach of J. Blau, "Sind uns Reste arabischer Bibelübersetzungen erhalten geblieben?" *Le Muséon* 86, 1973, 67–72. More recently S. Griffith again refutes this idea, showing in detailed fashion that the first evidence of an Arabic Bible dates only to the 'Abbāsid era. See S.H. Griffith, "The Gospel in Arabic: An inquiry into its appearance in the first Abbāsid century," *OC* 69, 1985, (126–67) 128.

109 Rudolph, *Abhängigkeit*, 25–6. For his part Schwally argues that there is hardly any religious idea in the Qur'ān that does not come from Judaism or Christianity. *GdQ2*, 121.

Jeffery, arguing that even Rudolph overestimates the evidence of Arab paganism in the Qur'ān, comments, "It comes, therefore, as no little surprise, to find how little of the religious life of this Arabian paganism is reflected in the pages of the Qur'an."[110]

Yet the notion of the pagan background to the Qur'ān has hardly gone away. In his 1936 article "Die Orginalität des arabischen Propheten", Johann Fück criticizes the efforts of scholars in his day to connect the Qur'ān to Biblical literature.[111] Toufiq Fahd presents the pagan background to Islam in his 1968 work *Le Panthéon de l'Arabie centrale à la veille de l'hégire.*[112] Later (1984) Alfred Beeston would claim to discover evidence for the development of an indigenous Arab monotheism (which he connects with the reports of the *ḥanīf*s in Islamic sources) in South Arabian inscriptions.[113]

110 *FV*, 1. Joseph Henninger observes, "Die Zeiten sind schon lange vorüber, da man im Islam eine Beduinenreligion sah, entstanden inmitten der Wüste, spontan hervorgebrochen aus den Tiefen der semitischen Seele." J. Henninger, *Spuren christlicher Glaubenswahrheiten im Koran*, Schöneck: Administration der Neuen Zeitschrift für Missionswissenschaft, 1951, 1. Henninger here is responding to Ernest Renan's emphasis on the Bedouin Arab background to the Qur'ān. See esp. E. Renan, "Nouvelles considérations sur le caractère général des peuples sémitiques," *Journal Asiatique* 13, 1859, 214–82; 417–50.

More recently Gerald Hawting argues that the pagan culture of the Prophet's Mecca, and indeed the very association of the Prophet with that city, are myths developed for the purpose of *Heilsgeschichte*. Hawting writes, "I suggest that the traditional descriptions of pre-Islamic Arab paganism – although their explicit references in the Qur'ān are limited – can be understood as a form of exegesis in that their primary purpose is to give substance to the idea that the Qur'ān (and therefore, in the traditional understanding, Islam) was revealed in a pagan Arab society." G. Hawting, "Qur'ānic exegesis and history," 415–16. Thereafter (p. 418) he continues "The most obvious of those considerations would be a need – conscious or unconscious – to emphasize the association of the Qur'ān with the activity of the prophet Muḥammad in western central Arabia." Cf. idem, *The Idea of Idolatry and the Emergence of Islam*.

111 J. Fück, "Die Orginalität des arabischen Propheten," *ZDMG* 90, 1936, 509–25.

112 T. Fahd, *Le Panthéon de l'Arabie centrale à la veille de l'hégire*, Paris: Geuthner, 1968. The title of Fahd's work is reminiscent of Henri Lammens' studies on the Prophet's historical context, although Lammens is concerned with Christianity, and Fahd with paganism. E. Gräf, for his part, attempts a theology of Meccan pagan religion. See "Zu den christlichen Einflüssen im Koran," esp. p. 121.

113 See A.F.L. Beeston, "The religions of pre-Islamic Yemen," in J. Chelhod (ed.), *L'Arabie du Sud: Histoire et civilisation*, Paris: Maisonneuve et Larose, 1984, 259–69; ibid., "Himyarite monotheism," *Studies in the History of Arabia II, Pre-Islamic Arabia*, Riyadh: King Saud University Press, 1984, 149–54. Regarding Beeston's arguments A. Rippin asks, "Do we have evidence that may be taken as historically firm that a group of monotheists, known as the *ḥanīfiyya*, existed in pre-Islamic times? If so, it may then be possible to interpret the inscriptions in light of that evidence. Or, approaching the issue the other way around, does the Epigraphical South Arabian material demand an interpretation of a non-Jewish, non-Christian monotheism? If that is the case, then it may be possible to interpret the Islamic literary evidence in light of the inscriptions. The problem here is a methodological one, involving the assessment of the nature of historical evidence and its interpretation." A. Rippin, "RḤMNN and the Ḥanīfs," in W.B. Hallaq and D.P. Little (eds.), *Islamic Studies Presented to Charles J. Adams*, Leiden: Brill, 1991, (153–68) 157; cf. idem, "Epigraphical South Arabian and Qur'ānic exegesis," *JSAI* 13, 1990, 155–74. Both reprinted in Rippin, *The Qur'ān and Its Interpretive Tradition*.

In the present work my study of the Qur'ān is not based at all on a historical context, whether pagan, Jewish, or Christian.[114] Accordingly this work is not an investigation into the sources of the Qur'ān. This search was often the explicit goal of earlier studies, as indicated by the titles of Abraham Geiger's *Was hat Mohammed aus dem Judenthume aufgenommen* and Clément Huart's "Une nouvelle source du Qorān."[115] As Geiger's title suggests, this idea was usually connected to the historical principle that Muḥammad was the sole author of the Qur'ān. This principle, meanwhile, was often shaded with the conviction that a merchant from an obscure corner of the Arabian Peninsula was incapable of composing narratives on Biblical themes. Thus Muḥammad was usually assumed to have borrowed material from Jews and Christians. The Qur'ān consequently was seen as something of a scrapbook of earlier religious ideas.

As I see it this pejorative approach to the Qur'ān was in large part a product of the historical optimism of nineteenth-century modernists, and in particular of their trust in the received biography of the Prophet. That biography goes to great lengths to emphasize Muḥammad's pagan context. Thereby it emphasizes the divine origin of the Qur'ān, by having Muḥammad far away from the traditional centers of Judaism and Christianity, in a city that was the last, proud metropolis of paganism. It even has the Prophet reared by a (pagan) Bedouin foster mother in middle of the desert. The acceptance of this biography as history led scholars to believe that Muḥammad could not have written the Qur'ān without help from the Jews and Christians whom he would later meet. It might be added, however, that behind this approach also lies the purely polemical portrayal of Muḥammad in pre-modern European writings, according to which he was no prophet but rather the protégé of a heretical Nestorian monk.[116] This approach is, of course, totally incompatible with the views I have introduced above on the problems of reading the Qur'ān through *sīra*.

114 Instead my approach might be compared to that of D. Masson. In introducing his work Masson explains: "Le présent ouvrage ne se place pas sur le plan historique; il se limite à l'examen des éléments proprement religieux et spirituels contenus dans le Coran. La Révélation s'inscrit dans l'histoire, mais elle la transcende aussi et elle s'ouvre sur des perspectives eschatologiques." D. Masson, *Le Coran et la révélation judéo-chrétienne*, Paris: Adrien-Maisonneuve, 1958, 10. In a footnote (p. 10, n. 1) he explains further: "Nous nous sommes abstenus de nous référer trop souvent à la Tradition musulmane, pour nous borner au texte coranique."

115 A more polemical example is the work of the Christian missionary Tisdall, *Original Sources of the Qur'an*. At one point (p. 55) Tisdall writes, "We now turn to the Jews from whom Muhammad borrowed so very much that his religion might almost be described as a heretical form of later Judaism."

116 In this regard it is worth noting that when Peter the Venerable, in 1143, commissioned the first Latin translation of the Qur'ān from Robert of Ketton, he also had translated the Christian Arabic work *Risālat al-Kindī*, in which the story of the heretical monk Baḥīra appears. On this see A. Abel, "L'Apologie d'al-Kindī et sa place dans la polémique islamo-chrétien," *L'Oriente cristiano nella storia della civiltà*, Rome: Academia dei Lincei, 1964, 501–23.

It still might be contended that sources for the Qur'ān can be pursued even if Muḥammad is not assumed to be its author. It may be enough to take a textual approach, comparing the Qur'ān with earlier works, in order to identify its sources. To this contention I have two objections. First, we have no pre-Qur'ānic Arabic literature, if any ever existed. This means, as I see it, that we cannot generally claim that the Qur'ān itself has borrowed foreign vocabulary, having no way to know whether this vocabulary entered into Arabic long before. Presumably the same must be said about texts and traditions.

Second, the Qur'ān's literary style is evidently allusive. The Qur'ān does not seem to quote texts, Biblical or otherwise, at all. Instead the Qur'ān alludes to them as it develops a unique religious message. The Qur'ān thus is one part of a dynamic and complicated literary tradition, marked not by strict borrowing but by motifs, topoi, and exegesis.

Accordingly I introduce in the following chapter the idea of the Qur'ān's subtext. By this I mean the collection of traditions that the Qur'ān refers to in its articulation of a new religious message. The key, then, is not what sources entered into the Qur'ān, but rather the nature of the relationship between the Qur'ānic text and its Jewish and Christian subtext. For this reason I speak of the Qur'ān in conversation with a larger literary tradition. The idea of the Qur'ān's conversation is not meant as a substitute for the idea of the Qur'ān's sources. It is meant to reflect the notion of the Qur'ān as a homiletic text (an idea that I will develop in the final chapter of this work) animated by its allusions to, and interpretation of, its literary subtext.

So while research on the Qur'ān cannot be limited to identifying its sources, it should not ignore the earlier literary and religious traditions to which the Qur'ān consistently alludes. The student of the Qur'ān should be always alert to the conversation that the Qur'ān conducts with earlier texts, and in particular to its intimate conversation with Biblical literature. The case studies of the following chapter might be seen as an exercise in listening closely to that conversation.

Excursus: regarding the dates of Jewish and Christian texts

Above I discuss briefly the problems in using Jāhilī poetry as an element of pre-Qur'ānic literature. The question of dating can no less be ignored when it comes to Jewish and Christian literature. For the most part, however, the Jewish and Christian works that I turn to in the following chapter date from well before the period of Islamic origins. Such is the case for the canonical Bible, of course, but also for narrative works such as *Jubilees* (3rd–1st century BC; a Jewish account of the revelation given to Moses on Mt. Sinai), the *Life of Adam and Eve* (ca. 1st century AD),[1] the *Gospel of Bartholemew*, the *Apocalypse of Abraham* (ca. 2nd century AD; a Jewish account of Abraham's rejection of idol-worship and reception of divine revelation), the *Gospel of Nicodemus* (3rd or 4th century AD), and the *Cave of Treasures* (a Christian account of sacred history from Adam to Christ; 4th–6th century AD).[2] Pre-Qur'ānic as well are the works of Philo (d. ca. AD 50), Josephus (d. AD 100), Ephraem (d. AD 373; although in his case close attention must be paid to the question of authenticity), and Jacob of Serūgh (d. AD 521). So too the Babylonian Talmud, which reached its final form (for all practical purposes) in the sixth century, can safely be counted pre-Qur'ānic.

However, the question of Jewish midrashic works and targums is more complicated. The great collection *Midrash Rabba*, for example, contains works from a wide variety of dates. *Genesis Rabba*, which dates from the fifth Christian century (ca. 450), is quite clearly pre-Qur'ānic, but most other volumes, including *Exodus Rabba* (11th–12th century) and *Numbers Rabba* (12th century) are post-Qur'ānic. *Leviticus Rabba* and *Ecclesiastes Rabba* date from around the period of the Qur'ān's origins, but they play no major role in the present work. *Esther Rabba* is a compilation of two works, one (*Esther 1*, covering the Book of Esther, chs. 1–2) quite early (early 6th century)

1 The origins of the *Life of Adam and Eve* are unclear. Some scholars hold that it was originally Jewish and later went through various Christian redactions. Today it is extant only in Christian recensions, including Greek, Latin, Armenian, Georgian, Slavonic, and Coptic versions.

2 These are the dates for the Syriac version of the text; the Arabic version dates only to the 8th century.

and one (*Esther 2*, covering Esther 3–8) quite late (ca. 11th century), but it likewise plays no major role in the present work.

Other Rabbinic works must be evaluated individually. The *Mekīltā de-Rabbī Shim'ōn b. Yoḥai*, a commentary on Exodus at once haggadic and halakhic, is quite early, dating from the early Amoraic period (probably 3rd–4th century AD).[3] More problematic is the evaluation of other Jewish works which reached their final form around the period of Islamic origins. The *Pirqē de-Rabbī Elī'ezer*, for example, was likely written in the eighth century and in places contains clear reflections of an Arab and Islamic historical context (esp. chs. 30, 32, in regard to Abraham, Hagar, and Ismā'īl). However, in other places it no less clearly preserves more ancient material.[4]

The question of the Hebrew *Pirqē de-Rabbī Elī'ezer*'s date is closely related to the question of the Aramaic Targum Pseudo-Jonathan's date. The two works share common material, but the direction of influence between the two works is a matter of scholarly dispute. The predominant scholarly view is that *Pirqē de-Rabbī Elī'ezer* is earlier and influenced the Targum of Pseudo-Jonathan.[5] Robert Hayward, however, argues that Pseudo-Jonathan is the earlier text; indeed he suggests that it is pre-Islamic.[6] James Kugel, while acknowledging that there are some post-Islamic references in Pseudo-Jonathan, argues that the basis of the work "goes back far earlier."[7] In light of this scholarly debate, which I have no authority to judge, it seems that caution should be exercised in using these two sources in a study of the Qur'ān. Accordingly, I include information from the *Pirqē de-Rabbī Elī'ezer* and the *Targum of Pseudo-Jonathan* only in footnotes, not in the main text. The question of the Aramaic *Targum Neofiti*, however, is quite different. It is of Palestinian provenance (whereas Pseudo-Jonathan is Babylonian) and was written well before the rise of Islam (ca. 1st century AD).[8]

3 On this see W.D. Nelson, "Mekhilta de R. Simeon b. Yohai," *Encyclopaedia of Midrash*, ed. J. Neusner and A.J. Avery-Peck, Leiden: Brill, 2005, 1:493.

4 See the introduction to *Pirke de-Rabbi Elieser*, ed. and trans. D. Börner-Klein, Berlin: de Gruyter, 2004, xxxix–xlvii.

5 Thus M. Ohana, "La polémique judeo-islamique d'Ismaël dans Targum Pseudo-Jonathan et dans Pirke de Rabbi Eliezer," *Augustinianum* 15, 1975, 367–87. This is also the view of M. Maher, who dates Pseudo-Jonathan to the seventh–eighth centuries. See *The Aramaic Bible*, Collegeville, MN: Liturgical Press, 1992, 1B:11–12.

6 See R. Hayward, "The date of Targum Pseudo-Jonathan: Some comments," *Journal of Jewish Studies* 40, 1989, 7–30.

7 *TB*, 944.

8 M. McNamara argues for a date of the fourth century AD. See *The Aramaic Bible*, Collegeville, MN: Liturgical Press, 1992, 1A:3; cf. E. Levine, *The Aramaic Version of the Bible*, Berlin: de Gruyter, 1988, 23–5. On this question more generally see D. York, "The dating of Targumic literature," *The Journal of Jewish Studies* 5, 1974, 49–62.

2 Qur'ānic case studies

CS 1 The prostration of the angels

Qur'ānic account

References to the prostration of the angels before Adam appear in no less than seven different Sūras,[1] suggesting that this is an account of fundamental importance to the Qur'ān. In part the Qur'ān uses this account as an etiology, to explain the devil's fall from heaven. Yet it also uses this account to make an anthropological point, to illustrate the high station of Adam, and thereby humanity.

It is this second aspect that is salient in *al-baqara* (2) 30ff. Here the Qur'ān has God announce to the angels His intention to create a *khalīfa* ("vicegerent") on earth.

> (2.30) When your Lord said to the angels, "I am making a *khalīfa* on earth," they said, "Will you make on it one who will be iniquitous and shed blood, while we praise your glory and sanctify you?" He said, "I know what you do not know."[2]

2.30 وَإِذْ قَالَ رَبُّكَ لِلْمَلاَئِكَةِ إِنِّي جَاعِلٌ فِي الأَرْضِ خَلِيفَةً ، قَالُواْ أَتَجْعَلُ فِيهَا مَن
يُفْسِدُ فِيهَا وَيَسْفِكُ الدِّمَاءَ ، وَنَحْنُ نُسَبِّحُ بِحَمْدِكَ وَنُقَدِّسُ لَكَ قَالَ إِنِّي أَعْلَمُ مَا لاَ تَعْلَمُونَ

Thereafter the Qur'ān turns to an account (Q 2.31–3) of God's (now in the third person singular) teaching the names of things to Adam. God challenges the angels to produce these names, and they are unable to do so. Thus while in verse 30 the Qur'ān insists that God knows what the angels do not, here it is revealed how Adam knows what the angels know not. Thereafter (Q 2.34, returning to the first person plural) the Qur'ān has God record that when He commanded the angels to prostrate to Adam, all of them did so except the devil.

1 Q 2.34; 7:11–12; 15:28–33; 17:61–2; 18:50; 20:115–6; 38:71–8.

2 In his translation Blachère puts this verse in italics, an indication that he believes it is a later insertion.

In different ways each element of this pericope emphasizes the high station of humanity. Humans are God's *khalīfa*. Humans (like God) know that which the angels do not. A human receives the veneration of angels.

The station of humans is further illuminated by a second Qur'ānic account of the prostration. In *al-ḥijr* (15) 29 (cf. Q 38.72), the Qur'ān has God relate (in the first person singular), "When I have made him, and breathed my spirit into him, then fall down prostrating to him." Here the presence of God's spirit in the human not only distinguishes him from the angels, it also seems to explain why the human should be venerated. Thus it is with no little irony that the devil says elsewhere, in *al-aʿrāf* (7) 12 (cf. 17.61), that he, who is made of fire, will not prostrate to Adam, who is made of clay. For if Adam was made from clay, he is brought to life with the very Spirit of God.

Elsewhere the Qur'ān elaborates on the tension between the devil and humanity. In *al-aʿrāf* (7) 13 (cf. Q 7.18; 15.35; 38.77) God banishes the devil from heaven, although the devil requests (Q 7.14; cf. 15.36; 17.62; 38.79) and receives (Q 7.15; cf. 15.37; 17.63; 38.80–1) a reprieve, some sort of liberty, until the Day of Resurrection. After his banishment the devil, who in heaven is Iblīs, is named Shayṭān. Iblīs is the rebel against God. Shayṭān is the tempter of humans. The Qur'ān is quite clear about this distinction. In *al-baqara* (2) 34 the devil is Iblīs, but two verses later, when he has entered into the garden, he is Shayṭān.[3]

As Iblīs refuses to acknowledge man's high station, so Shayṭān seeks to bring man down from that station.[4] Accordingly, when he enters the heavenly garden Shayṭān assaults Adam and his wife, who succumb to his deception (Q 2.36; 7.22; 20.121). At this they are literally brought down. God casts all of them (the devil, Adam, and his woman) from the heavenly garden to the earth below (Q 2.36, 39; 7.24; 20.123). Adam and the woman repent of their fault (Q 7.23) and God forgives them: "Adam received words from his Lord, who accepted his repentance. He is accepting and merciful" (Q 2.37; cf. 20.122).

Problems for interpreters

Khalīfa

As mentioned above, in *al-baqara* (2) 30 God declares to the angels his intention of creating a *khalīfa* on earth. According to classical Arabic lexicography *khalīfa* might mean either "representative" or "successor."[5] Most modern translators choose the first meaning. Pickthall translates "representative";

3 Likewise cf. Q 7.11 vs. 7.20; 20.116 vs. 20.120.

4 Thus the devil announces his intention to harass humans: "Since You have sent me astray, I will set an ambush for them on your righteous path" (Q 7.16, cf. 15.39).

5 Thus Lane: "A successor: and a vice-agent, vicegerent, lieutenant, substitute, proxy or deputy." *AEL*, 2:797c–798a.

Yusuf Ali, "vicegerent"; Blachère "vicaire"; Arberry, "viceroy"; and Fakhry, "deputy." Paret, however, opts for the second meaning, translating "Nachfolger," as does Abdel Haleem, "successor."[6]

Both meanings, however, present difficulties to Muslim *mufassirūn*. If God is thought to have created a "representative" or "vicegerent," then man would seem to have divine qualities. According to Islamic doctrine, however, God is absolutely superior to man, a position often supported with reference to *al-shūrā* (42) 11: "There is nothing like Him" (*laysa ka-mithlihi shay'*). On the other hand, if God is creating a "successor," whom is man succeeding?[7] This quandary might explain the appearance of the variant reading of *khalīfa* as *khalīqa* ("creature"),[8] a term which allows the interpreter to avoid both horns of the dilemma.

Most *mufassirūn*, however, accept the standard reading of *khalīfa* and explain that the term means "successor." Thereby they avoid the theological problem, and are left with only the problem of explaining how the first human could be a successor. *Tafsīr Muqātil* explains accordingly that God "created the angels and the *jinn* before He created Satan and humans."[9] The angels, *Tafsīr Muqātil* explains, were created to be residents of heaven and the *jinn* residents of earth. Yet the *jinn* began to fight amongst themselves and God sent angelic soldiers from the lowest heaven,[10] named "Jinn" (not to be confused with the creatures named *jinn*), among whom was "the devil, the enemy of God,"[11] to earth.[12] These "Jinn" however, were so impious that God decided to create humans as their successors, as the new residents of earth.[13]

Qummī's explanation is similar, although he insists that the devil is not an angel. Instead, he was one of the *jinn* who originally inhabited the earth. That is, the devil did not descend to earth to defeat the *jinn*. Instead, God sent angels to earth to defeat the devil. When they did so they took him prisoner to heaven, for which reason he was present there when God

6 W. Qadi avoids both meanings and translates simply "inhabitant, settler on earth." See "Caliph," *EQ*, 1:277a.

7 Paret explains in his commentary (*Der Koran. Kommentar und Konkordanz*, 16), that man is a successor to the angels. As will be seen below, this seems to be a version of the classical position of the *mufassirūn*.

8 *MQQ*, 1:40, on the authority of Zayd b. 'Alī.

9 Muqātil b. Sulaymān, *Tafsīr* (henceforth *Tafsīr Muqātil*), ed. 'Abdallāh Muḥammad al-Shiḥāta. Beirut: Dār al-Turāth al-'Arabī, 2002 (Reprint of: Cairo: Mu'assasat al-Ḥalabī, n.d.), 1:96, on Q 2.30.

10 *Samā' al-dunyā*, see Q 37.6; 41.12; 67.5.

11 On the devil's soldiers cf. Q 26.59.

12 *Tafsīr Muqātil*, 1.96, on Q 2.30. By naming the devil's group of angels "Jinn," *Tafsīr Muqātil* is able to explain why the Qur'ān includes the devil among the *jinn* (Q 18.50) even while it implies by the prostration scene that he was an angel.

13 When God relates "I know what you do not know," at the end of *al-baqara* (2) 30, what He means is "I know that you [angels] will be residents of heaven and Adam and his descendents residents of the earth and among them will be those who will praise my glory and sanctify me." *Tafsīr Muqātil*, 1.96, on Q 2.30.

commanded the angels to bow to Adam.[14] In a second tradition (on the authority of 'Alī b. Abī Ṭālib), Qummī relates that the *jinn* and the *nasnās*[15] inhabited the earth for 7000 years. When they became iniquitous and began to shed blood (cf. Q 2.30), God declared: "I want to create a creature with my hand, and make prophets, messengers, virtuous servants and rightly guided Imāms among his descendants."[16]

With these narratives Qummī seems to define *khalīfa* as successor, but soon thereafter he comments that the term *khalīfa* is a reference to Adam's role as the *ḥujja*, "proof" or "sign," of God on earth.[17] Thus he also entertains the alternative definition of *khalīfa* as "representative."

Ṭabarī similarly acknowledges both definitions. He first reports a version of the "successor" narrative (on the authority of Ibn 'Abbās) according to which God sent the devil and his soldiers to earth. They defeated the *jinn* and banished them to islands and distant mountains. He then created Adam as a successor to the *jinn*.[18]

Yet Ṭabarī also presents a tradition (likewise on the authority of Ibn 'Abbās),[19] according to which *khalīfa* means "representative." Adam, or "whoever rises to his station in obedience to God" (presumably a reference to the caliphs) is God's representative inasmuch as he is commanded to rule God's creation. Those authorities who support this tradition, however, are careful to insist that the end of *al-baqara* (2) 30 (i.e. that the *khalīfa* will be iniquitous in it and shed blood) applies only to Adam's descendents, not to Adam himself.[20] In the end Ṭabarī prefers the definition of *khalīfa* as "follower" or "successor." He explains that rulers are called *khalīfa* ("caliph") only because they follow a predecessor.[21]

Zamakhsharī defines *khalīfa* simply as the one who is designated.[22] He offers no story about the *jinn* who lived on earth before humans. Instead he considers two explanations for his definition: either Adam was a *khalīfa* because God designated him (and his descendents) above the angels, or simply because each prophet is designated by God.[23]

14 Abū l-Ḥasan Ibrāhīm al-Qummī, *Tafsīr*, Beirut: Mu'assasat al-A'lamī li-l-Maṭbū'āt, 1412/1991, 1:49, on Q 2.30–4.

15 A creature identified by Islamic tradition (although not mentioned in the Qur'ān) as a mix between ape and human.

16 Qummī, 1:50, on Q 2.30–4.

17 Ibid.

18 Ṭabarī, 1:200, on Q 2.30. According to a second tradition (this on the authority of al-Ḥasan al-Baṣrī), however, *khalīfa* is actually a reference to Adam's son, who is the successor to his father. Ibid.

19 Ṭabarī recognizes (1:202) that the traditions applied to Ibn 'Abbās are incompatible.

20 Ṭabarī 1:200, on Q 2.30.

21 Ibid., 1:199, on Q 2.30.

22 Muḥammad al-Zamakhsharī, *Al-Kashf 'an ḥaqā'iq ghawāmiḍ al-tanzīl*, ed. Muḥammad Ḥusayn Aḥmad, Cairo: Maṭba'at al-Istiqāma, 1365/1946, 1:124, on Q 2.30–3. Here Zamakhsharī also mentions the alternative reading *khalīqa*.

23 Zamakhsharī, 1:124, on Q 2.30–3.

Ibn Kathīr follows the position of Ṭabarī that *khalīfa* means successor,[24] but he rejects the idea that Adam could be God's successor. He argues instead that the *khalīfa* in *al-baqara* (2) 30 refers only to humans inasmuch as they "succeed one another, century after century, and generation after generation."[25]

To bow or not to bow

The religious instinct that discouraged the *mufassirūn* from defining *khalīfa* as "representative" also rendered problematic God's command to the angels to prostrate before Adam.[26] The Qur'ānic term for prostration (*sajada*) is closely associated with worship, as indicated by the word for mosque, "the place of prostration" (*masjid*).[27] Thus even if there is an example in the Qur'ān of prostration before a human (namely Joseph; Q 12.100), the idea of the angels prostrating before Adam was infelicitous, to say the least, to believers who insisted that nothing but God should be worshipped (cf. Q 2.105, 135, 221, passim).[28] The fact that certain mystics, among them

24 Ibn Kathīr agrees with the views of his predecessors, among whom he names Rāzī, Zamakhsharī, and Qurṭubī, that the angels were not speaking about Adam, but rather about humanity in general, with their question: "Will you make on it one who will be iniquitous and shed blood . . . ?" Ibn Kathīr also mentions the view of Rāzī that this question was the angels' way of requesting to live on earth in the place of humans. When God responds, "I know what you do not know," He means, "that it is better for you to remain in heaven." On this tradition Ibn Kathīr adds skeptically, "and God knows better" (*wa-Allāhu aʿlam*). He is also skeptical of a second view, related in a prophetic *ḥadīth*, according to which the word "earth" in Q 2.30 in fact means "Mecca," since the world was created beginning with the holy city. Ibn Kathīr, *Tafsīr*, ed. Muḥammad Bayḍūn. Beirut: Dār al-Kutub al-ʿIlmiyya, 1424/2004, 1:71, on Q 2.30.

25 Ibn Kathīr, 1:70, on Q 2.30. In support of this view Ibn Kathīr cites other instances of the root *kh.l.f.* in the Qur'ān (namely Q 6.165; 19.59; 27.62; 43.60; cf. also Q 10.14), arguing that it relates to the succession of human generations. He likewise cites, but does not favor, traditions which describe humans as successors to the *jinn* (Ibn Kathīr, 1:71–2, on Q 2.30). So too he cites a narrative, reported on the authority of the fifth Shīʿī Imām Muḥammad al-Bāqir, which attributes the angels' protest in *al-baqara* (2) 30 to the evil angels Hārūt and Mārūt (cf. Q 2.102). On this Ibn Kathīr comments that Muḥammad al-Bāqir "transmitted [this tradition] from the People of the Book. It includes a reprehensible point that must be refuted." Ibn Kathīr, 1:72, on Q 2.30. On a following narrative he comments: "This is also an Israelite [story] to be rejected, like the one before it."

26 On this question cf. L. Chipman, "Adam and the angels: An examination of the mythic elements in Islamic sources," *Arabica* 49, 2002, 4, 429–55.

27 See *AEL*, 1308a.

28 Adam might seem particularly unfit for the veneration, since the Qur'ān never names him a prophet or a messenger, while it alludes to his sin (cf. Q 7.23; 20:121). The *mufassirūn*, nevertheless, insist that he was a prophet (see, e.g. *Tafsīr Muqātil*, 1:97–8, on Q 2.30; Qummī, 1:52, on Q 2.30–4) and generally find a way to excuse his sin. They argue, for example, that it was unintentional, or took place before he descended to Earth, or before he was called to prophethood. On this see Ṭabarī 1:224, on Q 2.34; M.J. Kister, "Ādam: A study of some legends in *Tafsīr* and *Ḥadith* literature," *Israel Oriental Studies* 13, 1993, (113–74) 147–52.

Ḥallāj (d. 309/922), proposed that the devil did the right thing by *rejecting* God's command to prostrate before Adam[29] demonstrates just how difficult this problem was.

Moreover, in a well-known *ḥadīth*, reported in the *Musnad* of Aḥmad b. Ḥanbal (d. 241/855), the *Ṣaḥīḥ* of Bukhārī (d. 256/870) and the *Sunna* of ʿAbdallāh b. Aḥmad b. Ḥanbal (d. 290/903), the Prophet reports, "God created Adam in His image (*ṣuratihi*)."[30] This *ḥadīth*, and the anthropomorphism which it implies, was an apple of discord in Islamic theology. In his commentary to Muslim (d. 261/875), wherein a different version of this *ḥadīth* appears,[31] Yaḥyā b. Sharaf al-Nawawī (d. 677/1278) comments:

> Some of the scholars refrain from speculating about [this *ḥadīth*], saying, "We believe that it is true even if it appears to be undesirable. Its meaning corresponds to [its appearance]." This is the teaching of those who follow the forefathers. It is sounder and safer. A second group says that one should speculate on this according to what corresponds to appropriate language for God Most High, namely, "There is nothing like Him" (Q 42.11).[32]

Nawawi's comment seems to reflect the efforts of rationalist theologians to explain away an ancient view of Adam as *imago Dei*,[33] a view accepted by those scholars, presumably Ḥanbalīs, who followed a more literal reading of the Qur'ān. In fact, the historian Ibn Miskawayh (d. 421/1030) reports a speech made by the caliph al-Rāḍī (r. 322/934–329/940) in 323/935 against the Ḥanbalīs, in which the caliph condemns them for holding that

29 On this see P. Awn, *Satan's Tragedy and Redemption*, Leiden: Brill, 1983, 122–34.

30 Aḥmad b. Ḥanbal, *Musnad*, "Musnad Abī Hurayra," 8191, Beirut: Dār al-Kutub al-ʿIlmiyya, 1413/1993, 2:421; Bukhārī, *Ṣaḥīḥ*, 79, "Al-Istiʾdhān," 1, Beirut: Dār al-Kutub al-ʿIlmiyya, 1420/1999, 4:142; ʿAbdallāh b. Aḥmad, *al-Sunna*, 1171, Mecca: Al-Maṭbaʿa al-Salafiyya, 1349, 186. G. Juynboll attributes the origin of this *ḥadīth* to ʿAbd al-Razzāq. See G.H.A. Juynboll, *The Encyclopedia of Canonical Ḥadīth*, Leiden: Brill, 2007, 33.

31 "If one of you fights his brother let him avoid the face. For God created Adam according to His image (*ṣūratihi*)." The predominance of the first *ḥadīth* suggests that the description of Adam as *imago Dei* is an ancient one, and its application to the question of where to punch secondary. See Muslim, "*al-Birr wa-l-ṣila wa-l-ādāb*," 32, 115, Beirut: Dār al-Kutub al-ʿArabiyya, 1421/2000, 16:136.

32 Nawawī, printed in the margin of the ʿAbd al-Bāqī edition of Muslim, 16:136.

33 D. Gimaret describes the casuistic efforts of Muslim theologians to explain the pronoun "his" in "his image" as *raḥmān* (divine mercy) or Adam himself, or an anonymous bystander; alternatively some scholars worked around the anthropomorphic content of this *ḥadīth* by defining *ṣūra* in the manner of *ṣifa*, explaining that Adam was created with the divine qualities of life, knowledge, sight, speech, etc., but not with the divine form. See D. Gimaret, *Dieu a l'image de l'homme: les anthropomorphismes de la sunna et leur interprétation par les théologiens*, Paris: Cerf, 1997, 123–36. Cf. Kister, "Ādam: A study of some legends in *Tafsīr* and *Ḥadith* literature," 137–8.

their own ugly faces were created in the pattern (*'alā l-mithāl*) of God's face.[34]

For his part *Tafsīr Muqātil* relates that the devil was not happy with the notion that God would create man as his *khalīfa*, but he kept his anger hidden after noticing the obedience of the angels. Yet when God shaped Adam from dirt, and left him lifeless for forty years, the devil took to mocking him, entering into Adam's behind and emerging from his mouth,[35] and declaring "I am fire, this is hollow clay, and fire overcomes clay" (cf. Q 34.20). God noticed the pride that dwelt within the devil and for this reason commanded the angels to prostrate to Adam. "He wanted to expose to the angels that which [the devil] was concealing inside."[36]

Qummī provides a similar explanation.[37] He adds that when God commanded the angels to prostrate, the devil, looking for a way out, declared: "O Lord, excuse me from prostrating before Adam and I will worship you in a way that the highest angels do not worship you." God responded, "I have no need of your worship."[38] Ṭabarī records a number of similar narratives, all of which make the point that the angelic prostration had no meaning in itself; the whole business was a ploy arranged by God to trap the devil.[39]

Zamakhsharī, however, focuses not on narratives but on a doctrinal point, that there are two types of prostration. Prostrating before God is an act of worship, while prostrating to anything else is only *takrima*, an act of honoring. This applies to the prostration before Adam as it does to the prostration before Joseph (Q 12.100).[40] In a similar manner Ibn Kathīr describes the angelic prostration before Adam as a great honor (*karāma 'aẓīma*).[41] While

34 Ibn Miskawayh, *K. Tajārib al-Umam*, ed. H.F. Āmidrūz (Baghdad: Muthannā, 1332/1914), 1:322 (s.a. 323).

35 *Tafsīr Muqātil* 1:97, on Q 2.30; read *fammihi* for *fihi*.

36 Ibid., 1:9, on Q 2.34.

37 "When God commanded the angels to prostrate to Adam, he uncovered the envy in the heart of the devil. Thus the angels knew that the devil was not like them." Qummī, 1:49, on Q 2.30–4.

38 Ibid., 1:52, on Q 2.30–4.

39 Ṭabarī describes in detail the triumph of the devil's tribe of angels (the tribe named "al-Jinn") over the *jinn* on earth, and even quotes his private boast: "I have done something no one else has done." Ṭabarī, 1:202, on Q 2.30. He also describes God's choice to form Adam from dirt and leave him lifeless for forty days (not forty years as *Tafsīr Muqātil* has it) as a way to provoke the devil, who used to pass by and kick him every day. When God declared to the angels: "I know what you do not know" (Q 2.30), He was alluding to the devil's pride, which would only become apparent to the angels when the devil refused to prostrate before Adam. Ibid., 1:202–3, on Q 2.30.

40 Zamakhsharī, 1:126–7, on Q 2.34–6. He adds that the devil was a *jinnī*; he refused to bow to Adam since God commanded explicitly only the angels to do so. Ibid., 1:127, on Q 2.34–6. Later (2:90, on Q 7.12) Zamakhsharī explains, "He only disobeyed the command of his Lord since he believed it was not obligatory."

41 Ibn Kathīr, 1:76, on Q 2.34.

Ibn Kathīr reports a narrative on humanity's creation, which combines motifs from a number of the traditions seen above,[42] he finds it unbelievable.[43] He prefers the idea that the angelic prostration was only an act of salutation, as in the case of Joseph (Q 12.100).[44] This was a practice, Ibn Kathīr comments, "among earlier nations, but was abrogated for our community."[45] To prove the point he relates how one of the companions of the Prophet (Mu'ādh), who had observed Syrians prostrating before their bishops and scholars, told Muḥammad, "You, O messenger of God, are more deserving of prostration."[46] The Prophet responded, "If I were to command any human to prostrate before another, I would command a woman to prostrate before her husband, due to the magnitude of his authority over her."[47]

According to another tradition the angels were actually prostrating before God, and simply used Adam as a *qibla*. In other words, Adam served to indicate the direction of their prostration. This is a reasonable idea, Ibn Kathīr comments,[48] but (on the basis of *isnād*s) he maintains that the prostration was simply an act of "honor, veneration, respect and greeting" for Adam.[49]

Subtext

The final tradition above has Adam standing in between the angels and God, so that the angels are actually prostrating to God. The Qur'ān's subtext

42 This narrative records the creation of the angels from light, the place of Iblīs (who was originally named Ḥārith) in a tribe of angels named "al-Jinn," the creation of the *jinn* from the fire of *samūm* (see Q 15.27), the creation of a human from sticky clay (*lāzib*, see Q 37.11), and the campaign of the angels (led by Iblīs) against the *jinn* who had grown evil on earth. This same tradition also relates how Iblīs (due to his pride after his triumph over the *jinn*) would strike the lifeless body of Adam, which made the sound of rattling pottery (see Q 55.14), and how, when God finally breathed His spirit into him, Adam tried to stand up prematurely (see Q 17.11). Ibn Kathīr, 1:76, on Q 2.34. This narrative also has Iblīs give a number of reasons for his refusal to prostrate: "I will not prostrate before him because I am better than him, older than him and stronger than him. You created me from fire and you created him from clay." Ibid., 1:76, on Q 2.34.

43 Pace this narrative he insists (as Zamakhsharī does), for example, that Iblīs is a *jinnī* and not an angel, in deference to *al-kahf* (18) 50 ("Iblīs was from the *jinn*."). Ibn Kathīr, 1:78. He cites a number of traditions to support this view, among them a prophetic *ḥadīth*: "Iblīs was not an angel even for an instant. He was the first of the *jinn* as Adam was the first of humanity." Ibn Kathīr adds that this *ḥadīth* has a valid *isnād*. Iblīs was included with the angels in the command to prostrate before Adam, he later explains, only due to his similarity to the angels.

44 Ibn Kathīr, 1:78, on Q 2.34.

45 Ibid.

46 Ibid.

47 Ibid.

48 In this context Ibn Kathīr notes Q 17.78, in which the setting of the sun establishes the time of prayer.

49 Ibn Kathīr, 1:78, on Q 2.34.

suggests that there may be something to this idea, except that God was not on the other side of Adam, he was in him.

The Bible, of course, does not report the story of the angels' protesting God's plans to create a human. Their protest, however, is a prominent feature of Jewish exegesis, for classical Jewish exegetes often understood Psalm 8.4 ("What are human beings that you spare a thought for them, or the child of Adam that you care for him?") as the angels' response to God's declaration in Genesis 1.26 ("Let us make man in our own image, in the likeness of ourselves, and let them be masters of the fish of the sea"). This juxtaposition of otherwise independent Biblical verses led to the narrative to which the Qur'ān is referring.

Thus in the Babylonian Talmud (*Sanhedrīn* 38b) Gn 1.26 and Psalm 8.4 are joined together to form a coherent narrative:

> When the Holy One, blessed be He, wished to create man, He [first] created a company of ministering angels and said to them: Is it your desire that we make a man in our image? They answered: Sovereign of the Universe, what will be his deeds? Such and such will be his deeds, He replied. Thereupon they exclaimed: Sovereign of the Universe, What are human beings that you spare a thought for them, or the child of Adam that you care for him? Thereupon He stretched out His little finger among them and consumed them with fire. The same thing happened with a second company. The third company said to Him: Sovereign of the Universe, what did it avail the former [angels] that they spoke to Thee [as they did]? the whole world is Thine, and whatsoever that Thou wishest to do therein, do it.[50]

Other midrashic narratives relate that the angels were moved to wonder, even to worship, by Adam's countenance. Thus *Genesis Rabba* 8.9: "When the Lord created Adam, the angels mistook him [for a divine being]. What did the Holy One, blessed be He, do? He caused sleep to fall upon him, and so all knew that he was [but mortal] man." *Genesis Rabba* continues by explaining, "Thus it is written, 'Have no more to do with humankind, which has only breath in its nostrils. How much is this worth?'" (cf. Isaiah 2.22).[51]

50 Cf. Shabbāt, 88b. See also Geiger, *Was hat Mohammed*, 97.

51 All quotations from *Midrash R.* are from the translations of H. Freedman et al. London: Soncino, 1983 (here 1:61). I have, however, adjusted Biblical quotations therein according to the New Jerusalem translation. Cf. *Ecclesiastes R.* (ca. 6th–8th century) 6:9 (trans. Freedman et al., 8:163).

According to *BT Sanhedrīn* (59b) the concern of the angels for Adam led to the serpent's jealousy of him: "Adam reclined in the Garden of Eden, whilst the ministering angels roasted flesh and strained wine for him. Thereupon the serpent looked in, saw his glory, and became envious of him." Cf. D. Sidersky, *Les origines des légendes musulmanes dans le coran et dans les vies des prophètes*, Paris: Geuthner, 1933, 14. According to the Wisdom of Solomon (2.24), the devil (not the serpent) was jealous of Adam.

According to most Jewish traditions, however, the angels never actually worship Adam.[52] In *Genesis Rabba* God disabuses the angels of their notion that Adam is divine. In Christian traditions, however, the angelic prostration is a regular feature.[53]

To Christians Adam is the prototype of Christ, and the scene of the angels' prostrating before him is an anticipation of the angelic worship of Christ described in Hebrews: "Again, when He brings the First-born into the world, He says: Let all the angels of God pay him homage" (1.6).[54] In Philippians 2.6–11 Paul similarly describes how "all beings in the heavens, on earth and in the underworld, should bend the knee at the name of Jesus" (v. 10).[55] The larger theme here of Christ's humility ("he emptied himself, taking the form of a slave," v. 7) and glorification ("and for this God raised him high," v. 9) forms a contrast between Adam and Christ. Adam was human and desired to become divine. Christ is divine and was willing to become human.[56]

Yet in a significant tradition of Christian literature, including the *Life of Adam and Eve*,[57] the *Gospel of Bartholemew*,[58] the *Gospel of*

52 A prominent exception is the Hebrew apocalypse 3 Enoch. When Enoch is taken into heaven, the angels protest at first, referring explicitly to the earlier protest of angels at the creation of Adam. Like the earlier angels, however, they submit to God's will and worship the man: "They said before the Holy One blessed be he, 'Lord of the Universe, did not the primeval ones give you good advice when they said, Do not create man!' The Holy One, blessed be he, replied 'I have made him and will sustain him' . . . [the angels objected] 'What right has he to be in heaven?' Again the Holy One, blessed be he, replied . . . 'I have chosen this one in preference to all of you, to be a prince and a ruler over you in the heavenly heights'. At once they all arose and went to meet me and prostrated themselves before me, saying, 'Happy are you, and happy your parents, because your Creator has favored you' " (3 Enoch 4:6). Trans P. Alexander in J.H. Charlesworth (ed.) *The Old Testament Pseudepigrapha*, Vol. I: *Apocalyptic Literature and Testaments*, New York: Doubleday, 1983, 223–315.

53 Thus Speyer (*BEQ*, 58) concludes: "Die qoranische Sage ist also zweifellos christlicher Herkunft." Cf. Geiger, *Was hat Mohammed*, 98.

54 In a similar way the Gospel authors use the title Son of Man for Jesus and emphasize that, as the Son of Man, he is to be worshipped (Mt 16.27; Mk 8.38; Lk 9.26). This comparison evokes Daniel's vision (Daniel 7.13–4) of a heavenly "son of man" who is given "rule, honor and kingship." On this see Masson, *Le Coran et la révélation judéo-chrétienne*, 208.

55 This passage is often considered to be a quotation of an early hymn. On this see E. Scott, "Philippians," *The Interpreter's Bible*, New York: Abingdon, 1946, 11, 46–7.

56 Elsewhere Paul explicitly makes Adam into an anti-type of Jesus: "Just as all die in Adam, so in Christ all will be brought to life" (1 Corinthians 15.22). Cf. Romans 5.12, 14; Colossians 1.15–6.

57 Extant in Greek, Latin, Armenian, Georgian, Slavonic, and Coptic versions. These versions are edited and translated in parallel columns by G. Anderson and M. Stone: *A Synopsis of the Books of Adam and Eve*, Atlanta: Scholars Press, 1999. Cf. online http://www3.iath.virginia.edu/anderson/vita/vita.html. D. Bertrand introduces the work in *La vie grecque d'Adam et Ève*, ed. and trans. D. Bertrand, Paris: Adrien-Maisonneuve, 1987 (see esp. pp. 32–7). The story of the fall of Satan does not appear in the Greek version of the *Life of Adam and Eve* (but only in the Armenian, Georgian, and Latin versions thereof).

58 The *Gospel of Bartholemew* is edited in N. Bonwetsch, "Die apokryphen Fragen des Bartholomäus," *Nachrichten von der Gesellschaft der Wissenschaften zu Göttingen: Philologisch-*

Nicodemus[59] and the *Cave of Treasures*, the comparison in Philippians 2 is not a contrast but a parallel. Adam is not an anti-type but an ante-type of Jesus. Both Adam and Jesus came down from heaven to earth; both were raised up in worship. To this end they relate the story of the angels' bowing to Adam. The *Life of Adam and Eve*, for example, recounts:

> Satan also wept loudly and said to Adam. "All my arrogance and sorrow came to pass because of you; for, because of you I went forth from my dwelling; and because of you I was alienated from the throne of the cherubs who, having spread out a shelter, used to enclose me; because of you my feet have trodden the earth."
>
> Adam replied and said to him, "What are our sins against you, that you did all this to us?"
>
> Satan replied and said, "You did nothing to me, but I came to this measure because of you, on the day on which you were created, for I went forth on that day. When God breathed his spirit into you, you received the likeness of his image. Thereupon, Michael came and made you bow down before God. God said to Michael, 'Behold I have made Adam in the likeness of my image.' Then Michael summoned all the angels and God said to them, 'Come, bow down to god whom I made.' Michael bowed first. He called me and said. 'You too, bow down to Adam.' I said, 'Go away, Michael! I shall not bow down to him who is posterior to me, for I am former. Why is it proper for me to bow down to him?' The other angels, too, who were with me, heard this, and my words seemed pleasing to them and they did not prostrate themselves to you, Adam. Thereupon, God became angry with me and commanded to expel us from our dwelling and to cast me and my angels, who were in agreement with me, to the earth; and you were at the same time in the Garden.[60]

Still closer to the Qur'ān is the version of this legend in the *Cave of Treasures*, a Syriac text written some time between the fourth and sixth centuries AD.[61]

historische Klasse 1897, 1–42; English trans. in M.R. James, *The Apocryphal New Testament*, Oxford: Clarendon 1924, 166–81; *NTA*, 1:539–57 (see esp. p. 549 for the fall of Satan).

59 See *NTA*, 1:501–34, esp. pp. 522–3; cf. M. Simon, "Adam et la rédemption dans la perspective de l'église ancienne," in R.J.Z. Werblowsky and C.J. Bleeker (eds.), *Types of Redemption*, Leiden: Brill, 1970, 62–71 (esp. p. 68).

60 *The Life of Adam and Eve*, Armenian version, 12.1-16.1 (cf. Latin and Georgian versions); Anderson and Stone, *Synopsis of the Books of Adam and Eve*, 10–12. In the *Gospel of Bartholemew*, meanwhile, God Himself bows to Adam. See *NTA*, 1:549.

61 M.D. Gibson argues that the *Cave of Treasures* was written in the sixth century, but most scholars favor an earlier date. See *Apocrypha Arabica*, *Studia Sinaitica* 8, ed. and trans. M.D. Gibson, London: C.J. Clay, 1901. Simon holds that the text was written in Syria in the fifth or sixth century: "Adam et la rédemption", 67. S.-M. Ri, meanwhile, argues that the *Cave of Treasures* predates Ephraem (d. 373). See his *Commentaire de la* Caverne des trésors, *CSCO* 581, Leuven: Peeters, 2000, 86; idem, "La Caverne des trésors: problèmes

Here the Biblical imagery of bending the knee (cf. Philippians 2.10) appears:

> God formed Adam with his holy hands, in His image and in His likeness. When the angels saw the image and the glorious appearance of Adam, they trembled at the beauty of his figure. . . . Moreover, the angels and celestial powers heard the voice of God saying to Adam "See, I have made you king, priest and prophet, Lord, leader and director of all those made and created. To you alone have I given these and I give you authority over everything I have created." When the angels and the archangels, the thrones and dominions, the cherubims and seraphins, that is when all of the celestial powers heard this voice, all of the orders bent their knees and prostrated before him.[62]

The *Cave of Treasures* continues by explaining how, and why, the devil refused to join the worship of the angels:

> When the leader of the lesser order saw the greatness given to Adam, he became jealous of him and did not want to prostrate before him with the angels. He said to his hosts, 'Do not worship him and do not praise him with the angels. It is proper that you should worship me, since I am fire and spirit, not that I worship something that is made of dirt.[63]

d'analyse littéraire," *IV Symposium Syriacum, Orientalia Christiana Analecta*, 229, Rome: Pontificium Institutum Studiorum Orientalium, 1987, 188–90. G. Anderson places the text in the fourth or fifth century. See G. Anderson, "The garments of skin in apocryphal narrative," in J. Kugel (ed.), *Studies in Ancient Midrash*, Cambridge, MA: Harvard University Press, 2001, 135.

The *Cave of Treasures* also had an important literary history in Arabic. A. Dillman estimates that the Arabic version was written by an Egyptian monophysite between 750 and 760. See "Bericht über das äthiopische Buch Clementinischer Schriften," *Nachrichten von der G.A. Universität und der königl. Gesellschaft der Wissenschaften zu Göttingen* 17–19, 1858, 201ff. P. de Lagarde agrees that the original author of the Arabic text was an Egyptian monophysite but argues that it was written still earlier, soon after the death of the Byzantine emperor Heraclius (d. 641). See his *Mittheilungen*, Göttingen: Dieterich, 1884–91, 4:12. Such an early date is quite unlikely in light of what is now known of the rise of Arabic literature generally. Still the *Cave of Treasures* was widely read in Arabic, as is attested by the larger number of extant manuscripts thereof. The Arabic version of the *Cave of Treasures* has been edited twice: *Die Schatzhöhle* (including both the Arabic and Syriac versions), ed. and trans. C. Bezold, Leipzig: Hinrisch'sche Buchhandlung, 1888; *Apocrypha Arabica*, ed. and trans. Gibson. A. Mingana has translated the Karshūnī version of the *Cave of Treasures* as the *Apocalypse of Peter* (*Woodbrooke Studies* 3, Cambridge: Heffer, 1931), a name that appears in some Arabic manuscripts for a text that follows the *Cave of Treasures*.

62 *Cave of Treasures*, 2:12–13, 2:22–5 (R. Oc.) = *La caverne des trésors*, *CSCO* 486 (French trans., 487), ed. and trans. S.-M. Ri, Leuven: Peeters, 1987, 17–21 (trans., 9). The last phrase ("all of the orders bent their knees and prostrated before him" is found in a variant manuscript tradition, see n. 2e).

63 *Cave of Treasures*, 3:1–2, p. 21 (trans., 11).

This marks a distinct development in the narrative on the devil's rebellion. According to the *Life of Adam and Eve*, the devil's excuse for not worshipping Adam is that he was created first.[64] In the *Cave of Treasures*, however, the devil's excuse is that he was created from fire, while Adam was created from dirt. It is this tradition that is reflected in the Qur'ān: "I am better than he is. You created me from fire. You created him from clay" (Q 7.12; cf. 15.33; 17.61; 38.76).

The Qur'ān's close connection with the Adam tradition of the *Cave of Treasures* also explains why the God of the Qur'ān would demand that the angels bow to Adam and to no other human (before Christ, at least). For in this light it appears that God orders the angels to bow to Adam because Adam is created in His image. Thus the angels do not worship a man. They worship the divine glory within him.

Of course, and as mentioned above, the idea of humans as *imago Dei* is rejected by Islamic theology. Yet the Qur'ān itself hardly rejects it. The creation of Adam as the *khalīfa* of God (Q 2.30) can mean nothing else, if what is understood by *imago Dei* is nothing physical.[65] And indeed for the Church fathers this phrase cannot redound to Adam's looks. Origen comments: "But if anyone suppose that this man who is made 'according to the image and likeness of God' is made of flesh, he will appear to represent God himself as made of flesh and in human form. It is most clearly impious to think this about God."[66] The idea of *imago Dei* relates not to the human body but to man's particular relationship with God and His creation, namely his place as *khalīfa*, God's vicegerent. Indeed this seems to be the view of the *Cave of Treasures* itself. Therein the angels do not bow to Adam when they see his glorious appearance, but only when they hear the authority that God has given him. The prostration of the angels to Adam in the Qur'ān might be understood fruitfully from this perspective.[67]

It might be added that, Islamic doctrine notwithstanding, the Qur'ān never refers to Adam as a prophet (*nabī*) or messenger (*rasūl*). This may be

64 *The Life of Adam and Eve*, 14.3; Anderson and Stone, *Synopsis of the Books of Adam and Eve*, 11.

65 On the Qur'ānic use of the term *khalīfa* see especially R. Paret, "Signification coranique de *ḫalīfa* et d'autres dérivés de la racine *ḫalafa*," *SI* 31, 1970, 211–7; W. Qadi, "The term 'khalīfa,' in early exegetical literature," *Die Welt des Islams* 28, 1988, 392–411; reprint *The Qur'an: Formative Interpretation*, ed. A. Rippin, Aldershot: Ashgate, 1999, 327–46. Cf. also F. Steppat, "God's deputy: Materials on Islam's image of man," *Arabica* 36, 1989, 163–72.

66 Origen, *Homilies on Genesis and Exodus*, trans. R.E. Heine, Washington: Catholic University of America Press, 1982, 63.

67 This is also the conclusion of Masson: "Si donc il a ordonné aux anges, créés de feu [sic], d'honorer *Adam*, formé d'argile, c'est, parce qu'à travers ce premier homme, les anges auraient dû reconnaître une créature privilégiée: *image* de Dieu, home parfait, auquel Allāh a *soumis* l'univers créé pour lui" (*Le Coran et la révélation judéo-chrétienne*, 206–7). Cf. the reflection of Massignon: "C'est parce que cette image, vêtue de gloire, Le recouvrait, que Dieu invita les Anges à L'adorer sous la *nâsoût*, sous l'humanité préfigurée d'Adam." *La passion d'al-Ḥallāj*, Paris: Geuthner, 1922, 2:602.

purely accidental, or it may be an indication that Adam is something other than a prophet, something more than a prophet. The incident of the names is also suggestive in this regard. God concludes His address to the angels in *al-baqara* (2) 30 with the declaration "I know what you do not know." Where, one might ask, does the Qur'ān explain what it is that the angels do not know? According to the popular narrative among the *mufassirūn* God knows the pride that dwelt inside of Iblīs after he defeated the *jinn*. Yet the Qur'ān itself, only several verses later, seems to provide the answer. When God asks the angels about the names they reply, "Glory be to You! We have knowledge only of the things you taught us" (Q 2.32). Tellingly, the one who knows the names, the one who knows what the angels do not know, is Adam (Q 2.33).

Finally it is worth noting that the Qur'ān, like the *Cave of Treasures*, presents Adam as a prototype of Christ. In *āl 'Imrān* (3) 59, the Qur'ān relates: "The likeness (*mathal*) of Jesus before God is as the likeness of Adam. He created [Adam] from dirt and then said to him 'Be' and he was" (cf. Q 3.47). According to the traditional Islamic interpretation of this verse, found even from the time of Ibn Hishām (d. 218/833; he ascribes it to the meeting of Muḥammad with a delegation of Christians from Najrān),[68] the Adam/Christ comparison here is meant as a refutation of Christians,[69] since Christians claimed that the Virgin Birth proves Christ's divinity. But the larger context of this passage (from Q 3.45ff.) suggests that the Qur'ān's intent here is to venerate, not qualify, the attributes of Christ. Its comparison with Adam is the high point of this veneration.[70]

The interpretation of Ibn Hishām is anyway peculiar, since early Christians did not regularly use the Virgin Birth in their apologies for Christ's divinity (but turned instead to Christ's declarations, his miracles, his transfiguration, his resurrection, and so on). On the contrary, early Christians themselves emphasized the parallel between the births of Adam and Christ. Irenaeus, for example, relates, "the Word itself, taking its existence from Mary, who remained ever virgin, had a generation that recapitulates that of Adam."[71] Others, and in particular the Syriac Fathers, insisted that Adam was created

68 Ibn Hishām, *Sīrat Rasūl Allāh*, 409 (trans., 276).

69 Ibn Hishām's reading of this Qur'ānic verse is something like the view that Cassian (d. 435) attributes to Nestorius: "You assert the Lord Jesus to have been like in all and equal (*similem in omnibus et parum*) to Adam: Adam indeed [created] without seed and Jesus too without seed; the first only a man and the second, too, a man and nothing more." *De Incarnatione Christi* 7.6, *Corpus Scriptorum Ecclesiasticorum Latinorum* 17, ed. M. Petschenig, Vindobonae: Tempsky, 1888, 362.

70 Cf. the view of M. Sfar, who argues (*Le Coran, la Bible et l'orient ancien*, 120–7) that in the post-Biblical tradition the devil was increasingly understood by Jews and Christians as a deity ("une divinité ennemie du Dieu suprême," 122). Regarding Q 3.59 he concludes "Il est évident que le rapprochement fait plus tard par le Coran entre Adam et Jésus s'inspire de ce cycle judéo-chrétien" (p. 135).

71 *Contra Haereses*, 3.26.10–11.

in the image of Christ. In his *Homilies Against the Jews* Jacob of Serūgh (d. 521) challenges the Jews:

> Why did the Father say, 'let us make man in our image'?
> In whose likeness was Adam created?"[72]

Jacob continues by explaining that the human nature of Christ was, conversely, created in the image of Adam:

> Christ who became one of us, is the second Adam,
> who resembles the first, modeled according to his image.
> God contemplated how He should present His son,
> under what form He would come into the world, which He would save,
> and it was in this image, by which he made Adam, that He made [Christ],
> so that the master would take the form of the slave, when He would save [the world].[73]

If the Qur'ān does not have the same Christology, it does reflect this Adam-Christ typology. The Qur'ān has Christ, like Adam, created directly from the Spirit of God. Speaking of Mary's conception of Christ, the Qur'ān has God declare, "[She is the one who] preserved her chastity. We breathed Our Spirit into her and made her, and her son, signs to the worlds" (Q 21.91; cf. 66.12; Gn 2.7). On the creation of Adam the Qur'ān has God declare, "I shaped him and breathed into him My spirit, so fall down prostrate before him" (Q 15.29; cf. 32.9; 38.72; Lk 1.35).[74] Thus when the Qur'ān compares the birth of Christ with that of Adam in *āl 'Imrān* (3) 59 it is indeed making

72 *Homélies contre les juifs*, *PO* 174, ed. and trans. M. Albert, Turnhout, Belgium: Brepols, 1976, 46, ll. 33–4. Origen likewise has Adam created not in the image of God but in the image of Christ. *Homilies on Genesis and Exodus*, 12; cf. also Tertullian: "Id utique quod finxit, ad imaginem Dei fecit illum, scilicet Christi." *De Resurrectione Carnis* 6, *PL* 2, ed. J.-P. Migne, Paris: Migne, 1879, 848. In a second sermon Jacob addresses Christ directly:

> When your compassionate Father fashioned Adam in His image,
> it was You He depicted in him;
> for in You the dust that had multiplied would be adorned.
> He gave to Adam Your likeness when He created him,
> so that he might put it on,
> and by it reign over and possess all of creation.

Jacob of Serūgh in, "Jacob of Serūgh's Verse Homily on Tamar," ed. and trans. S. Brock, *Le Muséon* 115 (2002), (279–315) 281, ll. 41–4 (English trans., 294).

73 *Homélies contre les juifs*, 46, ll. 35–40.

74 For spirit Blachère translates here "souffle de vie."

a polemical point, only not against the Christians. On the contrary, it is arguing against the Jews, who deny the Virgin Birth and Christ himself.

The case of the angelic prostration is particularly illustrative of the virtue in appreciating the Qur'ān's subtext. If, as the *mufassirūn* have it, God ordered the angels to prostrate only to expose the pride of the devil, or to greet Adam in the way that Joseph's family bowed before him (Q 12.100) then the prostration in itself loses its meaning. The interpretations of certain western scholars have the same effect. Torrey, for example, argues that the angelic prostration of the Qur'ān reflects Oriental customs of salutation.[75] The current study suggests that it reflects instead a rich tradition of religious interpretation.

CS 2 *al-Shayṭān al-Rajīm*

Qur'ānic account

In the previous case study I note the manner in which the Qur'ān distinguishes between the devil as celestial rebel against God, as the leader of evil beings in heaven (see Q 26.59), whom it names Iblīs, and the devil as the tempter of humans on earth (see Q 7.20; 20.120; 41.36; 114.4), whom it names Shayṭān. To the name Shayṭān, but never to the name Iblīs, the Qur'ān often adds another term: *rajīm* (Q 3.36; 15.34; 16.98; 38.77). This term thus seems to be a mark of the devil's state after his banishment from heaven. When the devil refuses to bow before Adam (Q 15.33; cf. 26.210–2; 38.76), God turns to him and proclaims: "Leave here, you are *rajīm*" (Q 15.34; cf. 38.77).

In *al-ḥijr* (15) 17 the Qur'ān uses the term *rajīm* not for Satan (*shayṭān*) alone but for the *shayāṭīn*, or demons (i.e. the hosts of the devil), in general. Here the Qur'ān's concern is cosmology. It describes how God has placed towers (*burūj*; Q 15.16) in heaven to protect it from "every *shayṭān rajīm*" (Q 15.17; cf. 37.7; 41.12). Here again it appears that the *rajīm* is the one who is barred from entering heaven. This idea clarifies *al-takwīr* (81) 25, where the Qur'ān insists it has not been affected by any *shayṭān rajīm*; that is, no demon has influenced its composition.[76] The Qur'ān intends, in other words, that no demon is able to enter heaven, or the divine council, whence revelation originates (Q 26.210–2). Therefore no demon is able to mar the heavenly book.

75 C.C. Torrey, *The Jewish Foundation of Islam*, New York: Jewish Institute of Religion, 1933, 71. Tisdall contends that the appearance of this account in the Qur'ān is a product of Muḥammad's (wrong) assumption that Adam, and not Christ, is intended in Hebrews 1.6. Tisdall, *Original Sources of the Qur'an*, 197.

76 In these instances *rajīm* is parallel in syntactic terms to *mārid* or "rebellious," as in *al-ḥājj* (22) 3: "they follow every Satan *mārid*" (cf. Q 27.7). We will see below that the two terms are parallel as well semantically.

Problems for interpreters

If the meaning of *rajīm* thus seems evident, it did not always seem so to the interpreters. For the matter is rendered complicated by the base meaning of the Arabic root *r.j.m.*, namely, "to stone."[77] Thus in *al-ḥijr* (15) 17, where cosmology is the issue, Paret translates *kulli shayṭānin rajīm* as "jedem gesteinigten Satan." However, a bit further on in the same Sūra, when Satan's banishment from the garden is the issue, Paret translates *fa-innaka rajīmun* as "Du bist (von jetzt ab) verflucht." As though to reconcile the two ideas Pickthall and Abdel Haleem translate here "outcast," a word which conveniently has some sense of "stoned" (or at least "thrown") and some sense of "cursed." In *al-takwīr* (81) 25, however, Pickthall turns to the idea of stoning, translating *bi-qawli shayṭānin rajīm* as "utterance of a devil worthy to be stoned."[78]

The job of translation becomes yet more difficult with *al-mulk* (67) 5: The Qur'ān here remarks: "We have adorned the lowest heaven [*samā' al-dunyā*] with lamps and made them *rujūm* for demons [*shayāṭīn*]." If *rajīm* is understood as "outcast" or "cursed" then what to do with the related plural noun *rujūm*? Most follow Islamic tradition, and the standard Arabic meaning of the root, and translate "missiles" (thus Pickthall, Yusuf Ali, Fakhry, and Abdel Haleem). Thereby they connect this verse to other Qur'ānic passages which have a *shihāb* ("comet, firebrand") chase away the demons or jinn who try to enter heaven (cf. Q 15.18; 37.10; 67.7; 72.9). Paret adds a parenthetical explanation: "diese (zugleich) zu Wurfgeschossen für die Satane gemacht (um sie damit zu verjagen, wenn sie aus Neugierde zu nahe an den Himmel herankommen)." Paret again turns to this idea in his translation of *al-ṣāffāt* (37) 8, where the Qur'ān seems to relate that the demons "are thrown [from heaven] from every side" (*yuqdhafūna min kulli jānibin*). Paret, however, relates that it is the stars that are thrown: "Vielmehr wirft man von überallher (mit Sternen) nach ihnen."

As for the *mufassirūn*, *Tafsīr Muqātil* glosses *rajīm* with "cursed" (*mal'ūn*),[79] and remarks elsewhere that God made the stars into missiles (*ramiyyāt*) for the demons.[80] Qummī agrees, explaining that God did so because "the demons would continuously ascend to heaven and spy."[81] He adds an anecdote on the birth of the Prophet Muḥammad in the words of his mother, Āmina. When she was about to give birth, Āmina recounts, a light emerged from her that illuminated everything between heaven and earth. At that moment, "The demons were struck with stars and cut off from heaven."[82] At this, she

77 Lane defines the first form verbal noun *rajm* as "The throwing, or casting, of stones." *AEL*, 3:1047c.

78 In this latter sense M. Gaudefroy-Demombynes defines *rajīm* as "driven away and struck with projectiles of fire by the angels." M. Gaudefroy-Demombynes, "*Radjm*," *EI*[2], 8:379a.

79 *Tafsīr Muqātil*, 2:429.

80 Ibid., 4:390, on Q 67.5.

81 Qummī, 1:375, on Q 15.17.

82 Ibid., 1:376.

continues, the demons gathered around the devil complaining of their fate. In response the devil sought to enter the Ka'ba, but the angel Gabriel, wielding a spear, blocked his path and shouted: "Go away accursed one (*mal'ūn*)."[83] When Gabriel explained that the Prophet was about to be born, the devil asked: " 'Will I have any success with him?' [Gabriel] said, 'No.' He said, 'And with his community?' [Gabriel] said, 'Yes.' He said, 'Then I am satisfied.' "[84]

For his part Ṭabarī is unusually laconic in his commentary on *rajīm*. In his explanation of *al-ḥijr* (15) 34 Ṭabarī defines this term as "insulted" (*mashtūm*) or "cursed" (*mal'ūn*).[85] Yet he does not connect this meaning to the appearance of *rujūm* in *al-mulk* (67) 5. There he notes simply that God made stars for three purposes: as decorations for the sky, to stone demons, and as guiding signs (i.e. in navigation).[86]

Zamakhsharī defines *rajīm* as one who would be stoned with shooting stars (*shuhub*) or (idiomatically) one who is expelled from the mercy of God.[87] In his commentary on *al-mulk* (67) 5 Zamakhsharī repeats the same tradition of Ṭabarī on the three purposes of the stars. He adds, however, that it cannot be the stars themselves that are cast at demons, only a sort of firebrand (*qabs*) from them.[88] Ibn Kathīr follows Zamakhsharī closely here, repeating the "three purposes" tradition, and commenting: "He does not cast the stars that are in the sky but other shooting stars (*shuhub*), which might be extensions of [the stars]. God knows better."[89] Elsewhere Ibn Kathīr explains the fall of the devil with the comment, "God *ablasahu* (cf. Iblīs), which means 'made [the devil] despair of all goodness,' and made him a *shayṭān rajīm*, punished for his rebellion." In fact Iblīs does not come from the Arabic verb *ablasa*, but is an Arabized form of Greek διάβολος.[90] *Rajīm*, too, has a foreign origin, as we will see presently.

Subtext

In his *Neue Beiträge zur semitischen Sprachwissenschaft*, Nöldeke proposes that Qur'ānic *rajīm* is not to be understood in light of the standard Arabic root *r.j.m.* ("to stone") but rather in light of Ethiopic *ragama*, "to curse,

83 Ibid.

84 Ibid., 1:377.

85 Ṭabarī, 13:32, on Q 15.34.

86 Ibid., 29:3–4, on Q 67.5.

87 "For the one who is expelled is stoned. It means cursed, because a curse means being expelled from mercy and kept far away from it." Zamakhsharī, 2:577, on Q 15.34.

88 Ibid., 4:577, on Q 67.5.

89 Ibn Kathīr, 4:367, on Q 67.5. Ibn Kathīr also agrees with Zamakhsharī's basic definition of *rajīm*, glossing it with *marjūm*, "what is stoned." Ibn Kathīr, 2:522, on Q 15.34–8. Ibn Kathīr, 1:76, on Q 2.34.

90 See *FV*, 57–8.

insult."[91] It is a form of this term (*rəgəmt*) that is used in the Ethiopic Bible for the cursing of the serpent in Genesis 3.14 (אָרוּר; LXX ἐπικατάρατος), and for the casting of the condemned into the fire with the devil in Matthew 25.41 (Gk. κατηραμένοι). Moreover, in Ethiopic texts an adjectival form of this term is commonly used together with Satan in the phrase *sayṭān rəgūm* ("cursed Satan").[92] Since Qur'ānic *shayṭān* also seems to have an Ethiopic provenance,[93] there is reason to think that this phrase entered into Arabic (and eventually the Qur'ān) as the unit *al-shayṭān al-rajīm*.

91 T. Nöldeke, *Neue Beiträge zur semitischen Sprachwissenschaft*, Strassburg: Trübner, 1910, 25, 47; Jeffery (*FV*, 139–40) agrees.

92 On this cf. Ahrens, "Christliches im Qoran," 39; *FV*, 140.

93 Ar. Shayṭān, of course, is cognate with Heb. *śāṭān* (and thence Syr. *sāṭānā*, Gk. σατᾶν; see *FV*, 190). Yet as Nöldeke (*Neue Beiträge*) points out, the diphthong ("ay") in the first syllable points to an etymology through Ethiopic *sayṭān*. Most scholars follow him in this, including Rudolph (*Abhängigkeit*, 34–5), Horovitz (*KU*, 120), Speyer (*BEQ*, 70) and Jeffery (*FV*, 190). Recently, however, G. Puin has proposed that Qur'ānic Shayṭān may in fact be a misreading of Shāṭān (in which case an etymology Heb.>Syr.>Ar. would be preferable), noting that in early Qur'ān mss. medial *yā'* is occasionally used as a *mater lectionis* for *alif*. See G. Puin in "Neue Wege der Koranforschung," *Magazin Forschung* 1/1999, 39. M. Kropp counters that the presence of the diphthong in the first syllable of the Ethiopic form of the root renders such speculation unnecessary. See his "Der äthiopische Satan = *šayṭān* und seine koranischen Ausläufer; mit einer Bemerkung über verbales Steinigen," *OC* 89, 2005, (93–102) 93. C. Luxenberg responds by noting (with Puin) that medial *yā'* is used as a *mater lectionis* in early Qur'ānic manuscripts. He then argues (in a remarkably complicated fashion) that the pronunciation of Satan (written شيطن) as *shayṭān* developed due to the influence of the Syriac root *s.'.ṭ.* (which Luxenberg argues is behind the Syriac and Qur'ānic forms of Satan, see pp. 56–7) and the tendency in Eastern Syriac to suppress the pronunciation of the *'ayn*. Thus the classical Syriac term *sa'īṭā* (meaning "the detested" or "the rejected") was pronounced in the East with a diphthong: *sayṭā*. See C. Luxenberg, "Zur Morphologie und Etymologie von syro-aramäisch *sāṭānā*=Satan und koranisch-arabisch *šayṭān*," in Burgmer, *Streit um den Koran* (46–66) 46–59.

Long before this debate Wellhausen argued that Shayṭān is an Arabic term, pointing to the Arabic root *ṣ.ṭ.n.* (cf. *AEL*, 1552a; despite the difference in the first consonant), and the use thereof by Jāhilī poets including Umayya b. Abī l-Ṣalt. See his *Reste arabischen Heidentums*, Berlin: Reimer, 1897, 200, n. 1. Cf. also F. Praetorius, who argued that the Ethiopic *sayṭān* in fact came from Arabic: "Äthiopische Etymologien," *ZDMG* 61, 1907, 261–2. However, Horovitz (*KU*, 1201), Speyer (*BEQ*, 68–71), and Kropp ("Der äthiopische Satan") all argue against Wellhausen on linguistic grounds. There is also reason to suspect that Wellhausen's poetic witnesses are not pre-Islamic and likely influenced by the Qur'ān itself.

Finally, Horovitz (*KU*, 121), Jeffery (*FV*, 188), and Kropp ("Der äthiopische Satan," 93) note that the Arabic lexicographers (also on the basis of poetry) list "snake" as a meaning for *shayṭān*. Both Horovitz and Jeffery propose that this meaning is somehow influenced by the use of Shayṭān in the Qur'ān. Horovitz comments: "Und wie die Araber sich diese 'shayāṭīn' als Schlangen vorstellten, vielleicht gar sie nach ihnen benannten, so war umgekehrt die Schlange also Versucherin im Paradies in den christlichen Versionen und Ausbildungen der Erzählung zum Satan geworden" (*KU*, 121). Jeffery (*FV*, 189) wonders if the Arab belief in the supernatural power of snakes could have led to the use of Shayṭān as a name of the devil. Kropp, however, maintains that any original Arabic term Shayṭān with the meaning of snake has "nothing to do with Qur'ānic *Shayṭān* 'devil; Satan'" ("Beyond Single Words: *mā'ida – Shayṭān – jibt and ṭāghūt*," *QHC*, 204–16).

Now there are some problems with ascribing an Ethiopic origin to any Qur'ānic term. Christian Ethiopic literature appears by the late fourth century, but it largely consists of translations from Greek and Aramaic (esp. Syriac). Moreover, the great bulk of the Christian manuscripts (including the Bible) are post-Qur'ānic and indeed quite late (ca. 1300 onwards). Of course none of this precludes the possibility that Ethiopic *sayṭān rəgūm* is the immediate source of the Qur'ānic phrase *al-shayṭān al-rajīm*. Yet it is important to note that the root *r.j.m.* (Hebrew *r.j.n.* is likely related) is used in various Semitic languages with a meaning appropriate to the character of Satan.[94] In two different Mandaean incantations this root is used to describe the cursed state of demonic forces.[95] What the Qur'ān itself means by the term *rajīm* I will address presently.

Yet this matter is complicated by the appearance of *rujūm* in *al-mulk* (67) 5, which seems to make the stars into missiles cast at demons. By Nöldeke's explanation, this idea emerged from Muḥammad's misunderstanding of the term *rajīm*. If the term originates from Ethiopic (with a meaning "curse") Muḥammad understood it according to the Arabic root *r.j.m.*, which is related to stoning.[96] So he came up with the idea of God stoning *al-shayṭān al-rajīm* from heaven. The stars are the stones, or *rujūm*. It is this idea, of course, that presumably lies behind the tradition of stoning pillars associated with the devil during the *ḥājj*, a ritual that is not mentioned in the Qur'ān.

Thus Nöldeke proposes that the Qur'ān uses one sense of *r.j.m.* (related to cursing) in its reference to the banishment of Satan from the garden, and

94 Leslau notes that while Heb. *rāgam* has the meaning of "stone, imprecate," in other northern Semitic languages, including Aramaic/Syriac, Ugaritic, and Akkadian this root has a meaning related to "speak," "shout," or "accuse." Hence he suggests the semantic development of the root is: "speak, say > speak against, bring legal action against > abuse, curse > cast stones." *LCD*, 465. F. Rosenthal argues that the Hebrew cognate to the Akkadian and Ugaritic root *r.g.m.* is *r.g.n.* and points to its use of Proverbs (16.28; 18.8; 26.20, 22) with the meaning of "slanderer." On this basis, and in light of other Jewish writings that use the root in connection with the "rebellious talk of the snake in Genesis," he suggests that it might be understood as "slanderer" and thus essentially equivalent with διάβολος. See F. Rosenthal, "Some minor problems in the Qur'ān," *The Joshua Starr Memorial Volume*, New York: Conference on Jewish Relations, 1953, 67–84; reprint: *What the Koran Really Says*, ed. Ibn Warraq (322–42), 338.

95 I am grateful to Adam Silverstein of Oxford University for drawing my attention to these texts, which were discovered on bowls and date to ca. AD 600. The first text reads: "Bound and sealed and cut and muzzled and encompassed and whipped and blinded and stopped and deafened are the cures and incantation, and evil eye and the envious and dim-seeing eye of poverty. Muzzled and *rgīmā* [the translation has 'stoned'] and closed!" Trans. E.M. Yamauchi, *Mandaic Incantation Texts*, New Haven: Yale University Press, 1967, 226–9 (text 20, ll. 17–19). Cf. the similar second text on pp. 272–5 (text 27, l. 14).

96 *Neue Beiträge*, 25. G. van Vloten offers another opinion, arguing that in the days of Muḥammad Arabs would pelt snakes with rocks. Hence Muḥammad connected the idea of stoning with the cursing of the serpent (and thus Satan) in the Eden story. See G. van Vloten, *Feestbundel aan de Goeje*, Leiden: Brill, 1891, 35, 42; idem, "Daemonen, Geister und Zauber bei den alten Arabern," *Wiener Zeitschrift für die Kunde des Morgenlandes* 7, 1893, (169–87, 233–47) 175.

another sense of *r.j.m.* (related to stoning) in its cosmology. Yet, in the light of Jewish and Christian tradition, there is reason to think that the Qur'ān's story of Satan's banishment and the Qur'ān's cosmology are connected.

If Genesis has only a serpent in the garden, a number of Jewish texts suggest that the serpent is to be identified with Satan, and Christian texts make that identification explicit.[97] The Qur'ān seems to continue this exegetical development by doing away with the serpent altogether and having Satan alone in the garden.

Moreover, if Genesis seems to have the Garden of Eden in a well-watered valley or plain somewhere in Mesopotamia, a prominent exegetical tradition locates the Garden of Eden on a high mountain where heaven and earth meet, the "cosmic mountain," as Gary Anderson names it.[98] The notion of a cosmic mountain is suggested already in some Old Testament passages, such as 2 Kings 2, where Elijah is taken "*up* to heaven in the whirlwind" (2 Kings 2.11) and cannot be found by the fifty men who search for him over three days (v. 17). The prophecy of Ezekiel (ch. 26) against Tyre reflects the notion that when God curses humans – as he did Adam – He sends them *down*. Here Yahweh describes how he will, "fling you [Tyre] down with those

97 The main Jewish exegetical texts do not explicitly identify the serpent with Satan (although cf. the manner in which God rebukes Satan in Zechariah 3:1–2, which is reminiscent of Gn 3.14), but this association becomes increasingly apparent in later texts. Already in 4 Maccabees 18.7–8, the woman relates, "nor did the Destroyer, the deceitful serpent, defile the purity of my virginity." *Gn R.* (17:6; trans. Freedman et al., 1:137) mentions only that Satan was created along with the woman, but *Pirqē de-Rabbī Elī'ezer* (13) identifies the serpent with Samael, the angel of death. See *Pirke de-Rabbi Elieser*, ed. and trans. D. Börner-Klein, Berlin: de Gruyter, 2004, 135. The *Targum of Pseudo-Jonathan* similarly comments (on Gn 3.6) that Eve, when speaking to the serpent, saw Samael.

The Christian association of the serpent in Genesis with Satan is evident already with texts such as Romans 16.20 and Revelation 12.9. Justin Martyr refers to, "the devil himself, that is, the one whom Moses called the serpent" (*Dialogue with Trypho*, 103; trans. T.B. Falls, Washington: Catholic University of America Press, 1948, 309). Augustine (*City of God*, 14.11), describes the serpent as the tool of Satan. Ephraem calls Satan the one who bit Eve in the heel ("Hymn on the Nativity of Christ," *Hymni et Sermones*, ed. J. Lamy, Mechliniae: Dessain, 1886–1902, 2:457) and the serpent a "garment for the evil one to put on" (Ephrem, *Hymns on Paradise*, 15:24, trans. S. Brock, Crestwood, NY: St. Vladimir's Seminary Press, 1990, 187). Both the *Cave of Treasures* and Jacob of Serūgh, in his *Homily on the Departure of Adam from Paradise*, explain that Satan took possession of the serpent before entering the garden to tempt Adam and Eve. The *Cave* explains that Satan did so in order to hide his terrifying appearance, while Jacob concludes instead that he did so to hide *from* the glorious divine image of Adam. *Cave of Treasures*, ed. Bezold, 2:22; Jacob of Serūgh, *Quatre homélies métriques sur la création*, vv. 305–22, pp. 43–4 (trans., 48–9). Accordingly both Geiger (*Was hat Mohammed*, 99) and Speyer (*BEQ*, 70) argue that the presence of Satan in the Qur'ān's garden account indicates that it has a Christian origin. Cf. *TB*, 98–100.

98 On this see G. Anderson, "The cosmic mountain: Eden and its interpreters in Syriac Christianity," in G.A. Robbins (ed.), *Genesis 1-3 in the History of Exegesis: Intrigue in the Garden*, Lewiston: Mellen, 1988, 187–223.

who go down into the abyss, with the people of long ago, and put you deep in the underworld, in the ruins of long ago with those who sink into oblivion, so that you can never come back or be restored to the land of the living" (v. 20).

The New Testament suggests that the paradise above is nothing other than the Garden of Eden. In 2 Corinthians 12:2–4 Paul reports having met a man who was "caught *up* right into the third heaven . . . up into paradise." In Revelation 2.7 Jesus declares, "Those who prove victorious I will feed from the tree of life set in God's paradise."[99] Most significant, perhaps, is the manner in which the geography of heaven is reflected in Revelation 12.9. In Genesis 3.23, Adam is sent *out* of the garden (וַיְשַׁלְּחֵהוּ; LXX: ἐξαπέστειλεν; Psh. ܘܫܕܪܗ). In Revelation, however, Satan is sent *down*: "The great dragon, the primeval serpent, known as the devil or Satan, who had led all the world astray, was hurled down (ἐβλήθη; Psh. ܐܬܪܡܝ) to the earth and his angels were hurled down with him." In the same way the Qur'ān has God send Adam, Eve, and Satan *down* (*ihbiṭū*; Q 2.38).

The idea of the cosmic mountain is prominent in midrashic traditions, some of which connect the Temple mount with Eden.[100] Yet it is especially central to Syriac Christian tradition. The *Cave of Treasures* explains that "Paradise is in a high place. It is higher than all of the lofty mountains."[101] Ephraem, for his part, describes the mountain of paradise in detail towards the opening of his *Hymns on Paradise*:

> With the eye of my mind * I gazed upon paradise;
> the summit of every mountain * is lower than its summit,
> the crest of the Flood * reached only its foothills;
> these it kissed with reverence * before turning back,
> to rise above and subdue the peak * of every hill and mountain.
> The foothills of Paradise it kisses * while every summit it buffets.[102]

99 On this see *TB*, 105–7.

100 On this see Anderson, "The cosmic mountain." As Anderson explains, the notion of a cosmic mountain has deep roots in North-West Semitic religious traditions. In Jewish tradition Sinai is also presented as a cosmic mountain. A tradition in *Gn R.*, for example, explains that Moses fasted while on top of the mountain not due to some religious discipline, but rather because he had entered into the heavenly realm, where there is no eating or drinking. See *Gn R.* 48:14, trans. Freedman et al., 1.413; cf. *Leviticus R.* 34:8, trans. Freedman et al., 4:433.

101 Ed. Bezold, 2:20. As Anderson explains, the language here is shaped by Gn 7.19, which relates that the flood covered all of the lofty mountains. By making the cosmic mountain still higher, the *Cave of Treasures*, like Ephraem (see the following citation), implies that it was untouched by the Flood. Anderson, "Cosmic mountain," 220, n. 52.

102 Ephraem, *Hymnen De Paradiso und Contra Julianum*, 1:4; *CSCO* 174, ed. E. Beck, Louvain: Secrétariat du CorpusSCO, 1957, 2; English trans.: *Hymns on Paradise*, trans. S. Brock, Crestwood, NY: St. Vladimir's Seminary Press, 1990, 78–9.

By this tradition, prevalent in Syriac texts, the cosmic mountain is at once the lowest level of heaven and the highest level of earth. The devil is sent here when, after refusing to worship Adam, he is expulsed from the higher levels of heaven, along with his lower order of angels.[103] In the garden the devil enters into the body of the serpent, and proceeds in his jealousy to lead man astray.[104] When God punishes the serpent, he falls again. The serpent is punished to crawl on its belly, to eat dust, and to suffer the enmity of the woman and her offspring, who will bruise its head (Gn 3.14–5). The devil, meanwhile, is expulsed from the cosmic mountain: "For the serpent it was decreed that it and all its seed should be trampled – so it was decreed against Satan who was in the serpent that he should go to the fire along with all his hosts."[105]

Thus the devil is shut out from the heavenly garden forever.[106] Henceforth only those whom Christ raises up will be able to scale the mountain and enter the garden. Ephraem reflects:

> By those who are outside * the summit cannot be scaled,
> but from inside Paradise inclines its whole self * to all who ascend it;
> the whole of its interior * gazes upon the just with joy.
> Paradise girds the loins * of the world,
> encircling the great sea * neighbor to the beings on high,
> friendly to those within it * hostile to those without.[107]

The language of paradise encircling the world is particularly telling, since it suggests that the cosmic mountain is at once a peak and a firmament. It effectively blocks the devil and his hosts from entering the celestial realm. Its function, in other words, is not unlike that of the *burūj* (Q 15.16), the *kawākib* ("stars"; Q 37.6), or the *maṣābīḥ* ("lamps"; Q 67.5) of the Qur'ān, which block the demons and the jinn from entering heaven (or, in the case of 67.5, the lowest heaven: *samā' al-dunyā*). The celestial realm is blocked in this way because of the disobedience of Satan and Adam. In this tradition cosmology reflects sacred history. Jacob of Serūgh reflects:

103 N.b. the passage from the *Cave of Treasures* quoted above (CS 1; *Cave*, 3:1–2, p. 21; trans., 11), which continues: "Saying these things the rebel was disobedient. He separated himself from God by his own will and freedom. He was cast out and fell down, he and all of his company."

104 In the (post-Qur'ānic) Arabic version of the *Cave of Treasures* (see ed. Bezold, 23), Satan enters into the serpent, which (not yet being cursed to slither on its belly) had a body like a camel (*ba'īr*). Satan lifts it up and flies with it to the lowest part of paradise.

105 Ephraem, *Commentary on Genesis and Exodus. CSCO* 152–3, ed. R.-M. Tonneau, Leuven: Secrétariat du CorpusSCO, 1955, 44–5 (trans. in Brock, *Hymns of Paradise*, 222).

106 On this cf. the scene in Job 1.6–7. There the angels, or literally the "sons of God" (*bney ha-elohīm*), come before the Lord with Satan among them. When God asks Satan where he has been, Satan replies, "Prowling about on earth . . . roaming around there" (cf. Job 2:2) If this text suggests that Satan can still come before God it also reflects the notion that Satan's place is below, on earth.

107 *De Paradiso* 2:6 (ed. Beck, 6; trans. Brock, 87); cf. 1:17a (ed. Beck, 4–5; trans. Brock, 84).

When the deceiver attempted to knock down the house of Adam;
he himself fell from the celestial station.
His fall cast him into the deep. Once among the watchful,
he seized Adam and fell with him who had been weakened.[108]

In the Qur'ān Satan is likewise twice cast down. When he refuses to prostrate before man God declares to him: "Go down (*ihbiṭ*) from [heaven]!" (Q 7.13). Thereafter he is sent down from the garden when God punishes him along with Adam and Eve: "Go down (*ihbiṭū*) from [the garden], all of you" (Q 2.38; cf. 7.24). It is because of this banishment that the Qur'ān calls Satan and his hosts *rajīm* when it describes how their way to heaven is blocked (Q 15.17). Again the Qur'ān calls them *rajīm* in a passage on false revelation (Q 16.98; 81.25); demons always bear false revelation since, due to their banishment, they cannot hear the decrees of the divine council (*al-mala' al-a'lā*).

Thus in the Qur'ān heaven is something like a fortress. The stars are placed in the lowest heaven to act not only as decoration but also as protection (*ḥifẓ*; Q 37.6–7).[109] They form a barrier which frustrates the efforts of Satan and his hosts to listen in to the divine council.[110] Accordingly in *al-ḥijr* (15) 16–17 the Qur'ān declares: "We have made *burūj* in heaven and decorated it for onlookers. We protected it (*ḥafiẓnāhā*; cf. *ḥifẓ* in Q 37.7) from every *shayṭān rajīm*" (vv. 16–17)." *Burūj* here appears in the place of the "stars" (*kawākib*) in *al-ṣāffāt* (37) 6. It is often understood as "constellations" (thus, for example, Arberry). Paret, however, translates *burūj* literally as "Türme" ("towers"). This is also the understanding of Paul Eichler, who writes, "Burdschun [sic, i.e. *burūj*], πυργος, ist der Mauerturm. . . . Die Sterne werden also auf der Himmelskugel befindlich gedacht als Grenzschuß gegen die niedere Geisterwelt."[111]

Thus the Qur'ān paints a picture of the cosmos according to which spiritual beings, and heaven itself, exist in the same universe as this world.[112]

108 Jacob of Serūgh, *Homily on the Departure of Adam from Paradise*, in *Quatre homélies métriques sur la création*, *CSCO* 508 (French trans., 509), ed. and trans. K. Alwan, Leuven: Peeters, 1989, vv. 135–40, p. 36 (French trans., 40).

109 Paret's translation of these two verses expresses this idea well: "Wir haben den unteren Himmel mit dem Schmuck der Sterne versehen und (diese auch) zum Schutz vor jedem rebellischen Satan (bestimmt)."

110 On this see G. Hawting, "Eavesdropping on the heavenly assembly and the protection of the revelation from demonic corruption," in S. Wild (ed.), *Self-Referentiality in the Qur'ān*, Wiesbaden: Harrassowitz, 2006, (25–37) esp. pp. 30–1; Hawting follows in part P.A. Eichler, *Die Dschinn, Teufel und Engel im Qur'ān*, Leipzig: Klein, 1928. On the question of the High Council both Eichler and Hawting refer to the story, related in *BT Giṭṭīn* 68a, of the demon Asmodeus' participation in the "academy of the sky," where he received information on the destinies of human beings.

111 Eichler, *Dschinn, Teufel und Engel*, 31.

112 On Qur'ānic cosmology in general, and on the pathways to heaven in particular (Qur'ānic *asbāb*) see K. van Bladel, "Heavenly cords and prophetic authority in the Quran and its Late Antique context," *BSOAS* 70, 2007, 223–46.

The angels travel from earth into heaven (as they do in Jacob's vision at Bethel, Gn 28.11–7), but the demons cannot. If they manage to get close enough to hear something of the divine council, they come under fire. The Qur'ān explains that a *shihāb* ("comet" or "firebrand") pursues those demons (Q 15.18; 37.10; 67.7) or *jinn* (Q 72.9) who manage to steal something of the heavenly conversation.

It is worth noting, however, that this *shihāb* does not stone (*rajama*) the demons or *jinn*. It pursues (*atbaʿa*,) them. The stars, meanwhile, never perform this function. Far from being missiles which God casts at demons, they are set firmly, unmovable, at the boundary of heaven. It is accordingly the demons, not the stars, that are thrown (*yuqdhafūna*) from heaven in *al-ṣāffāt* (37) 8.

With this we arrive at the term *rujūm* in *al-mulk* (67) 5, which Nöldeke understands, in light of the Arabic root *r.j.m.*, to mean "missiles." In this verse the Qur'ān relates: "We have adorned the lowest heaven with *lamps* and made them *rujūm* for demons." It is parallel to *al-ṣāffāt* (37) 6: "We adorned the lowest heaven with the adornment of *stars*;" or *al-ḥijr* (15) 16: "We have made *towers* in the sky and adorned it for onlookers." When the Qur'ān describes "lamps" (i.e. "stars" or "towers") as *rujūm*, it does not mean that they are missiles to be cast at demons, but rather that they are part of the celestial fortress that protects heaven. The term *rujūm* in the Qur'ān is semantically connected to the term *rajīm*. It means something like *burūj*, "towers" (one might translate "barriers"), and reflects the particular role of the stars in protecting heaven, thereby enforcing the banishment of the demons.[113] In this their function is not unlike that of the "fiery flashing sword" of Genesis 3:24, which is held by the cherubim and blocks the entrance to the garden.[114]

Eichler describes the Qur'ān's references to demons being blocked from heaven as a nature myth. Inasmuch as these references reflect the Qur'ān's cosmology he is undoubtedly correct.[115] On the other hand there is reason to doubt that this myth is due to "der Reste arabischen Heidentums" as Eichler, following Sprenger and Wellhausen, concludes,[116] or that Muḥammad

113 A. Bausani comes to a similar conclusion on this point, but he does so on the basis of a Mazdaean myth in which certain stars guard the gates of heaven and bar demonesses, disguised as planets, from entering therein. See A. Bausani, *Persia religiosa*, Milan: Il Saggiatore, 1959, 157.

114 This parallel is drawn by Eichler, who notes in particular the fire of the sword in Gn 3.24 and the Qur'ān's use of the term *shihāb* (e.g. Q 15.18; 37.10; 72.9), the root of which is connected to fire, for the heavenly object that pursues demons or jinn who have heard something of the heavenly conversation. See Eichler, *Dschinn, Teufel und Engel*, 31–2.

115 "Dieser Mythos ist ein Naturmythos, durch ihn wird das Wirkungsbereich der Schaitane und Dschinn so abgrenzt, daß sie das Himmelsgewölbe von unten her nicht überschreiten können" (Eichler, *Dschinn, Teufel und Engel*, 30).

116 Ibid., 9; Sprenger, *Leben*, 2:245; Wellhausen, *Reste arabischen Heidentums*, 2:137.

intended thereby to combat pagan Arab worship of the *jinn*.[117] Instead, this myth is connected to a larger Judaeo-Christian cosmology, as Eichler elsewhere recognizes: "Er setzt auch die biblische Himmelsvorstellung voraus, denn die Geister wollen die Engel belauschen."[118]

Thus the term *rajīm* appears to hold much more significance than the traditional understanding thereof as "deserving to be stoned." *Rajīm* means banished, or outcast.[119] It reflects a larger religious cosmology whereby God established the stars in the lowest celestial sphere. Genesis 1.17 relates accordingly, "God set [the stars] in the vault [רָקִיעַ; LXX στερεώματι] of heaven to shine on the earth." This vault forms a barrier. Heaven, the divine council, and the presence of God lie beyond. This is the cosmology of the Psalmist when he writes, "Yahweh our Lord, how glorious is your name in all the Earth. Who has lifted your glory above the heavens" (Psalm 8.1).[120] So too it is the cosmology of literary apocalypses which employ the image of stars falling to the earth,[121] for nothing will remain hidden from man when the veil dividing heaven and earth is lifted.

CS 3 Adam and feathers

Qur'ānic account

After Adam is sent down from the Garden in *al-a'rāf* (7) 25, the Qur'ān addresses his offspring:

> O children of Adam, We sent down to you clothing to cover your shameful parts and *rīsh*. Yet the clothing of piety is better. That is a sign of God, if only they will remember.

> 7.26 يَابَنِي آدَمَ قَدْ أَنزَلْنَا عَلَيْكُمْ لِبَاساً يُوَارِي سَوْءَاتِكُمْ وَرِيشاً وَلِبَاسُ ٱلتَّقْوَىٰ ذٰلِكَ خَيْرٌ ذٰلِكَ مِنْ آيَاتِ ٱللَّهِ لَعَلَّهُمْ يَذَّكَّرُونَ

The present case study is focused on the term *rīsh*, a *hapax legomenon* in the Qur'ān. *Rīsh* is a collective plural which literally means "feathers." In its context above it appears awkward to both classical and modern interpreters. As we will see, most attempt to dispense with the literal sense of *rīsh* by understanding it as a metaphor. In a recent article James Bellamy concludes

117 Eichler, *Dschinn, Teufel und Engel*, 31.

118 Ibid.

119 In this light one might also reconsider the term *marjūm*, which appears in the course of the unbelievers' threatening address to Noah (Q 26.116). Most interpreters conclude that with *marjūm* the unbelievers are threatening to stone him, but if this term is related to *rajīm* they might rather be threatening him with banishment.

120 My translation, reflecting the verb ἐπήρθη (in place of Hebrew *tenā*) of the LXX.

121 See Daniel 8.10; Mt 24.29; Mk 13.25; Revelation 6.13; 8.12; 12.4.

that the word *rīsh* itself is wrong, proposing that the text be emended here to read instead *wirā'*, an unattested noun from the same root of the verb *yuwārī* (Q 7.26), which could mean "a covering." In defending the virtue of his emendation Bellamy begins with the comment: "First, we get rid of the feathers."[122] In the present study I will propose that we keep the feathers. Still more, I will argue below that the feathers are a key to a deeper understanding of the larger passage at hand.

Al-a'rāf (7) 26 is addressed to the "children of Adam." This phrase is something more than an idiomatic manner of addressing humanity. There are only six occurrences of it in the Qur'ān (Q 7.26, 27, 31, 35, 127; 36.60). Remarkably, four of them are grouped together in this passage connected to the story of Adam, and a fifth is in the same Sūra. The final occurrence (Q 36.60) appears in a verse, not unrelated to this passage, which warns of the snares of Satan. Thus the phrase "children of Adam" seems to be an idiom meant to connect the Qur'ān's audience with the story of Adam.

In *al-a'rāf* (7) 26 the Qur'ān reminds the "children of Adam" of the clothing and the feathers that God "sent down" (presumably from heaven) and urges them to put on piety.[123] Thereafter, changing to the third person, the Qur'ān adds, "That is a sign of God, if only they will remember." This last phrase is particularly telling, since in the Qur'ān the term translated here "sign" (*āya*, pl. *āyāt*) means more precisely an "evidentiary miracle," a divine act that testifies to God and His sovereignty. By remembering that God has performed such a sign people will know to fear divine judgment. The plagues sent down upon Pharoah's people (Q 8.52) and the miraculous sleep of the Companions of the Cave (Q 18.17) are among such miraculous signs. But, one might reasonably ask, what is so miraculous about clothing and feathers?

The answer seems to lie in the story of Adam, with which verse 26 is closely connected. The term for "shameful parts" (Ar. *saw'āt*) in this verse is precisely that which appears in verse 20, which describes Satan's intention to uncover the "shameful parts" of Adam and the woman, and verse 22a, which describes how he succeeded in doing so. It also appears afterwards, in verse 27, wherein the Qur'ān warns its audience, again called the "children of Adam," of Satan's wiles. At the same time, the clothing and feathers of verse 26 build on the reference in verse 22b to Adam and his wife covering themselves with leaves from the garden. According to verse 26, God gave them something better to wear.[124]

122 J. Bellamy, "Ten Qur'ānic emendations," *JSAI* 31, 2006, (118–38) 132.

123 Cf. *al-a'rāf* (7) 31: "O children of Adam, take your adornment (*zīna*) to every place of worship."

124 Cf. the Qur'ān's description of the silk garments (18:31; 22:23; 35:33, 44:53, passim) that God prepares for the believers in heaven. Thus Q 76.12: "Reward them for their patience with a garden and silk."

Problems for interpreters

But could they have put on feathers? This seems to be an impossibly awkward image. Accordingly, most modern translators conclude that the Qur'ān uses feathers only as a symbol, and translate *rīsh* in a metaphorical fashion:

Pickthall:	"splendid vesture"
Yusuf Ali:	"adornment"
Blachère:	"atours"
Paret:	"Schmuck"
Fakhry:	"finery"
Abdel Haleem:	"adornment"[125]

Only Arberry differs and translates *rīsh* literally: "feathers."

The other translators follow the precedent of the *mufassirūn*. *Tafsīr Muqātil* explains that the term *rīsh* actually refers to "possessions," (*māl*).[126] Qummī sees it as a reference to either "objects" (*matāʿ*) or "possessions," although he adds an esoteric interpretation: "The forbidden areas of the modest do not show even if one is stripped of clothing. The forbidden areas of the depraved are exposed even if one is covered with clothing."[127]

Ṭabarī, on the other hand, begins by describing the reason for the revelation of this verse. The Quraysh, he relates, used to perform the *ṭawāf* ("circumabulation") at the Kaʿba naked, and God revealed this verse to admonish them.[128] He then turns to the philological debates over *rīsh*, repeating first the opinion of *Tafsīr Muqātil* (citing the authority of Ibn ʿAbbās and Mujāhid) that *rīsh* means "possessions," and noting a tradition on the authority of Ibn Zayd that it means "beauty." Ṭabarī adds that some scholars (Suddī, Ḍaḥḥāk, and ʿUrwa b. Zubayr among others) follow an alternative reading: *riyāsh* (the standard plural form of the *nomen unitatis rīsha*).[129] Yet their definition of the term is still metaphorical (*amwāl*, "possessions," or *maʿāsh*, "livelihood").[130] The word for feathers acquired this metaphorical meaning, Ṭabarī explains, because feathers are often used for luxurious clothing, or to fill a mattress or blanket. Among the Bedouins, he adds, *rīsh* are the symbol of abundance (*khiṣb*) and luxury (*rafāha*).[131]

Thus Ṭabarī's analysis of *al-aʿrāf* (7) 26 suggests that in this verse God is speaking of clothing (*libāsan yuwārī saw'ātikum*) on the one hand, and material possessions (*wa-rīsh*) on the other. Zamakhsharī disagrees. Noting

125 In his article "Clothing," S.M. Toorawa translates *rīsh* as "attire." See *EQ*, 1:346b.

126 *Tafsīr Muqātil*, 2:33, on Q 7.26.

127 Qummī, 1:232, on Q 7.26.

128 Ṭabarī, 8:146, on Q 7.26.

129 This latter form in fact appears in most of the *qirā'āt* (ʿĀṣim, Abū ʿAmr, al-Ḥasan al-Baṣrī, Zirr b. Ḥubaysh, etc.) See *MQQ*, 2:350.

130 Ṭabarī, 8:148, on Q 7.26.

131 Ibid.

(as Ṭabarī does) that feathers are used in decorative clothing, he argues that *al-aʿrāf* (7) 26 refers to two types of clothing. By his reading this verse explains that God sent "clothing to cover your shameful parts (*libāsan yuwārī saw'ātikum*) and clothing for your decoration (*wa-rīsh*)."[132] This, Zamakhsharī notes, proves that it is licit for Muslims to wear clothing for the purpose of adornment.[133] Ibn Kathīr follows Zamakhsharī on this point, explaining, "*libās* is that which covers forbidden (or shameful) parts and *riṣh* is that which beautifies the appearance."[134] Otherwise Ibn Kathīr reports a number of explanatory traditions, similar to those cited by Ṭabarī, which insist that *rīsh* (or *riyāsh*) has a metaphorical meaning.[135]

Subtext

The *mufassirūn* thus take an atomistic approach to this question, focusing their attention almost exclusively on the verse in which *rish* occurs (Q 7.26), without concern for the relation of this verse to its literary context, namely the story of Adam and his woman in the garden. Ṭabarī instead connects *al-aʿrāf* (7) 26 with a report on the pagan Quraysh performing the *ṭawāf* naked. Thereby he removes the verse entirely from the story of Adam, and places it instead into the story of Muḥammad.

And yet the Qur'ān itself directs the reader to the story of Adam. The declaration in *al-aʿrāf* (7) 26 that God sent clothing "to cover your shameful parts" is explained by the following verse, wherein the Qur'ān admonishes, "Do not let Satan lead you astray as he sent your parents out of the garden when he tore off their clothing from them, in order to reveal to them their shameful parts" (Q 7.27). With this the Qur'ān reminds the audience how Satan lied to Adam and his wife, encouraging them to eat from the forbidden tree (Q 7.20–1). When they succumbed to his temptations and ate of the tree's fruit, "their shameful parts were revealed to them" (Q 7.22).

The place of Satan in the Qur'ān's garden account is of course different than that of Genesis, wherein only a serpent lurks in the garden. Yet Jewish exegetical texts increasingly suggest that the serpent is to be identified with Satan, while Christian exegetical texts make that identification explicit.[136] In the Qur'ān the serpent has completely given way to Satan. Thus Jewish and

132 Zamakhsharī, 2:97, on Q 7.26.

133 *Zīna*; he cites Q 16.8 and 16.6 as a further proof. Zamakhsharī, 2:97, on Q 7.26.

134 Ibn Kathīr, 2:200, on Q 7.26.

135 Ibid. Ibn Kathīr turns to traditions on decorative clothing. Among them is a *ḥadīth* in which the Prophet declares, "Whoever takes a new robe and wears it should say, when it reaches his collarbone, 'Praise be to God who has dressed me with that which covers my forbidden parts and beautifies my life.'" In a second version, on the authority of Aḥmad b. Ḥanbal, the Prophet is made to use the Arabic term for feathers in a metaphorical sense: "Praise be to God who provides me with *riyāsh* that beautify me among people and cover my forbidden parts." Ibn Kathīr, 2:200, on Q 7.26.

136 On this see CS 2, n. 97 above.

Christian midrash act as a sort of bridge between the Biblical and Qur'ānic garden accounts. The same might be said for the question of Adam and Eve's clothing. In Genesis Adam and Eve do not have clothing stripped off them when they eat from the tree. Instead, "The eyes of both of them were opened and they *knew* (וַיֵּדְעוּ; LXX ἔγνωσαν) that they were naked" (Gn 3.7). However, according to a prevalent tradition of Jewish midrash Genesis 3.7 is not about some change in Adam and Eve's vision or knowledge, but rather about their loss of an original, celestial garment.[137] In other words, they were really stripped naked, or as the Qur'ān has it, "their shameful parts were revealed to them."

Accordingly Jewish exegetes insist that when Genesis 2:25 mentions that Adam and Eve were naked in the garden it intends that they had no fabricated clothing.[138] Rather, according to *Genesis Rabba* (20:12), they wore a "garment of light,"[139] or (according to another tradition) a sort of skin that was as "smooth as a finger nail and as beautiful as a jewel."[140] This original clothing is often referred to as a garment of "glory,"[141] a term inspired by exegesis of Psalm 8:4–5: "What are human beings that you spare a thought for them, or the child of Adam that you care for him? * Yet you have made him little less than a god, you have *crowned him with glory* and beauty." In the Syriac Peshitta this last phrase appears as "clothed him with honor and glory" (*b-īqārā wa-b-shūbḥā a'ṭeftāh*).

Accordingly Ephraem relates that Adam and Eve were not ashamed of their nakedness because they were covered – before eating from the tree

137 Regarding this see H. Reuling, *After Eden: Church Fathers and Rabbis on Genesis 3:16–21*, Leiden: Brill, 2006, esp. 253–61.

138 On the question of Adam and Eve's skin in Jewish and Christian exegesis see above all Anderson, "Garments of skin"; cf. the briefer treatment of J.C. Reeves, "Some explorations of the intertwining of Bible and Qur'ān," in Reeves (ed.), *Bible and Qur'ān* (43–60) 56–8.

139 The idea of a garment of light is connected to the exegesis of Gn 3.21, which reports that God made "tunics of skin," in Hebrew *kotnōt 'ōr*, for Adam and Eve. Some exegetes read instead *kotnōt ōr* (with *alef* in place of *'ayin*) or "garments of light." This allowed them to avoid the unseemly notion that God killed and skinned an animal to make the tunic. But since a tunic of light would seem to be a blessed garment, it was usually argued (as in *Gn R.* 20:12) that Gn 3.21 should be understood to refer to the original clothing of Adam and Eve, not to the clothing (as the place of v. 21 in the text would suggest) that they wore on the way out of paradise. This is a case of Biblical *ta'khīr al-muqaddam*.

140 Trans. Freedman et al., 1:171. *Pirqē de-Rabbī Elī'ezer* (14) similarly explains that Adam wore "a skin of horn and the cloud of glory covered him. After he ate from the fruit of the tree, the skin of fingernail was stripped off of him." *Pirke de-Rabbi Elieser*, ed. and trans. D. Börner-Klein, 142. Similarly the *Targum of Pseudo-Jonathan* mentions that the clothing which Adam and Eve sowed from fig leaves (Gn 3.7) served as a replacement to "the garments of glory with which they had been created." *Targum of Pseudo-Jonathan* (on Gn 3.7), in *Targum du Pentateuque, Sources chrétiennes* 245, 256, 261, 271, 282, trans. R. Le Déaut, Paris: Cerf, 1978–81, 245:91. Cf. Anderson, "Garments of skin," 134.

141 Thus *Gn R.* 11:2, *Targum Neofiti* (Gn 3.21), and the Jewish texts *Apocalypse of Moses* (20:2), 3 Baruch (4:16), and 2 Enoch (22:8). On this see *TB*, 116–9.

– by a clothing of holiness (*qūdshā*) and glory (*shūbḥā*).[142] In the *Cave of Treasures*, Adam and Eve are likewise clothed in glory (*shūbḥā*), in royal vestments (*lbūshê malkūtā*; 2:17), before their fall. Satan, jealous of Adam, finds his revenge by convincing Eve to eat of the forbidden tree. When she does so (4:15) she is stripped naked of her celestial clothing. When Adam eats (4:18), he too is stripped.

In Jacob of Serūgh's *Homily on the Departure of Adam from Paradise*, the sin of Adam and Eve similarly strips them of the glorious (*shbīḥā*) garment in which God had clothed them and covers them instead in shame.[143] When the moment of their judgment arrives, the garment of leaves that Eve had sown for them dries up and falls off, leaving the two naked before their creator. God then creates new clothing for them, a sign that God's mercy is greater than His reproach.[144]

The sequence suggested by this exegetical tradition, therefore, is the following: Adam and Eve were created with heavenly garments; those garments were stripped off of them when they ate of the tree, and they made clothing from fig leaves in their place (Gn 3.7). Finally God, after announcing the decree of banishment (Gn 3.14–9), provided them with new clothing: "Yahweh God made tunics of skin (*kotnōt ʿōr*) and clothed them" (Gn 3.21) The Qur'ān follows this same sequence: Adam and Eve are stripped (Q 7.22a), they make clothing of fig leaves (Q 7.22b), God announces the decree of banishment (Q 7.24–5) and provides new clothing (Q 7.26). Indeed, the description of this clothing as a sign, or better a miracle (*āya*), which humans are to remember (Q 7.26b), suggests that the Qur'ān is not referring here to any ordinary clothing, but rather to the extraordinary clothing that God himself made for Adam and Eve.

The Qur'ān's participation in this larger exegetical tradition suggests that an explanation for the feathers might also be sought in these "tunics of skin." There is a significant tradition of speculation on the nature of these tunics among both Jewish and Christian exegetes. *Genesis Rabba* (18:6), for example, explains that by "tunics of skin" the Bible is not referring literally to skin, but rather to materials produced from skin, such as the pelts or wool of animals. Thus, *Genesis Rabba* reports, some authorities conclude that the "tunics of skin" were garments of Circassian wool, while others propose the

142 *De Paradiso* 15:8–9 (ed. Beck, 64); cf. G. Anderson, "The fall of Satan in the thought of St. Ephrem." *Hugoye: Journal of Syriac Studies* [http://syrcom.cua.edu/syrcom/Hugoye] 3, 2001, 1, 11, n. 48. When Ephraem elsewhere portrays the blessed in heaven he reflects: "Among the saints, none is naked, for they have put on glory * nor is any clad in those leaves or standing in shame * for they have found, through our Lord, the robe that belongs to Adam and Eve." *De Paradiso* 6.9 (ed. Beck, 21; trans. Brock, 112).

143 Jacob of Serūgh, *Quatre homélies métriques sur la création*, vv. 573–4, p. 55 (trans., 61). Cf. the Gnostic Christian text *Apocryphon of John* (24:6–8), which relates, "And He cast them out of paradise and clothed them in gloomy darkness." See *TB*, 133.

144 Jacob of Serūgh, *Quatre homélies métriques sur la création*, vv. 1025–26, p. 74 (trans., 84).

wool of camels or rabbit hair.[145] The *Cave of Treasures* presents still other ideas, that Adam and Eve were given garments made from the "skin" of trees (*qlāfê d-īlānê*), that is, bark,[146] or that they were given no garments at all. The "tunics of skin" were nothing other than human skin, which God created for them and stretched over their bodies.[147] Jacob insists only that they were *not* in fact made of skin but rather out of nothing. The Bible describes these garments metaphorically as skin (or hide), since they were thick and soft to the touch.[148]

All of these propositions might seem rather unusual interpretations of the phrase "tunics of skin" in Genesis 3.21. Certainly it would be more faithful to the text to propose that these tunics were indeed made of skin, that is, the hides of animals. Instead the exegetes propose instead that they were made only from wool or hair shaved from hide. The *Cave of Treasures*, in turn, offers the creative, if hardly obvious, explanations that God clothed them with the bark of a tree (the forbidden tree?) or with human skin. The idea that the "tunics of skin" were made of animal hides is nowhere to be found in the early exegetical tradition.

The reason for this is in a detail of Genesis. Blood is only shed after humanity leaves the garden. Only then does the woman give birth (Gn 4.1–2). Only then is an animal slaughtered in sacrifice to God (Gn 4.4). Only after the flood, meanwhile, are animals licit food. In Genesis 1.29, God specifies that "seed-bearing plants" and "trees with seed-bearing fruit" will be humanity's food. In Genesis 2.16 God tells Adam that he can eat from all of the trees, but does not mention eating animals. When Noah emerges from the ark, however, God gives him authority over animals: "Be the terror and the dread of all the animals on land and all the birds of heaven, of everything that moves on land and all the fish of the sea; they are placed in your hands" (Gn 9.2).[149] In the garden, in other words, an animal would not have been killed for its skin. Accordingly the exegetes speculate that the "tunics of skin" were made from "the skin" of a tree, or from wool, for which one need only shear a sheep, not slaughter it. So too these tunics could have been made

145 Trans. Freedman et al., 1:171. Cf. Reeves, "Explorations of the intertwining of Bible and Qur'ān," 57. The *Targum of Pseudo-Jonathan* (on Gn 3.21) suggests that God made clothing out of the skin the serpent had shed, an opinion shared by *Pirqē de-Rabbī Elī'ezer* (20; ed. Börner-Klein, 212).

146 This tradition is not preserved in the edition of Ri but rather in the earlier edition of C. Bezold. See *Die Schatzhöhle*, 2:28 (German trans., 1:6).

147 Ed. Ri, 4:22–3; p. 37 (trans., 17). On this cf. Anderson, "Garments of skin," 135–6.

148 Jacob of Serūgh, *Quatre homélies métriques sur la création*, v. 997, p. 72 (trans., 82) and vv. 1000–2, pp. 72–3 (trans., 82).

149 Cf. *LJ*, 5:104. The Babylonian Talmud (*Sanhedrin* 59b) explains: "Adam was not permitted to eat flesh, for it is written, [Genesis 2.16] to you it shall be for food, and to all the beasts of the earth, implying that the beasts of the earth shall not be for you. But with the advent of the sons of Noah, it was permitted, for it is said [Genesis 9.3], even as the green herb have I given you all things."

from feathers shed by or removed from a bird, so long as the bird is not plucked to death.

CS 4 Abraham the Gentile monotheist

Qur'ānic account

While the Adam of the Qur'ān is sent away from God, the Abraham of the Qur'ān, born in the midst of unbelief, comes to know God. According to *al-an'ām* (6) 76–9, Abraham learns to worship God only after worshipping heavenly bodies: first the stars, then the moon, then the sun. When each of these bodies sets in the western sky, Abraham realizes that it is unworthy of worship. Ultimately he decides to worship the creator alone. Thus Abraham appears in the Qur'ān as a rational monotheist, a believer who discovers the existence of one God through an examination of natural signs.[150]

The Qur'ān also describes how Abraham, after becoming a monotheist, opposes idolatry. In *al-ṣāffāt* (37) 82–91 Abraham first (v. 85) reprimands his own father (cf. Q 9.114) and his people for their devotion to idols and then (v. 93) destroys those idols, for which the people seek to kill him (vv. 97ff.).[151] Elsewhere (Q 26.70–81) the Qur'ān cites Abraham's interrogation of his father and his people:

> (26.70) . . . "What do you worship?"
> (71) They said, "We worship idols, and we serve them with devotion."
> (72) He said, "Do they hear you if you pray to them? (73) Do they benefit or harm you?"
> (74) They said, "This is what we found our fathers doing."
> (75) He said, "That which you have worshipped, (76) you and your fathers before you, (77) they are all enemies to me except the Lord of the worlds, (78) who created me and guided me, (79) who gives me to eat and drink, (80) who heals me when I am sick, (81) who will take my life and then give me life."

Thus the Abraham in the Qur'ān is a self-taught monotheist and an opponent to the idolaters. These qualities are presumably implied by the term *ḥanīf*,

150 It is precisely this activity that the Qur'ān so often asks of its audience, insisting that the existence of God is evident in the signs of nature. See, e.g., Q 7.57 (re: rain); 26.7 (fruit); 50.6–11 (the sky, mountains, rain, trees, etc.); 55.4–12 (sun, moon, stars, trees, crops), passim. On this see E. Gräf, who refers to these passages as the "Zeichen[*ayāt*]-Partien des Korans." Gräf, "Zu den christlichen Einflüssen im Koran," 118–23.

151 The Qur'ān refers to the same narrative in *al-anbiyā'* (21) 51–71 (cf. also Q 29.16–25) wherein Abraham, who is described as a young man (*fatā*, v. 60), declares boldly, "You and your fathers were in clear error" (v. 54).

which the Qur'ān applies to Abraham and no one else.[152] When Abraham embraces the worship of God alone, he announces that he is "a *ḥanīf*, not one of the idolaters (*mushrikīn*)" (Q 6.79), a phrase that becomes a refrain in the Qur'ānic material on Abraham (2.135; 3.67, 95; 6.79, 161; 16.120, 123). Among other things, it seems to be a way of separating Abraham from Judaism and Christianity, as when the Qur'ān declares: "Abraham was not a Jew, and not a Christian, but rather a *ḥanīf* and a *muslim*" (Q 3.67a).[153]

Problems for interpreters

Abraham and the heavenly bodies[154]

Tafsīr Muqātil begins the story of Abraham with an account of his birth. Abraham, *Tafsīr Muqātil* explains, was born in Kūtā (i.e. Kūthā, in southern Iraq), a city ruled by the pagan tyrant Nimrod. Before his birth Nimrod's priests warned him of a child to be born. This child, they told the tyrant, "will ruin the gods of the people and call them to something other than your gods. He will cause the destruction of your rule and the destruction of your family."[155] In response Nimrod ordered men and women kept apart, except during a woman's period, so that no children would be born. Yet a man named Āzar (cf. Q 6.74) disobeyed the tyrant's rule and his wife conceived Abraham.

When Āzar's wife gave birth to Abraham she dug a burrow in the ground, placed the baby therein, and covered it with a boulder to protect him from wild animals. She returned in secret to nurse Abraham, who grew in a day what other babies grow in a month, and in a month what they grow in a year. Ultimately,[156] the young Abraham grew curious about the outside world. He "approached the entrance of the burrow . . . and saw Venus at the beginning of the night from the midst of the burrow, behind the boulder."[157]

152 *Ḥanīf* appears in Q 2.135; 3.67, 95; 4.125; 6.79, 161; 10.105; 16.120, 123; 30.30. The plural form *ḥunafā'* appears twice: 22.31; 98.5.

153 So too the Qur'ān urges its audience to follow neither Judaism nor Christianity but rather the religion of Abraham. See Q 2.135; 16.120, 22.78.

154 On the history of exegesis on this episode see M. Grünbaum, *Neue Beiträge zur semitischen Sagenkunde*, Leiden: Brill, 1893, 90–8, 123–32; Calder, "Tafsir from Tabari to Ibn Kathir"; B.M. Hauglid, "On the early life of Abraham: Biblical and Qur'ānic intertextuality and the anticipation of Muḥammad," *Bible and Qur'ān*, 87–105.

155 *Tafsīr Muqātil*, 1.569–70, on Q 6.74.

156 Before describing Abraham's examination of the heavenly bodies, *Tafsīr Muqātil* records Abraham's interrogation of his parents: "He asked his mother, 'Who is my Lord?' She replied 'I am.' He asked, 'Then who is your Lord?' She replied, 'Your father.' He asked, 'Then who is my father's Lord?' She hit him and said to him, 'Be quiet' and he was quiet" (1.570, on Q 6.74). Abraham then approached his father: " 'O Father, who is my Lord?' " He replied, 'Your mother.' [Abraham] asked, 'Then who is my mother's Lord?' He replied, 'I am.' He asked, 'Then who is your Lord?' He hit him and said to him, 'Be quiet' " (1:570, on Q 6.74).

157 *Tafsīr Muqātil*, 1:571, on Q 6.75.

He contemplated worshipping Venus. When Venus set and the moon rose, however, he contemplated worshipping the moon, and when the moon set and the sun rose, the sun. When the sun set he finally realized that only the creator is to be worshipped. At this Abraham left his burrow and went into the city. There he discovered his people worshipping idols (cf. Q 6.78) and confronted them (cf. Q 6.79).[158]

Qummī relies on a different version of the same narrative to explain the Qur'ānic passage on Abraham and the heavenly bodies. According to Qummī's version, Abraham's father Āzar was himself an astrologer for Nimrod. He warned the tyrant that "a man will be born who will replace this religion and invoke a new religion," unaware that this man would be his own son.[159] Thus astrology is a central trope in this narrative. The stars predict the birth of Abraham, just as they guide him to the worship of one God.[160]

Ṭabarī offers still another version, on the authority of Ibn Isḥāq, in which Āzar is not an astrologer but an idol maker. Nimrod orders all pregnant women imprisoned and, when they give birth, has their children killed. However, God keeps the pregnancy of Abraham's mother from showing. She escapes to a cave, gives birth, hides the child, and tells her husband that the child has died. While in the cave the child Abraham spies the heavenly bodies and, knowing no better, considers worshipping them.[161]

A new controversy also appears in his commentary. Ṭabarī relates that some authorities refuse to accept the report that Abraham, even for a moment,

158 Ibid. Ultimately Abraham confronts Nimrod himself, declaring to him that the Lord is the one who controls life and death. At this Nimrod takes a free man and kills him, and takes a condemned man and spares him. But when Abraham adds that his Lord chooses to make the sun rise in the East and set in the West, and challenges Nimrod to do the opposite, the tyrant is confounded. *Tafsīr Muqātil*, 1:572. This narrative follows closely the allusions of Q 2.258.

159 Qummī, 1:213, on Q 6.75–7.

160 Qummī's version of this narrative also includes additional explanatory details. Abraham's mother was able to avoid the pogrom of the tyrant because her pregnancy did not show. She was able to give birth without the knowledge of her husband (who, after all, was an employee of the tyrant) with the excuse that she was menstruating, which, according to that country's customs, meant that she had to be separated from him (thus the opposite of the *Tafsīr Muqātil* account, where the king allowed women and men to meet only during the woman's period). Abraham was able to survive in a cave (not a burrow) because God made yogurt flow from his thumb. Qummī, 1:213–14.

Qummī continues his commentary with an account of Abraham's confrontation with his father Āzar (cf. Q 6.74). Thereby Āzar is not only an astrologer and advisor to the king but also an idol-merchant. When Āzar assigns his son to manage his business, Abraham ties a cord around the neck of the idols and drags them around, calling out to people, "Who will buy something that neither benefits nor harms them?" (Qummī, 1:215). After Abraham abuses the idols in various ways, his brothers tell on him and Āzar locks Abraham up in his house. Qummī 1:214–5.

161 Ṭabarī, 7:248–9, on Q 6.76. Ṭabarī is skeptical of the more fantastic details of the narrative. To the report that Abraham was nourished through his thumb Ṭabarī adds *wa-Llāhu a'lam* ("And God knows better").

worshipped the stars, moon, or sun.[162] Now the Qur'ān has Abraham say of each of them, "This is my Lord" (Q 6.76–8), but these exegetes insist that no prophet would fall into such grave unbelief. They therefore offer a number of alternative explanations: Perhaps Abraham was pretending to worship the heavenly bodies in order to highlight the error of his people, who worshipped simple idols, objects much less spectacular than the stars, moon, and sun; or perhaps his statements were actually rhetorical questions; that is, what he meant was: "Could such a thing be my Lord?"[163]

Zamakhsharī reports instead that Abraham's people in fact worshipped the sun, the moon, and the stars.[164] Therefore Abraham "wanted to warn them of their error in religion, to guide them on the path of contemplation and evidence, to make them understand how true contemplation teaches that none of these things can be a god, to present the evidence of their createdness."[165] Thus Zamakhsharī insists that Abraham did not really mistake the stars, the moon, and the sun as gods. When he cried out, "This is my Lord," he did so only in order to lead his opponents along.[166] In other words, Zamakhsharī does not connect this affair with Abraham's childhood narrative at all, but rather with a (rational) contest between Abraham and his pagan opponents later in life. His apparent worship of the heavenly bodies was a ruse.

Unlike Zamakhsharī Ibn Kathīr reports an abridged version of the Ibn Isḥāq narrative found in Ṭabarī's commentary.[167] In this version Abraham's mother gives birth to him in a den outside of the city. Yet, after noting laconically that Ibn Isḥāq reports miracles took place in this den,[168] Ibn Kathīr abruptly turns away from this narrative, and moves in the direction of Zamakhsharī's commentary. He declares: "The truth is that Abraham (peace be upon him) debated with his people in this place, demonstrating to them the falsehood of their worshiping heavenly bodies (*hayākil*) and idols."[169]

162 Ibid., 7:249. On this cf. Calder, "Tafsir from Tabari to Ibn Kathir," 116ff.

163 Others would concede that he worshipped the heavenly bodies, but only before he was called to be a prophet. Ṭabarī, 7:249–50, on Q 6.76.

164 Zamakhsharī begins his commentary on *al-an'ām* (6) 74 with a discussion on the name given here for Abraham's father, Āzar, noting that other sources name him Tāriḥ (indeed in Genesis [11.24, 25, 26, passim] it is *teraḥ*; Syr. *trāḥ*). Zamakhsharī, 2:39, on Q 6.74–9. This question has been a frequent subject of discussion in critical scholarship. See Geiger, *Was hat Mohammed*, 126–7; R. Dvořák, "Über die Fremdwörter im Korân," *Kaiserliche Akademie der Wissenschaften. Phil.-Hist. Classe. Sitzungsberichte* 109, 1, 1885, (481–562) 515–16; S. Fraenkel, "Miscellen zum Koran," *ZDMG* 56, 1902, 72; *FV*, 55; *KU*, 85.

165 Zamakhsharī, 2:40, on Q 6.74–9.

166 Ibid.

167 Like Zamakhsharī, Ibn Kathīr precedes his analysis with a discussion of the name of Abraham's father, noting, among other explanations, a report that *āzar* is not a name but a pejorative term with which Abraham insulted his idol-worshipping father. "It is a curse and an insult in their speech," explains one report. Another tradition insists: "It is the most severe word that Abraham ever spoke." Ibn Kathīr, 2:145–6, on Q 6.74–9.

168 Ibn Kathīr, 2:147, on Q 6.74–9.

169 Ibid.

Abraham only pretended to worship these heavenly bodies, Ibn Kathīr explains, in the course of these debates. Since Abraham's people considered the sun to be the most important heavenly body, Abraham began his scheme with the planet Venus (cf. Q 6.76), then the moon (Q 6.77), and culminated with the sun (Q 6.78). Thus he implemented a systematic strategy. By taking gradual, logical steps Abraham slowly demonstrated to his people the folly of their beliefs.

Thus Ibn Kathīr denies that Abraham ever considered worshipping the heavenly bodies.[170] In support of his position Ibn Kathīr quotes *al-anbiyā'* (21) 51–2 where the Qur'ān relates "We guided Abraham earlier" (implying that Abraham had from the beginning divine protection from error) and cites a *ḥadīth* where the Prophet declares: "Everyone is born according to the *fiṭra*." To Ibn Kathīr this *fiṭra*,[171] or "constitution," is Islam; in other words, everyone is born a Muslim. Ibn Kathīr comments: "If this is true for the rest of people, then how must it be for Abraham, the *khalīl* ('close friend of God'; Q 4.125) whom God made 'a community obedient to God and a *ḥanīf*' [Q 16.120]'?"[172]

Ḥanīf

But the term *ḥanīf* is itself problematic. The translators clearly struggle with this word, either leaving it untranslated or offering a translation on the basis of its Qur'ānic context:[173]

Pickthall:	"upright."
Yusuf Ali:	"firmly and truly."[174]
Blachère:	"*ḥanīf*."
Arberry:	"*ḥanīf*."
Paret:	"*ḥanīf*."
Fakhry:	"Upright man."[175]
Abdel Haleem:	"True believer."[176]

170 Ibid.

171 See *AEL*, 2416c. Cf. the verbal form in Q 30.30.

172 Ibn Kathīr, 2:147, on Q 6.74–9.

173 Here as they translate Q 6.79. The classical Arabic lexicographers seemed to have defined the word only on the basis of its Qur'ānic context. See *AEL*, 2:658b.

174 Elsewhere Yusuf Ali generally relies on some combination of "true" and "faith" to translate *ḥanīf* (cf. his translation of Q 30.30, "truly to the faith"; pace his translation in Q 10.105, "true piety"). In Q 3.95 he provides a curious translation of *ḥanīf* as "sane in faith."

175 On the ten occasions where *ḥanīf* appears in the singular in the Qur'ān, Fakhry translates it either as "Upright man," "upright," or "uprightly," except at Q 3.67, where he keeps *ḥanīf* untranslated and adds in a note: "This Arabic word means 'one who turned away from paganism'."

176 Abdel Haleem is the least consistent in his translation of this term. On two occasions (Q 2.135; 3.57) he translates "Upright." On one occasion (Q 3.95) "Had true faith." On two occasions (Q 4.125; 16.120) "true in faith." On one occasion (Q 6.79) "True believer." On four occasions (6.161; 10.105; 16.123; 30.30) "Pure faith."

The choice of Blachère, Arberry, and Paret to leave *ḥanīf* untranslated could simply reflect their uncertainty. On the other hand it might reflect an Islamic exegetical tradition by which certain lone individuals in pre-Islamic Arabia who had rejected the polytheism of their countrymen (very much like Abraham), but not become Jews or Christians, were known as *ḥanīf*s.[177] By this tradition *ḥanīf* is a proper name.

The other translators follow the medieval exegetes. *Tafsīr Muqātil* glosses *ḥanīf* with *mukhliṣ* ("devoted, faithful").[178] Ṭabarī defines *ḥanīf* as *mustaqīm*, "upright,"[179] even while he mentions alternative views. Some interpreters, Ṭabarī relates, hold that *ḥanīf* refers to one who performs the pilgrimage to Mecca, and that Abraham is so called because he was the first to do so. Others hold that it is related to the idea of following. Abraham is so called because he was the first to practice circumcision and others followed him in this. A third group hold the view of *Tafsīr Muqātil*, that it means *mukhlīṣ*, while a fourth group content themselves by defining *ḥanīf* as Muslim. Ṭabarī finds these latter two views acceptable, but he rejects the first two views. If *ḥanīf* simply means a pilgrim to Mecca, he notes, then the pre-Islamic pagans who also performed the Hajj must be given this title. If *ḥanīf* relates to circumcision, then the Jews must be given this title. Yet in the Qur'ān *ḥanīf* is used to distinguish Abraham from pagans (Q 6.79) and Jews (Q 3.67).

Zamakhsharī, for his part, turns not to traditions but to philology. The root *ḥ.n.f.*, he insists, is related to *m.'.l.* (or *m.y.l.*) and therefore means either to depart from (with *'alā* or *'an*) or to incline to (with *ilā*). Thus a *ḥanīf* is "one who departs from a false religion and inclines to the religion of truth."[180] When the Qur'ān adds "and he was not one of the polytheists"

177 Ibn Hishām refers to four such *ḥanīf*s (*Sīrat Rasūl Allāh*, 143; trans., 99): Waraqa b. Nawfal (the cousin of Muḥammad's first wife Khadīja), who verifies the authenticity of Muḥammad's first revelation by comparing it to the *nāmūs* (cf. Gk. νόμος, "the law") given to Moses; 'Ubayd Allāh b. Jaḥsh, who became a Muslim and then a Christian when he emigrated with the Muslims to Ethiopia; Zayd b. 'Amr b. Nufayl, who adopted neither Islam nor Christianity; and 'Uthmān b. Ḥuwayrith, who emigrated to Byzantium and became a Christian.

Ibn Hishām even uses this tradition to explain the report that Muḥammad, before his call to prophethood, would perform a religious exercise named *taḥannuth*. Ibn Hishām, *Sīrat Rasūl Allāh*, 152–3 (trans., 105). Ibn Hishām explains that *taḥannuth* is an Arabic verbal noun from *ḥ.n.f.*, meaning "following the religion of the *ḥanīf*s," since in the Meccan dialect the "*f*" was pronounced "*th*". In fact the root of *taḥannuth* is certainly *ḥ.n.n.* ("*th*" reflecting the feminine ending in Hebrew or Aramaic/Syriac) and related to Hebrew and Aramaic/Syriac terms meaning devotional prayer. See H. Hirschfeld, *New Researches into the Composition and Exegesis of the Qoran*, London: Royal Asiatic Society, 1902, 19 and the entry for Syriac *taḥnanthā*, "supplication" in *TS*, 1316. Cf. the more traditional approach of M.J. Kister, "*Al-taḥannuth*: An inquiry into the meaning of a term," *BSOAS* 31, 1968, 223–36.

178 *Tafsīr Muqātil*, 1:141, on Q 2.135. When the Qur'ān describes Abraham as "*ḥanīf*, not one of the polytheists (*mushrikīn*)," *Tafsīr Muqātil* glosses "not one of the polytheists," with "not a Jew or a Christian."

179 Ṭabarī, 1:565, on Q 2.135.

180 Zamakhsharī, 1:194, on Q 2.135. He quotes a line of anonymous poetry to prove his case.

(Q 2.135) to the description of Abraham as *ḥanīf*, Zamakhsharī explains, it is rebuking the People of the Book and others who claim to follow Abraham, although they are polytheists (cf. Q 3.67).[181] Ibn Kathīr agrees with Zamakhsharī's definition of *ḥanīf*.[182] However, in light of the prophetic *ḥadīth* on the *fiṭra* (quoted above), he insists that Abraham did not become a *ḥanīf* by inclining to the religion of truth. He was born a *ḥanīf*.

Subtext

Yet the Qur'ān is not alone in its report of Abraham's conversion from paganism to monotheism.[183] In the Jewish text *Jubilees* (3rd–1st century BC), for example, Abraham comes to believe in God although his father Terah is an idolater. Abraham confronts his father, presenting a series of proofs drawn from nature for the worship of God alone and asking, "What help or advantage do we have from these idols?" His father acknowledges that Abraham is right, but warns him of the wrath of the idolaters, "Be silent my son, lest they kill you" (*Jubilees* 12:2, 8).[184] However, not only does Abraham refuse to stay quiet, he also burns down the sanctuary of the idols. Terah (presumably afraid of the idolaters' vengeance) takes Abraham and Abraham's wife Sarah to Ḥarrān (*Jubilees* 12.14–15). In Ḥarrān one night Abraham goes out to observe the sky in order to find a sign that will foretell the rains for that year. While doing so he has a celestial experience:

> And he was sitting alone making observations [of the stars] and a voice came into his heart saying, "All the signs of the stars and the signs of the sun and the moon are all under the Lord's control. Why am I seeking [them out]? If He wishes, He will make it rain morning and evening, and if He desires He will not make it fall, for everything is under His control."
> (*Jubilees* 12:16–17)[185]

181 Ibid., 1:194–5.

182 Ibn Kathīr, 2:147, on Q 6.74–9. Elsewhere he provides a similar definition, explaining the *ḥanīf* as one who "turns away (*muḥtanifan*) from polytheism and heads towards faith." Ibid., 1:356, on Q 3.65–8.

183 Ginzberg identifies six different versions of this myth. *LJ*, 5:210, n. 16; cf. *BEQ*, 124. He proposes that it developed from small reports like that in *Genesis Rabba* (38.13), in which Abraham notices that the elements cancel one another (e.g. fire extinguishes water) and refuses to worship them on this basis (trans. Freedman et al., 1:311. Cf. the statement of R. Judah in *BT Babā Batrā* 10a). However, more detailed accounts of this story appear in texts written earlier than *Genesis Rabba*.

184 Trans. *TB*, 246, based on *The Book of Jubilees: A Critical Text*, *CSCO* 510–11, ed. and trans. J.C. Vanderkam, Leuven: Peeters, 1989.

185 *TB*, 250. Meanwhile the *tafsīr* traditions which place this account in Abraham's childhood are related to a tradition found in *Pirqē de-Rabbī Elī'ezer*: "When Abraham, our father, was born, all of the great kings wanted to kill him and he was hidden for thirteen years under the earth, so that he had seen neither sun nor moon" (26; ed. Börner-Klein, 262). A larger version of this story, which provides more of the details found in *tafsīr*, appears

Philo (d. AD 50) knew of this legend, although he does not present it *in toto*. Instead he describes, by way of condemnation, the practice of the Chaldeans to seek signs in natural phenomenon. He then comments:

> In this creed Abraham had been reared, and for a long time remained a Chaldean. Then opening the soul's eye as though after profound sleep, and beginning to see the pure beam instead of the deep darkness, he followed the ray and discerned what he had not beheld before, a charioteer and pilot presiding over the world and directing in safety His own work.[186]

With Philo, the role of this account in the Abraham story changes. In *Jubilees* Abraham already believes in the one God before he looks to the heavens for guidance; he learns, in effect, that a monotheist has no need of astrology. According to Philo, however, Abraham becomes a monotheist by looking to the heavens. So too Josephus (d. AD 100) explains that Abraham inferred the existence of one omnipotent God from "the changes to which land and sea are subject, from the course of sun and moon, and from all the celestial phenomena."[187]

In the *Apocalypse of Abraham* (ca. 2nd century AD) Abraham refers to the heavenly bodies in the context of confronting his father Terah. Here, unlike *Jubilees*, Terah is truly guilty of paganism (for which sin God destroys him and his house; *Apocalypse of Abraham* 8.5–6). Abraham, in order to save his father from his disbelief (cf. Q 9.114), presents (in vain) a logical argument for the existence of one God. He describes to his father how fire is subdued by water, water by earth, and earth by the sun (*Apocalypse of Abraham* 7.1–7). He continues:

> So I would call the sun nobler than the earth, since with its rays it illumines the inhabited world and the various airs. But I would not make it into a god either, since its course is obscured both at night and by the clouds. Nor, again, would I call the moon and the stars gods, since they too in their times at night can darken their light.
>
> (*Apocalypse of Abraham* 7.8–10)[188]

in a midrashic text known as *Ma'asē Abraham*. Speyer, however, points out that this work is late and likely itself influenced by *tafsīr*. See *Ma'asē Abraham* in *Bēt-Hammidrāsh*, ed. A. Jellinek, Jerusalem: n.p., 1938, 1:25; cf. Grünbaum, *Neue Beiträge*, 122–4; *BEQ*, 126.

186 *De Abrahamo*, 70, ed. and trans. F.H. Colson, *Philo in Ten Volumes*, Cambridge, MA: Harvard University Press, 1961–6, 6:41.

187 *Jewish Antiquities*, 1:7:1, ed. and trans. H. St.J. Thackeray, R. Marcus, A. Wikgreen, and L.H. Feldman, Cambridge, MA: Harvard University Press, 1967–9, 76. On this cf. Sidersky, *Les origines des légendes musulmanes*, 36; Grünbaum, *Neue Beiträge*, 131; *BEQ*, 124. Elsewhere Josephus reports that Abraham taught astronomy to the Egyptians. See Josephus, *Jewish Antiquities* 1:8:2, ed. Thackeray et al., 82.

188 English trans. in A. Kulik, *Retroverting Slavonic Pseudepigrapha: Toward the Original of the Apocalypse of Abraham*, Leiden: Brill, 2004, (9–36) 15.

Similar to this is the tradition in *Genesis Rabba* 39:1, according to which Abraham sees an impressive building and then meets its owner. He realizes that the world, too, must have an owner, at which point God calls out to Abraham and announces that He is the master of the entire world.

All of these traditions, it seems, are shaped by two verses. The first is Deuteronomy 4.19, which at once forbids astrology to Israel and makes it a feature of gentile practice: "When you raise your eyes to heaven, when you see the sun, the moon, the stars – the entire array of heaven – do not be tempted to worship them and serve them. Yahweh your God has allotted these to all the other peoples under heaven."[189] The second is Genesis 15.5, by which God takes Abraham outside and tells him, "Look up at the sky and count the stars if you can." The verse, of course, implies that Abraham is unable to do so, and indeed implies that humans must rely on God, not on science. Commenting on this verse a tradition in *Genesis Rabba* (44:12) has God then declare to Abraham: "Thou art a prophet, not an astrologer."[190]

In the infancy legend of Abraham the exegetes also use the traditional association of Chaldea with astrology in order to provide a narrative setting for the history of Abraham in Ur,[191] regarding which the Bible has precious little to say.[192] This legend also serves to illustrate the superiority of the prophet to the astrologer, inasmuch as Abraham begins with stellar observation and ends with the voice of God, in the way that he begins in Mesopotamia and ends in the Promised Land.

It is noteworthy that the legend of Abraham's contemplation of heavenly bodies does not have a prominent place in Christian exegesis.[193] In fact, early Christian authors tend to describe Abraham's conversion in terms of faith alone. Some conclude that Abraham's faith was in the Word of God who would become incarnate in Jesus. Thus Eusebius (d. ca. 342) writes:

189 It is no surprise, then, to find Philo report that the reason why Abraham left Ur was to get away from the impious science of astrology. Cf. *BEQ*, 145–6.

190 Trans. Freedman et al., 1:368. Cf. Kugel, *TB*, 263, who refers to a related tradition in *BT Shabbāt*, 156a. On Abraham as a prophet see Gn 20.7.

191 Kugel writes: "For the Chaldeans were famous at the time of the ancient interpreters for one thing: their mastery of astronomy and astrology (the two pursuits were a single field in ancient times). So exact were their calculations concerning the sun, the moon, and the stars that the word 'Chaldean' itself came to be a synonym for astrologer." J. Kugel, *How to Read the Bible*, New York: Free Press, 2007, 93.

192 Of course, the logic of the Biblical account suggests that Abraham's confrontation with his father should take place in Ḥarrān, since it is in Ḥarrān, not Ur, where God calls Abraham (Gn 12.1–4; cf. Gn 11.31). The location of the midrashic legend in Chaldea, i.e. Babylonia (southern Mesopotamia), and not in Ḥarrān (northern Mesopotamia), presumably reflects instead the references later in the Bible (Gn 15.7; Nehemiah 9.7) to God bringing Abraham out of Ur of Chaldea.

193 Although in his apologetical work *Praeparatio Evangelica* (9:17; *PG* 21, ed. J.-P. Migne, Paris: Migne, 1857, 708) Eusebius describes Abraham as the inventor of astrology.

> It was by faith towards the Logos of God, the Christ who had appeared to him, that he was justified, and gave up the superstition of his fathers, and his former erroneous life, and confessed the God who is over all to be one; and Him he served by virtuous deeds, not by the worship of the law of Moses, who came later. . . . It is only among Christians throughout the whole world that the manner of religion which was Abraham's can actually be found in practice.[194]

Eusebius' comments are inspired by Genesis 15, wherein God appears to Abraham (long after his departure from his father's city) and promises him that he will have descendents as numerous as the stars in the sky (Gn 15.5). In response, Genesis explains, Abraham "put his faith in Yahweh and this was reckoned to him as uprightness" (Gn 15.6). Eusebius proposes that not God Himself but His Logos appeared to Abraham on this occasion. Thereby he develops a larger theological theme (prominent too in the thought of his predecessor Origen) according to which the transcendent God is never seen or heard by His creation, only the mediating Logos.

More to the point, however, is Eusebius' focus on Abraham's faith. In this Eusebius is following Paul, who uses the figure of Abraham, and this verse in particular, to illustrate his conception of justification: "If Abraham had been justified because of what he had done, then he would have had something to boast about. But not before God: * does not scripture say: Abraham put his faith in God and this was reckoned to him as uprightness?" (Romans 4.2–3).[195] In this way Christianity, a religion of faith and not of law, becomes an Abrahamic religion. Paul accordingly describes Christians as the "progeny of Abraham, the heirs named in the promise" (Galatians 3.29; cf. Romans 4.1; 11.1).

For Christian authors the figure of Abraham is attractive because he lived before the Law of Moses and before (his grandson) Jacob, the father of Israel.[196] Indeed Paul points out that Abraham was justified (Gn 15.6; cf. Romans 4.2–3) even before he was circumcised:

> Now how did this come about? When he was already circumcised, or before he had been circumcised? Not when he had been circumcised, but while he was still uncircumcised * and circumcision was given to him later, as a sign and a guarantee that the faith which he had while still

194 *Ecclesiastical History*, 1:4:13–4, trans. K. Lake and J.E.L. Oulton, Cambridge, MA: Harvard University Press, 1964, 1:45.

195 At the same time, the author of the letter of James likewise calls on the figure of Abraham, but in a distinct manner. As though in response to Paul (although the chronological sequence of the two letters is disputed), James argues, "Was not Abraham our father justified by his deed, because he offered his son Isaac on the altar?" (James 2:21).

196 This phenomenon of claiming Abraham can also be observed with some Talmudic and midrashic texts, wherein Abraham is presented essentially as a Jew. See, e.g., *BT ʿAbōdā Zārā* 14b, *Yōmā* 28b, where he is said (anachronistically) to follow the law. Cf. also *Pirqē de-Rabbī Elīʿezer* 31; ed. Börner-Klein, 353. On this see *GdQ1*, 17, n. 2.

uncircumcised was reckoned to him as uprightness. In this way, Abraham was to be the ancestor of all believers who are uncircumcised, so that they might be reckoned as upright.

(Romans 4.10–1)

By claiming Abraham, Christian authors are thereby asserting that Christianity, far from being a perverse innovation of Judaism, is an ancient and primary religion (cf. also Jn 8.57–9; Romans 8.7–9). Indeed, Eusebius' insistence that Christ appeared to Abraham makes this especially clear. By his view Judaism would appear as the innovation, inasmuch as Moses came after Abraham. In the same way the Syriac father Aphrahat (d. ca. 345), insists, "The peoples which were of all languages were called first, before Israel, to the inheritance of the Most High, as God said to Abraham, 'I have made you the father of a multitude of peoples' [Gn 17.5]."[197]

This debate forms the background of the Qur'ān's position on Abraham. In *āl 'Imrān* the Qur'ān reprimands Jews and Christians for staking claims on Abraham (*yā ahla l-kitābi li-ma tuḥājjūna fī ibrāhīma*; Q 3.65a), noting that the Jewish and Christian scriptures were revealed after him (Q 3.65b; cf. 2.140).[198] The Qur'ān then concludes: "Abraham was not a Jew or a Christian but a *ḥanīf*, a *muslim*" (Q 3.67; cf. 2.135). The term *ḥanīf* would accordingly seem to be the key to understanding the manner in which the Qur'ān claims Abraham for its own.[199]

The meaning of this term has long been debated by scholars of the Qur'ān, and two different approaches to the problem have developed.[200] The first,

197 Aphrahat, *Homily 16 (On the Peoples Which Are in the Place of the People)*, para. 1, trans. in J. Neusner, *Aphrahat and Judaism: The Christian-Jewish Argument in Fourth-Century Iran*, Leiden: Brill, 1971, 60. Syriac text in W. Wright, *The Homilies of Aphraates, the Persian Sage*, London: Williams and Norgate, 1869, 320.

198 On this cf. Grünbaum, *Neue Beiträge*, 101. "Though the Jews followed the revelation as it had been delivered to Moses in the *Torah*, and the Christians that delivered to Jesus in the *Injīl*, both Jews and Christians claimed to have Abraham as their father." Jeffery, *Qur'ān as Scripture*, 75.

199 Ahrens ("Christliches im Qoran," 28, 190) points out the connection between the Qur'ān's description of Abraham as *ḥanīf* and the place of Abraham in Paul's argument.

200 Bibliographic references on earlier scholarship on the question of the *ḥanīf*s can be found in an article by N.A. Faris and H.W. Gilden, who present a detailed classification: "The various schools of thought regarding the *ḥanīf*s may be roughly grouped into the following categories: 1) They were either a Christian or a Jewish sect; 2) They were not a sect and had no specific cult; 3) They represented an Arabian movement under Christian or Jewish influence; 4) They represented an independent movement; 5) They were closely connected with the Ṣābians." Tellingly, Faris and Gilden never mention the possibility that the *ḥanīf*s are not a historical group at all. See N.A. Faris and H.W. Gilden, "The development of the meaning of Koranic *ḥanīf*," *Journal of the Palestine Oriental Society* 19, 1939/40, 1–18; reprint: *Der Koran*, ed. R. Paret, *Wege der Forschung* 326, Darmstadt: Wissenschaftliche Buchgesellschaft, 1975, 255–68 (quotation from 255–6). Faris and Gilden themselves argue, largely on the basis of Jāhilī poetry, that the *ḥanīf*s were a Hellenized, gnostic group present among the Nabateans who claimed a connection with Abraham (see esp. pp. 264–8).

and the more popular, involves an examination of the use of *ḥanīf* in biographical literature on Muḥammad, and the literature of Jāhilī poetry that would seem to support it. On this basis a number of scholars have argued that in the time of Muḥammad there was an independent, monotheistic sect whose members were known as *ḥanīf*s (pl. *ḥunafā'*).[201] Sprenger suggests that these *ḥanīf*s might have been associated with the Ṣābi'a.[202] Schulthess argues for the historical existence of the *ḥanīf*s on the basis of the poetry of Umayya b. Abī l-Ṣalt.[203] Rudolph describes the *ḥanīf*s as: "einzelne Männer, die, mit dem anererbten Heidentum unzufrieden, sich vom Götzendienst abwandten und etwas Neues, Besseres suchten."[204] This view, based firmly on Islamic tradition, becomes increasingly common among later scholars. Bell, for example, insists that the *ḥanīf*s were independent monotheists who happened to be around in the Prophet's place and time (he does not find any elsewhere). To this effect he even reproduces, almost verbatim, Ibn Hisham's report of the four most famous *ḥanīf*s: Waraqa b. Nawfal, Ubaydallāh b. Jaḥsh, Zayd b. 'Amr b. Nufayl, and 'Uthmān b. Ḥuwayrith.[205]

In addition to the sources mentioned elsewhere in this case study, notable works on the question of *ḥanīf* include D.S. Margoliouth, "On the origin and import of the names *muslim* and *ḥanīf*," *JRAS* 35, 1903, 467–93; C.J. Lyall, "The words 'hanīf' and 'Muslim'," *JRAS* 35, 1903, 771–84; Omer Bey, "Some considerations with regard to the *Hanīf* question," *MW* 22, 1932, 72–5; Y. Moubarac, *Abraham dans le Coran* (Paris: Vrin, 1958), 151–61; F. Denny, "Some religio-communal terms and concepts in the Qur'an," *Numen* 24, 1977, (26–59) 26–34; S. Bashear, *Studies in Early Islamic Tradition*, Jerusalem: The Hebrew University Press, 2004, ch. xiv.

201 Sprenger, *Leben*, 1:67–71; H. Hirschfeld, *Beiträge zur Erklärung des Ḳorāns*, Leipzig: Schulze, 1886, 46; Beeston, "The religions of pre-Islamic Yemen"; idem, "Himyarite monotheism." Wellhausen argues that the *ḥanīf*s were instead some sort of Christian penitential sect. See Wellhausen, *Reste arabischen Heidentums*, 207; *GdQ1*, 8. Nöldeke (*Neue Beiträge*, 30) comments elsewhere, "Es kann aber sehr wohl ein Einsiedler oder Büßer sein, wie Wellhausen annimmt." R. Dozy, noting the meaning "pagan" of the root *ḥ.n.p.* in Hebrew, argues that *ḥanīf* referred originally to those Jews who obeyed only the written law. See Dozy, *Die Israeliten zu Mekka von Davids Zeit*, 189. Margoliouth ("On the origin and import of the names *muslim* and *ḥanīf*") proposes that the word stems from the tribe B. Ḥanīfa, suggesting that they accepted monotheism with the false prophet Musaylima before Muḥammad. Cf. also Hirschberg, *Judische und christliche Lehren*, 33.

202 Sprenger, *Leben*, 1:45–7.

203 Schulthess, "Umajja ibn Abī ṣ Ṣalt," in C. Bezold (ed.), *Orientalische Studien, Th. Nöldeke zum 70. Geburtstag gewidmet*, Gieszen: Töpelmann, 1906, 1:(71–89) 86–7. Nöldeke doubts the historicity of references to the *ḥunafā'* and *ḥanīfiyya* in the poetry of Umayya b. Abī l-Ṣalt, stating, "Freilich ist das Meiste, was von diesen berichtet wird, mit Mißtrauen zu betrachten, und der oft zitierte Vers des Omaija b. Ṣalt, der الحنيفة als allein wahre Religion nennt . . . ist so verdächtig wie der größte Teil der diesem Dichter zugeschriebenen Verse." *Neue Beiträge*, 30.

204 Rudolph, *Abhängigkeit*, 70.

205 Bell, *Origin*, 57–8; cf. Ibn Hishām, *Sīrat Rasūl Allāh*, 143 (trans., 99). For a critique of the assumption that the *ḥanīf*s are figures of history, not literature, see Rippin, "RḤMNN and the Ḥanīfs," 161–4.

The strange thing about this sort of report is, in a word, *ḥanīf*. The root *ḥ.n.f(p)*. in Semitic languages, is not in fact connected to monotheism but rather, quite to the contrary, to paganism. In Syriac, for example, *ḥanpā* is the standard word for "pagan."[206] Yet in the Islamic accounts, such as that of Ibn Hishām, the *ḥanīf*s who existed in the time of Muḥammad were Abrahamic monotheists. To Jeffery these accounts are essentially exegetical; they are based on the use of the word *ḥanīf* in the Qur'ān.[207] François de Blois notes that there is nothing in the Qur'ān to suggest that there was ever a religious group that was known by this name.[208] I might add that there is nothing outside of the Qur'ān, either, to suggest this.

The second approach to address the term *ḥanīf* is, essentially, the approach of the current book: to examine the text and subtext of the Qur'ān, that is, to investigate what is written before (Jewish and Christian literature), not what is written after (*tafsīr*), the Qur'ān. Thus one might begin instead with the Qur'ān's own explanation that Abraham the *ḥanīf* is neither a Jew nor a Christian (e.g. Q 2.135; 3.67).[209] In a way one might end here. With *ḥanīf* the Qur'ān is not seeking to define a new religion or religious community. Instead it is simply insisting that Abraham does not belong to Jews or Christians. The Qur'ān is using the term in the context of sectarian polemic, not religious history.[210]

206 See *TS*, 1322; U. Rubin, "Ḥanīf," *EQ*, 2:403b (The root *ḥ.n.f.* is strangely absent from M. Zammit's *A Comparative Lexical Study of Qur'ānic Arabic*, Leiden: Brill, 2002). This lexical point did not escape the attention of later Syriac writers. Theodore bar Kōnī (fl. ca. 792), for example, regularly refers to Muslims as *ḥanpê*. S. Griffith comments, "It is likely that Bar Kônî was fully aware of the double entendre inherent in the term." *The Church in the Shadow of the Mosque: Christians and Muslims in the World of Islam*, Princeton: Princeton University Press, 2008, 43, n. 62. Cf. idem, "Chapter Ten of the Scholion: Theodore bar Kônî's Apology for Christianity," *Orientalia Christiana Analecta* 218 (1982), 169–91.

207 *FV*, 114, n. 4. Horovitz attempts (*KU*, 56–9) to save the historical value of these reports by suggesting that the *ḥanīf*s of Muḥammad's time were originally called so in derision. Later they adopted the term (in the way that Americans adopted the originally pejorative term Yankee). This is, of course, an *argumentum e silentio*. Still, speculation on the historical character of the *ḥanīf*s has hardly subsided in recent years. W.M. Watt's article on the term in the *Encyclopaedia of Islam* (2nd edition) is largely based on the "historical" reports of *ḥanīf*s in the time of Muḥammad. See W.M. Watt, "Ḥanīf," *EI²*, 3:165–6; Cf. also the speculative historiography on this point by Lüling, *Challenge to Islam for Reformation*, 340ff.

208 See de Blois, "*Naṣrānī* and *Ḥanīf*," 17.

209 This point is emphasized by Rippin in his article "RḤMNN and the Ḥanīfs." Horovitz, for his part, attempts to understand *ḥanīf* in the light of its appearance in Jāhilī poetry. See *KU*, 56–8.

210 Thus U. Rubin notes the "polemical context in which the use of this term in the Qur'ān should be understood." Rubin, "Ḥanīf," *EQ*, 2:402–3; J. Obermann comments, "There can be little doubt, at any rate, that in his own utterances Muhammad employs the word *ḥanīf* to describe persons who, although not belonging to the 'People of the Book,' and therefore properly classed as 'heathens,' penetrated to the belief in one God of the World." Obermann, "Islamic origins," 80–1; cf. R. Paret, "Ibrāhīm," *EI²*, 3:980b.

Yet there remains the problem of the relationship between *ḥanīf* and Syriac *ḥanpā*. Richard Bell (revising his earlier theory) suggests accordingly that it was the Syriac plural *hanpê* that was first taken into Arabic, as *ḥunafāʾ* (a standard Arabic plural form and in fact the plural of *ḥanīf* in Q 22.31; 98.5). From this plural form was derived the corresponding singular form *ḥanīf*.[211] François de Blois, while raising the possibility that *ḥanīf* is a genuine Arabic term that simply acquired the meaning of its Syriac cognate, suggests the same solution, referring to it as a "back-formation."[212]

Now when it comes to foreign words there is usually no compelling reason to claim that the Qur'ān has borrowed them directly, since we have no pre-Qur'ānic Arabic literature by which to control such a claim. However, *ḥanīf* may be an exception to this rule, since there is some internal evidence that the Qur'ān borrowed the term directly from Syriac *ḥanpā* (pl. *ḥanpē*). Christoph Luxenberg points out that in all of its ten appearances in the Qur'ān *ḥanīf never* appears with the definite article, and *always* appears with an *alif* appended to it.[213] This *alif* is commonly explained as an Arabic accusative marker (in most cases as an accusative of circumstance, or *ḥāl*). Yet this explanation is not always convincing. In at least two verses (Q 6.161; 30.30) the absence of a definite article, and the presence of the extra *alif*, is salient and awkward. On this matter Luxenberg provides an attractive solution: that the *alif* here is not an accusative marker, but in fact a remnant of the Syriac definite article.[214]

Whether or not his solution is correct, it remains to be explained why the Qur'ān would use Syriac *ḥanpā* for its discourse on Abraham. This explanation is elusive only if Syriac *ḥanpā* is understood according to its primary meaning of "pagan."[215] Yet *ḥanpā* also appears with a secondary meaning of "gentile." In this way it is used in the Peshitta to translate Ἕλλην ("Greeks")

211 R. Bell, "Who were the *Ḥanīfs*?" *MW* 29, 1949, (120–5) 120–1. Earlier (*The Origin of Islam in Its Christian Environment*, 1926, 58) Bell had argued that *ḥanīf* is a genuine Arabic word from the root *ḥ.n.f.*, meaning "to depart from."

212 De Blois, "*Naṣrānī* and *Ḥanīf*," 23. On this point I am grateful for the insight in the forthcoming paper by Munʿim Sirry, "The early development of the Qur'anic *hanīf:* An exegetical analysis," *Journal of Qur'anic Studies*.

213 *Die syro-aramäische Lesart des Koran*. Berlin: Schiler, 2002, 65.

214 Thus Q 6.161, which in the Cairo text reads *innanī hadānī rabbī ilā ṣirāṭin mustaqīmin dīnan qayyiman millata Ibrāhīma ḥanīfan wa-mā kāna min al-mushrikīn*, might actually be understood as *innanī hadānī rabbī ilā ṣirāṭin mustaqīmin dīnan qayyiman millata Ibrāhīma* ***al-ḥanīfī*** *wa-mā kāna min al-mushrikīn*. A much more harmonious reading is thereby achieved (likewise in regard to Q 30.30). See *Die syro-aramäische Lesart*, 63–6 and the precise analysis of Luxenberg's work by D. Stewart: "Notes on medieval and modern emendations of the Qur'ān," *QHC*, 223–48.

215 Thus Nöldeke, *Neue Beiträge*, 30; Mingana, "Syriac influence on the style of the Kur'ān," 97; *FV* 115; W.M. Watt, "Ḥanīf," *EI*², 3:165; Rubin, "Ḥanīf," *EQ*, 2:402; de Blois, "*Naṣrānī* and *Ḥanīf*," 18–9.

in Romans 1.16 ("For I see no reason to be ashamed of the gospel; it is God's power for the salvation of everyone who has faith – Jews first, but *Gentiles* [*ḥanpê*] as well").[216] Accordingly Payne Smith offers as a second meaning of *ḥanpā*: *gentilis, ethnicus*.[217]

In other words the term is essentially synonymous with the Arabic term that the Qur'ān uses to describe Muḥammad: *ummī* (e.g. Q 7.157: "Those who follow the messenger, the *ummī* ["gentile"] prophet. They find him in their Tawrāt and Injīl").[218] The Qur'ān itself consistently opposes the *ummī*s to the People of the Book (cf. esp. Q 3.20, 75; 62.2). Islamic tradition sees this as a sign that *ummī* means "illiterate," literally someone without a book. But if the "Book" (*kitāb*) in "People of the Book" is seen instead as a reference to a covenant with God, then this phrase would refer to a people with an earlier revelation and law. The term *ummī* would then mean someone thus far without a covenant, that is, a "gentile."[219] In this light it becomes clear why in one place the Qur'ān describes Abraham (Q 16.120) with the related term *umma*, a nation, a description which per se seems awkward.[220] In fact this description is meaningful in two ways. First, it reflects the Biblical description of Abraham as a nation (*gōy*; Gn 18.18), itself an epithet that reflects the divine promise of blessing. Second, it separates Abraham from the Jews and the Christians, making him – like the Qur'ān's own prophet – a prophet of the gentiles.[221] Accordingly the Qur'ān elsewhere (Q 2.135) declares: "They say, 'Be a Jew or Christian and you will find guidance.' Say, 'No. The community (*milla*) of Abraham the *ḥanīf*, who was not one of the idolaters.'"[222] Thus it is understandable why the Qur'ān insists that "the

216 Similarly the Peshīṭtā has *ḥanptā* for Greek 'Ελληνίς ("gentile woman") in Mark 7:26.

217 *TS*, 1322. De Blois ("*Naṣrānī* and *Ḥanīf*," 21) argues that this meaning is derived: "The fact that the Syriac Bible can designate the gentiles with a word, *ḥanpē*, which etymologically means 'deceitful ones', is clearly also a continuation of Jewish usage; the gentiles (*goyīm*) are by definition godless (*ḥānēf*)."

218 On *ummī* see Horovitz (*KU*, 52), who defines the term with Greek ἐθνικός (referencing Heb. *umma* and Aramaic *ummethā*), and notes, "Muhammad bezeichnet sich also als Prophet aus den Heiden und für den Heiden."

219 Cf. the analysis of this term, which leads to a similar conclusion, in the little known work of I. Daouk, *The Koran from a Vernacular Perspective: Vocabulary Strings and Composition Strata*, Erlangen: Daouk, 2004, esp. 80ff.

220 Accordingly J. Bellamy, in a recent article, proposes to emend the text here to read *mr'* instead of *umma*. Yet the correspondence of this verse with those verses (Q 2.135; 22.78) which describe Abraham with the synonymous word *milla* render such an emendation superfluous. See Bellamy, "Ten Qur'ānic emendations," 124.

221 Thus J. Bowman comments: "[Abraham] is the Gentile prophet, the prophet of the Gentiles in either the Old Testament or New Testament sense, and for the Gentile Arabs he is the national prophet, the prophet from among themselves." J. Bowman, "The debt of Islam to monophysite Syrian Christianity," in E.C.B. MacLaurin (ed.), *Essays in Honor of Griffithes Wheeler Thatcher*, Sydney: Sydney University Press, 1967, (191–216) 207.

222 Cf. Q 22.78: "The community of Abraham is yours."

closest people to Abraham are those who followed him and *this prophet*" (Q 3.68).

Jeffery concludes that the word *ḥanīf* was unfamiliar to the Qur'ān's audience. He notes that when *ḥanīf* appears in the Qur'ān it is usually followed by the added phrase, *wa-mā kānā min al-mushrikīn* (Q 2.135; 3.95; 6.161; 16.123; cf. 6.79; 10.105; 16.120). The larger phrase is commonly understood to mean: "a monotheist (*ḥanīf*) *and* he was not a polytheist."[223] That is, Jeffery understands the added phrase as a definition of *ḥanīf*, an explanation for an Arab audience unfamiliar with this Syriac term.[224] Yet this phrase now appears to be less a definition and more a qualification: this *ḥanīf*, this gentile, was not a polytheist; that is, Abraham was "a gentile *but* he was not a polytheist."

With this refrain the Qur'ān is insisting that Abraham was a *ḥanpā*, or a *ḥanīf*, in the ethnic sense of the word, not in the religious sense.[225] This suggests, of course, that the Qur'ān's audience, pace Jeffery, was eminently familiar with the term *ḥanpā/ḥanīf*, and that the Qur'ān was consequently anxious to specify in which sense it intends the term. De Blois goes still further than this, proposing that the Arabs at the time of the Qur'ān's proclamation, who at once identified themselves as gentiles and descendants of Abraham, would have been particularly eager to emphasize his gentile monotheism.[226] This is a speculative point, although it seems to me quite reasonable.

On the other hand no speculation is needed to see how the Qur'ān connects its own prophet to Abraham the gentile. In *al-baqara* (2) 127–9 the Qur'ān has Abraham implore God to send forth a prophet from among his descendents:

> When Abraham, with Ismāʿīl, was raising the foundations of the house, [he said] "O Lord, accept [this] from us. You are the seer, the knower. * O Lord make us submissive to you, and make a nation (*umma*) submissive to you from our descendents. Show our rites and return to us. You are the returner, the merciful. * O Lord send to them a messenger who will declare your signs to them, who will teach them the book and the wisdom, who will purify them. You are the powerful, the wise."

Thus it appears that the figure of Abraham in the Qur'ān is above all a symbol and a prototype for the Qur'ān's own prophet. The *ḥanīf* prophet

223 In the case of Q 6.79, for example, the particle *wa* is translated "and" by Pickthall, Yusuf Ali, Blachère (et), Paret (und), and Fakhry. This translation is also implied by both Arberry and Abdel Haleem, who begin a new sentence at this point.

224 *FV*, 112.

225 To this end de Blois points to the description of Abraham in the Syriac life of Clement: *haymen abrāhām l-alāhā kad ḥanpā wā*, which de Blois interprets as "Abraham was obedient to god, as a gentile." De Blois, "*Naṣrānī* and *Ḥanīf*," 23.

226 De Blois, "*Naṣrānī* and *Ḥanīf*," 23.

anticipates the *ummī* prophet. This idea might be taken still further in light of the Qur'ān's insistence that the *umma* to which its prophet is sent is that of the Arabs: "[God] is the one who sent a messenger from the gentiles, to the gentiles (*ummīyīn*), to declare His signs to them, to purify them, to teach them the book and the wisdom. Before this they were in obvious error" (Q 62.2). Elsewhere the Qur'ān indicates who these gentiles are, when it explains, "For this reason we have revealed to you an Arabic Qur'ān, that you might warn the mother of the villages and those around it" (Q 42.7). Thus it seems that the Qur'ān here is developing a nationalist discourse, insisting that the Arabs are a nation descended from Abraham, a nation to whom God has finally spoken. Accordingly the Qur'ān insists that the Jews and Christians have no special privilege: "The Jews and the Christians say, 'We are the sons of God and His beloved.' Say, 'Then why does He punish you for your sins? No, you are only humans, humans among the many whom He has created'" (Q 5.18a).

In this light it is telling that the Qur'ān has Abraham apply the term *ḥanīf* to himself. After rejecting the worship of the stars, the moon, and the sun, the Qur'ān has Abraham declare: "I have turned my face to the one who created the heavens and the earth, a gentile (*ḥanīf*), but not a polytheist" (Q 6.79). In this way the Qur'ān asserts that Abraham was in no way obliged to the People of the Book for his faith, and it thereby implies the same for its own Prophet.

CS 5 The laughter of Abraham's wife

Qur'ānic account

The Qur'ān's interest in Abraham, however, is not limited to his monotheism. The story of the annunciation of Isaac, Abraham's son, has a similarly prominent place in the Qur'ān. In three different places the Qur'ān refers to this narrative, most fully in *Hūd* (11) 69ff.:

> (69) Our messengers came to Abraham with good news. They said, "Peace." He said, "Peace," and hastened to bring them a <u>roasted</u> calf.[227] (70) When he saw that their hands did not touch it he became suspicious and fearful of them. They said, "Do not fear. We have been sent to the people of Lot." (71) His wife was standing by,[228] <u>then</u> she laughed. We gave her the good news of Isaac and, after Isaac, Jacob. (72) She said,

227 "Roasted" is the traditional translation. Zamakhsharī (1:410) defines *ḥanīdh* as something "roasted on a hot stone in a trench." Cf. Ibn Kathīr, 2:426, on Q 11.69–73. Yet *ḥanīdh* is an enigmatic term and a *hapax legomenon*.

228 *Imrā'atuhu qā'imatun*. The reading of Ibn Mas'ūd adds here *wa-huwa jālisun* ("and he was sitting") or, according to Zamakhsharī (1:410), *wa-huwa qā'idun* ("and he was sitting"). See *MQQ*, 3:123; Ibn Kathīr, 2:426, on Q 11.69–73.

"Woe is me! Shall I give birth as an old woman, when my master is aged? This is truly a strange thing."

11.69 وَلَقَدْ جَاءتْ رُسُلُنَا إِبْرَاهِيمَ بِالْبُشْرَى قَالُواْ سَلاَمًا قَالَ سَلاَمٌ فَمَا لَبِثَ أَن جَاء بِعِجْلٍ حَنِيذ

11.70 فَلَمَّا رَأَى أَيْدِيَهُمْ لاَ تَصِلُ إِلَيْهِ نَكِرَهُمْ وَأَوْجَسَ مِنْهُمْ خِيفَةً قَالُواْ لاَ تَخَفْ إِنَّا أُرْسِلْنَا إِلَى قَوْمِ لُوطٍ

11.71 وَامْرَأَتُهُ قَآئِمَةٌ فَضَحِكَتْ فَبَشَّرْنَاهَا بِإِسْحَاقَ وَمِن وَرَاء إِسْحَاقَ يَعْقُوبَ

11.72 قَالَتْ يَا وَيْلَتَى أَأَلِدُ وَأَنَاْ عَجُوزٌ وَهَذَا بَعْلِي شَيْخًا إِنَّ هَذَا لَشَيْءٌ عَجِيبٌ

Several preliminary observations can be made on these verses. First, the declaration of the messengers in verse 70 connects this pericope to that which immediately follows, on the destruction of Lot's people (Q 11.77–83). Thereby this pericope is connected to the larger Qur'ānic topos of divine punishment. Second, the verb *bashshara* in verse 71 connects this passage, on the other hand, with the Qur'ānic topos of annunciation. The Qur'ān (Q 57.12) describes the blessed in heaven as receiving a *bushrā*.[229] The Qur'ān even refers to itself as a *bushrā* (Q 2.91; 46.12). Third, it is noteworthy that the divine voice of the Qur'ān, in the first person plural, delivers the good news, since in the previous verse it is the messengers who speak, in the third person plural. Apparently God is present, somehow, in the midst of the messengers.

Finally, this pericope as a whole might be compared to that in *āl 'Imrān* (3) 39–40. Here angels call to Zechariah while he is standing (cf. Q 11.71, where Abraham's wife is standing) and praying. They announce that God gives him good news (*yubashshiruka*, v. 39). He responds: "O my Lord (*rabbī*)! How can I have a boy when I have already reached old age and my wife is infertile" (v. 40). The angels speak to Zechariah, but he addresses God. Once again, it seems that God is present, somehow, in the midst of the messengers. Similarly, in the annunciation to Mary (Q 3.45–7) angels speak to her (v. 45), but she addresses God directly (v. 47).

Two other Qur'ānic passages refer to the annunciation to Abraham, and thereby illuminate the Qur'ān's interest in it.[230] In *al-ḥijr* (15) 51–60, the Qur'ān refers to the messengers as the guests (*al-ḍayf*) of Abraham (v. 51). This passage is notably more succinct than that of *Hūd*. Here there is no mention of a meal. Instead, Abraham immediately declares that he is afraid of the visitors (v. 52). Here Abraham's wife does not appear at all. When the messengers give good news of a boy (v. 53), it is Abraham, instead, who expresses amazement (v. 54).

229 Cf. also Hebrew *bsūra* or *bsūra ṭōba* used in 2 Sam. 18.20, 27; 2 Kings 7.9. Cf. *BEQ*, 147.

230 In addition to the passages described below cf. Q 14.37–9, wherein Abraham thanks God for giving him Isaac and Ishmael in his old age, and Q 29.31.

More details can be found in *al-dhāriyyāt* (51) 24–34, where the visitors are again referred to as guests (v. 24). As in *Hūd*, Abraham is frightened when they do not eat the food he offers them (v. 27–8). At this the visitors immediately give him the news (here it is reported in the third person plural: *bashsharū*) of a son to be born, and Abraham's shocked wife emerges shouting (*fī ṣarratin*). She strikes her face (*ṣakkat wajhahā*), declaring: "An infertile old woman!" (v. 29).

Hūd (11) 69–72 reports the events of the visitation to Abraham in the following order: (1) the messengers refused to eat, (2) Abraham became fearful, (3) the messengers declared that their mission is to Lot's people, (4) Abraham's wife laughed, and (5) the angels announced that she would conceive Isaac. The problem with this order is that the laughter of Abraham's wife (4) appears *before* the annunciation (5). Why, then, does she laugh?[231] *Al-dhāriyyāt* implies that her laughter is in fact due to the annunciation, word order notwithstanding, since her function in the narrative is to express amazement at that annunciation, whether she does so through shouting, hitting herself or laughing.

Problems for interpreters

Most of the translators, however, follow the order of the Arabic text:

Pickthall:	"And his wife, standing by laughed when We gave her good tidings."
Yusuf Ali:	"And his wife was standing (there), and she laughed: But we gave her glad tidings."
Blachère:	"La femme [d'Abraham] rit, debout, tandis qu'il était assis,[232] et Nous lui annonçâmes."
Arberry:	"And his wife was standing by; she laughed, therefore We gave her the glad tidings."
Paret:	"Seine Frau, die dabeistand, lachte. Da verkündeten wir ihr."
Fakhry:	"His wife was standing by, so she laughed. Thereupon We announced to her the good news."
Abdel Haleem:	"His wife was standing [nearby] and laughed. We gave her good news."

Only Pickthall, with the use of "when," portrays the laughter of Abraham's wife as a result of the messengers' announcement. Yusuf Ali, quite on the contrary, seems to suggest with the use of "but" that the announcement occurred *despite* her laughter. With his use of "therefore" Arberry implies that the

231 For other instances of laughter in the Qur'ān see Q 53.43, 59–60.

232 In adding "tandis qu'il était assis," Blachère follows the variant reading of Ibn Mas'ūd. See *MQQ*, 3:123. Cf. A. Jeffery, *Materials for the History of the Text of the Qur'ān*, Leiden: Brill, 1937, 47.

announcement was a response to (or reward for?) her laughter. Otherwise the translators simply follow the word order of the Qur'ān, connecting the two events without implying any causal relationship.

The reluctance of the translators to attribute Abraham's wife's laughter to the annunciation of a son reflects the majority opinion of the *mufassirūn*.[233] *Tafsīr Muqātil*, for example, explains that her laughter was not related to that annunciation but rather to "Abraham's fear and terror of three individuals."[234] In other words, she did not realize – as Abraham did – that the messengers were celestial. Abraham's anxious behavior therefore seemed humorous.

Qummī explains this passage with a long narrative about a nearby city to which Lot had been sent. This city was known for its plentiful fruit, he explains, and those who passed it would inevitably steal from its orchards. When the devil sensed the frustration of its people at this thievery, he encouraged them to attack and sodomize those who passed by.[235] The residents of the city soon fell into hopeless depravity, and God sent Lot to warn them of His punishment. Soon thereafter four (not three as *Tafsīr Muqātil* has it)[236] messengers came to Abraham, who recognized them as divine messengers and rushed to offer them hospitality. When they did not eat, Abraham's wife, offended, shouted at them: "You do not partake in the food of the *khalīl* of God!?"[237] At this they explained that they were on a mission to destroy Lot's people (cf. Q 11.70), and thus it was revealed that the guests were angels. Suddenly Abraham's wife had her menses ("which had not come to her for a long time"). In response she covered her face with her hands (cf. Q 51.29) and cried "Woe is me!" (cf. Q 11.72). But she did not laugh. Qummī argues that Arabic *ḍaḥikat* (Q 11.71) here actually means *ḥāḍat* ("she menstruated").[238] Qummī's interpretation, of course, has an appealing logic

233 On Islamic exegesis of this passage cf. L. Ammann, *Vorbild und Vernunft. Die Regelung von Lachen und Scherzen im mittelalterlichen Islam*, Hildesheim: Olms, 1993, 19ff.; idem, "Laughter," *EQ*, 3:148; S. Stetkevych, "Sarah and the hyena: Laughter, menstruation, and the genesis of a double entendre," *Mélanges de Science Religieuse* 53, 1996, 13–41.

234 *Tafsīr Muqātil*, 2:290, on Q 11.69.

235 In fact, Qummī relates that the devil himself appeared to them as a beautiful boy, inviting the men to have intercourse with him, in order to encourage their sexual perversion. Qummī 1:334, on Q 11.69.

236 On this question Zamakhsharī relates one tradition (on the authority of Ibn ʿAbbās) that three angels visited Abraham: Gabriel, Michael, and Isrāfīl. Yet another tradition has nine and still another eleven. Zamakhsharī, 1:409, on Q 11.69–73. Ibn Kathīr argues that they were four: Gabriel, Michael, Isrāfīl, and Raphael. Ibn Kathīr, 2:426, on Q 11.69–73.

237 Qummī 1:335, on Q 11.69. The Qur'ān reports (Q 4.125) that God took Abraham as a *khalīl*, "trusted friend." Cf. 2 Chr. 20.7; Isaiah 41.8; James 2.23. For references to Abraham as "friend of God" in Jewish and Christian literature see *BEQ*, 173.

238 Qummī 1:335, on Q 11.69. Lane (*AEL*, 5:1771b) describes the debate among lexicographers over this alternative definition of *ḍaḥikat*, which I will discuss further below. According to two authorities (Ibn Sīda and Zabīdī [author of *Tāj al-ʿarūs*]) the word can be used in this way in regard to rabbits. These and other (Zamakhsharī, Ṣaghānī, Fayyūmī) authorities

to it, since the appearance of Abraham's wife's menses would correspond with her miraculous conception of a child in her old age.

This is only one of many explanations that Ṭabarī considers. According to the first explanation Abraham's wife laughed when she saw that his guests did not eat.[239] According to the second explanation, she laughed when she heard that the angels were to destroy the people of Lot, "pleased that God's punishment had come upon a heedless people."[240] According to the third explanation (stated with a circumlocution for modesty's sake), she laughed when she realized that the visitors would not do to them that which Lot's people were known to do. The fourth explanation is that of *Tafsīr Muqātil*, that she laughed when she saw Abraham's fear of the messengers.

According to the fifth explanation Abraham's wife laughed when she received the good news of Isaac and Jacob, that is, she laughed with joy because of the miracle granted to her. Ṭabarī immediately notes that this explanation contradicts the word order of the Qur'ān.[241] There is, he notes, a philological device (*ḥīla*) that could solve this difficulty, namely *ta'khīr al-muqaddam*: understanding later that which appears earlier. Ṭabarī, however, declares his preference to avoid using such devices.

The sixth explanation is that of Qummī, that she did not laugh at all but rather menstruated (*ḥāḍat*). Ṭabarī is likewise suspicious of this creative interpretation, noting that the grammarians of Kūfa reject entirely this secondary meaning for *ḍaḥikat*.[242] Finally, according to the seventh explanation

record that the root *ḍ.ḥ.k.* received this secondary meaning due to the *ḍaḥḥāk* ("interior") of a palm tree that splits open. A number of lexicographers (Ṣaghānī, Fayyūmī, Fīrūzābādī, Zabīdī) hold that it can be used for women in addition to rabbits and some of them (Ṣaghānī, Fīrūzābādī, Zabīdī) use it in their interpretation of Q 11.71. Stefan Wild mentions this example as a case of the Arabic lexicographical tradition relying on Qur'ānic exegesis. See his *Das Kitāb al-ʿAin und die arabische Lexikographie*, Wiesbaden: Harrassowitz, 1965, 50, n. 137. I found this reference thanks to A. Rippin, "Qur'ān 78/24: A study in Arabic lexicography," *JSS* 28, 1983, (311–320) 312; reprint: *The Qur'ān and Its Interpretive Tradition*, ed. Rippin.

239 Here Ṭabarī mentions a variant reading of *hūd* (11) 69, attributed to Ibn Masʿūd, which adds "When he offered [the calf] to them he said, 'Will you not eat?'" (*fa-lammā qarrabahu ilayhim qāla a-lā ta'kalūn*). Ṭabarī, 12:72, on Q 11.71.

240 Ṭabarī, 12:72, on Q 11.71.

241 Ibid.

242 Ṭabarī, 12:73, on Q 11.71. S. Stetkevych defends this reading of Q 11.71 in light of a line in a Jāhilī poem of the *Ḥamāsa* (attributed to Ta'abbaṭa Sharran), in which the poet announces his intention to avenge his uncle's blood and alludes to a hyena laughing (*taḍḥaku al-ḍabʿū*). She explains that Marzūqī (d. 421/1030) and Tibrīzī (d. 502/1109) consider the idea that Ta'abbaṭa is referring to menstruation, although neither of them accept it. Stetkevych counters: "The connection between menstruation and unavenged blood or defeat on the battlefield is too well established to leave any doubt that there is a pun at work here." S. Stetkevych, *The Mute Immortals Speak*, Ithaca: Cornell University Press, 1993, 66 (see p. 60 for the poetic verse, cited from Tibrīzī's version of the *Ḥamāsa*). She argues (p. 67) that there is similarly a "double entendre" in the case of Q 11.71.

Abraham's wife laughed when she heard that the angels were to destroy the people of Lot, out of relief that her own family was going to be safe.

Ṭabarī favors the explanation that Abraham's wife laughed out of satisfaction that Lot's people would be destroyed (the second view above).[243] This is the best explanation, Ṭabarī remarks, since the last phrase in the Qur'ān before *ḍaḥikat* (i.e. at the end of Q 11.70) is "Do not fear. We have been sent to the people of Lot." Ṭabarī concludes: "Thus the laughter and amazement can only have been due to the affair of Lot's people."[244]

Zamakhsharī, for his part, finds the key to understanding the laughter of Abraham's wife's in Abraham's fear (Q 11.70). Regarding that fear Zamakhsharī comments, "The apparent cause is that he felt they were angels. He became suspicious of them because he was afraid that they had come down with divine censure of him, or to punish his people."[245] For this reason, he explains, the angels said "do not be afraid" (Q 11.70), for "they saw signs of fear and change in his face."[246] When Abraham's wife saw the fear in her husband's face subsequently disappear, she laughed.[247]

Ibn Kathīr explains that when the messengers did not eat the food that he offered them, Abraham realized they were angels. Ibn Kathīr explains: "Angels have no interest in eating. They do not desire it and they do not eat."[248] It was this realization that frightened Abraham. As for the laughter of Abraham's wife, Ibn Kathīr reports seven different explanations, the last of which is that she laughed when she received the good news about Isaac.[249]

Meanwhile, R. Firestone discusses a tradition reported by Tha'labī in his *Qiṣaṣ al-anbiyā'* that *ḍaḥikat* came to have the secondary meaning of "she menstruated" due to the Bedouin belief that rabbits laugh when they menstruate. See R. Firestone, *Journeys in Holy Lands*, Albany: SUNY Press, 1990, 58; Tha'labī, *'Arā'is al-majālis fī qiṣaṣ al-anbiyā'*, ed. Ḥasan 'Abd al-Raḥmān, Beirut: Dār al-Kutub al-'Ilmiyya, 1425/2004, 74–6. Regarding the connection to rabbits see the references to *AEL* in n. 238 above.

243 Ṭabarī, 12:74, on Q 11.71.

244 Ibid.

245 Zamakhsharī, 1:410.

246 Ibid.

247 Zamakhsharī does cite alternative explanations: that she laughed at the coming destruction of the sinful people of Lot, or at their obliviousness of the punishment that had drawn near. According to another explanation, "She used to say to Abraham: 'Bring your nephew Lot here with you, for I know that a punishment will come down on this people.'" She laughed when the matter took place as she predicted. Zamakhsharī also notes that some scholars argue that *ḍaḥikat* means "she menstruated." He does not mention, however, the possibility that Abraham's wife laughed at the annunciation of a son. Zamakhsharī, 1:411.

248 Ibn Kathīr, 2:426, on Q 11.69–73.

249 According to the first explanation Abraham's wife, who was named Sarah, laughed when she saw that their guests did not eat, after all of the work they had done. According to a second explanation, however, Sarah laughed when she heard about the promised annihilation of Lot's people, due to their iniquity and obdurate unbelief. The tradition adds that because of this righteous laughter "she was rewarded with a son, after she had given up hope." According to a third explanation she laughed at the obliviousness of Lot's people to the imminent punishment. According to a fourth explanation, she did not laugh, but

Yet Ibn Kathīr finds this final explanation, which he reports on the authority of Wahb b. Munabbih (the prototypical transmitter of traditions from Jews; *isrā'īliyyāt*), unacceptable. He explains, "This is contrary to the syntax, for the announcement of the good news is clearly a consequence of her laughter."[250] Instead Ibn Kathīr favors the view (also that preferred by Ṭabarī) that Abraham's wife, whom he names Sarah, laughed at the coming annihilation of Lot's people.

Subtext

Nevertheless there are signs in *Hūd* that the Qur'ān is in conversation with the Biblical account that has Sarah laugh when she hears the news of Isaac. To begin with, the Qur'ān follows quite closely here the sequence of the Biblical account: from the visitation to Abraham (Gn 18.1–16; Q 11.69–73), to Abraham's plea for Lot's people (Gn 18.17–33; Q 11.74–6), to the destruction of Lot's people (Gn 19.1–29; Q 11.77–83). In doing so, however, the Qur'ān neither reproduces the Biblical account in full nor provides an alternative account. Instead the Qur'ān develops its own homily, or religious exhortation, using references to the Biblical story along the way. This suggests that the Qur'ān assumes that its audience is already familiar with this story.

Thus it is perfectly reasonable for the Qur'ān to allude to the laughter of Sarah without a detailed explanation thereof. It is also reasonable for the Qur'ān (in Q 11.71) to mention that laughter before the annunciation of Isaac's birth, and to expect the reader nevertheless to understand that the annunciation came first (as Ṭabarī puts it, through *ta'khīr al-muqaddam*). In fact, the Qur'ān has a perfectly good literary reason for doing so. For here as elsewhere the Qur'ān follows a rhyme scheme (Ar. *fāṣila*) according to the penultimate syllable of the last word of each verse. In this section of *Hūd* those syllables are marked by either *ī* or *ū*: *bi-'ijlin ḥanīdh* (69); *qawmi Lūṭ* (70); . . . (71); *la-shay'un 'ajīb* (72); *ḥamīdun majīd* (73).

Yet the statement on Sarah's laughter – *wa-imrā'atuhu qā'imatun fa-ḍaḥikat* – would break this scheme. So too, for that matter, would the name Isaac, *isḥāq*. For this reason the Qur'ān takes the extraordinary step of adding Jacob, Sarah's grandson, to the annunciation. In Jewish and Christian traditions on this annunciation (and indeed in other annunciations that follow this topos, e.g. to Manoah in Judges 13), the divine visitors announce only the birth of a son. Even the two other Qur'ānic passages that allude to this episode speak only of a single boy (*ghulām*; Q 15.53; 51.28). Yet by adding

rather menstruated. According to a fifth explanation she laughed (out of fear?) when she thought that the angels had come to do that which Lot's people do. According to a sixth explanation she laughed when she saw Abraham's terror. Ibn Kathīr, 2:426–7, on Q 11.69–73.

250 Ibn Kathīr, 2:427, on Q 11.69–73.

Jacob in *Hūd* – *wa-warā' isḥāqa ya'qūb* – the meaning of the annunciation is not altered but developed and the Qur'ān's rhyme scheme is obeyed.

In other ways, however, the Qur'ān departs from the Biblical story in a fashion that clearly reflects Jewish and Christian exegetical developments. In Genesis 18.2, for example, the Bible reports that three men (אֲנָשִׁים; LXX ἄνδρες) appeared to Abraham, but in *Hūd* the Qur'ān mentions instead three messengers (*rusul*). This is an apparent allusion to angels (Greek ἄγγελος might even be behind *rusul* here). The Qur'ān itself (Q 22.75) explains that God chooses *rusul* from among both angels and men. In any case this allusion is fully in accordance with Jewish and Christian tradition on this question.[251] Josephus identifies them as angels,[252] as does *Targum Neofiti*.[253] The same view is reflected in the exhortation to hospitality in the Book of Hebrews: "Remember always to welcome strangers, for by doing this, some people have entertained angels without knowing it" (Hebrews 13.1).[254]

Hūd also explicitly remarks that Abraham's visitors did not eat (Q 11.70), a rather extraordinary remark since the Bible states clearly, "They ate while he remained standing near them under the tree" (Gn 18.8). Other Biblical accounts, however, make it a point to insist that angels do not eat. When, in the Book of Tobit, the angel Raphael finally reveals his identity after the long journey to Iran with Tobias, he announces, "You thought you saw me eating, but that was appearance and no more" (Tobit 12:19). When, in Judges, the angel of Yahweh visits Manoah to foretell the birth of Samson, Manoah asks the visitor to receive his hospitality: "Allow us to detain you while we prepare a kid for you" (Judges 13.15). The angel retorts, "Even if you did detain me, I should not eat your food" (v. 16).

The anti-anthropomorphic idea about angels in the Manoah account appears in Jewish and Christian exegesis on Genesis 18. Philo, Josephus, and Justin Martyr all argue that the angels who visited Abraham did not actually

251 Cf. the description elsewhere (Q 15.51; 51.24) of Abraham's visitors as "guests" (*ḍayf*).

252 *Jewish Antiquities* 1:11:2, ed. Thackeray et al., 96–8.

253 Trans. Le Déaut, Paris: Cerf, 1978–81, 184–5.

254 With Christian commentators an additional interpretation of Genesis 18 appears. The Bible mentions here in one place (Gn 18.1) that Yahweh himself appeared to Abraham, but in another (Gn 18.2) that three people visited him. Again, while three people initially speak to Abraham (Gn 18.8), only one voice announces the promise of a son (Gn 18.10), and Yahweh himself speaks to Abraham about the laughter of Sarah (Gn 18.12). To Christian authors the ambiguity of the divine presence in the midst of three visitors is an indication of the triune nature of God. The polemical Arabic treatise attributed to al-Kindī employs this argument against a Muslim antagonist. See *Risālat 'Abdallāh b. Ismā'īl al-Hāshimī ilā 'Abd al-Masīḥ b. Isḥāq al-Kindī wa-risālat 'Abd al-Masīḥ ilā l-Hāshimī*, Damascus: al-Takwīn li-l-Ṭibā'a wa-l-Nashr wa-l-Tawzī', 2005 (reprint of ed. A. Tien, London: n.p., 1880), 43; trans.: *The Apology of al-Kindy*, trans. W. Muir, London: Society for Promoting Christian Knowledge, 1887, 42. The Qur'ān preserves this ambiguity. In *Hūd* (11) 69–70 the messengers speak, but in the next verse (Q 11.71) God Himself (in the first person plural) announces the promise of a son.

eat.[255] *Targum Neofiti* on Genesis 18:8 relates: "They seemed to [Abraham] as if they were eating and as if they were drinking."[256] A tradition in *Genesis Rabba* (48.14) relates that Abraham's visitors only pretended to eat in order to conform with human customs.[257] A second tradition in *Genesis Rabba* explains that Moses fasted on the top of Mt. Sinai (Deuteronomy 9.9) because in the divine realm there is no eating or drinking.[258] The legal inspiration for this exegetical reasoning can be found in the Babylonian Talmud (*Babā meṣī'ā* 86b; cf. *Ḥagīgāh* 16a), which uses the example of Genesis 18 to comment on a *mishnah* on following local custom.[259]

This tradition on eating is reflected in the account in Luke's Gospel of the travelers, on the road to Emmaeus, who meet Christ and insist that he join them for a meal (Lk 24.13–32). In Luke's account the celestial presence is again in human form, but the travelers do not recognize this presence until Christ breaks the bread. He does not eat, however, but vanishes from their sight (v. 31). In response the two travelers hurry to Jerusalem and find the apostles. When they tell their story Christ suddenly appears again, startling the apostles who mistake him for a ghost (v. 37). To prove that he is truly flesh and bones (v. 39; i.e. resurrected in the body) he asks "Have you anything here to eat?" (v. 41). They hand him a piece of fish, which he eats "before their eyes" (v. 43). To the same effect the Qur'ān insists that both Jesus and his mother ate food (Q 5.75), a proof, apparently, of their human nature.

Thus the Qur'ān's view on the nature of Abraham's visitors is common to Jewish and Christian texts. Yet on the question of Sarah's laughter Jewish and Christian readings divide. To Jews the report that Sarah laughed (Heb. *tiṣḥaq*; Gn 18.12) when she heard that they would have a boy named Isaac (*yiṣḥāq*) is a clear etiology for the name of their son.[260] This word play, of

255 Philo comments that the visitors to Abraham "gave the appearance of both eating and drinking." *De Abrahamo* 118, ed. Colson, 6:60; cf. Philo, *Questions and Answers on Genesis* 4:9, ed. R. Marcus, Cambridge, MA: Harvard University Press, 1961, 283. Josephus similarly insists that they only seemed to eat. *Jewish Antiquities* 1:11:2, ed. Thackeray et al., 96–8. Justin expresses the same view in his *Dialogue with Trypho* (ch. 57). Tertullian, however, uses the example of the celestial visitors eating in Genesis 18 to defend the idea of the Incarnation (*Ad Martyras* 3:9, *Corpus Christianorum Series Latina* 1, ed. E. Dekkers, Brepols: Turnhout, 1954). For if the angels were able to take on a carnal form and eat, so too could the Word of God.

256 Trans. *TB*, 344.

257 Trans. Freedman et al., 1:413; *Leviticus R.* 34:8, trans. Freedman et al., 4:433. Cf. *LJ*, 5:236; *BEQ*, 149.

258 Trans. Freedman et al., 1:415.

259 On this see *LJ*, 5:236; *BEQ*, 149.

260 In the Armenian version of Philo's *Questions and Answers on Genesis*, Philo, hinting at the etiology, describes the birth of Isaac as "the birth of joy." The editor explains that the word for laughter in Armenian is equivalent to the Aramaic word for Isaac. See *Questions and Answers on Genesis* 4:17, ed. Marcus, 291.

course, would be invisible to Christians reading the Bible in Greek.[261] It would also not appear in Syriac, where the verbal root for laughter (*g.h.k.*) does not match Isaac's name (*isḥāq*).

Christians accordingly found a different meaning for the laughter of Sarah. To Ephraem her laughter points to the birth of Christ: "Sarah did not laugh because of Isaac, but because of the One who is born from Mary."[262] He then likens Sarah's laughing to John the Baptist's leaping in Elizabeth's womb at the approach of Christ (Lk 1.44): "And as John by leaping, so Sarah by laughing revealed the joy."[263]

Ephraem's reading is encouraged by the Biblical portrayal of Mary as the new Sarah. In Genesis Sarah responds to the visitors' message, thinking, "Now that I am past the age of childbearing and my husband is an old man, is pleasure to come my way again?" (Gn 18.12). In Luke Mary's response is similar, "But how can this come about, since I have no knowledge of man?" (Lk 1.34). In Genesis the Lord replies to Sarah, "Nothing is impossible for the Lord" (Gn 18.14). In Luke the angel replies to Mary, "Nothing is impossible for God" (1:37). And while Sarah laughs in amazement at the annunciation, Mary sings of her joy in the Magnificat (Luke 1:46–55).

This Sarah/Mary typology is preserved in the Qur'ān. In *Hūd* (11) 71 the Qur'ān has God proclaim, "We gave [Sarah] the good news of Isaac" (*bashsharnāha bi-isḥāq*). In *āl 'Imrān* (3) 45 the angels foretell the birth of Jesus to Mary with the report, "God gives you good news of a Word from him" (*inna Llāha yubashshiruki bi-kalamatin minhu*). Both women react in amazement. Sarah shouts, "Woe is me. Shall I give birth in my old age, when my Lord is aged? This is an amazing thing" (Q 11.71; cf. Q 51.29). Mary wonders, "O My Lord, am I to have a child when no man has touched me?" (Q 3.47).

It is, I propose, in light of the Sarah/Mary typology that the Qur'ān's reference to Sarah's laughter should also be understood. The Qur'ān reflects the fullness of Christian veneration for Mary. The Qur'ān defends her from the calumny of Jews (Q 4.156), alludes to her birth without sin (Q 3.36–7), and describes her as a sign for the worlds (Q 21.91). Mary is not simply the only woman whom the Qur'ān refers to by name. She is, according to the Qur'ān, the perfect woman: "The angels said, 'O Mary, God has elected you and purified you. He has elected you over the women of the worlds'" (Q 3.42). As in the Syriac Bible, the laughter of Sarah in the Qur'ān cannot be understood in light of the Hebrew word play, since in Arabic

261 "She laughed" of Gn 18.12 in the LXX is ἐγέλασεν.

262 *Hymn on Abraham and Isaac* (§26), in *S. Ephraem Syri Opera*, ed. S.J. Mercati, Rome: Pontifical Biblical Institute, 1915, 49. Regarding the authenticity of this text, which is extant only in Greek, Mercati notes (5–6) that both the content and the style agree with the known Syriac works of Ephraem.

263 *Hymn on Abraham and Isaac* (§27), *S. Ephraem Syri Opera*, 49.

too the verbal root for laughter (*ḍ.ḥ.k.*) does not match Isaac's name (*isḥāq*).[264] Instead her laughter, and indeed the annunciation to Sarah as a whole, should be understood as an anticipation of the angelic annunciation to Mary.

CS 6 Haman and the tower to heaven

Qur'ānic account

Quite unlike the pious figure of Abraham is the impious Haman. In *ghāfir*[265] (40) 36–7 (cf. Q 28.38) Pharaoh, in an act of defiance, commands Haman to build him a tower that he might reach the ways (*asbāb*)[266] to heaven and look on the God of Moses. This he does because of – or perhaps, despite – his conviction that Moses is a liar (v. 37).[267] The image of building a tower to heaven, as will be discussed below, fits into a larger Qur'ānic trope of human insolence. Yet in this case study my primary concern is the identity of the one who is to build that tower: Haman.

The first thing to note in this regard is the consistency with which the Qur'ān associates Haman with Pharaoh. Thus *al-qaṣaṣ* (28) 5–6:

> (28.5) We wish to favor those who are the oppressed on earth, to make them leaders and make them heirs. (6) We will strengthen them on earth and show Pharaoh, Haman and their soldiers that which they take precautions against.

264 Regarding this L. Ammann makes a curious observation: "The loss of this detail need not be greatly regretted since the value of this folk etymology has been doubted anyway: the name Isḥāq is probably of theophoric origin and expressed the wish that God should either laugh, that is, welcome the new-born or grown-up bearer of the name, or make him laugh, that is, happy" (Ammann, "Laughter," 148b). Ammann is presumably correct regarding the etymology of Isaac (it is perhaps an abbreviation of *yiṣḥāq-ēl*: "God laughs." See *The Oxford Bible Commentary*, ed. J. Barton and J. Muddiman, Oxford: Oxford University Press, 2001, 52). Still it seems to me that the importance of this etymology is not in its scientific validity but in its role in the Abraham stories of Gn 17–18 and Jewish exegetical literature. That Christians and the Qur'ān alike lost this detail is, if not to be regretted, still of great significance for their exegeses.

265 Or *al-mu'min*, in certain Qur'ān manuscripts.

266 Pickthall: "roads"; Yusuf Ali: "ways and means"; Blachère: "les Cordes (*les Cordes du ciel*)"; Arberry: "cords"; Paret: "Zugänge"; Fakhry: "pathways"; Abdel Haleem: "ropes." Cf. the occurrences of this term in the Dhū l-Qarnayn narrative, Q 18.84, 85, 89, 92. *Tafsīr Muqātil* (3:713, on Q 40.36) defines *asbāb* as "the doors of the seven heavens." Ṭabarī (24:64–5) has, "roads, doors, houses, ropes, or ladders." Cf. Zamakhsharī, 4:167. For a fuller discussion of *asbāb* see K. van Bladel, "The legend of Alexander the Great in the Qur'ān 18:83–102," *QHC* (175–203), 182; and idem, "Heavenly cords and prophetic authority"; cf. *AEL*, 4:1285c.

267 Q 40.37: "*fa-aṭṭaliʿa ilā ilāhi mūsā wa-innī la-uẓunnuhu kādhiban.*" Most modern translators understand *wa* as "because" (e.g. Blachère: "car"; Arberry: "for"; Fakhry: "for") but Pickthall translates "though."

28.5 وَنُرِيدُ أَن نَّمُنَّ عَلَى الَّذِينَ اسْتُضْعِفُوا فِي الْأَرْضِ وَنَجْعَلَهُمْ أَئِمَّةً وَنَجْعَلَهُمُ الْوَارِثِينَ
28.6 وَنُمَكِّنَ لَهُمْ فِي الْأَرْضِ وَنُرِيَ فِرْعَوْنَ وَهَامَانَ وَجُنُودَهُمَا مِنْهُم مَّا كَانُوا يَحْذَرُونَ

The place of Haman in this passage suggests that he is the immediate colleague, or even the partner, of Pharaoh. He is again paired with Pharaoh two verses later, when the Qur'ān reports that "Pharaoh, Haman and their soldiers were sinners" (Q 28.8). Thus if Haman shared in Pharaoh's power, he also shared in Pharaoh's sin (28.4).

Elsewhere (Q 29.39; 40.24) the Qur'ān adds a third figure, Qārūn, to this pair, condemning the arrogance of all three (Q 29.39) and noting how they rejected the divine message of Moses (Q 40.23–4). In another place (Q 28.76) the Qur'ān relates that Qārūn abused Moses' people, even though he was one of them. In the same verse the divine voice of the Qur'ān notes: "We gave him so many treasures that its keys would have been a burden to a band of strong men." Thus Qārūn was blessed with wealth (cf. Q 29.39), but he arrogantly attributed this wealth to his own knowledge (Q 28.78). In retribution God had the earth swallow Qārūn even as he processed before the people in his luxury (Q 28.79–81; cf. Numbers 16.31–3; 26.10; Psalm 105:17).

This final report sheds some light on the Qur'ān's reference elsewhere (Q 29.40) to the deaths of Qārūn, Pharaoh, and Haman: "We took each of them according to his sin: We sent a storm against one. An earthquake (*ṣayḥa*) took another. We made the earth consume one. We drowned one of them." If Qārūn was swallowed by the earth, and Pharaoh drowned (cf. Q 7.136; 8.54; 17.103, passim), then the Qur'ān presumably intends that Haman was killed by a storm or an earthquake. In either case the Qur'ān thus places Haman within the larger topos of divine punishment through natural means. Thamūd, the people to whom the prophet Ṣāliḥ is sent, are destroyed by an earthquake (*al-rajfa* in Q 7.73–9 and 26.141–58; *al-ṣayḥā* in 11.67–8), while 'Ād, the people to whom the prophet Hūd is sent, are destroyed by a wind storm (*al-rīḥ al-'aqīm* in Q 51.41–2; *riḥ ṣarṣar* in 41.16; 54.19; 69.6).

The case of 'Ād is revealing, for the Qur'ān elsewhere has the Prophet Hūd challenge 'Ād: "You build factories thinking that you will become eternal" (Q 26.129). This rather cryptic verse seems to refer to the larger topos of humans erecting monuments in the hope that these will make them immortal, an image that illustrates human insolence before God. *Al-naḥl* (16) 26, for example, describes how God uprooted a building, crushing the unbelievers inside (cf. Q 22.45).

Pharaoh's command to Haman in *ghāfir* (40) 36–7 (and Q 28.38) to build a tower that will reach into heaven is thus part of a larger topos on human buildings and the civilizations which produce them. It is also parallel to *al-nisā'* (4) 153, where the Israelites insolently demand that Moses show them God. And it is completed by the Qur'ān's reference elsewhere (Q 7.137) to the destruction of the things that Pharaoh and his people constructed – presumably a reference to the tower of Haman – and to the demise of Pharaoh and Haman. Ironically, then, both perished by their attempt to reach immortality.

Problems for interpreters

The identity of Haman

Tafsīr Muqātil describes Haman with two Persian terms: *qahramānu fir'awn wa-dastūruhu*, "the steward and minister of Pharaoh."[268] This description seems to be extrapolated from the Qur'ānic references (e.g. Q 28.6, 8) to "Pharaoh, Haman and *their* soldiers." Presumably no importance should be placed on the use of Persian, although one is tempted to imagine that somehow Haman was more familiar to Persians, in light of the Biblical Esther story set in Susa. According to his traditional biography Muqātil b. Sulaymān was from Balkh and thus likely a Persian speaker. This (or the Persian background of a later editor of the work) would more likely explain the use of Persian here.

Neither Qummī nor Ṭabarī, for their part, attempt to identify Haman. Zamakhsharī, like *Tafsīr Muqātil*, names him the vizier and assistant of Pharaoh.[269] Ibn Kathīr expresses virtually the same opinion, describing Haman as Pharaoh's, "vizier, the director of his citizens and the advisor of his nation."[270] In other words, none of the *mufassirūn* in our survey provide outside information on Haman. They simply deduce his identity from the context of the Qur'ān. This is surprising. Even if some *mufassirūn*, most notably Ibn Kathīr, are clearly suspicious of outside information, none of them categorically excludes it. Presumably they do so in this case because the Biblical tradition on Haman is in apparent contradiction to the Qur'ānic account. In the Book of Esther Haman is in Iran, not Egypt, and is the vizier to Xerxes, not Pharaoh.[271]

The tower to heaven

Regarding Pharaoh's quest to build a tower reaching heaven,[272] Qummī describes how Haman's construction stretched so high into the air that it

268 *Tafsīr Muqātil*, 3:383, on Q 29.39.

269 Zamakhsharī, 3:415, on Q 28.38.

270 Ibn Kathīr, 3:364, on Q 28.38–42.

271 On Qorah as well the *mufassirūn* rely on stories inspired by Qur'ānic material. Qummī provides an extraordinary example thereof when he has Qorah (who in the Qur'ān is swallowed by the earth; Q 28.79–81) meet Jonah (who is swallowed by a fish) in the netherworld. See Qummī, 1:319–20, on Q 10.98. Cf. CS 8, note 376 below.

272 On this *Tafsīr Muqātil* (3:345, on Q 28.38) comments only that Pharaoh was the first to use baked bricks (*ajurr*) in construction.

reached a point above which no person could climb due to the powerful winds. Refusing to abandon their project, Pharaoh and Haman built an ark (*tābūt*),[273] to which they secured four wooden beams. They then took four strong eagles and tied one to the base of each beam. At the peak of each beam they attached a piece of meat. As the eagles sought in vain to reach the meat they lifted the craft in flight. Yet although they sailed upwards they came no closer to heaven. When Pharaoh asked Haman what he could see of heaven, Haman replied only, "I see the sky as I would see it on the ground from afar."[274] Soon thereafter a strong wind buffeted their craft and they fell to the ground.[275]

Ṭabarī also relates a fanciful tradition on Haman's building. After constructing a high tower, the tradition relates, Haman climbed up to its peak and launched an arrow into the sky. The arrow returned to earth stained with blood. Haman shouted, "I have killed the God of Moses." Ṭabarī comments: "God is far above what they say."[276]

Zamakhsharī reports a version of this same story,[277] although he reports that Pharaoh, not Haman, climbed to the top of the tower and fired an arrow into the sky. According to Zamakhsharī's version, moreover, this impudent act provoked God into sending the angel Gabriel to scuttle his work.[278] Ibn Kathīr, for his part, argues that the building (*ṣarḥ*; Q 28.38; 40.36) which Pharaoh sought to build was not a tower but "a lofty, elevated, high palace."[279]

273 The term also used in the Qur'ān for the ark of the covenant (Q 2.248; 20.39). The *mufassirūn* commonly use *tābūt* to describe the ark of Noah, although Qummī simply refers (1:328ff.) to the ark as "ship" (*safīna*; whereas the Qur'ān, e.g. 11.38, uses the term *fulk*). Its origin is Hebrew *tēbā* (although Jeffery [*FV*, 88] follows the conclusion of Nöldeke [*Neue Beiträge*, 49] that it reached Arabic through Ethiopic), used in the Bible for Noah's ark (Gn 6.14; 9.18; LXX κιβωτός) and the basket in which Moses is hidden (Ex 2.3, 5). As Jeffery notes (*FV*, 88), Heb. *tībā* is used in the Mishnah for the ark of the covenant, and it is this term that is reflected in the Qur'ān.

274 Qummī 2:118, on Q 28.38.

275 Ibid., 2:117–8.

276 Ibid., 20:78. Regarding the origin of this narrative in midrash see Grünbaum, *Neue Beiträge*, 126–7.

277 Regarding which cf. Grünbaum, *Neue Beiträge*, 164.

278 Zamakhsharī describes how Gabriel descended at sunset and cut the tower into three pieces with his wing; one piece landed on the soldiers of Pharaoh and killed a million of them, a second landed in the sea and a third in the Maghrib. Zamakhsharī remarks skeptically: "God knows better whether it is reliable." Zamakhsharī, 3:413, on Q 28.38. He also proposes an explanation of how Pharaoh might have been so deluded to think himself an equal of God (on which cf. Q 28.38): "If [Pharaoh] were excessively ignorant of [God] and His attributes, he could have considered that [God] is in a place as he is in a place, and that he would look at [God] as He would look at him when he sat in his high place, and that He is the king of the sky as he is the king of the earth." Zamakhsharī, 3:414, on Q 28.38.

279 Otherwise Ibn Kathīr asks what Pharaoh meant when he declared Moses a liar (Q 28.38; cf. 40.37). He could not have been denying Moses' claim of coming from God, since he did not acknowledge the existence of God in the first place. Instead Pharaoh was denying that his citizens (*ra'iyya*; Q 28.28 has instead "council," *mala'*) have a god other than him

Subtext

The most prominent Biblical image of a tower, of course, is that in the Babel story of Genesis 11. Here the people gathered in the land of Shinar declare: "Come . . . let us build ourselves a city and a tower with its top reaching heaven. Let us make a name for ourselves, so that we do not get scattered all over the world" (Gn 11.4). Their desire to be remembered is a desire to be immortal. Accordingly, God sees the tower as a menace and remarks: "This is only the start of their undertakings! Now nothing they plan to do will be beyond them" (Gn 11.6b). This story is evidently related to the Qur'ān's account of Pharaoh's tower. The Bible reports that the people in Shinar baked bricks (*lebēnīm*; Gn 11.3) for their tower. The Qur'ān has Pharaoh order Haman to bake clay (*ṭīn*; Q 28.38) for his tower.

Now in the Qur'ān (40:36–7) Pharaoh does so with the intent of climbing the tower and entering heaven itself. It is worth noting, accordingly, that a prominent exegetical tradition maintains that the ambition of those gathered in Shinar was just that. The book of *Jubilees* reports that they "built the city and the tower, saying, 'Let us ascend on it into heaven'" (*Jubilees* 10.19).[280] According to the *Sibylline Oracles*, "They were all of one language and they wanted to go up to starry heaven."[281] These traditions, of course, assume a cosmology in which heaven exists in the same material realm as the earth, but simply above it, on the other side of the firmament (on this see CS 2). Accordingly other traditions imagine that the builders of the Tower of Babel sought to pierce the firmament itself, with a drill or hatchets.[282]

Indeed according to some of these traditions these builders carried with them weapons of war, to fight against God himself. In the *Targum Neofiti* on Genesis 11:4 the people in Shinar say, "Come, let us build ourselves a city, and a tower whose top will reach to the heavens, and let us make for ourselves at its top an idol and we will put a sword in its hand, and it will make war against Him."[283] A tradition in the Babylonian Talmud (*Sanhedrīn* 109a) relates that one of three parties at the time of Babel desired to wage war with God.

In Genesis 11, of course, there is no king or tyrant to give orders. The tower appears to be a communal project of the people, who cooperate in their rebellious construction. It is this cooperation that leads God to scuttle their language (Gn 11.7–8). Yet in Jewish and Christian exegesis this project

(see Q 28.38a: "O council, I do not know that you have a god other than me."). To this effect Ibn Kathīr cites Q 26.23, 29. Ibn Kathīr, 3:364, on Q 28.38. Elsewhere (4:72–3, on Q 40.36–7) Ibn Kathīr concludes instead that Pharaoh denied God sent Moses to him. Ibn Kathīr, 4:72, on Q 40.36–7.

280 Trans. *TB*, 228.

281 Trans. *TB*, 229.

282 Thus 3 Baruch 3:7–8 and *BT Sanhedrīn* 109a. On this see *TB*, 229.

283 Trans. *TB*, 229.

is attributed to Nimrod, a figure whom the Bible describes in the previous chapter of Genesis as "a mighty hunter in the eyes of Yahweh" (Gn 10.9; cf. 1 Chr. 1.10). It also makes Nimrod the ruler of Babel, Erech and Accad, all of which are in the land of Shinar (Gn 10.10), where the tower would be built.

With some exegetes Nimrod becomes a Gilgamesh-like figure who maniacally constructs monuments on earth to spite heaven.[284] Philo describes the Tower of Babel as "a royal and impregnable castle for the evil tyrant."[285] According to Josephus, Nimrod sought to build the tower of Babel in response to the destruction of humanity in the flood:

> He persuaded them to attribute their prosperity not to God but to their own valour, and little by little transformed the state of affairs into a tyranny, holding that the only way to detach men from the fear of God was by making them continuously dependent upon his own power. He threatened to have his revenge on God if He wished to inundate the earth again; for he would build a tower higher than the water could reach and avenge the destruction of their forefathers.[286]

The Tower project, then, was a maneuver in a war between God and humanity. By having the Tower reach to heaven, Nimrod meant to have a position high enough to survive a second flood.[287] The image of Nimrod as opponent to God, incidentally, is expressed in the Arabic verb: *tanamrada*: "to be boastful, presumptuous."[288]

This tradition of Nimrod's rebellion against God seems to be reflected in the words of Isaiah to the king of Babylon:

> You who used to think to yourself: "I shall scale the heavens; higher than the stars of God I shall set my throne. I shall sit on the Mount of Assembly far away to the north. * I shall climb high above the clouds, I shall rival the Most High." * Now you have been flung down to Sheol, into the depths of the abyss!
>
> (Isaiah 14.13–5)

284 *Targum Neofiti* of Gn 10.9 relates that Nimrod "was mighty in sinning before the Lord." Trans. *TB*, 231.

285 *De Confusione Linguarum* 113, ed. and trans. F.H. Colson and G.H. Whitaker, *Philo in Ten Volumes*, 4:71.

286 Josephus, *Jewish Antiquities* 1:4:2, ed. Thackeray et al., 54. Similarly *Pirqē de-Rabbī Elīʿezer* (24; ed. Börner-Klein, 261) has the people at the time of Babel declare: "We want to build a great tower . . . in order to go up to heaven, for the power of God is only in the water."

287 Trans. Le Déaut, 143. Cf. *The Sibylline Oracles*, in *Die Apokryphen und Pseudepigraphen des Alten Testaments*, (2:177–217), 2:187.

288 See R. Dozy, *Supplément aux dictionnaires arabes*, Leiden: Brill, 1881; reprint: Beirut: Librairie du Liban, 1981, 2:733a.

Generally construction, the building of monuments, appears in the Bible as a topos of human rebellion against God (and against humanity's own mortality). This topos appears again with Pharaoh, who compels the Hebrews to build the cities of Pithom and Rameses (Ex 1.11), to dig clay (*ḥōmer*, cf. Q 28.38), and to make bricks (*lebēnīm*; Ex 1.14; cf. Gn 11.3). The Biblical Pharaoh is defined by his relentless campaign of building. In the Qur'ān, accordingly, Pharaoh is named *dhū l-awtād* (38:12; 89.10),[289] "the man of columns."

Like Nimrod, Pharaoh's obsession with building is inspired by his conviction that he is equal to God, that he, like God, is a creator. Thus the Book of Ezekiel relates:

> The Lord Yahweh says this: "Look, I am against you, Pharaoh king of Egypt – the great crocodile wallowing in his Niles who thought: My Nile is mine, I made it. * I shall put hooks through your jaws, make your Nile fish stick to your scales, and pull you out of your Niles with all your Nile fish sticking to your scales."
>
> (Ezekiel 29.3–4)

Later Ezekiel prophesies that when Yahweh carries out his threat the cities of Egypt "will be the most desolate of wasted cities" (Ezekiel 29.12). Israel's God will reduce to nothing all that which Pharaoh created to render himself eternal.

When the Qur'ān has Pharaoh demand that Haman build him a tower to heaven that he might look at God, it integrates Nimrod and Pharaoh traditions. From a literary perspective this is hardly inappropriate. The tower of Babel story itself nowhere appears in the Qur'ān, and so it might be used to advantage in the Pharaoh account, a myth of central importance to the Qur'ān.

On the other hand the Qur'ān does seem to refer to Nimrod, although not by name, as the boastful, blasphemous ruler par excellence. In *al-baqara* (2) 258 the Qur'ān speaks of a king with whom Abraham argued. When the king claims that he, and not God, has power over life and death, Abraham challenges him to make the sun rise from the West, as God makes it rise from the East. At this "the one who disbelieved in God was befuddled" (Q 2.258). In light of the traditional Jewish and Christian associations between Abraham and Babylon (cf. CS 4), the Qur'ān presumably intends that this disbeliever is Nimrod.

Thus Nimrod and Pharoah in the Qur'ān represent the same type, the ruler who challenges God's sovereignty. The two figures are, from a literary perspective, identical.[290] It is precisely the same sort of literary integration

289 *BEQ*, 117.

290 Indeed Grünbaum points out (*Neue Beiträge*, 52) that in Arab tradition these two figures became symbolic of the boastful and arrogant ruler: "Bei den Arabern sind Nimrod und

that accounts for the appearance of Haman with Pharaoh in the Qur'ān. The story of Esther appears nowhere in the Qur'ān, but its connection with the Pharaoh account is evident. In the Book of Esther Haman is the vizier of the king Xerxes (Ahaseurus) and the opponent of Mordecai, a leader of the Jews in Persia. When Mordecai refuses to prostrate before Haman (Esther 3.2), that is, when he refuses to treat him as he would treat God, Haman plans to kill not only Mordecai, but all of the Jews of Persia (Esther 3.6). Ultimately, and thanks to the cunning beauty of Mordecai's cousin Esther (Esther 5.1–3), Haman suffers the very fate that he had prepared for his nemesis. He is hanged on the gallows he had built for Mordecai (Esther 7.10). And on the day that Haman had assigned for the massacre of the Jews, it is instead the Jews who massacre their enemies (Esther 9.1).

The telling of the Esther story is thoroughly informed by the story of Moses and Pharaoh in Egypt. Once again the Israelites are in exile. Once again there is a ruler who demands to be treated like a god. Once again the Israelites escape massacre, and their oppressors are massacred instead.[291] If, unlike Exodus, the God of the Israelites is noticeably lacking from the original, Hebrew, version of Esther, He is prominent in the Greek additions thereto (in chs. 1, 3, 4, 5, 8, 10) and in later exegesis.

In its reference to Haman's tower, moreover, the Qur'ān is following a tradition found in the Assyrian legend of Aḥīqar, as Adam Silverstein has insightfully illustrated.[292] By this tradition Aḥīqar's treacherous nephew Nādān tells Pharaoh, the great antagonist of the Assyrian empire, that Aḥīqar is dead. At this Pharaoh challenges the Assyrian emperor Esarhaddon to send him a man who might build him a tower between heaven and earth, knowing that only the mighty hero Aḥīqar would be capable of such a feat. In fact Aḥīqar is still alive. He rushes to Egypt and builds the tower to heaven, while the Assyrian emperor reproaches the duplicitous Nādān.

As Silverstein points out, a connection between Aḥīqar and Haman can be found in the Septuagint version of the Book of Tobit. Therein Tobit counsels his son on his death bed, "Consider, son what was done by [H]aman to Achiacharus (Aḥīqar), who raised him up" (Tobit 14:10).[293] Thus in Tobit Haman enters into the Aḥīqar story in the place of Nādān. In the Qur'ān he takes the place of Aḥīqar himself. The literary logic in this latter shift is apparent. In the Qur'ān Pharaoh and his cohorts are all the enemies

Pharaoh insofern typische Personen, als ihre Namen appellativisch gebraucht werden und so auch im Plural vorkommen zur Bezeichnung übermüthiger und ungläubiger Tyrannen."

291 So too Esther (Esther 8.1) acquires the possessions of Haman, as the Israelites despoiled the Egyptians (Ex 12.36).

292 On this topic see also A. Silverstein, "Haman's transition from the jahiliyya to Islam," *JSAI* 34, 2008, 285–308.

293 The name appears as Αμαν in the LXX. Later manuscript traditions in both Greek and Aramaic (reflected in most English translations) have some form of the name Nādān.

of God. There is no place for the celebration of the Assyrian hero Aḥīqar's guile and prowess in outsmarting his nephew and building a tower. Instead the story of the tower is subsumed within the larger theme of humanity's rebellion against God, and the abominable Haman appropriately takes the place of the heroic Aḥīqar.

The Qur'ān's use of the Aḥīqar legend also emerges from a tradition, found in the Talmud but not in the Bible, that Pharaoh had certain helpers in Egypt. As noted by James Kugel, in two places (*Sōṭa* 11a; *Sanhedrīn* 106a) the Babylonian Talmud cites traditions by which Jethro, Balaam, and Job aided Pharaoh in Egypt.[294] This topos is continued by the Qur'ān, only now Pharaoh's helpers include Haman and Qorah. In the Bible, Qorah rebels against Moses only in the desert, after the Israelites' departure from Egypt (Numbers 16). In the Qur'ān, however, he is already working against Moses in Egypt (Q 29.39–40; 40.24), a development which reflects (or is reflected in) later Jewish exegesis.[295]

The pairing of Qorah and Haman, if not in line with the Biblical account, is hardly unreasonable in literary terms. Both acted as the nemesis of God's servant (Qorah of Moses, Haman of Mordecai). Qorah was extremely wealthy.[296] Haman was extremely powerful.[297]

The argument that the Qur'ān is somehow wrong or confused by placing Haman and Qorah in Egypt (or, for that matter, that the Talmud is wrong by placing Jethro, Balaam, and Job there) seems to me essentially irrelevant.[298] The Qur'ān's concern is not simply to record Biblical information but to shape that information for its own purposes. The more interesting question is therefore *why* the Qur'ān connects Haman and Qorah with the story of Pharaoh. The answer, it seems, is that the Pharaoh story is to the Qur'ān a central trope about human conceit and rebelliousness, on the one hand, and divine punishment, on the other. Accordingly the characters of Haman and Qorah,[299] and the legend of the Tower of Babel, find their way into the Qur'ān's account of Pharaoh. Thereby the Qur'ān connects this account to its lessons elsewhere on the mastery of God over creation. Thus while the Qur'ān never explains what happens to Pharaoh's tower, the reader might

294 *TB*, 507.

295 According to the *Targum of Pseudo-Jonathan* (on Numbers 16.19), Qorah grew wealthy by finding two of the treasures of Joseph (in Egypt). His wealth made him egotistical to the point that he sought to reduce Moses and Aaron to desperation. On this see Geiger, *Was hat Mohammed*, 153. Elsewhere Jewish exegetes associate Qorah with Haman, regarding which see *BEQ*, 343.

296 Regarding his treasure see *BT Pesaḥīm* 119a; *Sanhedrīn* 110a.

297 See Esther 3.1, 10.

298 For this argument see Geiger, *Was hat Mohammed*, 153; *KU*, 149; *BEQ*, 283; G. Vajda, "Hāmān," *EQ*, 3:110b; A.J. Wensinck and G. Vajda "Fir'aun," EI^2, 2:918a.

299 Speyer argues (*BEQ*, 283) that Muḥammad intended to place the prototypical enemy of Israel (Haman) together with the prototypical enemy of Abraham (Nimrod, represented here by Pharaoh).

imagine that its fate was something like that of the houses of the rebellious people of ʿĀd:

> When they saw something as a cloud heading to their valleys they said "This is a cloud that will bring rain." No, this is that which you hastened: a wind with a painful punishment that will destroy everything by the command of its Lord. In the morning their houses could no longer be seen. Thus we requite a guilty people.
>
> (Q 46.24–5)

CS 7 The transformation of Jews

Qur'ānic account

Quite unlike the fate of ʿĀd, but perhaps no better, is that assigned in the Qur'ān to a people who violated the Sabbath. In *al-aʿrāf* (7) 163 the Qur'ān alludes to the circumstances of their violation:

> Ask them about the town along the sea when they violated the Sabbath. On the Sabbath their fish would come to them openly, but on other days they would not come. Thus we tested them in the matter in which they were iniquitous.

7.163 وَاسْأَلْهُمْ عَنِ الْقَرْيَةِ الَّتِي كَانَتْ حَاضِرَةَ الْبَحْرِ إِذْ يَعْدُونَ فِي السَّبْتِ إِذْ تَأْتِيهِمْ
حِيتَانُهُمْ يَوْمَ سَبْتِهِمْ شُرَّعًا وَيَوْمَ لاَ يَسْبِتُونَ لاَ تَأْتِيهِمْ كَذَلِكَ نَبْلُوهُمْ بِمَا كَانُوا يَفْسُقُونَ

Thereafter the Qur'ān describes how the people of this town refused God's warnings (v. 165), and continued to perpetrate forbidden acts. In light of verse 163, it seems that these forbidden acts included fishing on the Sabbath. The Qur'ān implies that this people could not resist the temptation of fish that exposed themselves on that day. God therefore punished them with the curse: "Be despised monkeys" (v. 166).

In *al-baqara* (2) 65–6, the Qur'ān refers to this same account, which it declares well known to its audience:

> (65) You know about those among you who violated the Sabbath, how we said to them: "Be despised monkeys." (66) We made them into a warning for those of their time and those after them [or, "for all of those around them"] and an admonition for the pious.

2.65 وَلَقَدْ عَلِمْتُمُ الَّذِينَ اعْتَدَواْ مِنكُمْ فِي السَّبْتِ فَقُلْنَا لَهُمْ كُونُواْ قِرَدَةً خَاسِئِينَ

2.66 فَجَعَلْنَاهَا نَكَالاً لِّمَا بَيْنَ يَدَيْهَا وَمَا خَلْفَهَا وَمَوْعِظَةً لِّلْمُتَّقِينَ

In yet a third passage, *al-mā'ida* (5) 60, the Qur'ān seems to have this account in mind when it mentions those "with whom God grew angry."

Here, however, the Qur'ān reports that God "made some of them into monkeys and pigs." This is notably different from *al-a'rāf* (7) 166 and *al-baqara* (2) 65, where the Qur'ān reports only that God *said* "Be despised monkeys." In *al-mā'ida* (5) 60 the Qur'ān declares that God *made* (*ja'ala*) them into monkeys (and pigs).[300]

Elsewhere (Q 4.47) the Qur'ān uses the pitiable fate of the people whom God transformed to warn its audience:

> You who have been given the Book. Believe in what we have brought down, which confirms that which is already with you, before we transform figures, turning them inside out, or we curse you as we cursed the people of the Sabbath. The command of God was carried out.

4.47 يَا أَيُّهَا الَّذِينَ أُوتُواْ الْكِتَابَ آمِنُواْ بِمَا نَزَّلْنَا مُصَدِّقًا لِّمَا مَعَكُم مِّن قَبْلِ أَن نَّطْمِسَ
وُجُوهًا فَنَرُدَّهَا عَلَى أَدْبَارِهَا أَوْ نَلْعَنَهُمْ كَمَا لَعَنَّا أَصْحَابَ السَّبْتِ وَكَانَ أَمْرُ اللّهِ مَفْعُولاً

From this verse it emerges that the Qur'ān sees the story of the People of the Sabbath as an example par excellence of the sequence of divine prohibition, human violation, and divine punishment. The episode of the People of the Sabbath is thus not ultimately about the Sabbath prohibition.[301] Instead, it is about the fate of those who do not obey God. The notion of the Sabbath as a test of earlier peoples is again suggested by *al-nisā'* (4) 154, where the Qur'ān refers to the covenant on Mt. Sinai but only mentions two commandments explicitly. One of these is, "Do not violate the Sabbath."[302]

There is, however, another lesson in this account. In *al-a'rāf* (7) 164, a group among the People of the Sabbath counsel their companions to give up all hope in the transgressors: "Why do you preach to a people whom God will annihilate and punish severely?" Their companions respond: "In order to seek forgiveness from your Lord, and that they might become righteous" (Q 7.164). Thus the Qur'ān teaches that believers should preach to unbelievers in all cases, for the sake of their own salvation, and with the conviction that even those condemned might repent.

300 Later in that same Sūra the Qur'ān refers to "the unbelieving Israelites who were cursed by the tongue of David and Jesus" (Q 5.78). It is not clear, however, whether the Qur'ān is thereby harking back to verse 60.

301 It is not therefore in logical contradiction with passages that oppose this prohibition, such as *al-naḥl* (16) 124, in which the Qur'ān insists that the Sabbath "was only made for those who disagreed about it" (perhaps a reference to Jews and Christians) or *al-jumu'a* (62) 10, which explains that when prayer is finished on the day of congregation believers are free to pursue their affairs.

302 The other command is, "Enter the gate while prostrating" (*udkhulū al-bāba sujjadan*), an allusion to the narrative referred to in Q 2.58, i.e. the shibboleth episode of Judges 12.6. On this see U. Rubin, *Between Bible and Qur'an: The Children of Israel and the Islamic Self-Image*, Princeton: Darwin, 1999, 83ff.

Problems for interpreters[303]

Still the passages on the people of the Sabbath present a typical challenge to modern translators. Does the Qur'ān intend that these people were physically transformed into animals? If translators answer no, should they then provide only the metaphorical meaning? If so, what is the metaphorical meaning of "monkey" and how does it differ from that of "pig"?

In the case of *al-baqara* (2) 65, most, but not all, translators simply relate the literal sense.[304] Yet the two most recent translators are not content with this. Fakhry uses the word "like" to suggest a metaphorical meaning without specifying one: "Be [like] dejected apes."[305] Abdel Haleem similarly uses "like," but he also adds a phrase to suggest what the Qur'ān intends by its metaphor, translating, "Be like apes! Be outcasts." Abdeel Haleem also adds a footnote on this topic: "This is understood by some as 'physically turn into apes' but in fact it is a figure of speech."[306] For *al-mā'ida* (5) 60 Abdel Haleem translates "condemned as apes and pigs" and then adds another footnote (a):[307]

> Ṭabarī (in his commentary on 2:65) regards this as metaphorical in the sense of 'like apes, pigs'. Compare the metaphorical use of 'blind, deaf, dumb' – 2:18; 5:71; 8:22; 43:40; etc.

Yet Abdel Haleem's description of Ṭabarī's commentary is wrong.

In fact the great majority of the *mufassirūn*, Ṭabarī included, read the references to the transformation of people into animals as reports of an actual occurrence. *Tafsīr Muqātil* reports that there were two such occurrences. The first occurred in the time of David, when God transformed a people who refused to stop fishing on the Sabbath into monkeys. God revealed this story as a warning (*maw'iẓatan*; cf. Q 7.164) for the people in the Prophet Muḥammad's time. In particular, God intended this affair to be a warning not to hunt in the sacred *ḥaram* of Mecca.[308] The second transformation occurred in the time of Jesus. After God sent down a table from heaven, in answer to Jesus' prayer (see Q 5.112–5), Jesus forbade his disciples two things: eating from this table (cf. the disciples' request in Q 5.113) and disbelieving in God. When they did both, Jesus asked that they be cursed

303 Regarding Islamic commentary on this episode see especially M. Cook, "Ibn Qutayba and the monkeys," *SI* 89, 1999, (43–74) esp. 51ff.

304 Pickthall: "Be ye apes, despised and hated!"; Yusuf Ali: "Be ye apes, despised and rejected"; Blachère: "Soyez des singes abjects!"; Arberry: "Be you apes, miserably slinking!"; Paret: "Werdet zu abgestoßenen Affen!"

305 Although his translation of Q 5.60 ("transformed them into monkeys and swine") suggests a literal reading.

306 Abdel Haleem, 9, n. b.

307 Ibid., 74, n. a.

308 *Tafsīr Muqātil*, 1:113, on Q 2.65.

as the people of the Sabbath were cursed (cf. Q 5.115). God accordingly transformed them into pigs.[309] *Tafsīr Muqātil*'s report is evidently shaped by the Qur'ān's reference to "the unbelieving Israelites who were cursed by the tongue of David and Jesus" (Q 5.78).

Qummī, for his part, connects the various Qur'ānic references in one narrative about a village of Israelites near the sea. He explains:

> Water came to them according to the tide. It would enter into their rivers and fields. Fish would come out of the sea, even unto the end of their fields. Yet God had forbidden them to fish on the Sabbath. So they would place their nets on the evening before Sunday in the rivers and fish. Yet the fish would come out on Saturday but not on Sunday.

One group of people, Qummī continues, insisted on fishing on Saturday. As a punishment, God transformed them into monkeys and pigs.[310] Qummī, however, adds that it was anyway wrong to avoid work on the Sabbath: "The holiday of everyone, Muslims and non-Muslims,[311] was Friday. Yet the Jews opposed this. They said, 'Our holiday is Saturday.' So God forbade them to fish on Saturday and transformed them into monkeys and pigs."[312] Thus Qummī implies that the Sabbath prohibition was itself a penalty. God transformed the Jews into animals not only for breaking the prohibition, but also for their perverted ideas of the Sabbath in the first place.

Qummī then adds a second narrative, which he reports on the authority of the fifth Shī'ī Imām, Muḥammad al-Bāqir (d. 115/733), who claims to have found an explanation of these references in a book of the first Imām 'Alī b. Abī Ṭālib. Thereby the People of the Sabbath were not Jews but a tribe of Thamūd (Q 7.73; 9.70 passim), from the people of Ayka (Q 15.78; 26.176; 38.13; 50.14). God sent fish to them on Saturday to test their obedience. Initially they would close their gates and canals on the Sabbath (so that the fish would not swim into their traps), but then Satan said to them, "You are only forbidden to eat [fish] on Saturday but you are permitted to fish."[313] One group of people listened to Satan while another group remained obedient to God. The obedient group therefore left the city one night, performing a sort of *hijra* (as Muḥammad left the unbelieving Meccans for Yathrib/Medina). When they returned the next morning they found the gate of the city locked. One of them took a ladder, climbed over the wall, and discovered that the people therein had been changed into monkeys.[314]

309 Ibid., 1:488, on Q 5.60.
310 Qummī, 1:245, on Q 7.163.
311 Most of the *mufassirūn* refer to believers of any era, before or after Muḥammad, as Muslims.
312 Qummī, 1:246, on Q 7.163.
313 Ibid.
314 Ibid., 1:247, on Q 7.163.

In his commentary Ṭabarī (pace Abdel Haleem) continues this narrative tradition on the people of the Sabbath, opening with the declaration: "God transformed them into monkeys due to their rebelliousness."[315] On the authority of Ibn 'Abbās he relates, in accordance with Qummī, that God did not establish the Sabbath prohibition. When the Jews did so themselves, God added to it, punishing them by making it burdensome.

Ṭabarī relates that the village that figures in the People of the Sabbath account was located between Ayla and the Mount (*al-ṭūr*, i.e. Sinai), in Midian, that is, along the Red Sea. The problems there began when one man set a line on Saturday (when fish were easily caught) and brought it up on Sunday. His conduct tempted others to do the same until all but a small pious group were openly fishing on Saturday. One day this group found that all of the transgressors had locked themselves into their houses. Entering into those houses the pious group found not people but monkeys.[316]

Ṭabarī, like Qummī, then adds a second narrative, according to which some people of this town set traps to catch fish on the Sabbath.[317] Eventually the "Muslims," as Ṭabarī describes the group who refused to violate the Sabbath (although above he had described observation of the Sabbath as a Jewish excess), refused to live among the transgressors, and decided to divide the village in two with a wall. This wall was equipped with a door for each group, and every day they would pass back and forth, until one day the Muslims discovered that the transgressors refused to open their door. When the Muslims forced their way through they found a bunch of monkeys.[318]

While these narratives both speak of a physical transformation (although in each case the monkeys show the distinctly human quality of embarrassment), Ṭabarī does mention one tradition, on the authority of Mujāhid, that *al-baqara* (2) 65 should be read as a metaphor, that is, that the transgressors' "hearts were transformed but they were not actually transformed into monkeys." Yet Ṭabarī decisively rejects this opinion, commenting: "The statement of Mujāhid is in contradiction with the clear indication of the Book of God. For God relates in His book that He made them into monkeys and pigs."[319]

Zamakhsharī takes a different view. On *al-baqara* (2) 65, he relates a version of Qummī's and Ṭabarī's second narrative, in which the transgressors use traps.[320] In the conclusion of that narrative, however, Zamakhsharī insists

315 Ṭabarī, 1:330, on Q 2.65.
316 Ibid., 1:330–1.
317 Ibid., 1:331, on Q 2.65.
318 Ṭabarī, 1:331–2.
319 Ibid., 1:332. The comment on pigs relates to Q 5.60.
320 Thereby God arranged for all of the fish in the ocean to stick their heads out of the water on the Sabbath (and disappear on the other days of the week) as a test of the Jews' devotion. (Cf. Q 7.163, which concludes: "Thus we tested them in the matter in which they were iniquitous."). Zamakhsharī, 1:147, on Q 2.63–6.

that God did not physically transform the People of the Sabbath. When God told them: "Be despised monkeys" (Q 2.65), He meant, "Have the qualities both of monkeys and of the scorned, that is, be servile and exiled."[321]

When the Qur'ān reports (Q 5.60) that God made (*ja'ala*) some people into monkeys and others into pigs, Zamakhsharī concludes instead that this was a case of physical transformation (*maskh*). Thus Zamakhsharī follows the wording of the Qur'ān with care. Where the Qur'ān has God *say*, "Be monkeys" (Q 2.65) he finds room for a metaphorical interpretation. Yet where the Qur'ān reports that God *made* some people into monkeys and pigs (Q 5.60) he follows the literal meaning of the text. This leads Zamakhsharī to make the affair of the People of the Sabbath totally separate from the physical transformation referred to in *al-mā'ida* (5) 60. This physical transformation took place instead when the Jews insulted Jesus and Mary, and Jesus prayed: "O God, You are my Lord, You created me by your word [cf. Q 3.45; 4.171]. O God curse those who insult me and my mother."[322] God answered his prayer and transformed the Jews into monkeys and pigs.[323]

If Zamakhsharī shows curiosity in the narratives that would explain the Qur'ān's references to the People of the Sabbath, he is outdone by Ibn Kathīr. To begin with, Ibn Kathīr reports a version of the Ibn 'Abbās tradition (already seen in Ṭabarī's commentary), according to which the Jews' initial error was to consecrate the Sabbath:

> God imposed upon the Israelites the day which He imposed upon you, your Friday holiday. They opposed this with the Sabbath, venerating it and abandoning what they had been commanded. When they accepted only the Sabbath, God tested them on it. He forbade them what He had permitted them on other days.[324]

Thereafter Ibn Kathīr reports versions of both of the principal narratives found in Qummī and Ṭabarī.[325] He adds, however, a report that one day

321 Zamakhsharī, 1:147, on Q 2.63–6.

322 Ibid., 1:587, on Q 4.153–9.

323 Elsewhere, however, Zamakhsharī relates a tradition that in its reference to monkeys and pigs the Qur'ān intends two different groups. Those who hold this position, however, explain it in two different ways. Some scholars hold that the People of the Sabbath were transformed into monkeys but those who disbelieved in the *mā'ida* affair (cf. Q 5.115; *Tafsīr Muqātil* above) were transformed into pigs. In other words, Jews were turned into monkeys and Christians into pigs. Others argue that the young men among the People of the Sabbath were transformed into monkeys, but the old men thereof into pigs. Zamakhsharī, 1:653, on Q 5.60–1. Regarding this see Cook, "Ibn Qutayba and the monkeys" (esp. pp. 52–3) who notes the decree of Ibn Ṭālib (d. 275/888), judge of Qayrawān, that Jews attach an image of a monkey, and Christians an image of a pig, to their clothing.

324 Ibn Kathīr, 1:105, on Q 2.65–6.

325 According to the first the village in question in both *al-baqara* (2) 65 and *al-a'rāf* (7) 163 was named Midyan, and was located between Ayla and Mt. Sinai. God tried its citizens by having the fish come openly on the Sabbath, but disappear entirely on all other days.

'Ikrima, the slave of Ibn 'Abbās, discovered his master crying while reading the story of the People of the Sabbath from the Qur'ān.[326]

Ibn Kathīr also explains that there were in fact three groups in this unhappy village: one, those who transgressed; two, those who remained obedient and preached repentance to the transgressors; and three, those who remained obedient but found such preaching pointless. *Al-a'rāf* (7) 164, he explains, includes the question of the last group ("Why do you preach to a people whom God will annihilate and punish severely?") and the response of the second group ("In order to seek forgiveness from your Lord, and that they might become righteous.").[327]

Finally, Ibn Kathīr is particularly interested in the debate over the nature of the transformation, citing a number of different explanations thereof. According to the first:

> God transformed them into the shape of monkeys, which means He made the people look like something in their outer appearance, not in [their] human nature. Such were the deeds and the trickery of these people when they made the appearance of truth but were opposed to it inwardly.[328]

In other words, the transformation of the unbelievers was purely external. Essentially they continued to be humans. This transformation was a fitting punishment for their crime of hypocrisy. According to a second explanation, however, it was the other way around. The transformation was purely internal. One tradition to this effect explains that when God cursed them with the words, "Be despised monkeys" (Q 2.65) He meant, "Be subordinate and lowly."[329] A second tradition explains: "Their hearts were transformed but they were not transformed into monkeys. It is like the proverb of God: '. . . like donkeys carrying books [cf. Q 62.5].' "[330] On this tradition Ibn Kathīr comments that it has a good *isnād*, but that "it is a peculiar statement, contrary to the apparent context in this place and elsewhere."[331] Ibn Kathīr's

The events unfold as Ṭabarī presents them. A single man sets a fishing line, his neighbors imitate him, the believers leave the city and God punishes all of the transgressors by transforming them into monkeys. Ibn Kathīr, 1:105, on Q 2.65–6; cf. the Ibn 'Abbās tradition (1:106) and another version of the same narrative: 2:247, on Q 7.164–6. According to the second narrative, some devious citizens begin to trap fish in ditches on the Sabbath. The smell of fish tempts others to do the same. The believers divide the village in two with a wall. When the transgressors refuse to open the door of the wall one day, the believers climb over it and discover that the transgressors have been transformed into monkeys. Ibn Kathīr, 2:246, on Q 7.164–6.

326 Ibn Kathīr, 2:246, on Q 7.164–6.

327 Ibid.

328 Ibid., 1:105, on Q 2.65–6.

329 Ibid.

330 Ibid.

331 Ibid. Ibn Kathīr cites Q 5.60 to support his position.

opinion on this question emerges fully when he considers a third tradition, which states simply that the transformation was "in nature not in shape" (*ma'nawiyyan lā ṣūriyyan*). He comments: "In fact the correct answer is that it was in both nature and shape, but God knows better."[332] Thus he favors (against Zamakhsharī and with the other *mufassirūn*) the view that a physical transformation took place.[333]

As for the fate of those transformed, Ibn Kathīr relates a tradition that God turned the People of the Sabbath into monkeys and annihilated their children.[334] He means thereby to refute a rather logical, if hardly scientific, suggestion that the very species of monkeys and pigs were created in this incident.[335] To this end Ibn Kathīr also reports that when the Prophet was asked whether monkeys and pigs are the descendents of the cursed Jews, he replied: "When God annihilates or transforms a people he never gives them descendants or offspring. Monkeys and pigs already existed before this."[336]

Subtext

If Ibn Kathīr rejects the idea that all monkeys and pigs have Jews for ancestors, he accepts the idea that the People of the Sabbath were physically transformed into these animals. Indeed all of the *mufassirūn* in my survey, with the exception of Zamakhsharī, come to this conclusion. This is one case where recent translators, who generally conclude instead that the Qur'ān is here speaking metaphorically, do not follow *tafsīr*. Yet the Qur'ān is quite comfortable with narratives on supernatural phenomena. It relates, for example, how a group of youths and their dog slept for 309 years (Q 18.25), how a man and his donkey were brought back to life after a hundred years (Q 2.259), how a dead fish that Moses and his companion carried came back to life (Q 18.61), how the prophet Ṣāliḥ was accompanied by a "camel of God" (Q 7.73; 11.64; 91.13; cf. 26.155; 54.27), and how a fish swallowed, and later spat up, the prophet Jonah (Q 21.87–8; 37.139–48). These examples, in fact, suggest that the Qur'ān is particularly interested in narratives on animals that are controlled or created by God. A story on the transformation of humans into animals would presumably not be out of place.

Moreover, while this story is not extant in Jewish and Christian literature *in extenso*, the motif of human transformation is. According to the *Babylonian*

332 Ibn Kathīr, 1:106, on Q 2.65–6.

333 Thus the majority of the *mufassirūn*, see Cook, "Ibn Qutayba and the monkeys," 51–2.

334 Another tradition (on the authority of Ibn 'Abbās) explains that those who were transformed did not live longer than three days: "They did not eat. They did not drink. They did not have relations." Ibn Kathīr, 1:105, on Q 2.65–6.

335 On this debate see Cook, "Ibn Qutayba and the monkeys," 54–5.

336 Ibn Kathīr, 2:73, on Q 5.59–63. Here Ibn Kathīr relates as well a second *ḥadīth* (on the authority of Ibn 'Abbās): "The Messenger of God – God's blessing and peace be upon him – said, 'Snakes are transformed *jinn* [perhaps a reference to the curse of Satan] as monkeys and pigs are transformed [people].'" Ibn Kathīr comments: "This *ḥadīth* is very irregular."

Talmud (*Sanhedrīn* 109a), for example, when humans inclined towards evil at the time of the Tower of Babel, God transformed some of them into apes:

> They split up into three parties. One said, "Let us ascend and dwell there"; the second said, "Let us ascend and serve idols"; and the third said, "Let us ascend and wage war [with God]." The party which proposed, "Let us ascend, and dwell there" – the Lord scattered them; the one that said, "Let us ascend and wage war" were turned to *apes*, spirits, devils, and night-demons.[337]

A tradition in *Genesis Rabba* (23:6) relates that in the days of Enosh, that is, in the days between Adam and Noah when humans inclined towards evil, four things changed: "The mountains became [barren rocks], the dead began to feel [the worms], *men's faces became ape-like*, and they became vulnerable to demons."[338] From these references it appears that the humans who most disobey God are those transformed into apes. Presumably this reflects their loss of the divine image in which they were created. I imagine that these traditions use apes to illustrate this idea because they are the most human of all beasts (and yet as a rule have bad manners).

The place of pigs in the Qur'ānic material on human transformation may owe something to the account in Matthew (8:28–32) and Luke (8.30–3) according to which Jesus cast demons from a possessed man (or two possessed men, as Matthew has it) into a herd of pigs. These pigs "ran violently down a steep place into the sea, and perished in the waters" (Mt 8.32).[339] Thus while the demons believed they would find a refuge in the pigs, they found instead a punishment. Tellingly, in all three of these cases the transformation of humans into animals (or in the New Testament case, the casting of demons into animals) is a divine punishment.[340]

337 On this cf. *BEQ*, 313. J. Kugel points out a similar report in the *Biblical Antiquities* (7:5) of Pseudo-Philo. *TB*, 237.

338 Trans. Freedman et al., 1:196. Cf. *BEQ*, 313–14.

339 On this cf. Hirschfeld, *Beiträge*, 86. Elsewhere (*New Researches*, 108) Hirschfeld proposes that *qirada* ("monkeys"; Q 2.65; 5.60; 7.166) is a misreading of *qirdān* ("ticks," "vermin"), which is intended in a metaphorical sense.

340 I. Lichtenstadter finds these references insufficient to explain the Qur'ānic motif of transformation. She comments: "It seems that neither Muslim nor Western scholars ever considered this transmutation of sinners into apes worthy of special examination, let alone wondered whether it might not be more than an expression for 'apt punishment' of evil doers." I. Lichtenstadter, "And become ye accursed apes," *JSAI* 14, 1991, (153–75) 159–60; reprint: *The Qur'ān: Style and Contents*, ed. A. Rippin, Aldershot: Ashgate, 2001, 61–83. In fact both Muslim and Western scholars consider (and indeed Muslim scholars generally prefer) the idea that the Qur'ān intends a physical transformation. In any case, Lichtenstadter proceeds with a detailed study (pp. 162–75) of the motif of human transformation into animals in various classical texts, including myths from India, Egypt, Greece (especially Plutarch's *De Iside et Osiride*), and Christian legend (especially the legend of Christopher's

The connection between the Qur'ān's references to the People of the Sabbath and Biblical literature becomes more evident still in the light of a topos that appears in a second series of narratives. These latter narratives are all intended to illustrate the sanctity of the Sabbath, or the gravity of violating the Sabbath prohibitions. Thereby the Israelites are tempted by the presence of food, or supplies, available all around them but prohibited due to the Sabbath. In Exodus 16, for example, God provides the Israelites with manna that miraculously appears with the dew of each morning. However, Moses warns the Israelites not to collect any on the Sabbath (cf. Deuteronomy 8.16, which as Prof. Michael Tzvi Novick has pointed out to me, describes the manna as a "test"), the Lord's day (but instead to collect twice as much on the sixth day; Ex 16.23). When some people nevertheless go out to look for manna on the Sabbath, they find none (Ex 16.27). Their actions anger God, who asks Moses: "How much longer will you refuse to obey my commandments and laws?" (Ex 16.28). A similar incident occurs in Numbers 15. A man who was caught gathering sticks in the desert on the Sabbath is brought to Moses and God condemns him to death by stoning (Numbers 15.35).

In the Qur'ānic account of the People of the Sabbath, however, the temptation is not manna or sticks but fish. In this regard the Qur'ān reflects the opinion found in the Talmud in favor of eating fish on the Sabbath. According to the Babylonian Talmud (*Shabbāt*, 118b) when Rabbi Judah was asked how one should show delight in the Sabbath he replied: "With a dish of beets, *large fish*, and heads of garlic." Elsewhere (*Shabbāt*, 119a) the Babylonian Talmud tells the story of a pious man, known as Joseph-who-honors-the-Sabbaths, who bought a fish at the last moment before sunset on the Sabbath eve, and thus at a high price. When he opened the fish he found a jewel therein which he sold for thirteen roomfuls of gold dinars.[341]

Closer to the Qur'ānic account of the People of the Sabbath is a narrative in the Babylonian Talmud (*Qiddūshīn*, 72a) that follows the topos of Exodus 16 and Numbers 15, but with fish in the place of manna or sticks. It describes how the Jews of one town (cf. the *qarya* of Q 7.163) in Babylon took fish out of a ditch on the Sabbath, and for this were destroyed.[342] This report provides a setting for the narrative to which the Qur'ān is alluding: not the Red Sea, as most accounts of the *mufassirūn* have it, but rather Iraq. It also implies that the events recounted took place during the Babylonian exile, when Jews would have been hard pressed to remain faithful to the Mosaic law.

martyrdom under Decius). In this she is helped by a long and detailed letter from Prof. Brian Daley, which Lichtenstadter includes in her article (pp. 165–8). Ultimately Lichtenstadter concludes that the ape became the symbol of the devil in early Christian legend (especially in Egypt; see pp. 174–5).

341 Cf. *Gn R.* (11:4), which tells the story of a man who paid twelve dinars to purchase a fish on the eve of the Day of Atonement to show how much he honors that day. Trans. Freedman et al., 1:83.

342 On this cf. *BEQ*, 314.

The Qur'ān's account is also related to a larger Jewish tradition surrounding a legendary river referred to in Aramaic and Hebrew variously as Sanbaṭyōn, Sambaṭyōn, or Sabbaṭyōn.[343] Josephus, who refers to this river while describing the campaign of Titus, locates it in Lebanon, near the village of Arka northeast of Tripoli. He reports that this river flows only on the Sabbath, while on other days it "presents the spectacle of a dry bed."[344] Presumably the river Sabbaṭyōn became associated with the Sabbath because of its name, which in Greek (Josephus has σαββατικὸν) is close to the word for Sabbath (σάββατον).[345] Josephus' contemporary Pliny the Elder (d. AD 79) also knew of this miraculous river, which he places in Judaea. Pliny, however, records to the contrary of Josephus that the strange river dries up on the Sabbath and flows on the other days of the week.[346] *Genesis Rabba* (11:5) also connects this river with the Sabbath. A tradition therein reports, in line with Pliny, that the River Sambaṭyōn "carries stones the whole week but allows them to rest on the Sabbath."[347] The Babylonian Talmud (*Sanhedrīn*

343 The *Targum of Pseudo-Jonathan* (on Ex 34.10), for example, has God promise that when the Jews are taken away in exile to Babylon, He will remove them and make them dwell on the banks of the River Sabbaṭyōn. Trans. Le Déaut, 256:271.

344 Josephus, *The Jewish War*, ed. and trans. T.E. Page, E. Capps, and W.H.D. Rouse, London: Heinemann, 1928, 535. Lichtenstadter notes that certain later (post-Qur'ānic) rabbinic traditions relate not only that the river rests on the Sabbath, but that its fish do as well. On the Sabbath the fish of this river come up and rest on its banks. Here the connection with the Qur'ān is apparent. This indeed seems to be the very tradition to which the Qur'ān is referring when it mentions fish that appeared "openly" on the Sabbath (Q 7.163). While this innovation in the story does not appear, as far as I know, in any Jewish text that pre-dates the Qur'ān, the presence thereof in the Qur'ān suggests that it was already in circulation, although the influence certainly might have been the other way around. See Lichtenstadter, "And become ye accursed apes," 160, following Ginzberg, *LJ*, 6:408, n. 56. In these later traditions the River Sabbaṭyōn is connected to the Babylonian exile. According to these traditions, when the Jews were taken to Babylon, Nebuchadnezzar commanded that the Levites commit a sacrilege by playing music for his entertainment with the sacred harps that once belonged to the Temple. Some Levites refused to do so and were killed for their refusal. Others bit off their own fingers when Nebuchadnezzar demanded that they played harps, and showed their mutilated hands to the king. Others were led by a cloud and a pillar of fire (as the Israelites during the Exodus) to a tract of land that was surrounded by the sea on three sides. The River Sabbaṭyōn formed a boundary on the fourth side and protected them, and the holy objects of the Temple, from their oppressors. *LJ*, 4:317.

345 The Hebrew/Aramaic form Sabbaṭyōn bears little resemblance to Hebrew *shabbāt*.

346 *Natural History*, 31:18.

347 Trans. Freedman et al., 84. In *Lamentations Rabba* (7th century AD) this river has no connection with the Sabbath but instead marks a boundary. A tradition therein reports that Israel has experienced three exiles: one to the far side of the River Sambaṭyōn, one to Daphne (i.e. the grove where the nymph Daphne was turned into a laurel tree) of Antioch, and one "when the cloud descended upon them and covered them." *Lamentations R.* 2:9, trans. Freedman et al., 4:172. By this tradition *Lamentations R.* associates the River Sambaṭyōn with the Assyrian exile of the ten northern tribes (cf. the similar tradition in the Jerusalem Talmud, *Sanhedrīn*, 10:6), an association that is explicit in *Genesis Rabba* (73:6): "The ten tribes were exiled beyond the River Sambaṭyōn, whereas the tribes of

65b), for its part, cites this river as proof that Jews celebrate the Sabbath on the right day. "Who tells you that *this* day is the Sabbath," Rabbi Akiba is asked. "Let the river River Sabbaṭyōn prove it," he replies.[348]

Thus the story to which the Qur'ān is referring slowly emerges. It combines, on the one hand, the tradition of Jews of the Babylonian exile who were punished by taking fish on the Sabbath and, on the other hand, the tradition of the River Sambaṭyōn with its unusual Sabbath day habits. If the Qur'ān locates the settlement of the Jews along the *baḥr* (Q 7.163), the term should here be understood not as the sea but rather as a river. This is certainly well within its semantic range.[349]

Thus in its references to the People of the Sabbath the Qur'ān incorporates two motifs of Judaeo-Christian literature: transformation into animals as divine punishment, and restraint on the Sabbath as a divine test. The Qur'ān's development of this latter motif is particularly noteworthy. According to Exodus 16 manna appeared every day but the Sabbath. According to Numbers 15 sticks were available on the Sabbath, but they were available on other days as well.[350] According to *al-a'rāf* (7) 163, however, fish *only* came to the town along the sea on the Sabbath. With this detail the Qur'ān intensifies the tone of admonition. The people of this town did not simply break a rule that God had given them. Rather, God, knowing their weakness, set a trap for them. He "tested them in the matter in which they were iniquitous" (Q 7.163).

CS 8 Jonah and his people

Qur'ānic account

When the Qur'ān has believers among the People of the Sabbath ask their companions why they bother preaching to unbelievers whom God has vowed to punish, the companions respond, "In order to seek forgiveness from your Lord, and that they might become righteous" (Q 7.164). Thus they hope for the repentance of a condemned people. This hope, which might otherwise seem ridiculous, is meaningful in light of *yūnus* (10) 98:

Judah and Benjamin are dispersed in all countries." Trans. Freedman et al., 1:671. Again this river has a mysterious, legendary quality. Beyond it lie the ten tribes who never returned from their exile, and whose location was never discovered.

348 Trans. I. Epstein, London: Soncino, 1935, 1:445–6.

349 See *AEL*, 156b.

350 Although no direct relationship with the Qur'ānic material on the People of the Sabbath is evident, it is worth mentioning the prominence of New Testament narratives involving fish or fishing. These include the parable of heaven as a dragnet (Mt 13.47–9), the multiplication of the fish and loaves (Mt 14.14–22; 15.32–8; Mk 6.34–45; Lk 9.12–7; Jn 6.5–14), the miracle of a fish with a shekel in its mouth (Mt 17.27), and the apostles' catch of a great haul of fish (Lk 5.6; and after Christ's resurrection: Jn 21.3–11).

> If only another city came to believe, and benefited from its belief, other than the people of Jonah.[351] They believed and We lifted from them a shameful punishment in the life of this world. We gave them a respite, for a time.

10.98 فَلَوْلاَ كَانَتْ قَرْيَةٌ آمَنَتْ فَنَفَعَهَا إِيمَانُهَا إِلاَّ قَوْمَ يُونُسَ لَمَّا آمَنُواْ كَشَفْنَا عَنْهُمْ
عَذَابَ الخِزْيِ فِي الْحَيَاةَ الدُّنْيَا وَمَتَّعْنَاهُمْ إِلَى حِينٍ

Here, in the only verse that mentions Jonah in the Sūra that bears his name, the Qur'ān suggests ("We lifted from them . . .") that his people believed only *after* God had decided on their punishment, and that their belief saved them nevertheless. This report runs contrary to the standard Qur'ānic topos of prophetic history, according to which the prophet calls his people to repent and believe lest God punish them; the people refuse to believe and God destroys them.

The belief of Jonah's people is again referred to in a passage of *al-ṣāffāt* (37):

> (37.139) Jonah was indeed a messenger. (140) He escaped to a loaded ship. (141) They cast lots and he was the one reproved. (142) The fish swallowed him and he was blameworthy. (143) If he did not give praise, (144) he would have remained in its belly until the Day of Resurrection. (145) So we cast him to the barren land, and he was weak. (146) We caused a *yaqṭīn* tree to sprout above him. (147) We sent him to one hundred thousand and more. (148) They believed and We gave them a respite, for a time.[352]

37.139 وَإِنَّ يُونُسَ لَمِنَ الْمُرْسَلِينَ

37.140 إِذْ أَبَقَ إِلَى الْفُلْكِ الْمَشْحُونِ

37.141 فَسَاهَمَ فَكَانَ مِنْ الْمُدْحَضِينَ

37.142 فَالْتَقَمَهُ الْحُوتُ وَهُوَ مُلِيمٌ

37.143 فَلَوْلاَ أَنَّهُ كَانَ مِنْ الْمُسَبِّحِينَ

37.144 لَلَبِثَ فِي بَطْنِهِ إِلَى يَوْمِ يُبْعَثُونَ

37.145 فَنَبَذْنَاهُ بِالْعَرَاء وَهُوَ سَقِيمٌ

351 Or perhaps, "Why has no city come to believe, and benefited from its belief, other than the people of Jonah?"

352 To Speyer (*BEQ*, 410) the Qur'ān's note that Jonah's people were given a respite "for a time" (*ilā ḥīn*) is an allusion to the later destruction of Nineveh (by the Babylonians and others in 612 BC). Muḥammad added this note, he suggests, to preclude the possibility that someone who knew the history of the Assyrian Empire might use the report of Nineveh's destruction to question his preaching on Nineveh's salvation. More likely this note reflects less a concern with historical accuracy and more a concern with rhyme. Both verses in which this note occurs (Q 10.98; 37.148) are in passages where the Qur'ān's rhyme scheme (*fāṣila*) is based on penultimate ī or ū. By adding "*wa-mattaʿnāhum ilā ḥīn*" to the word *dunyā* (which would break the rhyme) the Qur'ān is able to continue this scheme.

37.146 وَأَنبَتْنَا عَلَيْهِ شَجَرَةً مِّن يَقْطِينٍ

37.147 وَأَرْسَلْنَاهُ إِلَى مِئَةِ أَلْفٍ أَوْ يَزِيدُونَ

37.148 فَآمَنُوا فَمَتَّعْنَاهُمْ إِلَى حِينٍ

According to this passage Jonah committed a blameworthy act (v. 142), one forgiven only by his praise in the belly of the fish (143–4). *Al-anbiyā'* (21) 87–8 adds some details to this account:

> (21.87) The Man of the Fish (*dhū l-nūn*) went off angry and thought We would have no power over him. He called in the darkness: "There is no god but You. Praise be to You. I have been a wrongdoer." (88) We responded to him and saved him from distress. Thus We will save the believers.

21.87 وَذَا النُّونِ إِذ ذَّهَبَ مُغَاضِبًا فَظَنَّ أَن لَّن نَّقْدِرَ عَلَيْهِ فَنَادَى فِي الظُّلُمَاتِ أَن لاَّ إِلَهَ
إِلاَّ أَنتَ سُبْحَانَكَ إِنِّي كُنتُ مِنَ الظَّالِمِينَ

21.88 فَاسْتَجَبْنَا لَهُ وَنَجَّيْنَاهُ مِنَ الْغَمِّ وَكَذَلِكَ نُنجِي الْمُؤْمِنِينَ

If indeed "darkness" (Q 21.87) is an allusion to the fish's belly, then the Qur'ān is here quoting the praise of Jonah alluded to in *al-ṣāffāt* (37) 143. Jonah's departure in anger (Q 21.87) would then seem to be the blameworthy act that was atoned for by his praise. Still this is a remarkably allusive passage. The Qur'ān does not explain whence he left, whither he went, and why he was going there in the first place.

For its part *al-qalam* (68) 48–50 seems to refer to a second blameworthy act of Jonah. In *al-ṣāffāt* (37) 143–4 we learn that Jonah would have remained in the belly of the fish if he did not praise God. In *al-qalam* we learn that the "Companion of the Fish" (*ṣāḥib al-ḥūt*; v. 48) would have been cast unto a barren land (cf. Q 37.145) in condemnation, had not "his Lord chose him and made him one of the righteous" (v. 50). In other words, this error was forgiven not by Jonah's praise but by God's grace. The Qur'ān thus suggests that Jonah sinned twice, and was forgiven twice.

Jonah is evidently a unique prophet in the Qur'ān. He flees from God in anger, doubting that God has the power to restrain him, and only returns to God when he is brought down to the bowels of the earth (Q 21.87).[353] The Qur'ān accordingly uses the example of Jonah to warn its audience: "Wait for your Lord's decree, and do not be like the Companion of the Fish, who cried out in desperation" (Q 68.48).[354]

353 Still the Qur'ān includes Jonah in two separate lists (Q 4.163; 6.86) of divine messengers.

354 The imagery of the Jonah narrative also seems to be connected to, if not formative of, other topoi in the Qur'ān. In *al-isrā'* (17) 66–9, for example, the Qur'ān laments that humans only recognize their dependence on God, and turn to Him in supplication, when at sea. Similarly, it is only when Pharaoh is faced with death in the sea that he repents and is saved, in the body at least, by God (Q 10.90–2).

Problems for interpreters

Jonah's faults

Of course, the idea of a sinful prophet is hardly felicitous to the *mufassirūn*, all of whom are influenced to different degrees by the dogmatic principle of prophetic infallibility.[355] Yet the *mufassirūn* had to deal with the Qur'ān's suggestion (Q 21.87) that Jonah grew angry with God, a sin not to be taken lightly. *Tafsīr Muqātil* explains that Jonah was not in fact angry with God but instead with king Hezekiah b. Aḥār[356] and other unbelieving Israelites.[357] Qummī reports in one place that Jonah was angry with the actions of his people.[358] In another place, however, he concludes instead that Jonah grew angry with God when the people to whom he was sent repented and God spared them His wrath.[359]

With Ṭabarī it is clear that the explanation of Jonah's anger had become an issue of contention. He presents four different opinions on this matter. According to a first opinion (for which he cites two traditions, one on the authority of Ibn 'Abbās), Jonah was angry at the impiety of his people. According to a second opinion, Jonah was angry at God for withholding His punishment. A tradition (also on the authority of Ibn 'Abbās) explains that Jonah was shamed when God relented from a punishment that Jonah had publicly predicted. He announced: "By God I will not ever go back to them as a liar."[360] Or, as another tradition has it, he was not shamed but afraid, since this people executed liars.[361]

According to a third opinion Jonah was angry with God, but only because of the fact that God burdened him with the weights of prophethood, "weights that only a few can bear."[362] Finally, according to a fourth opinion, Jonah was angry with God, but only because of the haste with which God insisted he depart on his mission. God did not even give Jonah time to put on his sandals.[363]

Ṭabarī concludes simply that Jonah was angry with God, without specifying a reason. If he were angry with his (sinful) people, Ṭabarī explains, God would not have punished Jonah (Q 37.142),[364] and the Qur'ān would

355 For a wider survey of exegetical views on this topic see H. Busse, "Jonah," *EQ*, 3:53–4.

356 Cf. 2 Kings 18.1; Heb. Ākhāz. Syr. Ahār. The edition of *Tafsīr Muqātil* reads Ajār.

357 *Tafsīr Muqātil*, 3:90, on Q 21.87.

358 Qummī, 2:49, on Q 21.87.

359 Ibid., 1:318–19, on Q 10.98.

360 Ṭabarī, 17:77, on Q 21.87.

361 Ibid. On this view see also Ṭabarī 11:170, on Q 10.98.

362 One tradition in support of this view (related on the authority of Wahb b. Munabbih) directly refutes the view that Jonah was angry with his people (the first opinion), insisting that those who follow it do so "only because they deny that a prophet might be angry with God." Ṭabarī, 17:77, on Q 21.87.

363 Ṭabarī, 17:77, on Q 21.87.

364 Busse notes that some *mufassirūn* who insist that Jonah was angry with his people and not God explain that the incident with the fish was not actually a punishment, but rather a "correction" (*ta'dīb*). Busse, "Jonah," *EQ*, 3:54b.

not have used him as a cautionary example for the Prophet Muḥammad (Q 68.48).[365]

Zamakhsharī, who agrees that Jonah was angry at God,[366] finds in the Qur'ān other indications of Jonah's faults. First, he notes that Jonah should not have left his people in anger (Q. 21.87a): "He should have been patient and waited for permission from God to leave them."[367] Second, Zamakhsharī remarks that Jonah was wrong to think that God had no power over him (*lan naqdira ʿalayhi*; Q 21.87b). On this second point Zamakhsharī notes that some scholars – presumably the opponents of the Muʿtazila – insist that Jonah did not doubt God's power but only the doctrine of divine preordainment (*qadar*). A tradition in support of this view describes how the caliph Muʿāwiya came to Ibn ʿAbbās for an explanation of this verse, saying:

> "Yesterday the waves of the Qur'ān struck me and I am drowning in them. You are my only hope for salvation." [Ibn ʿAbbās] said, "What is it O Muʿāwiya?" He read this verse and said, "Could a prophet of God think that He had no power (*lā yaqduru*) over him?" [Ibn ʿAbbās] said, "This is about *qadar* ("preordainment") and not *qudra* ("power")."[368]

Zamakhsharī, as one might expect from a Muʿtazilī, insists that *qudra* is intended. Still he proposes solutions to avoid the conclusion that so troubled Muʿāwiya. The meaning of the text could be that Jonah thought God would not *use* His power; or the Qur'ān might mean that the actions of Jonah were like those of one who really thought God had no power over him (but Jonah himself did not think such a thing);[369] or the Qur'ān might here be referring not to Jonah's convictions but to a Satanic temptation (*waswasat al-shayṭān*), a temptation that Jonah refuted, "as the careful believer does with the incitements of Satan, with the temptations that Satan whispers every moment."[370] This was, in other words, Jonah's version of the Satanic verses.

If Zamakhsharī seeks to defend the character of Jonah, Ibn Kathīr goes still further. He never admits the possibility that Jonah could have been angry at God, insisting that the prophet was angry with his people.[371] Still Ibn Kathīr is compelled to follow the text of the Qur'ān and admit that Jonah had at least done some wrong (cf. Q 21.87). Regarding this Ibn Kathīr relates a tradition meant to emphasize Jonah's repentence. When Jonah was swallowed by the fish, the tradition explains, the sound of Jonah worshipping God reached the angels in heaven. They asked God about this strange, distant sound and God responded:

365 Ṭabarī, 17:78, on Q 21.87.
366 Zamakhsharī, 3:131, on Q 21.87.
367 Ibid.
368 Ibid., 3:132.
369 Ibid.
370 Ibid.
371 Ibn Kathīr, 3:180, on Q 21.87–8. Cf. the similar tradition on p. 3:181.

> "That is my servant Jonah. He rebelled against me and so I have enclosed him in the belly of the fish." They asked: "You mean the virtuous servant from whom good work ascended to You every day and night?" He replied, "Yes." At this the angels interceded for Jonah and God commanded the fish to cast him on the shore.[372]

To the same effect Ibn Kathīr elsewhere quotes a *ḥadīth* in which the Prophet declares: "No servant of God should say, 'I am better than Jonah.'"[373]

The sequence of events

Yet the matter of Jonah's faults is not the only aspect of his account that challenges the *mufassirūn*. They also struggle to establish a basic sequence of events for that account. The problem in this regard is whether Jonah's mission to his people preceded, or followed, his stay in the fish. The difficulty begins with *al-ṣāffāt* (37) 139–48, which refers first to Jonah's departure from some place (140), then to the fish incident (142–5) and the tree incident (146), and *then* to his mission (147–8). The *mufassirūn* assume that the departure of verse 140 is Jonah's departure from his mission in Nineveh, which would make it before the fish incident. This assumption, however, seems to be belied by the reference to Jonah's mission at the end of the passage.

On this question *Tafsīr Muqātil* relates that Jonah went on his mission, to a city named Nineveh,[374] before he was swallowed by the fish.[375] Qummī agrees and relates Jonah's story in some detail. In Jonah's city there were two good men, one religious (*'ābid*), named Malīkhā, and the other knowledgeable (*'ālim*), named Rūbīl. Malīkhā encouraged Jonah to announce God's punishment to them, but Rūbīl insisted he not do so since God would ultimately withdraw His punishment. Jonah listened to Malīkhā. He announced God's punishment and fled the city before the dreadful hour. Yet Rūbīl stayed behind, implored the people to repent, and taught them how to pray. They did so earnestly, praying for God's forgiveness. As Rūbīl had predicted, God withdrew His punishment. In anger Jonah fled to the coast and boarded a boat (cf. Q 37.140), but God sent a great fish that trapped the boat at sea. When the sailors cast lots and Jonah was found to be responsible for their tight spot (cf. Q 37.141), they threw him into the water and the fish

372 Ibn Kathīr, 3:181, on Q 21.87–8. Ibn Kathīr reports a second version of this tradition, in the context of Q 37.143–4 ("If he did not give praise, he would have remained in its belly until the Day of Resurrection."). Here the angels make the reason for their intercession explicit: "Will you not have mercy on him and save him in a time of distress, in light of [the good that] he did in a time of comfort?" Ibn Kathīr 4:20, on Q 37.139–48.

373 Ibn Kathīr, 4:19, on Q 37.139–48.

374 *Tafsīr Muqātil*, 3:621, on Q 37.147.

375 Ibid., on Q 37.146.

swallowed him (cf. Q 37.142).[376] The fish later cast Jonah onto a barren land (cf. Q 37.145, which has God, not the fish, cast him), where God caused the *yaqṭīn* tree to sprout up (cf. Q 37.146).[377]

This narrative, however, does not incorporate the last two verses (147–8) of the passage in *al-ṣāffāt*, verses which suggest that Jonah's mission came after the fish incident. A different view, accordingly, appears in a narrative reported by Ṭabarī, according to which the Qur'ān's earlier reference to Jonah going off angry (Q 21.87; cf. 37.140) refers not to his leaving from Nineveh but to his leaving for Nineveh:

376 Qummī, 1:318–19, on Q 10.98. Qummī then continues (p. 319) with a remarkable tradition, according to which the Jews challenge ʿAlī b. Abī Ṭālib to describe where the fish took Jonah. He responds that the fish took him first to the Red Sea (*baḥr al-Qulzum*; presumably with the idea that Jonah sailed from the Ḥijāz), then to the Sea of Egypt (i.e. the Mediterranean), then to the Sea of Ṭabaristān (i.e. the Caspian), then to the Tigris, and then under the earth. There he met Qorah, who was swallowed by the earth (Q 28.79–81) and remained in its bowels as a punishment. When Qorah heard the sound of Jonah praying inside of the fish and called out to him. Jonah replied, "I am the wrongdoer, the sinner, Jonah b. Mattay." responded a voice. The two had a conversation, during which Qorah expressed remorse for what he had done to the people of Moses. At this God released him from his underground prison. With Qorah as his model Jonah called out to God in the darkness (cf. Q 21.87) "There is no God but you, praise be to you. I am a wrongdoer." God, answering his prayer, ordered the fish to bring Jonah up and spit him onto land. Cf. *Pirqē de-Rabbī Elīʿezer* (10; ed. Börner-Klein, 103), wherein Jonah meets the sons of Qorah who are praying directly underneath the temple.

377 Qummī, 1:319, on Q 10.98. There is great dissension among the interpreters over the identity of this tree which the Qur'ān names *yaqṭīn* (Pickthall: "a tree of gourd"; Yusuf Ali: "a spreading plant of the gourd kind"; Paret: "Kürbispflanze [?]"). *Tafsīr Muqātil* (3:621, on Q 37.146) describes it as a gourd tree that provided shade to Jonah, who also drank the milk of its fruit. Although *Tafsīr Muqātil* usually does not rely on traditions, three are cited here to validate his view, a sign that this was a much disputed exegetical point. For his part, Qummī glosses *yaqṭīn* with *dubbā'* (a type of gourd) in two places (1:319, on Q 10.98; 2:200, on Q 37.146). In a third (1:320, on Q 10.98) he does so with *qaraʿ* (another type of gourd), adding that it provided shade to Jonah after his hair had fallen out and his skin grown thin (and vulnerable to the sun in a barren place) due to his time inside the fish. Ṭabarī presents a broad survey of this debate (23:102–3, on Q 37.146). According to two traditions it is a plant that does not grow higher than one's leg. According to another it is any plant that grows and dies within one year. According to three traditions it is *dubbā'*. According to one tradition it is *baṭṭīkh* ("watermelon"). According to eight traditions it is *qaraʿ*. According to a final tradition it is not any of these, but a different tree called only *yaqṭīn* with which God chose to shade Jonah. Zamakhsharī (4:62, on Q 37.133–48) includes also fig and banana tree among the proposals. Ibn Kathīr (4:20, on Q 37.139–48) quotes a verse of poetry from Umayya b. Abī l-Ṣalt in his description of this tree.

Qummī also preserves material on the didactic purpose of this tree. According to Qummī, when Jonah became sad at the death of the tree, God asked him, "Are you saddened by a tree that you did not plant or water . . . but not saddened by the people of Nineveh, more than 100,000 [cf. Q 37.147] people upon whom I was going to send down destruction?" Qummī, 1:320, on Q 10.98. Similarly, Ṭabarī reports that when the tree died and Jonah complained of the heat God said to him: "Are you concerned with the heat of the sun but not concerned with the hundred thousand or more who have repented to me?" Ṭabarī, 23:104, on Q 37.146.

> Gabriel came to [Jonah], saying: "Go to the land of Nineveh and warn them of the punishment that has been prepared for them." [Jonah] said, "Allow me to seek out a mount." [Gabriel] replied, "The matter is too urgent for that." [Jonah] said, "Allow me to seek out shoes." He replied, "The matter is too urgent for that." . . . So Jonah grew angry, left and boarded a ship. Yet when he boarded, the ship became stuck. It would not advance or retreat. So they drew lots. . . . The fish came wagging its tail. It was told: "O fish, we do not give you Jonah as sustenance but we give you to him as a shelter and mosque." . . . The fish swallowed him and left that place with him until he passed Ayla, then he left with him until he passed the Tigris, and then he left with him until he cast him into Nineveh.[378]

The problem seems to be resolved. Jonah's departure in anger (v. 140) was not from Nineveh but from his disagreeable meeting with Gabriel. Thus the latter mention of the mission (vv. 147–8) is no longer redundant. And yet Ṭabarī elsewhere cites a tradition that puts things precisely the other way around. Therein Jonah's anger, as in the Qummī tradition, is due not to the pushiness of the angel Gabriel but to the stubbornness of the Ninevites.[379]

Zamakhsharī also concludes that the fish incident came only after Jonah departed in anger from his mission (v. 140). Regarding the reference to Jonah's mission at the end of *al-ṣāffāt* (37) 139–48, he explains pointedly: "The intention here is his earlier mission to his people, the residents of Nineveh."[380] Thus Zamakhsharī resolves the problem with grammar. The Qur'ān has simply mentioned a fact later that should be understood earlier (*taqdīm al-mu'akhkhar*).

Ibn Kathīr follows Zamakhsharī's sequence in his discussion of *al-anbiyā'* (21) 87–8. Jonah is swallowed by the fish only after leaving Nineveh.[381] Yet when Ibn Kathīr arrives at *al-ṣāffāt* (37) 139–48 he quotes a contradictory tradition that the mission of Jonah was after the fish incident.[382] To his credit

378 Ṭabarī, 23:105, on Q 37.147–9.

379 Ibid. Elsewhere (11:170 on Q 10.98) Ṭabarī expresses his preference for this latter view.

380 Zamakhsharī, 4:62, on Q 37.133–48.

381 Ibn Kathīr explains that Jonah left Nineveh in anger over his people's stubbornness and then boarded a ship. When a storm rose up, the sailors decided to choose someone to throw overboard, in order to lighten the ship, by casting lots. Jonah's lot came up and he threw himself overboard. Yet God sent a fish, from the outer ocean (*Al-baḥr al-akhḍar*; cf. D.M. Dunlop, "Al-Baḥr al-Muḥīṭ," *EI*[2], 1:934a) to swallow him. God instructed this fish: "Do not eat his flesh or smash his bones, for Jonah is not to be sustenance for you, but your belly is to be a prison for him." Jonah began to pray from the belly of the fish, declaring: "O Lord, I have made this place, which no other person has reached, a mosque for you." Ibn Kathīr, 3:181, on Q 21.87–8. Cf. 4:19–20, on Q 37.139–48.

382 Ibn Kathīr, 4:20, on Q 37.137–48. Ibn Kathīr also notes a tradition that the fish cast Jonah along the Tigris, the river associated (as in the Ṭabarī tradition above) with Nineveh where Jonah would conduct his mission. A second tradition, however, names Yemen. Ibn Kathīr concludes, "God knows better."

Ibn Kathīr recognizes the contradiction and proposes an explanation. He suggests that Jonah went to Nineveh twice: "There is no reason why he could not have returned to the people to whom he was first sent after he left the fish, and that they then believed him."[383] He also mentions a solution proposed by Baghawī (Abū Muḥammad al-Farrā', d. 516/1122), that Jonah was sent to a certain people before the fish incident, and a different people thereafter.

The salvation of Jonah's people

Of course, the very idea of the belief and salvation of Jonah's people is itself extraordinary, since the Qur'ān is filled with examples of peoples (of Noah, Lot, Hūd, Ṣāliḥ, and so on) who stubbornly refused to believe and were destroyed. Moreover, in *Yūnus* (10) 98 the Qur'ān suggests that the people of Jonah believed only *after* God had decided to destroy them. Just a few verses earlier (Q 10.90–2) the Qur'ān describes how Pharaoh repented and was saved *in extremis*, but his people drowned to death nevertheless (cf. Q 7.136; 8.54; 17.103). Ṭabarī remarks that the faith of Jonah's people benefited them, "whereas the faith of Pharaoh did not benefit him when he was drowning."[384] In light of the extraordinary nature of the salvation of Jonah's people, the *mufassirūn* use all of their creative energies to illustrate the exuberance with which they repented.

Tafsīr Muqātil relates that Jonah's people repented only when they actually saw the punishment descending upon their heads. They put on sackcloth, poured ashes on their heads, separated mothers from their children and women from their husbands, and cried out to God collectively. At this God lifted the punishment (Q 10.98).[385]

According to Ṭabarī, "The fear of divine punishment enveloped the people of Jonah as a funeral cloth envelops the tomb."[386] The whole city climbed up to a high place and prayed fervently;[387] "they put on sackcloth, divided every beast from its young and cried out to God for 40 days."[388] According to another tradition they sought out a wise man who taught them to pray in the following words, "O Living one, there is no God but You."[389]

Zamakhsharī relates in one place that the Ninevites repented only when they saw Jonah flee from the city.[390] In another place he explains that they

383 Ibn Kathīr, 4:21, on Q 37.137–48.

384 Ṭabarī, 11:170, on Q 10.98.

385 *Tafsīr Muqātil*, 2:250, on Q 10.98.

386 Ibid.

387 Ṭabarī, 11:171, on Q 10.98.

388 Ibid., 11:172.

389 Ibid. This last tradition has doctrinal significance, for it suggests that piety alone does not lead to salvation. Proper religious practice is needed, as well.

390 Zamakhsharī, 2:371, on Q 10.98.

ignored his preaching with the comment, "When we see the approach (*asbāb*) of annihilation we will believe in you."[391] Zamakhsharī continues:

> When thirty-five days had gone by a terrible black cloud, with intense smoke, covered the sky. It descended until it enveloped their city, blackening their roofs. At this they put on sackcloth and went out to a high point with their women, young and animals. They divided women from their children and animals from their children. They felt great compassion for each other. Their voices and their cries ascended on high. Thus they showed their faith, repentance and supplication. God had mercy on them and lifted the punishment from them. It was a Friday and the day of 'Ashūrā'.[392]

In his commentary on *Yūnus* (10) 98 Ibn Kathīr describes the conversion of Jonah's people in similar terms. He maintains that the people of Nineveh repented when they lost track of Jonah and God "cast fear into their hearts."[393] Elsewhere, however, Ibn Kathīr explains that they took Jonah's prophecies of doom seriously only when they learned that a prophet does not lie.[394]

Subtext

For the most part the Qur'ān follows closely the Biblical narrative of Jonah. Indeed the Qur'ānic references and allusions to the Jonah story pose no problem to someone familiar with the Biblical narrative. As for the question of Jonah's faults, the Biblical story not only accepts that Jonah is an imperfect prophet, it emphasizes – indeed exaggerates – his imperfections. The Biblical Jonah flees God and heads for Tarshish, the end of the world (Jonah 1.3), clearly convinced that God does not rule over the entire world (cf. Q 21.87).[395] When God responds by casting a storm upon the sea it is

391 Ibid.

392 Ibid., 2:371–2. The last note regarding 'Ashūrā' presumably reflects Zamakhsharī's familiarity with Shī'ī penitence practices on that day, which commemorates the martyrdom of Ḥusayn.

Zamakhsharī later (2:372) adds that the people of Jonah also sought out a wise man to teach them how to pray. He told them to say: "O Living one without whom there is no life, O Living one who brings the dead to life, O Living one there is no god but you."

393 They put on sackcloth, separated animals from their children and cried out to God for forty nights. They found a scholar who taught them to pray. Ibn Kathīr, 2:410, on Q 10.98.

394 Ibn Kathīr, 3:180, on Q 21.87–8.

395 The midrashic text *Mekīltā de-Rabbī Shim'ōn* (ca. 3rd–4th century AD) has Jonah imagine that Yahweh has power only on land: "But Jonah thought: I will go outside of the land, where the Shekinah does not reveal itself." *Mekīltā*, trans. J.Z. Lauterbach, Philadelphia: Jewish Publication Society of America, 1976, 1:7 (cf. 8). In the *Pirqē de-Rabbī Elī'ezer* (10, ed. Börner-Klein, 93) Jonah expresses a similar idea: "I will flee to a place where his glory is not mentioned. If I go to the heavens, it is said that his glory is there, for it is said 'His glory is above the heavens' (Ps 113.4). If on earth, it is said that this glory is there, for it is said, 'The entire earth is filled with his glory' (Isaiah 6.3)."

the gentile sailors, not Jonah, who fear the name of Yahweh (Jonah 1.9–10). When Jonah is swallowed by the fish he repents, praises God (Jonah 2.2–10; cf. Q 21.87–8; 37.143–4) and, once he is vomited onto land, proceeds to Nineveh (Jonah 3.3). Yet Jonah hardly preaches with great enthusiasm there. He goes only one day into a city that takes three days to cross (Jonah 3.3) and announces only a single sentence to its people (Jonah 3.4). Later Jonah regrets that he preached at all, and becomes furious when God spares the city (Jonah 4.1-2), furious to the point of death (Jonah 4.3). Jonah's fury, of course, is due in part to the symbolic identity of Assyria as the enemy and oppressor of Israel. The Qur'ān nowhere makes this point, but then neither does the Book of Jonah, at least not explicitly. In any case, the Qur'ān follows closely the Biblical portrayal of Jonah the recalcitrant prophet, and quite appropriately uses him as a cautionary example for its audience (Q 68.48).

Likewise the question of the sequence of events is resolved when the Qur'ān is read in conversation with its Biblical subtext. When the Qur'ān is read alone then *al-ṣāffāt* (37) 139–48 seems to suggest both that the mission came before (v. 140) and after (vv. 147–8) the fish incident. Ibn Kathīr accordingly wonders if Jonah had two different missions.[396] Yet when the Qur'ān's own references to the Biblical Jonah story are followed the impasse disappears altogether. Therein Jonah departs (Q 37.140) not from Nineveh but from wherever he was (presumably Palestine) when God first called him (Jonah 1.2–3). The fish incident follows (Q 37.142–5; Jonah 1–2), then the mission (Jonah 3) and then the tree/vine incident (Jonah 4).

Of course, *al-ṣāffāt*, pace the Biblical Jonah story, refers to the tree incident (Q 37.146) before referring to the mission (Q 37.147–8). But the conflict is only apparent, since the Qur'ān's reference to Jonah's mission here does not correspond to the narrative in Jonah 3 (a topic taken up instead in Q 10.98). Instead it corresponds to the epilogue of the story in Jonah 4. When the Qur'ān (Q 37.145) refers to God casting Jonah unto a barren place (cf. Q 37.145: *'arā'*) it is not alluding to the fish vomiting him on shore (cf. Jonah 2.11), as the *mufassirūn* have it, but rather to Jonah's sojourn to the east of Nineveh (Jonah 4.5). The barrenness of the place is implied by the report that Jonah built a shelter (Jonah 4.5) and that God provided him with a shade-giving vine (Q 4.146; Jonah 4.6). When God destroys this same vine (Jonah 4.7) and sends a scorching wind and a burning sun (Jonah 4.8), it is to teach Jonah a lesson in compassion:

> Yahweh replied, "You are concerned for the castor-oil plant which has not cost you any effort and which you did not grow, which came up in a night and has perished in a night. * So why should I not be concerned for Nineveh, the great city, in which there are more than *a hundred and*

396 Ibn Kathīr, 4:21, on Q 37.137–48.

> *twenty thousand people* who cannot tell their right hand from their left, to say nothing of all the animals?"
>
> (Jonah 4.10–1)

These are the words that are reflected in the conclusion of the passage on Jonah in *al-ṣāffāt*: "We sent him to *one hundred thousand and more*. * They believed and we gave them a respite, for a time" (Q 37.147–8).

Finally, as for the question of the extraordinary salvation of Jonah's people (cf. Q 10.98a), the Qur'ān is here developing an important Biblical theme. The Qur'ān's insistence (Q 10.98b) that Jonah's people were saved after God had determined to destroy them is troubling to the *mufassirūn*,[397] but it is an apt commentary on the Biblical story. Indeed in the Bible Jonah does not come to warn the people of Nineveh, but simply to announce the destruction of their city (Jonah 3.4). Still the people respond by believing in God and hoping in his mercy (Jonah 3.5). The king himself puts on sackcloth, sits on an ash heap (Jonah 3.6), and orders his people to show signs of repentance.[398] With this hyperbolic scene the Book of Jonah serves as a satire to humble Israel. The gentiles, who in the narratives of the Pentateuch and the Historical Books are the enemies of Yahweh,[399] fear the word of Yahweh more than the Israelite prophet.

When the Qur'ān cites the extraordinary example of the people of Jonah, however, it is concerned not with Israel but with its own audience. In *yūnus* (10) 93 the Qur'ān refers to the differences among the Jews that arose once God gave them revelation. Thence it turns to the audience, mentioning how many people deny the warnings of God until the moment of their doom (Q 10.95–7). Only then does the Qur'ān cite the example of Nineveh, lamenting, "If only another city came to believe, and benefited from its belief, other than the people of Jonah" (Q 10.98a).

At first glance this citation is extraordinary. Other than Jonah none of the major or minor Biblical prophets appear in the Qur'ān. And Jonah hardly

397 Speyer (*BEQ*, 410) imagines that Muḥammad found it difficult to comprehend the Jonah story, which is so unlike the standard Qur'ānic punishment story.

398 "No person or animal, herd or flock, may eat anything; they may not graze, they may not drink any water. * All must put on sackcloth and call on God with all their might; and let everyone renounce his evil ways and violent behaviour. * Who knows? Perhaps God will change his mind and relent and renounce his burning wrath, so that we shall not perish." Jonah 3.7b–9.

399 In Exodus, for example, the Israelites are attacked immediately after their departure from Egypt by the Amalekites (Ex 17.8–13). When Israel prevails Yahweh explains to Moses: "Write this down in a book to commemorate it, and repeat it over to Joshua, for I shall blot out all memory of Amalek under heaven" (Ex 17.14). Indeed, as the Book of Samuel explains, many generations later Yahweh sent Saul to annihilate the Amalekites (1 Samuel 15). Elsewhere in the Book of Samuel the Philistines defeat Israel and take the Ark of the Covenant, that is, the seat of Yahweh Himself, to their temple in Gaza. Yet Yahweh humiliates their God Dagon, who repeatedly falls over on his face, while He strikes the Philistines with tumors (1 Samuel 5). In the Book of Jonah, on the other hand, the Ninevites obey Yahweh and Yahweh expresses compassion for them, even for their animals (Jonah 4.11).

stands out as the most prominent of those prophets. Indeed in the Old Testament he is dwarfed by Isaiah, Jeremiah, Ezekiel, and others.

Not so, however, in the New Testament. Both Matthew and Luke have Jesus insist that the only sign that his generation will be given is the "sign of Jonah" (Mt 12.39; Lk 11.29). Although Matthew (12.40) has Jesus compare his death and resurrection to the sojourn of Jonah in the fish, the primary meaning of this expression for both Matthew and Luke seems to be the manner in which Jesus (like Elijah before him) is rejected by his own people. Thus Jesus proclaims: "On Judgement Day the men of Nineveh will appear against this generation and they will be its condemnation, because when Jonah preached they repented; and look, there is something greater than Jonah here" (Mt 12.41; cf. Lk 12.32). In *yūnus* (10) 98 the Qur'ān refers to the Jonah story in precisely the same way: to contrast the repentance of Jonah's people with the stubbornness of its audience. Thus the Qur'ān's references to the story of Jonah reflect the content of the Old Testament Book, but the homiletic interpretation of the New Testament.[400]

The philological evidence also suggests that the Qur'ān is in conversation with the Christian interpretation of the Jonah story. The Qur'ānic form of the name Jonah, Yūnus, is connected to Christian Palestianian Aramaic Yūnis (from Greek Ἰωνᾶς),[401] and not to Hebrew Yōnā.[402] The Qur'ānic epithet of Jonah, *dhū l-nūn* ("the Man of the Fish"; Q 21.87), also reflects a Christian subtext, inasmuch as *nūn* is related to Syriac *nūnā*, not to Hebrew *dāgā*.[403] It is then important to note the Christian homiletic tradition in which Jonah is an allegory for the stubborness of the Jews and mercifulness of God to the nations.[404] This tradition appears not only in the Gospels of Matthew and Luke, but also in a homily (*mēmrā*) of Ephraem on *The Repentance of Nineveh*.[405] Therein Ephraem relates how Jonah wondered at the hard hearts of the Jews, a trope that is also central to the Qur'ān (Q 5.13; cf. CS 10), and at God's mercy:

400 B. Heller and A. Rippin describe the Qur'ānic material on Jonah as a "periphrastic rendering of the story." "Yūnus b. Mattā," *EI*², 11:348b. In light of its relationship to the New Testament, however, this material might better be described as a "homiletic rendering" thereof.

401 See F. Schulthess, *Lexicon Syropalaestinum*, Berlin: Reimer, 1903, 82a.

402 On this see Jeffery (*FV*, 296). Others (Hirschfeld, *Beiträge*, 56; Rudolph, *Abhängigkeit*, 47; *KU*, 155; Mingana, "Syriac influence on the style of the Kur'ān," 83) are unaware of the Palestinian Aramaic form and consider only Syriac Yūnān (See *TS*, 1581). Because this Syriac does not match Qur'ānic Yūnus, they argue that the latter form comes directly from the Greek.

403 Cf. *FV*, 282; Mingana, "Syriac influence on the style of the Kur'ān," 84.

404 For a detailed review of Syriac commentaries on the Jonah story see J.M. Heisler, *Gnat or Apostolic Bee: A Translation and Commentary on Theodoret's Commentary on Jonah*, Ph.D. dissertation, Florida State University, 2006.

405 This homily is extant only in Greek form, but its authenticity is generally accepted. For the text see *S. Ephraem Syri opera omnia quae exstant graece, syriace, latine, in sex tomos distributa*, ed. J.S. Assemani, P. Mobarek, and S.E. Assemani, Rome: n.p., 1732–46, 2:359–87; English trans.: *The Repentance of Nineveh: A Metrical Homily on the Mission of Jonah, by Ephraem Syrus*, trans. H. Burgess, London: Blackader, 1853. Regarding the history and contents of the homily see D. Hemmerdinger-Illiadou, "Saint Éphrem le Syrien: Sermon sur Jonas (Texte grec inédit)," *Le Museon* 80, 1967, 47–74.

> He blushed for the children of his own people. He saw the Ninevites were victorious. And he wept for the seed of Abraham. He saw the seed of Canaan in sound mind, while the seed of Jacob was infatuated; He saw the uncircumcised cut to the heart, while the circumcised had hardened it.[406]

The Qur'ān, like Ephraem, uses the account of Jonah to deliver a message on human repentance and divine mercy. It is this message that ultimately explains the Qur'ān's interest in the figure of Jonah, to the exclusion of almost all of the other Biblical prophets.

CS 9 The nativity of Mary

Qur'ānic account

If the Qur'ān presents Jonah as the prime example of a disobedient prophet, it presents Mary as the prime example of a righteous woman. Mary is the only woman whom the Qur'ān mentions by name and the only woman whose birth the Qur'ān describes. This description occurs in *āl 'Imrān*, where the Qur'ān declares that God has selected Adam, Noah, the family of Abraham, and the family of 'Imrān above all others (Q 3.33). Thereafter the Qur'ān turns to 'Imrān's wife, and, without any other introduction, relates how she dedicated her unborn child to God:

> (3.35) The wife of 'Imrān said, "Lord, I have vowed to consecrate that which is in my womb to you. Accept it from me. You are the hearing, the knowing."

3.35 إِذْ قَالَتِ امْرَأَةُ عِمْرَانَ رَبِّ إِنِّي نَذَرْتُ لَكَ مَا فِي بَطْنِي مُحَرَّرًا فَتَقَبَّلْ مِنِّي إِنَّكَ أَنتَ السَّمِيعُ الْعَلِيمُ

The Qur'ān then jumps to the delivery of that child, emphasizing that 'Imrān's wife gave birth to a daughter:

> (3.36) When she delivered her [daughter] she said, "Lord I have delivered a female," (God is more knowledgeable about what she delivered) "and the male is not like the female. I have named her Mary. I commit her, and her offspring, to your protection from Satan the outcast."

3.36 فَلَمَّا وَضَعَتْهَا قَالَتْ رَبِّ إِنِّي وَضَعْتُهَا أُنثَى وَاللَّهُ أَعْلَمُ بِمَا وَضَعَتْ وَلَيْسَ الذَّكَرُ كَالأُنثَى وَإِنِّي سَمَّيْتُهَا مَرْيَمَ وِإِنِّي أُعِيذُهَا بِكَ وَذُرِّيَّتَهَا مِنَ الشَّيْطَانِ الرَّجِيمِ

406 *The Repentance of Nineveh*, 5:77–87, trans. Burgess, 58.

The Qur'ān here implies that 'Imrān's wife was not only surprised to discover that her child was a girl, she was also disappointed. For her comment (or alternatively that of the Qur'ān's narrator), "the male is not like the female," is connected to a larger discourse on male and female offspring in the Qur'ān. Elsewhere the Qur'ān, offended by those who imply that God be associated with goddesses, remarks caustically: "Inquire of them whether your Lord has daughters while they have sons" (37.149).[407]

Yet 'Imrān's daughter Mary is an exceptional female. Several verses later the Qur'ān reports how the angels declared to her: "God has singled you out, and purified you. He has singled you out above all of the women of the worlds" (Q 3.42; cf. 66.12). Mary's distinction above all other women is also suggested by the extent to which the report of her nativity and upbringing is connected to that of a man: John, the son of Zechariah (see Q 3.35–41; 19.1–33). In fact, the Qur'ān joins their stories completely by reporting that Zechariah, the father of John, was also the guardian of Mary (Q 3.37). At the same time the request of 'Imrān's wife (Q 3.36) that God protect both her child (Mary) and her child's offspring (Jesus) from Satan suggests that Mary is distinctive because of Jesus.

The description of Mary's nativity in *āl 'Imrān* is followed by allusions to her extraordinary upbringing:

> (3.37) Her Lord received her well, and brought her up well. He made Zechariah her guardian. Whenever Zechariah came to her in the *miḥrāb* he found sustenance there with her. He asked, "Mary how did this come to you?" She replied, "It is from God." God gives sustenance without end to whomever He wishes.

3.37 فَتَقَبَّلَهَا رَبُّهَا بِقَبُولٍ حَسَنٍ وَأَنبَتَهَا نَبَاتًا حَسَنًا وَكَفَّلَهَا زَكَرِيَّا كُلَّمَا دَخَلَ عَلَيْهَا زَكَرِيَّا
الْمِحْرَابَ وَجَدَ عِندَهَا رِزْقًا قَالَ يَا مَرْيَمُ أَنَّى لَكِ هَذَا قَالَتْ هُوَ مِنْ عِندِ اللّهِ إِنَّ اللّهَ يَرْزُقُ
مَن يَشَاء بِغَيْرِ حِسَابٍ

Mary, then, dwelt in a place the Qur'ān names the *miḥrāb* (cf. Q 19.11, which describes her emergence from the *miḥrāb*), the identity of which is clear only in light of the passage's subtext. There she received miraculous sustenance (*rizq*, presumably a reference to food) from God, while remaining under the care of her guardian Zechariah.

Several verses later, after a section on the annunciation of John, the Qur'ān returns to the story of Mary. The Qur'ān relates how the angels informed Mary that God has chosen and purified her (v. 42), and how they admonished her to be obedient and prayerful (v. 43). With this the Qur'ān turns again to the question of a guardian for Mary, declaring "You were not there when

407 Cf. 43.61; 52.39 and especially 53.21, where, after naming three goddesses, the Qur'ān asks: "Are you to have males but He females?"

they cast their pens to see which of them would become the guardian of Mary. You were not there when they quarreled" (v. 44b). Thus the Qur'ān seems to allude to a contest held to name Mary's guardian, but it leaves the *mufassirūn* to speculate over the details of this event.

Problems for interpreters

Mary the daughter of 'Imrān and sister of Aaron

In fact even the very identity of Mary is a problem for the *mufassirūn*, inasmuch as the Qur'ān makes her the daughter of 'Imrān. The *mufassirūn* were well aware of the Biblical report that Mary the daughter of 'Imrān (Heb. 'Amrām) was the sister of Moses and Aaron. The fact that the Qur'ān elsewhere (Q 19.28) refers to Mary the mother of Jesus as "sister of Aaron" made the problem still more pressing. For the *mufassirūn* were well aware that a long period of time (600 years, according to one tradition reported by Ṭabarī)[408] separated Aaron and Moses from Jesus.

Tafsīr Muqātil resolves this problem by insisting that Mary is only called the sister of Aaron in the Qur'ān because she is among his descendants.[409] Ṭabarī, however, cites three contrasting explanations. According to the first explanation, the phrase "sister of Aaron" is merely an epithet that the Israelites used to refer to a virtuous woman. There was among them an exceptionally virtuous man (although not the brother of Moses) named Aaron. Thus by calling Mary the "sister of Aaron" they were invoking her virtue.[410] According to the second explanation, the Israelites called Mary the sister of Aaron because he was her ancestor. His name became the patronym for all of his descendents, as though he were the founder of a tribe. Mary is called "sister of Aaron" as someone from the tribe of Tamīm (of which a man named Tamīm was the forefather) might be called, "O brother of Tamīm" or someone from the tribe of Muḍar, "O brother of Muḍar."[411] According to the third explanation (the inverse of the first), Aaron was the name of an immoral Israelite, and by calling Mary "sister of Aaron," the Israelites were associating her with vice, accusing her of fornication.[412]

408 Ṭabarī, 16:77, on Q 19.28.

409 *Tafsīr Muqātil*, 2:625–6, on Q 19.28. Elsewhere (1:271, on Q 3.35) *Tafsīr Muqātil* reports that Mary's father was 'Imrān b. Māthān and her mother Ḥanna bt. Fāqūz. Qummī relates only that Mary's mother was named Ḥanna. Qummī, 1:109, on Q 3.36. Ṭabarī presents detailed information on Mary's ancestors, listing her mother as Ḥanna bt. Fāqūdh b. Qatīl and her father as 'Imrān b. Yāshham. For the latter figure he presents a complete genealogy all the way back to David the son of Jesse (Īshā, cf. Mt 1.6–16).

410 Ṭabarī, 16:77, on Q 19.28.

411 Ibid.

412 Ibid. According to all three of these explanations, in other words, Mary the mother of Jesus was not the sister of Moses. To this same effect Ṭabarī adds a tradition according to which Ka'b al-Aḥbār (or al-Ḥabr [sing.], i.e. the "Rabbi," to whom many reports on

Zamakhsharī provides a logical refutation to those who would confuse the family of Mary mother of Jesus with the family of Aaron:

> You might say that since 'Imrān b. Y.ṣ.h.r.[413] had a daughter named Mary, who was older than Moses and Aaron, and 'Imrān b. Māthān had the Virgin Mary, then how do we know that this 'Imrān is the father of the Virgin Mary, not the 'Imrān who is the father of Mary the sister of Moses and Aaron. I would say: "That Zechariah was [her] guardian is enough of a proof to show that 'Imrān [b. Māthān] is the father of the Virgin. For Zechariah the son of Ā.dh.n. and 'Imrān b. Māthān lived at one time. Zechariah married ['Imrān b. Māthān's] daughter Elizabeth (Īshā'), the sister of Mary. John and Jesus were maternal cousins.[414]

On the appellation of Mary in *Maryam* (19) 28, "sister of Aaron," Zamakhsharī turns to a prophetic *ḥadīth* in which Muḥammad identifies Aaron as the Qur'ānic prophet. Zamakhsharī comments: "His descendents were in the category of siblings, even if there were one thousand or more years between her and him."[415]

In addressing this problem Ibn Kathīr reports the three explanations cited by Ṭabarī,[416] yet he also notes that some authorities insist Mary the mother of Jesus was indeed the sister of Aaron and Moses, the same woman "who used to play the tambourine with the women, praising God and thanking him for the way He blessed the Israelites."[417] This view, however, Ibn Kathīr describes as, "nonsense, a serious error."[418] He concludes instead that Mary

Jewish matters are attributed) makes this point to the Prophet's wife 'Ā'isha. 'Ā'isha retorts, "You lie," and Ka'b explains: "O mother of the believers, If the Prophet – God's blessing and peace be upon him – said [the contrary] then he is more knowledgeable and informed. But if not then I see that there are six hundred years between them." At this 'Ā'isha is silent.

According to the standard history Ka'b converted to Islam only during the caliphate of 'Umar (whom he accompanied to Jerusalem in 15/636). Therefore, even if he had a profound knowledge of prophetic history, he would not have had the authority of a companion of Muḥammad. Another tradition has the Prophet himself support Ka'b's statement. When al-Mughīra was in Najrān, the tradition relates, the Christians there asked him how Mary could be both the mother of Jesus and the sister of Aaron. Confused, al-Mughīra returned to the Prophet, who explains: "They would name [people] with the names of those before them." Ṭabarī, 16:77, on Q 19.28.

413 According to Ex 6.18 'Amrām (the father of Moses, Aaron and Miriam) was the son of Kohath.

414 Zamakhsharī, 1:355, on Q 3.33–7. According to Zamakhsharī Mary's father was 'Imrān b. Māthān (Ṭabarī reports b. Yāshham), and her mother Ḥanna bt. Fāqūdh.

415 Zamakhsharī, 3:14, on Q 19.27–8. She is called "sister of Aaron," Zamakhsharī explains, just as someone from Hamadhān might be called "O brother of Hamadhān." Thus the Iranian Zamakhsharī replaces the Arab examples of Tamīm and Muḍar with an Iranian one.

416 Ibn Kathīr, 3:112, on Q 19.27–33.

417 Ibid., 3:113. cf. Ex 15.20.

418 Ibn Kathīr, 3:113, on Q 19.27–33.

is called the "sister of Aaron" because the Israelites use to call people by the names of prophets and virtuous people.[419]

The birth of a female

The Qur'ān's allusion to the surprise of 'Imrān's wife at giving birth to a female presents a second interpretive problem to the *mufassirūn*, since the Qur'ān itself does not give any explanation for that surprise. *Tafsīr Muqātil* explains that only boys were consecrated in the days of 'Imrān. Mary's mother was accordingly worried that her child might be female, and for this reason she prayed to God: "Accept [the child] from me. You are the hearing, the knowing" (Q 3.35).[420]

According to Qummī 'Imrān's wife was confused. A female, Qummī notes, cannot be a prophet and is not worthy of a divine annunciation. Yet 'Imrān and his wife mistakenly assumed that God's promise referred to their child, when in fact it referred to their grandson: Jesus. This misunderstanding lies behind the Qur'ān's comment: "God is more knowledgeable about what she delivered" (Q 3.36).[421]

Ṭabarī comments, like *Tafsīr Muqātil*, that the custom in 'Imrān's day was to consecrate only boys. When 'Imrān's wife stated "the male is not like the female" (Q 3.36), she was referring to the prohibition of women in the holy place (*quds*) and/or synagogue (*kanīsa*) while they are in the state of impurity.[422] For this reason she was surprised to discover that the child she had dedicated to service there was female.

Zamakhsharī agrees with this view and provides an even more detailed narrative illustrating it. 'Imrān's wife had grown old without having a child. Moved by the sight of a bird feeding her chick, she made a vow to God that, if she were to have a child, she would consecrate him to service in Jerusalem as a *sādin* (a term that Christians use for a sacristan, and Muslims for the guardian of the Ka'ba).[423] Such service, however, was only for boys, for which reason 'Imrān's wife could not understand why God had given her a girl. Yet Zamakhsharī notes another view that the statement "the male is not like the female" (Q 3.36) was her way of saying: "Perhaps God

419 Ibid. In support of his opinion, Ibn Kathīr quotes the prophetic *ḥadīth* (seen with Ṭabarī above) in which Ka'b informs 'Ā'isha on this matter. He also quotes the tradition (likewise seen with Ṭabarī above) in which the people of Najrān challenge al-Mughīra on this question.

420 *Tafsīr Muqātil*, 1:271–2, on Q 3.35. Upon delivery, however, 'Imrān's wife was nevertheless surprised to discover that her consecrated child was indeed female. Yet God promised to protect the girl from Satan (cf. Q 3.36). 'Imrān's wife fulfilled the vow of consecration, wrapping the girl in a robe and delivering her to the *miḥrāb* (cf. Q 3.37) in Jerusalem. Ibid., 1:272, on Q 3.36.

421 Qummī, 1:109, on Q 3.36.

422 Ṭabarī, 3:236–7, on Q 3.35. Another tradition (p. 238) explains that this applies to women only when they are menstruating.

423 Zamakhsharī, 1:355, on Q 3.33–7. See *AEL*, 1335b.

Most High has a secret and wisdom in this. Perhaps this female will be better than a male."[424] By this view the Qur'ān's statement "Her Lord received her well" (Q 3.37) signifies God's acceptance of a female in the place of a male.[425]

Mary in the miḥrāb

By associating the consecration of Mary with religious service the *mufassirūn* make a link with *āl 'Imrān* (3) 37, where Mary is found in *al-miḥrāb*. Most interpreters assume that this term refers to a building, or part of a building, but its precise meaning is a point of contention, even among modern translators. Most of them (Pickthall, Blachère, Arberry, Fakhry, and Abdel Haleem) translate it "sanctuary." Paret translates "Tempel," a translation close in meaning to "sanctuary" but suggestive of the Jerusalem Temple. Yusuf Ali, quite unlike the others, has "chamber," implying that the *miḥrāb* was more a place of confinement than of religious service.

As for the *mufassirūn*, *Tafsīr Muqātil* implies that the *miḥrāb* was a sort of hut or enclosure. He relates that Zechariah *built* a *miḥrāb* for Mary in the middle of Jerusalem and locked her within, trusting no one with the key. Only when Mary had her period would Zechariah let her out to stay with her sister Elizabeth (Aylīshafa'a bt. 'Imrān), the mother of John.[426] *Tafsīr Muqātil*'s commentary is thus motivated by a concern to illustrate Mary's perfect chastity.[427] Qummī takes a similar approach. He locates the *miḥrāb* in Jerusalem, and insists that Mary only entered into the *miḥrāb* when she reached maturity.[428] (*Tafsīr Muqātil* implies the same with the references to Mary's menstrual cycle.) There she wrapped herself in a curtain so that no one would see her.

With Ṭabarī, on the other hand, it appears that the *mufassirūn* were deeply divided over the meaning of the *miḥrāb*. Some authorities hold it to have been a synagogue (*kanīsa*),[429] others an important place in mosques (*masājid*), prayer halls, or courts (*majālis*).[430] According to one tradition the *miḥrāb*

424 Zamakhsharī, 1:356, on Q 3.33–7.

425 Ibid., 1:357. Ibn Kathīr also cites a tradition in which 'Imrān's wife notices a bird feeding its child. By this version, however, she does not make a vow right away but only after sleeping with her husband and discovering she is with child. As for the surprise of 'Imrān's wife at delivering a female, Ibn Kathīr explains that she assumed a child dedicated in the womb to God's service would turn out to be a male, since men perform that service better. Ibn Kathīr, 1:244, on Q 3.35–6.

426 *Tafsīr Muqātil*, 1:273, on Q 3.36.

427 This report is also closely related to the narratives on the seclusion of Abraham in his infancy (see CS 4).

428 Qummī, 1:109, on Q 3.36.

429 Ṭabarī, 3:241, on Q 3.37.

430 Ibid., 3:246, on Q 3.37. Ṭabarī quotes a verse of the Jāhilī Christian poet 'Adī b. Zayd by way of explanation.

was simply Zechariah's house.[431] Still another tradition relates that Zechariah used to lock Mary in the *miḥrāb* with seven doors,[432] implying that it was a place where Mary was confined to protect her virginity, in line with the *Tafsīr Muqātil* and Qummī traditions above.

The uncertainty over the term *miḥrāb* is still evident in the commentary of Zamakhsharī, who notes three different views without expressing his preference. According to the first view, which follows the topos of Mary's chaste seclusion, the *miḥrāb* was an upper room in a mosque accessed only by a ladder. According to the second view it was an important court, since she was "placed in the most honorable location in Jerusalem."[433] According to the third view it was a mosque, which in those days was called a *miḥrāb*. Zamakhsharī does not attempt to choose between these views. Ibn Kathīr, for his part, makes no attempt to identify the *miḥrāb* at all.[434]

Yet on the Qur'ān's report in *āl 'Imrān* (3) 37 that Zechariah would find *rizq* ("sustenance") in the *miḥrāb* with Mary, the *mufassirūn* are suddenly less uncertain. *Tafsīr Muqātil* explains that Gabriel would bring her grapes from heaven.[435] Qummī reports that when Zechariah went to visit Mary in the *miḥrāb*, he would find there winter fruit in summer and summer fruit in winter.[436] Ṭabarī agrees with this report, quoting a large number of traditions with variations thereof.[437] He adds that since Zechariah would enclose Mary with seven doors, he was especially surprised to find that she had fruit in the *miḥrāb* (and fruit out of season, at that!), for which reason he asked her whence it came (Q 3.37). Zamakhsharī likewise quotes the tradition on Mary receiving fruit out of season. To this tradition he adds the comment: "Her sustenance came from the heavenly Garden, for she never once suckled."[438] Indeed all of the traditions which identify Mary's sustenance with fruit imply that she was fed from the Garden of paradise.[439]

431 Ṭabarī, 3:243, on Q 3.37.

432 Ibid., 3:244–5.

433 Zamakhsharī, 1:358, on Q 3.33–7.

434 Instead his comments on Q 3.37 are restricted to the reason for Zechariah's adoption of Mary. One tradition explains that she was an orphan, another that the Israelites suffered a drought that year (which led people to give their children away in adoption) and still another that Mary was related to Zechariah.

435 *Tafsīr Muqātil*, 3:244, on Q 3.37.

436 Qummī, 1:109, on Q 3.37. Perhaps this detail is connected to the way in which 'Imrān's wife and Mary bore the fruit of a child in a supernatural manner, or out of season, as it were.

437 Ṭabarī, 3:244–5, on Q 3.37.

438 Zamakhsharī, 1:358, on Q 3.33–7.

439 Zamakhsharī uses this context to report a tradition on one of Muḥammad's miracles. Here the Prophet's daughter Fāṭima takes the place of Mary: "When [Muḥammad] grew hungry during a time of drought, Fāṭima (may God be pleased with her) presented him with two loaves of bread and a bit of meat that she considered special. Yet he returned it to her and said, 'Come and see, little girl.' She uncovered the plate, and it was filled with copious bread and meat. She was perplexed at first but then understood that it came down from

Ibn Kathīr's reports on the question of Mary's *rizq* coincide with those of Zamakhsharī.[440] He adds, however, that the site of Mary's service was not a holy place or synagogue, but rather *al-masjid al-aqṣā*, presumably a reference to the Temple Mount/al-Ḥaram al-Sharīf in Jerusalem.[441]

The ordeal

As for the reference in *āl 'Imrān* (3) 44 to a contest over Mary ("You were not there when they cast their pens to see which of them would become the guardian of Mary. You were not there when they quarreled."), *Tafsīr Muqātil* explains that it took place because 'Imrān died before Mary was born. Thereby the rabbis (*aḥbār*) want to adopt her, and propose casting lots to see who would have this honor. Zechariah objects to this device, however, arguing: "I have the most right for her because her sister is the mother of my son John."[442] But the other rabbis insist, noting that if family relationship were the standard then Mary's mother should be her guardian. Thus they cast their pens (*aqlām*; cf. Q 3.44) as lots three times; each time Zechariah is indicated. Qummī is more succinct. He relates that the people of 'Imrān fought over who would be Mary's guardian when she was born. They cast lots with arrows and Zechariah was indicated.[443]

With Ṭabarī it emerges that the matter was not always this simple to the *mufassirūn*. He begins by insisting that even if lots were used, God was the one to join Zechariah with Mary.[444] In other words, he is not fully comfortable with the idea of a device that determined the fate of two holy figures that is based on chance, or worse, on magic or divination. Still he seeks to give the Qur'ānic references a narrative context, and therefore reports a group of traditions,[445] according to which priests or rabbis threw arrow shafts, or pens, into the Jordan River (or, alternatively, some other stream). The only one that stood motionless on the water (or, alternatively, moved upstream) was that of Zechariah, and thus he was vindicated.

God. He said to her – God's blessing and peace be upon him: 'Where did I get this from?' She said, 'It is from God. God gives sustenance without end to whomever He wishes [Q 3.37b].' He said – God's blessing and peace be upon him, 'Praise be to God who has made you like the best woman of the Israelites [i.e. Mary].' Then the Messenger of God – God's blessing and peace be upon him – gathered 'Alī b. Abī Ṭālib, Ḥasan and Ḥusayn and all of his family. They ate until they were full but the food remained as plentiful as it was." Zamakhsharī, 1:358–9, on Q 3.33–7. Cf. the Gospel narratives on the multiplication of fish and loaves: Mt 14.14–22; 15.32–8; Mk 6.34–45; Lk 9.12–7; Jn 6.5–14.

440 He quotes both the report that Mary received fruit out of season, and the tradition (quoted in the note above) in which the Prophet's family together receive God's "sustenance without end." Ibn Kathīr, 1:245, on Q 3.37.

441 Ibid., 1:244, on Q 3.35–6.

442 *Tafsīr Muqātil*, 1:272, on Q 3.36.

443 Qummī, 2:110, on Q 3.44.

444 Ṭabarī, 3:241, on Q 3.37.

445 Ibid., 3:242–3, on Q 3.37.

In another tradition these events take place in the temple (*haykal*; a term that does not appear in the Qur'ān), where the scribes often typically fought over children brought to them. When Zechariah claims Mary on the basis of family relationship,[446] the scribes insist on casting their pens as lots (in the *Tafsīr Muqātil* tradition). When they do so, the pen of Zechariah stands up, as though it were made of clay. Victorious, he takes Mary to the *miḥrab*.[447] Ṭabarī also reports a number of traditions which affirm that lots were cast by throwing pens – according to one tradition the very pens with which the rabbis would write the *tawrāt*.[448]

Yet according to still another tradition reported by Ṭabarī it was indeed due to family relationship that Zechariah became Mary's guardian. Both Mary's father *and* mother had died, this tradition relates, and Zechariah was married to her maternal aunt: Ayshā' bt. Fāqūdh. A similar tradition relates that Mary was given to Ashī' (sic) until she became mature, at which point Zechariah brought her to the synagogue in fulfillment of her mother's vow. Only then did the rabbis quarrel over the guardianship of Mary. Thus this tradition places the casting of lots much later in Mary's life. A final tradition implies the same, explaining that Zechariah gave Mary up only because Israel was suffering from hardship and he could no longer support her. The rabbis accordingly cast lots to see who would take his place, and the lots indicated a carpenter named George (*j.r.y.j*).[449] Through these latter traditions the possibility appears that the ordeal over the guardianship of Mary is not connected to her childhood, but to the time of her maturity.

Zamakhsharī, however, does not consider this possibility. He relates that when Ḥanna gave birth to Mary, she ('Imrān having died while she was still pregnant)[450] wrapped her in a cloak and took her to the "mosque". There she told the priests, "the children of Aaron,"[451] to compete over the girl. The children of Māthān, the paternal grandfather of Mary, he explains, were the kings and the priests of the Israelites, for which reason the child was coveted. As *Tafsīr Muqātil* and Ṭabarī relate, Zechariah claimed rights over her because of his family relationship, but the priests insisted on casting lots.

446 According to this tradition (on the authority of Ibn Isḥāq), however, Zechariah's wife Elizabeth is not the sister of Mary (as *Tafsīr Muqātil* relates) but rather her aunt, the sister of Mary's mother Ḥanna. The dispute over the precise relationship of Elizabeth and Mary appears again with Zamakhsharī and Ibn Kathīr. Zamakhsharī (1:355, on Q 3.33–7) argues that they were sisters. Ibn Kathīr (1:345, on Q 3.37) relates the narrative of Ṭabarī in which Elizabeth appears as Mary's aunt. Yet he also notes a prophetic *ḥadīth* which relates that "John and Jesus were sons of two sisters." As is his wont, he favors the authority of prophetic *ḥadīth* and concludes that Elizabeth was indeed the sister of Mary.

447 Ṭabarī, 3:243, on Q 3.37.

448 Ibid.

449 Ibid., 3:246, on Q 3.37.

450 Zamakhsharī, 1:355, on Q 3.33–7.

451 Ibid., 1:357. Zamakhsharī explains: "They were to Jerusalem what the guardians (*ḥajaba*) are to the Ka'ba."

Seventeen of them threw their pens into the river, and only that of Zechariah floated.[452]

Ibn Kathīr also puts the ordeal over Mary in her childhood. He reports from 'Ikrima that the mother of Mary brought her in a cloak to Jerusalem, where she offered the child to the priests, the descendents of Aaron, whom Ibn Kathīr likens to the guardians of the Ka'ba.[453] The priests cast lots with their pens and Zechariah was indicated.[454] Yet Ibn Kathīr is clearly uncomfortable with the manner in which Zechariah is said to have been chosen. He adds: "In addition to this, he was the oldest among them, the most noble, and the most learned. He was their prayer leader and their prophet – God's blessings and peace be upon him and upon the rest of the prophets."[455]

Mary above all other women

In the passage on Mary's nativity the Qur'ān also remarks that God "purified and chose Mary above the women of the worlds" (Q 3.42). Here the *mufassirūn* were confronted not by a problem of narrative but of doctrine: In what way was Mary superior to other women? *Tafsīr Muqātil* and Qummī explain that the Qur'ān means only to indicate that Mary is exceptional by virtue of being the only woman to give birth without knowing man.[456]

Ṭabarī argues instead that the Qur'ān intends only to make Mary the best woman of her time.[457] He proceeds to quote three *ḥadīth* in which the Prophet names both Mary and (his wife) Khadīja as the best women. In four further *ḥadīth* the Prophet names four women: Mary, Khadīja, the wife of Pharaoh (cf. Q 66.11), and (his daughter) Fāṭima.[458] On this Zamakhsharī relates a well-known *ḥadīth* in which the Prophet declares: "Whenever children are born Satan stings them, and they raise their voice screaming from the sting of Satan, except for Mary and her son."[459] He comments: "God knows

452 Zamakhsharī, 1:357, on Q 3.33–7. Later Zamakhsharī reports a dispute over the term *aqlām*. Some hold that they were in fact *azlām*, arrows used for divination, while others report that they were the very pens with which the rabbis wrote the Tawrāt. Ibid.

453 Ibn Kathīr locates them simply in a *kanīsa* (church or synagogue), not in the temple. Ibn Kathīr, 1:348, on Q 3.42–4.

454 In a second tradition Ibn Kathīr specifies that they cast lots by throwing their pens in the Jordan River. Only that of Zechariah stood motionless on the water. Ibn Kathīr, 1:245, on Q 3.37.

455 Ibid., 1:348, on Q 3.42–4.

456 *Tafsīr Muqātil*, 1:275, on Q 3.42; Qummī, 1:110, on Q 3.42.

457 Ṭabarī, 3:262, on Q 3.42.

458 Ibid., 3:263–4. In yet another *ḥadīth*, however, the Prophet declares to (his wife) 'Ā'isha: "You are the first among the women of paradise, except for the Virgin Mary." Ibid., 3:264. Ṭabarī also adds a tradition on the occasion for the revelation of this verse. When Mary was secluded in the synagogue, where she was guarded by a young man named Joseph, an angel spoke the words of *āl 'Imrān* (3) 42 to Mary. Zechariah overheard and declared, "The daughter of 'Imrān is of consequence." Ibid.

459 Zamakhsharī, 1:356–7, on Q 3.33–7.

better whether or not it is valid. If it is valid it means that Satan makes everyone who is born desire his temptations, except for Mary and her son, for they were infallible."[460] Zamakhsharī prefers the view that Mary was superior only in the manner in which God accepted her from her mother (although she was a female) and in the way that He provided her with sustenance from heaven.[461]

Like Zamakhsharī, Ibn Kathīr quotes the *ḥadīth* on the protection of Mary and Jesus from the sting of Satan.[462] Yet he attributes the superiority of Mary not to this fact but to her miraculous conception of Jesus and her piety: "He chose her due to her many acts of worship and asceticism, and due to her honor and purity above grief and temptations."[463] Ibn Kathīr also records a number of *ḥadīth* in which the Prophet explains that certain other women, notably Fāṭima and ʿĀ'isha, are equal to Mary. In one such *ḥadīth* ʿĀ'isha is her superior.[464]

Subtext

The foregoing discussion reflects the degree to which the *mufassirūn* struggled to establish a narrative for Mary's nativity, yet as with the case of Jonah that narrative can be rather easily established by following the Qur'ān's own references to its Judaeo-Christian subtext. In this case, however, the Qur'ān is alluding not to a narrative found in a Biblical book but rather to one found in an apocryphal Gospel: the *Protoevangelium of James*, a work which purports to be the product of James the (half-)brother of Jesus (from an earlier marriage of Joseph). The *Protoevangelium* was written in Greek in the second half of the second century and translated into Syriac in the fifth century.[465]

460 Ibid., 1:357. Zamakhsharī adds a report that Mary could speak as an infant, like Jesus in the cradle (Q 3.46). Ibid., 1:358.

461 He also proposes that this verse is a response to the accusations of the Jews against Mary, from which God defends her (cf. Q 4.156, "their statement against Mary is a terrible slander"). Zamakhsharī, 1:357, on Q 3.33–7.

462 Ibn Kathīr, 1:344, on Q 3.36–7, with numerous and various *isnāds*.

463 Ibid., 1:347, on Q 3.42–4. He later (1:348) records a tradition that "Mary (peace be upon her) would remain standing [in prayer] so long that her feet would swell up." Another tradition (ibid.) reports that she would perform a full ritual washing every night.

464 Ibn Kathīr 1:347, on Q 3.42–4. In one *ḥadīth* Mary and Khadīja are named; in two others: Mary, Khadīja, Fāṭima, and the wife of Pharaoh (here named Āsiya); in another: Mary, the wife of Pharaoh and Fāṭima, but ʿĀ'isha has a certain virtue above other women (as *tharīd*, a type of porridge, has virtue over other food). This last note presumably reflects Ibn Kathīr's anti-Shīʿī viewpoint.

465 On this see O. Cullmann, "The Protoevangelium of James," in W. Schneemelcher (ed.), *New Testament Apocrypha*, trans. R. Wilson, Cambridge: J. Clarke & Co., 1991, (421–37) 423. On the *Protoevangelium*'s relationship to the Qur'ān see C.B. Horn, "Mary between Bible and Qur'an: Soundings into the transmission and reception history of the *Protoevangelium of James* on the basis of selected literary sources in Coptic and Copto-Arabic and of art-historical evidence pertaining to Egypt," *Islam and Christian-Muslim Relations* 18, 2007, 509–38. Regarding the Syriac translation see O. Cullmann, "The Protoevangelium of James," 421–2.

The *Protoevangelium*, as its title suggests, relates the events before the ministry of Christ. It is devoted particularly to the story of Mary,[466] beginning with her conception and birth. The *Protoevangelium* is thus a sort of supplement to the narratives of the New Testament, which introduce Mary only at the moment of the Annunciation. In the *Protoevangelium* Mary's mother Anne is barren and, because of this, she is belittled when she goes to offer sacrifices to God (1.2), and even mocked by her maidservant (2.3). In her grief Anne puts on mourning garments and raises a prayer of lamentation to God (2.4–3.1). Hearing her prayer, God sends an angel to Anne who delivers to her the promise of a child. In thanksgiving Anne replies: "As the Lord my God lives, if I bear a child, *whether male or female*, I will bring it as a gift to the Lord my God, and it shall serve him all the days of its life" (*Protoevangelium* 4.1).[467]

The account of Anne's conception of a child in the *Protoevangelium* is largely modeled on the account of Hannah's (i.e. Anna/Anne) conception of a child in 1 Samuel 1. Here Hannah is barren and consequently belittled when she goes to offer sacrifices, and even mocked by the second wife of her husband (1 Samuel 1.4–6). On one point, however, the two accounts differ starkly. Hannah prays for a boy: "Yahweh Sabaoth! Should you condescend to notice the humiliation of your servant and keep her in mind instead of disregarding your servant, *and give her a boy*, I will give him to Yahweh for the whole of his life and no razor shall ever touch his head" (1 Samuel 1.11). In the *Protoevangelium*, however, Anne declares her willingness to conceive either a boy or a girl, and to dedicate her child, whatever the sex, to God's service. The *Protoevangelium* consequently explains that when Anna delivered, and her midwife told her she had given birth to a girl, Anna replied, "My soul is magnified this day" (*Protoevangelium* 5.2).[468]

The Qur'ān seems to be aware of the novelty of the *Protoevangelium*'s approach. Indeed this dedication of a female to God's service is especially noteworthy in the Qur'ān, a text that has no female prophets at all. Accordingly the Qur'ān has Anne (if we may now call her such) display concern (if not distress) at the birth of a daughter, declaring: " 'Lord I have delivered a female . . . and the male is not like the female' " (Q 3.36).

The *Protoevangelium* continues by describing how Mary, at the age of six months, took her first steps. After seven steps Anne took Mary in her arms

466 "The whole was written for the glorification of Mary." O. Cullmann, "The Protoevangelium of James," 425.

467 Trans. O. Cullmann in *New Testament Apocrypha*, 1:427. Text: E. de Strycker, *La forme la plus ancienne du Protévangile de Jacques. Recherches sur le Papyrus Bodmer 5 avec une édition critique du texte et une traduction annotée*, Brussels: Société des Bollandistes, 1961. Cf. the Syriac version: *The Protoevangelium of James, Apocrypha syriaca*, ed. and trans. A. Smith Lewis, *Studia Sinaitica* 11, London: Clay, 1902.

468 Trans. Cullman, 1:428.

and declared that her daughter would walk no more until she had been delivered to the Temple in fulfillment of her vow. Therefore Anne "made a sanctuary (κοιτῶν) in her bedchamber, and did not permit anything common or unclean to pass through it" (*Protoevangelium*, 6.1).[469] The sanctuary here is certainly behind the *tafsīr* traditions that explain Mary's *miḥrāb* as a chamber in which she is isolated and kept pure. Whether the Qur'ān itself is indicating this sanctuary with *miḥrāb*, however, is another matter. Wensinck concludes that it is,[470] but the Arabic term *miḥrāb* is associated not with a simple chamber, but with a temple. *Miḥrāb* is related to the Semitic root *ḥ.r.m.* ("forbidden, sanctified").[471] It is accordingly cognate with Ethiopic *meḥrām*: "sanctuary, shrine, temple, chapel."[472] Thus *miḥrāb* is etymologically related to the term *ḥaram* used in Islamic law to designate an area where impure activities and people are forbidden, including the areas surrounding Mecca and Medina, and, not coincidentally, the Temple Mount complex (containing the Dome of the Rock and the Aqṣā mosque) in Jerusalem.

Again in *maryam* (19) 11 the Qur'ān seems to use the term *miḥrāb* for the Temple sanctuary. Here the Qur'ān describes how Zechariah, having received the annunciation of the birth of John, comes out from the *miḥrāb* and encounters his people. In the Gospel of Luke Zechariah is in the sanctuary of the Temple when the angel Gabriel announces to him the birth of John (Lk 1.8–20). He comes out from the Temple and encounters his people (Lk 1.21–2).

A different sense of *miḥrāb*, however, seems to appear in *ṣād* (38) 21–2. Here the Qur'ān refers to "adversaries" (*ḥaṣm*) who cross into the *miḥrāb*, that is, into David's chamber, asking that he mediate between them (part of a passage related to the Prophet Nathan's parable to David in 2 Samuel 12). Similarly in *saba'* (34) 13, the Qur'ān recounts how Solomon employed *jinn* to build *maḥārīb* (pl. of *miḥrāb*), statues, basins, and boilers. In both of these passages *miḥrāb* would seem to mean "palace" or "fortress,"[473] although it is curious that even in this instance there seems to be a connection with the Temple, as David is the king who desired to build the Temple and his son (Solomon) the one who built it.

As for the *miḥrāb* of *āl 'Imrān*, the Qur'ān is in close conversation here with the Mary tradition found in the *Protoevangelium*. In the *Protoevangelium*

469 Ibid.

470 A.J. Wensinck and P. Johnstone, "Maryam," *EI*², 6:630b. B. Stowasser ("Mary," *EQ*, 3:289) strangely ignores this question altogether.

471 This point is evident from South Arabian, where the words *mḥrm*, and *mḥrb* are interchangeable. See Leslau (*LCD*, 242b), who refers to Nöldeke, *Neue Beiträge*, 52, n. 3; C. Landberg, *Glossaire Datinois*, Leiden: Brill, 1920, 396–8; R.S. Serjeant, "Mihrab," *BSOAS* 22, 1959, 439–53.

472 See *LCD*, 242b; cf. M. Zammit, *A Comparative Lexical Study of Qur'ānic Arabic*, Leiden: Brill, 2002, 139.

473 Fränkel argues that *maḥārīb* here derives from Ethopic *mĕkĕrāb*, meaning "palaces." *Die Aramäischen Fremdwörter in Arabischen*, Leiden: Brill, 1886, 274.

(7.2) Mary's parents deliver her to the priest of the Temple at the age of 3 in fulfillment of her mother's vow.[474] In the Temple Mary is under the charge of (the high priest) Zechariah (*Protoevangelium* 8.2–3; cf. Q 3.37a). There she receives miraculous sustenance from heaven, receiving food "from the hand of an angel" (*Protoevangelium*, 8.1; cf. Q 3.37).[475]

When Mary reaches puberty the priests of the Temple become concerned that she will profane the Temple (*Protoevangelium* 8.2). Accordingly Zechariah enters into the sanctuary (ἁγίασμα) to pray for direction on what to do with her (*Protoevangelium* 8.3).[476] An angel of the Lord tells him to assemble all the widowers of the land, and to have them bring a rod with them, so that God might designate a guardian for Mary from among them (*Protoevangelium* 8.3). When the widowers are assembled Zechariah takes their rods (ῥάβδοι) into the Temple and prays over them. Thereafter he hands the rods back to the widowers, one by one, until he comes to the final rod, which belongs to a man named Joseph. From this rod a dove miraculously appears and alights on Joseph's head (*Protoevangelium* 9.1; cf. Mt 3.16; Mk 1.10; Lk 3.22; Jn 1.32).

This is the account to which Qur'ān is alluding in *āl 'Imrān* (3) 44: "You were not there when they cast their *aqlām* to see which of them would become the guardian of Mary." Thus it emerges that with the term *aqlām* (sing. *qalam*) the Qur'ān does not intend pens, but rather "rods." This, in fact, matches the primary meaning of *qalam*, a word derived from Greek κάλαμος ("reed").[477]

More importantly, it emerges that the Qur'ān is not speaking of an ordeal that made Zechariah Mary's guardian, but rather an ordeal that made Joseph her fiancé.[478] This is indeed suggested by the context of the Qur'ān, which

474 The consecration of Mary in the Temple also entered into Christian worship. The Byzantine Rite includes a feast day dedicated to this event. In the prayers for that day it is remembered that even before her conception Mary was consecrated to God (cf. Q 3.35): "Avant votre conception, ô Pure, vous avez été consacrée à Dieu et, après votre naissance en ce monde, vous Lui êtes maintenant présentée comme un don, en accomplissement de la promesse de vos parents." Mercenier, "Matines pour la fête: Entrée au Temple de la Mère de Dieu," *La Prière des Églises de rite byzantin* 2, 1939, 1, 6.

475 Trans. Cullman, 1:429.

476 Cf. Lk 1.9, where Zechariah enters into the Holy of Holies [ναὸν] to perform his priestly duty.

477 Jeffery (*FV*, 243) follows Nöldeke (*Neue Beiträge*, 50), who argues that Qur'ānic *qalam* comes from Ethiopic *qalam*, which in turn is based on Gk κάλαμος. However, it seems to me more likely, in light of the greater influence of Syriac on Qur'ānic vocabulary, that it comes instead from the common Syriac term *qalmā* (see attestations in *TS*, 3635). Cf. *LCD*, 428–9.

478 Pace N. Geagea, who in a monograph devoted to the Mary of the Qur'ān follows the views of the *mufassirūn* that Q 3.44, although it appears seven verses after the naming of Zechariah as the guardian of Mary (Q 3.37), is nevertheless referring to his selection for that role. N. Gegea, *Mary of the Koran*, trans. L.T. Fares, New York: Philosophical Library, 1984, 72.

already names Zechariah her guardian several verses earlier (Q 3.37). In other words, in *āl ʿImrān* the Qur'ān follows closely the chronology of Mary's life. First Mary is born (Q 3.36), then Zechariah becomes her guardian (Q 3.37), then she is engaged to Joseph (Q 3.44), and finally (Q 3.45) an angel visits her to announce the conception of Jesus.

Thus in the case of Mary's nativity the Qur'ān is closely in conversation with the *Protoevangelium*, a work that was widely read and extremely influential in the Christian Near East.[479] There remain, however, two doctrinal questions to address: the Qur'ān's description of Mary as the daughter of ʿImrān and its elevation of Mary above all other women. In the first case the Qur'ān seems to violate standard Biblical history. In the second case the Qur'ān seems to undermine standard Islamic doctrine on the superiority of Muḥammad's family (n.b. the prophetic *ḥadīth* in Ṭabarī and Ibn Kathīr on the equality or superiority of Fāṭima and ʿĀ'isha to Mary). Yet the two questions are resolved when they are examined together.

As for the first question, in Exodus 6.20 Amram (Heb. ʿAmrām; cf. Syr. ʿAmrān) is described as the father of Moses and Aaron. In Exodus 15.20 Miriam (i.e. Mary) is described as the sister of Aaron (cf. 1 Chr. 5.29). In the *Protoevangelium of James* (and Christian tradition generally), meanwhile, the father of Mary (the mother of Jesus) is named Joachim, not Amram. Many scholars, therefore, logically suggest that the Qur'ān has confused the Mary of the New and the Mary of the Old Testament when it makes Mary the mother of Jesus the daughter of ʿImrān (Q 3.35–6) and the sister of Aaron (Q 19.28). Henninger calls this "ein enormer historischer Irrtum."[480] Jeffery refers to it as a "well known confusion."[481]

Yet more recently Suleiman Mourad has noted that that the Qur'ān not infrequently uses the terms "brother" and "sister" to signify general

479 The *Protoevangelium* was in a sense the Gospel of Mary, the standard reference work on her life and her role in salvation history. One hundred and forty manuscripts thereof are extant in Greek alone. See E. de Strycker, "Die griechischen Handschriften des Protevangeliums Jacobi," in D. Harlfinger (ed.), *Griechische Kodikologie und Textüberlieferung*, Darmstadt: Wissenschaftliche Buchgesellschaft, 1980, 577–612. Manuscripts of the *Protoevangelium* are also extant in Syriac, Georgian, Latin, Irish, Armenian, Arabic, Coptic, Ethiopic, and Slavonic. See O. Cullmann, "The Protoevangelium of James," 421–2.

The influence of the *Protoevangelium* is evident in later (post-Qur'ānic) pious works on Mary, including the *Gospel of Pseudo-Matthew* and the *Ethiopian Synaxar*. See O. Cullmann, "Later Infancy Gospels," *New Testament Apocrypha*, 457–8. For text see J. Gijsel, *Die unmittelbare Textüberlieferung des sog. pseudo-Matthäus*, *Proc. Royal Acad. Belgium* 43, Brussels: AWLSK, 1981. Text and trans.: E. Amann, *Le Protévangile de Jacques et ses remaniements latins*, Paris: Letouzey, 1910, 272–339. On the birth of Mary see *Pseudo-Matthew* 2.2; on the ordeal over Mary see *Pseudo-Matthew* 8.2. For the *Ethiopian Synaxar* see: *Le synaxaire éthiopien* 2, *PO* 15, ed. and trans. S. Grébaut, Turnhout: Brepols, 1973 (see pp. 570–4).

480 Henninger, *Spuren christlicher Glaubenswahrheiten im Koran*, 9; cf. Rudolph, *Abhängigkeit*, 76; Sidersky, *Les origines des légendes musulmanes*, 141.

481 *FV*, 217.

tribal/national relationships or religious bonds.[482] His insight complements the argument of Masson, who suggests that the Qur'ān's association of Mary the mother of Jesus with the Mary of Exodus could be essentially symbolic, in the way that Jesus in the New Testament (e.g. Lk 1.32) is named "son of David" and Elizabeth is named (Lk 1.5) among the descendents of Aaron.[483]

This latter point is worthy of more attention. Luke reports that "in the days of King Herod of Judaea there lived a priest called Zechariah who belonged to the Abijah section of the priesthood, and he had a wife, Elizabeth by name, who was a descendant of Aaron" (Lk 1.5). Presumably Luke makes Elizabeth a descendant of Aaron due to her husband's role as priest in the Temple, and Aaron's symbolic status as the Israelite priest par excellence. It is presumably not coincidental, then, that the Qur'ān calls Mary the "sister of Aaron" (Q 19.28) soon after it refers to her departure from the *miḥrāb* (Q 19.16), which might now be recognized as the sanctuary (or Holy of Holies) of the Temple, the same sanctuary where, according to Luke, Zechariah fulfilled his priestly office. In other words, the Qur'ān names Mary the "sister of Aaron" for the same reason that Luke names Elizabeth the descendent of Aaron: she is associated with the priestly office of Israel. That Mary was known as Elizabeth's cousin (Lk 1.36) may have led the Qur'ān to extend Aaron's association with Elizabeth to Mary as well.

Yet why does the Qur'ān also describe Mary as the daughter of 'Imrān, a figure who is not connected to the Temple? The answer to this question lies in the peculiar list with which the Qur'ān introduces the passage on Mary's nativity: "God has chosen Adam, Noah, the family of Abraham and the family of 'Imrān above all of the worlds, * descendents of one another. God is the hearing, the knowing" (Q 3.33–4). The peculiarity in this list is not the absence of Muḥammad, a name that appears only four times in the Qur'ān. Instead it is the absence of Moses and Jesus. Moses is the most frequently named character in the Qur'ān (136 times), and Jesus is (arguably) the most extraordinary (his birth and death are mysterious; he is the word and spirit of God, and so on). It seems unbelievable that the Qur'ān would fail to mention both of these figures in its list of those whom God has chosen above all others.

The reference to *āl 'Imrān* ("Family of 'Imrān;" whence the name of this Sūra) is also curious. Presumably the Qur'ān uses *āl Ibrāhīm* ("Family of Abraham") as a title which includes both Isaac and Ishmael, or both the Jews/Christians (who claim physical or spiritual descent from Isaac) and the

482 For example Q 3.103; 7.38, 73. See S. Mourad, "Mary in the Qur'ān: A reexamination of her presentation," *QHC*, 163–74.

483 Masson, *Le Coran et la révélation judéo-chrétienne*, 311. Masson (p. 314, n. 1) also argues that Christians assigned the name Anne (i.e. Hannah/Ḥannā) to the mother of Mary when they took the Hannah of 1 Samuel as the model for her biography, and contends that the Qur'ān could be doing something similar with Mary. This contention seems wayward, however, since there is no sign that the Qur'ān bases the story of Mary the mother of Jesus on the story of Mary the sister of Moses and Aaron.

Arabs (who were thought of as descendents of Ishmael). By this theory the Qur'ān may use the expression "family of" as a way of referring at once to protagonists who have some particular connection. *Āl 'Imrān* could accordingly refer to Amram's two sons Moses and Aaron. This view, however, would still leave Jesus unaccounted for. Indeed it is more likely, as Samir Khalil Samir argues,[484] that with the phrase *āl 'Imrān* the Qur'ān intends Moses and Jesus. Moses is the physical descendent of Amram, and the symbol of Jews. Jesus is Amram's spiritual descendent, the new Moses who brought a new covenant.[485] This would mean that the Qur'ān intentionally chose to combine Moses and Jesus rather than to list them separately. The Qur'ān's intent to identify Jesus with Moses may even be reflected in its unusual form of the name Jesus, 'Īsā, a form that seems to be shaped in order to provide assonance with the Qur'ān's name for Moses, Mūsā (cf. the other Qur'ānic name pairs: Iblīs/Idrīs, Ismā'īl/Isrā'īl, Hārūn/Qārūn, Hārūt/Mārūt, Yājūj/Mājūj, Ṭālūt/Jālūt).

In light of this identification it would be no surprise if the Qur'ān also chose to combine Moses' sister and Jesus' mother, both of whom are named Mary. The idea of Miriam as a type of Mary is detectable already in the Gospel of Luke. The *Magnificat*, Mary's song of joy with Elizabeth after the Annunciation (Lk 1.46–55), is reminiscent of Miriam's song of joy with the Israelite women after the splitting of the Sea (Ex 15.20–1). This is also a prominent topos with some Church fathers, among them the Syriac author Aphrahat.[486]

The idea of the Qur'ān joining two characters together into one will anyway not seem unbelievable to the reader after the study of the Qur'ān's presentation of Haman and Qorah (CS 6). Here as there, any dispute over the Qur'ān's historical accuracy begs the question of whether the Qur'ān is attempting to present history in the first place. The conflation of the two Marys, it seems, is not a historical confusion but rather a literary typology.[487]

Of course, and in this a distinction appears from the case of Haman and Qorah, it is a distinctly Christian typology. Hence the connection to the second doctrinal question, the elevation of Mary, appears. In this regard it

484 S.K. Samir, "The theological Christian influence on the Qur'ān: A reflection," *QHC*, 141–62.

485 Samir argues that the Qur'ān would then refer to five chosen figures (in chronological order): Adam, Noah, Abraham, Moses, and Jesus. This would match the traditional Christian doctrine (seen with Origen [d. ca. 254] and John Chrysostom [d. 407] among others) that humanity had five covenants, a doctrine sometimes illustrated with the parable of the workers who come in five shifts (Mt 20.1–15). Yet if the phrase *āl Ibrāhīm*, like *āl 'Imrān*, also refers to multiple figures (presumably Abraham, Isaac, and Ishmael) then the total number of chosen figures would be more than five. See Samir, "Theological Christian influence on the Qur'ān," 142–5.

486 On this see Henninger, *Spuren christlicher Glaubenswahrheiten im Koran*, 10.

487 Thus E. Gräf ("Zu den christlichen Einflüssen im Koran," 118), "Die Lösung der Rätsels liegt wohl darin, daß tatsächlich eine Gleichsetzung erfolgte, und zwar in der typologischen Auslegung des Alten Testaments, wie sie in der frühen Kirche gang und gäbe war."

should first be noted that the pericope involving Mary in *āl 'Imrān* is linked with the Annunciation to Mary (Q 3.45–49a) and thence with the life, miracles, and death of Jesus (Q 3.49b–59). The section on Mary thus appears above all as an introduction to the Qur'ān's discourse on Jesus. Hence it is not awkward but rather appropriate that the Qur'ān has references to the birth of John in the middle of that section (Q 3.38–41; cf. the similar juxtaposition of John and Mary in Q 19.2–23). Mary and John are the two figures who prepare the way for Jesus. Mary received the Word of God (see Q 3.45); John preached the Word of God (see Q 3.39).[488]

It is for this reason that the Qur'ān (Q 3.42) has the angels tell Mary that God has chosen her above all other women. It is not because of her virtue, nor because she is to conceive without knowing man, but rather because she is to be the mother of the Word of God (Q 3.45), who will create a bird from clay, as God created Adam, breathe into it and bring it to life (Q 3.49), who will heal the sick and raise the dead (Q 3.49), and whom God will raise to Himself (Q 3.55). The Qur'ān, in other words, is here alluding to the salutation of the angel Gabriel to Mary: "Rejoice, you who enjoy God's favour! The Lord is with you" (Lk 1.28).[489]

CS 10 "Our hearts are uncircumcised"

Qur'ānic account

Although the nativity of Mary is not among them, a number of the case studies above involve divine punishment (e.g. CS 2, 3, 6, 7). This is again the case with *al-nisā'* (4) 153–6, where the Qur'ān focuses on the transgressions of the Jews. In *al-nisā'* (4) 153 the Qur'ān mentions a request of the People of the Book that the Prophet bring them a "book" from heaven, likening it to an earlier demand that Moses show them God. Thus it appears that here the term "People of the Book" refers only to the Jews (in v. 160 they are referred to as *alladhīna hādū*). The Qur'ān hence moves into a longer

488 On John and the Qur'ān see esp. G. Basetti-Sani, *The Koran in the Light of Christ*, trans. W.R. Carroll and B. Dauphinee, Chicago: Franciscan Herald Press, 1977, 147, 154.

489 Cf. in this regard Q 3.36, where Mary's mother declares: "I commit her, and her offspring, to your protection from Satan the outcast" (Q 3.36). Here the Qur'ān seems to allude to the sinlessness of Mary and Jesus. The same doctrine is suggested by Q 21.91, which describes Mary and her son as "a sign for the worlds," and Q 23.50, which again describes them as a sign and adds an opaque reference to a special station the two have been given (*wa-āwaynāhumā ilā rabwatin dhāti qarārin wa-ma'īn*. Paret: "Und wir gewährten ihnen Aufnahme auf einem flachen Höhenzug (*rabwa*) mit (fruchtbarem) Grund (*qarār*) und Quellwasser." Arberry: "and gave them refuge upon a height, where was a hollow and a spring.").

To illustrate the prominence of this doctrine in the Eastern Church, Henninger quotes a prayer of Ephraem: "You and your mother are the *only people* who are blessed in every respect. You, O Lord, have no imperfection, and your mother has no blemish." Henninger, *Spuren christlicher Glaubenswahrheiten im Koran*, 10, n. 31. The citation can be found in Ephraem, *Hymni et Sermones*, ed. T. Lamy, Mechilinae: Dessain, 1886, 2:327.

discussion of Jewish transgressions. This serves ultimately to explain why God forbade them things previously permitted (v. 160), and why He has prepared a punishment for the unbelievers among them (v. 161). At the heart of the discussion is verse 155, wherein the Qur'ān lists in summary fashion the primary faults of the Jews:

> Thus for their violation of the covenant,
> and for their unbelief in the signs of God,
> and for their murder of the prophets,
> and for their statement, "Our hearts are *ghulf*,"
> <u>in fact</u> God has sealed [their hearts] with their unbelief,
> so that only a few of them believe.

4.155 فَبِمَا نَقْضِهِم مِّيثَاقَهُمْ وَكُفْرِهِم بَآيَاتِ اللّهِ وَقَتْلِهِمُ الأَنْبِيَاء بِغَيْرِ حَقًّ وَقَوْلِهِمْ قُلُوبُنَا
غُلْفٌ بَلْ طَبَعَ اللّهُ عَلَيْهَا بِكُفْرِهِمْ فَلاَ يُؤْمِنُونَ إِلاَّ قَلِيلاً

The primary focus of the present case study is the statement "Our hearts are *ghulf*," one of three statements that the Qur'ān attributes to the Jews in the larger pericope. In verse 156 the Qur'ān refers to "their statement" (*qawl*) against Mary (presumably an accusation of fornication), which it calls, "A terrible slander."[490] In verse 157 the Qur'ān cites (and then refutes) their statement: "We killed Christ Jesus the son of Mary." While these latter two statements are linked by syntax and by the theme of calumny, the statement "Our hearts are *ghulf*" is separate. It is instead a pretext to the conclusion of verse 155: "<u>in fact</u> God has sealed [their hearts] with their disbelief, so that only a few of them believe."

This statement appears also in a second passage, *al-baqara* (2) 87–8:

> (2.87) We brought the book to Moses and We arranged messengers after him. We brought clear signs to Jesus the son of Mary and We supported him with the Holy Spirit. Whenever a messenger delivered something you did not desire you became disdainful. You denied some of them and killed some of them.
>
> (88) They said "Our hearts are *ghulf*." <u>In fact</u>, God has cursed them with their unbelief and few of them believe.

2.87 وَلَقَدْ آتَيْنَا مُوسَى الْكِتَابَ وَقَفَّيْنَا مِن بَعْدِهِ بِالرُّسُلِ وَآتَيْنَا عِيسَى ابْنَ مَرْيَمَ الْبَيِّنَاتِ
وَأَيَّدْنَاهُ بِرُوحِ الْقُدُسِ أَفَكُلَّمَا جَاءكُمْ رَسُولٌ بِمَا لاَ تَهْوَى أَنفُسُكُمُ اسْتَكْبَرْتُمْ ، فَفَرِيقًا كَذَّبْتُمْ
وَفَرِيقًا تَقْتُلُونَ

2.88 وَقَالُواْ قُلُوبُنَا غُلْفٌ بَل لَّعَنَهُمُ اللَّه بِكُفْرِهِمْ فَقَلِيلاً مَّا يُؤْمِنُونَ

490 *Buhtān* connected to Syriac *bhūttānā*, not to the Arabic root *b.h.t.* (which is related to "confusion"). See *TS*, 37; *FV*, 84.

In both *al-nisā'* and *al-baqara* the statement "Our hearts are *ghulf*" is preceded by an indictment of the Jews' rejection, or killing, of messengers. In both cases it is followed by an affirmation of God's retributive punishment. According to *al-nisā'* (4) 155, He sealed the Jews' hearts with their unbelief. According to *al-baqara* (2) 88, He cursed their hearts with their unbelief.

In both cases, moreover, the "hearts" statement is linked to this affirmation by the particle *bal*, which I translate above, "in fact." This translation is intentionally ambiguous, since *bal* can be read in a number of different ways depending on how one imagines the statement "Our hearts are *ghulf*." If the Qur'ān intends that this was the Jews' pretense to the divine messengers whom they rejected (i.e. that a *ghulf* heart is a good thing), then *bal* presumably should mean "on the contrary" (i.e. the Jews' hearts are *not ghulf*). If the Qur'ān intends instead that this was the Jews' confession and explanation of their sin (i.e. that a *ghulf* heart is a bad thing), then *bal* would mean "indeed" (i.e. the Jews' hearts *are ghulf* and God therefore sealed or cursed them).

Finally, it should also be noted that the larger syntax of *al-nisā'* (4) 155 is parallel to the opening of *al-mā'ida* (5) 13: "For the violation of their covenant (*bimā naqḍihim mithāqahum*), we cursed them and made their hearts hard (*la'annāhum wa-ja'alnā qulūbahum qāsiyyatan*; cf. Q 2.74; 6.43; 22.53; passim)." Thus it becomes clear that the verse at hand is part of a larger Qur'ānic trope in which the Jews' violation of their covenant (i.e. their rejection of God) and their rejection of the messengers is associated with the condition of their hearts.

Problems for interpreters

Most of the translators see *ghulf* as an adjective meaning something like "sealed" or "covered." Paret translates the phrase *qulūbunā ghulfun* in *al-nisā'* (4) 155 with a prepositional phrase: "Unser Herz ist hinter einem Schleier." Fakhry translates, "Our hearts are sealed" (and thereby implies that this phrase simply anticipates the end of the verse: "God has sealed [*ṭaba'a*] them with their unbelief"). Abdel Haleem translates *ghulf* as an adjective, although in an idiomatic fashion: "Our minds are closed."[491] Pickthall likewise sees *ghulf* as an adjective but the meaning he assigns to it is notably different. He translates *qulūbunā ghulfun* as "Our hearts are hardened," apparently in light of *al-mā'ida* (5) 13 ("We made their hearts hard [*qāsiyyatan*]").

Yusuf Ali, for his part, translates, "Our hearts are the wrappings (which preserve God's Word; We need no more)." By his view *ghulf* is a plural noun for some sort of covers or containers, which, according to Yusuf Ali's parenthetical note, encompass God's word.

491 He adds in a footnote (p. 65, n. b): "Literally 'our hearts are covered,' or 'encased.'"

Finally, two translators have a distinctly different approach to the phrase *qulūbunā ghulfun* in *al-nisā'* (4) 155. Arberry translates, "Our hearts are uncircumcised." Blachère's translation is similar: "Nos cœurs sont incirconcis!" In other words, both Arberry and Blachère see the statement *qulūbunā ghulfun* as a metaphor, a well-known Biblical metaphor no less. This same view is apparent in Paret's translation of the phrase as it appears in *al-baqara* (2) 88: "Unser Herz ist (eben) unbeschnitten." However, in *al-nisā'* (4) 155 Paret translates *ghulf* in line with the popular view that it is an adjective meaning "sealed" or "covered."

This latter translation reflects the view of *Tafsīr Muqātil*. According to *Tafsīr Muqātil*, the Jews spoke the words "Our hearts are *ghulf*" to Muḥammad as a way of saying: "Our hearts have shelters and wrappings on them. They do not comprehend or understand what you say, O Muḥammad."[492]

With Ṭabarī it becomes apparent that this question was not so straightforward for most commentators. Some of the scholars, he relates, argue that *ghulf* is the plural of the adjective *aghlaf*, on the model of *aḥmar/ḥumr*.[493] Ṭabarī relates no less than twelve traditions in support of this opinion, and declares his own preference for it. Yet he also cites a second opinion (that reflected in Yusuf Ali's translation), namely that *ghulf* should actually be read *ghuluf*,[494] a noun (plural of *ghilāf*, on the pattern of *kitāb/kutub*) meaning "containers."[495] A tradition in support of this opinion explains that with this term the Jews were boasting to the Prophet that their hearts were already filled with knowledge. It was their way of saying, "They do not need you, Muḥammad."[496]

Zamakhsharī follows the first opinion mentioned by Ṭabarī, identifying *ghulf* as an adjective and the plural of *aghlaf*. Yet in Zamakhsharī's commentary it becomes clear that the use of *ghulf* to modify "heart" is unusual, for he provides a rather detailed explanation of what it might mean:

> In other words [the heart] is a character (*khilqa*) or disposition (*jibla*) that is wrapped in a cover. That which Muḥammad – God's blessing and peace be upon him – brought does not reach it and it does not comprehend him. [*Ghulf*] comes from *al-aghlaf*, which means one who

492 *Tafsīr Muqātil*, 1:419, on Q 4.155.

493 In support of this opinion Ṭabarī compares *ghulf* to plural *nouns* that mean "covers," such as *aghṭiya*, *akinna* (cf. Q 41.5), or *ghishāwa*. According to Ṭabarī, the Jews were thereby saying to Muḥammad, "There are veils and covers [between us] and that to which you are calling us. We do not comprehend what you say and we do not understand it." Ṭabarī, 6:10, on Q 4.155.

494 On this cf. *MQQ*, 2:178.

495 Ṭabarī compares *ghuluf* to *aw'iyya*. Ṭabarī, 1:408, on Q 2.88.

496 Ṭabarī, 1:408, on Q 2.88. Ṭabarī cites three other traditions in favor of this view.

is not circumcised. This is like their statement: "Our hearts are in shelters from that to which you call us" [Q 41.5].[497]

Zamakhsharī here makes a remarkable philological insight, that the Qur'ān is using *ghulf*, a word that properly means "uncircumcised," in a metaphorical sense. This is, of course, the key to understanding this term, yet without access to the Qur'ānic subtext Zamakhsharī is not able to see what sort of metaphor the Qur'ān is using. Thus he passes over this point and instead relies on a comparison between "Our hearts are *ghulf*" and the phrase in *fuṣṣilat* (41) 5 "Our hearts are in shelters (*qulūbunā fī akinna*)." This comparison, however, is not exact. *Akinna* is a plural noun, while *ghulf*, by his reading, is an adjective.

Like Ṭabarī, Ibn Kathīr notes two opposing views on this word.[498] He begins with the familiar view that *ghulf* is an adjective and the plural of *aghlaf*.[499] Ibn Kathīr then turns to Ṭabarī's second view (which he attributes in one place to Ibn 'Abbās and in another place to Zamakhsharī), that the word should be read *ghuluf* and understood as the plural of *ghilāf*, that is, "containers."[500] He explains this view with a tradition that the Jews believed they needed no knowledge other than the Tawrāt.[501]

Finally, Ibn Kathīr also mentions a single tradition (attributed to al-Ḥasan b. 'Alī b. Abī Ṭālib), that *ghulf* means "uncircumcised." The statement "our hearts are *ghulf*" would then be a metaphor with which the Jews acknowledged the impurity in their hearts. Yet Ibn Kathīr follows instead the opinion of *Tafsīr Muqātil*, Ṭabarī, and Zamakhsharī, that *ghulf* is an adjective meaning "sealed," and that the Jews' statement is an explanation they offered for not listening to Muḥammad. Ibn Kathīr comments: "The matter is not as they claim. Rather, their hearts are cursed and sealed."[502]

497 Zamakhsharī, 1:163–4, on Q 2.87–9. Zamakhsharī, however, also detects a particular theological conviction in the statement *qulūbunā ghulfun*. The Jews were arguing thereby, he insists, that God *created* their hearts in this condition. He compares their argument, on one hand, to the polytheists who credit their worship of female angels to the divine will (quoting Q 43.20: "If the Merciful had willed otherwise we would not have worshipped them") and on the other hand to his theological opponents on the question of free will, whom he labels the Mujbira ("believers in divine compulsion"). He adds for good measure, "May God humiliate them." Ibid., 1:586, on Q 4.153–9.

498 Like his predecessors Ibn Kathīr includes (on the authority of Ibn 'Abbās) the tradition that "our hearts are *ghulf*" means that they "do not comprehend." Ibn Kathīr, 1:122, on Q 2.88. A similar tradition, attributed to Ibn 'Abbās' slave 'Ikrima, follows.

499 To this view Ibn Kathīr adds a tradition (attributed to Ḥudhayfa) with the explanation: "The *aghlaf* heart has anger upon it. This is the heart of the unbeliever." Ibn Kathīr, 1:133, on Q 2.88.

500 Ibn Kathīr, 1:122, on Q 2.88.

501 In regard to this latter view Ibn Kathīr makes a comparison between *ghuluf* and the term *akinna* of *fuṣṣilat* (41) 5, which both Ṭabarī and Zamakhsharī connect instead to the view that this term is an adjective. While Ibn Kathīr's choice makes some grammatical sense (both *ghuluf* and *akinna* are plural nouns), it does not make logical sense, since *fuṣṣilat* (41) 5 does not have the Jews claim that their hearts *are akinna* but only that they are *in akinna*.

502 Ibn Kathīr, 1:122, on Q 2.88.

Subtext

The confusion of the *mufassirūn* over the term *ghulf* is a product of the Qur'ān's allusive style, on the one hand, and the gap between Qur'ān and *tafsīr*, on the other. That the Qur'ān makes no effort to explain the metaphor of uncircumcised (*ghulf*) hearts implies that at the time of the Qur'ān's composition/proclamation it was well known. That this metaphor was so mysterious to the *mufassirūn*, on the other hand, shows how much had been forgotten. This point has been made in previous case studies. Here, however, it is even more evident.

Ghulf, after all, is a clear Arabic term, the plural of the well-attested singular adjective *aghlāf*, "uncircumcised."[503] If it is grammatically abnormal to use a plural (and not singular feminine) adjective with a non-human (or *ghayr ʿāqil*) noun,[504] this could not have been a consideration for the *mufassirūn*, who are willing to consider that *ghulf* is a plural adjective meaning "sealed." Indeed the tradition cited by Ibn Kathīr implies that they were aware of the possibility that it means instead "uncircumcised." However they still rejected it, presumably because, being unaware of the metaphor, they found the idea of an uncircumcised heart nonsensical. Modern translators, on the other hand, have no such excuse. Thus it is amazing to see all of them (except Blachère, Arberry, and Paret in one case) follow the *mufassirūn* and ignore the metaphor.[505]

Indeed circumcision of the heart is a trope found often in the Bible to describe obedience to, and love of, God. When Moses urges the Israelites to live piously once they cross the Jordan River, he tells them, "Circumcise your heart then and be obstinate no longer" (Deuteronomy 10.16). Elsewhere Moses explains that God will perform this task for them, "Yahweh your God will circumcise your heart and the heart of your descendants, so that you will love Yahweh your God with all your heart and soul, and so will live" (Deuteronomy 30.6). The prophet Jeremiah, meanwhile, uses the same

503 On *ghulf* as a plural of *aghlaf*, see Lane, *AEL*, 6:2283. The phonologically related form *aqlaf* is also attested (Lane, *AEL*, 8:2292c). This couplet matches that in Syriac. *Qlap* is "to circumcise" and *qlāpā* (cf. Gk κέλυφος) can refer to various wrappings, including tree bark, egg shell, bean shell, fish scales, and the foreskin (see *TS*, 3639). Parallel meanings are found for the root *g.l.f.* (*TS*, 732). Presumably this latter root corresponds with Arabic *gh.l.f* (and Hebrew *ʿ.l.f.*; Cf. F. Brown, *The New Brown-Driver-Briggs-Genesius Hebrew and English Lexicon*, Peabody, MA: Hendrickson, 1979, 763a). Note, however, that the basic Syriac root for circumcision is *g.z.r.* (*TS*, 700), as seen in the Psh. (e.g. Acts 7.51, Romans 2.29).

504 Notice the feminine singular *qāsiyya* used to modify *qulūb* in Q 5.13; 22.53. However, in Q 59.14 *qulūb* is modified with the plural adjective *shattā*. On the classical rule of adjectival agreement see W. Wright, *A Grammar of the Arabic Language*, 3rd edition revised by W.R. Smith and M.J. de Goeje, London: Cambridge University Press, 1898, 1:195C.

The Qur'ān has examples (e.g. Q 2.80; 3.7) of plural feminine adjectives modifying feminine plural non-human nouns, but such cases are more acceptable to later grammarians.

505 Basetti-Sani (*Koran in the Light of Christ*, 157), who argues that Q 2.87–91 is a paradigmatic passage of the Qur'ān's condemnation of Jewish opposition to Jesus, identifies the Biblical metaphor of the uncircumcised heart in Q 2.88. Likewise J. MacAuliffe, "Heart," *EQ*, 408a.

trope in his prophetic exhortations: "Circumcise yourselves for Yahweh, apply circumcision to your hearts, men of Judah and inhabitants of Jerusalem" (Jeremiah 4.4).[506]

The prophets also use the trope of the circumcision of the heart in condemnation. When Ezekiel chastises the Israelites for letting gentiles enter the Temple, he proclaims: "The Lord Yahweh says this: 'You have gone beyond all bounds with all your loathsome practices, House of Israel, by admitting aliens, uncircumcised in heart and body, to frequent my sanctuary and profane my temple'" (Ezekiel 44.6b–7; cf. v. 9). Jeremiah includes Israel itself among the nations with uncircumcised hearts:

> Look, the days are coming, Yahweh declares, when I shall punish all who are circumcised only in the flesh: Egypt, Judah, Edom, the Ammonites, Moab, and all the men with shaven temples who live in the desert. For all those nations, and the whole House of Israel too, are uncircumcised at heart.
>
> (Jeremiah 9.24–5)

So the uncircumcised heart is an accusation directed at Israel itself. In this light it is understandable why the Qur'ān does not simply proclaim that the Jews have uncircumcised hearts. It makes this the proclamation of the Jews themselves (*qawlihim qulūbunā ghulfun*). Again, with the killing of Jesus the Qur'ān turns a Biblical accusation (cf. Acts 3.14; 4.10; 7.52) into a proclamation of the Jews (Q 4.157).

The Qur'ān's interest in this trope becomes more evident still in the light of the New Testament.[507] Paul, for example, repeatedly uses the image of the circumcised heart in his exhortations. In Romans he comments:

> Being a Jew is not only having the outward appearance of a Jew, and circumcision is not only a visible physical operation. * The real Jew is the one who is inwardly a Jew, and real circumcision is in the heart, a thing not of the letter but of the spirit. He may not be praised by any human being, but he will be praised by God.
>
> (Romans 2.28–9; cf. Philippians 3.3)

506 Cf. Jeremiah 6.10.

507 The same trope is continued in midrashic literature. *Genesis Rabba* (46.5) explains that there are four types of foreskin. In addition to the bodily foreskin there are the metaphorical foreskins of the "ear, mouth and heart." Trans. Freedman et al., 1:392. *Pirqē de-Rabbī Elī'ezer* has a similar explanation: "There are five kinds of foreskin in the world. Four relate to men and one to trees. Those that relate to men are: the foreskin of the ear [cf. Jeremiah 6.10], the foreskin of the lips [cf. Ex 6.12], the foreskin of the heart [cf. Deuteronomy 10.16], and the foreskin of the flesh" (29; ed. Börner-Klein, 317). Thereafter *Pirqē de-Rabbī Elī'ezer* clarifies, "The foreskin of the heart keeps [Israel] from doing the will of his creator" (ed. Börner-Klein, 319).

Elsewhere Paul develops the metaphor still further: "In him you have been circumcised, with a circumcision performed, not by human hand, but by the complete stripping of your natural self. This is circumcision according to Christ" (Colossians 2.11).

In these passages circumcision of the heart is an important image by which Christians illustrated their doctrine on the Law. The Qur'ān for its part uses this image not for its teaching on the Law, but for its anti-Jewish polemic.[508] Thus the appearance of the same image in an anti-Jewish passage of the *Acts of the Apostles* is of particular consequence. In Acts 7 Luke has the martyr Stephen condemn the Jews in a long speech before the Sanhedrin. At the climax of this speech Stephen proclaims:

> You stubborn people, *with uncircumcised hearts and ears*. You are always resisting the Holy Spirit, just as your ancestors used to do. * Can you name a single prophet your ancestors never persecuted? They killed those who foretold the coming of the Upright One, and now you have become his betrayers, his murderers. * In spite of being given the Law through angels, you have not kept it.
>
> (Acts 7.51–3)

The correlation between this passage and that of *al-nisā'* (4) 155–7 is significant. Stephen accuses the Jews of being uncircumcised in heart and ears (v. 71); the Qur'ān accuses them of the statement that they are uncircumcised in heart (4.155). Stephen accuses the Jews of opposing the Holy Spirit (v. 71); the Qur'ān accuses them of disbelief in the signs of God (4.155, 6). Stephen accuses the Jews of killing the prophets (v. 72; on which cf. Mt 23.31); the Qur'ān accuses them of killing the prophets (4.155). Stephen accuses the Jews of betraying and killing Christ (v. 72); the Qur'ān accuses them of claiming to have killed Christ (4.157). Stephen accuses the Jews of breaking the law (v. 73); the Qur'ān accuses them of breaking their covenant (4.155).[509]

Of course the Qur'ān does not simply reproduce Acts. Whereas Luke has Stephen proclaim that the Jews are uncircumcised in heart *and* ears, the Qur'ān (Q 2.88, 4.155) speaks only of their uncircumcised hearts. This fact should now come as no surprise, since it has repeatedly been shown that the Qur'ān's relationship to Biblical literature is characterized not by imitation but rather by allusion and homiletic.[510]

508 On this point Geiger comments (*Was hat Mohammed*, 195) that Muḥammad "wollte er eine Entfernung von diesen hassenswerten Menschen recht fest machen und so seine Moslemen durch völlig entgegengesetzte Gebräuche von ihnen trennen."

509 Notice also the parallels between Acts 7.41–2 and Q 4.153.

510 A similar phenomenon is seen with the metaphor of a hard heart. In *al-mā'ida* (5) 13a the Qur'ān, speaking of the Jews, proclaims: "For the violation of their covenant (*bimā naqḍihim mithāqahum*), we cursed them and made their hearts hard (*la'annāhum wa-ja'alnā qulūbahum qāsiyyatan*)." This reflects an idiom in Ezekiel, who complains that "All of the house of Israel have a stiff forehead and a hard (*qeshē*) heart" (Ezekiel 3.7; my translation).

In this light the homiletic use of this same trope by Aphrahat is worth noting. In his *Homily on Circumcision* Aphrahat is almost completely occupied with his argument that the Jews are uncircumcised in heart. Quoting Moses' address to the Israelites in Deuteronomy 10.16, Aphrahat comments, "So it is known that whoever does not circumcise the foreskin of his heart, then also the circumcision of his flesh is of no value to him."[511] Ephraem likewise repeats the accusation that the Jews are uncircumcised in heart. Speaking to God in his *Homily on Our Lord* he remarks, "Then you conferred your sign, circumcision of the heart, by which the circumcised were recognized as not being yours."[512] John Chrysostom (d. 407) uses the trope of the uncircumcised heart to describe the spiritual malaise of the Jews in Christ's time, and thus to warn his Christian audience.[513]

The Syriac author Isaac of Antioch (d. late 5th century), in his *Homily against the Jews*, describes the nature of his own circumcision:

> I am circumcised, not on (the) flesh
> But rather (with) circumcision which is not (done) with hands.
> Not with the removal of flesh but,
> in the Spirit, by a removal that (removes) from evil.[514]

In his *Epistula de hymno trisagio* John of Damascus (d. 749) addresses circumcision of the heart when he paraphrases Stephen's speech in Acts 7. Tellingly, John has Stephen accuse the Jews of being "uncircumcised in heart (ἀπερίτμητοι τῇ καρδιᾳ)" but like the Qur'ān he omits the end of the phrase, "and of ears (καί τοῖς ὠσίν)" as it appears in Acts 7.[515] This is understandable, since John's point is not to provide a precise quotation of the Bible, but rather to use a Biblical image that would resonate with his audience and contribute to his homily. Precisely the same might now be concluded about the Qur'ān.

511 Aphrahat, *Homily 11 (On Circumcision)*, para. 5, trans.: Neusner, *Aphrahat and Judaism*, 23; Syriac text: Wright, *Homilies of Aphraates*, 207. On this cf. A.L. Williams, *Adversus Judaeos*, Cambridge: Cambridge University Press, 1935, 96.

512 *Homily on Our Lord*, 7. Trans. in C. Shepardson, *Anti-Judaism and Christian Orthodoxy: Ephrem's Hymns in Fourth-Century Syria,* Washington, DC: Catholic University of America Press, 2008, 103. Cf. Ephraem, *Hymns on the Nativity*, 26:11 (trans. Shepardson, 102).

513 See John Chrysostom, *Adversus Judaeos, PG* 48, ed. J.-P. Migne, Paris: Migne, 1862, (843–942) 845; *Contra Judaeos, gentiles et haereticos, PG* 48, ed. J.-P. Migne, Paris: Migne, 1862, (1075–80) 1079. Before Chrysostom this trope is found with Origen, who writes: "If there is anyone who burns with obscene desires and shameful passions and, to speak briefly, who 'commits adultery in his heart' [Mt. 5.28] this man is 'uncircumcised in heart.' But he also is 'uncircumcised in heart' who holds heretical views in his mind and arranges blasphemous assertions against knowledge of Christ in his heart." Origen, *Homilies on Genesis and Exodus*, 98.

514 S. Kazan, "Isaac of Antioch's homily against the Jews [part 1]," *Oriens Christianus* 45, 1961, (30–78) 47, ll. 355–8.

515 John of Damascus, *Epistula de hymno trisagio*, *PG* 95, ed. J.-P. Migne, Paris: Migne, 1864, (22–62) 23.15.

CS 11 "Do not think those who were killed in the path of God dead"

Qur'ānic account

If the previous case study is focused on a group whom God punishes, the present case study is focused on a group whom God rewards. In *al-nisā'* (4) 74 the Qur'ān relates: "Let those who would sell the life of this world for the next world fight in the path of God. To him who fights in the path of God and is killed or overcome [*yughlab*; pace standard *yaghlib*] will we give a great reward." This reward is again the subject of *āl 'Imrān* (3) 157, where the Qur'ān asks: "And if you are killed or die in the path of God? The forgiveness and mercy of God is better than that which they might gather."

Thus the Qur'ān suggests that martyrs of the holy war will have their sins forgiven.[516] This suggestion is made explicit later in the same Sūra, when the divine voice of the Qur'ān announces, "As for those who fight and are killed, I will absolve them of their faults, and bring them into a garden under which rivers flow, a reward from God" (Q 3.195). In *al-tawba* the Qur'ān again relates that the reward of martyrdom is entrance into the heavenly garden: "God has purchased from the believers their selves and their possessions and the garden is theirs" (Q 9.111; cf. Q 47.4–6). The language here is mercantile: God has bought the martyrs' lives, offering them admission into paradise in return. But this verse seems to complement, not contradict, *āl 'Imrān* (3) 157 and 195. The sacrifice of martyrs wins them expiation of sins, which allows them to enter into the garden.

In this the martyrs are set apart from other believers. They will not be subject to the Day of Judgment, when human acts will be weighed on the divine scale and human destiny determined (Q. 7.8–9; 23.102–3; 101.6–9). They do not, in other words, wait for the resurrection to enter into the garden. They already enjoy their reward:

> (3.169) Do not think those who were killed in the path of God dead. They are alive and receive sustenance with their Lord.[517]

3.169 وَلاَ تَحْسَبَنَّ الَّذِينَ قُتِلُواْ فِي سَبِيلِ اللّهِ أَمْوَاتًا بَلْ أَحْيَاء عِندَ رَبِّهِمْ يُرْزَقُونَ

516 The standard Arabic term for martyr, *shahīd* (lit. "witness"; a calque on Greek μάρτυρ presumably through Syr. *sāhdā*, the term used to translate μάρτυρ in the Psh.; see *FV*, 187), does not appear in the above verses. When *shahīd* appears in the Qur'ān (e.g. 3.140; 4.69; 39.69; 52.19) it is not clear whether it carries the meaning of "martyr." In certain cases (2.282; 24.4) it can only have the primary meaning of "witness." Goldziher therefore suggests that *shahīd* only gained the secondary meaning of "martyr" in post-Qur'ānic literature, due to Syriac Christian influence. See *Muhammedanische Studien*, 2:350–1, cited by E. Kohlberg, "Shahīd," *EI*^{2}, 9:204a. W. Raven ("Martyr," *EQ*, 3:282a) repeats this statement – and Kohlberg's references.

517 Similarly, the Qur'ān elsewhere proclaims, "Do not say that those killed in the path of God are dead, but rather alive, even if you do not sense (it)" (Q 2.154).

The importance of this proclamation emerges in light of the eschatological descriptions elsewhere in the text. For the Qur'ān generally insists that those who die will only live again on the Day of Judgment, when soul and body will be reunited. According to the sequence presented in *qāf* (50), angels record the merits and faults of humans during their life (vv. 16–8), humans die (v. 19), the trumpet of the Day of Judgment is sounded (v. 20), and the dead come forth (v. 21) to be judged and rewarded or punished (v. 22–35). In other words, nothing will happen between death (v. 19) and the Day of Judgment (v. 20). There is, apparently, no individual judgment at death, and no immediate retribution.

This doctrine is also reflected in the Qur'ān's presentation of the Companions of the Cave narrative (Q 18.9–26; cf. CS 12). The youths are said to be asleep in the cave (Q 18.18), yet the Qur'ān strongly suggests (see e.g. Q 18.11–2, 21) that in fact they are dead. The entire episode points to God seizing souls at the body's death, then reuniting soul and body on the Day of Judgment, that is, to the resurrection of the body. It is therefore meaningful that the youths, after "waking up," have no memory of what happened during their "sleep" (indeed they think they have slept for a day [Q 18.19] but they have slept for 309 years [Q 18.25]). This suggests that humans will have no experience between the death of the body and its resurrection (cf. the similar account of the man and his donkey, Q 2.259; and the similar passage set on the Day of Resurrection, Q 23.111–4).

On the other hand, in *al-mu'minūn* (23), the Qur'ān portrays those who have died in sin pleading to return to life in order to make amends (v. 99). This is impossible, the Qur'ān insists, since there is a boundary (*barzakh*) between the living and the dead that will be removed only at the Day of Judgment (v. 100).[518] This passage might be taken as evidence of an existence after death but before the Day of Judgment. Yet the language here is strongly homiletic, the point being that humans must not postpone their repentance, and the following section (vv. 101–6) makes it clear that judgment and retribution come only on that Day.

The privilege of the martyr in this regard can also be deduced from the parable in *yā' sīn* (36) 13–36, according to which three messengers are sent to a city (vv. 13–5). Its residents threaten to stone them (v. 18), but one righteous citizen comes to their defense (vv. 20–5). Suddenly (v. 26) this citizen is told to enter the garden. Apparently, he has died and won a heavenly reward. At this he asks that his people might be informed of his blessed state (vv. 26–7). This parable indeed suggests immediate retribution. Yet there is a strong implication here that the righteous citizen has been killed by the iniquitous residents of his city, and thus has become a martyr.[519] Indeed it

518 *Barzakh* comes from the Pahlavi *frasang*, through Aramaic *farsā* and Syriac *farshā* (cf. also Gk παρασάγγης), meaning "boundary." Elsewhere (Q 25.53; 55.20) the Qur'ān uses *barzakh* to refer to the boundary between two seas. See *FV*, 77.

519 Rudolph comments on this passage: "Dagegen ist es einzelnen Bevorzugten vergönnt, sofort nach dem Tod in die Seligkeit zu gehen" (*Abhängigkeit*, 31).

would seem to support, not contradict, the Qur'ānic verses on martyrdom introduced above, and thus the conclusion of T. Andrae: "Les martyrs forment dans le Coran l'unique exception au sort attribué aux morts."[520]

Problems for interpreters

The martyr's privilege

On the martyrs' heavenly rewards *Tafsīr Muqātil* provides only some explanatory details, exhibiting no concern for the doctrinal issues raised by those passages.[521] Qummī explains that the martyrs who enjoy a heavenly reward are the members of the family of the Prophet, and those believers who have obeyed them (i.e. the Shī'a), who have been unjustly killed. Thus regarding those who are alive with God (Q 3.169) Qummī comments, "They are, by God, our party (*shī'atunā*). They entered heaven and received honor from God and were given good tidings [cf. Q 57.12] of their brother believers in this world who did not yet join them."[522]

There is none of this, of course, with Ṭabarī, who is concerned instead with elaborating the doctrine of immediate retribution. In his commentary on *al-baqara* (2) 154 Ṭabarī explains that the martyrs are alive because they have been spared *barzakh*. If in the Qur'ān (e.g. Q 23.100) the term *barzakh* means "boundary," with exegetes like Ṭabarī it means instead the period of time between the death of the body and its reunion with the soul on the Day of Resurrection. This period is usually thought to be accompanied by an inquisition and punishment in the tomb.[523] According to Ṭabarī verses such as *al-baqara* (2) 154 indicate the martyrs are entirely exempt from this.[524] Such verses, Ṭabarī insists elsewhere, are meant to incite believers to fight the *jihād* against unbelievers, and to humiliate the hypocrites who are unwilling to join this fight.[525]

520 *OIC*, 167.

521 Thus *Tafsīr Muqātil* relates (1:314, on Q 3.169) that *āl 'Imrān* (3) 169 was revealed when Muslim martyrs, having arrived in heaven, requested that God comfort their fellow believers about their fate, and thereby encourage them to fight the *jihād*. They also made a second request, which could not be granted: "Our Lord, we wish that You return our spirits to our bodies that we might fight in your way another time." On Q 2.154 *Tafsīr Muqātil* relates (1:150) only that this verse was revealed about the Muslims who died at the battle of Badr.

522 Qummī, 1:134, on Q 3.169.

523 Ṭabarī, 2:39, on Q 2.154. On *barzakh* Ṭabarī cites Q 3.169.

524 Hence his paraphrase of *al-baqara* (2) 154: "The one among my creation who is dead is the one whose life deprived him and his sensations destroyed him . . . but the one among you who has been killed . . . is alive with me in life, grace, and a lovely existence." Ṭabarī, 2:38, on Q 2.154.

525 Ṭabarī, 5:167, on Q 4.74. On this verse note the variant reading *yaqtul* (for *yuqtal*), which would mean that God promises a reward not to those who are killed, but to those who kill. See *MQQ*, 2:146. In his commentary on *āl 'Imrān* (3) 169 Ṭabarī records a debate over which martyrs the Qur'ān has in mind here, those of the battle of Badr or those of Uḥud. Ṭabarī, 4:170, on Q 3.169–70.

If Zamakhsharī shows no particular interest in this question,[526] Ibn Kathīr agrees with Ṭabarī that martyrs will enter heaven immediately after death. To this effect he reports a number of anecdotal *ḥadīth* surrounding the martyrdom at Uḥud of the father of Muḥammad's companion Jābir b. 'Abdallāh al-Anṣārī. In one such *ḥadīth* the Prophet consoles Jābir by saying: "Have I not informed you that God only speaks to people from behind a veil? But now He speaks to your father face to face."[527]

Ibn Kathīr also cites a prophetic *ḥadīth* in which Muḥammad explains that *āl 'Imrān* (3) 169 was revealed when the martyrs in paradise asked that their companions on earth be told of their pleasant existence, so that they would not shirk from fighting the *jihād* and seeking martyrdom themselves. God revealed this verse in fulfillment of their wish.[528]

On the souls of the martyrs in heaven

A second exegetical dispute, however, emerged from the reference in *āl 'Imrān* (3) 169 to martyrs receiving "sustenance (*rizq*) with their Lord." The mention of sustenance, apparently food (cf. CS 9), suggests that the martyrs exist with both a soul and a body in heaven. Hence a problem is raised for the *mufassirūn*, inasmuch as the bodies of the martyrs are known to lie in tombs on earth.

In one place *Tafsīr Muqātil* insists that the martyrs exist in heaven as souls (*arwāḥ*) residing in the lotus tree of the highest heaven (*sidrat al-muntahā*;

526 Regarding *āl 'Imrān* (3) 169 Zamakhsharī concludes simply that God honors martyrs over other believers. Zamakhsharī, 1:469, on Q 3.169–71.

527 Ibn Kathīr, 1:408, on Q 3.169–75. In a second *ḥadīth* Jābir relates how the Prophet saw him weeping at his father's funeral and told him: "Do not cry, for the angels will shade him with their wings until he is raised up." Ibid.

Ibn Kathīr also mentions here the opinion of Anas b. Mālik, that *āl 'Imrān* (3) 169 once consisted of a statement of the martyrs: "Inform our people that we have found our Lord. He is pleased with us and we are pleased with him." After a long time, however, this verse was abrogated and replaced with the words that are now read ("Do not think those who were killed in the path of God dead. They are alive and receive sustenance with their Lord."). Ibid., 1:407, on Q 3.169–75.

528 Ibid. Elsewhere Ibn Kathīr has the Prophet explain that the reward of the martyrs in heaven is so bountiful that the only thing they will still want is the chance to fight and die again: "Your Lord will look at them and ask, 'What do you desire?' They will reply, 'O our Lord, what could we desire? You have given us that which You have not given to anything else of your creation.' Then He will return to them with the same question. When they understand that they will continue to be asked they will say, 'We wish that You would send us back into the realm of the world that we might fight in Your path and be killed another time.' This will be after they have seen the reward of martyrdom. The Lord (Mighty and Powerful) will say, 'I have decreed that they will not return.'" Ibn Kathīr, 1:191, on Q 2.153–4. Similarly Ibn Kathīr elsewhere (1:407, on Q 3.169–75) has the Prophet declare: "Of those who die and receive God's bounty, no one but the martyr will desire to return to this world. He will desire to return to this world and be killed another time when he sees the merit of martyrdom."

cf. Q 43.14).[529] Elsewhere, however, *Tafsīr Muqātil* reports that God places the souls of the martyrs into the bodies of green birds, who nest in the lamps on the divine throne, and eat of the fruit of the heavenly garden.[530] This, then, is their sustenance.

In Ṭabarī's commentary it becomes evident that this question had become the subject of serious debate.[531] In his commentary on *al-baqara* (2) 154 he records three different opinions on the condition of the martyrs' souls. According to the first opinion (and in line with *Tafsīr Muqātil*), the souls of the martyrs exist in the bodies of birds (two traditions specify white birds, two green birds), nesting in the lotus tree of the highest heaven. According to a second opinion all that can be said is that martyrs do not experience *barzakh*. The tombs of believers, after death, are opened unto paradise, so that they smell its scent. The tombs of the unbelievers are opened unto hell, so that they see its fire. The martyrs, however, are spared entirely this period in the tomb. According to a third opinion, the souls of the martyrs exist in white domes in paradise, where they are accompanied by two heavenly wives and partake in all of the food and drink of the garden.[532]

As though the question still bothered him, Ṭabarī again addresses it in his commentary on *āl 'Imrān* (3) 169. Here he cites eight different traditions on the manner in which the souls of the martyrs exist in paradise.[533] Three of these traditions have the souls of the martyrs in the bodies of green birds, eating the fruit of the heavenly garden. Four traditions put them in green domes. A final tradition explains merely that the martyrs' sustenance is not food but a heavenly wind.[534]

Zamakhsharī, for his part, insists that the martyrs "are given sustenance like any other living thing, eating and drinking."[535] There is a parallel for this, Zamakhsharī notes elsewhere, in the Qur'ān's description of the eschatological suffering of the family of Pharaoh (Q 40.45–7). The souls of the martyrs are able to enjoy sustenance in the same way that the souls of Pharaoh's family are able to feel pain.[536] Of course, this hardly solves the

529 *Tafsīr Muqātil*, 1:151, on Q 2.154.

530 Ibid., 1:314, on Q 3.169.

531 On this see W. Raven, "Martyr," *EQ*, 3:284a.

532 Ṭabarī, 2:39–40, on Q 2.154.

533 In addition, Ṭabarī adds here five traditions with the request of the martyrs to return to earth and thus to fight and die another time (as seen with *Tafsīr Muqātil* and Ibn Kathīr above); four traditions with the further detail that this verse was revealed in order to inform the believers of the martyrs' fate, and thereby to encourage them to fight the *jihād*; and one tradition which counters that it was revealed when the martyrs insisted on sending greetings to their Prophet. Ṭabarī, 4:170–3, on Q 3.169–70.

534 Evidently this explanation is meant to explain how they could receive sustenance but have no body (although a body is presumably also needed to feel a breeze). Ṭabarī, 4:170–3, on Q 3.169–70.

535 Zamakhsharī, 1:429, on Q 3.169–71.

536 Ibid. 1:206, on Q 2.149–54. Zamakhsharī adds here a tradition that the martyrs are not actually in heaven, but still feel its breeze and eat from its fruit.

problem of the martyrs' bodies. The solution he offers is in a prophetic *ḥadīth*, namely that the souls of the martyrs are in the bodies of green birds; they "fly around the rivers of paradise, eat from its fruit, and shelter in lamps of gold suspended in the shade of the divine throne."[537]

Ibn Kathīr also reports the *ḥadīth* that the souls of martyrs dwell in the bodies of green birds in paradise.[538] But he adds a prophetic *ḥadīth* (through Aḥmad b. Ḥanbal) with another view that the martyrs are not actually in paradise, but dwell along a river near its gate. Through this gate food is brought out to them in the morning and in the evening (cf. Q 3.169).[539]

Another conflict emerges from a second *ḥadīth* (also through Aḥmad b. Ḥanbal), which Ibn Kathīr insists has a "valid, strong, and excellent *isnād*."[540] Therein the Prophet explains that "the essence of believers . . . will be in a bird attached to a tree in paradise."[541] In other words, the souls of all believers, not of martyrs alone, will exist in the bodies of birds in paradise even before the Day of Resurrection. Ibn Kathīr accepts this *ḥadīth*, and is thereby compelled to find some other advantage that the martyrs enjoy. The solution, Ibn Kathīr relates, is that only birds with the souls of martyrs will be permitted to fly around paradise; the others will be confined to a tree. The souls of the martyrs are therefore "like the stars in comparison with the souls of regular believers."[542]

Subtext

Ibn Kathīr's opinion that all believers will experience immediate retribution reflects his use of *ḥadīth* as a source of revelation essentially parallel to Qur'ān. This opinion is hardly evident in the Qur'ān. Instead the Qur'ān describes immediate retribution as a particular privilege of the martyrs. In this matter the Qur'ān might fruitfully be viewed within the context of its religious milieu, inasmuch as this doctrine is found among the Church fathers in general,[543] and among the Syriac fathers in particular.

The concepts of eschatological retribution and martyrdom are also present in Jewish texts, yet they are hardly of fundamental importance. The Hebrew

537 Zamakhsharī, 1:430, on Q 3.169–71.

538 Ibn Kathīr, 1:191, on Q 2.153–4.

539 As though to reconcile this conflict Ibn Kathīr also mentions a tradition attributed to Ibn Isḥāq that some of the martyrs are in paradise, but others only at its gate. Ibn Kathīr, 1:408, on Q 3.169–75.

540 Ibn Kathīr, 1:408, on Q 3.169–75.

541 Ibid.

542 Ibid.

543 Thus Rudolph (*Abhängigkeit*, 31) comments, "Aber gerade mit dem heiligen Krieg denken wir doch unwillkürlich an die bevorzugte Stellung der Märtyrer in der christlichen Kirche, die bei den arabischen Christen sicher dieselbe Verehrung wie in der sonstigen Kirche genossen."

Bible has few direct references to the afterlife at all.[544] The narrative of the martyrdom of seven brothers (and their mother) in the late (2nd cent. BC) book 2 Maccabees is eschatological, but it does not suggest that the martyrs will receive immediate retribution.[545] The idea is suggested only in later Jewish writings. The Babylonian Talmud (*Berakoth* 18a), for example, speaks of "the righteous who in their death are called living."[546] Still, the Talmud does not identify these righteous dead as martyrs.

The New Testament, however, seems to reflect the idea of the martyrs' immediate retribution. In the parable of Lazarus and Dives (Lk 16.19–31), for example, Luke describes the miserable existence of Lazarus, who suffered from hunger, sickness, and neglect in this life, and the comfortable existence of a rich man, who whiled away his life with luxury and feasts. When Lazarus died, "He was carried away by the angels into Abraham's embrace" (Lk 16.22a). When the rich man died, Luke explains, he was buried (Lk 16.22b). The parable thus seems to suggest that Lazarus was not buried, that is, that at his death he was taken body and soul into heaven. This extraordinary privilege apparently was granted on account of his suffering.

The scene that Luke portrays at Jesus' crucifixion is similar. When one of two crucified criminals abuses Jesus, the other reprimands him (Lk 23.41). This good criminal then declares, "Jesus, remember me when you come into your kingdom" (Lk 23.42). Jesus responds, "In truth I tell you, today you will be with me in paradise" (Lk 23.43). Again the New Testament suggests the idea of immediate retribution of those who suffer in this life.

The immediate retribution of martyrs in particular is signaled above all by the resurrection of Christ, the martyr par excellence. Indeed the portrayal of the resurrected Christ in the Gospels seems to provide a vision of the heavenly body of the martyr. In Luke 24, when the apostles and others are gathered, Christ suddenly stands among them (Lk 24.36). His body is

544 Masson (*Le Coran et la révélation judéo-chrétienne*, 592) argues that the famous episode in Daniel 3, in which Shadrach, Meshach, and Abed-Nego are cast into the furnace but protected from its fire, is a sort of allegory indicating the protection of the martyrs from death.

545 The author of 2 Maccabees has the martyrs, before they are cruelly put to death by Antiochus, declare their confidence that God will reward them. One of the seven brothers tells the king: "Cruel brute, you may discharge us from this present life, but the King of the world will raise us up, since we die for his laws, to live again for ever" (2 Maccabbees 7.9). Similarly their mother, encouraging her sons to be strong in the face of death, declares, "And hence, the Creator of the world, who made everyone and ordained the origin of all things, will in his mercy give you back breath and life, since for the sake of his laws you have no concern for yourselves" (2 Maccabbees 7.23).

546 A. Katsh, *Judaism and Islam: Biblical and Talmudic Background of the Qur'ān and Its Commentaries*, New York: New York University Press, 1954 (p. 115) points to another tradition in the Babylonian Talmud (*Sanhedrīn* 92a) that seems to reflect the idea of immediate retribution: "The righteous, whom the Holy One, blessed be He, will resurrect, will not revert to dust."

apparently supernatural, as he appears in a seemingly impossible fashion.[547] The disciples think that he is a ghost (Lk 24.37), yet Christ carefully demonstrates that he indeed has a physical body:

> "See by my hands and my feet that it is I myself. Touch me and see for yourselves; a ghost has no flesh and bones as you can see I have." * And as he said this he showed them his hands and his feet. * Their joy was so great that they still could not believe it, as they were dumbfounded; so he said to them, "Have you anything here to eat?" * And they offered him a piece of grilled fish, * which he took and ate before their eyes.
>
> (Lk 24.39–43)

For his part John has Christ display the wounds on his hands and his side to Thomas (Jn 20.27). Thus the marks of his martyrdom still appear on Christ's body.

The martyrdom of Christ is the central mystery of the New Testament. Christ's martyrdom is a victory over death (cf. Mt 27.52; 1 Corinthians 15.55–7). Those who believe in him will be saved from death by virtue of that martyrdom (Romans 3.22–8; Hebrews 1.1–3). Those who suffer martyrdom for him are joined to him in that act. For this reason Paul likens himself to Christ when he declares: "It makes me happy to be suffering for you now, and in my own body to make up all the hardships that still have to be undergone by Christ for the sake of his body, the Church" (Colossians 1.24). The martyr dies, one might say, as Christ. For this reason the martyr enjoys the same consolation at death.

In this light it is apparent why Luke presents Stephen, the first Christian martyr, as a second Christ. On the cross Christ prays, "Father, forgive them; they do not know what they are doing" (Lk 23.34). Stephen, before he is stoned, prays, "Lord, do not hold this sin against them" (Acts 7.60). Christ asks the Father to receive his spirit (Lk 23.46). Stephen asks the "Lord Jesus" to receive his spirit (Acts 7.59). Thus in his martyrdom Stephen has become a new Christ. Accordingly, before his death he is given a view of his heavenly reward: "'Look! I can see heaven thrown open,' he said, 'and the Son of man standing at the right hand of God'" (Acts 7.55).

The name Stephen (Gk Στέφανος) itself, which means "crown," appears to be an epithet. Eusebius writes that Stephen "was the first to carry off the crown, implied by his name, which was gained by the martyrs of Christ found worthy of victory."[548] In the New Testament and other early Christian writings the crown is the symbol of the martyr. Like the wreath that is presented to a champion athlete, the crown is presented to the martyrs, who

547 John is still more explicit on this point: "The doors were closed in the room where the disciples were, for fear of the Jews. Jesus came and stood among them" (Jn 20.19).

548 *Ecclesiastical History*, 2:1:1, trans. Lake and Oulton, 1:103–5.

have triumphed in their religious struggle. Thus Paul writes Timothy from jail, as he is awaiting his execution and martyrdom:

> As for me, my life is already being poured away as a libation, and the time has come for me to depart. * I have fought the good fight to the end; I have run the race to the finish; I have kept the faith; * all there is to come for me now is the crown of uprightness which the Lord, the upright judge, will give to me on that Day; and not only to me but to all those who have longed for his appearing.
>
> (2 Timothy 4.6–8)[549]

Similarly the visionary of Revelation has Christ, who himself bears a gold crown (Revelation 14.14), declare to his beleaguered flock: "Do not be afraid of the sufferings that are coming to you. Look, the devil will send some of you to prison to put you to the test, and you must face hardship for ten days. Even if you have to die, keep faithful, and I will give you the crown of life for your prize" (Revelation 2.10). Elsewhere the visionary himself sees underneath the divine altar "the souls of all the people who had been killed on account of the Word of God, for witnessing to it" (Revelation 6.9; cf. 19.16; 20.4).

Thus the New Testament authors recognized immediate retribution as a particular privilege of the martyrs. This notion became especially prominent among Syriac authors who belonged to the Churches that would be known as Jacobite and East Syrian. The standard eschatological teaching of these Churches was precisely that suggested by the Qur'ān: the soul will not be rewarded (or punished) before it is reunited with the body.[550] Aphrahat, for example, explains that at death the natural spirit is buried with the body and is awakened only when the trumpet is blown on the last day to face judgment.[551]

549 James similarly encourages the believers with the words, "Blessed is anyone who perseveres when trials come. Such a person is of proven worth and will win the prize of life, the crown that the Lord has promised to those who love him" (James 1.12). So too Peter writes: "When the chief shepherd appears, you will be given the unfading crown of glory" (1 Peter 5.4).

550 According to Andrae the eschatology of both Eastern Christian tradition and the Qur'ān reflects a larger Semitic anthropology by which the soul cannot survive without the body. Hence before the resurrection the soul can only live a shadowy existence (e.g. the Biblical *sheol*). Andrae, *OIC*, 161–2. The dream of Enkidu before his death in the *Epic of Gilgamesh* (tablet 7) seems to illustrate Andrae's point. Elsewhere (p. 111) Andrae argues that the early Christian insistence on the resurrection of the body was a reaction against the Hellenistic inclination to assert the superiority of the soul.

551 As quoted by Andrae, *OIC*, 162–3. For the just, Aphrahat continues, this period of sleep is restful, but for sinners it is restless. O. Carré notes Blachère's observation in this regard: "Pour ce qui est de 'l'élévation' corps et âme dans le Coran, R. Blachère ([*Le Coran*, Paris: Maisonneuve, 1949], 900, n. 163) la compare aux 'âmes mortes vivant devant Dieu' de certains écrits syriaques contemporains du Coran, expression contradictoire dans les termes et, je pense, compréhensible seulement si l'âme n'est pas séparable du corps." O. Carré, "Méthodes et débats, à propos du Coran sur quelques ondes françaises actuelles," *Arabica* 53, 2006, 3 (353–81) 363.

This same doctrine is taught by Ephraem and Babai the Great (d. 628). Babai, in fact, uses the story of the Seven Sleepers (or Youths) of Ephesus to illustrate this doctrine, a story that appears in the Qur'ān as the Companions of the Cave account in *al-Kahf* (CS 12).[552]

The martyr, however, will not experience this period of waiting, but will immediately ascend to heaven. Andrae explains that according to Jacobite and East Syrian thought, "Personne de ceux qui ont quitté la vie ne séjourne aussitôt auprès du Seigneur, s'il n'a pas obtenu par le martyre le privilège d'habiter dans le Paradis et non dans les enfers."[553] The view that the martyrs ascended immediately to heaven can also be found among Church fathers in the West.[554] For this reason early Christians in both the East and the West put particular emphasis on the intercession of martyrs,[555] and not infrequently claimed to receive visitations from them. Eusebius tells the story, for example, of a soldier in Egypt who escorted the virgin Saint Potamiaena (who was burned alive in oil) to her pitiable death.[556] This soldier had heard the teaching of Origen and therefore treated the Christian girl well. In return she promised that she would ask God to remember him.[557] Some time later, "Potamiaena appeared to him by night, wreathing his head with a crown and saying that she had called upon the Lord for him and obtained what

552 On this see Andrae, *OIC*, 166.

553 Andrae, *OIC*, 168. He refers to *Die syrische Didaskalia* (trans. H. Achelis and J. Flemming, Leipzig: Hinrichs, 1904, 317). Elsewhere (p. 121) Andrae comments, "Il contemple déjà l'invisible de ses propres yeux et marche dans le monde céleste. . . . Il n'est déjà maintenant plus sur terre; son corps s'attarde bien encore ici-bas, mais son esprit est déjà dans le monde céleste."

554 Thus speaking of paradise Tertullian comments, "Nullas alias animas apud se pareter martyrum ostendit." *De anima* 55, *PL* 2, ed. J.-P. Migne, Paris: Migne, 1879, 789. Soon thereafter he adds, "Si pro Deo occumbas, ut Paracletus monet, non in mollibus febribus et in lectulis, sed in martyriis, si crucem tuam tollas, et sequaris Dominum, ut ipse praecepit; tota paradisa clavis tuus sanguis est." Ibid., 789–90; Cf. Augustine, *City of God*, 13:8. On this point W. Rordorf comments, "Dans la tradition chrétienne apparaît très tôt la conviction que le martyr à la différence des autre chrétiens, n'attendra pas dans l'Hadès la résurrection finale, mais ira directement au paradis." W. Rordorf, "Martyre," *Dictionnaire de spiritualité*, Paris: Beauchesne, 1980, 10:726. R. Hedde reports that before dying Saint Flavian (d. 449), Patriarch of Constantinople, said to the pagans: "When you kill us, we will live. We are not defeated by death but defeat it." R. Hedde, "Martyre," *Dictionnaire de théologie catholique*, Paris: Letouzey et Anê, 1928, 10:251.

555 In this regard P. Allard notes the early Christian inscriptions on the tombs of children in Rome which record the prayers of their parents that the martyr Basilla will receive their child in heaven. P. Allard, *Dix leçons sur le martyre*, Paris: Gabalda: 1930, 360.

556 Eusebius refers to her martyrdom as ἆθλος, "a contest." In a similar fashion Tertullian writes, "Nos aeternam consecuturi carcerem nobis pro palaestra interpretamur, ut ad stadium tribunalis bene exercitati incommodes omnibus producamur, quia virtus duritia exstruitur, mollitia vero destruitur." *Ad Martyras* 3:5, ed. Dekkers, 6. Cf. ibid., 4:9, ed. Dekkers, 7.

557 "She on her part accepted his fellow-feeling for her and bade him be of good cheer, for that she would ask him from her Lord, when she departed, and before long would requite him for what he had done for her." *Ecclesiastical History*, 6:5:6, trans. Lake and Oulton, 2:27.

she requested, and that before long she would take him to herself."[558] He subsequently became a Christian and joined Potamiaena in martyrdom.

Nevertheless there is some reason to think that on the question of martyrs the Qur'ān is particularly in conversation with the Syriac Christian tradition, for even the language of the Qur'ān is cognate to that of the Syriac fathers. For example, speaking of the martyrs the East Syrian ("Nestorian") Mar Jesse (d. late 6th cen.) comments: "People believed that they are dead. But their death killed their sin and they are living in the presence of God (*be-ḥayyê lewāt alāhā*)."[559] As Andrae points out, this pious reflection, even in its vocabulary, anticipates the declaration of the Qur'ān: "Do not think those who were killed in the path of God dead. They are alive and receive sustenance with their Lord (*bal aḥyā'un 'inda rabbihim yurzaqūn*)" (Q 3.169).

Furthermore, Jesse's comments give a clear explanation for the martyrs' privilege: The sufferings of their martyrdom achieve expiation of sins ("their death killed their sin").[560] For the Qur'ān too the martyr's suffering is itself a redemptive sacrifice: "And if you are killed or die in the path of God? The forgiveness and mercy of God is better than that which they might gather" (Q 3.157).

Of course, for Christians this redemptive sacrifice is intimately connected to that of Christ. Thus in his *Letter to the Romans* (ch. 4), written as he traveled towards martyrdom in Rome, Ignatius of Antioch (d. 110) presents himself as a new Christ, indeed as a Eucharist to be offered as a sacrifice to God: "I am the wheat of God, and let me be ground by the teeth of the wild beasts, that I may be found the pure bread of Christ." Similarly Origen, after mentioning how Paul was caught up in the third heaven (2 Corinthians 12.2, 4), consoles Christians threatened with martyrdom by saying:

> You will presently know more and greater things than the unspeakable words then revealed to Paul, after which he came down from the third heaven. But you will not come down if you take up the cross and follow Jesus, whom we have as a great High Priest who has passed through the heavens (cf. Heb. 4.14).[561]

This much cannot be found in the Qur'ān. Even if the Qur'ān's reflection on the Crucifixion of Christ (Q 4.157–8) is not taken as a denial of his death

558 *Ecclesiastical History*, 6:5:6, trans. Lake and Oulton, 2:27. On this tradition see also Allard, *Dix leçons sur le martyre*, 336–8.

559 Mar Isaï, *Traités sur les martyrs*, *PO* 7:1, trans. A. Scher, Paris: Firmin-Didot, 1911, 32. Andrae, *OIC*, 168.

560 Rordorf comments (10:726): "La souffrance du martyr a valeur expiatoire: Dieu lui pardonne ses péchés. Dans la tradition chrétienne, on parlera volontiers du 'baptême du sang' . . . le sang du martyr purifie celui qui n'a pas reçu le baptême d'eau, et il efface les péchés de celui qui été déjà baptisé, par un 'second' baptême."

561 Origen, *An Exhortation to Martyrdom*, trans. R. Greer, London: SPCK, 1979, 50.

(but rather as a denial of the Jews' boast),[562] the Qur'ān still shows no particular concern for the suffering of Christ, let alone the redemptive value of that suffering. However, the Qur'ān is concerned with the ascension of Christ (cf. Q 3.55; 4.157–8), and is in agreement with Christian doctrine on the ascension of the martyr to heaven.

CS 12 The Companions of the Cave

Qur'ānic account

In the previous case study I mentioned the story of the Seven Sleepers (or the Youths) of Ephesus, a story which Babai the Great uses to illustrate the sleep of the soul between death and the Day of Judgment. The Qur'ān, as mentioned, addresses this story in *al-kahf* (18), a chapter named for the cave (*kahf*) in which the sleepers are hidden away. Andrae argues that Muḥammad used this account in much the same way as Babai.[563] Other scholars have analyzed the Qur'ānic version of this narrative at great length.[564] Here I will approach the account of the Seven Sleepers, or the "Companions of Cave" as the Qur'ān refers to them, only inasmuch as it illustrates the theme of the present work: the Qur'ān's homily on Biblical literature.

In this regard it is worth noting the observation of S. Griffith that the Qur'ān frames its discussion of this account with verses that not only emphasize God's transcendence, but also have an anti-Christian tone.[565] In *al-kahf*, (18) 4 the Qur'ān insists that God sent the book to His servant in

562 On this see G.S. Reynolds, "The Muslim Jesus: Dead or alive?" *BSOAS* 72, 2009, 237–58.

563 *OIC*, 166.

564 See especially the insightful article of S. Griffith: "Christian lore and the Arabic Qur'ān: The 'Companions of the Cave' in *al-Kahf* and in Syriac Christian tradition," *QHC*, 109–37; and the detailed work of P. Michael Huber: *Die Wanderlegende von den Siebenschläfern*, Leipzig: Harrassowitz, 1910. Cf. also B. Heller, "Éléments, parallèles et origine de la légende des Sept Dormants," *Revue des études juives* 49, 1904, 190–218; and the works of L. Massignon on this topic: "Les 'Septs Dormants' apocalypse de l'Islam," *Analecta Bollandiana* 68, 1950, 245–60 (reprint: *Opera Minora*, ed. Y Moubarac, Beirut: Dār al-Ma'ārif, 1963, 3:104–18); idem, "Les sept dormants d'Ephèse (*ahl al-kahf*) en islam et chrétienté," *Revue des études islamiques* 12, 1954, 61–110; idem, *Le culte liturgique et populaire des VII dormants, martyrs d'Ephèse (*ahl al-kahf*): trait d'union orient-occident entre l'islam et la chrétienté, Studia Missionalia*, Rome: Gregorian University, 1961. For a brief overview see G.S. Reynolds, "Seven Sleepers of Ephesus," *Medieval Islamic Civilization: An Encyclopedia*, London: Routledge, 2005, 2:719–20.

565 "Christian lore and the Arabic Qur'ān," 117–8. Note Griffith's conclusion (p. 118): "It is hard to avoid the thought that not only is the Qur'ān here using a familiar Christian narrative to enhance the understanding of the sense of the expression 'God's signs,' but that it is also proposing in the sequel that the true meaning of the Christian story corrects what the Qur'ān considers to be one of the major errors of the Christian understanding. Namely, the doctrine that God has a son and that he is Jesus, the Messiah."

order that "he might warn those who say God took a son." In verse 26 the Qur'ān insists that the Companions of the Cave "had no friend other than God. He takes no partner in His rule." Thus the Qur'ān's concern with the Companions of the Cave narrative seems to be broadly connected with religious competition.

Between these two frames the Qur'ān presents this narrative in three distinct sections. In the first section the Qur'ān provides an overview thereof.[566] In this (and the next) section the speaker is the divine voice of the Qur'ān (that is, the narrator and the principal protagonist are the same). In verse nine the divine voice begins by asking: "Did you count the Companions of the Cave and *al-raqīm* among Our wonderful signs?"[567] Thereafter the Qur'ān refers to three elements of the story: one, the youths' flight to the cave and supplication to God therein (v. 10); two, God's act of "closing their hearing" (v. 11), presumably a reference to their sleep, or to their death (if the reference to the youths' sleep in v. 18 is read as a metaphor); and three, God's act of waking the youths, or bringing them back to life (*ba'athnāhum*, v. 12),[568] and challenging them to calculate how long they remained in the cave.

566 On this section Ibn Kathīr comments: "This is God Most High's telling of the story of the Companions of the Cave in a condensed and abridged fashion." Ibn Kathīr, 1:70, on Q 18.9–12.

567 The term *al-raqīm* here has long been debated, and the views of contemporary critical scholars thereon are as diverse as those of the classical Muslim scholars to be discussed in the next section. Tisdall (*Original Sources of the Qur'an*, 143, n. 10) identifies *al-raqīm* as the name of the district in which the cave was located. Horovitz (*KU*, 95) rejects this identification and suggests instead "inscription," in line with the Arabic meanings from the root *r.q.m.* Torrey (*Foundation*, 46–7) argues that *al-raqīm* stands for Decius (who, according to the Syriac sources, was the emperor whose persecution led the youths to flee to the cave), being a misreading of Syriac *dqīs*. Jeffery (*FV*, 144) argues that it is probably a place name, representing Syriac *Raqm de-gāyā*, or *Raqm be-marr brā de-ṣīn*, a location in southern Palestine. More recently Bellamy has proposed that *al-raqīm* is a corruption of *ruqūd*, "sleeping" a term that appears in 18.18. J.A. Bellamy, "*Al-Raqīm* or *al-Ruqūd*? A note on Sūrah 18:9," *JAOS* 111, 1991, 115–7. Luxenberg (*Die syro-aramäische Lesart des Koran*, 66–7) modifies Bellamy's suggestion to read Syriac *ruqād*, "sleep" (thus Q 18.9 would read "the Companions of the Cave and of Sleep"). Griffith, finally, convincingly supports the view of Horovitz, that *al-raqīm* should be read "inscription," noting that an inscription figures twice in the Syriac version of the account told by Jacob of Serūgh. He adds that the peculiar Arabic form *raqīm* is likely a Syriacism, i.e. the Syriac passive participle form (*f'īl*), used as a substantive adjective (*fa'īl*). On this Griffith refers to T. Nöldeke, *Compendious Syriac Grammar*, trans. J.A. Crichton, Winona Lake, IN: Eisenbrauns, 2001, 218, # 278. On *al-raqīm* see also C.C. Torrey, "Three difficult passages in the Koran," in T.W. Arnold and R.A. Nicholson (eds.), *A Volume of Oriental Studies Presented to Edward G. Browne (. . .) on his 60th Birthday*, Cambridge: Cambridge University Press, 1922, 457–9; Stewart, "Notes on medieval and modern emendations of the Qur'ān," 112.

568 *Ba'atha* is the verb that the Qur'ān regularly employs for the waking of the dead on the Day of Resurrection (e.g. Q 2.56, 259; 6.36, passim). The Qur'ān also refers in one verse (Q 30.56) to the "the Day of *ba'th*".

In the second section, verses 13–20, the Qur'ān presents the same account but in more detail.[569] In verse 13, in fact, the Qur'ān seems to introduce the story anew, although its use of pronouns draws a link with the first section: "We narrate their account to you in truth. They were youths who believed in their Lord and We guided them greatly." The Qur'ān then quotes the youths' declaration of faith (v. 14) and their rejection of the polytheism that surrounded them (v. 15). In verse 16 the divine voice of the Qur'ān, which heretofore had been addressing the reader, suddenly turns to the youths directly (thus the Qur'ānic discourse shifts into the temporal setting of the events it had been recounting), encouraging them to seek refuge in the cave and assuring them of God's protection therein. In verse 17 the Qur'ān turns back to the audience, describing a miracle of the sun that occurred while the youths were in the cave, which it describes as "a sign of God."[570]

Again the audience is addressed in verse 18: "You would have deemed them awake while they were sleeping." The Qur'ān describes how God turned the sleeping bodies of the youths over, back and forth, while their dog remained at the entrance[571] of the cave. Thereafter the Qur'ān describes how God woke the youths, who were unsure of how long they had been asleep, although one unidentified group is made to say, "Your Lord knows best how long you have tarried." Thereafter someone (those who have just spoken? God?), recommends that one person go to a city to buy food, with the warning to be courteous and secretive (v. 19), lest the people of the city discover his identity and then stone him or compel him to apostatize (v. 20).

Finally, verse 21 begins with a statement centered on two third person plural pronouns: "We made them known, that they might know the promise of God is true and that there is no doubting the Hour."[572] The Qur'ān is presumably referring to the Companions of the Cave with the first pronoun ("them"). The second pronoun ("they") seems to refer to the people of the city referred to in verse 20. The verse ends with a reference to a group, also

569 Bell suggests that verses 9–12 and 13–20 are remnants of two different versions of the Cave story. R. Bell, *A Commentary on the Qur'ān*, ed. C.E. Bosworth and M.E.J. Richardson, Manchester: University of Manchester, 1991, 1:483. Blachère divides the text here into two different columns, reflecting his belief that vv. 8–11, 24–5 on the one hand, and vv. 12–15, on the other hand, were originally separate accounts. See Blachère, 318–9. On this question cf. also Griffith, "Christian lore and the Arabic Qur'ān," 118–9.

570 The text, which speaks of the sun moving to the right of the cave when it rose, and to the left of the cave when it set, suggests that God prevented sunlight from striking the entrance of the cave.

571 Ar. *waṣīd*. The *mufassirūn* also debate the meaning of this term, some suggesting "courtyard" (*finā'*) others "dirt" or "soil" (*turāb*), others "gate" or "door" (*bāb*). See, e.g., Ibn Kathīr, 3:73, on Q 18.18. The context, however, strongly suggests a meaning of "entrance."

572 By the rules of standard Arabic the verb here (*a'thara* "make known") should have both a direct and an indirect pronominal object, to indicate who is being acquainted with what (or whom). See *AEL*, 1952b.

unidentified but perhaps to be associated also with the people of the city, who plan to build a place of worship (*masjid*) over the youths. Thus many of the details of the Qur'ān's account of the Companions of the Cave are left unclear, but the purpose of the account is not: it is a lesson on the resurrection of the body.

In the third section, verses 22–6, the Qur'ān turns its attention from the story itself to controversies about the story. In other words, the Qur'ān is concerned not only with the account of the Companions of the Cave, but also with debates over its interpretation. This section is therefore noticeably different from the preceding two sections. The speaker is now the Prophet, although the imperative, "Say," that introduces verses 22 and 26 makes the Prophet's words into a quotation given to him from God.

Here the Qur'ān first (v. 22) addresses a controversy over the number of companions who were in the cave ("They will say three and the dog is the fourth. They will say five and the dog is the sixth. . . . They will say seven and the dog is the eighth"), concluding simply: "Say 'My Lord knows their number best.' " It is worth noting that the Qur'ān speaks here in the imperfect ("They will say"), thus clearly separating the time of the cave incident from the later time of the controversy. In verse 25 the Qur'ān specifies the number of years the companions tarried in the cave: 309. That this is the resolution to a second controversy is suggested by the refrain in verse 26: "God knows best how long they tarried."

In between these two verses is a homiletic reflection (vv. 23–4). The language therein is ambiguous, but the basic point is clear: nothing takes place without the will of God. Indeed this point corresponds well with the Qur'ān's account of the Companions of the Cave, according to which God is the protagonist at every point.

Problems for interpreters[573]

Occasion of revelation

Tafsīr Muqātil reports that God sent down the verses on the Companions of the Cave to Muḥammad when Abū Jahl, the Prophet's pagan Meccan nemesis, sent five men to the Jews to get their opinion on the Prophet. The Jews instructed them to test Muḥammad by asking him about three matters: one, the Companions of the Cave; two, Dhū l-Qarnayn (cf. Q 18.83: "They will ask you about Dhū l-Qarnayn"); and three, the Spirit (Q 17.85: "They will ask you about the Spirit"). When Abū Jahl confronted Muḥammad, the

573 Regarding Muslim exegesis on this passage see the recent article of B. Fudge, "The Men of the Cave: *Tafsīr*, tragedy and Tawfīq al-Ḥakīm," *Arabica* 54, 2007, 1, 67–93. Fudge exams the *tafsīrs* of Ṭabarī, Ṭabrisī (d. 548/1154), Qāsimī (d. 1332/1924), and Sayyid Quṭb (d. 1386/1966). Cf. R. Tottoli ("Men of the Cave," *EQ*, 3:274–5), whose article consists only of a brief overview of *tafsīr*.

Prophet replied that he would provide answers the following day, but the angel Gabriel did not come to give him the answers before three days. Thus a phrase in verse 23, "Do not say about anything, 'I will do this tomorrow,'" (cf. Mt 6.34) is explained.[574]

Qummī relates that the pagan Meccans sent three men to Najrān in Yemen to ask the Jews and Christians how they might interrogate the Prophet.[575] The Jews there told them that if Muḥammad were trustworthy he would have knowledge on three subjects: first, the sleepers' identity, their number, the length of their sleep, and what accompanied them during their sleep; second, the story of Moses and the knowledgeable man whom he followed (Q 18.60–82); third, the story of Dhū l-Qarnayn (Q 18.83–98). These subjects are, in other words, the three principal narratives of *al-kahf*. If Muḥammad is trustworthy, they continued, he should also deny having knowledge of a fourth subject: the timing of the apocalyptic Hour (cf. Q 31.34: "With Him is knowledge of the Hour"; cf. Q 41.37; 43.85). When these three men returned and confronted Muḥammad, he told them that he would answer their questions the next day, but the angel Gabriel did not come to give him the answers before 40 days (thus Q 18.23).[576]

Ibn Kathīr also presents a version of this same tradition.[577] To this he adds an explanation of the Qur'ān's report that the Companions of the Cave were youths (*fityā*; Q 18.10). Ibn Kathīr comments: "The great majority of the elders of Quraysh continued in their religion. Only a few of them became Muslims. For this reason He (Most High) reported that the Companions of the Cave were youths, young men."[578]

The meaning of al-raqīm

At the opening of the Companions of the Cave account the term *al-raqīm* appears ("Did you count the Companions of the Cave and *al-raqīm* among Our wonderful signs?" [Q 18.9]), a term unclear to both classical *mufassirūn* and modern translators. Pickthall and Yusuf Ali translate "Inscription." So does Paret ("Inschrift") although he (wisely) adds a parenthetical question mark to admit his uncertainty. The others (Blachère, Arberry, Fakhry, and

574 *Tafsīr Muqātil*, 2:574–6, on Q 18.9.

575 That both *Tafsīr Muqātil* and Qummī have stories of pagan Meccans traveling outside of Mecca for information is no coincidence. This reflects the doctrine, on the one hand, that *al-kahf* was revealed in Mecca (on this see *GdQ1*, 140–3), and the doctrine, on the other hand, that Mecca was a purely pagan city. Abdel Haleem follows this approach with the insistence in his translation (p. 183, n. a) that this account was revealed in response to pagan Meccans.

576 Qummī, 2:6, on Q 18.9.

577 He explains that the Quraysh sent a delegation to the Jews, who told them to ask the Prophet about the Companions of the Cave (along with Dhū l-Qarnayn and the Spirit). Ibn Kathīr, 1:71, on Q 18.13–6.

578 Ibn Kathīr, 1:71, on Q 18.13–6.

Abdel Haleem) avoid the issue by merely transliterating *raqīm*. Fakhry, however, defines *al-raqīm* in a note as, "The name of the mountain where the Cave was."[579] Abdel Haleem also adds a note, but therein he simply lists some classical opinions on the term: "Al-Raqim is variously interpreted as being the name of the mountain in which the cave was situated, the name of their dog, or an inscription bearing their names."[580]

As for the *mufassirūn*, *Tafsīr Muqātil* and Qummī provide straightforward, and similar, explanations of *al-raqīm*. *Tafsīr Muqātil* comments:

> It is a book that two virtuous rulers wrote, one of whom was Mātūs, the other Astūs. They concealed their faith while residing in the house of the tyrant Decius. He is the emperor from whom the young men fled. They wrote the account of the young men on a lead tablet and placed it in a copper tomb and then placed it in the structure with which the entrance of the cave was blocked.[581]

Qummī also reports that *al-raqīm* refers to a tablet (according to him copper, not lead), inscribed with the story of the Companions of the Cave. The word *raqīm*, he explains, is an alternative form of the passive participle *marqūm*, synonymous with *maktūb*, "what is written."[582]

With Ṭabarī's polyvalent commentary it becomes clear that this is not the only opinion the *mufassirūn* entertained. Ṭabarī, who introduces his discussion of *al-raqīm* with the admission, "The interpreters differ on its meaning,"[583] cites three different opinions. According to the first opinion, *al-raqīm* is a place name, either the name of a village or a valley near the cave. Ṭabarī cites six traditions to this effect, two of which – both on the authority of Ibn ʿAbbās – relate village, and four of which – one on the authority of Ibn ʿAbbās – relate valley.

According to a second opinion (that of *Tafsīr Muqātil* and Qummī), *al-raqīm* refers to some type of writing. Ṭabarī cites three different traditions to this effect – one on the authority of Ibn ʿAbbās.[584] According to a third opinion, however, *al-raqīm* is a place name, but not of a village or valley as in the first opinion. Instead it is the name of the mountain on which the cave was located. Ṭabarī cites three traditions to this effect – one on the authority of Ibn ʿAbbās.[585]

579 Fakhry, 178, n. 563.
580 Abdel Haleem, 183, n. b.
581 *Tafsīr Muqātil*, 2:574, on Q 18.9.
582 Qummī, 2:6, on Q 18.9.
583 Ṭabarī, 15:198, on Q 18.9.
584 One further tradition is in harmony with the opinions of *Tafsīr Muqātil* and Qummī, that *al-raqīm* was "a stone tablet on which they wrote the stories of the Companions of the Cave and placed at the entrance of the cave." Ṭabarī, 15:198, on Q 18.9.
585 According to one of them the mountain was also called *b.n.j.ū.s.* (another has *b.n.ā.j.l.ū.s.*).

Thus Ṭabarī presents traditions in support of all three opinions on the authority of Ibn ʿAbbās. Thereafter he turns yet again to Ibn ʿAbbās for two further traditions. Now, however, Ibn ʿAbbās does not propose new solutions but simply confesses his ignorance. In one tradition he declares: "I know all of the Qur'ān, except for *ḥanānā* [Q 19.13], *awwāh* [Q 9.114; 11.75], and *al-raqīm*;" in another: "I do not know what *al-raqīm* is. Is it a book or a structure?"[586] From the midst of this confusion Ṭabarī raises his voice to support the opinion that *al-raqīm* is something written.[587] The advantage of this opinion, he explains, is the connection of the Arabic root *r.q.m.* to writing.[588]

Zamakhsharī, however, offers an entirely new solution to this debate. He describes *al-raqīm* as the name of the Companions' dog, a view nowhere seen in the Ṭabarī traditions.[589] Ibn Kathīr, on the other hand, turns to many of the same opinions noted by Ṭabarī, many of which are attributed to Ibn ʿAbbās. Thus *al-raqīm*, he explains, refers either to a valley, a building, a village, a mountain, or a book.[590] Like Ṭabarī he inclines towards this final opinion.[591]

586 Ṭabarī, 15:198, on Q 18.9.

587 According to one report, Ṭabarī notes, *al-raqīm* was a tablet on which the story of the Companions and their names were written. Yet he adds that scholars differ over what was done with this tablet: "One said that this tablet was taken up to the storehouse of the king. Another said that it was put on the entrance of the cave. Another said, 'No, it was conserved among one of the people of their country.'" Ṭabarī, 15:198, on Q 18.9. Later (pp. 203–4) Ṭabarī relates a tradition similar to that of *Tafsīr Muqātil*, that two believers in the king's palace, named Bīdrūs and Rūnās (*Tafsīr Muqātil* has Mātūs and Astūs), recorded the story and the names of the Companions on lead tablets, placed these tablets in a copper container and put the container at the entrance to the cave.

588 Like Qummī he relates that the form *raqīm* is a secondary passive participle (meaning, as Qummī also explains, "what is written") just as *jarīḥ* is secondary to *majrūḥ*, and *qatīl* is secondary to *maqtūl*. Ṭabarī, 15:198, on Q 18.9.

589 Although he does note the views of other scholars that it is the name of their village, or of a place between Ghaḍbān and Ayla in Palestine. Zamakhsharī, 2:704–5, on Q 18.7–11.

590 Ibn Kathīr begins his discussion of *al-raqīm* with a report, on the authority of Ibn ʿAbbās, that it is the name of a valley near Ayla. Another tradition defines it as a building (presumably an allusion to the *masjid* referred to in Q 18.21). A second tradition from Ibn ʿAbbās has him relate the opinion of Kaʿb al-Aḥbār that it is a village. A third tradition from Ibn ʿAbbās has him relate still another opinion, that it is the mountain in which the cave was located. An additional tradition names the mountain *b.n.j.l.ū.s.* (cf. Ṭabarī above). An unrelated tradition provides more detail: the mountain was named *b.n.j.l.ū.s.*, the cave *ḥ.ī.z.m.* and the dog *ḥ.m.r.ā.n.* Ibn Kathīr, 3:70, on Q 18.9–12. Thereafter, Ibn Kathīr reports the two traditions found in Ṭabarī in which Ibn ʿAbbās confesses his ignorance of *raqīm*. Ibn Kathīr, 3:70, on Q 18.9–12. Finally, however, Ibn Kathīr promptly reports yet another Ibn ʿAbbās tradition in which he defines *raqīm* as a book.

591 The order of the Ibn ʿAbbās traditions in Ibn Kathīr's commentary might seem illogical, since Ibn ʿAbbās is called on to give a view that *raqīm* means "book" or "tablet" after he has been quoted denying any understanding of this word. Yet Ibn Kathīr has presumably adopted this strange order since he prefers the definition of "book," and thus would like to see it come at the end. Indeed he uses this last Ibn ʿAbbās tradition as a segue into a discussion of the grammar of *raqīm* and its relationship to *marqūm*, a discussion that is reminiscent of Ṭabarī.

The flight of the Companions

There is less confusion among the *mufassirūn* regarding the reason for the flight of the Companions to the cave. *Tafsīr Muqātil* relates that the youths fled in fear of the persecution of a tyrant named Decius.[592] Qummī provides a similar explanation, but with more details. The incident occurred in the period between Jesus and Muḥammad, during the reign of Decius. According to a tradition (on the authority of the sixth Imām, Ja'far al-Ṣādiq) Decius would not allow people to leave the city, on pain of death, without worshipping idols. The youths were able to avoid this condition, however, on the pretext that they were merely leaving the city for a hunting party. But once outside of the city they hid in a cave, where God cast sleep upon them.[593]

Ṭabarī comments that most interpreters explain the flight of the Companions in the manner of *Tafsīr Muqātil* and Qummī; that is, it was caused by the persecution of a pagan king. One tradition in support of this explanation relates that the youths "were Muslims following the religion of Jesus. The king at the time was an idol-worshipper and demanded that they worship idols. They fled from him for the sake of their religion."[594] According to a second tradition, on the authority of Ibn Isḥāq, most of the people of the Gospel (cf. Q 5.47) had grown corrupt, but a few of them remained faithful to the religion of Jesus (i.e. Islam) and committed to monotheism. Eventually a cruel king named Decius rose to power. He began to torture and kill those who followed the religion of Jesus, hanging pieces of their bodies on the city walls as a warning. Thus the Companions, who were faithful Muslims, fled to the cave.[595]

A third tradition (also on the authority of Ibn Isḥāq) is the most detailed. Here Ṭabarī provides the names of all of the youths (which he numbers at eight). When these youths learned of Decius' persecution they gathered together in prayer,[596] but eventually Decius summoned them before him and demanded that they worship his idols. One of the youths (named Maksilmīnā) stood before the king and declared: "We have a god whom we worship. The heavens and the earth are full of His majesty. We will not pray to any god other than Him."[597] The king released them with only a warning and they

592 *Tafsīr Muqātil*, 2:579, on Q 18.20.

593 Qummī, 2:6–7, on Q 18.9. Qummī later (2:8, on Q 18.9) adds that when the evil king discovered the cave, his companions began to argue over the number of youths inside. Some said three, their dog being a fourth. Others five, the dog being a sixth, and still others seven, the dog being an eighth (cf. Q 18.22). Yet no one would enter the cave, since God had cast a great fear over them (cf. Q 18.18). Meanwhile, inside the cave the youths, out of fear of Decius, asked God to cast sleep upon them.

594 Ṭabarī, 15:200, on Q 18.10.

595 Ibid., 15:201.

596 Ṭabarī, in fact, remarks that they would pray "prostrate on their faces," presumably an allusion to Islamic prayer practice. Ṭabarī, 15:201, on Q 18.10.

597 Ṭabarī, 15:202, on Q 18.10.

fled to a cave (on a mountain named *b.n.j.l.ū.s.*) near Ephesus. Later Decius passed by the city and learned of their refuge. He decided to have the cave sealed up, that the Companions might die of hunger and thirst.[598] After relating two further, similar traditions, Ṭabarī turns to an alternative explanation for the flight of the Companions, that the youths fled to the cave when they were (falsely) accused of a crime.[599]

This alternative view does not appear in the commentary of Zamakhsharī, who follows the tradition that the youths fled from an evil pagan king named Decius.[600] Zamakhsharī explicitly compares Decius and his associates with the pagan Meccans of Muḥammad's time. Thus the flight of the companions appears as a *hijra* from the unbelievers. He also adds that Decius' wickedness was in part due to the development of Christianity: "It is related that the sins of the People of the Gospel grew great. Their kings grew excessive to the point that they worshipped idols and compelled others to worship them."[601]

Ibn Kathīr, on the other hand, argues that the incident of the Cave must have taken place before Christianity existed. This he concludes from the report on the occasion of the revelation for this passage (see p. 171 above), wherein the Jews – not the Christians – appear to have knowledge of this incident.[602] This conclusion, however, does not deter Ibn Kathīr from associating this incident with the rule of Decius (r. AD 249–51).[603]

598 Ibid., 15:203.

599 The sole tradition in support of this opinion (on the authority of Wahb b. Munabbih) surrounds the visit of one of Jesus' disciples to the city where the youths lived. See Ṭabarī, 15:205.

600 Zamakhsharī, 2:707, on Q 18.13–5.

601 Ibid., 2:711, on Q 18.21.

602 Ibn Kathīr, 3:71, on Q 18.13–6.

603 The Companions, he explains, were the children of noble parents living in a pagan city, over which ruled a cruel tyrant named Decius. Once a year a festival was held in which the tyrant demanded that all people worship idols (*aṣnām*, "idols," and *ṭawāghīt*, plural of *ṭāghut*, a Qur'ānic term [Q 2.256; 4.51, 60, 76 passim], related to Aramaic *ṭā'ūthā* and Ethiopic *ṭa'ot*, also meaning "idol"). The youths refused to take part and, one by one, gathered under a tree apart from their people, although they did not know each other previously. The topos of a tree as the gathering point for faithful believers redounds to the account in the Prophet's biography of the Treaty of al-Ḥudaybiyya, during which Muḥammad's followers took a pledge (known as *bay'at al-riḍwān* "the pledge of satisfaction") of obedience under a tree. See Ibn Hishām, *Sīrat Rasūl Allāh*, 750 (trans., 506).

At first none of the Companions openly declared his faith, fearful that the others might condemn him for opposing the religion of the king, but soon, one by one, they courageously proclaimed their rejection of that religion (cf. Q 18.14: "We made their hearts strong when they stood up and said, 'Our Lord is the Lord of the heavens and the Earth.' "). Thus "they all agreed on one statement, and became a united band, faithful brothers." After an interrogation by the king the Companions decided to flee from the disorder (*fitna*) of unbelief. When the king heard that they took refuge in a cave he had it sealed, that the youths might die inside. God, however, had different plans and cast a deep sleep on them. Ibn Kathīr, 3:72, on Q 18.13–6.

Like Zamakhsharī, Ibn Kathīr also compares the flight of the Companions explicitly to the *hijra* of Muḥammad. He draws the parallel still further, in fact, noting how the Prophet and Abū Bakr also hid in a cave (named Thūr) from the pagan Quraysh.[604] Ibn Kathīr comments: "The story of this cave is more noble, sublime, impressive, and amazing than the story of the Companions of the Cave."[605]

Their dog

The account of the Prophet and Abū Bakr hiding in a cave is also connected to the Companions of the Cave account by the role of animals. In the first account a spider weaves a web, and two birds build nests, in front of the cave. Finding the web and the nests, the Quraysh are convinced that the Prophet and Abū Bakr are not inside the cave. In the Companions account (Q 18.18) a dog stretches its legs in front of the entrance to the cave. Yet the appearance of a dog in this account is problematic to the *mufassirūn*. Dogs, after all, are generally considered unclean in Islamic law.[606] This tension surrounding the dog in the cave story presumably accounts for the appearance of a variant reading (on the authority of Muḥammad al-Bāqir, the fifth Shīʿī Imām), according to which the text is properly read not *kalbuhum*, "their dog," but *kāliʾuhum*, "their guard."[607]

Tafsīr Muqātil, however, simply explains that the dog was there as a guard.[608] Qummī reports instead that the dog was used for shepherding. To this report he adds a tradition, on the authority of Jaʿfar al-Ṣādiq, that only three animals will be admitted to paradise: the donkey of Balaam, the wolf of Joseph (cf. Q 12.13, 14, 17), and the dog of the Companions of the Cave.[609]

Ṭabarī, in one place, relates that this animal was neither a guard dog nor a shepherd dog, but rather a hunting dog.[610] In another place, however, he mentions that not all scholars accept that the Qur'ān is actually referring here to a dog. Some held that this was a person, namely the Companions' cook. Presumably the idea is that Arabic *kalb* ("dog") is a proper name.[611]

604 See Ibn Saʿd, *K. al-Ṭabaqāt al-kabīr*, ed. E. Mittwoch and E. Sachau, Leiden: Brill, 1917–40, 1:1:153.

605 Ibn Kathīr, 3:72, on Q 18.13–6.

606 On the other hand, the dog's noble qualities are appreciated by Dāmirī, who introduces his commentary on the animal with the declaration, "The dog is an animal of great energy and exceeding fidelity." Al-Dāmirī, *Ḥayāt al-ḥayawān*, Cairo: Maṭbaʿat al-Istiqāma, 1374/1954, 2:278.

607 *MQQ*, 3:304.

608 "The dog was named Qamṭīr and belonged to Maksilmīnā, the leader of the companions. It stretched its paws over the entrance of the cave to protect it, and God cast the same sleep upon it as He did upon the Companions." *Tafsīr Muqātil*, 2:578, on Q 18.18.

609 Qummī, 2:7, on Q 18.18.

610 Ṭabarī, 15:204, on Q 18.10. Ṭabarī elsewhere (15:227, on Q 18.22) names the dog Itmār.

611 Although it hardly seems becoming, Kalb is a name commonly found in pre-Islamic records; an entire tribe, *Banū Kalb*, traces their lineage to a man of this name. Ṭabarī, 15:214, on

Zamakhsharī also suggests that the Qur'ān could be referring to a person, reporting a variant reading (which he attributes to Ja'far al-Ṣādiq) by which *kalbuhum* would be read *kālibuhum*, meaning "the owner of their dog."[612] Elsewhere, however, he relates a narrative in which the Companions meet a dog with a miraculous gift of speech: "They passed by a dog who followed them. When they pushed it away God gave the dog the ability to speak. It said, 'Why are you harassing me? I am the most beloved of the lovers of God. Sleep and I will protect you.' "[613]

Ibn Kathīr notes that some authorities hold that the Companions' dog was a hunting dog, while others explain that it was the dog of the king's chef (who was a Muslim).[614] He insists, however, that the function of the dog was to guard the Companions' cave. He adds that this dog must have lain down *outside* the door. This, he explains, is evident from the well-known *ḥadīth* that angels do not enter a house where there is a dog, a picture, an impure person, or an unbeliever.[615]

The waking of the Companions

Finally, the *mufassirūn* are as interested in the waking of the Companions as they are in their falling asleep. In fact, most conclude that God woke the Companions, as He put them to sleep, because of a particular political situation. If they slept due to the ambitions of an evil king to spread his pagan beliefs, they woke up due to the ambitions of a good king to spread his Islamic beliefs.

Ṭabarī, for example, reports a tradition that the followers of this good king were arguing over whether the soul alone, or both the soul and body, would be raised on the Day of Resurrection. Wary of their argument, the king prayed: "O Lord you see their disagreement. Send a sign to guide them."

Q 18.18. Dāmirī (2:278) relates that the Prophet's own ancestors bore this name. F. Viré ("Kalb," EI^2, 4:491a) has Ṭabarī describe the dog as, "The reincarnation of a human being." This conclusion presumably reflects his understanding of this same tradition.

612 Zamakhsharī, 2:709, on Q 18.18.

613 Ibid., 2:711, on Q 18.21. A variant of this narrative, Zamakhsharī remarks (2:711–2), has them meet instead a shepherd accompanied by a dog.

614 "God knows better," he concludes. Ibn Kathīr 3:72, on Q 18.18. Ibn Kathīr also notes two versions of the dog's name: *ḥ.m.r.ā.n* (Ibn Kathīr, 3:70, on Q 18.9–12.) and (on the authority of al-Ḥasan al-Baṣrī) Qiṭmīr (3:72, on Q 18.18). In this tradition al-Ḥasan names a number of animals that appear in the Qur'ān: Abraham's ram he names *jarīr* (the ram itself does not appear in the Qur'ān, but there is a reference to a sacrifice *dhibḥ*: Q 37.107), the hoopoe bird of Sulaymān (Q 27.20) *'.n.q.z.*, and the calf that the Israelites worshipped (Q 2.51, 54, 92, passim) *b.h.m.ū.t*.

615 Ibn Kathīr 3:72, on Q 18.18. According to another version of this *ḥadīth* the Prophet was distressed one day when the angel Gabriel did not appear as promised in his house. When Muḥammad discovered a puppy hidden under a bed and threw it out of the house, the angel arrived. Gabriel explained to him: "We do not enter a house in which there is a dog or a picture." See, e.g., Muslim, *Saḥīḥ*, "al-Libās wa-l-zīna," 26, Beirut: Dār al-Kutub al-'Arabiyya, 1421/2000, 14:69–70.

God responded by waking the Companions of the Cave.[616] A second tradition (on the authority of Ibn Isḥāq) is more detailed. The king's name was Theodore, the tradition relates. After he had reigned for 68 years,[617] some of his subjects began to deny the resurrection of the body.

> This was hateful to the virtuous king Theodore. He cried to God and implored Him. He grew greatly sad when he saw these false people increasing and going out to the people of truth, saying: "There is no life but the life of this world. Only souls are raised. Bodies are not raised." They neglected that which is in the Book.[618]

In response to Theodore's prayer God raised the Companions of the Cave as a proof to the people, demonstrating that "the Hour is coming, there is no doubt of it" (cf. Q 18.21).[619]

Zamakhsharī explains the incident of the Cave as a demonstrative miracle, a proof for the resurrection, since the state of the Companions "in sleeping and being woken up is like the state of one who dies and is brought back to life."[620] Accordingly Zamakhsharī explains, like Ṭabarī, that God woke the Companions because of a debate over the resurrection of the body (cf. Q 18.21b: "When they disputed the matter among themselves").[621] He relates:

616 Ṭabarī, 15:217, on Q 18.19–20.

617 In fact, Theodosius II, whom Ṭabarī has in mind here, had an exceptionally long reign of 42 years, from 408 (when he was 7 years old) to 450 (or 48 years, if his reign is calculated from 402 when he was named co-emperor).

618 Ṭabarī, 15:217, on Q 18.19–20.

619 Ibid. According to this tradition (p. 220), when the youths rose they sent one of their number, named Yamlīkha, into the city to buy food. There Yamlīkha met two virtuous believers. The names of these believers are conspicuous: Arius and Asṭīyūs (Nestorius?).

620 Ibid., 2:711, on Q 18.21.

621 Zamakhsharī relates that the Companions came to understand God's power to resurrect the dead through intellectual reflection: "They considered and investigated the greatness of God Most High's power and thus became certain." Zamakhsharī, 2:710, on Q 18.19–20. It is also worth noting Zamakhsharī's commentary on a remark in Q 18.21: "Their Lord knows best about them." After attributing this statement to those who believe in the resurrection (about those who do not), Zamakhsharī mentions an alternative possibility: that it is the statement of God about those among the People of the Book who dispute the length of the Prophet Muḥammad's [i.e. Islam's] era (*'ahd*). Ibid. 7:712, on Q 18.21. Thus he would compare the idle and impious speculation over the length of the Companions' sleep to the habit of Christians (and Jews?) in his day to prophesy an end to Islamic rule. In fact, eastern Christian authors not infrequently sought to place Islamic rule into a chronological scheme inspired by Daniel's visions of four beasts (Daniel 7) and Christ's description of the signs of the apocalypse in Matthew 24. This is prominent, for example, in the Syriac apocalypse of Pseudo-Methodius (ca. 691). See G.J. Reinink, *Die syrische Apokelypse des Pseudo-Methodios, CSCO* 540–1, Louvain: Peeters, 1993; R. Hoyland, *Seeing Islam as Others Saw It: A Survey and Evaluation of Christian, Jewish and Zoroastrian Writings on Early Islam*, Princeton: Darwin, 1997, 259ff.; S. Griffith, *The Church in the Shadow of the Mosque*, 34.

> In the time when God brought them back to life, the king of the city was a virtuous and believing man. The people of his kingdom disagreed over the resurrection, some acknowledging it and some denying it. The king entered his house, locked the door, put on sackcloth and sat on an ash heap. He asked his Lord to show them the truth. So God sent at that moment a shepherd who knocked down that which blocked the mouth of the Cave in order to use it as an enclosure for his sheep.[622]

Ibn Kathīr follows the same approach on this matter, reporting that God woke up the Companions at a time in which people began to doubt the resurrection of the body.[623]

Subtext

That the *mufassirūn* explain the Qur'ānic Companions of the Cave account with narratives on Decius (r. 249–51) and Theodosius II (r. 408–450) reflects their awareness of the Christian legend of the Seven Sleepers (or the Youths) of Ephesus. The origin and history of this legend, including its appearance in the Qur'ān, is analyzed in detail by Michael Huber in his remarkable work, *Die Wanderlegende von den Siebenschläfern*.[624] Furthermore, in a recent article, "Christian lore and the Arabic Qur'ān,"[625] Sidney Griffith offers a concise and insightful analysis of the relationship of the Qur'ānic account with the Syriac version of the legend. With these references as a pretext, I will discuss this relationship only as it is relevant to the thesis of the present work.

It might first be pointed out that the topos of God waking people from an impossibly long sleep, that is, of God bringing people back to life, does not begin with that legend. In the Book of Ezekiel the prophet relates how God took him to a valley full of dry bones. He then recounts:

622 Zamakhsharī, 2:710, on Q 18.19–20. Zamakhsharī here identifies the city in question as Tartus (a city on the Syrian coast) in one place (2:710, on Q 18.19–20), but elsewhere (2:713, on Q 18.22) as Ephesus.

A second tradition is similar: "They disputed the truth of the resurrection. Some of them said that souls are brought back to life but not bodies. Some said that both bodies and souls are brought back to life. So [the miracle took place] to resolve the argument and to show that bodies are brought back to life, living and feeling with their souls just as they were before death." Ibid.

623 He also notes a tradition (on the authority of 'Ikrima) that after the Companions were awakened one of them (named *d.q.s.ū.s.*) went into the city to buy food (cf. Q 18.19). When the people of that city saw the ancient coin that he presented as payment, and heard him claim that he lived in the time of Decius, they brought him to their king. The king, who was a good, faithful Muslim named Theodosius (*t.ī.d.ū.s.ī.s.*), believed his story and followed him to the cave. There he met the Companions and exchanged greetings of peace with them. Ibn Kathīr, 3:74, on Q 18.21.

624 Leipzig: Harrassowitz, 1910.

625 *QHC*, 109–37.

> [Lord Yahweh] said to me, "Son of man, can these bones live?" I said, "You know, Lord Yahweh." * He said, "Prophesy over these bones. Say, 'Dry bones, hear the word of Yahweh. * The Lord Yahweh says this to these bones: I am now going to make breath enter you, and you will live. * I shall put sinews on you, I shall make flesh grow on you, I shall cover you with skin and give you breath, and you will live; and you will know that I am Yahweh.'"
>
> * I prophesied as I had been ordered. While I was prophesying, there was a noise, a clattering sound; it was the bones coming together. * And as I looked, they were covered with sinews; flesh was growing on them and skin was covering them, yet there was no breath in them. * He said to me, "Prophesy to the breath; prophesy, son of man. Say to the breath, 'The Lord Yahweh says this: Come from the four winds, breath; breathe on these dead, so that they come to life!'" * I prophesied as he had ordered me, and the breath entered them; they came to life and stood up on their feet, a great, an immense army.
>
> (Ezekiel 37.3–10)[626]

The account of Ezekiel in part anticipates the return of Israel from exile, but it is also a vision of the general Resurrection itself, of the Day when all bones will be clothed with flesh, when the souls of the dead will again enter their bodies and stand before God. It is thus a vivid illustration of the creator's power over His creation. It is in this light that the New Testament authors present Christ's power over death. Those who are dead to others are merely asleep to Christ. When in Matthew's Gospel an official asks Jesus to save his dead daughter (Mt 9.18), Jesus explains "the little girl is not dead; she is asleep" (Mt 9.24a; cf. Lk 8.52). For this he is ridiculed (Mt 9.24b), until he indeed wakes the girl up from her "sleep" (Mt 9.25).

Similarly in John's Gospel, when the news reaches Jesus that Lazarus is ill, he tarries for two days (Jn 11.6), and then explains to the disciples, "Our friend Lazarus is at rest; I am going to wake him" (Jn 11.11). John comments, "Jesus was speaking of the death of Lazarus, but they thought that by 'rest' he meant 'sleep'" (Jn 11.13). Before raising Lazarus, Jesus proclaims to his sister Martha, "I am the resurrection. Anyone who believes in me, even though that person dies, will live" (Jn 11.25). Thus in the New Testament sleeping and waking are tropes for death and resurrection (on this cf. also 1 Thessalonians 4:13).[627]

626 On this cf. Masson, *Le Coran et la révélation judéo-chrétienne*, 442, n. 2.

627 Sidersky points to a number of other narratives as antecedents to the Qur'ānic Companions of the Cave account. These include a tradition in the Babylonian Talmud (*Ta'anīt* 23a), itself a haggadic commentary on Psalm 126.1 (pace Sidersky who has 106.1): "When Yahweh brought back Zion's captives we lived in a dream." The story is then told of a skeptic who doubted that it is possible to sleep for 70 years, the length of the Babylonian captivity (as a literal reading of Psalm 126.1 would imply). One day the skeptic met an old man who was planting a carob tree, the fruit of which will not be ready for 70 years. When

It is this metaphor that provides the fundamental direction of the legend known in the West as the Seven Sleepers of Ephesus and in the East as the Youths of Ephesus. While this legend was presumably first recorded in Greek,[628] the first extant account thereof is found in two Syriac homilies (*mēmrê*) attributed to Jacob of Serūgh.[629] Like other Syriac authors, Jacob refers to the protagonists of the story as the *ṭlāyê* ("youths"; cf. Ar. *fityā*, Q 18.10) of Ephesus. Presumably his homilies on this legend were well known.[630] Griffith, who suggests that Jacob wrote the homilies for the feast

he asked why the old man was bothering with such a tree, the old man replied that he should provide trees for his descendents, just as his ancestors provided trees for him. Suddenly the skeptic fell asleep and only woke up 68 years later. When he got up he saw the grandson of the old man eating from the tree. Cf. Sidersky, *Les origines des légendes musulmanes*, 153. Sidersky also notes a Christian legend according to which the apostle John did not die but disappeared in the mountains. This legend (which is connected to Jn 21.21–3) can be found in the Arabic work of Agapius (Maḥbūb) of Menbidj. *K. al-'Unwān*, part 2:1, *PO 7*, ed. A. Vasiliev, Paris: Firmin-Didot, 1948, 493. Sidersky (*Les origines des légendes musulmanes*, 154) argues that it is directly connected with the Companions of the Cave narrative, since the cave is generally thought to be on a mountain (and *al-raqīm* occasionally understood to be the name of a mountain).

628 Griffith explains: "The currently prominent opinion is that a record of their miraculous survival after more than three hundred years of entombment was first composed in Greek by Bishop Stephen of Ephesus between the years 448 and 450, albeit that the earliest extant texts are in Syriac and date from the sixth century. . . . Nevertheless, the alternative opinion of a Syriac original, strongly seconded by Theodor Nöldeke in 1886, and bolstered by the remark of St. Gregory of Tours (d. 594) that he owed his account of the 'Seven Sleepers' to a Latin translation from a Syriac original, still survives. The thought among those who support this opinion is that the legend arose in the Syriac-speaking churches in connection with the 'Origenist' controversies of the sixth century, in which differing opinions about the doctrine of the resurrection of the body were an issue." Griffith, "Christian lore and the Arabic Qur'ān," 120.

On the origin of the Seven Sleepers narrative see also Huber, *Wanderlegende von den Siebenschläfern*; A. Allgeier, "Der Ursprung des griechischen Siebenschläferlegende," *Byzantinische-neugriechische Jahrbücher* 3, 1922, 311–31; E. Honigmann, "Stephen of Ephesus (April 15, 448 – Oct. 29, 451) and the Legend of the Seven Sleepers," in E. Honigmann, *Patristic Studies, Studi e Testi* 173, Vatican City: Biblioteca Apostolica Vaticana, 1953, 17:125–68.

629 For both versions see I. Guidi, "Testi Orientali Inediti sopra I Sette Dormienti di Efeso," *Reale Accademia dei Lincei* 282 (1884–5), Roma: Tipografia della R. Accademia dei Lincei, 1885, 18–29. One of the versions is also published in H. Gismondi, *Linguae Syriacae Grammatica et Chrestomathia cum Glossario*, 4th edition, Rome: De Luigi, 1913, 45–53. Both versions are translated into German by Huber, *Wanderlegende von den Siebenschläfern*. For more details on the relationship of the two recensions of Jacob's homily see Griffith, "Christian lore and the Arabic Qur'ān," 120–1; A. Vööbus, *Handschriftliche Überlieferung der Mēmrē-Dichtung des Ja'qōb von Serūg*, *CSCO* 344 and 345, 421 and 422, Louvain: Secrétariat du CSCO 1973, 344 and 1980, 71–2.

630 The legend of the Youths of Ephesus is also preserved in two other early texts: a Syriac translation of the Greek *Ecclesiastical History* of Zacharias of Mitylene (d. 536), and the Syriac *Ecclesiastical History* of John of Ephesus (d. 586), as quoted by the *Chronicle* of Dionysius of Tell Maḥrē (d. 845) in the *Chronicle* of Michael the Syrian (d. 1199) and also by the *Ecclesiastical Chronicle* of Bar Hebraeus (d. 1286). The *Ecclesiastical History* of

day of the Youths (recognized as martyrs and saints in the Jacobite Church),[631] argues that his homilies would have been familiar to Christian Arabs, particularly to Jacobites such as the Christians of Najrān.[632]

Thus when the Qur'ān took up this tale it was commenting on a religious tradition of significant importance in its context. The Qur'ān's particular interest in this tale becomes evident when the nature of the legend is appreciated. For it is shaped as a response to the notion that there is no resurrection of the body.[633] The insistence on the resurrection of the body, of course, is one of the central themes of Qur'ānic discourse (see e.g. Q 17.49; 18.48; 21.104; passim). In this regard a brief survey of Jacob's rendition of the Youths legend is worthwhile, in order to highlight the cooperative relationship between that legend and the Qur'ān.

In Jacob's telling the Youths are imprisoned when they refused to offer incense at the altars of Zeus, Apollo, and Artemis (the patron god of Ephesus)[634] as ordered by the emperor Decius, who had convened a festival

Zacharias of Mytilene was translated, according to Griffith, by "an anonymous monk at Amida in the year 569" (Griffith, "Christian lore and the Arabic Qur'ān," 121). It is published in *Historia Ecclesiastica Zachariae Rhetori, vulgo Adscripta II, CSCO* 84, ed. E.W. Brooks, Paris: E Typographeo Reipublicae, 1921, 106–22; and *Anecdota Syriaca* 3, *Zachariae Episcopi Mitylenes aliorumque Scripta Historica Graece plerumque Deperdita*; ed. J.P.N. Land, Leiden: Brill, 1870, 87–99. For the *Ecclesiastical History* of John of Ephesus see J.J. van Ginkel, *John of Ephesus: A Monophysite Historian in Sixth-Century Byzantium*, Ph.D. dissertation, Rijksuniversiteit Groningen, 1995; W. Witakowski, *The Syriac Chronicle of Pseudo-Dionysius of Tel-Maḥrē: A Study in the History of Historiography*, *Studia Semitica Upsaliensia* 9, Stockholm: Almqvist and Wiksell, 1987. For the account of the "Youths of Ephesus" therein see Guidi, "Testi Orientali Inediti," 35–44 and P. Bedjan, *Acta Martyrum et Sanctorum Syriace I*, Paris: Otto Harrassowitz, 1890, 301–25.

631 "It was probably the feast day of the youths, who were considered to be martyrs; Jacob clearly expects his congregation, perhaps monks, to be familiar with the story. Nevertheless, he will recall the narrative outline for them, to refresh their memories, as if to summon the very presence of the youthful saints and martyrs into the minds of the congregation." S. Griffith, "Christian lore and the Arabic Qur'ān," 122–3.

632 Griffith, "Christian lore and the Arabic Qur'ān," 121–2. He notes that early Syriac recensions of this legend are all in the works of Jacobite authors. I. Guidi ("Seven Sleepers," 429) accordingly concludes that the story must have reached Muḥammad through its oral circulation among Syrian monks. Griffith also refers here to E.K. Fowden, *The Barbarian Plain: Saint Sergius between Rome and Iran*, Berkeley: University of California Press, 1999, esp. 25–6, in which Fowden describes how, in remembrance of St. Sergius' role in converting the Arabs, a homily of Jacob of Serūgh is recited. On the Christians of Najrān see Trimingham, *Christianity among the Arabs in Pre-Islamic Times*; Shahid, *The Martyrs of Najrân*; idem, *Byzantium and the Arabs in the Sixth Century*; and esp. Tardy, *Najrân*.

633 Griffith notes, "The account of the legend in the Syriac version/epitome of the *Ecclesiastical History* of Zacharias of Mytilene mentions as an occasion of the miracle, controversies over the fate of the human body after death sparked by works of Origen." Griffith, "Christian lore and the Arabic Qur'ān," 134, n. 37. See *Historia Ecclesiastica Zachariae Rhetori vulgo Adscripta II*, 114–5.

634 Griffith insightfully notes how, in Acts 19.28–35, Paul visits Ephesus during the festival of Artemis, a scene that presumably affected the development of the Seven Sleepers story. "Christian lore and the Arabic Qur'ān," 135, n. 57.

for these gods during a visit to Ephesus. Eventually the Youths escape prison and, fleeing the city, take refuge in a cave. There God casts a miraculous sleep upon them, taking their souls to heaven and leaving a watcher (*ʿīrā*) to guard their bodies.[635] When Decius returns to Ephesus he has their cave walled up in order to seal their doom. The report of this event spreads among Christian believers, and two of them – convinced that the Youths would some day be raised from the dead – travel to the cave and inscribe on lead tablets the names of the Youths, the date they fled from Decius, and the reason for their flight.[636]

When, many years later, a man who wants to build a sheepfold takes stones away from the entrance, light pours into the cave and the Youths awake. Still in fear of Decius, and unaware of the time that has passed, they decide to send one of their number to Ephesus to buy food. Entering into the city he is amazed to see crosses prominently displayed. When he tries to buy food with a now ancient coin, a curious crowd gathers around him. They bring him to a church, where a wise man recognizes that the coin is from the era of Decius, who was king 372 years earlier.[637] Eventually news of the miracle reaches the Christian Emperor Theodosius II, who travels to the cave of the Youths. There he reads the lead tablet and asks the Youths to come to Ephesus where he might build a temple (Syr. *hayklā*) over their bodies.[638] Yet the Youths choose instead to stay and die where they are, explaining that they have been brought back from the dead only in order that "you could see and affirm that there is truly a resurrection."[639]

The correlation between the protagonists of the Christian Sleepers account and the Qur'ānic Companions account is evident. In both cases they are youths (Syr. *ṭlāyê*; Ar. *fityā*) or companions (Syr. *ḥabrê*; Ar. *aṣḥāb*). Even the dog of the Qur'ānic account has a precedent in the Christian Sleepers account. When Jacob speaks of a "watcher" who protects the Youths, he is invoking the common Syriac Christian allegory of shepherding, based on the trope of Jesus as the Good Shepherd (see Jn 10). Thus he relates:

> They went up the mountain; they entered the cave and stayed there.
> They called out to the Lord in a doleful voice and spoke thus,
> "We beseech you, Good Shepherd, who has chosen His servants,
> guard your flock from this wolf who thirsts for blood."
> The Lord saw the faith of the blessed lambs,
> and He came to give a good wage for their recompense.
> He took their spirits and brought them up to heaven,
> and He left a *watcher* to be the guardian of their limbs.[640]

635 "Testi Orientali Inediti," 1:19–20, ## 58–62.
636 Ibid., 1:20, ## 69–73.
637 Ibid., 1:22, ## 152 & 154–5.
638 Ibid., 1:23, # 179.
639 Ibid., 1:23, # 184.
640 Ibid., 1:19–20, ## 55–61.

The watcher of Jacob's account is there to protect the body of the Youths from the "wolf" while their souls are in heaven. The watcher, in other words, is protecting the sheep of the Good Shepherd. In this light it appears that the dog of the Qur'ān is, in a manner of speaking, a sheepdog. The Qur'ān's remark that the dog stretched its legs over the entrance of the cave suggests precisely this role.[641]

The Qur'ānic discourse on raising a building above the Cave is likewise understandable through an appreciation of the Sleepers legend. The Qur'ān, in a passage that otherwise seems cryptic, relates: "They said, 'Build over them a building. Their Lord knows best about them.' Those who prevailed in their matter said, 'We shall build a place of worship (*masjid*) over them'" (Q 18.21b). Thus the Qur'ān reports that there was some dispute – in this case one is tempted to see the report as a reflection of an actual historical event – over the building of a shrine at the site of the Youths' cave. Jacob's *mēmrā* has the Youths reject the offer to build a temple in Ephesus for them. Similarly the Qur'ān reports that some people wanted to construct a "building" (*bunyān*; Q 18.21), but that instead a place of worship was built "over them" (Q 18.21). While Jacob does not explicitly state that a shrine was built "over them," that is, at the site of their cave, this might simply be taken for granted. His audience was presumably well aware of the shrine for the Youths that indeed existed in the outskirts of Ephesus from an early date, and still exists today.[642]

The *Ecclesiastical History* of Zacharias of Mitylene (d. 536) relates that "a great sanctuary has been built over the cave for honor's sake, and for a house of worship (*bayt ṣlūtā*), and for liturgy (*teshmeshtā*) over their bodies."[643] The Qur'ān's description of this building as a *masjid* reflects this tradition closely. It is thus rather unnerving to encounter the opinion of Ibn Kathīr, who argues that the building of this *masjid* was an act of infidelity, with reference to the prophetic *ḥadīth*: "May God curse the Jews and the Christians for making the graves of their prophets and holy people into places of prayer."[644]

For its part the Qur'ān uses the Companions account to convince its audience that God will clothe bones with flesh, in much the same way that it uses the example of life returning to the soil when it rains (e.g. Q 41.39;

641 Curiously the man who falls asleep for a hundred years, referred to elsewhere in the Qur'ān (Q 2.259), is likewise accompanied by an animal, a donkey. Regarding the relation of these two accounts see *KU*, 98–9.

642 For a description and photos of this shrine see, e.g., http://www.sacred-destinations.com/turkey/ephesus-cave-of-the-seven-sleepers.htm. Regarding popular devotion to the Youths and to their shrine at Ephesus see also M. Coleridge, *The Seven Sleepers of Ephesus*, London: Chatto & Windus, 1893; and more recently G. Avezzù, *I Sette Dormienti: Una Leggenda fra Oriente e Occidente*, Milano: Medusa, 2002.

643 Trans. Griffith ("Christian lore and the Arabic Qur'ān," 129) from *Historia Ecclesiastica Zachariae Rhetori*, 121–2.

644 Ibn Kathīr 3:75, on Q 18.21.

43.11). So too the Qur'ān concludes its account of a man who falls asleep with his donkey for one hundred years by connecting it to the resurrection of the body (Q 2.259). In both this account and that of the Companions of the Cave God asks the protagonists how long they have tarried. In their confusion they respond, "A day or part of a day." Both accounts thus point to the Qur'ān's discourse on the Day of Resurrection, according to which God will ask the people: "How many years did you tarry in the Earth [i.e. in the tomb]?" They will answer, "A day or part of a day. Ask those who count!" (Q 23.112–3).

The connection with the Resurrection is thus the Qur'ān's primary concern with the Cave story. Its resolution to the dispute over the period of time that the youths slept (309 years; Q 18.25) is secondary. Indeed in the next verse the Qur'ān implies that this sort of calculation is anyway unimportant: "God knows best how long they tarried" (Q 18.26). As for the other dispute, over the number of Companions, the Qur'ān offers no definitive answer at all. After noting that some argue there were three and the dog a fourth, others five and the dog a sixth, and still others seven and the dog an eighth, the Qur'ān simply relates: "Say, 'My Lord knows their number best'" (18.22).

The reason for the Qur'ān's concern with these matters emerges only when it is realized that both of these questions were issues of contention in Syriac Christian tradition on the Youths of Ephesus. The difficulty of calculating the distance between the reigns of Decius and Theodosius II led to various estimations (mostly overestimations) of the time which the youths spent in the cave.[645] Even the two different recensions of Jacob's homily differ on this point. The first (and more ancient) recension has 372 years; the second has 350 years.[646] The *Ecclesiastical History* of John of Ephesus (d. 586), meanwhile, has 370 years.[647] The Syriac Christian sources also disagree over the number of youths who were in the cave. In Jacob's *mēmrā* and the *Ecclesiastical History* of John of Ephesus they are numbered eight, but in the *Ecclesiastical History* of Zacharias of Mitylene, and in most later texts, they are seven. Thus the Qur'ān not only offers a commentary on a Christian tale, it also intervenes in Christian debates.

CS 13 Muḥammad

Qur'ānic account

The accounts in the previous case study in which the Jews tell the pagan Meccans to ask Muḥammad about the Companions of the Cave, Dhū

645 Although in the *Ecclesiastical History* of Zacharias of Mitylene the bishop of Ephesus accurately tells one of the youths that the emperor Decius reigned approximately 200 years ago.

646 See "Testi Orientali Inediti," 1:22, ## 154–5 and 2:28, ## 179–80, respectively.

647 *Acta Martyrum et Sanctorum Syriace* I, 1:320.

l-Qarnayn, the Spirit, and the Hour form part of a larger genre of Muslim exegesis marked by historical narratives. The appearance of the word *khalīfa* (Q 2.30) in the Qur'ān is explained through narratives of the *jinn* who lived on earth before humans (not strictly historical, of course; see CS 1). A verse on clothing and feathers (Q 7.26) leads to accounts of the pagan Quraysh performing circumambulation at the Ka'ba naked (see CS 3). The term *ghulf* (Q 2.88; 4.155) leads to a story of how the Jews refused to listen to Muḥammad (see CS 10). Even some modern translators, Muslim or otherwise, have inherited this interpretive habit. If they do not always accept the narratives as historically reliable, they nevertheless believe that the Qur'ān should be read in the light of these narratives.

At the same time the *mufassirūn*, notably Ṭabarī, admit (usually when contradictory narratives offer competing explanations of the same passage) that many received historical narratives are in fact ahistorical. Scholars today might place all exegetical narratives under scrutiny, knowing that exegetes had a particular desire to tell stories about their Prophet. Narratives biographical information on Muḥammad may seem to be especially suspect. For example, in *al-sharḥ* (94) 1–2 the Qur'ān asks: "Did we not expand your breast and take away your burden (or sin)?" The expansion of the breast referred to here is evidently a metaphor (cf. Q 6.125; 20.25; 39.22),[648] but it is widely interpreted through a historical narrative, according to which angels physically opened the chest of Muḥammad, removed an impure blood clot (n.b. the term *wazr* in Q 94.2), washed his heart in the water of Zamzam, and stamped a sign of his prophetic status between his shoulders (n.b. the term *khātam* in Q 33.40).[649]

Many other such examples could be named, such as the story of the invasion of a Yemeni king with an elephant during the year of Muḥammad's birth (cf. Q 105),[650] the narratives of Muḥammad's call to prophethood (cf. Q 96.1–5),[651] of his night journey to Jerusalem (cf. Q 17.1),[652] or even of his splitting the moon in two (cf. Q 54.1).[653] Thus the point might be conceded

648 Note that Pickthall, for example, translates this expression metaphorically in Q 20.25 as "relieve my mind," but in Q 94.1 he no longer sees a metaphor, translating: "Have We not caused thy bosom to dilate?"

649 Thus Ibn Kathīr (4:491–3, on Q 94.1–7). Cf. Ibn Hishām, *Sīrat Rasūl Allāh*, 263–71 (trans., 181–7). The other *mufassirūn*, while not rejecting the story of Muḥammad's blood clot, also understand this phrase as a metaphor. See esp. Ṭabarī, who paraphrases: "Did we not expand your breast, O Muḥammad, for guidance, faith in God and knowledge of the truth? Thus we soften your heart and make it a receptacle of wisdom." Ṭabarī 30:234, on Q 94.1–8. Cf. *Tafsīr Muqātil*, 4:741, on Q 94.1; Zamakhsharī 4:770, on Q 94.1–4.

650 Ibn Hishām, *Sīrat Rasūl Allāh*, 29–38 (trans., 21–8).

651 Ibid., 151–4 (trans., 105–7).

652 Ibid., 263–8 (trans., 181–4).

653 Ṭabarī, 27.84–7, on Q 54.1–2. Note also the tradition of Khadīja wrapping Muḥammad in a blanket after he received the first revelation and descended from Mt. Ḥirā' (cf. Q 73.1;

that, in certain places at least, non-historical phrases in the Qur'ān were read as historical witnesses to the biography of Muḥammad.

But what of the name Muḥammad itself? It has traditionally been read as a record of the proper name of a historical figure. But could it be a thing of literature and not history? Could Muḥammad be an epithet that only became a proper name in the historical narratives of later interpreters? There is indeed something anomalous about the appearance of this name in the Qur'ān. The Qur'ān names Moses 136 times, Abraham 69 times, and Jesus 25 times. But while the Qur'ān refers hundreds of times to a messenger (*rasūl*) or prophet (*nabī*), it uses the names Muḥammad only four times:

> (Q 3.144) Muḥammad is only a messenger. Messengers passed away before him.
>
> 3.144 وَمَا مُحَمَّدٌ إِلاَّ رَسُولٌ قَدْ خَلَتْ مِن قَبْلِهِ الرُّسُلُ . . .
>
> (Q 33.40) Muḥammad was not the father of any of your men but rather the messenger of God and the seal of the prophets. God was knowing in all things.
>
> 33.40 مَّا كَانَ مُحَمَّدٌ أَبَا أَحَدٍ مِّن رِّجَالِكُمْ وَلَكِن رَّسُولَ اللَّهِ وَخَاتَمَ النَّبِيِّينَ وَكَانَ اللَّهُ بِكُلِّ شَيْءٍ عَلِيمًا
>
> (Q 47.2) As for those who believed, acted virtuously and believed in what was brought down to Muḥammad, which is the truth from their Lord, He absolved them of their bad deeds and set their heart right.
>
> 47.2 وَالَّذِينَ آمَنُوا وَعَمِلُوا الصَّالِحَاتِ وَآمَنُوا بِمَا نُزِّلَ عَلَى مُحَمَّدٍ وَهُوَ الْحَقُّ مِن رَّبِّهِمْ كَفَّرَ عَنْهُمْ سَيِّئَاتِهِمْ وَأَصْلَحَ بَالَهُمْ
>
> (48.29) Muḥammad is the messenger of God. Those who are with him are severe to the unbelievers but compassionate to each other.
>
> 48.29 مُّحَمَّدٌ رَّسُولُ اللَّهِ وَالَّذِينَ مَعَهُ أَشِدَّاء عَلَى الْكُفَّارِ رُحَمَاء بَيْنَهُمْ. . .

Whether or not these verses cite Muḥammad as a proper name is unclear. The only apparently biographical information therein is the remark in *al-aḥzāb* (33) 40 that Muḥammad is "not the father of any of your men." Indeed Islamic historical traditions insist that Muḥammad had no son that survived into adulthood. According to Ibn Kathīr, Muḥammad had three sons by

74.1), or the tradition of Muḥammad moving his lips when he received revelation (cf. Q 75.16).

Khadīja: Qāsim, Ṭayyib, and Ṭāhir; and one son from Māriya (his Egyptian concubine): Ibrāhīm. Yet all four of them, tellingly, are said to have died as children. They did not grow up to be men (cf. Q 33.40).[654]

Indeed if these traditions could be seen as evidence that *al-aḥzāb* (33) 40 is a historical report, they could just as easily be seen as attempts to place that verse in a historical context. One might better explain the Qur'ān's insistence that Muḥammad is "not the father of any of your men" in light of the rest of the verse: "but rather the messenger of God and the seal of the prophets." In other words, the source of the prophet's authority is divine and not human.

Moreover, the above verses might be measured against *al-ṣaff* (61) 6a:

> (Q 61.6) Jesus the son of Mary said, "O Israelites, I am the messenger of God to you, confirming the Tawrāt before me, and giving the good news of a messenger to come after me. His name is Aḥmad.

61.6 وَإِذْ قَالَ عِيسَى ابْنُ مَرْيَمَ يَا بَنِي إِسْرَائِيلَ إِنِّي رَسُولُ اللَّهِ إِلَيْكُم مُّصَدِّقًا لِّمَا بَيْنَ
يَدَيَّ مِنَ التَّوْرَاةِ وَمُبَشِّرًا بِرَسُولٍ يَأْتِي مِن بَعْدِي اسْمُهُ أَحْمَدُ

If the words of Jesus here are intended as a reference to the Prophet of the Qur'ān, then his name would seem to be Aḥmad. This would mean that the Prophet is called Muḥammad in four places, but in the only place where his name is explicitly identified ("His name is . . ."), he is Aḥmad. On the basis of the Qur'ān alone one might contend that there is as much reason to name the Prophet Aḥmad as Muḥammad.

However, it is certainly possible, and in my opinion probable, that here the adjective *aḥmad* "more praiseworthy" is intended, and the phrase should be understood: "His name is more praiseworthy." But then that is precisely the point with the name Muḥammad, which could be read as the adjective *muḥammad*, "praiseworthy," and be seen as an honorary epithet. If both terms (*muḥammad* and *aḥmad*) are read as adjectives, then we would have two different honorary titles for the Prophet in the Qur'ān, but nowhere his proper name.

Problems for interpreters

Nevertheless the majority of the translators, including Yusuf Ali, Arberry, Paret, Fakhry, and Abdel Haleem, present *aḥmad* as a proper name ("Aḥmad"). Only Pickthall sees the term as a substantive adjective, translating: "whose name is the Praised One." Blachère, for his part, offers two alternative translations, the first of which is simply the proper name "Aḥmad." The second is based on an unusually long Qur'ānic variant attributed to Ubayy. Thereby *al-ṣaff* (61) 6 reads "giving the good news of a messenger

654 Ibn Kathīr, 3:459, on Q 33.39–40. Cf. Zamakhsharī, 3:544, on Q 33.40.

to come after me," but then continues (in place of "His name is Aḥmad"), "whose community will be the last community and by whom God will place the seal on the prophets and messengers."

As for the *mufassirūn*, *Tafsīr Muqātil* reports that *aḥmad*, in Syriac, is "paraclete" (*fārqlīṭā*).[655] Thereby he puts *al-ṣaff* (61) 6 to apologetic use. He connects the announcement by Jesus of a messenger to come after him in the Qur'ān to the promises by Jesus of the Paraclete in the Gospel of John (14.16, 26; 15.26; 16.7).[656]

Qummī relates a tradition that suggests both Muḥammad and Aḥmad are among the Prophet's religious epithets:

> One of the Jews asked the Messenger of God, "Why are you named Muḥammad and Aḥmad and Bashīr ['bearer of good news'] and Nadhīr ['warner']?" He said, "As for Muḥammad, I am praised on the earth. As for Aḥmad, I am more praised in heaven. As for Bashīr, I give the good news of heaven to those who obey God. As for Nadhīr, I warn those who disobey God of hellfire."[657]

Ibn Kathīr relates a similar tradition in a prophetic *ḥadīth*:

> The Messenger of God said, "I have various names. I am Muḥammad. I am Aḥmad. I am al-Māḥī ['the eraser'] by which God erases unbelief. I am al-Ḥāshir ['the gatherer'] for the people will be gathered in front of me and I will be at the end."[658]

Thus even among the *mufassirūn* the idea that Muḥammad is one of the Prophet's religious epithets is entertained, even if none of the *mufassirūn* draws the conclusion that this was not, therefore, his proper name.

Subtext

However, the question of whether Muḥammad is the proper name of the Qur'ān's prophet has a long history in western scholarship. In the middle of the nineteenth century the Austrian scholar Aloys Sprenger argued that

655 *Tafsīr Muqātil*, 1:316, on Q 61.6.

656 Ibn Hishām employs a similar strategy. In his discussion of the Prophet's call he presents a version of Jn 15.26. For Paraclete (Gk παράκλητος) Ibn Hishām reports *m.n.ḥ.m.n.ā*, which he insists is the Syriac term for Muḥammad. In fact it is the term that appears in the Christian Palestinian Aramaic lectionary for Paraclete. See Ibn Hishām, *Sīrat Rasūl Allāh*, 153 (trans., 107); Schulthess, *Lexicon Syropalaestinum*, 122a; *GdQ1*, 9, n. 1.

657 Qummī, 2:346, on Q 61.6. Regarding this tradition cf. Grünbaum, *Neue Beiträge*, 30.

658 Ibn Kathīr, 4:332, on Q 61.6 (on the authority of Bukhārī). A similar tradition follows: "The Messenger of God called himself by various names for us, some of which we memorized. He said, 'I am Muḥammad. I am Aḥmad. I am al-Ḥāshir, al-Muqfī ("The one who follows") and the Prophet of Mercy, Repentance and Battle (*malḥama*).' "

it is not.[659] Sprenger argues that the Muslim Prophet adopted the name Muḥammad (which, he points out, appears only in Qur'ānic passages traditionally dated to the Medinan period) around the time of his migration from Mecca to Yathrib.[660] This he did because the Arabic root *ḥ.m.d.*, associated with "praise" in classical Arabic, is associated with "longing" in certain Arabic dialects. The Prophet, in other words, named himself "the one longed-for" and this in the hope of being acknowledged by the Jews as their Messiah.[661]

In support of his case Sprenger notes that in Islamic sources the name Muḥammad appears only rarely in the onomastica of Jāhilī Arabs.[662] In response to this point Ernest Renan notes that a Greek inscription in Palmyra, dated AD 115, includes the name θαιμοαμεδου, presumably the genitive form of θαιμοάμεδος.[663] Renan argues that this name represents Arabic *taym Muḥammad* or *taym Aḥmad* and testifies to the pre-Islamic use of the Prophet's name.[664] Sprenger, in turn, counters that the Greek μοαμεδος might represent another Arabic term, perhaps *muʿammad* ("The Baptized One").[665]

Sprenger's argument is followed in its broad outlines by Hartwig Hirschfeld, who notes that there is more evidence for the pre-Islamic use of the name Aḥmad, and thus more reason to assume that this was the Prophet's given name, and Muḥammad a variation thereof.[666] Another development of Sprenger's argument is found in a little known article by Gustav Rösch, who insists that the Palmyrene inscription is indeed a witness for the pre-Islamic, pagan use of the name Muḥammad.[667] But when Muḥammad made claims to prophethood, Rösch argues, he associated this pagan name with the appearance of the root *ḥ.m.d.* in the Hebrew Bible (Haggai 2.7; Song

659 See the addendum to the second chapter of his *Das Leben und die Lehre des Moḥammad* (1:155–62), entitled "Hiess der Prophet Moḥammad?"

660 Sprenger, *Leben*, 1:156–9.

661 Ibid., 1:155–62.

662 Ibid., 1:161.

663 See Augustus Böckh, *Corpus Inscriptionum Graecarum*, Berlin: Reimeri, 1828–77, # 4500; cf. E. Ledrain, *Dictionnaire des noms propres palmyrenians*, Paris: Leroux, 1886, 55.

664 See Sprenger, *Leben*, 1:581.

665 Ibid. In fact, in his *Dictionnaire des noms propres palmyrenians*, Eugene Ledrain transliterates (into Hebrew characters) the Greek inscription in this manner: *t.y.m.ʿ.m.d.* However, he interprets the root *ʿ.m.d.* in the name as a reference to "support" and translates the name, "celui que [the god] Thaimi soutient" (p. 55).

666 Hirschfeld, *Jüdische Elemente im Koran*, Berlin: Schulze, 1878, 70–7. In a later publication Hirschfeld notes that the appearance of the name Muḥammad in the Prophet's biography hardly resolves the issue. If the name Muḥammad appears in material that is presented as secular history, such as the Prophet's letters to world leaders, the authenticity of that material is far from certain. See Hirschfeld, *New Researches*, 137–40.

667 G. Rösch, "Die Namen des arabischen Propheten Muḥammed und Aḥmed," *ZDMG* 46, 1892, (432–40) 433–4. In the pagan context, Rösch contends, the name Muḥammad referred not to its bearer but rather to a patron god (in this case, he suggests, the moon-god Hubal, who is associated with Mecca in Islamic accounts) and it is in this sense that the future Prophet's father – or more likely, his grandfather – gave him the name. Ibid., 436.

of Solomon 2:3) in passages which – according to Rösch – Jews considered messianic.[668]

Nöldeke, however, emphatically rejects Sprenger's theory. In defense of the traditional notion of the name Muḥammad he notes: First, in historical records such as the treaty of Ḥudaybiyya and the Constitution of Medina the Prophet's name appears as Muḥammad; second, if the name were an epithet it should appear with the definite article; third, Jewish tradition does not use the idiom "the one longed-for" as an epithet for the Messiah; and four, Muḥammad was a name used by Arabs in pre-Islamic Arabia.[669] Meanwhile Nöldeke describes Sprenger's premise that in Jewish interpretation passages with the root *ḥ.m.d.* developed a messianic sense as "aus der Luft gegriffen."[670]

The academic debate over this issue is complicated still further by an addendum that appears at the end of the issue of *Die Zeitschrift der deutschen morgenländischen Gesellschaft* with Rösch's article. Therein Rösch explains that on October 19, 1892, he was able for the first time to examine the text of the Palmyrene inscription. After studying the text, Rösch reports, and consulting none other than Nöldeke himself, he became convinced that θαιμοαμεδου does not represent a form of the name Muḥammad but rather *taym ʿamed*, meaning (in Aramaic) "[the god] Taym supports" (Rösch, apparently following Nöldeke, reads *taym* as a divine name whereas it usually means "servant").[671]

For his part Nöldeke elsewhere speculates that Muḥammad might be an abbreviation of a theophoric Nabatean name.[672] Some years later Hubert Grimme proposed a similar theory, apparently without any knowledge of Nöldeke's remark, arguing that Muḥammad is an abbreviation for an Old North Arabian (Safaitic) theophoric name such as *muḥammad-īl*, "the praiseworthy God."[673] Grimme argues that the name Muḥammad could

668 On the messianic interpretation of these passages see also Sprenger, *Leben*, 1:159–60. As for the name Aḥmad ("The most praised"), Rösch argues that Muḥammad himself coined this variation, in order to associate himself with the παράκλητος predicted by Jesus (Jn 14.16). Rösch, following Luigi Marracci (*Refutatio Alcorani in qua ad Mahumetanicae superstitionis radicem securis apponitur*, Padua: ex typographia seminarii, 1698, 1:27), proposes that Muḥammad confused παράκλητος and περικλυτός ("the praised one") for which reason the Qur'ān (Q 61.6) has Jesus predict the coming of *aḥmad*. On this argument Nöldeke wonders how Muḥammad learned Greek at all. *GdQ1*, 10, fn. 1 (from page 9).

669 *GdQ1*, 9, fn. 1.

670 Ibid., 10, fn. 1.

671 G. Rösch, "Die Namen des arabischen Propheten Muḥammed und Aḥmed; Zu S. 432," *ZDMG* 46, 1892, 580. I am grateful to Prof. Manfred Kropp for his insight on this matter.

672 In a comment on an occurrence of the name *ʿAlī'īl* in a Nabatean inscription (which would seem to mean "God [El] is exalted"), Nöldeke speculates that the name ʿAlī could be an abbreviation thereof, and Muḥammad an abbreviation of a parallel name (*muḥammad'īl*, "God is praiseworthy"). Nöldeke's remark is in J. Euting, *Nabatäische Inschriften aus Arabien*, Berlin: Reimer, 1885, 67. A. Fischer refers to this remark in, "Muhammad und Ahmad, die Namen des arabischen Propheten," *Berichte über die Verhandlungen der Sächsischen Akademie der Wissenschaften zu Leipzig, phil.-hist. Klasse* 84, 1932, (3–27) 3.

673 H. Grimme, "Der Name Moḥammad," *Zeitschrift für Semitistik und verwandte Gebiete* 6, 1928, 24–6.

only properly be assigned to a god (who is worthy of praise or, according to the root *ḥ.m.d.* in Ancient South Arabian, thanksgiving). He also notes a Safaitic inscription with the name *m.s.b.ḥ.-il*, meaning likewise "the praise-worthy God" (from the root *s.b.ḥ.*, a calque with Arabic *ḥ.m.d.*). The Muslim prophet, Grimme concludes, must have intentionally taken on this name, since his fundamental religious message was to praise God alone. In a later work, moreover, Grimme claims to have found an instance of the name *muḥammad-īl*.[674]

On Grimme's theory August Fischer comments, "Wer mit dem klassisch-arabischen und den alt-arabischen Verhältnissen etwas genauer vertraut ist, der kann über diese ganze Argumentation nur den Kopf schütteln."[675] Fischer contends, with copious examples from Arabic lexicography, that the second form of *ḥ.m.d.* (of which *muḥammad* is the passive participle) is *not* generally used for praising God (which is instead the common use of the first form);[676] instead it is used in early Arabic texts for praising people, and indeed (Islamic) Arabic literature contains numerous references to individuals named Muḥammad before Islam.[677] Accusing Grimme of "Entdeckerfreude," Fischer adds that Muḥammad was not Safaitic but a Qurayshī Arab, and that these "echten Arabern" did not have theophoric names.[678]

Finally Fischer points to the occurrence of the name *m.ḥ.m.d.ā.* in the Syriac *Book of the Himyarites* (on the Christian martyrs of Najrān; probably 6th century).[679] Fischer concludes that this Syriac form must be a reproduction of the feminine Arabic form of Muḥammad, that is, Muḥammada, which would have been used by pre-Islamic Arabs (although why this name would fall completely out of use Fischer does not explain). This name proves that the proper name Muḥammad was used in pre-Islamic times, and that it was not theophoric (since it exists in a feminine form, and Arabs did not use theophoric names in the feminine).[680]

After Fischer's trenchant article, written in 1932, the question of the name Muḥammad would not again be raised for some time. Watt, for example, simply follows Nöldeke in insisting that the Prophet is named Muḥammad in those texts which comprise (for him) a reliable historical core of his biography. According to the report of the treaty at Ḥudaybiyya the pagan Quraysh objected to the Prophet signing the treaty document with the title "Messenger of God," but they accepted that he sign the document

674 H. Grimme, *Texte und Untersuchungen zur ṣafatenisch-arabischen Religion, mit einer Einführung in die ṣafatenische Epigraphik*, Paderborn: Schöningh, 1929, 63.

675 Fischer, "Muhammad und Aḥmad," 5.

676 "Insonderheit erscheinen für 'gepriesen' auf Gott bezüglich, immer nur *maḥmūd* oder *ḥamīd*, nirgends *muḥammad*." Fischer, "Muhammad und Aḥmad," 10.

677 See ibid., 11–3.

678 Ibid., 19.

679 See *The Book of the Himyarites*, ed. and trans. A. Moberg, Lund: Gleerup, 1924, 92. This work is examined in detail by Shahid, *The Martyrs of Najrân*.

680 Fischer, "Muhammad und Aḥmad," 26.

"Muḥammad."[681] No Muslim would fabricate such a report, he argues, since it casts Muḥammad in an unfavorable light.

Nöldeke's position appears also in Franz Buhl's article "Muḥammad" in the first *Encyclopaedia of Islam*,[682] and the expansion of that article by Alfred Welch in the second *Encyclopaedia of Islam*.[683] Buhl and Welch point to the name *m.ḥ.m.d.ā.* in the *Book of the Himyarites* and to lists provided by Ibn Sa'd (d. 230/845) and Ibn Durayd (d. 321/933) of individuals before Islam named Muḥammad.[684] Yet at the same time they note that Ibn Sa'd's list is prefixed by a title which hardly bespeaks historical reliability: "Account of those who were named Muḥammad in the Jāhiliyya in the hope of being called to the Prophethood which had been predicted." Buhl and Welch also remark that, according to one tradition, the Prophet was called Amīn in his youth. On this basis they argue that Amīn might indeed have been the Prophet's given name, due to its similarity to Āmina, the name of his mother. To my knowledge, however, Islamic tradition contains only the report that the Prophet was given the name *al-amīn*, that is, "the reliable," and this among many other names. This report appears in a widespread *ḥadīth* (cf. its appearance above in the *tafsīr*s of Qummī and Ibn Kathīr) which presents the various symbolic names (including Muḥammad) of the Muslim Prophet.[685] According to a version of this *ḥadīth* reported by Ibn al-Jawzī (d. 597/1200) the Prophet had twenty-three names, among them *muḥammad* ("the praised-one"), *aḥmad* ("the most-praised one"), and *al-amīn*.[686]

One of the few recent attempts to address this question is that of Claude Gilliot, who notes both the argument of Sprenger (which he describes as "malheureusement presque tombé dans l'oubli"[687]) and that of Hirschfeld.[688]

681 Watt, *Bell's Introduction to the Qur'ān*, 53.

682 F. Buhl, "Muḥammad," *Encyclopaedia of Islam*, 1st edition, Leiden: Brill, 1913–34, 3:685–6.

683 EI^2, 7:361b. Note also the short article of E.J. Jurji, "Pre-Islamic use of the name Muḥammad," *MW* 26, 1936, 389–91.

684 Ibn Sa'd, 1:1:111–2. Ibn Durayd, *Ishtiqāq*, ed. F. Wüstenfeld, Göttingen: Dieterichsche Buchhandlung, 1854, 6–7.

685 Versions of this *ḥadīth* are found in the *Ṣaḥīḥ*s of Bukhārī and Muslim and numerous other sources. See Wensinck, *Concordance de la tradition musulmane*, Leiden: Brill, 1936, 1:470b.

686 See Ibn al-Jawzī, *al-Wafā' bi-aḥwāl al-muṣṭafā*, Cairo: Dār al-Kutub al-Ḥadītha, 1386/1966, 103–5. The last name in this list is *al-qutham* ("the generous"), a name that appears in Islamic sources on pre-Islamic Arabs (e.g. the Prophet's paternal cousin Qutham b. al-'Abbās). Furthermore, a tradition in the *sīra* of Ḥalabī (d. 1044/1635) relates that this was the name that 'Abd al-Muṭṭalib intended to give to his grandson. See 'Alī b. Burhān al-Dīn al-Ḥalabī, *al-Sīra al-Ḥalabiyya*, Beirut: Dār al-Ma'rifa, n.d., 1:128. Accordingly Lammens wonders if this could have been the Prophet's given name. See Lammens, "Qoran et tradition," 29–30 (English trans., 171–2). See also Sprenger, *Leben*, 1:155–6; Rösch, "Namen des arabischen Propheten," 432–3.

687 C. Gilliot, "Une reconstruction critique du Coran ou comment en finir avec les merveilles de la lampe d'Aladin," in Kropp (ed.), *Results of Contemporary Research on the Qur'ān*, (33–137) 77, n. 304.

688 Ibid. Gilliot also argues that reports (like those found in Ibn Sa'd) of pre-Islamic figures who took the name Muḥammad in the hope of becoming prophets are fully legendary.

He concludes: "Ce nom très peu répandu avant l'islam n'apparaît que dans les sourates médinoises et il n'était probablement pas le sien. Ce serait un titre qu'il se serait attribué ou qu'on lui aurait décerné par la suite."[689] Gilliot thus rejects the traditional position of Nöldeke, but like Nöldeke he bases his arguments on traditional reports regarding the biography of Muḥammad and pre-Islamic Arabia. Indeed both the Sprenger/Gilliot position and the Nöldeke/Watt position rely fundamentally on such reports. Sprenger bases his argument on reports of the Prophet's eagerness to be accepted by a Jewish community in Medina, a fundamental feature of the *sīra*. Nöldeke (and after him Bell and Watt) accordingly counters with evidence from the *sīra*. Gilliot in turn responds with another argument based on the *sīra*, namely that the Qur'ān can be read according to the chronology of the Prophet's life and that the name Muḥammad appears only in later verses.

More recently, however, a number of studies have appeared in which the question of the term *muḥammad* is considered independently from the reports of Islamic tradition. In *Crossroads to Islam*, Yehuda Nevo and Judith Koren contend, on the basis of epigraphic evidence (above all the Dome of the Rock inscriptions), that *muḥammad* is an adjective meaning not "the praised one" (since praise in classical Arabic is associated rather with *s.b.ḥ.*) but rather "the chosen one." Thus they make the name Muḥammad an epithet synonymous with Muṣṭafā, another name commonly used for Islam's Prophet.[690]

Volker Popp agrees with Nevo and Koren (although he does not reference their work) that *muḥammad* means "chosen."[691] Yet Popp goes still further, contending that at the time of the Dome of the Rock Islam itself had not yet developed. The Umayyad Arabs were in fact Christians, although their hostility towards Byzantium led them to adopt a Nestorian Christology which they found in Persia, the ancient nemesis of Byzantium. Jesus, they maintained, was a mere human whom God chose to make his servant, Prophet, and Christ. In other words, the term *muḥammad*, the "chosen one," was originally used (for example, in early inscriptions) not for an Arab prophet but rather for Jesus.[692]

Popp is not alone is this view. It is supported by two other scholars who, with Popp, are active in a circle of European scholars that has recently produced a series of volumes of collected articles on Late Antiquity and

Gilliot notes that a similar list can be found in Ibn Ḥabīb, *Muḥabbar* (d. 245/860), ed. I. Lichtenstaedter, Hyderabad: n.p., 1942, 130.

689 "Une reconstruction critique du Coran," 77, n. 304.

690 See Y. Nevo and J. Koren, *Crossroads to Islam: The Origins of the Arab Religion and the Arab State*, Amherst, NY: Prometheus, 2003, 263–7.

691 V. Popp, "Die frühe Islamgeschichte nach inschriftlichen und numismatischen Zeugnissen," in K.-H. Ohlig and G.-R. Puin (eds.), *Die dunklen Anfänge: Neue Forschungen zur Entstehung und frühen Geschichte des Islam*, Berlin: Schiler, 2005, (16–123) 38.

692 Ibid., 60–5. In this section Popp relies above all on the inscriptions and iconography of Umayyad coins.

early Islam.[693] Christoph Luxenberg explains the Dome of the Rock inscription *muḥammadun ʿAbdu Llāhi wa-rasūluhu* as "The servant and messenger of God [i.e. Jesus] is praiseworthy."[694] The servant of God, he continues, is an early Christian trope for Jesus (rooted in the servant-messiah of Isaiah). This trope is to be found in the Qur'ān when the infant Jesus begins his discourse in *Maryam* (19) 30 with the phrase, *inni ʿAbdu Llahi* ("I am the servant of God").[695]

If Luxenberg understands *muḥammad* as "praiseworthy," Karl-Heinz Ohlig agrees instead with Nevo and Popp that its proper meaning is something like Greek ἐκλεκτός, "the chosen one" (cf. Lk 23:35).[696] The use of such a term for Christ was favored by Arabs, who had a Semitic, pre-Byzantine Christology focused on *heilsgeschichte* (as opposed to the natural/ontological Christology of the Greek Church fathers). When, after the conquests, the Arabs entered into formerly Byzantine areas, the Christians there were unfamiliar with this title and assumed that it represented a proper name of a different person.[697] Still the Qur'ān itself preserves evidence of the original meaning of *muḥammad*. In *ālʿImrān* (3) 144 the Qur'ān declares, "*muḥammad* [by Ohlig's reading, 'The chosen one'] was only a messenger. Messengers passed away before him." This passage, Ohlig contends, is parallel to *al-mā'ida* (5) 75, where the Qur'ān proclaims "*al-Masīḥ* [Christ] the son of Mary was only a messenger. Messengers passed away before him."[698]

These arguments, it seems to me, are worthy of some consideration. It is telling, for example, that the name Muḥammad for Islam's Prophet does not appear in any form before two Arab-Sasanian coins minted in AH 66 (AD 685–6) and 67 (686–7).[699] In the earliest textual witnesses to the rise of Islam, such as the Greek *Doctrina Jacobi* (ca. 634), the AD 634 Christmas sermon of Sophronius, and the Syriac dialogue with a Muslim Emir of John

693 These volumes are the work of the recently founded scholarly society *Inârah*: Institut zur Erforschung der frühen Islamgeschichte und des Koran.

694 C. Luxenberg, "Die arabische Inschrift im Felsendom zu Jerusalem," in Ohlig and Puin (eds.), *Dunklen Anfänge*, (124–47) 129–31.

695 Thus the phrase *muḥammadun ʿAbdu Llāhi wa-rasūluhu* is parallel to the Christian Arabic liturgical proclamation (derived from Mt 21.9, itself a quotation of Psalm 118.25–6), *mubārakun al-ātī bi-smi l-rabbi*. See Luxenberg, "Die arabische Inschrift," 131.

696 K.-H. Ohlig, "Von muḥammad Jesus zum Propheten der Araber: Die Historisierung eines christologischen Prädikats," in K.-H. Ohlig (ed.), *Der frühe Islam*, Berlin: Schiler, 2007, (327–76) 332–3.

697 Ibid., 346.

698 Ibid., 361.

699 See R. Hoyland, "New documentary texts and the early Islamic state," *BSOAS* 69, 2006, 397. See also idem, "The content and context of early Arabic inscriptions," *JSAI* 21, 1997, 77–102. A revisionist view is found in Y. Nevo, "Towards a pre-history of Islam," *JSAI* 17, 1994, 108–41, and in the more ambitious work, completed by Y. Nevo's assistant J. Koren, *Crossroads to Islam*. Therein (p. 247) Nevo and Koren argue that the earliest appearance of Muḥammad is on an Umayyad coin dated AH 71 (BC 690) and in an inscription on the Dome dated AH 72 (BC 691).

of Sedreh (644), it is nowhere to be found.[700] Yet ultimately all of these arguments are based on historical (re-)constructions. The present study, however, is based on the Qur'ān.

From this perspective it should first be noted that the Qur'ān repeatedly refers to the principal characters of its discourse with epithets. In the Qur'ān Jesus is commonly called *al-masīḥ*, a term which appears in the Qur'ān simply as a sort of honorary title, not as an indication of any particular religious role. Pharaoh (cf. CS 6) is referred to as *dhū l-awtād* (Q 38.12; 89.10). Jonah (cf. CS 8) is referred to as *dhū l-nūn* (Q 21.87) and *ṣāḥib al-ḥūt* (Q 68.48).

In all of these cases, of course, the Qur'ān provides a proper name as well, so that the reader is able to connect the epithets or nicknames with that name. Yet this is not always the case. The epithet *dhū l-kifl* (Q 21.85; 38.48), for example, is not easily identified with any other figure in the Qur'ān.[701] *Dhū l-qarnayn* ("Two-Horned"; Q 18.83, 86, passim) is easily identified with Alexander (who represented himself with iconography of the two-horned Egyptian god Ammon), but the name Alexander appears nowhere in the Qur'ān.[702]

The case of *al-ʿazīz* is similar. This title appears twice in the Qur'ān (Q 12.30, 51) for the man who bought Joseph (cf. Q 12.21), that is, Potiphar (see Gn 37.36), a name that appears nowhere in the Qur'ān. The epithet *al-ʿazīz*, "the powerful one," seems to reflect the role of Potiphar (the "commander" of Pharaoh's guard; Gn 39.1). The *mufassirūn*, aware of the Biblical story, generally make the connection,[703] even though ʿAzīz was a common

700 On this topic generally see Hoyland, *Seeing Islam as Others Saw It*. For the relevant excerpt of the *Doctrina Jacobi* see pp. 56–8. See also H. Usener, "Weihnachtspredigt des Sophronios," *Rheinisches Museum für Philologie* 41, 1886, 500–16; A.-M. Saadi, "The letter of John of Sedreh: A new perspective on nascent Islam," *Karmo* 1, 1998, 1, 18–31 (Arabic and Syriac); 1, 1999, 2, 46–64 (English trans.); F. Nau "Un colloque du patriarche Jean avec l'émir des Agaréens," *Journal asiatique* 11, 1915, 225–79; cf. also S. Griffith, "The Prophet Muḥammad, his scripture and his message according to the Christian apologies in Arabic and Syriac from the first Abbasid century," *Vie du prophète Mahomet, Colloque de Strasbourg (23–24 octobre 1980)*, Paris: Presses universitaires de France, 1983, 99–146.

701 J. Walker ("Who is Dhū 'l-Kifl?," *Muslim World* 16, 1926, 399–401) argues that *dhū l-kifl* should be identified as Job. Noting that the root *k.f.l.* has the meaning of doubling, Walker points out that in the epilogue of the Biblical book of the same name God gives Job *twice* what he once had (Job 42.10). M. Schub, on the other hand, identifies *dhū l-kifl* as Melchizedek (cf. Gn 14.18), noting that Melchizedek is said to have dwelt in the valley of *shāwēh* (Gn 14.17), a term meaning "equal" which he contends is also related to the meaning of *k.f.l.* See M. Schub, "The secret identity of Dhū l'Kifl," in Ibn Warraq (ed.), *What the Koran Really Says*, 394–5. Perhaps the most reasonable proposal is that of Jeffery, who suggests that *dhū l-kifl* does not refer to an otherwise unnamed figure but is rather, in light of its appearance next to the name Elisha (e.g. Q 38.48), a second name for Elijah, just as *dhū l-nūn* is a second name for Jonah. See Jeffery, *Qur'ān as Scripture*, 38.

702 See *KU*, 111–3; van Bladel, "The legend of Alexander the Great in the Qur'ān," 119, n. 18; cf. idem, "Heavenly cords and prophetic authority."

703 Thus Ṭabarī (12:175, on Q 12.21) writes: "The name of the one who bought [Joseph] was *q.ṭ.f.ī.r.* (presumably this is a corruption of *f.ṭ.f.ī.r.*). It is also said that his name was *i.ṭ.f.ī.r.*

Muslim name, and al-ʿAzīz (with the definite article) a name commonly taken by rulers.

It seems possible, then, that the Qur'ān reports the name Muḥammad ("the praised one") as an epithet in the way that it reports the name *al-ʿAzīz*. Because the proper name of Muḥammad does not appear elsewhere in the Qur'ān (as with Jonah) or in the Biblical subtext (as with Potiphar), the *mufassirūn* had no way of recognizing the epithet. However (and as Nöldeke points out),[704] the presence of the definite article with *al-ʿAzīz* suggests it is an epithet. The name Muḥammad, by contrast, never appears with the definite article.

There are, however, two cases that represent closer parallels. The first case is Ṣāliḥ (Q 7.73, 75; 11.61, passim), a word meaning "righteous" that is usually taken as the proper name of the prophet sent to a people called Thamūd. According to the *mufassirūn* Ṣāliḥ is one of the Arabian prophets unknown to the Jews and Christians. Geiger, however, suggests that Ṣāliḥ is not a proper name at all.[705] Horovitz accordingly points out that otherwise the Qur'ān uses the adjective *ṣāliḥ* to describe those who are obedient to God, especially the prophets (e.g. Q 2.130; 3.39, 46, 114 passim).[706] Thus he concludes that the name Ṣāliḥ "scheint eigene Schöpfung Muhammads zu sein."[707]

The case of Ṣāliḥ would seem to suggest that the name Muḥammad might also be a literary creation. True, *ṣāliḥ* is a common adjective in classical Arabic, while *muḥammad* is not. Yet there is nothing irregular about the form *muḥammad* (Form 2 passive participle of *ḥ.m.d.*), and presumably the infrequent use thereof as an adjective in Islamic literature is attributable to the inevitable associations that it carried with the Prophet.[708]

The second case is Ṭālūt, a character to whom the Qur'ān refers on two occasions (vv. 247, 249) in *al-baqara*. On closer inspection it is evident that

b. *r.ū.ḥ.ī.b.* He is *al-ʿazīz*." Ibn Kathīr, for his part, remarks, "The one who bought [Joseph] from Egypt was *ʿazīzuha* [i.e. *ʿazīz Miṣr*]. He is the vizier." Ibn Kathīr, 2:447, on Q 12.21–2. By Ibn Kathīr's day the title ʿAzīz Miṣr had become a standard title for the governor of Egypt, due to the Qur'ānic Joseph account. See B. Lewis, "ʿAzīz Miṣr," *EI*^{2}, 1:825b.

704 "Wäre der Name ursprünglich ein Epitheton, so würde die Tatsache, daß er nicht ein einziges Mal mit dem Artikel vorkommt, unverständlich sein." *GdQ1*, 10, n. 1.

705 "Überhaupt ist das Wort in seiniger Bedeutung 'ein Frommer' so allgemein, dass man es nicht mit Gewissheit hier ursprünglich als Eigennamen betrachten kann." Geiger, *Was hat Mohammed*, 118. Geiger argues that all of the so-called Arabian prophets of the Qur'ān are in fact Biblical figures. Thus he identifies, for example, Hūd as the Biblical Eber (cf. Gn 10.21, 24, 25; 11.14–7; Numbers 24.24). Ibid., 112–6. Notice, incidentally, the resemblance of the name Ṣāliḥ with the name of Eber's father, Shelah (Gn 10.24; 11.12). Speyer, for his part, argues that the name Ṣāliḥ is an epithet for Melchizedek (cf. Gn 14.18). See *BEQ*, 119.

706 See *KU*, 50.

707 *KU*, 123. Cf. A. Rippin: "The name Ṣāliḥ itself may well be a formation from the time of Muḥammad himself, from the root *ṣ.l.ḥ.* with the connotation of 'to be pious, upright.'" A. Rippin, "Ṣāliḥ," *EI*^{2}, 8:984b.

708 For a few examples of its use see *AEL*, 640a.

the Qur'ān intends thereby Saul, for Ṭālūt is the king who brings his army to face Goliath (Jālūt, Q 2.250) whom David defeats (Q 2.251). That the name Ṭālūt is purely literary seems apparent. On the one hand it provides assonance with Goliath's name (Jālūt). On the other hand, being related to the Arabic root for "height" (*ṭ.w.l.*), Ṭālūt is also a reflection of the Biblical reference to the stature of Saul, who was "head and shoulders" taller than his people (1 Samuel 10.23).[709]

With this example, then, it seems that the possibility of the name *muḥammad* likewise being an epithet cannot be ruled out. Indeed its relationship with the root for "praise" (*ḥ.m.d.*) makes this possibility quite compelling. The root *ḥ.m.d.* is widely attested in South Arabian and Northwest Semitic languages, and with a meaning close to Arabic *ḥ.m.d.*[710] This suggests that the word *muḥammad* would have been a meaningful epithet in the Qur'ān's context. Yet one Northwest Semitic language in which the root *ḥ.m.d.* does not appear is Syriac, the language which so often unlocks the sense of Qur'ānic vocabulary. Arabic *ḥ.m.d.* corresponds instead with Syriac *sh.b.ḥ.* (cognate with Arabic *s.b.ḥ.*).[711] Qur'ānic *muḥammad* is thus parallel to, if not a calque on, the Syriac passive participle *shbīḥ/shbīḥā*, an adjective consistently used in the Peshitta (e.g. Gn 45.22; Isaiah 23.9; Philippians 4.8) and in Syriac Christian literature to describe anyone, or anything, that is worthy of praise.[712] In this light, as well, the term *muḥammad* appears as a meaningful epithet.

The hypothesis that *muḥammad* is a literary epithet, furthermore, accords with the Biblical topos by which God's chosen ones receive a new name at the moment of their call (thus, e.g., Abram>Abraham, Sarai>Sarah, Jacob>Israel). This topos tellingly appears with both of the primary apostles of Jesus in the New Testament. Simon is named Peter (πέτρος, the "rock" on which Jesus will build his church) after he recognizes that Jesus is the Christ (cf. Mt 16.16–8; cf. Jn 1.42), while Saul is referred to by his Roman name Paul (παῦλος, "small," perhaps because he is the last of the apostles) after his conversion (Acts 13.9). The case of Paul is particularly interesting, since in Christian literature he is generally referred to simply as the τὸ ἀπόστολος (i.e. "the messenger"; cf. Syr. *shlīḥā*), just as the Qur'ān so often refers to its Prophet simply as *al-rasūl* ("the messenger").

Finally it might be noted that the Qur'ān has little concern with the proper names of its own place and time. The Qur'ān mentions Mecca once (Q 48.24; Q 3.96 notwithstanding), Badr once (Q 3.123), Ḥunayn once (Q 9.25), and the ruined city of Lot once (Q 37.137–8). Even then the Qur'ān does not

709 On this point cf. Geiger, *Was hat Mohammed*, 179; *KU*, 84, 123.

710 According to Zammit (p. 148) the root *ḥ.m.d.* has the following connotations: South Arabian, "to praise"; Aramaic, "to desire, covet"; Hebrew, "to desire; take pleasure in"; Phoenician, "to desire"; Ugaritic, "to be pleasant, covet."

711 Note, for example, the verbal noun *shūbḥ/shūbḥā* used in the Psh. with the meaning "laus, gloria" in Psalms 7.5; 8.1; 19.1; 24.10, passim. *TS*, 4026. Cf. *LCD*, 483b.

712 See *TS*, 4025. Cf. J.E. Manna, *Vocabulaire chaldeen-arabe*, Mosul: n.p., 1900; reprint: ed. R.J. Bidawid, Beirut: Babel Center, 1975, 762b.

identify Mecca as a city, but simply speaks of the "hollow" or the "heart" (*baṭn*) of *makka*. Nor does it make it clear that Badr or Ḥunayn were the sites of battles. Similarly, the Qur'ān names only two peoples – the Byzantines (Q 30.2) and the Quraysh (Q 106.1) – but gives no details on either one.

The Qur'ān never mentions by name Yathrib, Uḥud, Ṭā'if, Arabia, Egypt, Yemen, Persia, or the Red Sea.[713] More to the point, it mentions none of the protagonists of the *sīra* by name, not the Prophet's wives Khadīja or 'Ā'isha, not his daughter Fāṭima, his uncle Abū Ṭālib, his cousin 'Alī, or his companions Abū Bakr, 'Umar, and 'Uthmān. The Qur'ān, in other words, is not interested in the proper names of its historical context. It should not be a great surprise, then, that the Qur'ān never provides the proper name of its own Prophet.

713 The Qur'ān's use of *al-madīna* ("the city"; see Q 9.101, 120; 33.60; 63.8) is too general to assume that it is a proper name.

3 Qur'ān and *tafsīr*

The case studies of the previous chapter serve in part to illustrate the struggles of the classical *mufassirūn* to understand significant elements of the Qur'ān. Indeed it should be noticed that these case studies, for the most part, are not limited to isolated phrases, *hapax legomena*, or foreign vocabulary. Instead they largely address narratives or themes that lie at the heart of the Qur'ān's discourse. The struggles of the exegetes are therefore all the more curious.

The present chapter follows from this observation. Here I will consider in a more focused manner what our case studies suggest about the relationship of *tafsīr* and Qur'ān. This chapter is not meant as an exhaustive analysis of *tafsīr* literature. Instead I mean above all to show how the classical *mufassirūn* use certain key exegetical mechanisms to shape the Qur'ān according to their particular purposes. I will focus on five such mechanisms in particular:

a. Story-telling
b. Occasion of revelation
c. *Variae lectiones*
d. *Ta'khīr al-muqaddam*
e. Judaeo-Christian material

These five mechanisms are not intended as a classification or typology of *tafsīr* literature, but rather as a collection of select interpretive devices that are particularly salient in our case studies.[1] Together they are meant to provide examples of how the *mufassirūn* bridge the gap that separates them from the Qur'ān.

After an analysis of these elements I will turn to a brief diachronic study of the *mufassirūn* who appear in the second chapter. In particular I will

1 Indeed I do not suggest that the above list is a complete catalogue of exegetical mechanisms. One notable absence, for example, is the phenomenon of poetic citations as *shawāhid* ("testimonies") on the meaning of obscure Qur'ānic vocabulary. This interpretive technique, however, is absent in the two earliest *tafsīr*s (*Tafsīr Muqātil* and Qummī) and generally not as prominent as others in our case studies. Cf. Wansbrough's more thorough categorization of twelve "procedural devices." *QS*, 121.

analyze how knowledge of, and attitudes towards, the Biblical subtext of the Qur'ān varies from *Tafsīr Muqātil* to Ibn Kathīr. This analysis, which leads into the fourth and final chapter of this work, will suggest that while the *mufassirūn* were aware of that subtext to varying degrees, they generally did not rely on it as a key for unlocking the meaning of the Qur'ān. Certain *mufassirūn*, most notably Ibn Kathīr, developed a fundamentally antagonistic relationship with the Qur'ān's Biblical subtext. The traditions in *ḥadīth* come from Muḥammad, the greatest Prophet of God. Biblical traditions, on the other hand, come from those who have falsified the Islamic revelation given to the earlier prophets Moses and Jesus.

Thus this chapter is meant to uncover the manner in which Muslim scholars used *tafsīr* in the articulation of their particular religious teaching. Put in another way, this chapter will show how Muslims used *tafsīr* to claim the Qur'ān as their own. In so doing they tended to distance it from the narratives and doctrines of Jews and Christians.

Exegetical devices

Story-telling

Wansbrough sees haggadic, or narrative, exegesis as a primary stage of *tafsīr*, inasmuch as it was directed towards the goal of *Gemeindebildung* ("communal formation"). His use of the properly Jewish term haggadic is not accidental, since he contends that the early Muslim community's use of exegesis in the process of *Gemeindebildung* might be profitably compared with that of the post-exilic Jewish community. In both cases the development of stories and myths, of a communal narrative (or a *Heilsgeschichte*), was central to this process.[2] By way of example Wansbrough cites, among other things, *Tafsīr Muqātil*'s tendency towards *tasmiya* ("naming"). In particular he notes how *Tafsīr Muqātil* provides names for the various characters – even the dog – in the account of the Companions of the Cave (cf. CS 12). These names appear to be fully decorative. They do not serve in any way to explain the passage. They do, however, improve the story.[3]

Thus Wansbrough places haggadic exegesis within a chronological or quasi-chronological framework, inasmuch as he sees it as a phenomenon distinctive of the early Islamic community.[4] He asserts that the development

2 *QS*, 148.

3 Wansbrough comments, "The quality of the narrative was enhanced thereby and particularly, I suspect, for the purpose of oral delivery." *QS*, 136.

4 Wansbrough proposes an "exegetical typology" with five different elements: haggadic, halakhic, masoretic, rhetorical, allegorical. He comments: "From the point of view of function, by which I mean the role of each in the formulation of its history by a self-conscious religious community, these exegetical types exhibit only a minimum of overlapping and, save for the last-named, might almost be chronologically plotted in the above sequence." *QS*, 119. Later,

of a coherent narrative was the earliest interest of Muslim scholars in the elucidation of their scripture. This assertion seems to me quite reasonable. However, the interest in coherence was in no way limited to the early stages of exegesis, and, as the previous case studies show, later exegetes often recorded or enhanced the narratives of earlier exegetes.

Very often these narratives are a means of identifying ambiguous material in the text: *ta'yīn al-mubham*.[5] This is seen in the standard interpretation of *al-nisā'* (4) 157, where the Qur'ān famously quotes the Jews' claim to have killed Jesus and counters, "They did not kill him or crucify him but rather *shubbiha la-hum*." This last phrase can be read as either "The affair was made unclear to them" or "He was made to resemble [something or someone] to them." If the first reading is correct then the Qur'ān would here be making a religious point about the crucifixion of Jesus, not proposing an alternative narrative about that crucifixion. Yet the great majority of *mufassirūn* (and many modern translators, including Blachère, Arberry, and Paret) adopt the second reading.[6] In explanation of this reading a widespread tradition explains that God made someone else look like Jesus. This other figure, usually considered to be a faithful disciple willing to sacrifice himself (but sometimes, as in the Gospel of Barnabas, described as an enemy of Jesus – usually Judas – whom God wished to punish), was crucified in his place.[7]

The phenomenon of *ta'yīn al-mubham* is seen repeatedly in the accounts discussed in the present work. When the Qur'ān relates that God "created the human out of clay, like that of a potter" (Q 55.14) the story appears in *tafsīr* that Adam lay lifeless on the ground before God breathed His spirit into him. When Iblīs, out of envy, struck his body it made the sound of rattling pottery. When the Qur'ān relates that "the human was hasty" (Q 17.11; here a comment on human impatience generally), the detail is added that when Adam was brought to life he rushed to stand up (cf. CS 1).[8]

Again narrative exegesis serves this purpose in regard to *Yūnus* (10) 98 (cf. CS 8), where the Qur'ān refers to the belief of Jonah's people and then has God declare, "We lifted from them a shameful punishment." With this

however, he adds that the later redaction of early *tafsīrs* "have contributed to a degree of stylistic and methodological uniformity throughout the range of exegetical literature that makes difficult, if not quite impossible, description of the *Sitz im Leben* of any of its types." *QS*, 144. Apparently unaware of the nuance in Wansbrough's argument, C. Versteegh insists that Wansbrough places these different types of exegesis in a chronological order, and then refutes this idea. See C. Versteegh, *Arabic Grammar and Qur'ānic Exegesis in Early Islam*, Leiden: Brill, 1993, 47–8.

5 Rippin ("The function of *asbāb al-nuzūl* in Qur'ānic exegesis," 6) quotes Blachère's argument that haggadic exegesis is above all motivated by the "horror of the uncertain." See Blachère, *Introduction au Coran*, 233.

6 See *Tafsīr Muqātil*, 1:421, on Q 4.157; Ṭabarī, 6:12–7, on Q 4.157; Zamakhsharī, 1:586–7, on Q 4.153–9; Ibn Kathīr, 1:550–2, on Q 4.156–9.

7 On this question see Reynolds, "The Muslim Jesus: Dead or alive?"

8 See Ṭabarī, 1:201–2, on Q 2.30; Ibn Kathīr, 1:76, on Q 2.34.

declaration the divine voice of the Qur'ān seems to be recalling the salvation of Jonah's people in general terms. The *mufassirūn*, however, actualize this phrase in their stories. When the Qur'ān speaks of "lifting" or "uncovering" a punishment (Ar. *kashafa*), *Tafsīr Muqātil* reports that the residents of Nineveh actually saw the punishment in physical form above their heads, before it was lifted away.[9] Zamakhsharī describes what they saw in detail: "A terrible black cloud, with intense smoke, covered the sky. It descended until it enveloped their city, blackening their roofs."[10]

At other times narrative exegesis is a means to connect the text to the biography of Muḥammad, a process which Rippin names historicization.[11] This is the case, for example, in the common interpretation of the opening lines in *al-sharḥ* (94): "Did We not expand your breast?" with a story from Muḥammad's childhood (see CS 13).

The narrative found in the commentaries of *Tafsīr Muqātil*, Qummī, and Ibn Kathīr on the circumstances under which God revealed the Qur'ānic account of the Companions of the Cave seems to serve the same purpose. This narrative is evidently inspired by the Qur'ān's proclamation in *al-kahf* (18) 13: "We narrate their account to you in truth." The *mufassirūn* understand the speaker here to be God (or the angel Gabriel), and the intended audience to be Muḥammad. The concluding words "in truth" seem to imply that Muḥammad's correct knowledge of this account had been challenged, and that God (or Gabriel) was revealing this account to vindicate him. The *mufassirūn* accordingly found a historical narrative involving Muḥammad behind this phrase, namely the plot of Abū Jahl (*Tafsīr Muqātil*) or pagan Meccans (Qummī) or the Quraysh (Ibn Kathīr) to challenge the Prophet with information gathered from the Jews.[12]

When *Tafsīr Muqātil* and Ibn Kathīr relate that the Jews told the pagans to challenge Muḥammad also on his knowledge of Dhū l-Qarnayn and the Spirit, they use this story to explain two additional verses: "They will ask you about Dhū l-Qarnayn" (Q 18.83); "They will ask you about the Spirit" (Q 17.85). Evidently they were led to make a connection with these two

9 *Tafsīr Muqātil*, 2:250, on Q 10.98.

10 Zamakhsharī, 2:371–2, on Q 10.98. Zamakhsharī is presumably helped in his description by the Qur'ānic topos of destructive winds, as in *al-aḥqāf* (46) 24–5, where the Qur'ān describes how the people of 'Ād, whom the prophet Hūd had warned of divine punishment, saw that punishment come upon them: "When they saw something as a cloud heading to their valleys they said 'This is a cloud that will bring rain.' No, this is that which you wanted to hasten: a wind with a painful punishment" (cf. Q 41.16; 51.41–2; 54.19; 69.6).

11 Thus Rippin comments: "Designed both to prove the fact of revelation and to embody an interpretation that would relate the text to a context, historicisation grounded the text in the day-to-day life of the Muslim community. In that manner, the extraction of law was facilitated, the sense of moral guidance was emphasised and the 'foreign' made Islamic." "Tafsir," *EI*[2], 10:85a.

12 *Tafsīr Muqātil*, 2:574–6, on Q 18.9; Qummī, 2:6, on Q 18.9; Ibn Kathīr, 1:71, on Q 18.13–6.

verses due to a common rhetorical phrase ("They will ask you about . . ."). Qummī, on the other hand, relates instead that the Jews also told the pagans to challenge Muḥammad on Dhū l-Qarnayn and the story of Moses in *al-kahf* (Q 18.60–82). Thereby he uses this story instead to link the three main accounts of this Sūra.

Incidentally, the place of the Jews in this narrative is conspicuous, since both the account of the Companions of the Cave (in the Seven Sleepers/Youths of Ephesus literature) and the account of Dhū l-Qarnayn (in the Romance of Alexander literature) are prominent in Christian, not Jewish, literature. Abū Jahl, apparently, should have found some Christian informants. Perhaps aware of this inconsistency, Qummī locates these Jews in the quintessential Christian city of Najrān.[13] Nevertheless, the motive for making Jews the antagonists in this story is clear, in light of the exegetical tradition that Gabriel is their enemy.[14] Moreover, the Qur'ān itself (Q 5.82) describes the Jews and the polytheists as the greatest enemies to the believers. Accordingly in these narratives Gabriel foils the combined plot of the Jews and the polytheists by visiting Muḥammad and revealing to him the account of the Companions of the Cave.[15]

Still another detail in the Qur'ān is explained by this story. Both *Tafsīr Muqātil* and Qummī have Muḥammad promise his pagan Meccan opponents that he will inform them of the Companions of the Cave the next day. The angel Gabriel, however, arrives late (according to *Tafsīr Muqātil* by three days; according to Qummī by 40 days) and Muḥammad cannot keep his promise. This detail might strike the reader as peculiar since it puts the Prophet in a bad light. But the point of the story is neither to praise nor to belittle the Prophet, but rather to explain a phrase in the passage on the Companions of the Cave ("Do not say about anything, 'I will do this tomorrow'" [Q 18.23]) with an anecdote about Muḥammad.

It is telling that this detail is found in *Tafsīr Muqātil* and Qummī, the earliest *tafsīr*s in our survey. These works were apparently composed at a time when strict dogmas on the infallibility (*'iṣma*) of the prophets had not yet been developed, at a time when (as Wansbrough proposes) the community was above all interested in haggadic exegesis, in developing coherent stories to explain their scripture. They show no particular dismay that a prophet appears less than perfect in such narratives. The important thing is the story.[16]

13 Qummī, 2:6, on Q 18.9.

14 On this see Ṭabarī, *Jāmi' al-bayān*, 1:433–4 on Q 2.97.

15 On the theme of pagan/Jewish cooperation Wansbrough comments: "It is one of many but typical of all literary devices which implied a historical link between two sources of resistance to the Arabian prophet." *QS*, 123.

16 In this regard it is perhaps worth mentioning also the standard narrative reported in *tafsīr* literature to explain a passage later in *al-kahf*, namely the account of Moses and the wise, unnamed servant of God (Q 18.60–82; regarding which cf. *KU*, 141–3). Moses appears therein as a (impatient) disciple of the mysterious servant, who is named by tradition

That the early *mufassirūn* gave priority to narrative above dogma is not without consequence for a more famous example of historicization, the case of the so-called satanic verses. Early *mufassirūn* widely report the account in which the Prophet Muḥammad is tricked by Satan, who relates to him verses praising female deities.[17] Muḥammad assumes these verses to be divinely revealed, until God abrogates them with *al-najm* (53) 19–23 (although it is the question of abrogation raised by Q 22.52 that seems to have inspired the story). Most later *mufassirūn* reject this report, in deference to the dogmatic principle of the prophet's infallibility.[18] Most western scholars accept the account, arguing that no Muslim would invent a story in which the Prophet appears so unseemly.[19] Yet the cases discussed above strongly suggest that

al-Khiḍr (or Khaḍir). His role as a disciple seems to violate the later dogmatic principle that prophets are superior to all other humans. Indeed some *mufassirūn* argue that the protagonist of this account was not the prophet Moses, but someone else of the same name. Zamakhsharī, for example, notes (2:733–4, on Q 18.66) the argument that the account concerns not Mūsā b. ʿImrān but Mūsā b. Mīshā (i.e. Moses the son of Manasseh the son of Joseph, cf. Gn 41.51), "since a prophet is necessarily the most knowledgeable person of his era." A second argument, that al-Khiḍr was also a prophet (Zamakhsharī, 2:733–4, on Q 18.66; cf. Ibn Kathīr, 3:89–90, on Q 18.60–5), is directed towards the same end.

Tafsīr Muqātil, however, not only accepts that the prophet Moses is intended here, he also emphasizes Moses' arrogance in an explanatory narrative:

> When Moses (peace be upon him) learned the Tawrāt, which contains everything in detail, one of the Israelites said to him: "Is there anyone on earth who is more knowledgeable than you are?" He said, "No. None of the servants of God is more knowledgeable than I am." Then God (Powerful and Mighty) revealed to him: "There is a man, one of my servants, who lives in the islands of the sea, who is called al-Khiḍr, who is smarter than you are." [Moses] asked, "How can I meet him?"
>
> (*Tafsīr Muqātil*, 2:592–3, on Q 18.60)

This narrative, which reflects the classical topos of a search for the wisest man (cf., e.g., Plato, *The Apology*, 21a–22e), is related to Gn 18.17–27 and the story of Moses and Akiba in *BT*, *Menaḥōt*, 29b. On this see H. Schwarzbaum, "The Jewish and Moslem versions of some theodicy legends," *Fabula* 3, 1959, (119–69) 142–8; B. Wheeler refutes Schwarzbaum's conclusions in "The Jewish origins of Qur'ān 18:65–82," *JAOS* 118, 1998, 153–71. Cf. *QS*, 128 and the versions of this account in Ṭabarī 15:276–7, on Q 18.64–5; Zamakhsharī 2:732–3, on Q 18.60–5; Ibn Kathīr, 3:88, 89 on Q 18.89–90.

17 Among the *mufassirūn* in our survey see *Tafsīr Muqātil* 4:162, on Q 53.23; Ṭabarī 17:186–9, on Q 22.52; Zamakhsharī, 4:422–3, on Q 53.19–23; cf. also Ibn Hishām, *Sīrat Rasūl Allāh*, 239–40 (trans., 165–7). For a broader review of *tafsīr* on this question see S. Ahmed, "Satanic verses," *EQ*, 4:531–5. As mentioned in CS 8, Zamakhsharī also considers the possibility that the Qur'ān refers to a Satanic temptation of the prophet Jonah. See Zamakhsharī 3:131, on Q 21.87.

18 Thus Ibn Kathīr, 4:231–2, on Q 53.19–26.

19 This is the position of William Muir (*The Life of Mohamet from Original Sources*, London: Smith, 1877, 103) and, most famously, of W.M. Watt, who comments, "It is unthinkable that the story could have been invented by Muslims, or foisted upon them by non-Muslims." Watt, *Muhammad at Mecca*, 103; cf. idem, *Companion to the Qur'ān*, 245. M. Rodinson, *Mahomet*, 3rd edition, Paris: Éditions de Seuil, 1974, 135–7; F.E. Peters, *Muhammad and*

this account is to be rejected, not from any dogmatic principle, but rather because the early *mufassirūn* were not unwilling to present prophets in an unfavorable light when a good story was at stake.[20]

Occasion of revelation

The story of the pagans and the Companions of the Cave is an example of a particular sort of narrative exegesis, namely a report on the "occasion of revelation" (*sabab al-nuzūl* or *khabar al-nuzūl*).[21] Such stories explain when and why God revealed the passage at hand to Muḥammad. Through such stories individual Qur'ānic passages gain not only a narrative context but also a particular place in Muḥammad's prophetic career.

With the device of "occasion of revelation" the exegetes gain an organizational principle which allows them to control the text. The text can now be judged according to a chronology of Muḥammad's career, even if the Qur'ān itself does not follow any chronological order.[22] Even more, the text is now interwoven with the story of Muḥammad. Read by itself the Qur'ān says almost nothing about Muḥammad's biography. Read in light of the occasion of revelation, however, the Qur'ān becomes a book that is fundamentally shaped by that biography. Thus it seems to be distinctive of a more developed, and sectarian-minded, stage of exegesis.[23]

The impact of this device is reflected in a detail of the narrative on the pagans and the Companions of the Cave. According to this narrative the

the Origins of Islam, Albany, NY: SUNY Press, 1994, 160–1; M. Forward, *Muhammad*, Oxford: Oneworld, 1997, 34–6; R. Bell, and W.M. Watt, *Introduction to the Qur'ān*, Edinburgh: Edinburgh University Press, 2001, 55–6; F. Esack, *The Qur'an*, Oxford: Oneworld, 2002, 43–4. Other contemporary scholars (primarily but not exclusively Muslim) follow Islamic scholarship and discard the story for apologetic reasons. See, e.g., Haykal, *Life of Muḥammad*,105–14; M. Hamidullah, *Le prophète de l'islam*, Beirut: Özcan, 1395/1975; A.H. Siddiqui, *The Life of Muhammad*, Beirut: Dār al-Fatḥ, n.d.; M. Lings: *Muhammad: His Life Based on the Earliest Sources*, London: Unwin Hyman, 1983.

20 Cf. the comments of S. Ahmed: "The widespread acceptance of the incident by early Muslims suggests, however, that they did not view the incident as inauspicious and that they would presumably not have, on this basis at least, been adverse to inventing it." Ahmed, "Satanic verses," 535.

J. Burton contends, however, that the concerns of the exegetes regarding this passage were fundamentally halakhic, since the anecdote of the Satanic verses provides an example where both the wording and the juridical force of a Qur'ānic verse are abrogated. See J. Burton, "Those are the high-flying cranes," *JSS* 15, 1970, 246–65; reprint: *The Qur'an: Formative Interpretation*, ed. Rippin, 347–65.

21 On this topic see A. Rippin, "The function of *asbāb al-nuzūl* in Qur'ānic exegesis," *BSOAS* 51, 1988, 1–20; reprint: *The Qur'ān and Its Interpretive Tradition*, ed. Rippin. Therein Rippin argues (see especially the conclusion, p. 19) against Wansbrough that reports on the occasion of revelation are directed towards haggadic, not halakhic, exegesis. Cf. *QS*, 141–2, 177–85.

22 Wansbrough: "Historical order could thus be introduced into what was essentially literary chaos." *QS*, 177.

23 Cf. *QS*, 141.

pagans had to send a delegation away to seek the advice of the Jews.[24] This detail is necessary because *al-kahf* was understood to have been revealed during the early Meccan period of Muḥammad's life,[25] and Mecca was not a Jewish city like Medina, but the pagan city par excellence.

The use of occasion of revelation to connect the material of the Qur'ān to the biography of Muḥammad is likewise apparent in *tafsīr* on *al-aʿrāf* (7) 26 (cf. CS 3), in which the Qur'ān mentions God's provision of clothing and feathers to humans. In its textual context this verse is intimately connected with the story of Adam in the garden, in particular with the manner in which Satan stripped Adam and his wife of their heavenly clothing (cf. Q 7.20, 22, 27). Ṭabarī, however, reports that God revealed this verse as an admonition to the pagan Quraysh, who used to perform the circumambulation of the Kaʿba naked.[26] Thereby he connects this verse instead with the story of Muḥammad in Mecca.

Rippin argues that such anecdotes about pagans are a primary feature of occasion of revelation reports:

> This adducing of the Jāhilī "foil" or background is, in my estimation, one of the most significant elements of the *asbāb* reports. Provided in these reports is an implicit evaluation of the Islamic dispensation; it is saying: "this is how things were before Islam but now Islam has arrived and things have improved substantially."[27]

The Jews, on the other hand, tend to have a different function in reports on the occasion of revelation. The pagans are foils to the Prophet inasmuch as they allow the exegete to portray the evolution and advancement offered by Islam (apology). The Jews are foils to the Prophet inasmuch as they allow the exegete to illustrate the perversity behind the People of the Book's rejection of Muḥammad (polemic).[28]

This function is evident in the reports on the occasion of revelation for the statement, "Our hearts are *ghulf*" (Q 2.88; 4.155). In the Qur'ān this statement is part of a larger reflection on the transgressions of the Jews. The reference to their uncircumcised (*ghulf*) hearts (Q 4.155) is joined to references to the Jews' demand to see God (Q 4.153), to their worship of the calf (Q 4.153), violation of the covenant (Q 4.155), unbelief in the signs of God (Q 4.155), killing of the prophets (Q 2.87; 4.155), unbelief (Q 4.156), calumny against Mary (Q 4.156), and claim to have killed Jesus (Q 4.157). Through

24 Qummī, as mentioned previously, specifies that they traveled to (the Christian city) of Najrān. *Tafsīr Muqātil* and Ibn Kathīr remark simply that they sent a delegation to the Jews. Presumably by this they intend the Jews of Yathrib. Ibn Hishām (*Sīrat Rasūl Allāh*, 192; trans., 136) identifies Yathrib (Medina) explicitly.

25 On this see Ibn Hishām, *Sīrat Rasūl Allāh*, 192–7 (trans., 136–9).

26 Ṭabarī, 8:146, on Q 7.26.

27 Rippin, "The function of *asbāb al-nuzūl* in Qur'ānic exegesis," 10.

28 Ibid., 11.

the device of occasion of revelation, however, the focus turns to a new transgression: the Jews' rejection of Muḥammad. According to *Tafsīr Muqātil*, Ṭabarī, and Ibn Kathīr,[29] the Jews proclaimed, "Our hearts are *ghulf*," only when they rejected Muḥammad's invitation to become Muslims.

*Variae lectiones (*qirā'āt*)*

The matter of *variae lectiones* ("variant readings") would seem to most observers quite different from story-telling or occasion of revelation. Indeed, by the standard logic of critical scholarship *variae lectiones* would not belong in a study of *tafsīr* at all, inasmuch as they are thought to redound to the Qur'ān itself and not to the exegesis thereof.

Scholars usually divide *variae lectiones* into two groups.[30] The first type, what I have named earlier canonical *qirā'āt*, are those collections of variants – variously numbered at seven, ten, and fourteen – that were canonized in part through the efforts of Ibn Mujāhid (d. 324/936) in the early fourth/tenth century.[31] These canonical *qirā'āt*, according to the claims of tradition, are all valid methods of pronouncing the Qur'ān. They do not involve differences with the consonantal text codified by the caliph ʿUthmān. The second type are variations, (also referred to in Arabic as *qirā'āt*) very often of the consonantal text itself, which are purported to be historical records of divergent codices of the Qur'ān (*maṣāḥif*; sing. *muṣḥaf*) that existed before the caliph ʿUthmān established an authoritative text. According to the standard narrative, various Companions (most famously Ibn Masʿūd, Ubayy, and Abū Mūsā, whose texts are associated with Kūfa, Damascus, and Baṣra respectively) began their own collection of Qur'ānic verses during the lifetime of the Prophet and ultimately codified their own texts. These Companions all resisted, to different degrees, the later decree of the caliph ʿUthmān that all codices but his own be destroyed.[32]

This second type of *variae lectiones* would seem to be of greater interest to the critical scholar of the Qur'ān, as they represent reports of codices that differ from ʿUthmān's codex even in regard to the consonantal text. Not only are the variations attributed to the Companion codices significant (at times

29 *Tafsīr Muqātil*, 1:419, on Q 4.155; Ṭabarī, 1:408, on Q 2.88; Ibn Kathīr, 1:122, on Q 2.88.

30 On this topic see F. Leemhuis, "Readings of the Qur'ān," *EQ* 4:353–63.

31 Ibn Mujāhid famously argued that seven such readings were equally canonical. On the other hand it is not clear, as is often asserted, that he justified this argument with a famous *ḥadīth* which relates that the Qur'ān was revealed in seven "letters" (*aḥruf*). See C. Melchert, "Ibn Mujāhid and the establishment of seven Qur'ānic readings," *SI* 91, 2000, (5–22) 19–20. Still others, however, proposed ten or even fourteen canonical readings, end even then various versions of each individual reading. For a general introduction to the question of *qirā'āt* see Bell and Watt, *Introduction to the Qur'ān*, 44–50; Blachère, *Introduction au Coran*, 102–35; R. Paret, "Ḳirā'a," *EI²*, 5:127–9.

32 None more so than Ibn Masʿūd, who, according to Yaʿqūbī, got into a scuffle when the caliph demanded he surrender his codex in the mosque at Kūfa. See Yaʿqūbī, *Ta'rīkh*, ed. Khalīl Manṣūr, Beirut: Dār al-Kutub al-ʿIlmiyya, 1419/1999, 2:118.

including even additional sentences), the standard narrative makes these codices more ancient even than that of 'Uthmān.

They thus would seem to be a valuable tool for establishing the most ancient form of the Qur'ān. Indeed this is the assumption that informs Bergsträsser and Pretzl in the third volume of *Geschichte des Qorans*, which opens with a review of the standard *maṣāḥif* narrative and continues with descriptions of the canonical Qur'ānic variants reported in Islamic literature.[33] This was the assumption that inspired Gotthelf Bergsträsser, Otto Pretzl, and Arthur Jeffery, to work on both Qur'ānic manuscripts *and* traditional reports of Qur'ānic variants.[34] Together Bergsträsser and Jeffery, and later (after Bergsträsser's death) Pretzl and Jeffery, planned to produce a critical edition of the Qur'ān on this basis,[35] but their project was undermined by a ruinous series of events.[36]

33 See esp. *GdQ3*, 116–9. Paret follows their precedent in his *Encyclopaedia of Islam* article "Ḳirā'a." *EI*^{2}, 5:127–9.

34 In addition to *GdQ3* (esp. 60–97) see G. Bergsträsser, "Die Koranlesung des Ḥasan von Baṣra," *Islamica* 2, 1926, 11–57; O. Pretzl, "Die Wissenschaft der Koranlesung," *Islamica* 6, 1934, 1–47, 230–46, 290–331; A. Jeffery, "Progress in the study of the Qur'ān text," *MW* 25, 1935, 4–16; reprint: *Der Koran*, ed. Paret, 398–412; idem, "The Qur'ān readings of Zaid b. 'Alī," *Rivista degli Studi Orientali* 16, 1936, 249–89; idem, *Materials for the History of the Qur'ān: The Old Codices*, Leiden: Brill, 1937, vii; idem, "Abu 'Ubaid on the verses missing from the Koran," *MW* 28, 1938, 61–5; reprint: *What the Koran Really Says*, ed. Ibn Warraq, 150–3; idem, "A variant text of the Fatiha," *MW* 29, 1939, 158–62; reprint: *What the Koran Really Says*, ed. Ibn Warraq, 145–9; idem, "Further Readings of Zaid b. 'Alī," *Rivista degli Studi Orientali* 18, 1940, 218–36; idem, "The Qur'ān readings of Ibn Miqsam," *Ignace Goldziher Memorial Volume*, Budapest: n.p., 1948, 1–38.

In a series of articles in the journal *Orientalia* Edmund Beck added significantly to their catalog of *variae lectiones*. See E. Beck, "Der 'uṯmānische Kodex in der Koranlesung des zweiten Jahrhunderts," *Orientalia* 14, 1945, 355–73; idem, "Die Kodizesvarianten der Amṣār," *Orientalia* 16, 1947, 353–76; idem, "Studien zur Geschichte der Kūfischen Koranlesung in den beiden ersten Jahrhunderten I," *Orientalia* 17, 1948, 326–54; idem, "Studien zur Geschichte der Kūfischen Koranlesung in den beiden ersten Jahrhunderten II," *Orientalia* 19, 1950, 328–50; idem, "Studien zur Geschichte der Kūfischen Koranlesung in den beiden ersten Jahrhunderten III," *Orientalia* 20, 1951, 316–28; idem, "Studien zur Geschichte der Kūfischen Koranlesung in den beiden ersten Jahrhunderten IV," *Orientalia* 22, 1953, 59–78; idem, "Die Zuverlässigkeit der Überlieferung von ausser'uṯmānischen Varianten bei al-Farrā'," *Orientalia* 23, 1954, 412–35.

35 A description of their project can be found in G.S. Reynolds, "Introduction: Qur'ānic studies and its controversies," *QHC* (1–25), 2–5 and C. Gilliot: "Une reconstruction critique du Coran." See also the statements of the project participants themselves: G. Bergsträsser, *Plan eines Apparatus Criticus zum Qoran, Sitzungsberichte der Bayerischen Akademie der Wissenschaften 1930 (Heft 7)*, Munich: Verlag der Bayerischen Akademie der Wissenschaften, 1930; reprint: *Der Koran*, ed. Paret, 389–97; idem, "Über die Notwendigkeit und Möglichkeit einer kritischen Koranausgabe," *ZDMG* 84, 1930, 82–3; O. Pretzl, *Die Fortführung des Apparatus Criticus zum Koran*; A. Jeffery, "The textual history of the Qur'ān," *Journal of the Middle East Society* (Jerusalem) 1, 1947, 35–49; reprint in: A. Jeffery, *The Qur'ān as Scripture*, New York: Moore, 1952, 89–103; idem, "The present status of Qur'ānic studies," *Middle East Institute: Report of Current Research*, Spring 1957, 1–16.

36 Bergsträsser died in a mysterious hiking accident in August 1933; Pretzl died in a plane crash while serving in the Second World War in October 1941; Jeffery was told (falsely) by Pretzl's successor, Anton Spitaler, that their collection of manuscripts had been destroyed

The larger number of *variae lectiones* in Islamic literature may come as a surprise to contemporary readers, as the impression that Islamic tradition knows only one text of the Qur'ān seems to be ever more prevalent. This impression, however, is due primarily to the success of the text known as the Cairo, or King Fārūq, edition. This edition is virtually ubiquitous today, and it is often presented as the unanimous and ancient text of the Qur'ān, although it was first arranged in 1924.[37] Yet there is some reason to believe that the *variae lectiones* are not in fact historical records of ancient textual variants.

As for the reports of variants in pre-'Uthmānic codices (the second type above), they tend to appear in greater, not lesser, numbers in later works. Variants are rare in *Tafsīr Muqātil*, for example, but they are quite frequent in the *tafsīr*s of Ṭabarī, Zamakhsharī, and Ibn Kathīr.[38] Accordingly they seem to be products of exegesis more than records of ancient pre-'Uthmānic documents.[39] No sign of them is to be found in Qur'ān manuscripts. In this light it is worth noting the recent observation of Intisar Rabb, in her detailed article on an ancient Qur'ān manuscript in the British library: "A comparison of our manuscript to records of early codices reveals that ours – like all other extant copies of the Qur'ān of which we are currently aware – definitively hails from the 'Uthmānic recension."[40] Now it could be, of course, that 'Uthmān really succeeded in destroying every folio of variant manuscripts. But it also could be that they never existed.

But then reports of canonical *qirā'āt* (the first type of variant mentioned above), which may or may not be found in manuscript evidence, likewise do not seem to provide historical evidence for the ancient shape of the Qur'ān. For these reports are inevitably based on the same consonantal text. Accordingly they seem to be the result of the process of speculation on that text that accompanied the development of a fully vocalized Qur'ān. So codex variants – which involve profound changes to the standard text – seem to be the result of exegetical speculation where the interpretation and sense of the text is at issue.[41] Canonical *qirā'āt* variants seem to be the result of textual

during allied bombings of Munich towards the end of the war. For more detail see G.S. Reynolds, "Introduction: Qur'ānic studies and its controversies," 1–6.

37 Regarding which see G. Bergsträsser, "Koranlesung in Kairo," *Der Islam* 20, 1932, 1–42.

38 Versteegh (*Arabic Grammar*, 79) calculates that in all of *Tafsīr Muqātil* (about 3000 pages in the printed edition) there are sixteen variant readings attributed to Ibn Mas'ūd, four to Ubayy and two to anonymous sources.

39 Regarding this cf. the argument of Michael Cook, that the manuscript evidence seems to confirm the traditional claim that one manuscript (namely that of 'Uthmān) was distributed to four different cities. See M. Cook, "The stemma of the regional codices of the Koran," *Graeco-Arabica* 9–10, 2004, 89–104.

40 I. Rabb, "Non-Canonical readings of the Qur'ān: Recognition and authenticity (the Ḥimṣī reading)," *Journal of Qur'ānic Studies* 8, 2006, (84–127) 86.

41 Regarding this point A. Rippin notes how "the variants still show traces of their original intention: to explain away grammatical and lexical difficulties." "Qur'ān 21:95: A ban is upon any town," *JSS* 24, 1979, (43–53) 53. In another place he concludes: "Variants such

speculation, where the proper orthography and grammar of the text is at issue.[42] Neither type of *variae lectiones*, in other words, provides a basis for the development of a critical edition of the Qur'ān. Pretzl himself came to realize this point towards the end of his life, concluding that the *variae lectiones* are for the most part proposals by later scholars for readings of the Qur'ān that seemed to them improved in terms of grammar, syntax, or meaning.[43] This was likewise the position of Pretzl's student and successor at Munich, Anton Spitaler, and presumably explains why he did not continue the work of his predecessors on a critical edition of the Qur'ān.[44]

as those for Sūrah 7:40 were created when polemically based pressures on the exegetes were the strongest and the attitudes towards the Qur'ānic text less confining." "Qur'ān 7:40, until the camel passes through the eye of the needle," *Arabica* 27, 1980, (107–13) 113. On the exegetical nature of the variants see also F. Leemhuis, "Ursprünge des Korans als Textus receptus," in S. Wild and H. Schild (eds.), *Akten des 27. Deutschen Orientalistentages*, Würzburg: Ergon, 2001, 301–8, esp. 307.

42 On this point Gilliot notes that medieval Muslim scholars by no means saw the existence of *variae lectiones* as an inconvenience to Islamic apology: "Ce qui pourrait être vu comme un argument contre l'origine divine du Coran, la multiplicité des lectures, est considéré comme un indice supplémentaire en faveur de son caractère miraculeux. Les *variae lectiones* deviennent une preuve de la richesse de la langue coranique; plus les hommes y trouvent de problèmes, plus il est vu comme miraculeux." Gilliot, *Exégèse, langue, et théologie en Islam*, 163.

43 At one point Pretzl considered a detailed study of *variae lectiones* to be an essential scholarly task. In 1930 he wrote: "Wie bei keinem anderen Buche gingen im Koran zwei Wesensbestandteile, Konsonantentext und Lesung desselben, wie Materie und Form, wie Körper und Seele zusammengehörig nebeneinander her, ohne jemals ihr Eigenleben aufzugeben." *Die Fortführung des Apparatus Criticus zum Koran*, 1. Later, however, Pretzl came to believe that Islamic reports on the proper reading of the Qur'ān represent efforts at emendation, not an ancient oral tradition. Therefore scholars are left only with the written record of the Qur'ān, a record that is necessarily problematic due to the imperfect nature of the Qur'ānic script. Thus the very idea of a critical edition of the Qur'ān is problematic. Pretzl, who was killed in a plane crash while in combat in the Second World War, never had the opportunity to record his intellectual conversion on this point. It is known, however, from an account given by Pretzl's friend August Fischer: "Von den, 'Koran-Lesarten,' die m.E. großenteils weiter nichts sind als Emendationsexperiments philologisch geschulter Koran-Forscher an schwierigeren Stellen des 'oṯmānischen Koran-Textes, ist in den letzten zwei Jahrzehnten unter dem Einflusse Bergsträsser's, seines Schülers und Mitarbeiters Pretzl und Jeffery's wohl zu viel Aufhebens gemacht worden. Pretzl war, wie ich in wiederholten mit ihm in Kairo über diese Dinge geführten Gesprächen feststellen konnte, in den letzten Jahren seines – leider wie das seines Lehrers zu früh tragisch abgeschlossenen – Lebens von der generellen hohen Bewertung der Koran-Handschriften und Koran-Lesarten, wie er sie zunächst von seinem Lehrer übernommen hatte, stark zurückgekommen, und es ist höchst bedauerlich, daß er uns seine letzten Anschauungen von diesen Fragen (wie sie also noch nicht in Bd. III der 'Geschichte des Qorans' vorliegen) nicht mehr literarisch mitteilen." A. Fischer, "Grammatisch schwierige Schwur- und Beschwörungsformeln," *Der Islam* 28, 1948, (1–105) 5, n. 4. A second witness (also *post mortum*) to Pretzl's conversion on this matter is that of his student Spitaler. See A. Spitaler, "Otto Pretzl," *ZDMG* 96, 1942, 163–4.

44 See A. Spitaler, "Die Nichtkanonischen Koranlesarten und ihre Bedeutung für die arabische Sprachwissenschaft," *Actes du XXe Congrès International des Orientalistes, Bruxelles 5–10 Septembre 1938*, Louvain: Bureaux du muséon, 1940, 314–5; reprint: *Der Koran*, ed. Paret, 413.

Wansbrough is still more explicit on this matter, arguing that all of the reports of variants in Islamic literature are exegetical.[45] Indeed, he concludes that such reports are distinctive of a later stage of Islamic exegesis, when exegetes began to use the (new) science of Arabic linguistics to support particular exegetical positions.[46] Thus Wansbrough comments, "It will, however, be useful to remember that the existence of textual variants presupposed rather than prefigured divergent interpretations."[47]

The use of *variae lectiones* to legitimize a particular interpretation seems evident in the case of feathers (CS 3). The idea of God sending down feathers (*rīsh*) to Adam (Q 7.26) seems bizarre. Zamakhsharī accordingly proposes that the Arabic *rīsh* here is only a metaphor for *zīna* ("adornment"; cf. CS 3).[48] It can hardly be coincidental that other traditions report that the word *zīna* appeared in place of *rīsh* in the codex of Ubayy.[49]

The same dynamic appears in a more subtle manner in the *tafsīr* of *al-nisā'* (4) 155 (cf. Q 2.88; CS 10). Ṭabarī and Ibn Kathīr both mention the variant reading of *ghuluf* for *ghulf*, thus changing a plural adjective (meaning "sealed") to a plural noun (meaning "containers").[50] This emendation matches nicely a narrative used to contextualize this verse, that when the Jews refused to listen to Muḥammad they proclaimed, "Our hearts are containers of knowledge."[51]

In other cases *variae lectiones* serve to add narrative detail to a passage, as with two different variants in the passage on Abraham's visitors (cf. CS 5) attributed to Ibn Mas'ūd. The first relates to *Hūd* (11), verse 69–70: "Our messengers came to Abraham with good news. They said, 'Peace.' He said, 'Peace,' and hastened to bring them a roasted calf. * When he saw that their hands did not touch it, he became suspicious and fearful of them." According to Ṭabarī, Ibn Mas'ūd's *muṣḥaf* had an additional phrase which fits the context nicely: "When he offered [the calf] to them he said, 'Will you not eat?'"[52] The second variant relates to verse 71, which begins: "His wife was

45 "Of genuinely textual variants exhibiting material deviation from the canonical text of revelation, such as are available for Hebrew and Christian scripture, there are none. The Quranic masorah is in fact entirely exegetical, even where its contents have been transmitted in the guise of textual variants." *QS*, 203. Wansbrough also expresses here his belief that the primary purpose for the development of the traditions on the *variae lectiones* was to support the legendary account of the 'Uthmānic codification of the Qur'ān. In this regard I believe he underestimates the degree to which exegetical speculation itself could fuel the production of variants.

46 In earlier *tafsīrs*, then, the *variae lectiones* "represent intrusions." *QS*, 132.

47 *QS*, 190.

48 Zamakhsharī, 2:97, on Q 7.26.

49 Regarding which see Jeffery, *Materials*, 131; Bellamy, "Ten Qur'ānic emendations," 130.

50 Ṭabarī, 1:408, on Q 2.88; Ibn Kathīr, 1:122, on Q 2.88; cf. *MQQ*, 2:178.

51 Ṭabarī, 1:408, on Q 2.88. With this narrative, moreover, the topos of Jewish arrogance is emphasized (cf. Q 4.157; 5.64).

52 Ṭabarī, 12:72, on Q 11.71.

standing." According to Zamakhsharī and Ibn Kathīr, Ibn Mas'ūd's *muṣḥaf* added here: "and he was sitting."[53] In both cases the variants to the standard text differ radically in their orthography and phonology. In both cases the variants help fill out the narrative.

Yet the interest of the *mufassirūn* in *variae lectiones* is not always limited to clarification or elaboration. The case of the dog in *al-kahf* (vv. 18, 22; cf. CS 12), for example, illustrates how *variae lectiones* is used to reconcile the text with doctrine.[54] To some *mufassirūn* it is hard to imagine a dog, a ritually unclean animal, in a cave with the pious companions. Accordingly Zamakhsharī reports *kālibuhum*, "the owner of their dog" or "their dog-trainer" as a variant to *kalbuhum* "their dog."[55] A more salient example of this phenomenon is the variant *khalīqa* ("creature") for *khalīfa* ("vicegerent," "successor") in *al-baqara* (2) 30 (cf. CS 1). With this variant all of the theological problems involved with God having a vicegerent or successor are eliminated.[56]

For *al-ṣaff* (61) 6 (cf. CS 13) Zamakhsharī reports a tradition that *siḥr*, "magic," should be read *sāḥir* "magician."[57] This variant means only that the Israelites, instead of calling the miracles of Jesus "magic," are made to call him a magician. Yet a second, remarkable, variant to this verse includes an intrusive and detailed doctrinal statement. The standard text has Jesus announce "a messenger to come after me. His name is *aḥmad.*" The variant (attributed to the *muṣḥaf* of Ubayy), however, has Jesus announce "a messenger to come after me whose community will be the last community and by whom God will place the seal on the prophets and messengers."[58] With this long addition a sectarian position is vigorously defended.

53 Zamakhsharī (1:410): *wa-huwa qā'idun*; Ibn Kathīr, 2:426, on Q 69–73; cf. *MQQ*, 3:123: *wa-huwa jālisun.*

54 In this regard note as well the variant to Q 4.74b, which according to the standard text reads: "To him who fights in the path of God and is killed (*yuqtal*) or overcome [*yughlab*; pace standard *yaghlib*] will we give a great reward." The variant substitutes *yaqtul* for *yuqtal* and therefore has the one who kills receives the reward. *MQQ*, 2:146.

55 Zamakhsharī, 2:709, on Q 18.18. Zamakhsharī's variant is reported on the authority of Ja'far al-Ṣādiq. Another variant – *kāli'uhum*, "their guard" – is reported elsewhere on the authority of Ja'far's father Muḥammad al-Bāqir. *MQQ*, 3:304.

Note also a variant (attributed to Ubayy), again reported by both Zamakhsharī and Ibn Kathīr, for *al-nisā'* (4) 159a: "Every one of the People of the Book will believe in him before his death (*mawtihi*)." The pronouns here trouble the *mufassirūn* (see *Tafsīr Muqātil*, 1:421, on Q 4.159; Ṭabarī 6:18–23, on Q 4.159; Zamakhsharī, 1:588–9, on Q 4.153–9; Ibn Kathīr, 1:553–4, on Q 4.159). The first pronoun ("him" or "it") would seem to mean Jesus in light of the preceding context (i.e. Q 4.157–8), but some commentators nevertheless suggest it means Muḥammad, or the Qur'ān. The second pronoun ("his") is more difficult. It might again refer to Jesus or to the individual from the People of the Book. When Zamakhsharī and Ibn Kathīr report *mawtihim* ("their death") as a variant, it appears to be an effort to resolve this ambiguity in favor of the latter option.

56 *MQQ*, 1:40, on the authority of Zayd b. 'Alī.

57 Zamakhsharī, 4:525, on Q 61.6.

58 Blachère, 593, n. 6.

Regarding *variae lectiones*, the English scholar Richard Bell comments: "The variants hardly ever affect the consonantal outline of the text. They give the impression of being largely attempts by exegetes to smooth out the grammar."[59] While this is apparently the case for the canonical *qirā'āt*, it is decidedly not so for the *muṣḥaf* variants, which the *mufassirūn* use not only for the sake of grammar, but also for the sake of their religious doctrine.

Ta'khīr al-muqaddam

Wansbrough, as mentioned, proposes that *variae lectiones* belong to a later stage of exegesis, a stage which is distinguished in particular by masoretic concerns. In describing this stage,[60] however, not once does Wansbrough address a grammatical, or more properly hermeneutical, device that is significant in several of our case studies, namely *ta'khīr al-muqaddam* (or, expressed in contrary fashion, *taqdīm al-mu'akhkhar*), which might be paraphrased: "understanding later that which is written earlier."[61] By this device the Qur'ān is read, as it were, backwards.[62]

It may be surprising to find that the *mufassirūn* are not in principle opposed to reading the Qur'ān out of order. Sometimes they seem to find this device unavoidable. This is seen, for example, with the question of Jonah and the fish. Most of the *mufassirūn* conclude that Jonah was swallowed by the fish after his mission to Nineveh (CS 8).[63] Their conclusion is suggested by the word order of *al-anbiyā'* (21) 87: "The Man of the Fish went off angry and thought We would have no power over him. He called in the darkness: 'There is no god but You. Praise be to You. I have been a wrongdoer.'" According to the standard interpretation of this verse, Jonah first went off from his mission in Nineveh and later called out in the darkness of the fish.

Yet a related passage, *al-ṣāffāt* (37) 139–48, complicates this interpretation. Here the Qur'ān likewise refers first to Jonah going off (v. 140) and then to the fish incident (v. 142). However, several verses later (vv. 147) the Qur'ān refers directly to his mission. In light of this passage Ibn Kathīr speculates that Jonah went on two missions: one before the fish incident and one

59 Bell, *Introduction to the Qur'ān*, 50.

60 *QS*, 202–27.

61 In his section on haggadic exegesis, however, Wansbrough does refer to the use of the term *taqdīm* in *Tafsīr Muqātil* where it is suggested a word should be understood as though it appeared later in the text. *QS*, 143.

62 Versteegh points out that there are two versions of this technique (which he refers to as *muqaddam wa-mu'akhkhar*): *hysteron proteron*, which involves a restoration of the logical order of a passage, and *hyperbaton*, which involves transposing a word or phrase for the sake of syntax, not logic. The cases I mention below are all of the first type. Versteegh, *Arabic Grammar*, 122–3, 140–1.

63 *Tafsīr Muqātil* (3:621, on Q 37.147), Qummī (1:318–9, on Q 10.98), Ṭabarī (23:105, on Q 37.147–9), Zamakhsharī (4:62, on Q 37.133–48), and Ibn Kathīr (3:181, on Q 21.87–8; 4:19, on Q 37.139–48), all consider also the possibility that it was before his mission.

thereafter.[64] Zamakhsharī, however, argues that this passage should be read with *ta'khīr al-muqaddam*. While the reference to a mission (v. 147) appears after the reference to the fish (v. 142), things should be understood the other way around.[65]

This device appears again with the matter of Mary's guardian (CS 9). In *āl 'Imrān* (3) 37 the Qur'ān describes Zechariah as her guardian. Several verses later (Q 3.44), however, the Qur'ān alludes to the ordeal over who would become her guardian. In the light of the Qur'ān's subtext there is no confusion, since the ordeal relates not to Mary's adoption by Zechariah but to her engagement to Joseph. Although Ṭabarī is aware of traditions that explain the ordeal in this way, neither he nor the *mufassirūn* in our survey follow this explanation.[66] Instead they read this passage with *ta'khīr al-muqaddam*. The Qur'ān's reference to the ordeal (Q 3.44) is to be understood before the description of Zechariah as Mary's guardian (Q 3.37);[67] indeed this is how he became her guardian.

In these two cases the recourse to *ta'khīr al-muqaddam* is purely haggadic; it is a device that facilitates the development of a narrative used to explain Qur'ānic material. At other times, however, *ta'khīr al-muqaddam* becomes a device to justify a certain doctrine. In *āl 'Imrān* (3) 55, for example, the Qur'ān has God address Jesus directly, announcing to him, "O Jesus, I will make you pass away (*innī mutawaffīka*) and raise you up to me (*wa-rāfi'uka ilayya*)." The problem here for the *mufassirūn* is the question of Jesus' death. The term *tawaffā* in the Qur'ān indeed refers to God (or God's angels) taking the soul from the body, that is, making someone die.[68] Yet the *mufassirūn* generally held that Jesus did not die, that he was raised up body and soul to heaven, whence he will return to earth in the eschaton.[69] This position was advantageous for sectarian controversy, but it seemed to contradict *āl 'Imrān* (3) 55, where God is said to make Jesus die *before* He raises him up.

In other words, a way had to be found around *āl 'Imrān* (3) 55. Most scholars found it by redefining *tawaffā* – but only for those cases where it

64 Ibn Kathīr, 4:21, on Q 37.137–48.

65 Zamakhsharī, 4:62, on Q 37.133–48.

66 Ṭabarī, 3:246, on Q 3.37.

67 *Tafsīr Muqātil*, 1:272, on Q 3.36; Qummī, 2:110, on Q 3.44; Ṭabarī, 3:262–6, on Q 3.37; Zamakhsharī, 1:355–7, on Q 3.33–7; Ibn Kathīr, 1:348, on Q 3.42–4.

68 It appears twenty-five times in all. See, e.g., Q 7.126; 10.46; 16.28, 32; 47.27.

69 Thus *Tafsīr Muqātil* 1:279, on Q 3.55; Ṭabarī, 3:290, on Q 3.55; Ibn Kathīr, 1:553–4, on Q 4.159. Cf., among other works, Reynolds, "The Muslim Jesus: dead or alive?"; K. Cragg's introduction to M.K. Ḥusayn, *City of Wrong*, trans. K. Cragg, Amsterdam: Djambatan, 1958; H. Räisänen, *Die koranische Jesusbild*, Helsinki: Missiologian ja Ekumeniikan, 1971, 68ff.; Basetti-Sani, *Koran in the Light of Christ*, 163–79; M. Ayyoub, "Towards an Islamic Christology II: The death of Jesus, reality or delusion?" *MW* 70, 1980, 91–121; K. Cragg, *Jesus and the Muslim*, London: George Allen & Unwin, 1985, 271–332; W.M. Watt, *Muslim-Christian Encounters*, Routledge: London, 1991, 22ff.; N. Robinson, "Jesus," *EQ*, 3:17–21.

applied to Jesus (!) – as God's casting sleep on someone, or seizing both body and soul into heaven.[70] Yet, and with this we arrive at the point, according to Ṭabarī some scholars accepted the standard meaning of *tawaffā* but proposed reading *āl 'Imrān* (3) 55 with the device of *ta'khīr al-muqaddam*, that is, understanding the raising up of Jesus before his death (which might now be postponed to the eschaton), even if the Qur'ān puts it the other way around. *Tafsīr Muqātil* resolves the problem of Jesus' death in precisely this fashion.[71]

On the question of Sarah's laughter (CS 5) Ṭabarī considers but decisively rejects the use of *ta'khīr al-muqaddam*. In *Hūd* (11) 71 the Qur'ān reports her laughter *before* it reports the annunciation of a son and grandson. This left the *mufassirūn* seeking an explanation for that laughter. In the course of his analysis, Ṭabarī notes the opinion of some scholars that *ta'khīr al-muqaddam* should be applied here,[72] that the Qur'ān intends that Sarah laughed due to the annunciation of a son, even if it mentions the annunciation after her laughter.

Unlike the case of *āl 'Imrān* (3) 55, however, Ṭabarī rejects this view.[73] He concludes instead that Sarah laughed out of satisfaction when she learned that the people of Lot (who had it coming to them) were about to be destroyed. Ṭabarī bases his case on the word order of the Qur'ān, noting that the last thing the Qur'ān mentions before Sarah's laughter is the angels' statement to Abraham: "Do not fear. We have been sent to the people of Lot" (Q 11.70b).

Thus in none of the cases mentioned above – the story of Jonah, the ordeal over Mary, the death of Jesus, and the laughter of Sarah – do the *mufassirūn* use the Judaeo-Christian subtext of the Qur'ān as an aid to help them read the Qur'ān in the proper order. The *mufassirūn* were certainly not unaware of Biblical material, yet in these cases where *ta'khīr al-muqaddam* is applied, cases where the very meaning of the Qur'ān is at stake, this material has little impact on them. In fact, for all four cases of *ta'khīr al-muqaddam* discussed above the *mufassirūn* make decisions that run precisely contrary to the Biblical subtext.[74] Jonah was swallowed by the fish after he went to

70 Thus the majority of traditions related by Ṭabarī, see 3:289–90, on Q 3.55; cf. Ibn Kathīr, 1:350, on Q 3.55–8.

71 *Tafsīr Muqātil*, 1:279, on Q 3.55; cf. Ṭabarī 3:291, on Q 3.55.

72 Ṭabarī, 12:72, on Q 11.71.

73 Ibid. Ibn Kathīr does the same, noting that it "is contrary to the syntax." Ibn Kathīr, 2:427, on Q 11.69–73.

74 Ibn Kathīr also follows this trend in his commentary on *al-anbiyā'* (21) 63 ("He said, 'No, this one, the largest one of them, did it. Ask him about it if they are able to speak.'"). In this verse Abraham, after destroying a set of idols but leaving the largest of them untouched, lies about his deed when challenged. Yet Ibn Kathīr (3:172, on Q 21.57–63), who does not accept that a prophet might commit such a sin, suggests that this verse might be read with *ta'khīr al-muqaddam*, i.e. Abraham was actually saying that *if* idols are able to speak then the largest of them did it. In Jewish midrash Abraham's denial of the deed comes first. See, e.g., *Gn Rab.* 38:19; *BT Pesaḥīm* 118a; *'Erūbīn* 53a; *Jubilees* 12:1–5; Cf. Calder, "Tafsir from Tabari to Ibn Kathir," 108.

Nineveh. The ordeal over Mary was for her adoption, not engagement. Jesus did not die. Sarah's laughter was not due to the annunciation of a son.

Judaeo-Christian material

In other ways, however, the *mufassirūn* relied heavily on Biblical material. This was, one might say, an inevitable recourse for the early *mufassirūn*, in light of the Qur'ān's allusive style. Because the Qur'ān so often provides allusions to Biblical narratives but not the narratives themselves, the exegetes had to turn to the Jews and Christians in order to make sense of their own scripture.[75] Our case studies are replete with examples of this phenomenon and it would seem superfluous to list them. But the precise manner in which the *mufassirūn* use this Biblical material is worth noting. For Biblical material plays a role in Islamic exegesis that is at once significant and limited.[76]

In the case of Jonah, for example, all of the *mufassirūn* in our survey make use of the Biblical report that Jonah was sent to Nineveh.[77] Most of them, moreover, mention the report that the people of Nineveh put on sackcloth (*misḥ*) as a sign of their repentance.[78] Ṭabarī, Zamakhsharī, and Ibn Kathīr even add that as a sign of their repentance the people of Jonah separated not only human mothers from their children, but also animals from their offspring.[79] This report appears to be a reflection of Jonah 3.7, in which the king of Nineveh demands that animals join in the fast of repentance, and perhaps even of Jonah 3.8, which, according to both the masoretic text and the Septuagint, has the king demand that both humans and animals put on sackcloth.

In the debate over the meaning of the *yaqṭīn* tree (Q 37.146), the *mufassirūn* clearly incline to the view that it is some type of a gourd (*dubbā'*, *qara'* or even *baṭṭīkh*),[80] presumably in light of Jonah 4.6 (Heb. קִיקָיוֹן; LXX

75 On this point see A. Rippin, "Interpreting the Bible through the Qur'ān," in Hawting and Shareef (eds.), *Approaches to the Qur'an* (249–59) 251; reprint: *The Qur'ān and Its Interpretive Tradition*, ed. Rippin.

76 On this question cf. W. Saleh's recent edition of a treatise on the permissibility of using the Bible for religious purposes by Ibrāhīm al-Biqā'ī (d. 885/1480): W. Saleh, *In Defense of the Bible: A Critical Edition and an Introduction to al-Biqā'ī's Bible Treatise*, Leiden: Brill, 2008.

77 *Tafsīr Muqātil*, 3:621, on Q 37.147; Qummī, 1:318–9, on Q 10.98; Ṭabarī, 23:105, on Q 37.147–9; Zamakhsharī, 3:131, on Q 21.87; 4:62, on Q 37.133–48; Ibn Kathīr, 4:19, on Q 37.139–48.

78 *Tafsīr Muqātil*, 2:250, on Q 10.98; Ṭabarī, 11:171, on Q 10.98; Zamakhsharī, 2:371, on Q 10.98; Ibn Kathīr, 2:410, on Q 10.98.

79 Ṭabarī, 11:171, on Q 10.98; Zamakhsharī, 2:371, on Q 10.98; Ibn Kathīr, 2:410, on Q 10.98.

80 *Tafsīr Muqātil*, 3:621, on Q 37.146; Qummī, 1:319–20, on Q 10.98; 2:200, on Q 37.146; Ṭabarī, 23:102–3, on Q 37.146; Zamakhsharī, 4:62, on Q 37.133–48; Ibn Kathīr, 4:20, on Q 37.139–48.

κολοκύθη; Psh. *qirtā*).[81] Regarding this tree Qummī remarks that God had made it sprout in order to shade Jonah (cf. Jonah 4.6),[82] since Jonah had lost his skin due to his travails in the fish. He then adds the Biblical detail that God later had the tree wither (cf. Jonah 4.7). Qummī also uses Biblical material to explain the place of the tree in this account. By Qummī's telling, when Jonah complains that his tree is gone, God proclaims: "O Jonah, why should I not have mercy on the 100,000 or more while you are anxious from the pains of an hour?" (cf. Jonah 4.10–1).[83]

Tafsīr Muqātil turns to another Biblical episode in order to explain Jonah's anger (Q 21.87, "The Man of the Fish went off angry"). Jonah was not angry with God, *Tafsīr Muqātil* explains, but rather with King Hezekiah (!). Behind this explanation is 2 Kings 20.1–5, wherein the prophet Isaiah departs from Hezekiah after delivering a message of condemnation (v. 1). When Hezekiah repents (vv. 2–3), however, God stops Isaiah (before he even makes it out of the palace; v. 4), telling him to return and announce to the king that God has relented (v. 5). Thus the topos found in the Jonah account of condemnation, repentance, and clemency appears in the Hezekiah account. *Tafsīr Muqātil* accordingly puts Jonah in the place of Isaiah.

Thus there is a tendency for the *mufassirūn* to rely on details from Judaeo-Christian material that might contribute to the effectiveness of their narratives. This is seen again with the commentaries on the laughter of Abraham's wife (cf. CS 5). The *mufassirūn* unanimously name his wife Sarah, even though she is not named in the Qur'ān. Likewise they are all agreed that the messengers to Abraham (Q 11.69), elsewhere referred to as his guests (Q 15.51; 51.24), were in fact angels.[84] The Qur'ān itself never calls them angels, but the Bible does (Gn 19.1; cf. v. 15).

The same point might be demonstrated from the *mufassirūn*'s narratives on the infancy of Abraham. In order to contextualize passages such as *al-an'ām* (6) 74–83 (cf. CS 4), *al-shu'arā'* (26) 69–104, and *al-ṣāfāt* (37) 82–91, the *mufassirūn* weave these passages into the midrashic traditions on Nimrod's kingdom. They make Nimrod the perfect foil to Abraham, a king whose cruelty is matched only by his infidelity.[85]

81 Jeffery suggests (*FV*, 292) that the word *yaqṭīn* resulted when the Hebrew *qīqāyōn* was "heard during an oral recitation of the story, and then reproduced from memory in this garbled form."

82 Cf. *Tafsīr Muqātil*, 3:621, on Q 37.146.

83 Qummī also adds a conclusion not found in the Biblical account: Jonah repents and God, in return, heals his body. Qummī, 1:319–20, on Q 10.98.

84 *Tafsīr Muqātil*, 2:290, on Q 11.69; Qummī 1:335, on Q 11.69; Ṭabarī, 12:72–3, on Q 11.71; Zamakhsharī (1:409, on Q 11.69–73) refers to three angels: Gabriel, Michael, and Isrāfīl; Ibn Kathīr (2:426, on Q 11.69–73) speaks of four angels: Gabriel, Michael, Isrāfīl, and Raphael. Cf. *BT*, *Babā meṣī'a*, 86–7, where the messengers are said to be the angels Michael, Gabriel, and Raphael. The Qur'ān does specify elsewhere that angels might act as God's messengers; see Q 22.75; 35.1.

85 See *Tafsīr Muqātil*, 1:569–71, on Q 6.74; Qummī, 1:213–4, on Q 6.75–7; Ṭabarī, 7:248–50, on Q 6.76; Zamakhsharī, 2:39–40, on Q 6.74–9; Ibn Kathīr, 2:147, on Q 6.74–9.

Yet suspicion of Judaeo-Christian traditions generally increases among the later *mufassirūn*, and is particularly apparent with Ibn Kathīr. For Ibn Kathīr such traditions can play only a purely ornamental role. He reports, for example, the standard Christian tradition on the Companions of the Cave, complete with the anti-Christian emperor Decius. At the same time, however, Ibn Kathīr concludes that this affair must have taken place before Christianity, since, according to the occasion of revelation narrative, the Jews were the ones in Muḥammad's day who knew the story.[86]

Ibn Kathīr's suspicion appears again in his commentary on the ordeal over the guardianship of Mary (Q 3.44; cf. CS 9). He is not the only exegete to connect this passage to Zechariah's adoption of Mary, of course, but he is the only one to show anxiety over the very idea of an ordeal. Ibn Kathīr insists that if Zechariah defeated his competitors in this contest, he was also superior to them in virtue: "He was the oldest among them, the most noble, and the most learned. He was their prayer leader and their prophet – God's blessings and peace be upon him and upon the rest of the prophets."[87]

Thus there is a certain tension in the relationship between the *mufassirūn* and Judaeo-Christian narrative. That narrative is sought out for helpful details, but it is put aside again when it comes to fundamental questions of interpretation. This tension is perhaps most evident in the case of the creation of Adam (CS 1). While all of the *mufassirūn* borrow details from Jewish and Christian traditions on the prostration of the angels before Adam, none of them embraces the fundamental premise of those traditions – even if it has some echo in a prophetic *ḥadīth* – that Adam was created in the image of God.

The *mufassirūn*

Yet there are of course differences between the *mufassirūn*. Indeed the case studies of the previous chapter serve among other things to highlight those differences. *Tafsīr Muqātil* manifests certain unique features which reflect an early stage of *tafsīr*, even if the work as a whole cannot safely be attributed to Muqātil b. Sulaymān himself (a view supported by passages relevant to our case studies).[88] Still, even a cautious view on the question of authorship would place it around 200/815.[89] The internal evidence of *Tafsīr Muqātil*

86 Ibn Kathīr, 3:71, on Q 18.13–6.

87 Ibid., 1:348, on Q 3.42–4.

88 In one place (e.g. 2:625–6, on Q 19.28, regarding the genealogy of Mary) *Tafsīr Muqātil* has an *isnād* to Muqātil. In another place (3:620, on Q 37.142, regarding Jonah and the fish) the author (or editor) of the *tafsīr* specifies, "And now we return to the statement of Muqātil."

89 The extant recension of *Tafsīr Muqātil* is commonly attributed to Hudhayl b. Ḥabīb (d. after 190/805). Wansbrough argues that *Tafsīr Muqātil* and early *tafsīr*s in general, "despite biographical information on its putative authors, are not earlier than the date proposed to mark the beginnings of Arabic literature, namely 200/815." *QS*, 144.

suggests that it represents a stage of exegesis different from that seen with Ṭabarī in the early 4th/10th century.

Whereas Ṭabarī generally begins his commentary on each passage with a summary of scholarly views, *Tafsīr Muqātil* has no interest in summarizing, let alone resolving, scholarly disputes. Instead *Tafsīr Muqātil* explains Qur'ānic references, defines obscure words, and provides stories to contextualize allusions. It is a work, in other words, meant to render the Qur'ān comprehensible and approachable. *Tafsīr Muqātil*, it might be said, reads almost as a translation of the Qur'ān, from the language of revelation into the language of its intended audience. Wansbrough accordingly attributes to *Tafsīr Muqātil* an "unhurried, almost chatty style."[90] Regarding the question of *al-raqīm* (Q 18.9), for example, *Tafsīr Muqātil* explains simply, "It is a book that two virtuous rulers wrote, one of whom was Mātūs, the other Astūs."[91] Ṭabarī, on the other hand, reports fourteen different traditions (comprising at least six different opinions) on this question, before giving his own opinion and justifying it with grammatical examples.[92]

In *Tafsīr Muqātil* there is virtually no attention paid to debates over grammar, *variae lectiones*, or legal matters, and no particular concern with dogmatic principles. The report of Muḥammad's boastful (and false) declaration that he would receive information on the Companions of the Cave in a day hardly makes the Prophet look good. It does, however, turn a line in the Qur'ān (Q 18.23) into an entertaining story.

Tafsīr Muqātil's devotion to developing a Qur'ānic narrative also involves Biblical material. On Jesus' announcement of a messenger to come after him named Aḥmad (Q 61.6; cf. CS 13), Ṭabarī and Zamakhsharī have essentially no comment. Qummī and Ibn Kathīr present prophetic *ḥadīth*s on the Prophet's names.[93] *Tafsīr Muqātil*, however, reports that in Syriac Aḥmad means "paraclete" (*fārqlīṭā*).[94] Thereby *Tafsīr Muqātil* integrates *al-ṣaff* (61) 6 into a well-known Biblical tradition about Jesus (based on Jn 14 and 16). Similarly *Tafsīr Muqātil* provides a Biblical context to the story of the People of the Sabbath by insisting that their transformation into monkeys took place in the time of David (cf. CS 7).[95]

Tafsīr Muqātil's obliviousness to dogmatic principles and liberal use of Biblical material led later scholars to suspect the work and to associate Muqātil b. Sulaymān with various reviled sects.[96] Nevertheless *Tafsīr Muqātil*'s

90 *QS*, 133. Elsewhere Wansbrough comments that to the author of *Tafsīr Muqātil*, "the scriptural text was subordinate, conceptually and syntactically, to the *narratio*." *QS*, 127.

91 Tafsīr Muqātil, 2:574, on Q 18.9.

92 Ṭabarī, 15:198–204, on Q 18.9.

93 Qummī, 2:346, on Q 61.6; Ibn Kathīr, 4:332, on Q 61.6.

94 *Tafsīr Muqātil*, 1:316, on Q 61.6.

95 Ibid., 1:113, on Q 2.65.

96 Among other things he is accused of being a Zaydī and a Murji'ī. On this topic see M. Plessner and A. Rippin, "Muḳātil b. Sulaymān," *EI*[2], 7:508–9; I. Goldfeld, "Muqātil Ibn

relationship with Biblical material should not be exaggerated. The Bible is not used in this work as a guide for understanding the Qur'ān, but simply as a resource for adding interesting or explanatory details.

Regarding the identity of the Qur'ānic Haman (cf. CS 6), for example, *Tafsīr Muqātil* does not introduce traditions on the Biblical Haman. Such introductions would presumably confuse the primary goal of developing a narrative, seeing that the Biblical Haman is in Persia, not Egypt. Regarding *al-nisā'* (4) 157 and the case of *shubbiha la-hum*, *Tafsīr Muqātil* does not, in light of the Bible, conclude that Jesus was indeed crucified (although God – not the Jews – was responsible for his death). Instead *Tafsīr Muqātil* reports the standard Islamic doctrine that on the day of the Crucifixion God took Jesus into heaven, body and soul, and someone else died in his place. To this report, however, *Tafsīr Muqātil* adds Biblical details, reporting that Jesus was 33 years old at the time of the crucifixion, which took place on a mountain in Jerusalem.[97]

The *tafsīr* of Qummī is likewise directed towards the development of a coherent Qur'ānic narrative. Yet Qummī's work is also marked throughout by distinctly Shī'ī interpretations.[98] One might even say that whereas Biblical literature provides *Tafsīr Muqātil* with the details that enhance his narrative, 'Alīd traditions do so for Qummī. Qummī relates, for example, that the parable of the good and evil trees in *Ibrāhīm* (14) 24–6 refers to the Shī'a (*ahl al-bayt*) and the unbelievers, that is, the Umayyads.[99] The Shī'ī nature of Qummī's work is evident even in its basic structure, as Qummī credits most interpretations either to Ja'far al-Ṣādiq, the sixth Shī'ī Imām, or to his father Muḥammad al-Bāqir, the fifth Shī'ī Imām.

Regarding *al-'ankabūt* (29) 39 ("When Moses came with clear signs to Qārūn, Pharaoh, and Haman, they were arrogant on Earth but did not prevail"; cf. CS 6), Qummī directs his comments to a theological controversy. This verse, he explains, was revealed to counter the position of the *Mujbira*, since it shows that humans are free to rebel against God.[100] In this case, then, Qummī uses exegesis to support the Imāmī/Mu'tazilī teaching on free will and divine justice. Yet his primary concern is to develop a coherent narrative that illustrates the Qur'ān in Shī'ī colors.[101]

Sulaymān," *Bar-Ilan Arabic and Islamic Studies* 2, 1978, 13–30; C. Gilliot, "Muqātil, grand exégète, traditionniste et théologien maudit," 39–92.

97 *Tafsīr Muqātil*, 1:421, on Q 4.157.

98 Wansbrough comments that Qummī's *tafsīr* "consists entirely of haggadic elements applied to sectarian theology." *QS*, 146.

99 Qummī, 1:371, on Q 14.26. On the symbolic nature of Qummī's *tafsīr* Wansbrough remarks: "The device by which agency in the *narratio* was transformed into imagery appropriate to the Islamic theodicy could be construed as allegory, but because of the specifically historical mention in such exegesis, it may more accurately be described as typology." *QS*, 245.

100 A pejorative title that the Mu'tazila and Imāmī Shī'a used for those who taught a doctrine of divine determination. Qummī, 2:127, on Q 29.39.

101 Bar-Asher (p. 79) identifies a "limited interest in issues not directly related to the Shī'a" as a typical feature of early (pre-Būyid) Imāmī Shī'ī exegesis.

In this regard Qummī's narrative on Jonah's underworld encounter with Qārūn, which he attributes to 'Alī b. Abī Ṭālib, is particularly enlightening (cf. CS 6, 8).[102] In this narrative the Qur'ān's reference to God having the earth swallow Qārūn (Q 28.79–81) becomes a historical (and geographical!) fact. Therefore it is perfectly logical that Jonah would meet Qārūn during his sojourn under the earth in the belly of the fish. But the account of their meeting is not only a story, it is also exegesis. Qummī has Qārūn explain to Jonah that he now feels sympathy for Moses and his people (whom he had wronged, cf. Q 28.76). At this God orders an angel to set Qārūn free from his underground prison. This scene explains why Jonah decided to pray to God for forgiveness (cf. Q 21.87).

Of particular interest for our purposes is the report which introduces this narrative. Qummī relates that 'Alī b. Abī Ṭālib disclosed this account only when the Jews challenged him to explain where exactly Jonah went with his fish. In other words, Qummī employs precisely the same motif, complete with the Jews as opponents, that appears in the report on the revelation of the Companions of the Cave account. Here, however, 'Alī takes the place of Muḥammad.

The main focus of Qummī's contemporary Ṭabarī is quite different. In our case studies Ṭabarī appears to be above all concerned to present and resolve scholarly debates on disputed passages. For each individual passage Ṭabarī concerns himself first with recording traditions containing the views of earlier and contemporary scholars on a certain question. Only thereafter does he express his own opinion, an opinion generally based on his evaluation of the preceding traditions.[103] Not only does Ṭabarī admit of opposing views, he seeks to catalog as many of them as possible. Accordingly his *tafsīr* has been justly described as polyvalent.[104] In Ṭabarī's *tafsīr*, unlike those of Muqātil and Qummī, the reader is faced with the depth of disagreement in early Muslim interpretation of the Qur'ān.

But for Ṭabarī there is nothing scandalous about the scholarly confusion of his day. Indeed Ṭabarī often begins his commentary on a passage by admitting: "The interpreters differ over its interpretation" (*ikhtalafū ahlu l-ta'wili fī tawīli dhālik*). He is also perfectly willing, for example, to cite conflicting traditions, both of which claim Ibn 'Abbās as an authority (e.g. on *khalīfa*, CS 1; on with whom Jonah was angry, CS 8; on the meaning of *al-raqīm*, CS 12).[105] He is likewise willing, almost eager, to show the extent

102 Qummī, 1:319, on Q 10.98.

103 On Ṭabarī Gilliot comments: "L'histoire est pour lui une science de tradition dans laquelle l'induction et la déduction n'ont qu'une place réduite. Il en est de même, *mutatis mutandis*, pour son Commentaire." Gilliot, *Exégèse, langue, et théologie en Islam*, 166.

104 On this see Calder, "Tafsir from Tabari to Ibn Kathir," 103–4.

105 On the figure of Ibn 'Abbās as an authority of *tafsīr* see especially C. Gilliot, "Portrait 'mythique' d'Ibn 'Abbās," *Arabica* 32, 1985, 62–7. Elsewhere he notes, "In the functioning of a tradition the old *auctores* are also *auctoritates*, to whom later generations attribute, without feeling any discomfort at all, theses and interpretations which are those of the

of disagreement over the Qur'ān's interpretation. On the meaning of *al-raqīm* Ṭabarī reports fifteen different traditions. On the interpretation of *āl 'Imrān* (3) 169–70 and the question of the eschatological status of martyrs (cf. CS 11), Ṭabarī reports nineteen different traditions, comprising at least eight different views. Quite often the different views he reports are fully incompatible. *Al-raqīm*, for example, is said to mean a village, valley, book, tablet, mountain, or to be simply incomprehensible. The souls of martyrs either exist in domes near a river in paradise, where they are accompanied by young women, or in the bodies of birds.

Other traditions that Ṭabarī reports are themselves narratives.[106] Indeed in most of our case studies Ṭabarī provides detailed haggadic commentary: on the prostration before Adam (CS 1), on Abraham and the heavenly bodies (CS 4), on the transformation of the People of the Sabbath (CS 7), and so on. Yet Ṭabarī's recounting of these narratives is something like his report of scholarly opinions on an unclear term. He often reports a number of different stories – including stories he does not trust – to explain a single passage.

Ṭabarī indeed tends to read an individual passage, often an individual verse, independently both of the larger context and of parallel passages in the Qur'ān. He may turn to parallel passages when he is confronted with a rare word or a confusing grammatical sequence but otherwise his method is atomistic.[107] This atomism, it seems, is encouraged by the very format of *tafsīr*, in which the Qur'ān is approached piece by piece in its canonical order, Sūra by Sūra, verse by verse.[108] In this aspect *tafsīr* appears to be a more limited genre than its much maligned relative, the "Stories of the Prophets" (*qiṣaṣ al-anbiyā'*), which proceed in a quasi-chronological format.

Ṭabarī's atomism is evident, for example, in his commentary on the laughter of Sarah (CS 5). Here he concludes, on the basis of the immediate sequence of Q 11.70–1, that Sarah laughed due to the imminent extermination of the People of Lot.[109] Yet the parallel passage of *al-dhāriyyāt* (51) 24–34 strongly suggests that her laughter (Q 11.71), like her screaming (Q 51.29), is a response to the annunciation of a son.

group itself." C. Gilliot "The beginnings of Qur'ānic exegesis," trans. M. Bonner, in Rippin (ed.), *The Qur'an: Formative Interpretation*, (1–27) 10; trans. of "Les débuts de l'exégèse coranique," *Revue Monde Musulman et de la Méditerranée*, 58, 1990, 82–100.

106 On this see Calder, "Tafsir from Tabari to Ibn Kathir," 108.

107 On this term see J. Burton, "Law and exegesis: The penalty for adultery in Islam," *Approaches to the Qur'an*, 280.

108 In this regard the format of Qummī's *tafsīr* is worthy of mention. He tends to address themes or accounts in the Qur'ān all at once. Thus he analyzes *in toto* the angelic prostration before Adam account, which appears in seven different Sūras, in his commentary on the first appearance thereof (Q 2.30–4; Qummī, 1:49–50). At other times Qummī postpones his analysis of an account to a place that he finds *à propos*. Thus Qummī's analysis of the People of the Sabbath account, which appears in Q 2.65–6, 4.47, and 5.60, is to be found only in his commentary on Q 7.163.

109 Ṭabarī, 12:74, on Q 11.71.

Ṭabarī is ultimately committed to finding the precise, literal meaning of the text and filters traditions with this in mind. Thus he rejects a tradition attributed to Mujāhid that the transformation of the People of the Sabbath was only metaphorical, commenting: "The statement of Mujāhid is in contradiction to the clear indication of the Book of God."[110] Ṭabarī often turns to grammatical and semantic analysis in his search for the literal meaning of the Qur'ān. In the case of Sarah's laughter, for example, Ṭabarī considers closely the opinion of some grammarians that *ḍaḥikat* ("she laughed") might mean here, "she menstruated." He rejects this view, but not before adding a note that the Kūfan grammarians do not recognize this alternative meaning.[111]

Ṭabarī's commentary on the problematic term *ghulf* and the proposed variant *ghuluf* (Q 2.88; 4.155; CS 10) is dominated by grammatical debates over the form of these words, and includes a verse of Jāhilī poetry as a witness to their meaning.[112] His conclusion that *al-raqīm* must refer to a book or a tablet is in part based on grammar, namely the view that *raqīm* is a variant form of the passive participle *marqūm*, and thus synonymous with *maktūb*, "something written." In this case Ṭabarī cites a Bedouin expression to support his case.[113]

Thus Ṭabarī's *tafsīr* is not primarily distinguished by narrative, but rather by his concern with the literal meaning of the immediate passage at hand. According to Gilliot, this approach is ultimately inspired by Ṭabarī's position on the inimitability of Qur'ānic language.[114]

Zamakhsharī's *tafsīr* marks a significant development from this approach. In our case studies Zamakhsharī appears to be primarily concerned with the interpretation of the Qur'ān in light of an independent standard of reason. Thus he is generally suspicious of illogical or fantastic interpretations. On the report that the angel Gabriel cut up Haman's tower with his wings (cf. CS 6), for example, Zamakhsharī comments skeptically: "God knows better whether this is reliable."[115] On the idea of God casting stars at demons (Q 67.5; cf. CS 2) he comments that the Qur'ān could not be speaking of the stars themselves, but rather a sort of firebrand (*qabs*) from them.[116] Similarly, and in opposition to Ṭabarī, he insists that the Qur'ān is speaking

110 Ibid., 1:332.
111 Ibid., 12:73, on Q 11.71.
112 Attributed to Ṭarafa b. al-'Abd. Ṭabarī, 1:406, on Q 2.88.
113 Ṭabarī, 15:199, on Q 18.9.
114 "Mais d'autre part, l'utilisation du savoir grammatical et philologique y apparaître non seulement comme enracinée en tradition (quoi de plus traditionnel que la langue, dans une société classique, tout au moins!), mais aussi comme naturelle. Naturelle, elle le devient, en effet, dès lors qu'on a décrété que la langue du Coran est l'archétype, le modèle de l'arabe. Les règles qui valent pour la langue ordinaire s'appliquent éminemment à la langue sacrée. On ne devra jamais oublier les prolégomènes de son Commentaire dans lesquels il a déclaré que la langue du Coran est l'arabe par excellence, par voie d'éminence." Gilliot, *Exégèse, langue, et théologie en Islam*, 166.
115 Zamakhsharī, 3:413, on Q 28.38.
116 Ibid., 4:577, on Q 67.5.

only metaphorically when it mentions the transformation of the People of the Sabbath (CS 7).[117]

Zamakhsharī's concern with reason appears in a question of history, not biology, when he reports that the opponents of the Companions of the Cave were not pagans but Christians. Zamakhsharī relates that the Christian kings, "grew excessive to the point that they worshipped idols and compelled others to worship them."[118] This idea may be influenced by Islamic theories of the Christian falsification (*taḥrīf*) of Jesus' Islamic religion, or even by historical reports on the Byzantine Iconodule emperors. Yet more likely Zamakhsharī arrives at this idea due to the common tradition (seen also with *Tafsīr Muqātil*, Qummī, and Ṭabarī) that Decius was the emperor at the time of the Cave incident. Zamakhsharī recognizes (pace Ibn Kathīr) that Decius reigned in the Christian era, which makes it reasonable (if wrong) to conclude that he was, in fact, a Christian.

Finally, Zamakhsharī's rationalism is particularly prominent in his comments on the account of Abraham and the heavenly bodies (Q 6.76–9; cf. CS 4). *Tafsīr Muqātil*, Qummī, and Ṭabarī all connect this incident to the childhood narrative of Abraham. Zamakhsharī, however, insists that it took place instead when Abraham, as an adult, engaged the pagans in a rational contest.[119] This account is the Qur'ān's record of Abraham's efforts to explain Islam in a reasonable manner. That, one might say, is exactly what Zamakhsharī himself seeks to do in his *tafsīr*.[120]

Thus Zamakhsharī's exegetical task consists essentially of comparing two basic sources: the revelation of the Qur'ān and human reason. Ibn Kathīr's method is similar, but his sources are different. He compares instead the revelation of the Qur'ān with the revelation of the *ḥadīth*.[121] To Ibn Kathīr *ḥadīth* is a parallel path of revelation. The difference between the two sources is formal: Only the Qur'ān was revealed for public and liturgical recitation. As an epistemological source, however, *ḥadīth* is in no way inferior to the Qur'ān.

117 Ibid., 1:587, on Q 4.153–9.

118 Ibid., 2:711, on Q 18.21.

119 Abraham, Zamakhsharī concludes, pointed to heavenly bodies in order "to guide them on the path of contemplation and evidence, to make them understand how valid contemplation teaches that none of these things can validly be a god, to present the evidence of their createdness." Zamakhsharī, 2:40, on Q 6.74–9.

120 Zamakhsharī also seems to privilege interpretations which lend a certain coherence or symmetry to the Qur'ān. To this end he concludes that *al-raqīm* was the name of the dog of the Companions of the Cave (CS 12). Thereby *al-kahf* (18) 9, where the Companions and *al-raqīm* are mentioned together ("Did you count the Companions of the Cave and *al-raqīm* among Our wondrous signs?"), matches *al-kahf* (18) 22, where the Companions and the dog are mentioned together ("They will say three and the dog is the fourth. They will say five and the dog is the sixth. . . . They will say seven and the dog is the eighth.").

121 Thus Calder: "Any systematic reading of his work will reveal that his primary objective is to measure the text of the Qur'ān against the established collections of prophetic *ḥadīth*." Calder, "Tafsir from Tabari to Ibn Kathir," 130.

Accordingly the *ḥadīth* are the only reliable standard for the interpretation of the Qur'ān.[122] Rational speculation is not only unreliable, it is a dangerous temptation. The devil himself, Ibn Kathīr explains (cf. CS 1), fell victim to it: "He was the angel most devoted to independent reasoning (*ijtihād*) and greatest of them in knowledge, which led him to become arrogant."[123]

As might be expected, throughout our case studies Ibn Kathīr uses prophetical *ḥadīth* as his guide for interpreting the Qur'ān. In deciding whether Mary is the niece or sister of Zechariah's wife (Elizabeth), for example, Ibn Kathīr turns to a prophetic *ḥadīth* and concludes, in contradiction to most narratives on the topic, that the two are sisters.[124] Regarding the Companions of the Cave account, Ibn Kathīr insists that the dog must have remained outside of the cave, since according to a prophetic *ḥadīth*, angels do not enter houses where there is a dog, a picture, an unbeliever, or an unclean person.[125]

The influence of *ḥadīth* also explains Ibn Kathīr's suspicion of those who, according to the Qur'ān, desired to build a place of worship (*masjid*) over the Companions (Q 18.21; CS 12). The Qur'ān suggests that this is a pious act, and indeed it is just that in the Qur'ān's Judaeo-Christian subtext.[126] Yet Ibn Kathīr cites a *ḥadīth* in which the Prophet curses the Jews and Christians for praying at graves. To this same effect he reports with approbation a tradition that 'Umar b. al-Khaṭṭāb, when he discovered the grave of Daniel in Iraq during the conquests, buried it and hid it from the people.[127]

Elsewhere Ibn Kathīr's devotion to *ḥadīth*, a body of literature that emphasizes the infallibility of Prophets, leads him to emphasize the virtue of prophets in general, and the status of Muḥammad in particular. He reports, for example, that the people of Nineveh feared divine punishment only when they learned that a prophet does not lie (CS 8).[128] Elsewhere he insists that the biographical account of Muḥammad's flight with Abū Bakr to a cave is more "noble, sublime, impressive, and amazing" than the Qur'ānic account of the Companions of the Cave (CS 12).[129]

Yet Ibn Kathīr's reliance on *ḥadīth* as a second source of revelation also renders his exegetical task more difficult. For thereby he is often faced with

122 On Ibn Kathīr Calder comments ("Tafsir from Tabari to Ibn Kathir," 130), "The authorities to whom he looks for support are not those who work in the great intellectual traditions of exegesis or law or *kalām* but those responsible for the great collections of *ḥadīth* and those who figure in their *isnāds*."

123 Ibn Kathīr, 1:76, on Q 2.34.

124 Ibid., 1:345, on Q 3.37.

125 Ibid. 3:72, on Q 18.18. Cf. Muslim, "al-Libās wa-l-zīna," 26, Beirut: Dār al-Kutub al-'Arabiyya, 1421/2000, 14:69–70.

126 In the version of Jacob of Serūgh it is the pious emperor Theodosius himself who proposes building a temple (Syr. *hayklā*) over the bodies of the youths. "Testi Orientali Inediti," 2:23, # 179. Cf. Griffith, "Christian lore and the Arabic Qur'ān," 124.

127 Ibn Kathīr, 3:75, on Q 18.21.

128 Ibid., 3:180, on Q 21.87–8.

129 Ibid., 3:72, on Q 18.13–16.

uncomfortable conflicts between the two sources that must be resolved, ironically, through rational deduction. This is the case with his commentary on those passages (Q 3.157, 169; 4.74 passim; cf. CS 11) that emphasize the unique state of the martyrs in paradise. Ibn Kathīr follows the standard narrative that the souls of martyrs will exist in the bodies of birds between their death and the resurrection of their bodies. Yet a prophetic *ḥadīth* – with a "valid, strong, and excellent *isnād*"[130] – explains that the souls of *all* believers will be in the bodies of birds. Ibn Kathīr is thereby compelled to find a new privilege that the martyrs will enjoy. He resorts to the creative, if peculiar, solution that only the martyrs will be free to fly around paradise. The others will be stuck in a tree.[131]

As this last example suggests, Ibn Kathīr's use of *ḥadīth* as an interpretive standard requires him to pay close attention to the question of *isnād*s. In our case studies Ibn Kathīr consistently refers not only to the content of a *ḥadīth* (i.e. the *matn*), but also to the quality of its *isnād.*[132] He notes with satisfaction when a *ḥadīth* is present in the *Ṣaḥīḥ*s of both Bukhārī and Muslim.[133] He notes with suspicion when a tradition is based on the reports of non-Muslims. When he rejects a tradition on the authority of Muḥammad al-Bāqir, for example, Ibn Kathīr comments: "He transmitted it from the People of the Book. It includes a reprehensible point that must be refuted."[134] On the following tradition he comments, "This is also an Israelite [story] to be rejected, like the one before it."[135] So too Ibn Kathīr is skeptical of all traditions from Wahb b. Munabbih,[136] the prototypical transmitter of tales from Jews, the so-called *isrā'īliyyāt*. Ibn Kathīr's skepticism reflects a larger trend in Islamic scholarship. When *ḥadīth* collections had been formed and canonized, scholars were eventually expected to justify the Islamic orthodoxy of their sources.[137]

130 Ibid., 1:408, on Q 3.169–75.

131 Ibid.

132 Thus Ibn Kathīr favors (1:78, on Q 2.34) the view that the angels prostrated before Adam (CS 1) as a sign of honor, and not as a way of indicating the *qibla*, due to the reliable *isnād*s for the *ḥadīth* supporting the first view, even though he finds the second view logically appealing. On a *ḥadīth* regarding Jonah, which he traces back to the Companion Anas b. Mālik, Ibn Kathīr confidently adds: "I am sure that Anas attributed this *ḥadīth* to the Messenger of God – God's blessing and peace be upon him" (3:181, on Q 21.87–8; cf. CS 8). Regarding a *ḥadīth* on the transformation of the People of the Sabbath (CS 7), Ibn Kathīr concedes (1:105, on Q 2.65–6) that one *ḥadīth* which contradicts his opinion has a good *isnād.*

133 For example, on Abraham (2:147, on Q 6.74–9; 3:172, on Q 21.57–63; cf. CS 4); on Jonah (4:19, on Q 37.139–48; cf. CS 8); on the Companions of the Cave (3:75, on Q 18.23–4; cf. CS 12).

134 Ibn Kathīr, 1:72, on Q 2.30.

135 Ibid.

136 For example, on the laughter of Sarah (2:427, on Q 11.69–73; cf. CS 5); on the Crucifixion (1:552, on Q 4.156–9).

137 On this process see J. McAuliffe, "The prediction and prefiguration of Muḥammad," in Reeves (ed.), *Bible and Qur'ān* (107–31) 127–31. McAuliffe relies in part on F. Rosenthal,

Ibn Kathīr's emphasis on *ḥadīth* not infrequently leads him away from the literal meaning of the Qur'ān. If Ibn Kathīr might be justifiably called a fundamentalist,[138] his fundamentalism does not involve literalism. Among our *mufassirūn* only Ṭabarī might be called a literalist. Ibn Kathīr is too concerned with *ḥadīth* to merit such a title. This concern often leads him to conclusions that are in no way obvious from the text: that the Companions' dog remained outside of the cave, or that building a *masjid* at the site of the Companions' cave was irreligious, or that the souls of dead believers will be in the bodies of birds, yet confined to a tree and unable to fly.

Tafsīr and Qur'ān

The foregoing analysis is meant above all to emphasize the distinctive qualities of the *mufassirūn* in our survey. Thereby it displays the creativity and virtuosity of the *mufassirūn* in shaping the Qur'ān in light of their particular concerns, whether haggadic, sectarian, literalist, rationalist, or fundamentalist. At the same time, however, this analysis suggests that *tafsīr* is less a historical record that stretches back (parallel to the Qur'ān itself) to the time of the Qur'ān's origins, and more the product of individual scholars and the (much later) context in which they worked.

In this regard it is telling that Ibn Kathīr, with all of his impressive *ḥadīth* and accompanying evaluation of *isnād*s, appears no closer to understanding the Qur'ān than *Tafsīr Muqātil*, who rarely includes either. This point should not be missed. The implication of Ibn Kathīr's constant reference to prophetic *ḥadīth* is that the Islamic community has faithfully preserved not only the text of the Qur'ān but also the prophetic interpretation thereof. As the popular saying has it, Muḥammad himself is the first *mufassir*.

Over fifty years ago Jeffery, discussing his efforts to understand the Qur'ān, acknowledged this point:

> Neither the *Sīra* nor *Tradition* is of much help to us in this matter, and though the exegetes have preserved in their work good evidence of what was thought in their day to be the meaning of words and phrases in the Qur'ān, the bewildering array of variant opinions they record on almost every crucial point of interpretation, makes it quite clear [that] even the very early circle of exegetes was as much in doubt as we are as to the exact meaning of many of the terms that interest us the most.[139]

"The influence of the biblical tradition on Muslim historiography," in B. Lewis and P.M. Holt (eds.), *Historians of the Middle East*, London: Oxford University Press, 1962, 35–45.

138 Calder comments: "He and his mentor Ibn Taymiyya are in the strictest sense of the word fundamentalist: distrustful of the intellectual tradition of Islam and of the accumulated experience of the community, they look for salvation to a new (!) reading of the fundamental texts." Calder, "Tafsir from Tabari to Ibn Kathir," 131.

139 Jeffery, *Qur'ān as Scripture*, 7.

Since the time of Jeffery, however, the tendency among critical scholars to rely on "*sīra* and tradition" for the original meaning of the Qur'ān has in no way decreased.[140] This is explicit in the two most recent Qur'ān translations in our survey: Fakhry and Abdel Haleem. Both Fakhry and Abdel Haleem present their works as critical, not pious, studies. Still they are committed to the idea that the medieval *tafsīr*s are the key to establishing the original meaning of the Qur'ān. Fakhry comments, "For purposes of accuracy, we have often had to rely on the most authoritative commentaries, especially where the meaning of the text was either obscure or controversial, as the notes will show."[141] Abdel Haleem similarly explains that "ambiguous passages are made clear in the Arabic commentaries on the Qur'ān."[142]

Yet this chapter is certainly not meant to be a polemic against the medieval *mufassirūn*. Quite to the contrary, their use of exegetical devices – such as story-telling, occasion of revelation, *variae lectiones*, *ta'khīr al-muqaddam*, and Biblical material – shows not only the *mufassirūn*'s originality, but also their skill in shaping the text according to their particular goals. This accomplishment, however, can only be appreciated when their work is acknowledged to be fundamentally original. To this effect Andrew Rippin reflects:

> The role of the interpretation – which can be witnessed in other religious traditions as well – can be better understood when it is viewed in light of a Qur'ān which has been liberated from the shackles of the exegetical tradition which makes certain presumptions about the text seem "natural" or matters of "common sense" to the reader. This has been accomplished precisely because the interpretative tradition has been so successful in its approach to the text. To appreciate this accomplishment, we must first be able to read the Qur'ān with a background freed of the Muslim construct. Then, in returning to the works of *tafsīr*, we can achieve a better measure of the incredible creativity and accomplishment of the past masters of the exegetical imagination.[143]

140 For a recent study on the question of the relationship of Qur'ān to *tafsīr* see N. Sinai, *Fortschreibung und Auslegung: Studien zur frühen Koraninterpretation*. Wiesbaden: Harrassowitz, 2009.

141 Fakhry, 3–4.

142 Abdel Haleem, xxxv. Abdel Haleem announces that the superiority of his translation is based on his knowledge of the occasions of revelation. In his prolegomenon he gives an example to this effect, explaining that the "sword verse" (Q 9.5) has been "misinterpreted and taken out of context." When the Qur'ān here proclaims "so kill the polytheists wherever you find them" (*fa-qtulū l-mushrikīna ḥaythu wajadtumūhum*), this verse must be understood in its original context. Thereby it is seen that the Qur'ān means only to threaten the "hardened polytheists in Arabia, who would accept nothing other than the expulsion of the Muslims or their reversion to paganism, and who repeatedly broke their treaties." Abdel Haleem, xxxi.

143 Rippin, *The Qur'ān and Its Interpretive Tradition*, xviii–xix.

4 Reading the Qur'ān as homily

The relationship between the Qur'ān and *tafsīr* might be compared, *mutatis mutandis*, to the relationship between the *Iliad* and the *Aeneid*. When Virgil has Aeneas recount the story of the fall of Troy in Dido's court (Books 2–3), he is not revealing faithfully preserved details of events that took place centuries earlier, details that will allow the student to understand the true meaning of the *Iliad*. Instead Virgil is developing a new interpretation of the story of Troy, an interpretation motivated by his particular partisan agenda (above all the glorification of Augustan Rome). In the same way the details that the *mufassirūn* relate about the Qur'ān are a product of their intellectual and literary creativity, a creativity often, although not always, motivated by a sectarian agenda. Their accomplishment would seem to be much less if *tafsīr* were reduced to a sort of confused record of events and speeches that really took place.

Nevertheless, the method of reading the Qur'ān through *tafsīr*, which John Burton has called the "sanctification of tafsir,"[1] dominates the field of Islamic studies (regarding which see Ch. 1 above). Rippin notes how one of the pioneers of a critical approach to the Islamic sources, Joseph Schacht, anticipated this trend towards the end of his life:

> One thing disturbs me, however. That is the danger that the results achieved by the Islamic scholars, at a great effort, in the present generation, instead of being developed and being made the starting point for new scholarly progress might, by a kind of intellectual laziness, be gradually whittled down and deprived of their real significance, or even be turned inside out by those who themselves had taken no part in achieving them.[2]

1 Burton, "Law and exegesis," 271.

2 J. Schacht, "The present state of studies in Islamic Law," *Atti del terzo Congresso di Studi Arabi e Islamici*, Naples: Istituto Universitario Orientale, 1967, 622. Cited by Rippin, "Literary analysis of Qur'ān, *Tafsīr* and *Sīra*," 156; reprint: *The Qur'ān and Its Interpretive Tradition*, ed. Rippin. In this same article Rippin himself observes that "basic literary facts about the material are frequently ignored within the study of Islam in the desire to find positive historical results" (p. 153).

Schacht's point about "intellectual laziness" may seem gratuitous, but it is illustrative of my personal experience. As a Ph.D. student I tended to follow a positivist method. I learned to pursue an account of Islam's historical origins through a critical reading of the Islamic sources, and I learned that the Qur'ān should be read through those sources. This was in part due to the convenience and ease of the method. The manner in which Bell and Watt, for example, link up passages in the Qur'ān to incidents in Muḥammad's prophetic career is easy to follow and offers endless possibilities for the student's own reflection. Wansbrough's literary criticism, on the other hand, is complicated and, to those who hope to find out what really happened, frustrating. If these obstacles are overcome, the student still must wrestle with Wansbrough's difficult prose.

The problem of translating the Qur'ān

Nevertheless, the decision whether to read the Qur'ān through *tafsīr* or in the light of its subtext should not be taken lightly. The effects of this decision are particularly evident in the work of the modern translators to whom I refer in the course of the case studies. On the meaning of *miḥrāb* (Q 3.37; cf. CS 9), for example, the majority of translators look to *tafsīr*. The *mufassirūn*, however, are decidedly confused over the meaning of this term. They offer a number of explanations (and stories to accompany them) ranging from a sort of outdoor shelter to a chamber in Zechariah's house to an upper room in a mosque. The explanations are evidently extrapolations from the Qur'ānic verse itself.

On this basis it would seem prudent for a scholar to bypass these opinions entirely, and instead pursue an independent philological and literary study on the term *miḥrāb* and earlier stories of Mary's infancy. Only Paret's translation, "Tempel," unambiguously reflects such a study. The other translations "sanctuary" (Pickthall, Blachère, Arberry, Fakhry, and Abdel Haleem) and "chamber" (Yusuf Ali) appear to be a sort of distillation of the main *tafsīr* traditions. The effect is profound. Paret's choice connects the Qur'ānic passage to the larger tradition on Mary in Jerusalem to which the Qur'ān itself is alluding. The reader is then brought into the midst of the Qur'ān's profound religious conversation. The choice of the other translations is not only vague, it also prevents the reader from understanding the larger religious tradition in which the Qur'ān is participating. The text is thus isolated and reduced.

A similar phenomenon appears with the phrase *qulūbunā ghulf* (Q 2.88; 4.155; cf. CS 10). Both Arberry and Blachère recognize that this phrase is a particular religious trope – the uncircumcised heart – that transcends the Qur'ān. The other translators in our survey resort to the traditions found in *tafsīr*, according to which *ghulf* is either an adjective meaning "covered" or a noun meaning "containers." The very fact that these two interpretations are incompatible should serve as a warning that the *mufassirūn* have no privileged knowledge on this matter. By following the *mufassirūn*, the translators in turn prevent readers today from recognizing the trope.[3] In this light the value of the work of the earlier philologists (Geiger, Speyer, Jeffery et al.) should not be underestimated. Their work acts as a bridge, allowing readers to appreciate the Qur'ān's intimate relationship with earlier religious traditions. Mohammed Arkoun accordingly writes: "It is important to articulate what is really at stake in this quest in order to put an end to, if possible, the sterile out-of-date polemics against the Orientalist philologists."[4]

Homiletic features of the Qur'ān

On the other hand the philologists tend to limit their interest in the Qur'ān to the question of sources. In particular, they show little concern for the Qur'ān's literary genre. I do not pretend myself to present a detailed literary analysis of the Qur'ān. Still in this final chapter I would like to emphasize certain literary features of the Qur'ān that suggest it has a homiletic relationship to Biblical literature.

Now the philologists generally assume that the Qur'ān was written to rival the Bible. By this view the project of writing the Qur'ān – usually assumed to be undertaken by one man, Muḥammad – involved picking up (Geiger uses the verb *aufnehmen*) bits of religious tradition (or laws etc.) and using them to craft a new book that would replace the old one. Occasionally the insinuation is made (often with reference to Q 16.103)[5] that Muḥammad wanted to pass these traditions off as his own. In this way the philologists' hunt becomes more exciting; they are now uncovering the traces that the (pseudo-)Prophet attempted to erase.

Yet it would hardly be extraordinary if the Qur'ān was instead written in harmony with Biblical literature. The Gospels, for example, ask the reader to know the traditions of the Hebrew Bible. In the same way the present work suggests that the Qur'ān asks the reader to know the traditions of Biblical literature. Indeed, from a literary standpoint the relationship between the Qur'ān and Biblical literature is significantly closer than that between

3 Pickthall's translation of "Our hearts are hardened" is particularly curious. It seems to be his idiomatic interpretation of the views of the *mufassirūn*, in language borrowed from the anti-Jewish verse Q 5.13 ("We made their hearts hard."). A further example of this phenomenon can be found in translations of the term *umma* with which the Qur'ān describes Abraham (Q 16.120). In itself the phrase seems awkward, and indeed the translators attempt to avoid this word. Yusuf Ali translates *umma* instead as "model." Paret adds *für sich* in parentheses. In fact the Qur'ān seems to be alluding to the Biblical trope of Abraham as a nation (*gōy*; Gn 18.18).

4 M. Arkoun, "Introduction: An assessment of and perspectives on the study of the Qur'ān," trans. S. Lucas, in Rippin (ed.), *The Qur'ān: Style and Contents*, (297–331) 301. Translation of the Introduction to M. Arkoun, *Lectures du Coran*, Paris: Maisonneuve et Larose, 1982.

5 "We know how they say that a person is informing him. But the one to whom they refer speaks a foreign language, while this is clear Arabic language." Note the debate between Sprenger (*Leben*, 2:348–90) and Nöldeke ("Hatte Muḥammad christliche Lehrer?," 706–8; *GdQ1*, 17–8) regarding this verse.

the New Testament and the Hebrew Bible. For in a fundamental fashion the Qur'ān excuses itself from the task of narrative and depends instead on the narratives of Biblical literature.[6] Accordingly Reuven Firestone notes that the Qur'ān "contains so many parallels with the Hebrew Bible and New Testament that it could not possibly exist without its scriptural predecessors as subtexts."[7] The Qur'ān's relationship to its subtext, I would add, is like the relationship of homily and scripture.

The clearest indication that the Qur'ān is a sort of homily is its frequent recourse to allusions. Rather than retell a story the Qur'ān often employs a single word, or a simple phrase, that should bring the entire story to the mind of a Biblically-minded audience. The case of Sarah's laughter (Q 11.71; CS 5) is particularly illustrative of this quality. The Qur'ān explains neither the reason for nor the meaning behind her laughter. It only alludes to it with a passing phrase (*fa-ḍaḥikat*). In other words, the Qur'ān is not so much informing the audience that Sarah laughed as it is bringing to mind the audience's knowledge of her laughter. Thence the Qur'ān turns immediately to the religious dimension of this account: "They said, 'Do you wonder at the decree of God? May the mercy and blessings of God be upon you and your house. God is praiseworthy, glorious'" (Q 11.73). In the case of Sarah's laughter the Qur'ān's reliance on the audience's knowledge of the story is particularly salient, since for the sake of the rhyme the Qur'ān reports her laughter before it reports the annunciation of a son. Without knowledge of the Biblical account the audience is left in a state of bewilderment. Indeed the *mufassirūn* are found to be in precisely that state.

The case of Jonah on the barren land (*al-'arā'*; Q 37.145; cf. CS 8) is similar. The Qur'ān refers to God casting Jonah on *al-'arā'* immediately after it mentions his dwelling in the belly of the fish (Q 37.142–4). It does not mention his mission to Nineveh in between. In fact the Qur'ān alludes to this mission (Q 37.147–8; cf. Jonah 3) only after it speaks of the barren land and the vine that God made sprout up there (Q 37.145–6; cf. Jonah 4). If the audience is familiar with the Biblical story, however, the passage presents no problems whatsoever. The Qur'ān refers to those elements of the story that are relevant to its exhortation, in the order that is most convenient to that task. Neither the nature of the events in the Jonah story nor even their very sequence can be extrapolated from the Qur'ān itself. Instead the Qur'ān, much like a homilist, reports certain elements of the narratives, alludes to others, and skips others, since narrative is not the goal but only the means.[8]

6 As Wansbrough puts it, in the Qur'ān Biblical traditions "are not so much reformulated as merely referred to." *QS*, 20.

7 R. Firestone, "The Qur'ān and the Bible: Some modern studies of their relationship," *Bible and Qur'ān* (1–22), 3.

8 Thus Horovitz (*KU*, 8), "Muhammad ist das Erzählen meist nicht Selbstzweck, und so eilt häufig genug die Erzählung über die Einzelheiten des Geschehens den Lehren zu, die einzuprägen sie vor allem bestimmt ist."

Thus it seems that the Qur'ān is a book that expects the reader to be familiar with Jewish and Christian traditions. This is, *mutatis mutandis*, not unlike the expectations of the Christian homilist. In Christian liturgy the homily is given only once the relevant Biblical passages are recited to the congregation. The homilist will then expect the congregation to have a basic knowledge of those passages as he presses forward with a religious exhortation or teaching. The Qur'ān expects no less.

So too the Qur'ān, like a good homilist, has a particular concern for rhetorical effect. When it (Q 21.87; cf. CS 8) describes Jonah calling out to God not from the belly of a fish (cf. Jonah 2.2) but from "the darkness" (*al-ẓulumāt*) the language is less explicit but more evocative. The same effect is achieved through its use of epithets. If at times the Qur'ān refers to Jonah by name (Q 4.163; 6.86; 10.98; 37.139), elsewhere it names him "the Man of the Fish (*dhū l-nūn*)" (Q 21.87) or "the Companion of the Fish" (*ṣāḥib al-ḥūṭ*)" (Q 68.48). Pharaoh is similarly given an epithet, the "Man of Columns (*dhū l-awtād*)" (Q 38.12; 89.10). Other figures, such as Alexander, are never referred to by their proper name, but only by an epithet ("Two-Horned" *dhū l-qarnayn*; Q 18.83, 86, passim). The Qur'ān mentions neither the name of Lot's wife nor her relationship to the prophet, but simply calls her – in an evidently pejorative fashion – an "old woman" (*'ajūz*; Q 26.171), just as it never names Saul but simply calls him a "tall one" (Ṭālūt; Q 2.247, 249; n.b. the assonance with Jālūt; Q 2.250). The use of epithets, of course, implies that the audience is able to connect the symbolic name with the character's proper name. At the same time they are a literary flourish proper to an effective homily.

In a similar manner the Qur'ān often employs pronouns with no clear nominal antecedent. In referring to the ordeal over Mary, for example, the Qur'ān relates, "You were not there when *they* threw *their* rods" (Q 3.44; cf. CS 9), but never identifies the *they* or the *their*. But then every pronoun has an antecedent somewhere. In this case the antecedent is in the *Protoevangelium of James*.

At times the Qur'ān itself explicitly evokes the audience's knowledge of Biblical traditions. In introducing a passage on the transformation of the People of the Sabbath (cf. CS 7) the Qur'ān remarks, "*You know* about those among you who violated the Sabbath, how we said to them: 'Be despised monkeys'" (Q 2.65). Elsewhere the Qur'ān does the same with rhetorical questions. It asks the audience, "Has the story of Moses reached you?" (Q 20.9; 79.15). Regarding the story of Nathan's rebuke of David for his conduct with Uriah (2 Samuel 12), the Qur'ān asks: "Has the story of the dispute reached you?" (Q 38.21). The introduction to the Qur'ān's discourse on the Companions of the Cave (cf. CS 12) is quite similar: "Did you count the Companions of the Cave and *al-raqīm* among Our wondrous signs?" (Q 18.9). The subsequent account is thus introduced as a reflection on the meaning of a story that is already well known.

In a number of other cases the Qur'ān introduces its reflections on Biblical traditions with the imperative *udhkur*.[9] This command is sometimes translated "mention," but the root *dh.k.r.* seems to convey this sense only to the degree that mentioning is associated with recalling, remembering, or reminding.[10] In the Qur'ān this formula seems to carry out the same function as the rhetorical questions above; it brings a story into the audience's mind, and thus seems to mean "remember." With a similar meaning the Qur'ān refers to itself as a *dhikr*: "This is what we recite to you, signs and a wise reminder (*dhikr ḥakīm*)" (Q 3.58). More explicit is the opening of *ṣād*: "The Qur'ān is the reminder" (*wa-l-qur'āni dhī l-dhikr*; Q 38.1). This Sūra tellingly ends with a similar statement: "This is nothing but a reminder (*dhikr*) to the worlds" (Q 38.87; cf. the endings of Sūras 68 and 81).

Now the Qur'ān means above all to remind its audience of divine judgment. But it is for this very purpose that it also reminds its audience of the stories of sacred history, stories which act as proofs that the threat of divine judgment should be taken seriously. In *Hūd* (11; cf. Q 7; 26) the Qur'ān refers to the stories, in quick succession, of Noah (Q 11.25ff.), Hūd (Q 11.50ff.), Ṣāliḥ (Q 11.61ff.), Lot (Q 11.77ff.), Shu'ayb (Q 11.84ff.), and Moses (11.96ff.). These accounts, often referred to in western scholarship as "Straflegenden" or "punishment stories,"[11] are shaped for paraenesis. Alfred Welch comments, "Anyone reading these accounts or hearing them recited is immediately struck by their formulaic features – repeated elements that convey added force to passages that are already powerful in their warnings to those who reject God's messengers."[12] The formulaic nature of these

9 In *Maryam*, for example, a series of accounts begin with this formula, including those of Mary (Q 19.16), Abraham (Q 19.41), Moses (Q 19.51), and Ishmael (Q 19.54). Similar is *ṣād* (38), with accounts of David (Q 38.17), Job (Q 38.41), Abraham, Isaac, and Jacob (Q 38.45), and Ishmael, Elisha, and Dhū l-Kifl (Q 38.48).

10 In fact this root is used primarily with the meaning of "to remember" in both South Semitic (Ethiopic, South Arabian) and Northwest Semitic (Hebrew, Phoenician, Aramaic, Syriac) languages. See *LCD*, 636; Zammit, *Comparative Lexical Study of Qur'ānic Arabic*, 183.

11 On these accounts see Horovitz, *KU*, 10–32, and more recently A. Welch, "Formulaic features of the punishment-stories," in I.J. Boullata (ed.), *Literary Structures of Religious Meaning in the Qur'ān*, Richmond: Curzon, 2000, 77–116. In light of the appearance of seven such accounts in Q 26, Sprenger (*Leben*, 1:462) argues that they should be identified with the seven *mathānī* referred to in Q 15.87. Geiger notes (*Was hat Mohammed*, 57) that the term *mathānī* is related to Aramaic *mathnīthā* and Hebrew *mishnā*, or "report." On this basis Horovitz (*KU*, 26–7), following at once Sprenger and Geiger, proposes that the phrase seven *mathānī* (Q 15.87) be understood as the "seven reports" on divine punishment.

12 Welch, "Formulaic features of the punishment-stories," 77. In each of the punishment stories God sends a warner (*nadhīr*; thus Noah, Q 11.25) to a heedless people. They reject his warning and God destroys them for their contumacy. The Qur'ān even has the Prophet Shu'ayb himself invoke the repetitive cycle of divine warning and destruction, telling his people, "Do not let your split with me make you sin to the point that you are struck by that which struck the people of Noah, the people of Hūd, the people of Ṣāliḥ. The people of Lot are not different from you" (Q 11.89).

accounts, in other words, is a reflection of the Qur'ān's interest in religious exhortation.

Khaleel Mohammed, in his recent study on *ahl al-dhikr*, points out the Bible's frequent use of *zākhor* (cognate to Arabic *dh.k.r.*) in the Deuteronomic history.[13] The Bible recounts, for example, how God told the Israelites in the desert, "Remember (*zākhor*) how Yahweh your God treated Pharaoh and all Egypt" (Deuteronomy 7.18). This is indeed similar to the manner in which the prophets of the Qur'ān's punishment stories remind their people of God's actions. Hūd reminds his people 'Ād of how God favored them when Noah's people were destroyed, "Remember (*udhkurū*) how He put you in the place of Noah's people" (Q 7.69), and (after Hūd's people are destroyed) Ṣāliḥ reminds his people Thamūd of how God favored them after 'Ād, "Remember (*udhkurū*) how He put you in the place of 'Ād" (Q 7.74).

But the Qur'ān does not only recount the words of the prophets. It speaks as a prophet, reminding its own audience of divine punishment.[14] After the punishment stories in *Hūd*, the Qur'ān turns to its audience and proclaims: "Do not be like the wrong-doers, or the Fire will get you. You have no friends but God. You will find no other help" (Q 11.113). In this light it is understandable why the Qur'ān so often connects sacred history with eschatology, or reminding with warning.[15] Thereby the Qur'ān, "the reminder," fulfills the role of the homilist. The homilist brings to mind that which his audience once knew but, due to the human tendency to forget (Q 2.44; 6.68; 7.53; 9.67, passim), no longer heeds. After mentioning God's provision of clothing to Adam and Eve (cf. CS 3), for example, the Qur'ān adds: "That is a sign of God, if only they will remember" (Q 7.26).

In this light the Qur'ān's habit of repeating the same accounts, in a manner that is occasionally inconsistent or even contradictory, is also understandable. The Qur'ān, for example, refers to the account of the Devil's fall in seven different Sūras (Q 2.34; 7.11–12; 15.28–33; 17.61–2; 18.50; 20.115–16; 38.71–8; cf. CS 1), and the annunciation of Isaac's birth in three different Sūras (Q 11.69–72; 15.51–60; 51.24–34; cf. CS 5). In two of these passages (Q 11.71–2; 51.29) the Qur'ān has Abraham's wife call out in amazement at the news, while in a third (Q 15.54) she is nowhere to be found. It is instead Abraham who himself takes over her role.

13 K. Mohammed, "The Identity of the Qur'ān's *ahl al-dhikr*," in K. Mohammed and A. Rippin (eds.), *Coming to Terms with the Qur'ān*, North Haledon, NJ: Islamic Publications International, 2007, (33–45) 36.

14 Thus the Qur'ān names its own Prophet a "warner" (*nadhīr*; Q 2.119; 7.118; 11.2, passim). On this see *KU*, 47.

15 Thus Horovitz comments (*KU*, 4): "Daß so häufig – wir haben schon eine Reihe von Beispielen dafür kennen gelernt – die Erzählungen in Verbindung mit eschatologischen Schilderungen auftreten und nicht selten in sie ausmünden oder auch von ihnen umrahmt werden, hat innere Gründe. Viele dieser Erzählungen dienen Muhammad dazu, seine Landsleute vor dem zu warnen, was ihnen bevorsteht, wenn sie in ihrem Unglauben verharren."

The presence of such variations has long seemed odd to western scholars. They were often imagined to reflect different stages of Muḥammad's personal religious development, and in particular his increasing knowledge of Biblical stories.[16] This approach, of course, presumes the traditional position on the authorship and chronology of the Qur'ān. On Youakim Moubarac's use of this approach in his study on the Qur'ānic material on Abraham,[17] Wansbrough remarks pointedly:

> Demonstration of the "historical development of Abraham in the Qur'ān," for Moubarac the evolution of a composite figure out of an originally dual image, required not only a verifiable chronology of revelation but also the structural unity of the canon. Both were asserted; neither was proved."[18]

In turn Wansbrough suggests that the repetition and variation of Qur'ānic accounts reflects not the story of the author but the story of the book. Like Bell before him,[19] Wansbrough argues that these sort of variations are a typical sign (found likewise in the Bible) of a conservative redaction process. The redactors were unable or unwilling to choose one version of an account, and so chose to incorporate all of them.[20]

Wanbrough's approach to this problem, however, does not match the method of the present work. Here I am concerned with the Qur'ān as scripture, that is, with the canonical text of the Muslim community (even while I do not intend thereby to reject historical-critical approaches that would suggest multiple authors or literary layers and so forth). Yet neither is the method of the present work the sort of apology for the canonical text that is increasingly

16 Andrew Rippin, in his review of Richard Bell's theories (along with Duncan Black McDonald's reply to those theories), reflects, "But it is worth asking why there is this emphasis on the psychology of Muḥammad to begin with." Rippin, "Reading the Qur'ān with Richard Bell," 645.

17 Moubarac, *Abraham dans le Coran*; cf. the similar approach of E. Beck, "Die Gestalt des Abraham am Wendepunkt der Entwicklung Muhammeds," *Le Muséon* 65, 1952, 73–94.

18 *QS*, 21.

19 R. Bell, *The Qur'ān: Translated with a Critical Re-arrangement of the Suras*, Edinburgh: Clark, 1937.

20 Speaking of two variant passages on the heavenly garden Wansbrough comments, "More likely, however, is juxtaposition in the canon of two closely related variant traditions, contaminated by recitation in identical contexts, or produced from a single tradition by oral transmission." *QS*, 27.

To this effect Wansbrough examines three different versions of the Shuʿayb account (Q 7.85–93; 11.84–95; 26.176–90). After analyzing the features and peculiarities of each version he concludes: "The Shuʿayb traditions exhibit little by way of historical development but ample evidence of literary elaboration, drawn from recognizable and well-established types of prophetical report. Such elaboration is characteristic of Muslim scripture, in which a comparatively small number of themes is preserved in varying stages of literary achievement." *QS*, 35.

seen in recent publications, according to which any literary peculiarity – such as the repetition of accounts – necessarily redounds to the Qur'ān's literary brilliance.[21]

Instead, it seems to me that the Qur'ān's repetition of accounts must be approached as a feature of its homiletic interests. Because the Qur'ān has so little interest in narrative per se, there is nothing defective or inconvenient with returning to the same account on multiple occasions. Indeed the task of paraenesis is directed at the audience's conscience as much as it is at the audience's intellect. The Qur'ān accordingly has no intention of proceeding through an organized or logical re-telling of well-structured narratives. Instead it brings those narratives to the audience's mind (or better, conscience) whenever such a move corresponds to the task of reminding and warning. This is precisely what one might expect from a homily. It is not, incidentally, what one might expect of a folk tale, a literary genre which a number of recent scholars have used to analyze the Qur'ān.[22]

Now I am no expert in literary criticism and I do not mean to place the Qur'ān into a strict literary genre. The Qur'ān is, after all, a diverse book. Alfred Welch, for example, lists six different literary forms in the Qur'ān, while acknowledging still others.[23] Muḥammad Arkoun lists five different types of text in the Qur'ān.[24] My point is not to refute Welch or Arkoun by classifying all of the Qur'ān as homiletic, for my concern is not at all the classification of the text per se. Instead my concern is the relationship of the text with its subtext of Biblical literature. For my argument is that the Qur'ān

21 M. Mir, for example, writes: "The Qur'ān does not share the view that repetition is necessarily a demerit. There is considerable repetition in the Qur'ān – both of theme and expression – as one would expect from a book that calls itself *dhikr* ("remembrance, reminder") and is preoccupied with the task of explicating its message to doubters and objectors no less than to believers and submitters. From a Qur'ānic standpoint, the only relevant question is whether repetition serves a purpose, and there is sufficient reason to believe that repetition in the Qur'ān is purposeful." M. Mir, "Language," *The Blackwell Companion to the Qur'ān*, (88–106) 100–1. Cf. the ideas of M. Abdel Haleem on *iltifāt* in *Understanding the Qur'an*, ch. 13; M. Sells on *al-qadr*: "Sound, spirit, and gender in *al-qadr*," *JAOS* 111, 1991, 239–59 (reprint: *The Qur'ān: Style and Contents*, ed. Rippin, 333–53); H. Abdul-Raof, *Qur'ānic Translation: Discourse, Texture, and Exegesis*, Richmond: Curzon, 2001; A. Achrati, "Arabic, Qur'ānic speech, and postmodern language: What the Qur'ān simply says," *Arabica*, 2008, 161–203.

22 See H. Schwarzbaum, *Biblical and Extra-Biblical Legends in Islamic Folk Literature*, Walldorf-Hessen: Verlag füf Orientkunde, 1982; J. Stetkevych, *Muḥammad and the Golden Bough: Reconstructing Arabian Myth*, Bloomington and Indianapolis: Indiana University Press, 1996 (which addresses the Qur'ān only in passing); and most recently A. Dundes, *Fables of the Ancients? Folklore in the Qur'ān*, Lanham, MD: Rowman & Littlefield, 2003. Regarding the last work see the critical review of A. Rippin in *BSOAS* 68, 2005, 120–2.

23 Oaths, sign-passages, say-passages, narratives, regulations, and liturgical forms. A. Welch, "Ḳur'ān," *EI*[2], 5:421–6.

24 Prophetic, legislative, narrative, sapiential, and hymnal (poetic). See M. Arkoun, *Rethinking Islam*, trans. R. Lee, Boulder, CO: Westview, 1994, 38.

does not seek to correct, let alone replace, Biblical literature, but instead to use that literature for its homiletic exhortation.[25]

Like its repetition of accounts, the Qur'ān's peculiar character descriptions should be seen as a feature of homily. The Qur'ān places Haman in Egypt with Pharaoh when he should be in Persia with Xerxes (Cf. CS 6). The Qur'ān conflates Mary the mother of Jesus with Mary the sister of Moses and Aaron (cf. CS 9). Yet for the Qur'ān there is no question of historical accuracy in such matters.[26] These characters and these places are all topoi at the service of homily. Pharaoh in the Qur'ān is closely associated with self-deification and opposition to God's people, and Haman is the anti-Israelite villain par excellence. Mary in the Qur'ān is closely associated with the Temple, and Aaron (the brother of Miriam) is the Israelite priest par excellence.

Thus to suggest that the Qur'ān has missed the identity of these characters is the sort of judgment which, although strictly correct, hardly leads to a better understanding of the book. Indeed it is to suggest that these characters and places are part of a well-recorded history, the precepts of which should not be violated. If they are seen instead as topoi, then they have one function in their Biblical context and another function in their Qur'ānic context. Neither is right and neither is wrong. For the Qur'ān all that matters is the impact on the reader, the degree to which its discourse on these characters and places might lead the reader to repentance and obedience.

This same goal is evident in the Qur'ān's literary style. The Qur'ān itself, of course, insists that it is not poetry (Q 21.5; 36.69; 69.41), and this point accordingly became a point of traditional Islamic doctrine. Strangely, this doctrine is also followed among modern scholars, who often imagine that Muḥammad was in a sort of competition with the pre-Islamic poets. Thus Navid Kermani writes:

> The danger of being wrongly identified as poetry forced the Qur'ān to distance itself from it. The poets were, after all, direct rivals, since they both used the same formal language, the *ʿarabiyya*, both invoked heavenly powers and, like the prophet, both claimed to be the supreme authorities of their communities. "And the poets – the perverse follow

25 Cf. the comments of N.H. Abu Zayd: "Now, the point I would like to indicate is that the Qur'ān never repudiated the Jewish and Christian Scriptures; they are both revealed through the same channel as the Qur'ān: *waḥy*. What is always disputed is the way the people of the book understood and explained these scriptures." "Rethinking the Qur'ān," *Rethinking the Qur'ān: Towards a Humanistic Hermeneutics*. Amsterdam: Humanistics University Press, 2004, 43.

26 Compare the reflection of Horovitz (*KU*, 9): "So wird auch das Individuelle der Erzählungen oft verwischt, und die Helden werden einander angeähnelt. Freilich ist es nicht überall so, es fehlt keineswegs an Beispielen, wo Muhammad im wesentlichen der Überlieferung folgt und allenfalls kleinere Anpassungen an seine persönlichen Bedürfnisse vornimmt."

> them" (Q 26.24). The polemic against poets can only be understood in this context, and a good example can be found in *sūra* 26. The argument had nothing to do with literary rivalry. It was a contest for leadership, but not just the leadership of a single tribe, as enjoyed by the poets.[27]

Kermani's historical imagination is as vivid as it is creative. The Qur'ān itself has none of this riveting stand-off for leadership. Instead the Qur'ān seems to distance itself from poetry due to the belief that poets are inspired by demons or jinn (Q 26.221–6; 37.36). What is at stake in this question for the Qur'ān is its claim of divine (and not demonic) revelation. It is no more concerned with a fight against the poets then it is with its categorization into the literary genre of poetry.

So it is odd that most present-day scholars are so quick to insist that the Qur'ān is not poetry (an insistence that usually lacks a clear definition of what exactly poetry consists of), although Thomas Hoffman is a notable exception to this trend.[28] Otherwise critical scholars generally maintain that the language of the Qur'ān is the language of pre-Islamic poetry, that is, the famous poetic *koinē*,[29] but that the style of the Qur'ān is not poetry but rhymed prose, or *saj'*, the "medium of the ancient Arabian soothsayers."[30] Needless to say, perhaps, these soothsayers are found nowhere earlier than the Islamic works of the 'Abbāsid period.

Now I do not mean myself to make a detailed judgment of what, per se, poetry consists of and whether or not the Qur'ān fits properly into this category. These are matters involving theories of meter, style, and so on that are well beyond my critical abilities, and which Thomas Hoffman addresses

27 Kermani, "Poetry and language," 109.

28 See his work, *The Poetic Qur'ān: Studies on Qur'ānic Poeticity*, Wiesbaden: Harrassowitz, 2007; cf. also the recent Qur'ān translation of F. Nikayinu: *The Qur'ān: A Poetic Translation*, Ultimate Book, 2000.

29 On this point see especially Blachère, *Introduction*, 156–69. The background to his argument is Karl Vollers' critique of the traditional Islamic contention that the Qur'ān was revealed in pure classical Arabic. In his *Volksprache und Schriftsprache im alten Arabien* (Strassburg: Trübner, 1906) Vollers contends that the Qur'ān was first revealed in a colloquial dialect and later amended (mainly through the addition of case endings) to correspond to classical Arabic. Both Nöldeke (*Neue Beiträge*, 1–5) and Blachère argue instead that the Qur'ān was from the first revealed in the classical Arabic language of the poets.

30 Neuwirth, "Structural, linguistic and literary features," 98; Cf. Blachère, *Introduction*, 177–8; I. Goldziher, *Abhandlungen zur arabischen Philologie*, Leiden: Brill, 1896, 2:59; Welch, "Ḳur'ān," 5:420–1, J. Retsö, *The Arabs in Antiquity: Their History from the Assyrians to the Umayyads*, London: Routledge, 2003, 45–7. Regarding *saj'* see especially the detailed article by D. Stewart: "Saj' in the Qur'ān: Prosody and structure," *Journal of Arabic Literature* 21, 1990, 101–39; reprint: *The Qur'ān: Style and Contents*, ed. Rippin, 213–52. Stewart notes (pp. 102ff.) that most Muslim scholars deny the presence of *saj'* in the Qur'ān since, in light of the doctrine of the Qur'ān's inimitability, they refuse to accept the association of the Qur'ān with any mundane literature.

in an immensely more detailed manner.[31] Anyway it is hard for me to imagine any definition of poetry that would avoid entirely subjectivity or arbitrariness. Can poetry be defined in some essential way that is absolutely valid across cultures, languages, and epochs? Even if it can, here I mean only to make a rather simple point, namely that as a homiletic work the Qur'ān is profoundly interested in the effectiveness of its rhetoric.

Now one of the features the Qur'ān uses towards this end is a feature frequently, although of course not necessarily, found in poetry: rhyme.[32] Even on this point, incidentally, Muslim scholars insisted on distancing the Qur'ān from poetry. They reserve the word *qāfiya* for poetic rhyme and apply the word *fāṣila* ("division") to the Qur'ān's rhyme. Nevertheless, in places the Qur'ān's devotion to rhyme is so strong that it seems to reveal an underlying strophic structure, a structure that was later diffused by editing and emendation. This point has been argued forcefully by Rudolph Geyer,[33] and taken to rather improbable conclusions by Gunter Lüling.[34]

In any case the Qur'ān's concern with rhyme is significant.[35] It is evident in personal names, which tend to appear in rhyming pairs: Iblīs/Idrīs, Ismāʿīl/Isrā'īl, Mūsā/ʿĪsā, Hārūn/Qārūn, Hārūt/Mārūt, Yājūj/Mājūj, Ṭālūt/Jālūt (cf. Hūd/Lūṭ/Nūḥ). In fact, the Qur'ān's insistence on rhyme might explain the peculiar forms of certain personal names which deviate from the standard Semitic versions thereof.[36] In the course of our case studies, moreover, we have seen

31 Whereas below I will focus only on rhyme, Hoffman considers, among other things, various forms of recurrence, techniques of defamiliarization, semantic ambiguities, iconicity, entextualization, deictic volatility, self-referentiality, and cantillation.

32 Stewart ("Sajʿ in the Qur'ān," p. 108; cf. Appendix, pp. 135–7) calculates that 85.9 percent of Qur'ānic verses rhyme. M. Mir, commenting on the term *sajʿ*, notes: "The usual translation of this word, 'rhymed prose,' while not entirely incorrect, places Qur'ānic language in the category of prose, denoting, additionally, that that language happens to be rhymed. This description runs the risk of compromising the rhythmic quality of Qur'ānic language. The language of the Qur'ān partakes of both poetry and prose and is certainly more poetic in some parts and more prose-like in others, but it is difficult to generalize and say that it is primarily prose or poetry." Mir, "Language," 93.

33 R. Geyer, "Zur Strophik des Qurans," *Wiener Zeitschrift für die Kunde des Morgenlandes* 22, 1908, 265–86; trans.: R. Geyer, "The strophic structure of the Koran," trans. G.A. Wells in Ibn Warraq (ed.), *What the Koran Really Says*, 625–46.

34 Namely that behind the Qur'ān is an Ur-text, which was the hymnal of a Christian community in Mecca. See Lüling, *Über den Ur-Qur'ān*; trans.: *A Challenge to Islam for Reformation.*

35 Horovitz sees the Qur'ānic rhyme as an obstacle to Muḥammad's clear presentation of narratives: "Bedeutend erschwert hat er sich die Aufgabe durch Beibehaltung des Reimes. In der älteren Zeit und solange er in kurzen Sätzen redet, ist Muhammad der Zwang freilich kaum lästig. Aber wo die Sätze länger werden und die Erzählung mehr ins Breite geht, erweist der Reim sich als Hindernis." *KU*, 9.

36 In most Semitic languages the penultimate letter of Abraham's name is *ā*. By having an *ī* the name becomes parallel to Ismāʿīl. Meanwhile, in all Semitic languages – and indeed in Christian Arabic – the name Jesus has the ʿ. at its end not at its beginning. By shifting its place the Qur'ān makes it parallel to Mūsā. On this see *FV*, 44–6 and 218–20, respectively. Cf. D. Margoliouth, "Textual variations of the Koran," *MW* 15, 1925, 334–4; reprint: *The Origins of the Koran*, ed. Ibn Warraq, Amherst, NY: Prometheus, 1998, (154–62) 160.

the question of rhyme play a decisive role in the Qur'ān's articulation of religious accounts. For this reason the Qur'ān adds Jacob to its account of the annunciation of Isaac in *Hūd* (Q 11.69–72; cf. CS 5). Jacob does not appear in the two other Qur'ānic passages on this account, or, of course, in the Biblical version thereof. But in this section of *Hūd* the rhyme calls for a penultimate *ī* or *ū*, and *ya'qūb* accordingly appears.

Nöldeke himself noticed the prominent role that rhyme played in the shaping of the Qur'ānic text, providing as an example the Qur'ān's eschatological language:

> Die Einwirkung des Reimes auf die Redeweise des Qorans ist übrigens nicht ohne Bedeutung. Um des Reimes willen wird bisweilen die gewöhnliche Gestalt der Wörter und selbst der Sinn verändert. Wenn z. B. in der 55 Sura von zwei himmlischen Gärten (v. 46) die Rede ist, mit je zwei Quellen (v. 50) und zwei Arten von Früchten (52) und noch von zwei anderen ähnlichen Gärten (v. 62), so sieht man deutlich, daß hier die Duale dem Reime zu Liebe gebraucht sind; ebenso würde Sur. 69, 17 schwerlich die seltsame Zahl von acht Gottes Thron tragenden Engeln gewählt sein, wenn nicht zum Reime paßte. Von nicht geringer Wichtigkeit die Wirkung, welche der Reim auf die Komposition des Qorans ausgeübt hat.[37]

Here, however, my interest in the Qur'ān's use of rhyme is what it shows of the Qur'ān's interest in the attractiveness of its style, since this is the sort of thing that would concern a homilist.[38] In fact the Arabic rhyme helps provide the Qur'ān with a quality that provides awe in the believers and contributes to the sense that any translation of the Qur'ān is necessarily a compromise. The very sonority of the text recited cooperates with the vivid images conveyed by the text to produce an effective homily.

Michael Sells writes in detail about the importance of sonority to the Qur'ān, going far beyond the question of rhyme to other aspects of the text, namely its overall arrangement (*naẓm*) and its balance, or, as he puts it "textual harmonics" (*tawāzun*).[39] Sells writes in a fashion that is as obscure

37 *GdQ1*, 40.

38 Cf. the argument of Jan Retsö who, in his lengthy historical study of Arabs and Arabic, contends that by describing itself with the adjective *'arabī* the Qur'ān intends thereby rhymed speech. In his discussion of the Qur'ān's references to Arabs and Arabic, Retsö argues that the Qur'ān's distinction between the adjectives *'arabī* and *'ajamī* is not a distinction between Arabic and foreign languages (as is maintained by the *mufassirūn* and modern scholars who follow them). Instead *'arabī* is a formal qualification. It refers to rhymed prose, while *'ajamī* is a pejorative reference to vulgar or vernacular Arabic. See Retsö, *The Arabs in Antiquity*, 40–53; cf. the comments of Madigan, *Self Image*, 135, and the pointed response to Retsö of S. Wild, "An Arabic recitation: The meta-linguistics of Qur'ānic revelation," in Wild (ed.), *Self Referentiality in the Qur'ān*, (135–57) 152–6.

39 See Sells, "Sound, spirit, and gender in *al-qadr*," 240.

as it is creative. Angelika Neuwirth emphasizes in much clearer language the Qur'ān's sonority as a fundamental aspect of its moral discourse.[40]

Neuwirth also places the particular literary style of the Qur'ān into a religious context, arguing that the text is shaped by liturgical concerns.[41] This approach, which is central to the work of Erwin Gräf before her,[42] leads Neuwirth to argue that the Sūras should be seen as cohesive literary units, shaped for the sake of liturgical recitation. In this regard Neuwirth cites the traditional doctrine that the Sūra "was intended by the Prophet as the formal medium for his proclamation."[43] She also contends (more convincingly) that the canonical form of the text itself reveals something of the text's origins, inasmuch as the Sūra is the unit that the believing community itself canonized.[44]

At the same time, Neuwirth pointedly denies that the Qur'ān can be considered homiletic:

> Above all, it is not to be understood by the term "sermon" in the precise sense of rhetoric that expresses a truth that has already been announced and attempts to urge that truth upon the listener. The Qur'ān may contain some elements of homily along with its many other elements, but it yields just as few examples of these as it yields of the catch-all categories of hymns, narratives or legislation.[45]

40 Neuwirth writes: "In the Qur'ān what is repeated is not only the identical musical sound, but a linguistic pattern as well – a widely stereotypical phrasing. The musical sound pattern enhances the message encoded in the Qur'ānic cadenza phrase that, in turn, may introduce a meta-discourse. Many cadenza-phrases are semantically distinguished from their context and add a moral comment to it, such as 'verily, you were sinning (*innaki kunti min al-khāṭi'īn*, Q 12.29). They thus transcend the main – narrative or argumentative – flow of the Sūra, introducing a spiritual dimension, i.e. divine approval or disapproval." Neuwirth, "Structural, linguistic and literary features," 103.

41 See A. Neuwirth, "Einige Bemerkungen zum besonderen sprachlichen und literarischen Charakter des Koran," *Deutscher Orientalistentag 1975*, Wiesbaden: Steiner, 1977, 736–9; trans.: "Some remarks on the special linguistic and literary character of the Qur'ān," trans. G. Goldbloom, in Rippin (ed.), *The Qur'ān: Style and Contents*, 253–7.

42 Notice in particular Gräf's analysis of Q 74.1–7 ("Zu den christlichen Einflüssen im Koran," 123–33), a passage traditionally seen as God's exhortation to Muḥammad, soon after the first revelation, to begin his prophetic proclamations. Yet Gräf notes that "Die Angaben der Exegeten ergeben einen leidlichen Zusammenhang, obwohl sie verraten, daß diese Gelehrten keine exakte Kenntnis der ursprünglichen Bedeutung dieser Verse und ihres 'Sitzes im Leben' haben" (p. 129). Gräf argues instead that this is an address, from the Prophet to the faithful, which reflects Christian liturgical tropes. Thus, for example, a reflection of Christian baptism is visible in Q 74.4–5: "Purify your attire * and flee from impurity." Attire (Ar. *thiyāb*), by Gräf's reading, is a reference to the baptismal garment.

43 Neuwirth, "Some remarks," 254.

44 Pace El-Awa, who argues on linguistic grounds that the Sūras in fact "have a distinctly loose structure" ("Linguistic structure," 70).

45 Neuwirth, "Some remarks," 253. On this point Neuwirth refers to L. Baeck, "Griechische und jüdische Predigt," *Aus drei Jahrtausenden, wissenschaftliche Untersuchungen und Abhandlungen zur Geschichte des jüdischen Glaubens*, Tübingen: Mohr, 1958, 142.

In the place of sermon Neuwirth suggests that the Qur'ān should be understood in the literary genre of the Psalms. "The Sūra," she comments, "is a 'mixed composition,' that is to say, a complex later stage, coming after a longer process of religious and historical development."[46] This, Neuwirth continues, is similar to the manner in which "complex compositions in the Psalms, referred to in Old Testament studies as 'Mischgedichte', join together several of these originally separate genres into a larger unity."[47] In both cases, she suggests, the purpose of joining together diverse material is liturgy. The Sūra, like the Psalm, is a necessarily hybrid literary unit; it is intended to combine various aspects of religious proclamation for the purpose of liturgical recitation. More recently Neuwirth takes this argument still further, arguing that certain Sūras from the middle to late Meccan period, from the time which (according to the traditional doctrine) the community changed the direction of prayer to Jerusalem, actually reflect the first Muslim community's liturgy.[48]

Neuwirth's liturgical vision for the Qur'ān is not unreasonable, although her attempts to connect this to the development of a historical community, and especially her reliance on the traditional notion of Meccan and Medinan Sūras, is necessarily speculative. The parallel with the Psalms, however, is not entirely convincing. With few exceptions (e.g. Psalms 78, 105, 106) the Psalms do not depend on the audience's knowledge of an earlier narrative to communicate their message. The Qur'ān, on the other hand, depends regularly on such knowledge.

Neuwirth emphatically rejects the notion of Qur'ān as homily, noting that a sermon, "expresses a truth that has already been announced and attempts to urge that truth upon the listener." And yet this, it seems to me, is a lovely description of Qur'ānic discourse. The Qur'ān continually insists that it brings no new truth, but rather the same truth that has been proclaimed by all of the earlier prophets. Speaking to its own Prophet the Qur'ān declares, "We brought down the Book in truth to you, confirming that which was before it from the Book" (Q 5.48a). Elsewhere the Qur'ān insists that this revelation is like the revelation to Moses and Jesus: "He brought down the Book to you, confirming that which was before it, as he brought down the Torah and the Gospel" (Q 3.3). It is in this light that the Qur'ān addresses the believers: "O you who believe, believe in God and His Messenger, in the Book that he brought down to His messenger, and in the Book that He

46 Neuwirth, "Some remarks," 256; cf., more recently, A. Neuwirth, "Psalmen – im Koran neu gelesen (Ps 104 un 136)," in Hartwig et al. (eds), *Im vollen Licht der Geschichte*, 157–91.

47 Neuwirth, "Some remarks," 256.

48 "It comes as no surprise that the bulk of the middle and late Meccan Sūras seem to mirror a monotheistic service, starting with an initial dialogical section (apologetic, polemic, paranetic) and closing with a related section, most frequently an affirmation of the revelation. These framing sections have been compared to the Christian Orthodox *ecteniae*, i.e., initial and concluding *responsoria* recited by the priest or deacon with the community." Neuwirth, "Structural, linguistic and literary features," 110.

brought down earlier" (Q 4.135). In this light, as well, it makes sense when the Qur'ān proclaims to the Prophet (unless it is the Prophet proclaiming to his audience): "If you are in doubt of something that was brought down to you, then ask those who have been reading the Book before you" (Q 10.94; cf. 16.43). Many more such examples could be cited (cf., e.g., Q 2.177; 21.24–5 40.70–2, and so on) but the point should be clear. The truth proclaimed in the Qur'ān has indeed been previously announced. The job of the Qur'ān's Prophet is accordingly to urge that "old" truth upon the listener:

> Say: "We believe in God and what was brought down to us, and to Abraham, Ishmael, Isaac, Jacob, the Tribes, what was brought to Moses and Jesus, and what was brought to the Messengers by their Lord. We make no difference between them. And we are submissive to Him."
>
> (Q 2.136)

The Qur'ān and Christian homily

This point, however, in no way compromises the Qur'ān's originality. On the contrary, homily is not imitation. Even more, the idea of Qur'ān as homily precludes the possibility of judging the Qur'ān by Biblical standards. It is completely antithetical, for example, to the judgment of Henninger, who writes:

> Was wir an Christlichem (und Jüdischem) im Koran findet, stammt meistens aus solchen verworrenen oder schlecht aufgefaßten Erzählungen, zum großen Teil nicht aus echten biblischen Zeugnissen, sondern aus Apokryphen und anderen Legenden, aus der nachbiblischen rabbinischen Literatur und aus häretischen Spekulationen.[49]

Henninger seems to have viewed the Biblical material in the Qur'ān as a sort of periphrasis, an imperfect reproduction of the original narrative. This approach, ironically, is analogous to the traditional Islamic view of the Bible, namely that it is a falsified (*muḥarraf*) form of the original revelations to Moses, David, and Jesus. Yet this approach misses entirely the possibility that the Bible and the Qur'ān belong to two quite different literary genres. In the case studies of the present work the Qur'ān repeatedly appears to be not so much misunderstanding Biblical narratives as using Biblical material for its own homiletic purposes. As Jaroslav Stetkevych puts it, "In the Qur'ān, narrative, and indeed everything else, is subordinated to the overarching rhetoric of salvation and damnation."[50]

49 Henninger, *Spuren christlicher Glaubenswahrheiten im Koran*, 2.

50 J. Stetkevych, *Muḥammad and the Golden Bough: Reconstructing Arabian Myth*, Bloomington: Indiana University Press, 1996, 10–1.

If the Qur'ān is to be compared with earlier literature it should not be compared with the Bible itself, but rather with other homiletic works on Biblical literature. The Qur'ān itself suggests that it is particularly connected to the Christian homiletic tradition. Of course, the Qur'ān includes accounts, such as that on the People of the Sabbath (cf. CS 7), that are exclusive to Jewish tradition.[51] In other words, the Qur'ān is not a text which, for any dogmatic reason, is exclusively concerned with Christian traditions.

Nevertheless, the Qur'ān generally reflects Christian traditions.[52] Not only are many of the accounts to which the Qur'ān refers exclusively Christian,[53] but when an account is common to both Jewish and Christian tradition, such as the angelic prostration to Adam (cf. CS 1), the Qur'ān is generally concerned with the Christian rendition thereof. In the Jewish rendition of the angelic prostration the angels never in fact worship Adam, while in the Christian and the Qur'ānic rendition they most certainly do, with divine approbation.[54] Similarly, in Jewish tradition on the Garden of Eden, with few exceptions, the serpent is only a serpent. In Christian tradition the serpent is a symbol, or bearer, of Satan. In the Qur'ān the serpent has fully given way to Satan (cf. CS 2).[55]

Moreover, the very vocabulary of the Qur'ān suggests that it is closely involved with Christian tradition. As Horovitz and Rudolph point out, the great majority of Biblical names in the Qur'ān, such as Sulaymān, Ilyās, and Yūnus, clearly reflect a Christian (i.e. Syriac or Christian Palestinian Aramaic) and not a Jewish (Hebrew or Aramaic) provenance.[56] To these examples others that have arisen in the course of our case studies might be added,

51 The same might be said for accounts not found in our case studies, such as the account of Moses and the servant of God (Q 18.65–82), which is closely related to the Jewish legend of Rabbi Joshua b. Levi. On this see A.J. Wensinck, "Al-Khaḍir," *EI*², 4:902–5. Cf. the alternative argument of B. Wheeler, "The Jewish origins of Qur'ān 18:65–82? Reexamining Arent Jan Wensinck's theory," *JAOS* 118, 1998, 153–71.

52 As Grünbaum points out, those who would connect the Qur'ān primarily to Jewish narratives fail to recognize that many of those very narratives were later developed by Syriac Christian authors, and this developed form is more closely reflected in the Qur'ān. Thus he comments (*Neue Beiträge*, 54), "Die syrischen Legenden, die sich alle auf die Bibel beziehen, haben mehr aus dem Judenthum aufgenommen als die arabischen, deren manche übrigens syrischen Ursprungs sind."

53 Thus, for example, the Youths/Seven Sleepers of Ephesus ("Companions of the Cave"; see CS 12) and the Legend/Romance of Alexander (*dhū l-qarnayn*; cf. Q 18.83–98). On this see K. Czeglédy, "Monographs on Syriac and Muhammadan sources in the literary remains of M. Kmoskó," *Acta Orientalia Academiae Scientiarum Hungaricae* 4, 1954, (19–91) 31–9; van Bladel, "Legend of Alexander the Great in the Qur'ān."

54 See Geiger, *Was hat Mohammed*, 98; Grünbaum, *Neue Beiträge*, 60–1; *BEQ*, 55; *OIC*, 201–3.

55 See Geiger, *Was hat Mohammed*, 99; Grünbaum, *Neue Beiträge*, 61; Sidersky, *Les origines des légendes musulmanes*, 14; *BEQ*, 58–69.

56 *KU*, 80–1; Rudolph, *Abhängigkeit*, 47. Jeffery connects Sulaymān to Syriac *shlaymūn* ("conclusive proof of Christian origin"; *FV*, 178), Ilyās to Syriac *ēlyās* ("The name was no uncommon one among Oriental Christians before Islam"; *FV*, 67–8), and Yūnus to Christian Palestinian Aramaic *yūnus* ("The form of the word is conclusive evidence that it came to Muḥammad from Christian sources"; *FV*, 295–6).

including Iblīs (cf. CS 1),[57] *ḥanīf* (cf. CS 4),[58] Isḥāq (cf. CS 5),[59] Fir'awn (cf. CS 6),[60] Maryam (cf. CS 9),[61] Zechariah (cf. CS 9),[62] and *shuhadā'* (cf. CS 11).[63] These are all words that are common to Jewish and Christian Semitic languages, but in each case their Qur'ānic form reflects the Christian version thereof.

It is also worth noting the manner in which the Qur'ān echoes controversial themes central to Christian anti-Jewish rhetoric. In *al-nisā'* (4) 153–7, the Qur'ān recites a litany of accusations against the Jews much like that which Stephen proclaims in front of the Sanhedrin (Acts 6–7). Most telling is the idiomatic slander that the Jews are uncircumcised of heart (Acts 7.51; Q 2.88; 4.155; cf. CS 10). In this same passage the Qur'ān also refers to the Jews' statement against Mary, which it calls a "great slander" (*buhtānan 'aẓīm*; Q 4.156). In this the Qur'ān is following a traditional point of Christian apologetic, the defense of Mary against Jewish attacks on her purity. Finally, if Islamic scholars traditionally make the accusation of falsifying revelation (*taḥrīf*) against both Jews and Christians, the Qur'ān itself primarily makes this accusation against the Jews (Q 2.75; 4.46; 5.13, 41). In this the Qur'ān is likewise following a frequent theme of Christian anti-Jewish polemic.[64]

These points have led periodically to the argument that the Qur'ān is an essentially Christian book that was misunderstood by early Muslims. The Mu'tazilī Qāḍī 'Abd al-Jabbār (d. 415/1025), for example, writes in his *Tathbīt dalā'il al-nubuwwa* that Christians in his day claim, "Muḥammad conveyed Christianity and our teachings, but his companions did not understand him."[65] Indeed this approach is evident in the apology attributed to John of Damascus (d. 749)[66] and the *Risāla ilā aḥad al-muslimīn* of Paul of

57 From Greek διάβολος through Syriac *d.b.l.s.* (as *dīblūs* or *diyābūlūs*). See *FV*, 48–9; Reynolds, "A reflection on two Qur'ānic words."

58 From Syriac *ḥanpā* (*FV*, 112–5).

59 From Syriac *isḥāq* ("The Arabic form which lacks the initial [*yod*] of the *O.T.* forms . . . would seem to point to a Christian origin"; *FV*, 60).

60 From Syriac *fir'ūn* ("The probabilities are that it was borrowed from Syriac"; *FV*, 225).

61 From Syriac *maryam* ("The vowelling of the Arabic . . . would point to its having come from a Christian source rather than directly from the Hebrew"; *FV*, 262).

62 From Syriac *zakriyā* ("The name . . . must have been well known to Arabian Christians in pre-Islamic times"; *FV*, 151).

63 Connected to Syriac *sahdā* ("The word itself is genuine Arabic, but its sense was influenced by the usage of the Christian communities of the time"; *FV*, 187).

64 A point made forcefully by Andrae, *OIC*, 203; cf. (following Andrae) Bowman, "Debt of Islam," 200.

65 See 'Abd al-Jabbār, *The Critique of Christian Origins*, ed. and trans. G.S. Reynolds and S.K. Samir, Provo, Utah: Brigham Young Press, 2009, 38 (part 2, verse 88).

66 See chapter 100/1 (the authenticity of which is disputed) of his *De haeresibus*, in which he writes: "How, when you say that the Christ is the Word and Spirit of God, do you revile us as associators? For the Word and the Spirit are inseparable . . . So we call you mutilators [κόπτας] of God." Translation from R. Hoyland, *Seeing Islam as Others Saw It*, Princeton: Darwin Press, 1997, 486. Cf. the more complete translation in D.J. Sahas, *John of Damascus on Islam*, Leiden: Brill, 1972, 133–41.

Antioch (d. 1180).[67] This argument has also appeared, in different forms, in the recent works of Giuglio Bassetti-Sani, Georges Tartar, and Christoph Luxenberg.[68]

Bassetti-Sani contends that when the Qur'ān refers to *ahl al-kitāb* ("People of the Book") in a pejorative sense (e.g. Q 4.171; 29.46), it intends only the Jews (in fact he sees *ahl al-kitāb* as a calque on Hebrew *soferīm*, the Jewish scribes).[69] For Christians, he continues, the Qur'ān uses the phrase *ahl al-injīl* ("People of the Gospel"), a phrase that appears only once and then in a positive sense (Q 5.47). Even if this rather speculative point is granted, however, it must still be conceded that the Qur'ān intends Christians of some sort with the term *naṣārā*. While this term is connected in its etymology with Greek Ναζωραῖοι, it does not seem to designate the Judaeo-Christian sect of this name referred to by Epiphanius (d. 403), Theodoret of Cyrrhus (d. ca. 466), and John of Damascus. For the Qur'ān uses this term together with *yahūd* ("Jews") to refer to two major religious communities, as in *al-tawba* (9) 30: "The *yahūd* say, 'Uzayr is the son of God.' The *naṣārā* say, 'Christ is the son of God.' This is the statement of their mouths, by which they imitate the statement of earlier unbelievers. May God fight them and their perversity."

In its religious message the Qur'ān separates itself from both the Jewish and the Christian communities. It does not, however, separate itself from

67 Paul of Antioch, "*Risāla ilā aḥad al-muslimīn*," in L. Cheikho (ed.), *Vingt traités théologiques d'auteurs arabes chrétiens (IXe–XIIIe siècles)*, Beirut: Imprimerie Catholique, 1920, 15–26; trans.: "Lettre aux musulmans," trans. P. Khoury, *Paul d'Antioche*, Beirut: Imprimerie Catholique, 1964, 169–87.

68 Basetti-Sani, *Koran in the Light of Christ*; G. Tartar, *Connaitre Jésus-Christ: Lire le Coran à la lumière de l'Évangile*, Combs-la-Ville: Centre évangélique de témoignage et de dialogue, 1985; Luxenberg, *Die syro-aramäische Lesart des Koran*. Basetti-Sani argues that the Qur'ān presents the Christian kerygma in a manner that was understandable to the pagan Arabs and Jews of Muḥammad's context. The Qur'ān, he explains accordingly, focuses on the humanity of Jesus as a sort of *praeparatio evangelium*. By neglecting the more challenging doctrine of Jesus' divinity the Qur'ān intends to lead a skeptical audience slowly to Christian truths, in the way that Augustine recommends (*De Trinitate*, 1:12): "Believe in Christ born in the flesh and you shall reach the Christ born of God, God in God." Basetti-Sani, *Koran in the Light of Christ*, 180. Thus the Qur'ān is "the special 'revelation' destined for the pagan Arabs, Ishmael's descendants. It is the beginning of a journey in the direction of God." Ibid., 137.

For his part Tartar writes in the Introduction, "J'ai étudié le Coran et l'Islam dans un esprit de foi, de piété et de recherche sincère de la 'Vérité' révélée; et je me serais converti, si j'étais parvenu à la conviction que l'Islam représente la vraie religion; mais je n'y ai trouvé rien qui dépasse l'enseignement de l'Evangile, le complète ou l'enrichit" (p. 3). In the following pages he emphasizes above all the Qur'ānic material on the birth and ascension of Christ, along with the titles that the Qur'ān offers Christ. Cf. his earlier work *Le Coran rend témoignage à Jésus-Christ*, Paris: Témoignage évangélique et dialogue islamo-chrétien, 1980. Much earlier I. di Matteo developed a similar argument, in a more scholarly and sober tone, in his *La Divinità di Cristo e la Dottrina della Trinità in Maometto e nei Polemisti Musulmani*, Rome: Pontifical Biblical Institute, 1938.

69 Bassetti-Sani, *Koran in the Light of Christ*, 123.

the Bible. On the contrary, through consistent references to Biblical literature the Qur'ān claims a status as the proper interpreter of the Bible. Thus the Qur'ān develops independently from, but parallel to, Christian homily. As a parallel work, however, the Qur'ān shares a number of telling commonalities with Christian homiletic, in particular with the tradition of Syriac Christian homilies.

The classical Syriac homily, for example, is marked by an inconsistent rhyme (usually with a final *ā*, due to the common Syriac nominal form) and a regular metrical form.[70] This meter facilitates the chanting, or recitation, of the homily, in the same way that the Qur'ān's more consistent rhyme facilitates its recitation. The Syriac homily is not a record of an extemporaneous oral sermon, but rather a formal work meant for repeated public recitation. These elements are prominent in a work that I have already introduced, Jacob of Serūgh's (cf. CS 1, 12) Homily (Syr. *mēmrā*; pl. *mēmrê*) on the Youths of Ephesus. Jacob's homily, which Sidney Griffith describes as "liturgically inspired,"[71] was presumably composed in celebration of the ecclesiastical feast of those Youths. It opens with a formal invocation, in precise twelve syllable meter: "About the children, the sons of the princes of Ephesus, I have a homily to declaim before the hearers. * Pay attention to me, laborers; sing praise, sons of the bridal chamber."[72] The Qur'ān similarly opens its account of the same affair not with any detailed description but with a religious invocation: "Did you count the Companions of the Cave and *al-raqīm* among Our wonderful signs? * When the youths took refuge in the Cave, they said, 'send us Your mercy, provide us with guidance in our plight'" (Q 18.9–10).

In their ordering, too, the *mēmrê* and the Qur'ān demonstrate similar characteristics. The sequence of argument in the *mēmrê* is often extemporaneous; they tend not to follow a clear chronology or even a neat sequential progression. Instead certain points, or allusions, may be presented and revisited several times throughout a sermon. The editor of Jacob's *Homilies* (*mēmrê*) *against the Jews* accordingly notes, "Comme dans le reste de son œuvre, l'auteur y est fort prolixe et aucun plan rigoureux n'est suivi."[73]

Jacob's *Homilies against the Jews* move freely between religious, eschatological, legal, and sectarian topics. In order to make sense of these *Homilies*, in fact, the editor finds it necessary to provide both a sequential overview (*exposé*) of the seven homilies and, in light of the their non-sequential nature, an analysis of the various themes therein. These include law, circumcision, the

70 This metrical form is prominent both with Jacob of Serūgh and in Ephraem's *mēmrê*, e.g. in the aforementioned work *The Repentance of Nineveh*. Regarding this see Hemmerdinger-Illiadou, "Saint Éphrem le Syrien."

71 Griffith, "Christian lore and the Arabic Qur'ān," 122.

72 Trans. Griffith ("Christian lore and the Arabic Qur'ān," 122) from "Testi Orientali Inediti," 2:18.

73 M. Albert, Introduction to Jacob of Serūgh, *Homélies contre les juifs*, 10.

Sabbath, the Trinity, faith, universalism, the Church, love, anti-intellectualism, symbolism, and earlier scriptures. If an individual homily is examined in detail the same point is evident. In the third of his homilies, for example, Jacob first addresses his Jewish discussant,[74] and then discusses God's rest from the work of creation on the seventh day,[75] prophecy,[76] Jewish myopia,[77] the Crucifixion,[78] the history of Israelite disobedience,[79] the futility of the Sabbath observance,[80] God's unceasing work in nature,[81] the history of the patriarchs,[82] and the glorification of Christ as Son of God.[83]

The Qur'ān displays the same sort of topical wandering. Accordingly, and just like the editor of Jacob's *Homilies*, Andrew Rippin finds it necessary to provide both a topical and a sequential introduction to the Qur'ān. After introducing the main themes of the Qur'ān he notes, "A summary of the contents of the Qur'ān, such as that just provided, while necessarily incomplete, glosses over an important point about the composition of the book itself – its apparent random character and seemingly arbitrary sense of organization."[84] In defense of this point Rippin provides the following outline of the contents of *al-baqara* (2): vv. 1–29, faith and disbelief; vv. 30–9, creation, Adam, Satan; vv. 40–86, Biblical history – Moses; vv. 87–103, Biblical history – Jews, Jesus, Moses; vv. 104–21, polemic – Muslim, Jewish, Christian; vv. 122–41, Biblical history, Abraham; vv. 142–67, Islamic identity (direction of prayer, prayer itself, pilgrimage); vv. 168–203, juridical problems (food, wills, fast, pilgrimage, and so on); vv. 204–14, salvation history; vv. 215–42, juridical problems (holy war, marriage, divorce, and so on); vv. 254–60, mixed; vv. 261–83, juridical problems (charity, usury); vv. 284–6, faith.[85]

This remarkably unpredictable ordering is often, and reasonably, explained as a product of a conservative and/or a hurried editing process.[86] The present work, however, suggests a different explanation. The Qur'ān's format reflects a homiletic tradition in which such ordering is par for the course. The comments of Tor Andrae on the Qur'ān and Syriac homilies thus seem

74 Jacob of Serūgh, *Homélies contre les juifs*, 86 (Homily 3, ll. 1–14).
75 Ibid., 86–8 (Homily 3, ll. 15–26).
76 Ibid., 88 (Homily 3, ll. 27–32).
77 Ibid., 88 (Homily 3, ll. 33–44).
78 Ibid., 88 (Homily 3, ll. 45–58).
79 Ibid., 90–2 (Homily 3, ll. 59–118).
80 Ibid., 92–4 (Homily 3, ll. 119–50).
81 Ibid., 96–8 (Homily 3, ll. 151–82).
82 Ibid., 98–100 (Homily 3, ll. 183–240).
83 Ibid., 100–10 (Homily 3, ll. 240–358).
84 A. Rippin, *Muslims: Their Religious Beliefs and Practices*, London: Routledge, 1990, 1:22–3.
85 Ibid., 1:23.
86 "To the source critic, the work displays all the tendencies of rushed editing with only the most superficial concern for the content, the editors/compilers apparently engaged only in establishing a fixed text of scripture." Ibid.

appropriate: "A mon avis, les choses se présentent de telle manière qu'il ne s'agit pas en tout cas simplement de l'emprunt d'une tendance religieuse ou d'un état d'esprit général; il me semble qu'il y a essentiellement à la base *un seul et même schéma homilétique*" (emphasis mine).[87]

The Qur'ān's relationship to the Syriac Christian homiletic tradition is evident also in regard to content. The Qur'ān's anti-Jewish rhetoric, for example, parallels the anti-Jewish rhetoric in Syriac Christian works. Ephraem's aforementioned (c.f. CS 8) homily on the *Repentance of Nineveh* is fundamentally shaped by such rhetoric, as is (and this will be no surprise) Jacob's *Homilies against the Jews*. Like the Qur'ān (cf., e.g., Q 4.155–7) Jacob emphasizes the Jews' inability to recognize the signs of God:

> He commanded a man [Adam], who gave birth to Eve in a great miracle,
> He commanded a virgin, who gave her fruit without a union.
> O Jew, the two things are most certainly true,
> But you pretend one is false and admit the other, which is no truer than the first.[88]

Jacob's argument on this count (i.e. that the virgin birth of Christ is anticipated by the creation of Eve) emerges from his larger polemical vision in the *Homilies*, that the Jews do not understand their own scriptures. This is a common theme in the Syriac homiletic tradition,[89] and no less so in the Qur'ān: "Among the Jews are those who falsify (*yuḥarrifūna*) the meanings of words . . . while they twist their tongues (*layyān bi-alsinatihum*) and speak evil of the faith" (Q 4.46; cf. 2.75; 5.13, 41).

To the matter of anti-Jewish polemic a second example might be added. In the Syriac homilies, as in the Qur'ān, the fundamental medium of exhortation is eschatology. Moreover, the Qur'ān's eschatological imagery, both in regard to the Day of Judgment (regarding which cf. CS 11) and in regard to heaven and hell, follows closely that found in the writings of the Syriac fathers, and of Ephraem in particular.[90] The Qur'ān's logical proofs for the resurrection

87 *OIC*, 145. Cf. the conclusion of Gräf: "Wenn wir also nach Parallelen suchen, sollten wir uns nicht in erster Linie direkt an Bibel, Apokryphen etc. halten, sondern an die liturgische und auch *die homiletische* (exegetische) *Literatur*, die das damalige kirchliche Leben illustriert, und an die Art, wie sie die kanonischen Texte nutzt" (emphasis mine). Gräf, "Zu den christlichen Einflüssen im Koran," 133.

88 *Homélies contre les juifs*, 48, ll. 77–80.

89 "The early Christians in general and Syrians in particular regarded the Jews as heretics and as completely wrongly interpreting the Old Testament." Bowman, "Debt of Islam," 200.

90 On this see Andrae, *OIC*, 145–55. Andrae concludes, "Les citations ci-dessus doivent avoir clairement montré la parenté indéniable entre les descriptions du Coran et celles du Père syrien" (*OIC*, 154). Gräf also emphasizes the correspondence between the eschatological imagery of Ephraem and the Qur'ān. See Gräf, "Zu den christlichen Einflüssen im Koran," 115–7.

of the body, including the description of the resurrection as a second creation (Q 32.9–10; 53.45–7), also follow closely the Syriac homiletic tradition.[91] As Andrae demonstrates, even specific details of the Qur'ān's eschatology, such as the angels which drive the soul away at the moment of death (Q 8.50; 16.29; 47.27),[92] the two trumpet blasts (Q 39.68),[93] and the fruits of the heavenly garden (Q 2.266; 37.41–2; 38.51, passim),[94] have salient precedents in the writing of the Syriac fathers. Andrae accordingly notes that those who imagine the Qur'ān's materialistic eschatological imagery is far removed from Christian conceptions have not appreciated the Syriac tradition: "Le jugement Chrétien a toujours essayé de prouver les insuffisances morales de Mahomet par les joies sensuelles de son Paradis. Comme la déesse de l'histoire doit en avoir ri!"[95]

For Syriac fathers such as Ephraem the point of eschatological imagery is not simply to paint a picture of paradise and hell, but rather to inspire in the audience a fear of God.[96] In the same way the Qur'ān speaks of a God who is "mighty and invokes a severe revenge" (Q 3.4; 5.95) and of a "painful torture" on the Day of Resurrection (Q 2.10, 104, 175, passim, thirty-four times in all). For this the Qur'ān describes in gory detail the tree of *zaqqūm* from which the damned will eat in hell, a tree with fruit like the heads of

91 "Chez les Pères de l'Eglise syrienne, ces preuves appartiennent aux éléments rigides de la prédication, et elles sont presque toujours avancées, isolément ou successivement quand il est question de la Résurrection." Andrae, *OIC*, 170.

92 See *OIC*, 158–9.

93 *OIC*, 148.

94 *OIC*, 153. To this point one might add the curious controversy over an argument that Andrae makes regarding a line in Ephraem's *De Paradiso*. Therein (7:18) Ephraem proclaims that those who have abstained from wine on earth will receive pure wine in heaven, while the monk who has protected his chastity on earth will be embraced by "pure arms" (*'ūbhīn dakhyā*). Andrae argues (*Mahomet, sa vie et sa doctrine*, Paris: Adrien-Maisonneuve: 1945, 87–8) that this passage, if it was interpreted in a literal manner, could be an antecedent to the Qur'ān's description of the pleasures of wine and sex (both pleasures forbidden, or limited, on earth) in the heavenly garden. E. Beck, the editor of Ephraem's *De Paradiso*, argues in response that Ephraem intends nothing more with the reference to arms than a personification of the grape vine (he seems to have missed the nuance in Andrae's argument). See Ephraem, *Hymnen De Paradiso und Contra Julianum*, *CSCO* 174, ed. E. Beck, Louvain: Secrétariat du CorpusSCO, 1957, 29; E. Beck, "Eine christliche Parallele zu den Paradiesjungfrauen des Koran?" *Orientalia Christiana Periodica* 14, 1948, 398–405; idem, "Les Houris du Coran et Ephrem le Syrian," *MIDEO* 6, 1961, 405–8; cf. J. Horovitz, "Die paradiesischen Jungfrauen im Koran," *Islamica* 1, 1925, 543; reprint: *Der Koran*, ed. Paret, 74. Andrae's reading is followed by Bowman ("Debt of Islam," 208). Beck's response is cited by Luxenberg in his own argument that the Qur'ān's reference to *ḥūrs* (Q 2.25; 3.15; 4.57; 44.54, passim) indicates not virgins but grapes. See his *Die syro-Aramäische Lesart*, 236 (trans., 258–9). Cf. J. van Reeth, "Le vignoble du paradis et le chemin qui y mène. La thèse de C. Luxenberg et les sources du Coran," *Arabica* 53, 2006, (511–24) 515–6. For a lucid description of this confused matter see Griffith, "Christian lore and the Arabic Qur'ān," 112–3.

95 *OIC*, 155.

96 Thus Andrae: "Ephrem commence ordinairement sa prédication sur le Jugement avec conviction, comme si l'idée du Jugement l'envahissait de Crainte." Ibid., 146.

demons (Q 37.62–6), which will scorch their bowels like boiling water (Q 44.43–6; cf. Q 56.2–5). But the Qur'ān, like Ephraem, turns to such details due not to some morbid fascination, but rather to religious zeal.[97]

In light of the Qur'ān's commonalities with this homiletic tradition, it is perhaps not insignificant that Syriac *mēmrê* were particularly widespread in the period and in the context of Islam's origins. Jacob of Serūgh alone is said to have composed 763 homilies. His homilies were particularly well known in Jacobite circles, including circles in which the literary and religious language was Syriac but the population Arab.[98] This connection is suggested by a letter of consolation Jacob wrote to the Arab Christians of Ḥimyar who had suffered persecution under the Jewish ruler Dhū Nuwās.[99]

But I do not mean to argue that Jacob is the source of the Qur'ān (as Huart once argued that Umayya is its source). After my insistence on the Qur'ān's unique interpretation of Biblical traditions, it would be strange to speak now of his *mēmrê* as a source of the Qur'ān. In fact, Jacob's *mēmrā* on Jonah, which is filled with Christian typology,[100] has little material in common with the Qur'ānic references to the Jonah story. Syriac homilies are not an antecedent to the Qur'ān, but rather a parallel body of religious literature. Both the *mēmrê* and the Qur'ān point with allusions to Biblical traditions in order to deliver their religious exhortation. Both the *mēmrê* and the Qur'ān have a marked concern for the literary form of that exhortation.

The Qur'ān and its Biblical subtext

Consequently there is no reason to think that the Qur'ān belongs any less to the Biblical tradition than the *mēmrê* do. If the Qur'ān is rarely thought of in this manner this is due to the trend in critical scholarship to accept the connection made in the medieval Islamic sources between the biography of Muhammad and the Qur'ān. Curiously enough this has been challenged recently in the Islamic world by the Syrian scholar Muḥammad Shaḥrūr.

97 To this might be added the observations of E. Gräf who contends that the Qur'ān's frequent references to natural phenomena as proofs for the existence of the Creator and the resurrection of the dead reflect a trope in eastern Christian liturgy. Thus he writes, "Auch die monotone Wiederholung gleicher Gedankenreihen, ein Todfeind jeder Rede und Predigt, ist der Liturgie (Litanei!) eigentümlich und angemessen, will sie eine besondere erbauliche Wirkung erzielt bzw. erzielen soll." Gräf, "Zu den christlichen Einflüssen im Koran," 121.

98 On this point see Albert, Introduction to Jacob of Serūgh, *Homélies contre les juifs*, 9; Griffith, "Companions of the Cave," 121.

99 *Iacobi Sarugensis epistulae quotquot supersunt*, *CSCO* 110, ed. G. Olindar, Louvain: Secrétariat du CorpusSCO, 1952, 87–102 (German trans.: R. Schröter, "Trostschreiben Jacob's von Sarug an die himjaritischen Christen," *ZDMG* 31, 361–405).

100 Jacob of Serūgh, *Homiliae Selectae*, ed. P. Bedjan, Paris: Via Dicta de Sevres, 1905–10 (reprint: Piscataway, NJ: Gorgias, 2006), 4:368–90 (*mēmrā* 122). See the study of R.A. Kitchen, "Jonah's oar: Christian typology in Jacob of Serūgh's *Mēmrā* 122 on Jonah," *Hugoye* [http://syrcom.cua.edu/syrcom/Hugoye] 11, no. 1 (2008).

Shaḥrūr, however, only goes halfway: he challenges the use of medieval Islamic sources in reading the Qur'ān, but does not consider the Qur'ān's place in the Biblical tradition.[101]

Wansbrough goes all the way. The basic challenge raised by Wansbrough is not, as is often suggested, a point of history, that is, that the Qur'ān was codified at a late date or that Islam developed in Mesopotamia. Instead the basic challenge raised by Wansbrough is a point of method, namely that critical scholars, instead of reading the Qur'ān through *tafsīr*, should read the Qur'ān within a larger tradition of Biblical literature. Rippin notes accordingly:

> So the question raised by some critics concerning whether it is accurate to view Islam as an extension of the Judeo-Christian tradition cannot be considered valid until the evidence and the conclusions put forth in Wansbrough's works have been weighed. The point must always be: Is the presupposition supported by the analysis of the data? To attack the presupposition as invalid is to miss the entire point. To evaluate the work one must participate within its methodological presuppositions and evaluate the final results.[102]

The present study is intended to show, on the one hand, how much our understanding of the Qur'ān stands to gain from reading the text in light of its Biblical subtext and, on the other hand, that the Qur'ān itself points us to this reading.[103]

101 In his *Al-Kitāb wa-l-Qur'ān: qirā'a muʿāṣira*, Shaḥrūr argues that the Qur'ān must be read as though the Prophet had just died (p. 41), i.e. without the interference of medieval Islamic tradition. This leads him to reject certain traditional interpretations that are not evident in the Qur'ān, for example that *ummī* means illiterate (he counters it means that he was outside the faiths of Judaism and Christianity). However, he makes no effort to read the Qur'ān in conversation with earlier literature, and so uses traditional notions (ironically, the very notions of *tafsīr*) about Arab society and culture at the time of the Prophet to develop liberal interpretations (insisting, for example, that pre-Islamic culture was oppressive towards women while the Prophet sought their liberation; see pp. 564, 595). On this work see P. Clark, "The Shaḥrūr phenomenon: A liberal Islamic voice from Syria," *Islam and Christian-Muslim Relations* 7, 1996, 337–41.

102 Rippin, "Literary analysis of Qur'ān, *tafsīr*, and *sīra*," 157–8; reprint: *The Qur'ān and Its Interpretive Tradition*, ed. Rippin.

103 To this end Andrae comments, "Il faudrait d'abord s'acquitter de très vastes travaux préparatoires. Il faudrait demander en premier lieu une nouvelle 'théologie du Coran,' qui devrait satisfaire aux exigences de la méthode moderne de l'histoire des religions dans l'analyse du contenu des idées religieuses. Ensuite il faudrait une étude très poussée de toute la langue théologique du Coran compare à la langue religieuse des Eglises chrétiennes contemporaines en Syrie et en Abyssinie." *OIC*, 9. Cf. the comments of Masson: "Si le Coran se place dans la ligne de la Révélation monothéiste, on est autorisé à l'apprécier, non seulement à la lumière des textes bibliques, mais encore, en le comparant avec la doctrine de l'Eglise au stade dogmatique et théologique auquel elle était parvenue à l'époque où le Coran parut, et avec certains écrits rabbiniques." Masson, *Le Coran et la révélation judéo-chrétienne*, 11.

The fruit of this approach is perhaps most evident in Max Grünbaum's 1893 work, *Neue Beiträge zur semitischen Sagenkunde*. Therein Grünbaum does not follow the precedent of Geiger, that is, he does not go through the Qur'ān passage by passage and search through earlier literature to find likely sources. Nor does he follow the precedent of Nöldeke et al., by explaining the Qur'ān with constant reference to the *sīra*. Instead Grünbaum proceeds through narratives as they appear in Hebrew, Aramaic, Syriac, and Arabic (with occasional references to Greek and Latin versions) on the common protagonists of Jewish-Christian-Islamic tradition, from Adam to Solomon. He thus exhibits the remarkable conversation that the Qur'ān conducts with the various texts of that tradition, along with the manner in which the *mufassirūn* integrated Biblical traditions in their efforts to interpret the Qur'ān. The pre- and post-history of each Qur'ānic narrative thereby emerges, as does the degree to which the Qur'ān has a cooperative relationship with Jewish and Christian texts. In comparison, an approach which ignores those texts appears to be severely lacking.

While Grünbaum wrote his work well over a hundred years ago, a small group of recent publications likewise are focused on the Qur'ān's relationship with Biblical literature. Two different francophone scholars have recently published such works. The first is the Tunisian scholar Mondher Sfar, who shows a particular concern for the Qur'ān's reception of Biblical traditions that evolved from Ancient Near East mythology.[104] The second is Michel Cuypers, whose work *Le festin: Une lecture de la sourate al-Mâ'ida* is a close reading of the fifth chapter of the Qur'ān. Therein Cuypers employs rhetorical analysis in order to uncover the strategies behind the Qur'ān's turns of phrase and use of Biblical traditions.[105]

Yet more similar to Grünbaum's work is James Kugel's *In Potiphar's House*. Therein Kugel examines the Qur'ānic account of Joseph as one element of the larger midrashic tradition.[106] Thus Kugel addresses the reference in the

104 See especially *Le Coran, la Bible et l'orient ancien*. Sfar's ideas on the Qur'ān are articulated most clearly in ch. 4, where he comments "Une chose est sûre, c'est que l'on ne peut se rendre à la vérité d'une pensée aussi élaborée et complexe que celle du Coran sans lui restituer sa dimension temporelle, sa place dans l'histoire" (p. 427). This follows from his earlier conclusion regarding the manner in which Islamic tradition shaped the Qur'ān: "Telle est l'ironie de l'Histoire: la distance prise par l'Islam orthodoxe par rapport à l'expérience coranique est plus grande que la distance millénaire qui sépare le Coran des anciennes religions orientales. Le Coran apparaît alors dans ces conditions comme le dernier témoin vivant, authentique et éclairant de l'ancien civilisation orientale" (p. 351).

105 See M. Cuypers, *Le festin: Une lecture de la sourate al-Mâ'ida*, Paris: Lethellieux, 2007; English trans.: *The Banquet: A Reading of the Fifth Sura of the Qur'an*, Miami: Convivium Press, 2009. Note also the recent work that Cuypers has co-authored with G. Gobillot, *Le Coran: Idées reçues*, Paris: Le cavalier blue, 2007. The strategy of Cuypers and Gobillot in this work is to raise, and then refute through a critical examination, commonly held ideas about the Qur'ān (e.g. "le texte du Coran est fixe, depuis l'origine," or "Le Coran s'adresse à des païens incultes" or "Il n'y a aucun ordre dans le texte du Coran").

106 For a more recent intertextual reading of the Joseph story see M. Bal, *Loving Yusuf: Travels from Present to Past*, Chicago: University of Chicago Press, 2008.

Qur'ānic account of Joseph to women cutting themselves with knives (Q 12.31; nowhere to be found in the Biblical account) in light of a long tradition of Jewish speculation on the words *akhar ha-debārīm* "after these things" in Genesis 39.7.[107] In the Qur'ān the appearance of knives in the hands of the women is a non sequitur. Yet in light of the midrashic account it makes sense.

Thereby Potiphar's wife, usually named Zuleika, passes out knives that the woman might peel oranges (or other fruit) served at her banquet.[108] The knives, then, are a typical example of the Qur'ān penchant for allusions.[109] Meanwhile, the entire episode demonstrates the Qur'ān's intimate involvement in the tradition of midrashic development of the Biblical text. In fact the Qur'ān itself, in turn, seems to have exerted an influence on later Jewish exegesis. The *Midrash ha-Gadol*, for example, a post-Qur'ānic work (14th century) that stems from Yemen, reflects the Qur'ān's idiosyncratic sequencing of the Joseph account.[110] In a similar fashion to Kugel's work, the present work has repeatedly turned to Jewish and Christian midrash as a bridge to connect Bible and Qur'ān.[111]

It is telling that this sort of methodological approach to the Qur'ān, where it is seen for its participation in both earlier and later renditions of the Joseph

107 The Jewish exegetes either understand *dbārīm* with the meaning of "words" and provide a conversation for Joseph and Potiphar's wife, or they understand it to mean "things" (or "events") and provide the narrative of the women and their knives. This narrative also works as an appropriate pretext to the attempted seduction of Joseph by Potiphar's wife (Gn 39.7b ff.; although in the Qur'ān the order is in reverse). J. Kugel, *In Potiphar's House*, San Francisco: Harper, 1990, 42.

108 See *LJ*, 2:50.

109 Kugel comments (*In Potiphar's House*, 55): "It is indisputable that the Qur'ān, which has no interest in biblical exegesis *as such*, has thus simply taken over a bit of traditional exegesis that was also a good story, and woven it into its retelling of the doings of the hero Yusuf." The present work, however, suggests that the Qur'ān's relationship to Biblical exegesis is closer than that which Kugel assumes.

110 "Mrs. Potiphar seizes Joseph in the garment scene, and he flees; *then* comes the accusation of attempted rape, which is immediately, and publicly, disproved; then comes the assembly of ladies; then Joseph, as something of an afterthought, is jailed in spite of the fact that he has been proven innocent." Kugel, *In Potiphar's House*, 53.

111 For example, the angels' protest at God's plan to create a human, nowhere in the Bible, appears in midrash due to the juxtaposition of Gn 1.26 and Psalm 8.4; CS 1. The provision of feathers to Adam and Eve (CS 3), Abraham's observation of the celestial bodies (CS 4) and the refusal of Abraham's guests to eat (CS 5) all reflect themes which are not apparent in the Bible but are prominent in midrash. J. Obermann makes the same argument in regard to the Qur'ānic account of the Israelites at Mt. Sinai. He notes, "More deliberately perhaps than has been proposed in previous studies of the subject, the foregoing remarks tend to postulate the Agada, over against the Old Testament proper, as an indispensable, methodological criterion for literary and religious-historical criticism of the Koran." J. Obermann, "Koran and Agada: The events at Mt. Sinai," *American Journal of Semitic Languages and Literatures* 58, 1941, (23–48) 29. On Qur'ān and midrash see also Katsh, *Judaism and Islam*, xvii; Glaser, "Qur'ānic challenges for Genesis," *Journal for the Study of the Old Testament* 75, 1997, (3–19) 4.

story, appears in the work of a scholar of Biblical Studies. When we turn to the *Encyclopaedia of the Qur'ān*, the cardinal work of Qur'ānic Studies, the approach to the Qur'ān's account of Joseph is different.

In his article on Joseph, Shalom Goldman presents this account as though it emerged *ex nihilo*.[112] There is no consideration whatsoever of its pre-history, or of the Qur'ān's conversation with the midrashic tradition on the Joseph story. Instead Goldman turns directly to the opinions of *mufassirūn*, namely (and in the following order) Tha'labī (d. 427/1036), Bayḍāwī (d. ca. 685/1286), and Ṭabarī (d. 310/923). Thus there is no suggestion that the Qur'ān itself points its audience to the Biblical narrative with allusions (such as the knives of Q 12.31); neither is there an indication of the motives that shaped the historical development of *tafsīr* on this account. Instead the traditions of the *mufassirūn*, in a seemingly synchronic way, are presented as the ultimate source for a critical understanding of it.[113] Thus neither the Qur'ān nor *tafsīr* receives critical attention.

This approach is found frequently in the *Encyclopaedia of the Qur'ān*. In her article on Adam and Eve, Cornelia Schöck mentions only the classical Islamic interpretations of the Adam story (cf. CS 1).[114] In her article on Mary, Barbara Stowasser makes no mention of the subtext to which the Qur'ān itself is alluding.[115] The story of the ordeal, which in light of the subtext is understood to relate to Mary's engagement to Joseph, is left to the speculation of the *mufassirūn*. Indeed, time and again the *Encyclopaedia of the Qur'ān* appears to be instead the *Encyclopaedia of Tafsīr*. Of course, *tafsīr* is an important subject of critical research and, in my opinion, deserves its own encyclopedia. Yet to reduce the study of the Qur'ān to the study of *tafsīr* is to do a discredit to both.

Perhaps it is for this reason that doctoral students of the Qur'ān today are required to study Arabic (and modern European languages), and often Persian, but rarely Hebrew, Aramaic, Syriac, Ethiopic, Greek or Latin (let alone Ancient North/South Arabian), that is, the languages of the pre-Qur'ānic

112 S. Goldman, "Joseph," *EQ*, 3:55–7.

113 Goldman (ibid., 3:55–6) writes: "Joseph can thus be seen as exemplifying the basic paradigm of the Qur'ān: he is a prophet (*nabī*) who is derided and exiled, but is eventually vindicated and rises to prominence. As such, he serves as a model for the life of Muḥammad and many of the Qur'ānic commentaries see this as a central theme and function of the sūra. This interpretation is strengthened by the 'occasions of revelation' tradition, which places the circumstance of Yūsuf's revelation at the point where Muḥammad is challenged by skeptics who doubt his knowledge of the narrative of the Children of Israel. The sūra is one response to this challenge, and is thus greatly detailed and includes information not known from earlier tellings of the stories of Jacob's family."

114 C. Schöck, "Adam and Eve," *EQ*, 1:22–6. Much preferable is the approach of M.J. Kister, whose article on the Islamic Adam is by the author's explicit confession limited to the study of Islamic traditions. See Kister, "Ādam: A study of some legends in *Tafsīr* and *Ḥadith* literature."

115 B. Stowasser, "Mary," *EQ*, 3:288–95.

Judaeo-Christian tradition. In this regard our field has taken a great step backwards. Not only are students today not being trained to write philological works like those of Nöldeke, Grünbaum, Jeffery, and Speyer, very few of them are able to understand those works.

Yet on what grounds have contemporary scholars chosen to isolate the Qur'ān from earlier literary and religious traditions? Of course, a religious Muslim might, quite legitimately, make such a choice on the basis of dogma, just as certain Christian religious scholars find critical studies of the Bible or the historical Jesus taboo, or certain Hindu scholars find critical studies of the *Mahabharata* taboo. If the professors of al-Azhar do not ask their students to study pre-Islamic languages or, for example, to read *al-kahf* (Q 18) in the light of the narratives of the Sleepers of Ephesus, they might be excused on dogmatic grounds. Yet do scholars at liberal universities dedicated to critical study enjoy the same excuse?

The present work has hopefully provided a modest example of how much is to be gained by making a different choice, by reading the Qur'ān in the light of its Biblical subtext. With this method the depth and the skill of the Qur'ān's allusions appear. With this method, moreover, it emerges that Qur'ān and Bible, far from being incompatible or in opposition, are very much in harmony. In fact, this method demands that the student of the Qur'ān be no less a student of the Bible. So too it has implications for the student of the Bible. The Qur'ān can no longer be seen as a foreign or irrelevant book. It now appears as a work very much within the tradition of Biblical literature, and should be considered such at universities and seminaries alike.

Bibliography

The bibliography is divided into the following sections:

A. Qur'ān translations
B. Islamic sources
  a. *Tafsīr*
  b. Other
C. On the Islamic sources
D. Jewish and Christian sources
E. On the Jewish and Christian sources
F. Qur'ān and Biblical literature
  a. Dictionaries and grammars
  b. Studies
G. Other Qur'ānic, Religious, and Historical Studies

A. Qur'ān translations

Abdel Haleem, M. *The Qur'ān*. Oxford: Oxford University Press, 2004.
Arberry, A. *The Koran Interpreted*. London: Allen & Unwin, 1955.
Bell, R. *The Qur'ān. Translated with a Critical Re-arrangement of the Suras*. Edinburgh: Clark, 1937.
Blachère, R. *Le Coran*. Paris: Maisonneuve, 1949.
Fakhry, M. *The Qur'ān*. Reading: Garnet, 1996.
Paret, R. *Der Koran. Übersetzung*. Stuttgart: Kohlhammer, 1962.
Pickthall, M. *The Meaning of the Glorious Qur'ān*. London: Knopf, 1930.
Yusuf Ali's, A. *The Holy Quran*. Lahore: Muḥammad Ashraf, 1938.

B. Islamic sources

a. *Tafsīr*

Ibn Kathīr. *Tafsīr*. Ed. Muḥammad Bayḍūn. Beirut: Dār al-Kutub al-ʿIlmiyya, 1424/2004.
Muqātil b. Sulaymān, Abū l-Ḥasan. *Tafsīr*. Ed. ʿAbdallāh Muḥammad al-Shiḥāta. Beirut: Dār al-Turāth al-ʿArabī, 2002 (Reprint of: Cairo: Mu'assasat al-Ḥalabī, n.d.).

Al-Rāzī, Fakhr al-Dīn. *Mafātīḥ al-ghayb*. Ed. Muḥammad Bayḍūn. Beirut: Dār al-Kutub al-ʻIlmiyya, 1421/2000.

Al-Ṭabarī, Abū Jaʻfar Muḥammad. *Jāmiʻal-bayān fī ta'wīl al-Qur'ān*. Ed. Muḥammad Bayḍūn. Beirut: Dār al-Fikr, 1408/1988. (The pagination of this edition follows the thirty equal-part division of the Qur'ān, although it is bound in fifteen volumes.)

Al-Qummī, Abū l-Ḥasan Ibrāhīm. *Tafsīr*. Beirut: Mu'assasat al-Aʻlamī li-l-Maṭbūʻāt, 1412/1991.

Al-Zamakhsharī, Muḥammad. *Al-Kashf ʻan ḥaqā'iq ghawāmiḍ al-tanzīl*. Ed. Muḥammad Ḥusayn Aḥmad. Cairo: Maṭbaʻat al-Istiqāma, 1365/1946.

b. Other

Al-Dāmirī. *Ḥayāt al-ḥayawān*. Cairo: Maṭbaʻat al-Istiqāma, 1374/1954.

Ibn Hishām. *Sīrat Rasūl Allāh*. Ed. F. Wüstenfeld. Göttingen: Dieterich, 1858–60. English trans.: Ibn Isḥāq, *The Life of Muḥammad*. Trans. A. Guillaume. Oxford: Oxford University Press, 1955.

Ibn Kathīr. *Qiṣaṣ al-anbiyā'*. Ṭantā: Dār al-Ṣaḥāba li-l-Turāth, 1995.

Ibn Manẓūr. *Lisān al-ʻarab*. Beirut: Dār Iḥyā' al-Turāth al-ʻArabī, 1418/1997.

Ibn Saʻd. *K. al-Ṭabaqāt al-kabīr*. Ed. E. Mittwoch and E. Sachau. Brill: Leiden, 1917–40.

Al-Kulaynī, Muḥammad b. Yaʻqūb. *Uṣūl al-kāfī*. Tehran: Dār al-Uswa, 1418.

Muslim. *Ṣaḥīḥ*. Ed. Muḥammad ʻAbd al-Bāqī. Beirut: Dār al-Kutub al-ʻIlmiyya, 1421/2000.

Sahl al-Tustari. *Laṭā'if qiṣaṣ al-Anbīyā'*. Ed. Kamāl ʻAllām. Beirut: Dār al-Kutub al-ʻIlmīyah, 2004.

al-Thaʻlabī, Abū Isḥāq. *ʻArā'is al-majālis fī qiṣaṣ al-anbiyā'*. Ed. Ḥasan ʻAbd al-Raḥmān. Beirut: Dār al-Kutub al-ʻIlmiyya, 1425/2004.

al-Yaʻqūbī, Abū l-ʻAbbās. *Ta'rīkh*. Beirut: Dār al-Kutub al-ʻIlmiyya, 1419/1999.

C. On the Islamic sources

Abdul-Raof, H. *Qur'ānic Translation: Discourse, Texture, and Exegesis.* Richmond: Curzon, 2001.

Bar-Asher, M. *Scripture and Exegesis in Early Imāmī Shīʻism*. Leiden: Brill, 1999.

Barth, J. "Studien zur Kritik und Exegese des Qorans." *Der Islam* 6, 1916, 113–48.

Berg, H. *The Development of Exegesis in Early Islam*. Richmond: Curzon, 2000.

Berg, H. "Weaknesses in the arguments for the early dating of Qur'ānic commentary." In J.D. McAuliffe, B. Walfish, J. Goering (eds.), *With Reverence for the Word: Medieval Scriptural Exegesis in Judaism, Christianity and Islam*. Oxford: Oxford University Press, 2003, 329–45.

Birkeland, H. *Old Muslim Opposition against Interpretation of the Koran*. Oslo: Almqvist and Wiksells, 1956.

Burton, J. "Those are the high-flying cranes." *JSS* 15, 1970, 246–65. Reprint: *The Qur'an: Formative Interpretation*. Ed. A. Rippin. Aldershot: Ashgate, 1999, 347–65.

Calder, N. "Tafsir from Tabari to Ibn Kathīr: Problems in the description of a genre, illustrated with reference to the story of Abraham." In G.R. Hawting and A.A. Shareef (eds.), *Approaches to the Qur'an*. London: Routledge, 1993, 101–40.

Ess, J. van. *Theologie und Gesellschaft im 2. und 3. Jahrhundert Hidschra*. Berlin: Walter de Gruyter, 1991–7.

Firestone, R. *Journeys in Holy Lands: The Evolution of the Abraham-Ishmael Legends in Islamic Exegesis*. Albany, NY: SUNY Press, 1990.

Gilliot, C. "Portrait 'mythique' d'Ibn 'Abbās." *Arabica* 32, 1985, 62–7.

Gilliot, C. "Les débuts de l'exégèse coranique." *Revue Monde Musulman et de la Méditerranée* 58, 1990, 82–100. English trans.: "The beginnings of Qur'ānic exegesis." Trans. M. Bonner. In A. Rippin (ed.), *The Qur'an: Formative Interpretation*. Aldershot: Ashgate, 1999, 1–27.

Gilliot, C. *Exégèse, langue, et théologie en Islam*. Paris: Vrin, 1990.

Gilliot, C. "Muqātil, grand exégète, traditionniste et théologien maudit." *Journal asiatique* 279, 1991, 39–92.

Gilliot, C. "Exégèse et sémantique institutionnelle dans le commentaire de Ṭabarī." *SI* 77, 1993, 41–94.

Goldfeld, I. "Muqātil Ibn Sulaymān." *Bar-Ilan Arabic and Islamic Studies* 2, 1978, 13–30.

Hawting, G. "Qur'ānic exegesis and history." In J.D. McAuliffe, B. Walfish and J. Goering (eds.), *With Reverence for the Word: Medieval Scriptural Exegesis in Judaism, Christianity and Islam*. Oxford: Oxford University Press, 2003, 408–21.

Heath, P. "Creative hermeneutics: A comparative analysis of three Islamic approaches." *Arabica* 36, 1989, 173–210.

Leemhuis, F. "Ursprünge des Korans als Textus receptus." In S. Wild and H. Schild (eds.), *Akten des 27. Deutschen Orientalistentages*. Würzburg: Ergon, 2001, 301–8.

McAuliffe, J.D. "Qur'ānic hermeneutics: The views of al-Ṭabarī and Ibn Kathīr." In A. Rippin (ed.), *Approaches to the History of the Interpretation of the Qur'ān*. Oxford: Clarendon, 1988, 46–62.

McAuliffe, J.D. "The tasks and traditions of interpretation." In J.D. McAuliffe (ed.), *The Cambridge Companion to the Qur'ān*. Cambridge: Cambridge University Press, 2006, 181–209.

Motzki, H. "Dating the so-called *Tafsīr Ibn 'Abbās*: Some additional remarks." *JSAI* 31, 2006, 147–63.

Muranyi, M. "Visionen des Skeptikers." *Der Islam* 81, 2004, 206–17.

Paret, R. "Signification coranique de *ḫalīfa* et d'autres dérivés de la racine *ḫalafa*." *SI* 31, 1970, 211–7.

Qadi, W. "The term 'khalīfa' in early exegetical literature." *Die Welt des Islams* 28, 1988, 392–411. Reprint: *The Qur'an: Formative Interpretation*. Ed. A. Rippin. Aldershot: Ashgate, 1999, 327–46.

Rippin, A. "Qur'ān 21:95: A ban is upon any town." *JSS* 24, 1979, 43–53. Reprint: *The Qur'ān and its Interpretative Tradition*. Ed. A. Rippin. Aldershot: Ashgate, 2001.

Rippin, A. "Qur'ān 7:40, until the camel passes through the eye of the needle." *Arabica* 27, 1980, 107–13. Reprint: *The Qur'ān and its Interpretative Tradition*. Ed. A. Rippin. Aldershot: Ashgate, 2001.

Rippin, A. "The exegetical genre of *asbāb al-nuzūl*: A bibliographical and terminological survey." *BSOAS* 48, 1985, 1–15. Reprint: *The Qur'ān and its Interpretative Tradition*. Ed. A. Rippin. Aldershot: Ashgate, 2001.

Rippin, A. "Literary analysis of Qur'ān, *tafsīr* and *sīra*: The methodologies of John Wansbrough." In R.C. Martin (ed.), *Approaches to Islam in Religious Studies*.

Tucson: University of Arizona Press, 1985, 151–63. Reprint: *The Qur'ān and its Interpretative Tradition*. Ed. A. Rippin. Aldershot: Ashgate, 2001.

Rippin, A. "Al-Zuhrī, *naskh al-Qur'ān* and the problem of early *tafsīr* texts." *BSOAS* 47, 1985, 22–43. Reprint: *The Qur'ān and its Interpretative Tradition*. Ed. A. Rippin. Aldershot: Ashgate, 2001.

Rippin, A. "RḤMNN and the ḥanīfs." In W.B. Hallaq and D.P. Little (eds.), *Islamic Studies Presented to Charles J. Adams*. Leiden: Brill, 1991, 153–68.

Rippin, A. "Interpreting the Bible through the Qur'ān." In G.R. Hawting and A.A. Shareef (eds.), *Approaches to the Qur'an*. London: Routledge, 1993, 249–59. Reprint: *The Qur'ān and its Interpretative Tradition*. Ed. A. Rippin. Aldershot: Ashgate, 2001.

Rippin, A. "*Tafsīr Ibn 'Abbās* and criteria for dating early *Tafsīr* texts." *JSAI* 18, 1994, 38–83. Reprint: *The Qur'ān and its Interpretative Tradition*. Ed. A. Rippin. Aldershot: Ashgate, 2001.

Rippin, A. "Studying early *tafsīr* texts." *Der Islam* 72, 1995, 310–23. Reprint: *The Qur'ān and its Interpretative Tradition*. Ed. A. Rippin. Aldershot: Ashgate, 2001.

Rippin, A. "*Quranic Studies*, part IV: Some methodological notes." *Method and Theory in the Study of Religion* 9, 1997, 39–46. Reprint: *The Qur'ān and its Interpretative Tradition*. Ed. A. Rippin. Aldershot: Ashgate, 2001.

Rippin, A. "The designation of 'foreign' languages in the exegesis of the Qur'ān." In J.D. McAuliffe, B. Walfish, J. Goering (eds.), *With Reverence for the Word: Medieval Scriptural Exegesis in Judaism, Christianity and Islam*, Oxford: Oxford University Press, 2003, 437–44.

Rubin, U. *Eye of the Beholder*. Princeton: Darwin, 1995.

Rubin, U. *Between Bible and Qur'an: The Children of Israel and the Islamic Self-Image*. Princeton, Darwin, 1999.

Saleh, W. *In Defense of the Bible: A Critical Edition and an Introduction to al-Biqā'ī's Bible Treatise*. Leiden: Brill, 2008.

Sinai, N. *Fortschreibung und Auslegung: Studien zur frühen Koraninterpretation*. Wiesbaden: Harrassowitz, 2009.

Versteegh, C. "Grammar and exegesis: The origins of Kufan grammar and the *Tafsīr* Muqātil." *Der Islam* 67, 1990, 206–42.

Versteegh, C. *Arabic Grammar and Qur'ānic Exegesis in Early Islam*. Leiden: Brill, 1993.

D. Jewish and Christian sources

Acta Martyrum et Sanctorum Syriace I. Ed. P. Bedjan. Paris: Otto Harrassowitz, 1890.

Agapius (Maḥbūb) of Menbidj. *K. al-'Unwān*, Part 2:1. Ed. A. Vasiliev, *Patrologia Orientalis* 7. Paris: Firmin-Didot, 1948.

Aphrahat. *Homilies*. Ed. and trans. in W. Wright, *The Homilies of Aphraates, the Persian Sage*. London: Williams and Norgate, 1869; English trans. in J. Neusner, *Aphrahat and Judaism: The Christian-Jewish Argument in Fourth-Century Iran*. Leiden: Brill, 1971; French trans.: *Les Exposés. Sources Chrétiennes* 359. Trans. M.-J. Pierre. Paris: Cerf, 1988–9.

Apocalypse of Abraham. Ed. G.N. Bonwetsch. Trans. (German) G.H. Box. Leipzig: Deichert, 1897; English trans. in A. Kulik, *Retroverting Slavonic Pseudepigrapha: Toward the Original of the Apocalypse of Abraham*. Leiden: Brill, 2004, 9–36; earlier

English trans.: *The Apocalypse of Abraham*. Trans. G.H. Box and J.I. Landsman. London: Society for Promoting Christian Knowledge, 1919.

Augustine. *City of God*. Trans. D.B. Zema and G.G. Walsh. Washington: Catholic University of America Press, 1950.

The Book of the Bee. Ed. and trans. E.A.W. Budge. Oxford: Clarendon, 1886.

The Book of the Himyarites. Ed. and trans. A. Moberg. Lund: Gleerup, 1924.

Cassian. *De Incarnatione Christi. Corpus Scriptorum Ecclesiasticorum Latinorum* 17. Ed. M. Petschenig. Vienna: Tempsky, 1888.

The Cave of Treasures. Syriac version (and French translation): *La caverne des trésors. CSCO* 486 (French trans.: 487). Ed. and trans. S.-M. Ri. Leuven: Peeters, 1987. Syriac and Arabic version (with German translation of Syriac version): *Die Schatzhöhle* (text vol. 2). Ed. and trans. C. Bezold. Leipzig: J.C. Hinrisch'sche Buchhandlung, 1888; English translation of the Arabic version: *Apocrypha Arabica. Studia Sinaitica* 8. Ed. and trans. M.D. Gibson. London: C.J. Clay, 1901.

Enoch. Trans. P. Alexander in J.H. Charlesworth (ed.), *The Old Testament Pseudepigrapha*, Volume I: *Apocalyptic Literature and Testaments*. New York: Doubleday 1983, 223–315.

Ephraem. *Hymnen De Paradiso und Contra Julianum. CSCO* 174. Ed. E. Beck. Louvain: Secrétariat du CorpusSCO, 1957. English trans. of *De Paradiso*: *Hymns on Paradise*. Trans. S. Brock. Crestwood, NY: St. Vladimir's Seminary Press, 1990.

Ephraem. *Hymni et Sermones*. Ed. T. Lamy. Mechilinae: Dessain, 1886.

Ephraem. *On the Repentance of Nineveh*. In *S. Ephraem Syri Opera Omnia quae Exstant Graece, Syriace, Latine, in Sex Tomos Distributa*. Ed. J.S. Assemani, P. Mobarek, and S.E. Assemani. Rome: n.p., 1732–46, 2:359–87. English trans.: *The Repentance of Nineveh: A Metrical Homily on the Mission of Jonah*. Trans. H. Burgess. London: Blackader, 1853.

Ephraem. *Sancti Ephraem Syri in Genesim et in Exodum Commentarii. CSCO* 152–3. Ed. and trans. R.-M. Tonneau. Leuven: Secrétariat du CorpusSCO. 1955.

Ephraem. *Sermo in Abraham et Isaac*. In *S. Ephraem Syri Opera*. Ed. S.J. Mercati. Rome: Pontifical Biblical Institute, 1915, 43–83.

Eusebius. *The Ecclesiastical History*. Ed. K. Lake and H.J. Lawlor, trans. K. Lake and J.E.L. Oulton. Cambridge, MA: Harvard University Press, 1964.

Eusebius. *Praeparatio Evangelica. PG* 21. Ed. J.-P. Migne. Paris: Migne, 1857.

Ginzberg, L. *Legends of the Jews*. Trans. H. Szold. Philadelphia: Jewish Publication Society of America, 1988.

Irenaeus. *Contra Haereses. PG* 7. Ed. D.R. Massueti. Paris: Migne, 1857.

Isaac of Antioch, *Homily against the Jews*. In S. Kazan, "Isaac of Antioch's homily against the Jews [part 1]." *Oriens Christianus* 45, 1961, 30–78.

Jacob of Serūgh. *Homélies contre les juifs. PO* 174. Ed. and trans. M. Albert. Turnhout, Belgium: Brepols, 1976.

Jacob of Serūgh. *Homily on the Seven Sleepers of Ephesus*. In I. Guidi, "Testi Orientali Inediti sopra i sette Dormienti di Efeso." *Reale Accademia dei Lincei* 282 (1884–5). Roma: Tipografia della R. Accademia dei Lincei, 1885, 18–29. Trans. P. Michael Huber. *Die Wanderlegende von den Siebenschläfern*. Leipzig: Harrassowitz, 1910.

Jacob of Serūgh. *Homiliae Selectae*. Ed. P. Bedjan. Paris: Via Dicta, 1905–10. Reprint: Piscataway, NJ: Gorgias, 2006.

Jacob of Serūgh. *Iacobi Sarugensis Epistulae quotquot Supersunt. CSCO* 110. Ed. G. Olindar. Louvain: Secrétariat du CorpusSCO, 1952, 87–102. German trans.:

R. Schröter. "Trostschreiben Jacobs von Sarug an die himjaritischen Christen." *ZDMG* 31, 1877, 361–405.
Jacob of Serūgh. *Jacob of Serugh: Select Festal Homilies*. Trans. T. Kollamparampil. Bangalore: Dharmaram Publications, 1997.
Jacob of Serūgh. "Jacob of Serugh's verse homily on Tamar." Ed. and trans. S. Brock. *Le Muséon* 115, 2002, 279–315.
Jacob of Serūgh. *Quatre homélies métriques sur la création*. *CSCO* 508–9. Ed. and trans. K. Alwan. Leuven: Peeters, 1989.
Jerusalem Talmud. Trans. J. Neusner et al. Chicago: University of Chicago Press, 1983–9.
Jesse of Edessa (Mar Isaï). *Traités sur les martyrs*. *PO* 7:1. Trans. A. Scher. Paris: Firmin-Didot, 1911.
John Chrysostom. *Adversus Judaeos*. *PG* 48. Ed. J.-P. Migne. Paris: Migne, 1862, 843–942.
John Chrysostom. *Contra Judaeos, Gentiles et Haereticos*. *PG* 48. Ed. J.-P. Migne. Paris: Migne, 1862, 1075–80.
John of Damascus. *Epistula de Hymno Trisagio*. *PG* 95. Ed. J.-P. Migne. Paris: Migne, 1864, 22–62.
Josephus, Flavius. *Jewish Antiquities*. Ed. and trans. H. St. J. Thackeray, R. Marcus, A. Wikgreen, and L.H. Feldman. Cambridge, MA: Harvard University Press, 1967–9.
Josephus, Flavius. *The Jewish War*. Ed. and trans. T.E. Page, E. Capps, and W.H.D. Rouse. London: Heinemann, 1928.
Jubilees. *The Book of Jubilees. A Critical Text*. *CSCO* 510–1. Ed. and trans. J.C. Vanderkam. Leuven: Peeters, 1989; earlier trans.: trans. R.H. Charles. New York: Macmillan, 1917.
Justin Martyr. *Dialogue with Trypho*. Trans. T.B. Falls. Washington: Catholic University of America Press, 1948.
Legends of Our Lady Mary, The Perpetual Virgin and Her Mother, Hanna. Trans. E.A. Wallis Budge. London: Oxford University Press, 1933.
The Life of Adam and Eve. In E. Kautzsch. *Die Apokryphen und Pseudepigraphen des Alten Testaments*. Tübingen: Mohr, 1900. English trans.: G. Anderson and M. Stone. *A Synopsis of the Books of Adam and Eve*. Atlanta: Scholars Press, 1999. French trans. in *La vie grecque d'Adam et Ève*. Ed. and trans. D. Bertrand. Paris: Maisonneuve, 1987.
Linguae Syriacae Grammatica et Chrestomathia cum Glossario. Ed. H. Gismondi. Rome: C. De Luigi, 1913.
Mekīltā. Trans. J.Z. Lauterbach. Philadelphia: The Jewish Publication Society of America, 1976.
Midrash Rabba: Genesis, Exodus, Leviticus, Numbers, Deuteronomy, Lamentations, Ruth, Ecclesiastes, Esther, Song of Songs. Trans. H. Freedman et al. London: Soncino, 1983.
Mujādalat Abī Qurra maʿa al-mutakallimīn al-muslimīn fī majlis al-khalīfat al-Maʾmūn. Ed. I. Dick. Aleppo: Ignatius Dick, 1999.
Al-Naṣrāniyya wa-adabuhā bayna ʿarab al-jāhiliyya. Ed. L. Cheikho. Beirut: Dar al-Machreq, 1912–23. Trans.: *Le christianisme et la littérature chrétienne en Arabie avant l'Islam*. Beirut: Imprimerie Catholique, 1923.
New Testament Apocrypha. Ed. W. Schneemelcher. Trans. R. Wilson. Cambridge: J. Clarke & Co., 1991.

Origen. *An Exhortation to Martyrdom*. Trans. R. Greer. London: SPCK, 1979.

Origen. *Homilies on Genesis and Exodus*. Trans. R.E. Heine. Washington: Catholic University of America Press, 1982.

Philo. *De Abrahamo*. Ed. and trans. F.H. Colson. *Philo in Ten Volumes*. Cambridge, MA: Harvard University Press, 1961–6, 6:4–135.

Philo. *De Opificio Mundi*. Ed. and trans. F.H. Colson and G.H. Whitaker. *Philo in Ten Volumes*. Cambridge, MA: Harvard University Press, 1961–6, 1:6–137.

Philo. *Questions and Answers on Genesis*. Ed. R. Marcus. Cambridge, MA: Harvard University Press, 1961.

Pirke de-Rabbi Elieser. Ed. and trans. D. Börner-Klein. Berlin: de Gruyter, 2004.

Protoevangelium of James. Ed. and trans. in: E. de Strycker, "La forme la plus ancienne du Protévangile de Jacques. Recherches sur le Papyrus Bodmer 5 avec une édition critique du text et une traduction annotée." *Subsidia hagiographica 33*. Brussels: Société des Bollandistes. English trans. in W. Schneemelcher (ed.), *New Testament Apocrypha*. Trans. R. Wilson. Cambridge: J. Clarke & Co., 1991, 421–37. Syriac version: *Apocrypha Syriaca*. Ed. and (English) trans. A. Smith Lewis. *Studia Sinaitica* 11. London: Clay, 1902.

Questions of Bartholomew. Ed. N. Bonwetsch in "Die apokryphen Fragen des Bartholomäus." *Nachrichten von der Gesellschaft der Wissenschaften zu Göttingen: Philologisch-historische Klasse*, 1897, 1–42.

Risālat ʿAbdallāh b. Ismāʿīl al-Hāshimī ilā ʿAbd al-Masīḥ b. Isḥāq al-Kindī wa-risālat ʿAbd al-Masīḥ ilā l-Hāshimī. Damascus: al-Takwīn li-l-Ṭibāʿa wa-l-Nashr wa-l-Tawzīʿ, 2005 (reprint of ed. A. Tien. London: n.p., 1880). English trans.: *The Apology of al-Kindy*. Trans. W. Muir. London: Society for Promoting Christian Knowledge, 1887. French trans.: *Dialogue Islamo-chrétien sous le calife al-Ma'mûn (813–834): les épitres d'al-Hashimî et d'al-Kindî*. Trans. G. Tartar. Paris: Nouvelles Éditions Latins, 1985.

Sammlung kleiner Midraschim. Ed. C.M. Horovitz. Berlin: Itzkowski, 1881.

The Soncino Talmud. London: Soncino, 1948.

Sibylline Oracles. In *Die Apokryphen und Pseudepigraphen des Alten Testaments*. Ed. E. Kautzsch. Tübingen: Mohr, 1900, 2:177–217. Trans.: *The Old Testament Pseudepigrapha*. London: Darton, Longman and Todd, 1983–5, 1:317–472.

Le synaxaire éthiopien. *PO* 15. Ed. and trans. S. Grébaut. Turnhout: Brepols, 1973.

Die syrische Didaskalia. Trans. H. Achelis and J. Flemming. Leipzig: Hinrichs, 1904.

Targum of Neofiti 1. French trans.: *Targum du Pentateuque*. *Sources chrétiennes* 245, 256, 261, 271, 282. Trans. R. Le Déaut. Paris: Cerf, 1978–81.

Targum of Pseudo-Jonathan. French trans.: *Targum du Pentateuque*. *Sources chrétiennes* 245, 256, 261, 271, 282. Trans. R. Le Déaut. Paris: Cerf, 1978–81.

Tertullian. *Ad Martyres*. *Corpus Christianorum Series Latina* 1. Ed. E. Dekkers. Turnhout: Brepols, 1954.

Tertullian. *De Anima*. *PL* 2. Ed. J.-P, Migne. Paris: Migne, 1879.

Tertullian. *De Resurrectione Carnis*. *PL* 2. Ed. J.-P. Migne. Paris: Migne, 1879.

The Testament of Adam. In M. Kmosko, "Testamentum Patris Nostri Adam." *Patrologia Syriaca* 2. Turnhout: Brepols, 1907, 1339–46.

"Testi Orientali Inediti sopra i Sette Dormienti di Efeso." Ed. I. Guidi in *Reale Accademia dei Lincei* 282 (1884–1885). Roma: Tipografia della R. Accademia dei Lincei, 1885, 18–29.

Zacharias of Mytilene. *Historia Ecclesiastica Zachariae Rhetori Vulgo Adscripta II. CSCO* 84. Ed. E.W. Brooks. Paris: E Typographeo Reipublicae, 1921.

Zacharias of Mytilene. *Zachariae Episcopi Mitylenes aliorumque Scripta Historica Graece plerumque Deperdita*. Ed. J.P.N. Land. *Anecdota Syriaca* 3. Leiden: Brill, 1870.

On the Jewish and Christian sources

Allard, P. *Dix leçons sur le martyre*. Paris: Gabalda, 1930.

Allgeier, A. "Der Ursprung des griechischen Siebenschläferlegende." *Byzantinische-neugriechische Jahrbücher* 3, 1922, 311–31.

Anderson, G. "The cosmic mountain: Eden and its interpreters in Syriac Christianity." In G.A. Robbins (ed.), *Genesis 1–3 in the History of Exegesis: Intrigue in the Garden*. Lewiston: Mellen, 1988, 187–223.

Anderson, G. "The fall of Satan in the thought of St. Ephrem." *Hugoye: Journal of Syriac Studies* [http://syrcom.cua.edu/syrcom/Hugoye] 3, 2001, 1.

Bou Mansour, T. *La théologie de Jacques de Saroug. Bibliothèque de l'Université Saint-Esprit* 16 and 40. Kaslik, Lebanon: L'Université Saint-Esprit, 1993 and 2000.

Brock, S.P. "The 'Nestorian' Church: A lamentable misnomer." *Bulletin of the John Rylands University Library of Manchester* 78, 1996, 23–35.

De Lagarde, P. *Mittheilungen*. Göttingen: Dieterich, 1884–91.

Honigmann, E. "Stephen of Ephesus (April 15, 448–Oct. 29, 451) and the legend of the Seven Sleepers." In E. Honigmann, *Patristic Studies. Studi e Testi* 173. Vatican City: Biblioteca Apostolica Vaticana, 1953, 17:125–68.

Horovitz, J. "Judaeo-Arabic relations in pre-Islamic times." *Islamic Culture* 3, 1929, 161–99.

Kazan, S. "Isaac of Antioch's homily against the Jews [part 2]." *Oriens Christianus* 46, 1962, 87–98; 47, 1963, 89–97; 49, 1965, 57–78.

Kollamparampil, T. *Salvation in Christ according to Jacob of Serugh: An Exegetico-theological Study on the Homilies of Jacob of Serugh (451–521 AD) on the Feasts of Our Lord*. Bangalore: Dharmaram Publications, 2001.

Kugel, J. *In Potiphar's House*. San Francisco: Harper, 1990.

Kugel, J. *Traditions of the Bible: A Guide to the Bible as It Was at the Start of the Common Era*. Cambridge, MA: Harvard University Press, 1998.

Kugel, J. *How to Read the Bible*. New York: Free Press, 2007.

Loofs, F. *Leitfade zum Studium der Dogmengeschichte*. Halle: Niemeyer, 1893.

Neusner, J. *Aphrahat and Judaism: The Christian-Jewish Argument in Fourth-Century Iran*. Leiden: Brill, 1971.

Reuling, H. *After Eden: Church Fathers and Rabbis on Genesis 3:16–21*. Leiden: Brill, 2006.

Ri, S.-M. *Commentaire de la Caverne des tresors: Étude sur l'historie du texte et de ses sources. CSCO* 581. Leuven: Peeters, 2000.

Ruzer, S. "The Cave of Treasures on swearing by Abel's Blood and expulsion from paradise: Two exegetical motifs in context." *Journal of Early Christian Studies* 9, 2001, 251–71.

Shepardson, C. *Anti-Judaism and Christian Orthodoxy: Ephrem's Hymns in Fourth-Century Syria*. Washington, DC: The Catholic University of America Press, 2008.

Simon, M. *Recherches d'histoire judéo-chrétienne*. Paris: Mouton, 1962.

Simon, M. "Adam et la rédemption dans la perspective de l'église ancienne." In R.J.Z. Werblowsky and C.J. Bleeker (eds.), *Types of Redemption*. Leiden: E.J. Brill, 1970, 62–71.

Vanderkam, J. *Textual and Historical Studies in the Book of Jubilees*. Missoula: Scholars Press, 1997.

Qur'ān and Biblical literature

Dictionaries and grammars

Ambros, A. and S. Prochazka. *Concise Dictionary of Koranic Arabic*. Wiesbaden: Reichert, 2004.

Ambros, A. and S. Prochazka. *Nouns of Koranic Arabic Arranged by Topics*. Wiesbaden: Reichert, 2006.

Brown, F. *The New Brown-Driver-Briggs-Genesius Hebrew and English Lexicon*. Peabody, MA: Hendrickson, 1979.

Dozy, R. *Supplément aux dictionnaires arabes*. Leiden: Brill, 1881. Reprint: Beirut: Librairie du Liban, 1981.

Kazimirski, A. de Biberstein. *Dictionnaire arabe-français*. Paris: Maisonneuve, 1860.

Lane, E. *An Arabic-English Lexicon*. London: Williams and Norgate, 1863–93.

Ledrain, E. *Dictionnaire des noms propres palmyrenians*. Paris: Leroux, 1886.

Leslau, W. *Comparative Dictionary of Ge'ez*. Wiesbaden: Harrassowitz, 1987.

Nöldeke, T. *Compendious Syriac Grammar*. Trans. J.A. Crichton. Winona Lake, IN: Eisenbraun's, 2001.

Payne Smith, R. *Thesaurus Syriacus*. Oxford: E Typographeo Clarendoniano, 1879–1901 (two volumes numbered consecutively).

Rūḥānī, Maḥmūd. *Al-Muʿjam al-iḥṣā'ī. A Statistical Dictionary of Qur'ānic Words*. Mashad: Razavi, 1420/1990.

Schulthess, F. *Lexicon Syropalaestinum*. Berlin: Reimer, 1903.

Studies

Ahrens, K. "Christliches im Qoran." *ZDMG* 84, 1930, 15–68, 148–90.

Anderson, G. "The exaltation of Adam and the fall of Satan." In G. Anderson, M. Stone, and J. Tromp (eds.), *Literature on Adam and Eve*. Leiden: Brill, 2000, 83–110.

Anderson, G. "The garments of skin in apocryphal narrative." In J. Kugel (ed.), *Studies in Ancient Midrash*. Cambridge, MA: Harvard University Press, 2001, 101–43.

Andrae, T. *Les origines de l'islam et le christianisme*. Trans. J. Roche. Paris: Adrien-Maisonneuve, 1955. Originally published in German as "Der Ursprung des Islams und das Christentum." *Kyrkshistorisk årsskrift* 23, 1923, 149–206; 24, 1924, 213–25; 25, 1925, 45–112.

Avezzù, G. *I sette dormienti: Una leggenda fra Oriente e Occidente*. Milano: Medusa, 2002.

Azzi, J. See al-Ḥarīrī, Abū Mūsā.

Bart, J. *Etymologische Studien zum Semitischen*. Leipzig: Hinrichs, 1893.

Basetti-Sani, G. *The Koran in the Light of Christ*. Trans. W.R. Carroll and B. Dauphinee. Chicago: Franciscan Herald Press, 1977.

Bashear, S. *Studies in Early Islamic Tradition*. Jerusalem: Hebrew University Press, 2004.

Baumstark, A. "Arabische Übersetzung eines altsyrischen Evangelientextes und die Sure 21, 105 zitierte Psalmenübersetzung." *OC* 3, 1934, 165–88.

Beck, E. *Das christliche Mönchtum im Koran*. Helsinki: Studia Orientalia, 1946.

Bell, R. *The Origin of Islam in Its Christian Environment*. London: Macmillan, 1926.

Bell, R. *The Qur'ān: Translated with a Critical Re-arrangement of the Suras*. Edinburgh: Edinburgh University Press, 1937.

Bell, R. "Who were the *Ḥanīfs*?" *MW* 29, 1949, 120–5.

Bellamy, J.A. "*Al-Raqīm* or *al-Ruqūd*? A note on *Sūrah* 18:9." *JAOS* 111, 1991, 115–7.

Bellamy, J.A. "Some proposed emendations to the text of the Koran." *JAOS* 113, 1993, 562–73.

Bellamy, J.A. "More proposed emendations to the text of the Koran." *JAOS* 116, 1996, 196–204.

Bellamy, J.A. "Textual criticism of the Koran." *JAOS* 121, 2001, 1–6.

Bellamy, J.A. "A further note on 'Īsā." *JAOS* 122, 2002, 587–8.

Bonanate, U. *Bibbia e Corano: I testi sacri confrontati*. Turin: Bollati Boringhieri, 1995.

Bousquet, G.-H. *Remarques critiques sur le style et la syntaxe du Coran*. Paris: Maisonneuve, 1953.

Bowman. J. "The debt of Islam to monophysite Syrian Christianity." In E.C.B. MacLaurin (ed.), *Essays in Honor of Griffithes Wheeler Thatcher*. Sydney: Sydney University Press, 1967, 191–216.

Bravmann, M.M. *The Spiritual Background of Early Islam*. Leiden: Brill, 2009.

Busse, H. *Die theologischen Beziehungen des Islam zu Judentum und Christentum*. Darmstadt: Wissenschaftliche Buchgesellschaft, 1988.

Chabbi, J. *Le Coran décrypté: Figures bibliques en Arabie*. Paris: Fayard, 2008.

Clemen, C. "Muhammeds Abhängigkeit von der Gnosis." *Harnack-Ehrung: Beiträge zur Kirchengeschichte*. Leipzig: Hinrichs, 1921, 249–62.

Coleridge, M. *The Seven Sleepers of Ephesus*. London: Chatto & Windus, 1893.

Cragg, K. *Jesus and the Muslim*. London: George Allen & Unwin, 1985.

Crone, P. and M. Cook. *Hagarism: The Making of the Islamic World*. Cambridge: Cambridge University Press, 1977.

Cuypers, M. *Le festin: Une lecture de la sourate al-Mâ'ida*. Paris: Lethellieux, 2007; English trans.: *The Banquet: A Reading of the Fifth Sura of the Qur'an*. Trans. M. Sherry. Miami: Convivium Press, 2009.

Czeglédy, K. "Monographs on Syriac and Muhammadan sources in the literary remains of M. Kmoskó." *Acta Orientalia Academiae Scientiarum Hungaricae* 4, 1954, 19–91.

de Blois, F. "Elchasai – Manes – Muhammad: Manichäismus und Islam in religionshistorischen Vergleichs." *Der Islam* 81, 2004, 31–48.

de Blois, F. "*Naṣrānī* and *Ḥanīf*: Studies on the religious vocabulary of Christianity and Islam." *BSOAS* 65, 2004, 1–30.

di Matteo, I. *La Divinità di Cristo e la Dottrina della Trinità in Maometto e nei Polemisti Musulmani*. Rome: Pontifical Biblical Institute, 1938.

Denny, F. "Some religio-communal terms and concepts in the Qur'an." *Numen* 24, 1977, 26–59.

Din, M. "The crucifixion in the Koran." *MW* 14 1924, 23–9.

Dundes, A. *Fables of the Ancients? Folklore in the Qur'ān*. Lanham, MD: Rowman & Littlefield, 2003.

Dvořák, R. "Über die Fremdwörter im Korân." *Kaiserliche Akademie der Wissenschaften. Phil.-Hist. Classe. Sitzungsberichte* 109, 1, 1885, 481–562.

Eichler, P.A. *Die Dschinn, Teufel und Engel im Qur'ān*. Leipzig: Klein, 1928.

Faris, N.A. and H.W. Gilden. "The development of the meaning of Koranic *ḥanīf*." *Journal of the Palestine Oriental Society* 19, 1939/40, 1–13. Reprint: *Der Koran*. Ed. R. Paret. *Wege der Forschung* 326. Darmstadt: Wissenschaftliche Buchgesellschaft, 1975, 255–68.

Firestone, R. "The Qur'ān and the Bible: Some modern studies of their relationship." In J.C. Reeves (ed.), *Bible and Qur'ān: Essays in Scriptural Intertextuality*. Atlanta: Society of Biblical Literature, 2003, 1–22.

Fraenkel, S. *De Vocabulis in antiquis Arabum carminibus et in Corano peregrinis*. Leiden: Brill, 1880.

Fraenkel, S. *Die aramäischen Fremdwörter im Arabischen*. Leiden: Brill, 1886.

Frank-Kamenetzky, I. *Untersuchungen über das Verhältnis der dem Umajja b. Abi ṣ Ṣalt zugeschriebenen Gedichte zum Qorān*. Doctoral Dissertation, Königsberg, 1911.

Fück, J. "Die Originalität des arabischen Propheten." *ZDMG* 90, 1936, 509–25.

Fudge, B. "The men of the cave: *Tafsīr*, tragedy and Tawfīq al-Ḥakīm." *Arabica* 54, 2007, 67–93.

Gallez, É.-M. *Le messie et son prophète: Aux origines de l'Islam*. Paris, Éditions de Paris, 2005.

Geagea, N. *Mary of the Koran*. Trans. L. Fares. New York: Philosophical Library, 1984.

Geiger, A. *Was hat Mohammed aus dem Judenthume aufgenommen*. 2nd edition. Leipzig: Kaufmann, 1902.

Glaser, I. "Qur'ānic challenges for Genesis." *Journal for the Study of the Old Testament* 75, 1997, 3–19.

Gnilka, J. *Die Nazarener und der Koran: Eine Spurensuche*. Freiburg: Herder, 2007.

Goitein, S.D. *Jews and Arabs*. New York: Schocken, 1955.

Gräf, E. "Zu den christlichen Einflüssen im Koran." *Al-Bāḥith* 28, *Festschrift Joseph Henninger zum 70 Geburtstag*, 1976, 111–44.

Griffith, S. "Christian lore and the Arabic Qur'ān: The 'Companions of the Cave' in *Sūrat al-Kahf* and in Syriac Christian tradition." In G.S. Reynolds (ed.), *The Qur'ān in Its Historical Context*. London: Routledge, 2007, 109–37.

Griffith, S. "The Gospel in Arabic: An inquiry into its appearance in the first Abbāsid century." *OC* 69, 1985, 126–67.

Grünbaum, M. *Neue Beiträge zur semitischen Sagenkunde*. Leiden: Brill, 1893.

Guzzetti, C.M. *Bibbia e Corano: Un Confronto Sinottico*. Cinisello Balsamo: Edizioni San Paolo, 1995.

al-Ḥaddād, Yūsuf. *Al-Qur'ān da'wā naṣrāniyya*. Jounieh: Librairie pauliste, 1969.

al-Ḥaddād, Yūsuf. *Al-Injīl fī-l-Qur'ān*. Jounieh: Librairie pauliste, 1982.

al-Ḥarīrī, Abū Mūsā. *Qass wa-nabī*. Beirut: n.p., 1979. French trans.: J. Azzi. *Le Prêtre et le Prophète*. Trans. M.S. Garnier. Paris: Maisonneuve et Larose, 2001.

Hauglid, B.M. "On the early life of Abraham: Biblical and Qur'ānic intertextuality and the anticipation of Muḥammad." In J.C. Reeves (ed.), *Bible and Qur'ān:*

Essays in Scriptural Intertextuality. Atlanta: Society of Biblical Literature, 2003, 87–105.

Hawting, G. "Eavesdropping on the heavenly assembly and the protection of the revelation from demonic corruption." In S. Wild (ed.), *Self-Referentiality in the Qur'ān*. Wiesbaden: Harrassowitz, 2006, 25–37.

Hawting, G. *The Idea of Idolatry and the Emergence of Islam*. Cambridge: Cambridge University Press, 1999.

Heller, B. "Éléments, parallèles et origine de la légende des Sept Dormants." *Revue des études juives* 49, 1904, 190–218.

Heller, B. "Éléments juifs dans les termes religieux du Koran." *Revue des études juives* 4, 1928, 51–5.

Henninger, J. *Spuren christlicher Glaubenswahrheiten im Koran*. Schöneck: Administration der Neuen Zeitschrift für Missionswissenschaft, 1951. Originally published in *Neue Zeitschrift für Missionswissenschaft/Nouvelle Revue de Science Missionnaire* 1, 1945, 135–40, 304–14; 2, 1946, 56–65, 109–22, 289–304; 3, 1947, 128–40, 290–301; 4, 1948, 129–41, 284–93; 5, 1949, 127–40, 290–300; 6, 1950, 207–17, 284–97.

Hirschberg, H.Z. *Jüdische und christliche Lehren im vor-und frühislamischen Arabien*. Krakow: Nakl. Polskiej Akademii Umiejętności, 1939.

Hirschfeld, H. *Jüdische Elemente im Koran*. Berlin: Schulze, 1878.

Hirschfeld, H. *Beiträge zur Erklärung des Ḳorāns*. Leipzig: Schulze, 1886.

Hirschfeld, H. *New Researches into the Composition and Exegesis of the Qoran*. London: Royal Asiatic Society, 1902.

Horn, C.B. "Mary between Bible and Qur'an: Soundings into the transmission and reception history of the *Protoevangelium of James* on the basis of selected literary sources in Coptic and Copto-Arabic and of art-historical evidence pertaining to Egypt." *Islam and Christian-Muslim Relations* 18, 2007, 509–38.

Horovitz, J. "Das koranische Paradies." *Scripta Universitatis atque Bibliothecae Hierosolymitanarum*. Jerusalem: Hebrew University Press, 1923. Reprint: *Der Koran*. Ed. R. Paret. *Wege der Forschung* 326. Darmstadt: Wissenschaftliche Buchgesellschaft, 1975, 53–73.

Horovitz, J. "Jewish proper names and derivatives in the Koran." *Hebrew Union College Annual* 2, 1925, 145–227. Reprint: Hildesheim: Olms, 1964.

Horovitz, J. "Die paradiesischen Jungfrauen im Koran." *Islamica* 1, 1925, 543. Reprint: *Der Koran*. Ed. R. Paret. *Wege der Forschung* 326. Darmstadt: Wissenschaftliche Buchgesellschaft, 1975, 74.

Horovitz, J. *Koranische Untersuchungen*. Berlin: de Gruyter, 1926.

Huart, C. "Une nouvelle source du Qorān." *Journal Asiatique* 10, 1904, 125–67.

Huber, P. Michael. *Die Wanderlegende von den Siebenschläfern*. Leipzig: Harrassowitz, 1910.

Hurgronje, C.S. *Het Mekkaansche Feest*. Leiden: Brill, 1880.

Jeffery, A. *Foreign Vocabulary of the Qur'ān*. Baroda: Oriental Institute, 1938.

Jeffery, A. *The Qur'ān as Scripture*. New York: Moore, 1952. Originally published in four parts in *Muslim World* 40, 1950, 41–55, 106–34, 185–206, 257–74.

Jeffery, A. "The present status of Qur'ānic studies." *Middle East Institute: Report of Current Research*, Spring 1957, 1–16.

Johnston, D. "The human *khilāfa*: A growing overlap of reformism and Islamism on human rights discourse?" *Islamochristiana* 28, 2002, 35–53.

Jourdan, F. *La tradition des Sept Dormants: Une rencontre entre chrétiens et musulmans*. Paris: Maisonneuve et Larose, 2001.

Kandler, H. *Die Bedeutung der Siebenschläfer (Ashab al-kahf) im Islam: Untersuchungen zu Legenden und Kult in Schrifttum, Religion und Volksglauben unter besonderer Berücksichtigung der Siebenschläfer-Wallfahrt.* Bochum: Universitätsverlag, 1994.

Katsh, A. *Judaism and Islam: Biblical and Talmudic Background of the Qur'ān and Its Commentaries.* New York: New York University Press, 1954.

Khoury, R.G. "Quelques réflexions sur la première ou les premières Bibles arabes." In T. Fahd (ed.), *L'arabie préislamique et son environnement historique et culturel. Actes du colloque de Strasbourg 24–27 juin 1987.* Leiden: Brill, 1989, 549–61.

Knieschke, W. *Die Erlösungslehre des Korans.* Berlin: Runge, 1910.

Kropp, M. "Der äthiopische Satan = *šayṭān* und seine koranischen Ausläufer; mit einer Bemerkung über verbales Steinigen." *OC* 89, 2005, 93–102.

Kropp, M. "Beyond single words: *mā'ida – Shayṭān – jibt and ṭāghūt.*" In G.S. Reynolds (ed.), *The Qur'ān in Its Historical Context.* London: Routledge, 2007, 204–16.

Lichtenstadter, I. "And become ye accursed apes." *JSAI* 14, 1991, 153–75. Reprint: *The Qur'ān: Style and Contents.* Ed. A. Rippin. Aldershot: Ashgate, 2001, 61–83.

Lüling, G. *Über den Ur-Qur'ān: Ansätze zur Rekonstruktion vorislamischer christlicher Strophenlieder im Qur'ān.* Erlangen: Lüling, 1974 (2nd edition: Erlangen: Lüling, 1993). Recently translated and expanded as *A Challenge to Islam for Reformation.* Delhi: Molital Banarsidass, 2003.

Lüling, G. *Der christliche Kult an der vorislamischen Kaaba.* Erlangen: Lüling, 1977.

Lüling, G. *Die Wiederentdeckung des Propheten Muḥammad: Eine Kritik am "christlichen" Abendland.* Erlangen: Lüling, 1981.

Lüling, G. "Preconditions for the scholarly criticism of the Koran and Islam, with some autobiographical remarks." *Journal of Higher Criticism* 3, Spring 1996, 1, 73–109.

Lüling, G. "A new paradigm for the rise of Islam and its consequences for a new paradigm of the history of Israel." *Journal of Higher Criticism* 7, Spring 2000, 1, 23–53.

Luxenberg, C. *Die syro-aramäische Lesart des Koran.* Berlin: Das arabische Buch, 2000. 2nd edition: Berlin: Schiler, 2002 (3rd edition: Berlin: Schiler, 2007). English trans.: Berlin, Schiler, 2007.

Luxenberg, C. "Zur Morphologie und Etymologie von syro-aramäisch *sāṭānā*=Satan und koranisch-arabisch *šayṭān.*" In C. Burgmer (ed.), *Streit um den Koran.* Berlin: Schiler, 2004, 46–66.

Luxenberg, C. "Nöel dans le Coran." In A.-M. Delcambre et al. (eds.), *Enquêtes sur l'Islam.* Paris: Éditions Desclée de Brouwer, 2004, 117–38. Cf.: "Weihnachten im Koran." In C. Burgmer (ed.), *Streit um den Koran*, Berlin: Schiler, 2005, 35–41.

Luxenberg, C. "Die arabische Inschrift im Felsendom zu Jerusalem." In K.-H. Ohlig and G.-R. Puin (eds.), *Die dunklen Anfänge: Neue Forschungen zur Entstehung und frühen Geschichte des Islam.* Berlin: Schiler, 2005, 124–47.

Margoliouth, D.S. "On the origin and import of the names *muslim* and *ḥanīf.*" *JRAS* 1903, 467–93.

Margoliouth, D.S. "Old and New Testament in Muhammedanism." *Encyclopedia of Religion and Ethics.* Ed. J. Hastings. New York: Scribner, 1909, 9:480–3.

Margoliouth, D.S. "The origins of Arabic poetry." *JRAS*, 1925, 415–49.

Margoliouth, D.S. "Textual variations of the Koran." *MW* 15, 1925, 334–44. Reprint: *The Origins of the Koran.* Ed. Ibn Warraq. Amherst, NY: Prometheus, 1998, 154–62.

Margoliouth, D.S. "Some additions to Jeffery's *Foreign Vocabulary*." *JRAS*, 1939, 53–61.

Massignon, Louis. "Les 'Septs Dormants': Apocalypse de l'Islam." *Analecta Bollandiana* 68, 1950, 245–60. Reprint: *Opera Minora*. Ed. Y. Moubarac. Beirut: Dār al-Ma'ārif, 1963, 3:104–18.

Massignon, Louis. "Les sept dormants d'Ephèse (*ahl al-kahf*) en islam et chrétienté." *Revue des Études Islamiques* 12, 1954, 61–110.

Massignon, Louis. *Le culte liturgique et populaire des VII dormants, martyrs d'Ephèse (*ahl al-kahf*): Trait d'union orient-occident entre l'islam et la chrétienté. Studia Missionalia*. Rome: Gregorian University Press, 1961.

Masson, D. *Le Coran et la révélation judéo-chrétienne*. Paris: Adrien-Maisonneuve, 1958. 2nd edition: *Monothéisme coranique et monothéisme biblique*. Paris: Desclée de Brouwer 1976.

Mingana, A. "Syriac influence on the style of the Kur'ān." *Bulletin of the John Rylands Library* 11, January 1928, 1, 77–98. Reprint: *What the Koran Really Says: Language, Text, and Commentary*. Ed. Ibn Warraq. Amherst, NY: Prometheus, 2002, 171–92.

Moubarac, Y. *Abraham dans le Coran*. Paris: Vrin, 1958.

Mourad, S. "Mary in the Qur'ān: A reexamination of her presentation." In G.S. Reynolds (ed.), *The Qur'ān in Its Historical Context*. London: Routledge, 2007, 163–74.

Newby, G. "The drowned son: Midrash and myth making in the Qur'ān and Tafsīr." In W.M. Brinner and S.D. Ricks (eds.), *Studies in Islamic and Judaic Traditions*. Atlanta: Scholars Press, 1986.

Nöldeke, T. "Hatte Muḥammad christliche Lehrer?" *ZDMG* 12, 1858, 699–708.

Nöldeke, T. *Neue Beiträge zur semitischen Sprachwissenschaft*. Strassburg: Trübner, 1910.

Nöldeke, T. "Umaija b. AbiṣṢalt." *Zeitschrift für Assyriologie* 27, 1912, 159–72.

Nöldeke, T. et al., *Geschichte des Qorāns* Göttingen: Verlag der Dieterichschen Buchhandlung, 1860; 2nd edition, Nöldeke's revised work being titled therein *Über den Ursprung des Qorāns* [referred to in the present work as *GdQ1*] and including, F. Schwally, *Die Sammlung des Qorāns* [*GdQ2*], ed. and revised F. Schwally, Leipzig: T. Weicher, 1909, 1919; second edition including G. Bergsträsser and O. Pretzl, *Die Geschichte des Koran-texts* [*GdQ3*], Leipzig: T. Weicher, 1938; reprint: 3 vols. in 1, Hildesheim: Olms, 1970.

Obermann, J. "Koran and agada: The events at Mt. Sinai." *American Journal of Semitic Languages and Literatures* 58, 1941, 23–48.

Obermann, J. "Islamic origins: A study in background and foundation." In J. Friedlander (ed.), *The Arab Heritage*. New York: Russell and Russell, 1963, 58–120.

Ohlig, K.-H. "Von muhammad Jesus zum Propheten der Araber: Die Historisierung eines christologischen Prädikats." In K.-H. Ohlig (ed.), *Der frühe Islam*. Berlin: Schiler, 2007, 327–76.

O'Shaughnessy, T. *The Koranic Concept of the Word of God*. Rome: Pontifical Biblical Institute, 1948.

O'Shaughnessy, T. *The Development of the Meaning of Spirit in the Koran*. Rome: Pontifical Biblical Institute, 1953.

Paret, R. *Der Koran. Kommentar und Konkordanz*. Stuttgart: Kohlhammer, 1971.

Parrinder, G. *Jesus in the Qur'ān*. London: Faber and Faber, 1965.

Rabin, C. "Islam and the Qumran Sect." In C. Rabin (ed.), *Qumran Studies*. London: Oxford University Press, 1957, 112–30.

Räisänen, H. *Das koranische Jesusbild: Ein Beitrag zur Theologie des Korans*. Helsinki: Missiologian ja Ekumeniikan, 1971.

Reeth, J. van. "L'Évangile du Prophète." In D. de Smet et al. (eds.), *Al-Kitâb: La sacralité du texte dans le monde de l'Islam. Acta Orientalia Belgica Subsidia 3*. Brussels: Société belge d'études orientales, 2004, 155–74.

Reeth, J. van. "Le vignoble du paradis et le chemin qui y mène. La thèse de C. Luxenberg et les sources du Coran." *Arabica* 53, 2006, 511–24.

Reeves, J.C. "Some explorations of the intertwining of Bible and Qur'ān." In J.C. Reeves (ed.), *Bible and Qur'ān: Essays in Scriptural Intertextuality*. Atlanta: Society of Biblical Literature, 2003, 43–60.

Reynolds, G.S. "A reflection on two Qur'ānic words (*iblīs* and *jūdī*) with attention to the theories of A. Mingana." *JAOS* 124, 2004, 675–89.

Reynolds, G.S. "The Qur'ānic Sarah as prototype of Mary." In D. Thomas (ed.), *The Bible in Arab Christianity*, Leiden: Brill, 2006, 193–206.

Reynolds, G.S. (ed.) *The Qur'ān in Its Historical Context*. London: Routledge, 2007.

Reynolds, G.S. "Qur'ānic studies and its controversies." In G.S. Reynolds (ed.), *The Qur'ān in Its Historical Context*. London: Routledge, 2007, 1–25.

Reynolds, G.S. "The Muslim Jesus: Dead or alive?" *BSOAS* 72, 2009, 237–58.

Robinson, N. "Jesus and Mary in the Qur'ān: Some neglected affinities." *Religion* 20, 1990, 161–75. Reprint: *The Qur'ān: Style and Contents*. Ed. A. Rippin. Aldershot: Ashgate, 2001, 21–35.

Robinson, N. *Christ in Islam and Christianity*. London: Macmillan, 1991.

Robson, J. "Stories of Jesus and Mary." *MW* 40, 1950, 236–43.

Roncaglia, M.P. "Éléments ébionites et elkésaïtes dans le coran: Notes et hypothèses." *Proche Orient chrétien* 21, 1971, 101–26.

Rösch, G. "Jesusmythen des Islam." *Theologische Studien and Kritiken*, 1876, 409–54.

Rosenthal, F. "Some minor problems in the Qur'ān." *The Joshua Starr Memorial Volume*. New York: n.p., 1953, 68–72. Reprint: *What the Koran Really Says*. Ed. Ibn Warraq. Amherst, NY: Prometheus, 2002, 322–42.

Rudolph, W. *Die Abhängigkeit des Qorans von Judentum und Christentum*. Stuttgart: Kohlhammer, 1922.

Samir, S.K. "The theological Christian influence on the Qur'ān: A reflection." In G.S. Reynolds (ed.), *The Qur'ān in Its Historical Context*. London: Routledge, 2007, 141–62.

Schall, A. "Die Sichtung des Christlichen im Koran." *Mitteilungen und Forschungsbeiträge der Cusanus-Gesellschaft* 9, 1971, 76–91.

Schapiro, I. *Die haggadische Elemente im erzählenden Teil des Korans*. Leipzig: Gustav Fock, 1907.

Schedl, C. *Muhammad und Jesus. Die christologisch relevanten Texte des Korans*. Wien: Herder, 1978.

Schedl, C. "Die 114 Suren des Koran und die 114 Logien Jesu im Thomas-Evangelium." *Der Islam* 64, 1987, 261–4.

Schlatter, A. "Die Entwicklung des jüdischen Christentums zum Islam." *Evangelisches Missionsmagazin* 62, 1918, 251–64.

Schulthess, F. "Umajja ibn Abī ṣ Ṣalt." In C. Bezold (ed.), *Orientalische Studien: Th. Nöldeke zum 70. Geburtstag gewidmet*. Gieszen: Töpelmann, 1906, 1:71–89.

Schulthess, F. *Umajja ibn Abī ṣ Ṣalt: Die unter seinem Namen überlieferten Gedichtfragmente gesammelt und übersetzt*. Leipzig: Hinrichs, 1911.
Schützinger, H. *Ursprung und Entwicklung der arabischen Abraham-Nimrod-Legende*. Bonn: n.p., 1961.
Seale, M. *Qur'an and Bible*. London: Croom Helm, 1978.
Seidensticker, T. "The authenticity of the poems ascribed to Umayya Ibn Abī al-Ṣalt." In J.R. Smart (ed.), *Tradition and Modernity in Arabic Language and Literature*. London: Curzon, 1996, 87–101.
Sfar, M. *Le Coran, la Bible et l'orient ancien*. Paris: Sfar, 1998.
Siddiqi, A. *Studien uber die persischen Fremdwörter im klassischen Arabisch*. Göttingen: Vandenhoeck and Ruprecht, 1919.
Sidersky, D. *Les origines des légendes musulmanes dans le coran et dans les vies des prophètes*. Paris: Geuthner, 1933.
Silverstein, A. "Haman's transition from the jahiliyya to Islam." *JSAI* 34, 2008, 285–308.
Smith, H. *Bible and Islam*. New York: Scribner, 1897.
Speyer, H. *Die biblischen Erzählungen im Qoran*. Gräfenhainichen: Schulze, 1931 (reprint: Hildesheim: Olms, 1961). F. Rosenthal notes in his "The history of Heinrich Speyer's *Die biblischen Erzählungen im Qoran*" (see bibliographic entry below) that the original publication information is false. The printing was only completed in 1937, and then under the direction of Theodor Marcus in Breslau.
Sprenger, A. "Foreign words occurring in the Qôran." *JRAS of Bengal* 21, 1852, 109–14.
Syez, S. *Ursprung und Wiedergabe der biblischen Eigennamen im Qoran*. Frankfurt: Kauffmann, 1903.
Thyen, J.-D. *Bibel und Koran: Eine Synopse gemeinsamer Überlieferungen*. Cologne/Vienna: Böhlan, 2003.
Tisdall, W. St. Clair. *The Original Sources of the Qur'an*. London: Society for Promoting Christian Knowledge, 1905.
Torrey, C.C. "Three difficult passages in the Koran." In T.W. Arnold and R.A. Nicholson (eds.), *A Volume of Oriental Studies Presented to Edward G. Browne (. . .) on his 60th Birthday*. Cambridge: Cambridge University Press, 1922, 464–71.
Torrey, C.C. *The Jewish Foundation of Islam*. New York: Jewish Institute of Religion, 1933.
Tartar, G. *Le Coran rend témoignage à Jésus-Christ*. Paris: Témoignage évangélique dialogue islamo-chrétien, 1980.
Tartar, G. *Connaitre Jésus-Christ: Lire le Coran à la lumière de l'Évangile*, Combs-la-Ville: Centre évangélique de témoignage et de dialogue, 1985.
Tottoli, T. *Biblical Prophets in the Qur'an and Muslim Literature*, Richmond: Curzon, 2001.
van Bladel, K. "Heavenly cords and prophetic authority in the Quran and its late antique context." *BSOAS* 70, 2007, 223–46.
van Bladel, K. "The legend of Alexander the Great in the Qur'ān 18:83–102." In G.S. Reynolds (ed.), *The Qur'ān in Its Historical Context*. London: Routledge, 2007, 175–203.
Walker, J. *Bible Characters in the Koran*. Paisley: Gardner, 1931.
Wansbrough, J. *Quranic Studies: Sources and Methods of Scriptural Interpretation*. Oxford: Oxford University Press, 1977. Reprint: Amherst, NY: Prometheus, 2004.

Weil, G. *Biblische Legenden der Muselmänner*. Frankfurt: Rütten, 1845. English trans.: *The Bible, the Koran, and the Talmud or Biblical Legends of the Mussulmans*. New York: Harper, 1846.
Wheeler, B. *Prophets in the Quran*. London: Continuum, 2002.
Wimmer, S.J. and S. Leimgruber. *Von Adam bis Muhammad. Bibel und Koran im Vergleich*. Stuttgart: Katholisches Bibelwerk, 2005.
Zammit, M. *A Comparative Lexical Study of Qur'ānic Arabic*. Leiden: Brill, 2002.
Zwemer, S. "The worship of Adam by angels." *MW* 27, 1937, 115–27.

Other Qur'ānic, religious and historical studies

Abdel Haleem, M. *Understanding the Qur'an*. London: Tauris, 1999.
Abdul-Raof, H. "On the stylistic variation in the Quranic genre." *JSS* 52, 2007, 79–111.
Abu Zayd, N. *Rethinking the Qur'ân: Towards a Humanistic Hermeneutics*. Amsterdam: Humanistics University Press, 2004.
Achrati, A. "Arabic, Qur'ānic speech, and postmodern language: What the Qur'ān simply says." *Arabica*, 54, 2008, 161–203.
Allard, M. et al. *Analyse conceptuelle du Coran sur cartes perforées*. Paris: Mouton, 1963.
Ammann, L. *Vorbild und Vernunft. Die Regelung von Lachen und Scherzen im mittelalterlichen Islam*. Hildesheim: G. Olms, 1993.
Andrae, T. *Mahomet, sa vie et sa doctrine*. Paris: Adrien-Maisonneuve, 1945. Trans.: *Mohammed: The Man and His Faith*. Trans. T. Menzel. New York: Barnes and Noble, 1935.
Arkoun, M. *La pensée arabe*. Paris: Presses Universitaires Françaises, 1979.
Arkoun, M. *Lectures du Coran*. Paris: Maisonneuve et Larose, 1982. Trans. of Introduction: "Introduction: An assessment of and perspectives on the study of the Qur'ān." Trans. S. Lucas. In A. Rippin (ed.), *The Qur'an: Style and Contents*. Aldershot: Ashgate, 2001, 297–331.
Arkoun, M. *Rethinking Islam*. Trans. R. Lee. Boulder, CO: Westview Press, 1994.
Armstrong, K. *Muḥammad: A Biography of the Prophet*. London: Phoenix, 2003.
Awn, P. *Satan's Tragedy and Redemption*. Leiden: Brill, 1983.
Ayoub, M. "Towards an Islamic Christology II: The death of Jesus, reality or delusion?" *MW* 70, 1980, 91–121.
Al-Azami, M.M. *The History of the Qur'ānic Text from Revelation to Compilation: A Comparative Study*. Leicester: UK Islamic Academy, 2003.
Baljon, J. "The '*amr* of God' in the Koran." *Acta Orientalis* 23, 1959, 7–18.
Bashaer, S. "The title *fārūq* and its association with 'Umar I." *SI* 72, 1990, 65–70.
Bausani, A. "On some recent translations of the Qur'ān." *Numen* 4, 1957, 75–81.
Bausani, A. *Persia religiosa*. Milan: Il Saggiatore, 1959.
Beeston, A.F.L. "The religions of pre-Islamic Yemen." In J. Chelhod (ed.), *L'Arabie du Sud: Histoire et civilisation*, Paris: Maisonneuve et Larose, 1984, 259–69.
Bell, R. *Introduction to the Qur'ān*. Edinburgh: Edinburgh University Press, 1963.
Bell, R. *A Commentary on the Qur'ān*. Ed. C.E. Bosworth and M.E.J. Richardson. Manchester: University of Manchester, 1991.
Bell, R. and W.M. Watt. *Introduction to the Qur'ān*. Edinburgh: Edinburgh University Press, 2001.

Bellamy, J. "Ten Qur'ānic emendations." *JSAI* 31, 2006, 118–38.

Ben-Shemesh, A. "Some suggestions to Qur'ān translators." In Ibn Warraq (ed.), *What the Koran Really Says: Language, Text, and Commentary*. Amherst, NY: Prometheus, 2002, 238–44.

Bergsträsser, G. *Plan eines Apparatus Criticus zum Qoran. Sitzungsberichte der Bayerischen Akademie der Wissenschaften 1930 (Heft 7)*. Munich: Verlag der Bayerischen Akademie der Wissenschaften, 1930. Reprint: *Der Koran*. Ed. R. Paret. *Wege der Forschung* 326. Darmstadt: Wissenschaftliche Buchgesellschaft, 1975, 389–97.

Bergsträsser, G. "Über die Notwendigkeit und Möglichkeit einer kritischen Koranausgabe." *ZDMG* 84, 1930, 82–3.

Blachère, R. *Introduction au Coran*. 2nd edition. Paris: Maisonneuve, 1959. Reprint: Paris: Maisonneuve, 1991.

Buhl, F. *Das Leben Muhammeds*. Trans. H.H. Schaeder. Heidelberg: Quelle and Meyer, 1930.

Burton, J. *Collection of the Qur'ān*. Cambridge: Cambridge University Press, 1977.

Caetani, L. *Annali dell'Islam*. Milano: Hoepli, 1905–26.

Carré, O. "À propos du coran sur quelques ondes françaises actuelles." *Arabica* 53, 2006, 353–81.

Chipman, L., "Adam and the angels: An examination of the mythic elements in Islamic sources." *Arabica* 49, 2002, 429–55.

Conrad, L. "Qur'ānic studies: A historian's perspective." In M. Kropp (ed.), *Results of Contemporary Research on the Qur'ān: The Question of a Historio-Critical Text of the Qur'ān*. Beirut: Ergon, 2007, 9–15.

Cook, M. "Ibn Qutayba and the Monkeys." *SI* 89, 1999, 43–74.

Cook, M. "The stemma of the regional codices of the Koran." *Graeco-Arabica* 9–10, 2004, 89–104.

Crone, P. *Meccan Trade and the Rise of Islam*. Princeton: Princeton University Press, 1987.

Crone, P. "The first-century concept of Higra." *Arabica* 3, 1994, 352–87.

Crone, P. "Two legal problems bearing on the early history of the Qur'ān." *JSAI* 18, 1994, 1–37.

Cuypers, M. and G. Gobillot. *Le Coran: Idées reçues*. Paris: Le cavalier blue, 2007.

Daouk, I.B.T. *The Koran from a Vernacular Perspective: Vocabulary Strings and Composition Strata*. Erlangen: Daouk, 2004.

de Caprona, P.C. *Le Coran: Aux sources de la parole oraculaire, structures rythmiques des sourates mecquoises*. Paris: Publications Orientalistes de France, 1981.

de Prémare, A.-L. *Les fondations de l'Islam. Entre écriture et histoire*. Paris: Seuil, 2002.

Derenbourgh, H. "Bibliographie primitive du Coran." In R. Guiffrida (ed.), *Scritti per il centenario della nascita di Michele Amari*. Palermo: Società siciliana per la storia patria, 1990, 1:1–22. Reprint: *Sources de la transmission manuscrite du texte coranique, I. Les manuscrits de style hiğāzī, Le manuscrit Or. 2165 (f. 1 à 61)*. Ed. F. Déroche and S.N. Noseda. Lesa, Italy: Fondazione F. Noja Noseda, 2001, xxxix–lv.

Donner, F. "The historical context." In J.D. McAuliffe (ed.), *The Cambridge Companion to the Qur'ān*. Cambridge: Cambridge University Press, 2007, 23–39.

Dozy, R. *Die Israeliten zu Mekka von Davids Zeit*. Leipzig: Engelmann, 1864.

Esack, F. *The Qur'an*. Oxford: Oneworld, 2002.

Ess, J. van. *Theologie und Gesellschaft im 2. und 3. Jahrhundert Hidschra*. Berlin: de Gruyter, 1991–7.

Fahd, T. *Le Panthéon de l'Arabie centrale à la veille de l'hégire*. Paris: Geuthner, 1968.

Fischer, A. "Muhammad und Ahmad, die Namen des arabischen Propheten." *Berichte über die Verhandlungen der Sächsischen Akademie der Wissenschaften zu Leipzig, phil.-hist. Klasse* 84, 1932, 3–27.

Fischer, A. "Grammatisch schwierige Schwur- und Beschwörungsformeln." *Der Islam* 28, 1948, 1–105.

Fowden, E.K. *The Barbarian Plain: Saint Sergius between Rome and Iran*. Berkeley: University of California Press, 1999.

Geyer, R. "Zur Strophik des Qurans." *Wiener Zeitschrift für die Kunde des Morgenlandes* 22, 1908, 265–86. Trans.: R. Geyer, "The strophic structure of the Koran." Trans. G.A. Wells in Ibn Warraq (ed.), *What the Koran Really Says*. Amherst, NY: Prometheus, 2002, 625–46.

Gilliot, C. "Deux études sur le Coran." *Arabica* 30, 1983, 1–37.

Gilliot, C. "Une reconstruction critique du Coran ou comment en finir avec les merveilles de la lampe d'Aladin." In M. Kropp (ed.), *Results of Contemporary Research on the Qur'ān: The Question of a Historio-Critical Text of the Qur'ān*. Beirut: Ergon, 2007, 33–137.

Gimaret, D. *Dieu a l'image de l'homme: les anthropomorphismes de la sunna et leur interprétation par les théologiens*. Paris: Cerf, 1997.

Glaser, E. *Skizze der Geschichte und Geographie Arabiens*. Berlin: Weidmann, 1890.

Goldziher, I. *Muhammedanische Studien*. Halle: Niemeyer, 1888–90. English trans.: *Muslim Studies*. Trans. C.R. Barber and S.M. Stern. New Brunswick, NJ: Aldine, 2006.

Goldziher, I. *Die Richtungen der islamischen Koranauslesung*. Leiden: Brill, 1920. English trans.: *Schools of Koranic Commentators*. Trans. W. Behn. Wiesbaden: Harrasowitz in Kommission, 2006.

Grimme, H. "Der Logos in Südarabien." In C. Bezold (ed.), *Orientalische Studien: Th. Nöldeke zum 70. Geburtstag gewidmet*. Gieszen: Töpelmann, 1906, 1:453–61.

Grimme, H. "Über einige Klassen südarabischer Lehnwörter im Qoran." *Zeitschrift für Assyriologie* 26, 1912, 158–68.

Grimme, H. "Der Name Moḥammad." *Zeitschrift für Semitistik und verwandte Gebiete* 6, 1928, 24–6.

Grimme, H. *Texte und Untersuchungen zur ṣafatenisch-arabischen Religion, mit einer Einführung in die ṣafatenische Epigraphik*. Paderborn: Schöningh, 1929.

Groß, M. and K.-H. Ohlig (eds.) *Schlaglichter: Die beiden ersten islamischen Jahrhunderte*. Berlin: Schiler, 2008.

Hawting, G.R. "Eavesdropping on the heavenly assembly and the protection of the revelation from demonic corruption." In Stefan Wild (ed.), *Self-Referentiality in the Qur'an*. Wiesbaden: Harrassowitz, 2006, 25–37.

Haykal, M.H. *The Life of Muḥammad*. Trans. I.R.A. al-Fārūqī. Indianapolis: American Trust Publications, 1976.

Horovitz, J. "Judaeo-Arabic relations in pre-Islamic times." *Islamic Culture* 3, 1929, 161–99.

Hoyland, R.G. "The content and context of early Arabic inscriptions." *JSAI* 21, 1997, 77–102.

Hoyland, R.G. *Seeing Islam as Others Saw It: A Survey and Evaluation of Christian, Jewish and Zoroastrian Writings on Early Islam*. Princeton: Darwin, 1997.

Hoyland, R.G. "New documentary texts and the early Islamic state." *BSOAS* 69, 2006, 395–416.

Hoyland, R.G. "Writing the biography of the Prophet Muhammad: Problems and solutions." *History Compass* 5, 2007, 581–602.

Hurgronje, C.S. *Het Mekkaansche Feest*. Leiden: Brill, 1880.

Ḥusayn, M.K. *City of Wrong*. Trans. K. Cragg. Amsterdam: Djambatan, 1958.

Jeffery, A. "Progress in the study of the Qur'ān text." *MW* 25, 1935, 4–16. Reprint: *Der Koran*. Ed. R. Paret. *Wege der Forschung* 326. Darmstadt: Wissenschaftliche Buchgesellschaft, 1975, 398–412.

Jeffery, A. *Materials for the History of the Text of the Qur'ān*. Leiden: Brill, 1937.

Jeffery, A. "The textual history of the Qur'an." *Journal of the Middle East Society* (Jerusalem) 1, 1947, 35–49. Reprint: *The Qur'ān as Scripture*. Ed. A. Jeffery. New York: Moore, 1952, 89–103.

Kister, M.J. "Ādam: A study of some legends in *tafsīr* and *ḥadīth* literature." *Israel Oriental Studies* 13, 1993, 113–74.

Lammens, H. "Qoran et tradition: Comment fut composée la vie de Mahomet." *Recherches de Science Religieuse* 1, 1910, 25–51; English trans.: "The Koran and tradition: How the life of Muhammad was composed." In Ibn Warraq (ed.), *The Quest for the Historical Muhammad*. Amherst, NY: Prometheus, 2000, 169–87.

Lammens, H. "L'Age de Mahomet et la chronologie de la *sīra*." *Journal Asiatique* 17, 1911, 209–50; English trans.: "The Koran and tradition: How the life of Muhammad was composed." In Ibn Warraq (ed.), *The Quest for the Historical Muhammad*. Amherst, NY: Prometheus, 2000, 188–217.

Lammens, H. *Fāṭima et les filles de Mahomet*. Rome: Sumptibus pontificii instituti biblici, 1912.

Lammens, H. *La Mecque à la veille de l'hégire*. Beirut: Imprimerie Catholique, 1924.

Lammens, H. *L'Arabie occidentale avant l'hégire*. Beirut: Imprimerie Catholique, 1928.

Leszynsky, R. *Die Juden in Arabien zur Zeit Mohammeds*. Berlin: Mayer and Müller, 1910.

Lohmann, T. "Die Nacht al-Qadr: Übersetzung und Erklärung von Sure 97." *Mitteilungen des Instituts für Orientforschung* 15, 1969, 275–85.

Madigan, D. *The Qur'ān's Self-Image: Writing and Authority in Islam's Scripture*. Princeton: Princeton, 2001.

Madigan, D. "Themes and topics." In J.D. McAuliffe (ed.), *The Cambridge Companion to the Qur'ān*. Cambridge: Cambridge University Press, 2007, 79–95.

Margoliouth, D.S. *The Relations between Arabs and Israelites Prior to the Rise of Islam*. London: Oxford University Press, 1924.

Massignon, L. *La passion d'al-Ḥallāj*. Paris: Geuthner, 1914–1921; English trans.: *The Passion of al-Ḥallāj*. Trans. H. Mason. Princeton: Princeton University Press, 1982.

McAuliffe, J. "The prediction and prefiguration of Muḥammad." In J.C. Reeves (ed.), *Bible and Qur'ān: Essays in Scriptural Intertextuality*. Atlanta: Society of Biblical Literature, 2003, 107–31.

Melchert, C. "Ibn Mujāhid and the establishment of seven Qur'ānic readings." *SI* 91, 2000, 5–22.

Mohammed, K. "The identity of the Qur'ān's *ahl al-dhikr*." In K. Mohammed and A. Rippin (eds.), *Coming to Terms with the Qur'ān*. North Haledon, NJ: Islamic Publications International, 2007, 33–45.

Molitor, J. "Urchristliches Kerygma in seiner Abhängigkeit von der Aramäischen Verkehrs und Kanzleisprache und seine Nachwirkung im Koran." In R.H. Fischer (ed.), *A Tribute to Arthur Vööbus*. Chicago: Lutheran School of Theology, 1977, 97–108.

Muir, W. *The Life of Mohamet from Original Sources*. London: Smith, Elder, and Co., 1877.

Muth, F.-C. "Reflections on the relationship of early Arabic poetry and the Qur'ān: Meaning and origin of the Qur'ānic term *ṭayran abābīla* according to early Arabic poetry and other sources." In M. Kropp (ed.), *Results of Contemporary Research on the Qur'ān: The Question of a Historio-Critical Text of the Qur'ān*. Beirut: Ergon, 2007, 147–56.

Nau, F. *Les arabes chrétiens de Mésopotamie et Syrie du VIIe au VIIIe siècle*. Paris: Imprimerie Nationale, 1933.

Neuwirth, A. "Einige Bemerkungen zum besonderen sprachlichen und literarischen Charakter des Koran." *Deutscher Orientalistentag 1975*. Wiesbaden: Steiner, 1977, 736–9. Trans.: "Some remarks on the special linguistic and literary character of the Qur'ān." Trans. G. Goldbloom. In A. Rippin (ed.), *The Qur'ān: Style and Contents*. Aldershot: Ashgate, 2001, 253–7.

Neuwirth, A. *Studien zur Komposition der mekkanischen Suren*. Berlin: de Gruyter, 1981 (2nd edition 2007).

Neuwirth, A. "Qur'ānic literary structure revisited." In S. Leder (ed.), *Story-Telling in the Framework of Non-Fictional Arabic Literature*. Wiesbaden: Harrassowitz, 1998, 388–420.

Neuwirth, A. "Qur'ān and history – a disputed relationship. Some reflections on Qur'ānic history and history in the Qur'ān." *Journal of Qur'anic Studies* 5, 2003, 1–18.

Neuwirth, A. "Zur Archäologie einer Heiligen Schrift: Überlegungen zum Koran vor seiner Kompilation." In C. Burgmer (ed.), *Streit um den Koran*. Berlin: Schiler, 2004, 82–97.

Neuwirth, A. "Structural, linguistic and literary features." In J.D. McAuliffe (ed.), *The Cambridge Companion to the Qur'ān*. Cambridge: Cambridge University Press, 2007, 97–113.

Neuwirth, A. "Im vollen Licht der Geschichte: Die Wissenschaft des Judentums und die Anfänge der kritischen Koranforschung." In D. Hartwig, W. Homolka, M. Marx, and A. Neuwirth (eds.), *Im vollen Licht der Geschichte: Die Wissenschaft des Judentums und die Anfänge der kritischen Koranforschung*. Würzburg: Ergon, 2008, 25–39.

Neuwirth, A. "Psalmen – im Koran neu gelesen." In D. Hartwig, W. Homolka, M. Marx, and A. Neuwirth (eds.), *Im vollen Licht der Geschichte: Die Wissenschaft des Judentums und die Anfänge der kritischen Koranforschung*. Würzburg: Ergon, 2008, 157–91.

Nevo, Y. and J. Koren. "Methodological Approaches to Islamic Studies." *Der Islam* 68, 1991, 87–107.

Nevo, Y. and J. Koren. *Crossroads to Islam: The Origins of the Arab Religion and the Arab State*. Amherst, NY: Prometheus, 2003.

Nöldeke, T. *Geschichte der Perser und Araber zur Zeit des Sasaniden*. Leiden: Brill, 1879.

Ohlig, K.-H. (ed.) *Der frühe Islam*. Berlin: Schiler, 2007.

Ohlig, K.-H. and G.-R. Puin (eds.) *Die dunklen Anfänge: Neue Forschungen zur Entstehung und frühen Geschichte des Islam*. Berlin: Schiler, 2005.

Paret, R. (ed.) *Der Koran. Wege der Forschung* 326. Darmstadt: Wissenschaftliche Buchgesellschaft, 1975.

Popp, V. "Die frühe Islamgeschichte nach inschriftlichen und numismatischen Zeugnissen." In K.-H. Ohlig and G.-R. Puin (eds.), *Die dunklen Anfänge: Neue Forschungen zur Entstehung und frühen Geschichte des Islam*. Berlin: Schiler, 2005, 16–123.

Pretzl, O. *Die Fortführung des Apparatus Criticus zum Koran. Sitzungsberichte der Bayerischen Akademie der Wissenschaften 1934 (Heft 5)*. Munich: Verlag der Bayerischen Akademie der Wissenschaften, 1934.

Pretzl, O. "Die Wissenschaft der Koranlesung." *Islamica* 6, 1935–6, 1–47; 230–46; 290–331.

Pretzl, O. "Aufgaben und Ziele der Koranforschung." *Actes du XXe Congrès International des Orientalistes, Bruxelles 5–10 Septembre 1938*. Louvain: Bureaux du muséon, 1940, 328–9. Reprint: *Der Koran*. Ed. R. Paret. *Wege der Forschung* 326. Darmstadt: Wissenschaftliche Buchgesellschaft, 1975, 411–2.

Rabb, I. "Non-canonical readings of the Qur'ān: Recognition and authenticity (The Ḥimṣī reading)." *Journal of Qur'ānic Studies* 8, 2006, 84–127.

Rabbath, E. *L'orient chrétien à la veille de l'islam*. Beirut: Université Libanaise, 1980.

Renan, E. "Nouvelles considérations sur le caractère général des peuples sémitiques." *Journal Asiatique* 13, 1859, 214–82; 417–50.

Retsö, J. *The Arabs in Antiquity: Their History from the Assyrians to the Umayyads*. London: Routledge, 2003.

Rippin, A. "The Qur'ān as literature: Perils, pitfalls and prospects." *British Society for Middle Eastern Studies Bulletin* 10, 1983, 38–47. Reprint: *The Qur'ān and Its Interpretative Tradition*. Ed. A. Rippin. Aldershot: Ashgate, 2001.

Rippin, A. *Muslims: Their Religious Beliefs and Practices*. London: Routledge, 1990.

Rippin, A. "Reading the Qur'ān with Richard Bell." *JAOS* 112, 1992, 639–47.

Rodinson, M. *Mahomet*. 3rd edition. Paris: Éditions du Seuil, 1974.

Rösch, G. "Die Namen des arabischen Propheten Muḥammed und Aḥmed." *ZDMG* 46, 1892, 432–40.

Rosenthal, F. "The influence of the biblical tradition on Muslim historiography." In B. Lewis and P.M. Holt (eds.), *Historians of the Middle East*. London: Oxford University Press, 1962, 35–45.

Rosenthal, F. "The history of Heinrich Speyer's *Die biblischen Erzählungen im Qoran*." In D. Hartwig, W. Homolka, M. Marx, and A. Neuwirth (eds.), *Im vollen Licht der Geschichte: Die Wissenschaft des Judentums und die Anfänge der kritischen Koranforschung*. Würzburg: Ergon, 2008, 113–6. This is the transcript of an address that Prof. Rosenthal delivered in Berkeley, California in 1993.

Rubin, U. "Abū Lahab and Sūra CXI." *BSOAS* 42, 1979, 13–28. Reprint: *The Qur'ān: Style and Contents*. Ed. A. Rippin. Aldershot: Ashgate, 2001, 269–83.

Rubin, U. "Ḥanīfiyya and Ka'ba – an inquiry into the Arabian pre-Islamic background of Dīn Ibrāhīm." *JSAI* 13, 1990, 85–112.

Rubin, U. *The Eye of the Beholder*. Princeton: Darwin, 1995.

Saeed, A. *Interpreting the Qur'ān: Towards a Contemporary Approach*. London: Routledge, 2006.

Schacht, J. "A reevaluation of Islamic traditions." *JRAS* 49, 1949, 143–54.

Schacht, J. *The Origins of Muhammadan Jurisprudence*. Oxford: Oxford University Press, 1950.

Schöck, C. *Adam im Islam: ein Beitrag zur Ideengeschichte der Sunna*. Berlin: Schwarz, 1993.

Sells, M. "Sound, spirit, and gender in *sūrat al-qadr*." *JAOS* 111, 1991, 239–59. Reprint: *The Qur'ān: Style and Contents*. Ed. A. Rippin. Aldershot: Ashgate, 2001, 333–53.

Sfar, M. *Le Coran, est-il authentique?* Paris: Sfar, 2000.

Shahid, I. *Byzantium and the Arabs in the Sixth Century*, Washington, DC: Dumbarton Oaks, 1995–2002.

Shaḥrūr, M. *Al-Kitāb wa-l-Qur'ān: qirā'a mu'āṣira*. Damascus: Ahālī, 1990.

Sinai, N. "Orientalism, authorship, and the onset of revelation: Abraham Geiger and Theodor Nöldeke on Muḥammad and the Qur'ān." In D. Hartwig, W. Homolka, M. Marx, and A. Neuwirth (eds.), *Im vollen Licht der Geschichte: Die Wissenschaft des Judentums und die Anfänge der kritischen Koranforschung*. Würzburg: Ergon, 2008, 145–54.

Spitaler, A. "Die Nichtkanonischen Koranlesarten und ihre Bedeutung für die arabische Sprachwissenschaft." *Actes du XXe Congrès International des Orientalistes, Bruxelles 5–10 Septembre 1938*. Louvain: Bureaux du muséon, 1940, 314–5. Reprint: *Der Koran*. Ed. R. Paret. *Wege der Forschung* 326. Darmstadt: Wissenschaftliche Buchgesellschaft, 1975, 413.

Sprenger, A. *Das Leben und die Lehre des Moḥammad*, Berlin: Nicolai'sche Verlagsbuchandlung, 1861–5.

Stetkevych, J. *Muḥammad and the Golden Bough: Reconstructing Arabian Myth*. Bloomington: Indiana University Press, 1996.

Stetkevych, S. *The Mute Immortals Speak*. Ithaca: Cornell University Press, 1993.

Stewart, D. "Saj' in the Qur'ān: Prosody and structure." *Journal of Arabic Literature* 21, 1990, 101–39. Reprint: *The Qur'ān: Style and Contents*. Ed. A. Rippin. Aldershot: Ashgate, 2001, 213–52.

Stewart, D. "Notes on medieval and modern emendations of the Qur'ān." In G.S. Reynolds (ed.), *The Qur'ān in Its Historical Context*. London: Routledge, 2007, 223–48.

Tardy, R. *Najrân: Chrétiens d'Arabie avant l'Islam*, Beyrouth: Dar al-Machreq, 1999.

Trimingham, J.S. *Christianity among the Arabs in Pre-Islamic Times*. London: Longman, 1979.

Wansbrough, J. *The Sectarian Milieu: Content and Composition of Islamic Salvation History*. Oxford: Oxford University Press, 1978.

Watt, W.M. *Companion to the Qur'ān*. London: Allen and Unwin, 1967.

Watt, W.M. *Muhammad's Mecca: History in the Quran*. Edinburgh: Edinburgh University Press, 1988.

Watt, W.M. *Muslim-Christian Encounters*. Routledge: London, 1991.

Watt, W.M. and R. Bell. *Bell's Introduction to the Qur'ān*. Edinburgh: Edinburgh University Press, 1977.

Weil, G. *Historisch-kritische Einleitung in den Koran*. Bielefeld: Velhagen and Klasing, 1844.

Welch, A. "Formulaic features of the punishment-stories." In I.J. Boullata (ed.), *Literary Structures of Religious Meaning in the Qur'ān*. Richmond: Curzon, 2000, 77–116.

Wellhausen, J. *Reste arabischen Heidentums*. Berlin: Reimer, 1897.
Wensinck, A.J. *Mohammed en de Joden te Medina*. Leiden: Brill, 1908. Trans.: *Muhammad and the Jews of Medina*. Trans. W. Behn. Freiburg: Schwarz, 1975.
Widengren, G. *Mohammed, the Apostle of God and His Ascension*. Uppsala: Lundequistska bokhandeln, 1955.
Zaehner, R.C. *At Sundry Times: An Essay in Comparative Religions*. London: Faber and Faber, 1958.

Index of Qur'ānic Verses

Index of Biblical Verses

Deuteronomy

4.19 79
7.18 236
9.9 95
10.16 152–5
30.6 152

Judges

12.6 107 (n. 302)
13.15 94

1 Samuel

1.4–6 141
1.11 141
10.23 198
5 128 (n. 399)
15 128 (n. 399)

2 Samuel

12 142, 234

2 Kings

2.11, 17 59
7.9 88 (n. 229)
18.1 120 (n. 356)
20.1–5 218

1 Chronicles

1.10 102
5.29 144

2 Chronicles

20.7 90 (n. 237)

Nehemiah

9.7 79 (n. 192)

Tobit

12.19 94
14.10 104

Esther 99

3.1, 10 105 (n. 297)
3.2, 6 104
5.1–3 104
7.10 104
8.1 104 (n. 291)
9.1 104

Job

1.6–7 61 (n. 106)
2.2 61 (n. 106)
42.10 196 (n. 701)

Psalms 20–1 (n. 71), 244

7.5 198 (n. 711)
8.1 198 (n. 711)
19.1 198 (n. 711)
24.10 198 (n. 711)
78 244
105 244
106 244
113.4 126 (n. 395)

Proverbs

16.28 58 (n. 94)
18.8 58 (n. 94)
26.20, 22 58 (n. 94)

Song of Solomon

2.3 191

Wisdom of Solomon

2.24 47 (n. 51)

Isaiah

2.22 47
6.3 126 (n. 395)
14.13–5 102
23.9 198
41.8 90 (n. 237)

Jeremiah

4.4 153
6.10 153 (nn. 506–7)
9.24–5 153

Ezekiel

3.7 154 (n. 510)
26 59
29.3–4, 12 103

Index of People Places and Subjects